ARMIES OF THE SEVEN YEARS WAR

Armies of the Seven Years War

Commanders, Equipment, Uniforms and Strategies of the 'First World War'

Digby Smith

Spellmount

First published 2012 by
Spellmount, an imprint of
The History Press
The Mill, Brimscombe Port
Stroud, Gloucestershire, GL5 2QG
www.thehistorypress.co.uk

British Library Cataloguing in Publication Data.
A catalogue record for this book is available from the British Library.

ISBN 978 0 7524 5923 3

Typesetting and origination by The History Press
Production managed by Jellyfish Print Solutions
Printed in India

CONTENTS

Foreword   6

1   Political Background   7

2   Military Tactics, Weapons and Equipment   9

3   Naval Warfare   20

4   The Austrian Empire   23

5   The Holy Roman Empire   43

6   The Ducal Electorate of Bavaria and the Palatinate   59

7   The Duchy of Brunswick   61

8   The Kingdom of France   65

9   The Kingdom of Great Britain   96

10   The Electorate of Hanover (Braunschweig-Lüneburg)   139

11   The Landgravate of Hessen-Kassel   150

12   The County of Lippe-Detmold and Schaumburg-Lippe   154

13   The Kingdom of Portugal   157

14   The Kingdom of Prussia   161

15   The Empire of all the Russias   207

16   The Electorate of Saxony   219

17   The Kingdom of Spain   224

18   The Kingdom of Sweden   226

19   The Duchy of Württemberg   236

20   The Bishopric of Würzburg   241

Appendix 1   Key Battles   243

Appendix 2   Key Places   291

Appendix 3   Key People   293

Bibliography   328

Index   329

FOREWORD

Any historical work of this type is only as good as the sources used in its composition. Over many years, I have been lucky enough to have been able to collect much data, the true value of which I often did not realise at the time, as my main field of interest then was the Napoleonic era. Luckily, this data was retained and only recently resurfaced to be included in this book. One resource of outstanding scope, depth and quality is the website Project Seven Years War (Kronoskaf), run by Richard Couture in Canada, to whom a great deal of credit must be given for opening up many obscure sources to the general public. The volunteer contributors to this site give their time, efforts and linguistic skills freely, to expand and improve the content continuously. It now represents the best asset on all aspects of the Seven Years War that I have seen. Richard has my thanks for allowing me free use of his creation, as have Colonel Michael Zahn, Christian Rogge, Fredric Aubert and many others, who contributed so much detailed information to the site.

Most of the major battles and sieges of the Seven Years War were fought in Silesia (which is now part of Poland) and all the old German names have been changed, making modern maps more of a hindrance than a help when trying to follow the campaigns. To ease this difficulty, a German–Polish register of the major military sites has been included.

Units of palace life guards, garrison regiments and militia (home guard) regiments are not included in this work, unless – as in the case of Prussia – they were mobilised and went on campaign.

1

POLITICAL BACKGROUND

Up to 1740, Prussia was a second-rate state within Europe, but in that year her new king Friedrich II (Frederick the Great as he came to be known) attacked Austria in the opening round of the Wars of the Austrian Succession.

The struggle took its name from the failure of Carl VI, Holy Roman Emperor (1711–1740), to father a male heir. Under Salic Law a woman could not rule the Empire, which had been in Habsburg hands since the fifteenth century and was seen in Vienna as a hereditary title. The succession of Carl VI's eldest surviving daughter, Maria Theresa, to the family possessions (principally the Austrian provinces, the Bohemian crown lands and the kingdom of Hungary, together with the outlying territories of the Duchy of Milan and the Austrian (southern) Netherlands) was provided for by a family agreement, the so-called Pragmatic Sanction, which had been agreed to by the other crowned heads of Europe in 1713. Two middle-sized German states, Bavaria and Saxony, had their own claims to the Holy Roman Empire's throne, but when Carl VI died suddenly in October 1740, Maria Theresa took the throne on 20 October. An unexpected challenge to Maria Theresia's accession swiftly came from the new, ambitious Prussian king, who harboured years of resentment against Austria's power and unwelcome influence in Prussian domestic affairs. He also coveted the wealth of the Austrian province of Silesia; it was rich in coal, copper, silver, cadmium, zinc and lead, and had a thriving agricultural industry, watered and powered by the river Oder.

Frederick invaded Silesia in 1740; the war lasted for two years. Austrian efforts to recover the northern parts of the province failed and the war was ended by the Peace of Breslau (now Wroclow), signed in Berlin on 11 June 1742. Based on the terms of the treaty, Maria Theresa ceded most of the Silesian duchies to Prussia except for the Duchy of Teschen, the districts of Troppau and Krnov south of the Opava river as well as the southern part of the Duchy of Nysa (Neisse), that were all to become the province of Austrian Silesia. Furthermore Frederick annexed the Bohemian county of Kladsko.

In the Second Silesian War (1744–1745), Austria attempted – and failed – to recover Silesia. The conflict was ended by the Peace of Dresden on 25 December 1745. By the terms of the treaty, Frederick the Great acknowledged Franz I – husband of Maria Theresa – as Holy Roman Emperor. In return, he maintained control over Silesia. The real loser was Saxony, who had to pay Prussia one million Thaler in reparations. The Third Silesian (Seven Years') War, completed the Wars of the Austrian Succession and confirmed Prussia as one of the most powerful nations in Europe.

But it was not only in Europe that this conflict was played out. The old enemies, Britain and France, were at this time engaged in a race to establish colonial empires, mainly in North America and

India, where both had existing footholds. This meant that much of their 'private war' was carried out by their respective fleets, who fought for control of the oceans and carried their armies, supplies and settlers to the territories in contention. It was during this war that Britain grasped the importance of command of the seas. Once that lesson had been well and truly learned, it was to shape her strategy for centuries to come. Through the Napoleonic era and two world wars, Britain's primary defence strategy was to maintain the supremacy of the Royal Navy.

2

MILITARY TACTICS, WEAPONS AND EQUIPMENT

Throughout history, military battlefield tactics have been dictated by the weapons available. In 1756 it was usual for an army to march divided into an advanced guard, the main body, the left and right flank guards and a rearguard. On the field of battle they would deploy, usually into two lines of infantry, one behind the other about 200m apart, with the cavalry on either wing, or one wing if the other was anchored on some obstacle like a river or a town. If both wings were so anchored, the main body of the cavalry would be behind the infantry. In all cases, only light cavalry scouting patrols would have been deployed before the line. The senior infantry regiment would be on the right of the first line, the next senior regiment on the extreme left, the other arranged between them, in descending order of seniority from the right. Each battalion had its own light artillery pieces under command. The reserve (heavy) artillery would be held in rear until the commander decided where and when to use them. When setting up camp in the field, the opposed armies would be arrayed in this formation, facing the expected direction of any enemy assault.

Infantry

Infantry of the line of battle (line infantry) were the most numerous presence on the battlefield, as they were the cheapest and most easily trained, equipped and replaced. They fought in close order, usually in ranks three or four men deep. The basic tactical infantry unit was the battalion of 600–900 men. Two or more battalions might be grouped together as a regiment, two or three regiments formed a brigade and two or three brigades formed a division. Confusingly, two companies of infantry or two squadrons of cavalry also formed a 'division'.

Regiments were 'sold' to their Colonel-in-Chief ('Chef' in Prussia, 'Inhaber' in Austria) by the sovereign and bore the colonel's name as their title. The Chef then drew an agreed allowance from the state for the upkeep of his regiment. Careful economy meant that a regiment could became a good source of income. Each regiment was distinguished by the colour of its facings (collar, cuffs, lapels, shoulder straps) and by its buttons, which were either of pewter or brass. The numbering of infantry and cavalry regiments was in its infancy at this point in history; it was not until about 1780 that numbers were widely applied. They are used here to enable further research by interested readers.

Battalions were sub-divided into companies of about 100 men, which were again divided, generally into two platoons. The great virtue of infantry was that although cavalry and artillery were able to force an enemy to cede ground, only infantry could effectively hold it against enemy assault or counter-attack.

In 1756, it was common for each company of infantry to carry a flag or colour. This was reduced to two per battalion by 1792. One of these colours was the sovereign's colour, the others the company – later battalion – colour. Each company usually had two drummers for the transmission of orders. The drummers wore special livery and decorations to their uniforms. Every infantry battalion also had its section of pioneers, or carpenters, equipped with axes, saws and other tools. Their task was to prepare the path for the battalion, clearing obstacles and building roads and simple bridges. They wore leather aprons and usually went unshaven.

Apart from line infantry, the Seven Years War was to see the emergence of light infantry and light cavalry regiments, with Austria leading the way with their Croat border infantry and their Hungarian hussars. These men were specially trained to fight in open order, to skirmish, to patrol and cover areas flanking the position of the main body of the army, to act with the advanced and rear guards. They were usually armed with shorter muskets or rifles and wore lightweight uniforms and equipment, often in sombre colours, to aid camouflage – then a new concept. These battalions carried no colours and commanders' signals were transmitted with hunting horns (later some units used bugles) instead of using bulky drums.

Breech-Loading Rifles

Although a French engineer is generally given credit for the development of this successful system, its origins date back to late sixteenth-century Spain. The system utilised a screw-threaded plug which, by being screwed and unscrewed vertically at the rear of the barrel, sealed and unsealed the breech for loading with powder and ball. Throughout the seventeenth century this system was experimented with in Germany, England and Denmark but was finally developed with success by Isaac de la Chaumette in France in 1704. The inventor was a protestant Huguenot, however, and fled to England where he took out a patent to protect his invention in 1721. For the next 50 years screw-plug breech-loading muskets and rifles were made in England as sporting guns but, in 1776, Captain Patrick Ferguson – a Scot and one of the best shots in Britain – took out a patent for an improved version which he intended for military use. Subsequent trials impressed British military authorities and 100 were manufactured to equip a corps of riflemen to be led by Ferguson on campaign in America. Although successful at Brandywine in 1777, Ferguson's corps was broken up after he was wounded, and his subsequent death at King's Mountain in 1780 ended Britain's experiment with military breech-loaders for the next 50 years.

Line infantry were armed with the muzzle-loading, smoothbore musket, with a rate of fire of about two to three rounds a minute. No one nation had muskets of any better performance than any other. Each soldier usually carried 40–60 paper cartridges in his cartridge pouch; each cartridge held a musket ball and the correct charge of powder. A further 60 cartridges per man Were held on his battalion's artillery wagons.

The initial rate of fire decreased progressively during action, due to misfires and errors made by the men in the reloading ritual, and the fouling of the barrel, caused by the burning of the black powder propellant charge. This meant that a musket barrel would have to be thoroughly cleaned out after firing about 30 rounds.

Under the fierce drilling of the 'Old Dessauer' (Prince Leopold von Anhalt-Dessau), Prussian infantry on the parade ground could reach the incredible rate of 'firing' five times in a minute. Being a smoothbore weapon, the musket was relatively inaccurate and the effective range was only about 300m, although the balls would often carry much further.

The advantages of rifling (cutting spiral grooves along the inside of the barrel of a musket or cannon, in order to improve the accuracy of the weapon by spinning the projectile), had long been known, and rifled small arms had been produced as early as 1520 by Gaspard Koller of Vienna and by an anonymous gunsmith in Nuremberg. Hunting rifles were also in production and were so accurate that a marksman could regularly hit a target the size of a man's chest at 150 paces. But it was difficult and costly to produce and the rate of fire was only about one shot every two or three minutes. After 20 shots the rifleman would have to withdraw and clean out the fouling in the barrel. This low rate of fire meant that the rifle was no good for general military use in 1756 and they were issued only to a few specialist crack shots. Technical improvements were made to the design of rifled infantry firearms, and the first weapon to be introduced into general service in 1835 was that designed by Nikolaus Dreyse for the Prussian Army.

Types of Musket Fire

Infantry battalions in combat mostly formed up in lines three or four ranks deep. The rank was the long line, the 'file' was the three or four men, one behind another in that rank. It was usual for the front rank to kneel down to fire, allowing the second and third ranks to fire over them. The fourth rank did not fire. Injuries caused by this system led to the third rank not firing either and battalion frontages were extended as armies slowly adopted a three-rank formation. By the time of the Napoleonic Wars, the British infantry formed only two ranks on the battlefield. The musket was so inaccurate that soldiers just pointed it in the general direction of the enemy and pulled the trigger, then stood up (if they had been kneeling) and reloaded at top speed, in order to be ready to fire again. Prior to such firing, the NCOs and officers took post in pre-determined positions to the flanks and rear of the battalion.

Due to the fact that the musket was a weapon with a relatively low rate of fire, it was unusual for a whole battalion to fire at once, as this would have left it unable to fire again for 20–30 seconds. Such a general salvo would only have been fired at very close range, just before a bayonet charge. Consequently, it was most common for a battalion to fire by *peleton* or platoon, i.e. by half company.

A Prussian battalion of four musketeer companies was subdivided into eight *peletons* in line; if we number them from left to right, the theoretical firing sequence went as follows: 1, 3, 5, 7, 2, 4, 6, 8. This could be achieved at speed on the parade ground, but, in the heat and terror of battle, the firing quickly became very ragged. *Peleton* fire was also used on the move, in the advance or withdrawal, with the platoon that was to fire, halting to fire and reload, then stepping off together to repeat the process. It was also possible to fire by ranks, companies or files.

Steady infantry, deployed in lines 3–4 deep, were usually impervious to cavalry charges from the front. If cavalry were able to charge a line from the rear, or from one end or the other, the result was almost always total destruction of the infantry. Thus, it was essential to anchor the ends of an infantry line on an obstacle, such as a river, ravine, thick wood or town. One infantry formation that had no ends, wherever it was formed, was the square. But the square reduced the number of muskets facing in any one direction, it was clumsy to move and, whilst being excellent defence against cavalry, it presented enemy artillery with an easy target.

Cavalry

The characteristics of cavalry are mobility, fire power and protection. The cavalry of 1756 could move relatively rapidly on the battlefield and deliver crushing blows against enemy infantry if it caught them unawares or in disorder. It is, however, a mistake to believe that the cavalry charge was always the thrilling, uncontrolled spectacle that Hollywood would have us believe. Many charges were delivered at the walk or trot, the speed often dictated by the physical state of the horses. In Russia in 1812, it is recorded that many 'charges' were delivered at the walk, due to the exhaustion and pitiful condition of the animals. On the march, cavalry usually moved at much the same rate as the infantry. The horses had to be carefully and regularly tended, watered and correctly fed if they were to be effective on the battlefield for more than a few days.

Heavy Cavalry

Heavy cavalry regiments (regiments of horse) were the heirs of heavily-armoured knights. Heavy cavalry rode large horses over 16 hands high (1 hand = 4 inches) and frequently wore metal cuirasses (breastplates), or at least the front plates. They were used en mass on the battlefield, to break enemy infantry in formal charges. It was usual for each squadron of cavalry to carry a square standard, usually borne at the front and centre of the unit, as a tactical marker and rallying point. Trumpeters were used to transmit orders; they often rode grey horses and were usually dressed in reversed colours, or in livery designed by the colonel-in-chief.

Cavalry charges were delivered usually by one squadron at a time. The unit moved at a walk, then a trot until very close to the enemy, fired their pistols into the opposing ranks, then drew their swords and tried to hack their way through. Heavy cavalry charges might be delivered by a regiment with the four squadrons in line, in echelon (with three squadrons to the flank and rear of the leading unit), or *en echiquier*, with alternate squadrons in the front rank and the rear rank. A charge by an entire cavalry regiment, *en masse*, in one line was quite rare at this time. After delivering their charge, a cavalry regiment was to rally (ideally out of enemy gunshot range) and reform, before charging again. It was the general rule that for every cavalry regiment involved in a charge, there would be at least as many regiments standing to the rear in reserve.

Light Cavalry

Light cavalry rode small horses (about 14 hands high) and were used – mainly off the battlefield – for patrolling, scouting, intelligence gathering and raiding. At this time they did not take part in formal battlefield charges. Light cavalry regiments included hussars, chasseurs-à-cheval (mounted rifles), lancers and – in Britain – light dragoons. Light cavalry regiments carried swallow-tailed banners – guidons – rather than standards. Trumpets were used for the transmission of orders. Light cavalrymen were armed with a light, curved sabre, a short-barrelled carbine and a brace of pistols. The front ranks of a lancer regiment (of which there were still very few in this war) were armed with lances and pistols, the rear ranks with a carbine and pistols.

Dragoons

Dragoons were originally conceived as mounted infantry. They rode small horses and their equitation skills were not highly developed. They were designed to move to a selected spot on the battlefield relatively quickly, then to dismount and fight on foot as infantry. To this end, they were equipped with drummers for signalling instead of trumpeters, and one man in four had to act as horse-holder for his fighting comrades when the unit dismounted for combat. Dragoon regiments usually carried one, swallow-tailed guidon per squadron. They were armed with swords and short muskets. Instead of the heavy, cuffed boots of the regiments of horse, they usually wore lighter, leather gaiters, fastened with buckles, so that their mobility on foot would be less compromised.

Many light and heavy cavalry regiments used kettle drums on ceremonial parades, but these instruments were not always taken on campaign. In the British Army, it became the tradition for kettle drummers to ride piebald horses. Britain was slow to adopt the title of hussars for their light regiments, preferring to dub them 'light dragoons'.

Field Artillery

By 1756, field artillery was emerging as its own military genre, distinct from fixed or fortress artillery. The difficulties of moving cumbersome, heavy guns over primitive roads and across open country with the available traction (horses, mules or oxen), severely limited its employment on campaign.

In 1756, all field artillery pieces were muzzle-loading smoothbores. This did not mean that breech-loading, rifled guns were not yet thought of. Hunters used rifles well before the Seven Years War, but they were prohibitively expensive weapons to produce in large numbers. The ideas and possibilities of rifled, breech-loading artillery guns had been explored on many international drawing boards for many years – Leonardo da Vinci designed one version – and some 6-pounder, breech-loading fortress guns had been produced in Austria; it was the technical limitations of the tools and materials then available which delayed their introduction.

Quick-Firing Guns

The Imperial Austrian Army in Italy had some in 1702/1703. They could be loaded and fired 'before a cavalryman could draw his sabre and swing it' – a rather inexact measure. These six 2-pounders were built in the style of the old '*Kammerschlange*' (chambered cannon) of artificer Vögler's design and had a removable breech block, which, when loaded, was inserted into the breech of the gun and locked in with a wedge. They seem to have been invented by the Austrian *Altfeuerwerker* (senior artillery artificer) Johann Georg Trompeter, as a file note (Imperial Austrian Hofkammer Archiv, June 1702) states that 'for the invention of the geschwinden Schuss', he received a gratification of 300 Guilders, a pay rise of 50 Guilders per month and travel expenses, so that he might travel to Italy to demonstrate how to use the weapon to the army there. Unfortunately, these weapons proved to be of limited use on the battlefield. Some interesting surviving examples may be seen in the collection of Prince Leichtenstein in Feldsberg and in the Esterhazy family's Schloss Forchtenstein.

In 1750, the Imperial *Zeugschlossermeister* (Master Artificer) Georg Johann Peyrl also invented a quick-firing, breech-loading gun and another such weapon was produced at the same time by the Imperial Austrian *Zeug-Lieutenant* M. von Eisenstein. Both weapons were 1-pounders, 5.2cm calibre and cast in bronze. Both weapons had ratchet-actioned sights. On 28 September 1860 both these weapons – amongst other breech-loaders – were test-fired; both tended to jam and to fill up with powder debris.

The Swedish king, Gustav Adolph II (1594–1632), was especially industrious in improving his field artillery, as he had made it his goal to make his entire army light and agile. In this project he was ably assisted by the commander of his artillery, General Baron Carl Cronstedt. The conventional, lumbering, large-calibre artillery stood in the way of this goal; as it was essential to the successful field operations of his army, the King concentrated upon improving it. He began with the lighter calibre field guns and in 1625, after many experiments, he produced a light 6-pounder. Dollaczek tells us that it supposedly weighed only 625lbs (350kg) but the barrel often split when fired. Gustav Adolph also tested the leather cannon (1628–1631) together with a Colonel Hamilton, and eventually a light field gun was developed.

The barrel was of iron, 1.5m long with sides of 14/16 and 7/18 thickness at the chamber and muzzle respectively. It had an angled touchhole and fired a 1.5kg ball, with a charge of 500g of powder. This charge was contained in a linen cartridge. Another projectile fired from this piece was the wooden grape cartridge. Both the ball and the grape container were attached to the charges by wire. This improved the rate of fire enormously and the gun could be loaded and fired three times before a musketeer could get off a single shot (a musket might be fired at two or three rounds per minute). The gun could easily be drawn by two horses.

Gustav Adolph sought to exploit this weapon to the limit by increasing the numbers of regimental guns with the infantry; each regiment had two or three such guns and there was also the reserve artillery, consisting of 6-, 12- and 24-pounder weapons. At the First Battle of Breitenfeld (17 September 1642), this artillery was decisive. At the Battle of Frankfurt/Oder (13 April 1631) there were over 200 guns with the Swedish Army. This successful increase in the artillery-to-infantry ratio forced Gustav's enemies to emulate him. After the events on the river Lech, the Austrians increased the number of their guns and at the Battle of Lützen (16 November 1632) Wallenstein's artillery outnumbered that of the Swedes.

For economic reasons, Gustav Adolph had his regimental guns crewed by detached infantrymen, which saved on the double salaries paid to the artillery specialists, the *Büchsenmeister* and the

Schlangenschützen (gun crew). This custom was copied by all other nations as was the entire Swedish system, and many professional gun commanders were made redundant. Following the end of the Thirty Years' War in 1648, artillery faded again into the background due to the shortage of funds and changing government priorities.

The relationship between the length of the bore of the barrel of a cannon and range that could be achieved was one that exercised artillery designers. For over 200 years, artillerists had been debating how to calculate the size of the charge, so that the projectile left the muzzle just at that point when all the powder had been burned.

Originally, it was thought that longer barrels meant longer range and greater accuracy and before the reign of the Holy Roman Emperor Carl V (1519–1556), there were guns built with barrel bores of 40–45 calibre length. An accidental discovery changed all this. At the siege of Philippsburg (1734) three Austrian guns, including a *demi-Karthaune*, were damaged at the muzzles. Imperial *Stückhauptmann* (artillery captain) Wenzel Wiskoczill, had the damaged muzzles sawn off and iron reinforcing rings welded to the new muzzles in order to restore the old centres of gravity. To the amazement of all concerned, the truncated guns had a longer range than before and had to be aimed at a point 200 paces in front of the wall in order to hit its crest. Thus began the era of shorter gun barrels.

Rates of fire were increased by various innovations, such as cartridges and fire lance fuzes. Meynert tells us that in 1748 a field gun was fired 13–14 times in a minute, without mopping out, aiming or running the gun forward. Rapid firing became an exercise in its own right under Austria's Fürst Liechtenstein and a report of one such event in the camp at Moldauthein (from the diary of the Württemberg artillery Captain Schmidt, an official observer) tells us that a detachment of six 6-pounder guns and six 3-pounder guns, were fired against an earthen rampart with aimed fire. After every 3–5 shots the barrels were mopped out and the pieces were run forward again. Each gun could fire 5–7 shots per minute. After 15 minutes 'cease fire' was drummed and in this time, the guns had fired a total of 1200 rounds. On the same day, they fired 40 hand grenades from a Coehorn mortar in nine minutes. Field guns now fell into two categories.

Artillery Ammunition

Until about 1700, the gunpowder charge was generally ladled into the barrel of a gun in a wooden spoon, then the powder was rammed to the rear of the chamber, a wad rammed on top of it and the projectile added. It seems likely (from Dollaczek) that the Swedes may have been the first to develop a method of pre-packing powder charges into cloth, leather or a pig's bladder container by 1625, the first step towards production of the artillery cartridge, often containing both the projectile and the charge.

Canister

A metal drum, filled with lead balls or pieces of metal, was fired from howitzers, against enemy infantry or cavalry at the same range as grape from cannon. As the container left the muzzle of the gun, it burst apart and the contents were thrown into the enemy in a lethal cloud.

Cannon

These were weapons designed to be fired in near-flat trajectories. They fired solid shot (ball) at longer ranges and grape (see below) when the appropriate target was close. The ranges achieved depended – amongst other things – upon the quality and amount of the powder in the charge, the length of the barrel and the windage (the gap between the projectile and the inside surface of the barrel).

In 1762, the maximum ranges of guns (with solid shot) were roughly as follows: 3-pounder – 1200 paces; 6-pounder – 1400 paces; 12-pounder – 1600 paces. With grape it was 300, 500 and 700 paces respectively. A pace is taken to be 30 inches long.

Grape

This was a collection of iron balls in a fabric container, which would be fired from cannon at hostile infantry or cavalry at closer ranges of up to 300m.

Howitzers

Howitzers were designed to be fired at high angles, so that their projectiles could reach targets hidden behind cover, be it natural, like woods and hills, or artificial, such as houses and walls. They fired hollow shells (see below) or canisters – tin containers filled with balls or chunks of metal – which was the equivalent of the grape fired by cannon. The Russians introduced a hybrid weapon in 1756; it was a long-barrelled howitzer, called a unicorn. The length of the barrel varied from 7.5 to 12.5 calibres.

Incendiaries

These projectiles, also known as carcasses, were used by large-calibre siege artillery, to be thrown into fortresses to start fires. Rockets were, as yet, unknown in European warfare. It would not be until about 1780 that the British would begin to dabble with William Congreve's weapons, copied from those used by Indian armies.

Mortars

Mortars were very large calibre, short-barrelled weapons, designed for high-trajectory siege work and were used to bombard cities into submission. They fired shell and incendiary ammunition. The Coehorn mortar was a lightweight weapon, capable of being moved by two men and firing a projectile of six pounds. This weapon was originally designed by the Dutchman Baron Menno van Coehorn and used by him against the French in 1673. It was used extensively by the British Army in the eighteenth century.

Round Shot

These were solid, forged iron balls, the main projectiles fired by cannon. They were often gathered up after battles and re-used.

Shells

These comprised hollow iron spheres containing a gunpowder charge and a fuse. The aim was to fire the shell on a high trajectory through the air, so that the fuse (cut to the desired length) would detonate the charge, just over the heads of enemy infantry or cavalry. The resultant explosion would break the casing into several lethal fragments, causing many casualties. Shells were also fired into towns and fortresses, to cause random fires when they exploded.

It was not until the Napoleonic Wars that the 'spherical case shot' – invented by Britain's Captain Henry Shrapnel – would come into use. This was much more destructive against men and horses than conventional shells, due to the fact that it was filled with a mixture of gunpowder and small metal balls, thus producing far more lethal fragments than a conventional projectile.

Trench Balls

These were wooden containers, holding several hand grenades, which were fired from a defender's mortar to disrupt working parties in a besieger's trenches.

Firing Procedure

The hazardous practice of spooning loose powder into gun barrels gave way (in most armies) to pre-packaged charges in linen bags (or pigs' bladders), painted with oil paint to protect against damp. To fire the loaded piece, a spike would be pushed through the touch-hole to pierce the casing of the charge, and some fine powder would be poured into the touch-hole and ignited by the burning linstock. This ignition would cause the main propellant charge to explode.

This system was soon replaced by the use of copper tubes, filled with powder and with a very sharp end, which was driven through the touch-hole and into the cartridge. These devices were called 'Schlagrohr' in Prussia, 'Brandel' in Austria. The touch-hole was angled forwards, so that the tube would be thrown clear of the crew when the gun was fired.

The cartridges were now so clean-burning, that a piece might be fired many times without being washed out with a mop. With all these improvements, well-trained Austrian gun crews could attain and maintain a rate of fire of up to four rounds a minute – as fast as infantry musket fire. The Austrian Prinz Wenzel Liechtenstein calculated that light field pieces might fire 100 rounds in 24 hours. One gun was recorded as having fired 1070 rounds over 17 consecutive days, but suffered bore erosion of 2mm. The other negative effects of prolonged firing were that the barrel would droop and the touch-hole would become enlarged, thus reducing the accuracy and effective range of the weapon.

Moving guns once they were on the battlefield was done by manpower. When the gun closed up to the action, the horse team would be unhitched and held in a sheltered position and the piece would be moved across country by the crew (and one horse) using bandolier-style leather belts with drag-ropes attached, and by poles placed through rings on the trail cheeks. Some claim that the famous French artillerist Gribeauval invented this device (which he called the 'bricole'), but evidence exists to show that the Austrians, amongst others, were using them long before the date claimed for Gribeauval.

The race was on to simplify and lighten the guns, in order to make their destructive power more readily available to commanders in the field. Considerable improvements were made to the composition of the metal of the barrels, so that less metal had to be used for the same calibre barrel. Improvements in the composition of gunpowder and experimentation with reducing the charges used, resulted in better ballistic performance, allowing the barrels to be lightened again. Better engineering techniques meant reduced 'windage' between the projectile and the inside of the barrel, giving improved range and accuracy. The elaborate heraldic decoration, which traditionally covered gun barrels was stripped away; functionality replaced appearance as the top priority. A virtuous circle of design had been established.

As barrels were lightened, the carriages could also be made lighter, the mobility of the piece improved and the teams of horses, used to pull the guns could be reduced. As the guns became more mobile, so to did the ammunition, crews, forges, spare gun carriages and equipment. Prince Wenzel Liechtenstein and his team re-designed and standardised Austria's field artillery material in 1751; it was the best on the field during the Seven Years War. In 1753, the Liechtenstein field artillery system replaced the existing guns of the 1716 design, which used the same pieces for fortress and field operations. After years of experimentation, Liechtenstein's design team came up with a family of three groups of relatively lightweight guns. He also introduced the screw-driven wedge sight alignment device. Austrian gun carriages of the Liechtenstein system were much lighter than previous models, the cheeks of the trails having been reduced to one calibre thickness and reinforced with iron bands. On heavy guns, a second trunnion position was incorporated on top of the cheeks, behind the firing-position trunnion sites, into which the barrel was moved for road transport. This placed the centre of gravity of the piece more in the centre of the gun/limber combination. The quadrant, heretofore used to establish elevation angle, was replaced by a graduated scale on the elevation device. Uniformity of design and manufacture were emphasised, thus increasing inter-changeability of components from various arsenals. Wheels for all field guns and the 7-pound howitzer were standardised at 50 inches diameter, with rims 2.25 inches wide. The same wheels were used on the rear of the ammunition carts. The French artilleryman Gribeauval never achieved such standardisation in his well-known 'system'; he had over 20 different wheel designs.

The Austrian gun limber was merely a two-wheeled axle, with a vertical spike projecting upwards, onto which a hole in the lower end of the gun-trails fitted. These, and the front axles of the ammunition carts, used wheels 36 inches in diameter. All axles were of wood, with a diameter of 4.25 inches, the ends fitting into the hubs of the wheels with brass bushes to reduce wear. A small wooden box (Lafettentrüchel), containing the first line supply of ammunition, was fitted onto the cheeks of the trail.

The ammunition wagons of this Austrian system had four wheels and the bodies were made of wicker-work, with a waterproof oilskin cover, to reduce their weight as much as possible. All items of a gun and supporting vehicles were branded with the same serial number, to aid accounting procedures. The guns and vehicles were painted in dark yellow, with black ironwork, to protect them against the weather.

Liechtenstein's Artillery Pieces

These included the light 1-pounder *amusettes* to be used as regimental guns for the *Grenzer* (aka Croats) infantry regiments and the 3-pounder, standard regimental guns for the line infantry. Field artillery included 6- and light 12-pounder cannon, whose barrels measured 16 calibres in length, and the 7-pound howitzers. Then there were the 'Battery Pieces' (long and short-barrelled guns): 12-, 18- and 24-pounder pieces. Heavy mortars: 10-, 30-, 60- and 100-pound mortars firing iron shot and a 100-pound, stone-throwing piece.

Gun	Barrel Weight	Range in Paces		
		Effective	Maximum	Canister
3-pounder gun	240kg	500	1600	400
6-pounder gun	414kg	600	2000	500
12-pounder gun	812kg	800	2300	700
7-pounder howitzer	280kg	1800–2000		600–700

Horse Artillery

In 1729 the Russians had equipped their dragoon regiments with two light, mobile cannon and associated vehicles, for their use when fighting on foot. The crews of these guns were mounted, as opposed to marching on foot. When Fredrick II of Prussia saw this equipment, he at once recognised its mobility as being of tactical importance and lost no time in introducing similar items in his army. A battery of these guns was captured by the Austrians at Maxen on 20 November 1759 by Field Marshal Leopold Graf von Daun, and the concept was brought to the Austrian Army. Within weeks, a battery of twelve 3-pounder cannon, together with the teams and crews, had been assembled.

These light, regimental or battalion guns were under the tactical control of their battalion commanders, which meant that most of the fire from the artillery pieces on the battlefield was dispersed along the line of battle, was of relatively limited effective range (below 500m) and could not be concentrated or controlled in the optimum manner by the army commander. The tactical use of these light regimental guns was explained in the *Schwäbischen Dienstvorschriften* (Swabian Service Regulations), or '*Reglement für die Truppen von den Fürsten und den Städten des schwäbischen Kreises*', confirmed by the Schwäbischen Kreiskonvention in 1795. As the enemy came into cannon range, the guns (which were now deployed about 200m ahead of their own infantry line) were to start firing at a slow rate. When the enemy had closed to 300 paces, the guns were to fall back into the intervals (between the battalions) and the enemy were to be kept under continuous fire of grape, the guns ensuring that they did not hinder the musket fire of the infantry, which by now would have begun. The reserve artillery would meanwhile have opened up on the enemy's main body, the infantry not advancing too quickly, so as not to obscure the target.

Apart from these light guns, there were the heavier-calibre pieces, the 6-, 8-, 12- and 24-pounder cannon and the howitzers and mortars, which were concentrated into the 'reserve artillery' under command of the army commander. Ideally, it was to be sited to a flank, so that their fire would strike the enemy line at an acute angle, to cause more damage than if fired from directly in front. If the artillery could be posted to the flank of the enemy line, it could rake it with most destructive 'enfilading fire'.

Some army commanders had already realised the advantages of concentrating several heavy guns into a 'battery' and directing their fire to optimal effect; Frederick the Great did this to great effect in his victory at Rossbach on 5 November 1757. It was, however, not until the era of Napoleon that massed batteries of guns would become the battlefield norm.

In 1747, Colonel Müller of the Royal Artillery had enumerated the equipment and train of artillery accompanying the British Army as including the following vehicles. The list is of interest, as it shows the immense size of the caravan involved. The columns of vehicles must have clogged the rear areas, consumed vast amounts of fodder and slowed the marches of all the armies during the Seven Years War.

Equipment	Number	Number of Horses	Total Horses
Kettle drum wagon	1	4	4
Tumbrils	2	2	4
12-pdr guns	6	15	90
9-pdr guns	6	11	66
6-pdr guns	14	7	98
3-pdr guns	26	4	104
Ammunition carts	20	3	60
Field forges	2	2	4
Pontoon wagons	30	7	210
Spare pontoon wagons	3	7	21
Spare 12-pdr gun carriages	1	7	7
Spare 9-pdr gun carriages	1	5	5
Spare 6-pdr gun carriages	2	5	10
Spare 3-pdr gun carriages	4	3	12
Spare 12-pdr limbers	3	2	6
Spare 9-pdr limbers	3	2	6
Spare 6-pdr limbers	2	1	2
Spare 3-pdr limbers	3	1	3
Spare horses	–	20	20
Colonel's baggage wagons	3	3	10 (sic)
Comptroller's baggage wagons	3	3	11 (sic)
Major's baggage wagons	2	3	7 (sic)
Captains' baggage wagons	4	4	16
Captain-lieutenants' (5) baggage wagons	5	3	15

Lieutenants and colonel's clerk (16) baggage wagons	6	3	18
Quartermaster's baggage wagons	1	3	3
Surgeon's baggage wagons	1	3	3
Paymaster's baggage wagons	1	3	3
Assistant paymaster and surgeon's mate baggage wagons	1	3	3
Chaplain and comptroller's clerk baggage wagons	1	3	3
Commissary and wagon master baggage wagons	1	4	4
Assistants (2) baggage wagons	1	3	3
Commissaries of stores (2) baggage wagons	2	3	6
Officers of 5 companies baggage wagons	5	3	15
Contractors and artificers baggage wagons	6	3	18
Army artillery flag wagon	1	3	3
Guard picket and provost store wagon	1	3	3
12-pdr guns stores wagons	9	3	27
9-pdr guns stores wagons	7	3	21
6-pdr guns stores wagons	12	3	36
3-pdr guns stores wagons	10	3	30
40 rounds for howitzer and petards store wagon	4	3	12
90 rounds Royal stores wagons	2	3	6
Ammuntion for 35,000 men stores wagons	122	3	360
Entrenching tools store wagons	24	3	72
Laboratory stores wagon	1	3	3
Gun wagon	1	3	3
Small stores and artificers' tools	20	3	60
Spare wagons	10	3	30
Total	**414**	**–**	**1509**

3

NAVAL WARFARE

Artillery

All the characteristics of naval cannon were as for land artillery. Ships' guns could be heavier than those used in field artillery, as the pieces were static within the vessel. Apart from shot and shell, the projectiles fired from naval guns included bar shot and chain shot, designed to cause maximum damage to the rigging of enemy ships. The heaviest naval guns were mounted on the lower gun deck, so as not to compromise the stability of the ship.

During the Seven Years War the importance of naval supremacy to the European colonial powers became clear. Following her victory at the Battle of Quiberon Bay on 20 November 1759, Britain had designed and implemented a blockade of French harbours, which practically swept the world's seas clean of French naval shipping. This ruined France's trade and economy, leading to her defeat in 1763, sealed at the Treaty of Paris and Peace of St Hubertusberg.

Whilst St Hubertusberg regulated the future of Franco-Prussian relationships, the Treaty of Paris was of global dimensions, ending what is sometimes seen as the first world war. It was signed by Britain on the one side, with France and Spain on the other, with Portugal on the sidelines. This treaty ushered in the long period of British dominance of global affairs. Whilst she agreed to return most of the colonies that she had captured to their former owners, she kept several key territories. In the far east, Britain asserted her dominance in India. In the New World she retained all of French Canada and her territories east of the Mississippi river. The islands of St Vincent, Dominico, Tobago, Grenada and the Grenadines also went to Britain. Of the old French colonies that had been taken, France recovered Guadaloupe, Martinique, Mariagalante, Desrade and St Lucia. Spain ceded Florida, St Augustin, Pensacola and all lands to the east and southeast of the Mississippi to Britain in exchange for Cuba, and she gained Louisiana from France. Britain was allowed to maintain a forestry undertaking in Honduras.

Rating System of Warships

Jean-Baptiste Colbert (1619–1683) was considered to be the father of the French Navy; he worked under King Louis XIV (the Sun King) and as well as introducing the notorious French practice of sending convicted criminals to the galleys, introduced the system of grading warships according to the number and weight of their cannon, details of which are shown below. Ships in the three largest categories were classed as 'Ships-of-the-Line', powerful enough to take a place in the line of battle, the conventional naval fighting formation. The number of carronades (short-barrelled, large calibre cannon, introduced into the Royal Navy in the 1770s) carried was not considered in this classification.

Ships in the 1st – 6th rates were commanded by post captains, minor rated vessels were commanded by commanders, and unrated ships were commanded by lieutenants or midshipmen according to size.

Rate	Guns Carried	Crew
1st	100 and more	850–875★
2nd	84–99	700–750
3rd	70–83	500–650
4th	50–69	320–420
5th	32–49	200–300
6th	18–31	140–200
Unrated vessels, sloops, brigs, cutters	6–17	5–25

★This number was increased by 20 when the ship was used as an admiral's flagship, 20 for a vice admiral and 15 for a rear admiral.

Apart from the crew of sailors, who manned and sailed the vessel and its artillery, there was also a complement of marines or sea-going soldiers on the larger ships. The first marines were raised for the Spanish Navy in 1537 by King Charles I of Spain, who was also Charles V, the Holy Roman Emperor. They provided armed protection for landing parties, as well as fire support in close range, ship-to-ship combats. Many line infantry regiments of the major maritime powers were sent to serve as marines during times of war.

HMS *Victory's* guns (1805)	
Forecastle	two 13-pounder cannon
	quarter deck – twelve 12-pounder cannon and six 18-pounder carronades
Upper gun deck	30 12-pounders
Middle gun deck	28 24-pounders
Lower gun deck	30 32-pounders

Typical French 110-gun ship	
Forecastle	four 8-pounder cannon
	quarter deck – twelve 8-pounder cannon and four 36-pounder carronades
Upper gun deck	32 12-pounders
Middle gun deck	32 12-pounders
Lower gun deck	30 36-pounders

Navigation

Sailors of the time were without the benefits of satellite navigation and radio beacons; they had to place their faith in the accuracy of the available marine charts and their knowledge of astronomy, winds and currents. Armed with this data it was theoretically possible to plot one's course. The tools needed were the requisite marine charts, accurate chronometers, the compass, the sextant, declinational tables and astrological charts. The information contained in these documents was treated as highly classified. The compass had been in use for thousands of years and Englishman John Hadley had produced a sextant in 1731. Marine charts had been accumulated after many years of daring exploration by navigators, the latest and best known of whom was Britain's Captain Cook (1728–1779). With these tools, it was possible to establish one's latitude and longitude every day at midday. Thus the effects of unknown currents and winds could be measured and compensated for.

Calculating the speed of the ship was done by dropping a piece of wood off the stem and measuring the time it took to reach a point at the stern. It could also be done by dropping a buoy on a string off the stern and counting how many knots passed over the stern of the ship in a certain time. These methods would give the ship's speed in 'knots' or nautical miles, each of which was 6080 feet.

By dropping a lead weight on a line off the bows, it was possible to tell if the water was getting shallow, as the line was marked off by pieces of coloured cloth to show the depth in fathoms (six feet). As the bottom of the weight was greased, it picked up a sample of the sea bottom and could be used to find good anchorages.

4

THE AUSTRIAN EMPIRE

In 1756 Austria was the controlling power of the Holy Roman Empire, which was made up of many countries and smaller states, bishoprics and principalities. The states were organised into the geographical areas known as the '*Kreise*', which supplied arms or money in times of war. The details of these military units are discussed in Chapter 5. Austria had no guards which took the field; they were only palace security troops and are not considered here.

Infantry

The infantry of the Austrian Empire fell into two classes: German and Hungarian. The organisation was the same for both, but they differed in their uniforms quite dramatically. From 1748, each line regiment consisted of sixteen fusilier companies in four battalions, and two grenadier companies. The two grenadier companies operated away from their parent regiments, combined with two other grenadier companies into elite battalions. These elite battalions had, as yet, no permanent nature; it was not until 1769 that this step was taken.

German Uniforms

All coats, waistcoats, breeches and belts were white unless otherwise stated. Fusiliers wore tricorns, edged and laced in white and with a regimental button. A sprig of oak or pine leaves was worn in the hat in the field. Grenadiers wore bearskins with a small brass front plate and a bag in the facing colour, tassel in the button colour. Packs were of calfskin. The black leather cartridge case had a small brass plate bearing the crowned initials 'MT'. The off-white coat had no collar and an off-white shoulder strap on the left shoulder only. It was double-breasted and the lapels were turned back to show the facings, which were also worn on the plain, round cuffs. The turnbacks of the coat were in the facing colour in 1756, but in the coat colour by 1762. Long white gaiters were worn in summer, black ones in winter. Only grenadiers wore moustaches, and hair had to be powdered, curled and plaited into a pigtail, a detested daily ritual that lasted until the Napoleonic era.

Officers' uniforms were of finer cloth and cut than those of the men; they wore gold lace trim to their tricorns, and green and white cockades. They had no shoulder strap to the coat and wore yellow and black waist sashes under their coats, the skirts of which were not turned back; they also had gold and black sword knots.

Officers of German infantry, 1740–1767. To the right is a grenadier. (Rudolf von Ottenfeld)

There was a rudimentary system of rank badges, shown by an officer's cane: colonels had a Malacca cane with a gold knob and cord with tassel; lieutenant-colonels had a cane with a large silver knob; majors had cane with a small silver knob; captains had cane with a bone knob; lieutenants and second-lieutenants had simple canes. Musketeer company officers also carried spontoons, grenadier company officers carried short-barrelled muskets in the field. Sergeants carried canes and halberds, corporals had hazelnut sticks; they both had yellow and black sabre straps. Drummers wore swallows' nests in the facing colour, and their drums were brass, with a black double eagle on a yellow ground; the rims were painted, usually in red, white, black and yellow flames.

Hungarian Uniforms

Hungarian regiments wore a much more colourful uniform in 1756 than their German colleagues. This costume was in transition, becoming simpler and more regularised as the years went on. There is much that we do not know about the development and the details. In 1745 they wore black mirlitons or winged caps, and the coat was decorated with coloured lace and tassels. The lace later became reduced to the *Bärentatzen* (bear's claws) worn on the pointed cuff. Instead of the white breeches and long gaiters, they wore ankle-length coloured breeches and short boots to just above the ankle. Their waistcoats were also in a variety of colours, usually matching their breeches, and they wore hussar-style barrel sashes. By 1762 all the coats were white, the mirlitons had been replaced by the tricorn and the amount of lace worn had been much reduced.

Austrian border infantry. Left to right: Bannalist and a Pandur of von Trenck's Freikorps. (David Morier (403392) from the Royal Collection)

Colours

There is much that we do not know about the colours and standards carried by the Austrian Army in the Seven Years War. When Maria Theresa became empress in October 1740, the state finances were in such a bad way that new colours and standards became the victims of cutbacks. Old pattern items, with the cipher of Maria Theresa's predecessor Carl VI, were carried for years afterwards.

Many battalion (or 'ordinary') colours were decorated in the regimental Inhaber's (colonel-in-chief's) own crests, ciphers and heraldic designs and many older pattern colours were carried in 1756. The colours of the newly-raised regiments were in grass green as ordered on 19 October 1743. This was when Austria lost the crown of the Holy Roman Empire, only to regain it in December 1745. These grass green colours had green and white flamed edges. The Hungarian regiments raised in 1741 (2, 31, 32, 33, 37 and 52) were ordered to carry red ordinary colours instead of yellow.

The first company of the 1st battalion of a regiment carried a white '*Leibfahne*' or sovereign's colour, bearing the imperial coat of arms on one side and the blessed virgin on the other. All other companies bore (theoretically) yellow '*Ordinair-fahnen*', with the double eagle on both sides. We know, however, that in Carl VI's reign, yellow, green, red or red-white-red colours were carried. These bore the cipher 'CVI'.

On the obverse of the new Ordinair-fahnen were the arms of Lothringen/Toscana, with the initials 'MT'. On the reverse were the arms of Hungary and Bohemia, with the initials 'FC' (Franciscus Corregens) and 'IM' (Imperator). The gilt finials were engraved to show the double eagle or the imperial cipher. Cords and cravats decorated the finials. Colour bearers' bandoliers were in the facing colour, decorated in the button colour.

A numbering system for infantry regiments was introduced in 1769; it is used in the list below, and the regiments are named for their Inhaber in 1756. These often changed during the war, and later Inhabers are also listed. The regiments of Austrian infantry were recruited from different areas of the empire. That ethnic flavour is indicated by a two-letter code. For uniform purposes, Germany includes BO, FR, GA, KA, KR, MS, NO, OO, ST, TY, VL and WL. The colours listed after the raising date are those of the facings and the buttons.

BO	Bohemia
FR	Friaul (north western Italy)
GA	Galicia
GE	Germany
GR	Grenz-Regimenter (regiments raised in the military border areas, mainly Croatia)
IT	central northern Italy
HU	Hungary
KA	Karinthia (southern Austria)
KR	Krain (Carniola)
MS	Moravia/Silesia
NO	Lower Austria
OO	Upper Austria
SB	Siebenburgen (Romania)
SL	Slavonia
ST	Steyermark
TY	Tyrol
VL	western Austria
WL	Walloon (Belgium)

Hungarian infantry, 1745–1768. (Rudolf von Ottenfeld)

Hungarian infantry regiments. Left to right: private of Kökényesdi Nr 34; officer of Ujvàry Nr 2; officer of Trenck's Pandurs Nr 53; private of Trenck's Pandurs; officer of Josef Esterhàzy Nr 37. Until 1743 all 'Hayduk' (Hungarian) infantry regiments wore their colourful national costume, with the well-known hussar flavour. In that year, the tunic, as worn by German regiments, was introduced. (Knötel, XI, 2)

Fusilier and grenadier of the mercenary unit Batallion Anhalt-Zerbst in imperial service, 1761. This unit was one of the many fragmentary contributions made to Austria's imperial war effort. The plate is based on a contemporary recruiting poster, preserved in the German Museum in Nuremberg. In 1798 the battalion became the 11th (Austrian) Light Infantry Battalion; the cavalry went into what later became the 12th Dragoons. (Knötel, XII 4)

Infanterie-Regiment Kaiser Nr 1
Raised in 1715. Pompadour, yellow. (GE MS).

Infanterie-Regiment Erzherzog Carl Nr 2
Raised in 1741. 1761 Erzherzog Carl. In 1745 they wore a dark blue dolman and breeches, with officers wearing white pelisses, black and yellow barrel sashes. In 1762 the coat was white with yellow facings, the dark blue waistcoat and breeches were laced yellow with yellow buttons and the barrel sash was yellow and white. They wore a dark blue sabretasche, with yellow, scalloped edging and an eagle. (HU)

Infanterie-Regiment Carl Lothringen Nr 3
Raised in 1715. Sky blue, white. (GE NO)

Infanterie-Regiment Deutschmeister Nr 4
Raised before 1683. Sky blue, yellow. (GE NO)

Infanterie-Regiment Nr 5
Raised in 1764. Disbanded in 1808. Garrison infantry regiment; no Inhaber and did not take the field. Dark blue, white. (GE GA)

Infanterie-Regiment Nr 6
Raised in 1795. Disbanded in 1808. Garrison infantry regiment; no Inhaber and did not take the field. Black, white. (GE WL)

Infanterie-Regiment Neipperg Nr 7
Raised in 1691. Dark brown, white. (GE MS)

Infanterie-Regiment Hildburghausen Nr 8
Raised in 1642. Poppy red, yellow. (GE MS)

Infanterie-Regiment Los Rios Nr 9
Raised in 1725. Apple green, yellow. (GE WL)

Infanterie-Regiment Jung- Wolfenbüttel Nr 10
Raised in 1710. Poplar green, white. (GE BO)

Infanterie-Regiment Wallis Nr 11
Raised in 1673. Pink, white. (GE BO)

Infanterie-Regiment Botta Nr 12
Raised in 1702. Dark brown, yellow. (GE MS)

Infanterie-Regiment Moltke Nr 13
Raised in 1664. Grass green, yellow. (GE FR)

Infanterie-Regiment Salm Nr 14
Raised in 1733. Black, yellow. (GE OO)

Infanterie-Regiment Pallavicini Nr 15
Raised in 1701. Madder red, yellow. (GE BO)

Infanterie-Regiment Königsegg Nr 16
Raised in 1703. Violet, yellow. (GE ST)

Infanterie-Regiment Kollowrat Nr 17
Raised in 1676. Light brown, yellow. (GE BO)

Infanterie-Regiment Marschall Nr 18
Raised in 1628. (GE BO)

Infanterie-Regiment Leopold Pálffy Nr 19
Raised in 1734. Sky blue, yellow. (HU)

Infanterie-Regiment Alt-Colloredo Nr 20
Raised in 1683. Lobster red, white. (GE MS)

Infanterie-Regiment Arenberg Nr 21
Raised in 1735. Sea green, yellow. (GE BO)

Infanterie-Regiment Hagenbash Nr 22
Raised in 1709. 1757 Salomon Sprecher; 1758 Franz Moritz Lascy. Emperor yellow, white. (GE MS)

Infanterie-Regiment Baden-Baden Nr 23
Raised in 1673. Disbanded in 1809; re-raised in 1814. 1707 Margrave Ludwig George Simpert von Baaden-Baaden; 1761 Margrave August Georg Simpert von Baaden-Baaden. Poppy red, yellow. GE NO)

Infanterie-Regiment Starhemberg Nr 24
Raised in 1652. Dark blue, white. (GE NO)

Infanterie-Regiment Piccolomini Nr 25
Raised in 1673. 1757 Franz Ludwig Thürheim. Sea green, white. (GE BO)

Infanterie-Regiment Puebla Nr 26
Raised in 1717. Poplar green, yellow. (GE KA)

Infanterie-Regiment Baden-Durlach Nr 27
Raised in 1682. (GE ST)

Infanterie-Regiment Wied Nr 28
Raised in 1698. Grass green, white. (GE BO)

Infanterie-Regiment Alt- Wolfenbüttel Nr 29
Raised in 1704. 1760 Infanterie-Regiment Laudon. (GE MS)

Infanterie-Regiment Sachsen-Gotha Nr 30
Raised in 1725. Pike grey, yellow. (GE WA)

Infanterie-Regiment Haller Nr 31
Raised in 1741. In 1762 they wore white coats, sky blue facings, lace, waistcoat (laced red) and breeches, red and sky blue barrel sash. This later became emperor yellow facings, white buttons. (HU SB)

Infanterie-Regiment Forgách Nr 32
Raised in 1741. Sky blue, yellow. (HU)

Infanterie-Regiment Nikolaus Esterházy Nr 33
Raised in 1741. Dark blue, white. (HU)

Infanterie-Regiment Batthyányi Nr 34
Raised in 1733. In 1745 it wore a dark blue jacket, waistcoat and breeches, yellow facings, buttons and lace, red and yellow barrel sash. By 1762 the coat was white with yellow laces and tassels, the waistcoat and breeches were dark blue with yellow lace. (HU)

Infanterie-Regiment Waldeck Nr 35
Raised in 1682. Lobster red, yellow. (GE BO)

Infanterie-Regiment Browne Nr 36
Raised in 1660. 1756 Ulysses Browne; 1757 Joseph Browne; 1761 Ulrich Kinsky. Light purple, white. (GE BO)

Infanterie-Regiment Joseph Esterházy Nr 37
Raised in 1741. 1762 Joseph Siskovics. White jacket, poppy red facings, lace, tassels, waistcoat and breeches, yellow buttons, green and white barrel sashes. (HU)

Infanterie-Regiment de Ligne Nr 38
Raised in 1713. Disbanded in 1809; re-raised in 1815. Pink, yellow. (GE WA)

Infanterie-Regiment Johann Pálffy Nr 39
Raised in 1756. 1758 Joseph Preysach. Poppy red, white. (HU)

Infanterie-Regiment Jung-Colloredo Nr 40
Raised in 1733. Crimson, white. (GE MA)

Infanterie-Regiment Bayreuth Nr 41
Raised in 1701. Sulphur yellow, white. (GE VL)

Infanterie-Regiment Gaisruck Nr 42
Raised in 1685. Orange, white. (GE BO)

Infanterie-Regiment Platz Nr 43
Raised in 1718. Disbanded in 1809; re-raised in 1814. Sulphur yellow, yellow. (GE KR)

Infanterie-Regiment Clerici Nr 44
Raised in 1744. Madder red, white. (IT)

Infanterie-Regiment Heinrich Daun Nr 45
Raised in 1661. Disbanded in 1809; re-raised in 1814. 1761 O'Kelly. Crimson, yellow. (GE ST)

Infanterie-Regiment Macquire Nr 46
Raised in 1745. Disbanded in 1809. Dark blue, yellow. (GE TY)

Infanterie-Regiment Harrach Nr 47
Raised in 1682. Steel green, yellow. (GE BO)

Infanterie-Regiment Luzan Nr 48
Raised in 1721. Disbanded in 1796; re-raised in 1798. Light brown, yellow. (IT)

Infanterie-Regiment Kheul Nr 49
Raised in 1715. 1758 Johann Ludwig Angern. Pike grey, white. (GE NO)

Infanterie-Regiment Harsch Nr 50
Raised in 1647. Violet, white. (GE OO)

Infanterie-Regiment Gyulay Nr 51
Raised in 1702. 1759 Franz Guilay. In 1745 they wore dark blue facings, waistcoat and breeches, yellow lace, yellow and white barrel sash. By 1762 the coat was white with red lace and tassels, facings, waistcoat and breeches were dark blue, the latter two laced with red and the barrel sash was dark blue and red. (HU SB)

Infanterie-Regiment Bethlen Nr 52
Raised in 1741. Pompadour, yellow. (HU)

Infanterie-Regiment Simbschen Nr 53
Raised in 1756. In 1745 they wore dark green coats, faced and laced red, yellow buttons. Bright red waistcoat and breeches laced dark green, dark green and red barrel sash. By 1762 it was a white coat with bright red facings, waistcoat and breeches, yellow lace and buttons, yellow and white barrel sash. (HU SL)

Infanterie-Regiment Sincère Nr 54
Raised in 1659. Apple green, white. (GE BO)

Infanterie-Regiment d'Arberg Nr 55
Raised in 1742. Light purple, yellow. (GE WA)

Infanterie-Regiment Mercy-Argenteau Nr 56
Raised in 1684. Steel green, yellow. (GE MA)

Infanterie-Regiment Andlau Nr 57
Raised in 1688. Violet grey, yellow. (GE BO)

Infanterie-Regiment Vierzet Nr 58
Raised in 1763. Black, white. (GE WA)

Infanterie-Regiment Leopold Daun Nr 59
Raised in 1682. Orange, yellow. (GE OO)

Border Infantry Regiments
These 'Grenz-Infanterie-Regimenter' were raised from amongst the settlers in the areas that bordered the Turkish (Ottoman) Empire. This area ran along the southern banks of the Danube, across the Theiss river (now the Tisa) which joins the Danube at Belgrade, and eastwards into the Banat (now Romania). It also extended along the Adriatic coast to include Croatia and Dalmatia. These regiments

Austria-Hungary border infantry regiments, 1762. Left to right: (foreground, white breeches) St Georger; (mid-ground, light blue breeches and dolman) Szluiner; (background, brown coat) Brooder; (foreground, white with dark green facings) Creutzer; (background, red dolman) Ottochaner; (background, blue dolman, red cloak) Oguliner; (foreground, red breeches and dolman) Liccaner. (Knötel, IV 43)

had no *Inhaber*. After the Seven Years War, the border infantry regiments were taken out of the line and received their own numbering system. The uniforms of these regiments reflected much of the local colour of the national costume and there was much less uniformity than for the line infantry. Many details of the colour, cut and style of these uniforms changed in the period 1756–1763; simplification and regulation was gradually imposed and it is impossible to be clear as to what was actually the status of their dress during the conflict. They wore black, peakless shakos, sometimes with a black-within-yellow pompon, sometimes with a brass front plate, and Hungarian-style coats, waistcoats, breeches and barrel sashes. They wore red cloaks and carried sabres.

Grenz-Infanterie-Regiment Licaner Nr 60
Raised in 1746. Red coat and breeches, green cuffs and waistcoat, yellow braid.

Grenz-Infanterie-Regiment Ottochaner Nr 61
Raised in 1746. Red coat, light blue cuffs, waistcoat and breeches, yellow braid.

Grenz-Infanterie-Regiment Oguliner Nr 62
Raised in 1746. Blue coat and waistcoat, yellow cuffs and braid, red breeches.

Grenz-Infanterie-Regiment Szluiner Nr 63
Raised in 1746. Light blue coat and breeches, red cuffs and waistcoat, yellow braid.

Grenz-Infanterie-Regiment Creuzer Nr 64
Raised in 1746. White coat, braid and breeches, green cuffs and waistcoat.

Grenz-Infanterie-Regiment St Georger Nr 65
Raised in 1746. Blue-green coat and waistcoat, white cuffs and braid, white breeches.

Grenz-Infanterie-Regiment Brooder Nr 66
Raised in 1756. Dark brown coat with yellow cuffs and lace, light blue waistcoat and breeches.

Grenz-Infanterie-Regiment Gradiscaner Nr 67
Raised in 1756. Facings purple grey, white buttons and lace.

Grenz-Infanterie-Regiment Peterwardeiner Nr 68
Raised in 1756. Facings pike grey, yellow buttons and lace.

Grenz-Infanterie-Regiment 1st Ansiedler Nr 69
Raised in 1746. Facings crimson, buttons and lace yellow.

Grenz-Infanterie-Regiment 2nd Ansiedler Nr 70
Raised in 1746. Facings crimson, white buttons and lace.

Infanterie-Regiment Rot-Würzburg (Imperial Regiment)
Austrian-style uniforms; white hate edging, red facings yellow buttons.

Feldjäger
Raised only in time of war, initially in 1760. Pike grey coats, grass green facings, yellow buttons.

Invaliden-Corps
White coats, lobster red facings, white buttons.

Cavalry

From 1769 to 1798, all mounted regiments of the Austrian Army shared a common numbering system. There were frequent, repetitive changes of role and titles. For ease of comprehension, the regiments are grouped according to type (kürassiers, dragoons, hussars) in order of seniority within that group.

Kürassiers
In 1756 each kürassier regiment had six squadrons, each of two companies, and an elite company of carabiniers, armed with rifled carbines. During the Seven Years War, the carabiniers were increased to a squadron. When in the field, these carabinier companies were detached from their parent regiments and combined with those of other regiments, to form elite units. After the war, they were reduced to the pre-war level of a company. In 1768 the carabinier companies of the kürassier regiments and the grenadier companies of the dragoon regiments were concentrated into two carabinier regiments.

The kürassier uniform coat was off white, with poppy red facings; the shoulder strap (on the right shoulder only) was off-white, edged red, and the turnbacks were red. Regiments were differentiated by their buttons, waistcoats, breeches and by the edging to their red shabraque and holster covers. A black cuirass was worn; on the breastplate of field officers there was a gilt keel down the centre, to the waistline. Those of junior officers had a smaller keel, reaching only half way down.

From 1751 each cavalry squadron bore a rectangular standard, fringed in the button colour; the senior (*Leibkompanie*) bore a *Leibestandarte* with a white field, the imperial arms on one side and the virgin within a baroque cartouche on the other. The other squadrons had (since 1745) *Ordinairestandarten*, with fields in the facing colour and the imperial arms on one face, various crests

Troopers of various kürassier regiments, 1762. Left to right: De Ville; Anhalt-Zerbst Nr 25; Brettlach Nr 29 (standing); Trauttmannsdorf Nr 21 (seated); Stampach Nr 10. To the right is a mounted kürassier of an unspecified regiment. (Knötel, V 30)

and heraldic beasts on the other. The gilt finials were pierced to show the double eagle or the imperial cipher. Cords and cravats decorated the finials. Standard bearers' bandoliers were in the facing colour, edged and fringed in the button colour.

Apart from the elaborate and costly standards, each regiment had its equally decorative trumpet banners and kettle drum aprons, complete with heraldic embroidery, fringes and tassels.

The regiments below are listed in order of their regimental numbers allocated in 1769, but named for their Inhaber in 1756. Each regiment went through name changes which reflected their changing Inhabers, and these are listed for the period. Many were assigned new numbers/roles in 1798, but fought as kürassiers during the Seven Years War.

Kürassier-Regiment Erzherzog Leopold Nr 3
Raised on 24 October 1685, in the Bishopric of Würzburg. 1750 Erzherzog Leopold; 1798 2nd Dragoons. Disbanded in 1801. Uniform: white coat and waistcoat, red facings and breeches, yellow buttons. Shabraque edging: equal red and white oblongs with red edges.

Kürassier-Regiment Erzherzog Ferdinand Nr 4
Raised on 16 March 1619 by Grand Duke Cosmo of Medici. Taken into Austrian service in 1621. 1756 Erzherzog Ferdinand; 1761 Erzherzog Maximilian; 1798 8th Kürassiers. Uniform: white coat, and waistcoat, red facings and breeches, yellow buttons. Shabraque edging: white with a wavy red central line.

Kürassier-Regiment Emanuel Infant von Portugal Nr 5
Raised on 6 March 1682. 1719 Emanuel, Infant of Portugal; 1798 3rd Dragoons. Uniform: white coat, red facings, red waistcoat and breeches, white buttons. Shabraque edging: white with red edging and red discs along its length.

Kürassier-Regiment von Pálffy Nr 8
Raised in 1679 in Lothringen by Baron Peter Ernst Mercy de Billets. 1734 Carl Paul Graf Pálffy ab Erdod. Disbanded in 1775. Uniform: white coat, waistcoat and buttons, red breeches. Shabraque edging: white with two red stripes.

Kürassier-Regiment von Stampach Nr 10
Raised on 6 February 1682. Carl Baron Kager von Stampach; 1798 5th Kürassiers. Uniform: white coat, red facings and waistcoat, white breeches, yellow buttons. Shabraque edging: red with a double row of white squares.

Kürassier-Regiment de Serbelloni Nr 12
Raised on 2 December 1672 by Baron Wilhelm von Harrant. 1756 Johann Baptist Graf Serbelloni; 1798 12th Kürassiers. Uniform white coat and buttons, poppy red racings, waistcoat and breeches. Shabraque edging: red with narrow white bars across it.

Kürassier-Regiment O'Donell Nr 14
Raised on 28 September 1721. Raised from three Spanish regiments (Cordoba and Vasques Cuirassiers and the Galbes Dragoons) brought to Austria by Kaiser Carl VI. 1756 Caspar Ferdinand Count Cordova; 1756 Carl Claudius Graf O'Donell; 1798 9th Kürassiers. Uniform: white coat and waistcoat, red facings and breeches, yellow buttons. Shabraque edging white with black edging and central zig-zag.

Kürassier-Regiment von Schmerzing Nr 20
Raised on 13 May 1701. Hannibal Baron von Schmerzing; 1798 10th Kürassiers. Uniform: white coat and waistcoat, red facings and breeches, yellow buttons. Shabraque edging: red with white oblongs, each having two red dots along the central axis.

Kürassier-Regiment von Trauttmansdorf Nr 21
Raised in November 1663. Franz Carl Graf Trauttmansdorf; 1798 7th Kürassiers. Uniform: white coat, waistcoat and buttons, red facings and breeches. Shabraque edging: red with two rows of white squares.

Kürassier-Regiment von Kalckreuth Nr 22
Raised in 1657. 1750 Georg Christian Baron Kalckreuth; 1760 Albert Casimir Herzog von Sachsen-Teschen. Disbanded in 1775. Uniform: white coat, red facings and waistcoat, buff breeches. Shabraque edging: red with two white stripes.

Kürassier-Regiment von Birkenfeld Nr 23
Raised in 1636. 1740 Wilhelm Prinz Pfalz-Birkenfeld; 1761 Cajetan Graf Stampa. Disbanded in 1775. Uniform: white coat and waistcoat, red facings and breeches, yellow buttons. Shabraque edging: red with a wide white central stripe and a red 'X' pattern.

Kürassier-Regiment von Anhalt-Zerbst Nr 25
Raised in 1682. 1753 Friedrich August Fürst Anhalt-Zerbst. Disbanded in 1775. Uniform: white coat, buff waistcoat and breeches, red facings, yellow buttons. Shabraque edging: red with a wide, white central band having red discs along it.

Kürassier-Regiment von Löwenstein Nr 27
Raised on 7 March 1682. 1751 Julius Caesar Graf Radicati; 1756 Christian Fürst Löwenstein-Wertheim; 1758 Benedict Graf Daun; 1798 4th Kürassiers. Uniform: white coat and waistcoat, red facings and breeches, yellow buttons. Shabraque edging: red with a ladder pattern of white oblongs.

Kürassier-Regiment von Bretlach Nr 29

Raised on 22 December 1672 as a dragoon regiment until 1798. 1745 Ludwig Karl Freiherr von Bretlach; 1798 2nd Kürassiers. Uniform: white coat and buttons, red facings, buff waistcoat and breeches. Shabraque edging: white with red diamonds.

Kürassier-Regiment von Anspach Nr 33

Raised on 4 May 1702 by the margrave Georg Friedrich von Anspach-Bayreuth. 1751 Markgraf Christian Friedrich von Brandenburg-Anspach und Bayreuth; 1798 11th Kürassiers. Disbanded in 1802. Uniform: white coat, waistcoat and buttons, red facings and breeches. Shabraque edging: white central band with a red ziz-zag pattern, narrow red edges.

The following kürassier regiments were disbanded in 1768, and thus never received numbers, being known only by the names of their various Inhabers.

Kürassier-Regiment de Ville

Raised in 1682 for Hermann Otto Graf Limburg-Styrum. 1751 Carl Ludwig Baron von Gelhay; 1759 Carl Marquis de Ville. Uniform: white coat and waistcoat, red facings and breeches, yellow buttons. Shabraque edging: red with two white stripes.

Kürassier-Regiment von Buccow

Transferred into Austrian service in 1684 as the kürassier regiment of Friedrich August Prinz von Braunschweig-Lüneburg. 1743 Joseph Count Lucchesi d'Abarra; 1757 Adolf Nikolaus Baron von Buccow. Uniform: white coat and buttons, red facings, waistcoat and breeches. Shabraque edging: red edging and red diamonds on a wide white central band.

Kürassier-Regiment Modena

Raised in 1701 from part of the Caprara Kürassiers. 1755 Franz III d'Este Modena. Often designated 'Alt Modena' to differentiate it from the 'Jung Modena' Dragoons. Uniform: white coat, waistcoat and buttons, royal blue facings and breeches. Shabraque: royal blue with royal blue edging having white oblongs along its length.

Dragoons

Each regiment consisted of six squadrons, each of two companies, and a company of horse grenadiers. From 1757, it was ordered that all dragoon regiments were to wear dark blue coats with poppy red lapels, cuffs and turnbacks and brass buttons. Breeches were also to be dark blue. This uniform change was introduced only slowly as clothing wore out and was replaced. Regiments were distinguished by the colour of their waistcoats, breeches, aiguillettes and edging to shabraque and holster covers. During the war, a dragoon regiment consisted of six normal squadrons and a company of horse grenadiers, which was usually detached from its parent regiment and combined, with other such squadrons, into elite regiments. Horse grenadiers wore bearskin caps with small brass plates bearing a grenade, a bag in the facing colour and lace and tassel in the button colour. In 1762 a Siebenburger (Walachisches) Grenz-Dragoner-Regiment (border dragoon regiment) was raised and as quickly disbanded. Moustaches were worn, except by the 31st/14th regiment, to commemorate their bravery as beardless youths in battle early in their career. By 1762, dragoon uniform coats were again white and facings were red for all regiments except Modena, Nr 13, who wore dark blue.

Guidons

From 1751, each squadron bore a swallow-tailed guidon; the *Leibkompanie* bore a white guidon, fringed in the button colour, with the virgin on one side and the imperial crest on the other. The other squadrons had *Ordinairestandarten*, in the facing colour, also fringed in the button colour, the imperial crest on one side and the Inhaber's crest on the other. The gilt finials were pierced to show the double eagle or the imperial cipher. Cords and cravats decorated the finials. Apart from the elaborate and costly standards, each regiment had its equally decorative trumpet banners and kettle drum aprons, complete with embroidery, fringes and tassels. Chevauxleger regiments carried guidons. The regimental numbers in the following list are those allocated in 1769.

Dragoner-Regiment Erzherzog Joseph Nr 1

Raised in 1688 by Gustav Hannibal Graf Löwenschild. 1748 Erzherzog Joseph (Kaiser from 1765); 1798 1st Dragoons. Uniform: dark green coat and waistcoat, red facings, yellow buttons, buff breeches. Shabraque: dark green with red edging, having two white stripes.

Dragoner-Regiment von Liechtenstein Nr 6

Raised on 11 February 1682 by Graf Saurau. 1725 Joseph Wenzel, Fürst Liechtenstein. Disbanded in 1775. Uniform: dark blue coat, waistcoat and breeches, poppy red facings, yellow buttons. Shabraque: dark blue with a red edging with a wide white central stripe.

Dragoner-Regiment von Batthyányi Nr 7

Raised in 1640 by Johann de la Corona. 1731 Carl Joseph Fürst Batthyányi; 1798 12th Dragoons. Uniform: dark blue coat, waistcoat and breeches, red facings, yellow buttons. Shabraque: dark blue with a red edging, having two white stripes.

Dragoner-Regiment Prinz Savoyen Nr 9

Raised on 7 February 1682 by Obrist Graf Küffstein. 1736 Ferdinand Carl Graf Aspremont-Linden; 1798 15th Dragoons. Uniform: red coat, waistcoat and breeches, black facings, yellow buttons. Shabraque: red with a black edging, having a series of white squares with black squares in their centres.

Dragoner-Regiment Jung-Modena Nr 13

Raised in 1706 by the Elector of Mainz, Franz Lothar von Schönborn, and rented out to Austrian service. 16 April 1710 taken into the Austrian Army; 1756 Hercules Erbprinz von Modena (Jung Modena); 1798 5th Dragoons. Uniform: red coat, light blue waistcoat, breeches, and facings, white buttons. Shabraque: red, with a light blue edging, having a white ladder pattern along it.

Dragoner-Regiment Jung-Löwenstein Nr 18

Raised in 1725. 1757 Graf Daun; 1 February 1758 Philipp Fürst von Löwenstein-Wertheim (who was Inhaber until 1781 as a chevauxleger regiment); 1759 Josef Graf St Ignon; 1798 4th Dragoons. Uniform: dark green coat with red facings, waistcoat and breeches and yellow buttons. Shabraque: red, with a white edging, having dark green edges and a row of dark green diamonds along its length.

Dragoner-Regiment Hessen-Darmstadt Nr 19

Raised on 4 November 1733 by Graf Alexander d'Ollone. 1746 Ludwig Landgraf Hessen-Darmstadt; 1798 14th Dragoons. Uniform: red coat, light green facings, yellow buttons, buff waistcoat and breeches, the former edged light green. Shabraque: red, with a tricolour; edging: light green, white, yellow, from the outer edge inwards.

Dragoner-Regiment Sachsen-Gotha Nr 28

Raised on 29 January 1718 by Friedrich Wilhelm Landgraf von Brandenburg-Anspach. 1726 Johann August Prinz von Sachsen-Gotha; 1798 10th Dragoons. Uniform: red coat, light blue facings and waistcoat, yellow buttons, buff breeches. Shabraque: red, with a light blue edging, with a white central band, having alternate light blue oblongs and discs along it.

Dragoner-Regiment de Ligne Nr 31

Raised 1 May 1725. 1732 Ferdinand Prinz de Ligne; 1757 Benedict Graf Daun; 1758 Christian Philipp Fürst zu Löwenstein-Wertheim; 1759 Joseph Graf St Ignon; 1798 11th Dragoons. Uniform: from 1732 they wore dark green coats, red facings and waistcoat, yellow buttons, buff breeches. In 1757 they were ordered to change to blue coats, waistcoats with red facings, but this was not executed. This regiment did not wear moustaches. Shabraque dark green, with red edging, having twin rows of white squares along it.

Dragoner-Regiment von Kolowrat-Krakowski Nr 37

Raised 15 March 1683. 1753 Emanuel Graf Kolowrat-Krakowski; 1798 6th Dragoons. Disbanded in 1802. Uniform: dark blue coat, red facings, waistcoat and breeches, white buttons. Shabraque: dark blue, having a red edging with two white stripes along it. On 25 June 1760, in the Battle of Landshut, this regiment captured the silver kettle drums of the Prussian 8th Dragoons (Alt Platen).

Dragoner-Regiment von Württemberg Nr 38

Raised 20 December 1688, by General Donat Heissler. 1740 Carl Eugen Herzog Württemberg; 1798 8th Dragoons. Uniform: red coat, buff waistcoat and breeches, black facings, yellow buttons. Shabraque: red, with a white edging, having narrow black sides and black discs along it.

Dragoner-Regiment von Porporatti Nr 39

Raised in 1701, by the Landgraf Christian Ernst von Brandenburg-Bayreuth. 1753 August Graf von Porporatti (killed at Reichenberg, 1757); 1758 Friedrich Pfalzgraf Zweybrücken-Birkenfeld; 1760 converted to a chevauxleger regiment; 1798 7th Dragoons. Uniform: dark blue coat and waistcoat, red facings, yellow buttons, buff breeches, Shabraque: dark blue with a white edging, having red outer edges and red diamonds along the centre.

Trooper, Austrian Husaren-Regiment Kálnoky, 1750. (David Morier (406850) from the Royal Collection)

The following regiment was disbanded in 1768, and thus never received a number.

Dragoner-Regiment Koháry

Raised 4 November 1733 by Graf Koháry, who was also the Inhaber until 1758. 1758 Michael Graf Althann. Uniform: white coat, waistcoat and breeches, yellow buttons. Shabraque: red, with a red edging having two white stripes.

Chevauxlegers

The first chevauxleger (light cavalry) regiment was raised in 1758 as part of Dragoner-Regiment Löwenstein-Wertheim. In early 1760, five more dragoon regiments were converted to chevauxlegers, but from 1760 to 1765 they were converted back to dragoons, and thus are included in the list above. Chevauxleger regiments wore grass green coats with poppy red facings, shoulder straps and lining. The officers wore the tricorn, the men wore black felt 'Casquets' with a brass front plate bearing the imperial cipher 'MJ'. At the top left hand side of the Casquet was a black-within-yellow pompon.

Hussars

Each hussar regiment had ten companies in five squadrons. They wore the complex and colourful national costumes of their homeland, Hungary, which became popular internationally following the dashing exploits of these troops during the war. After 1751, each squadron bore one guidon. The *Leibeskadron* bore a white, swallow-tailed guidon, with the imperial eagle and the virgin. Each other squadron bore a swallow-tailed guidon of double taffeta silk in the colour of the bag of the kalpak, fringed in the button colour and embroidered with a wide variety of crests and allegorical figures. The gilt finials were pierced to show the double eagle or the imperial cipher. Cords and cravats decorated the finials. Apart from the guidons, each regiment had its equally decorative trumpet banners, complete with embroidery, fringes and tassels. The regimental numbers in the following list are those allocated in 1769, the names those of the regimental Inhaber in 1756.

Husaren-Regiment Kaiser Franz I Nr 2

Raised in 1756. Kaiser; 1798 1st Hussars. Uniform in 1756: kalpak, red pelisse, dolman and breeches, yellow cuffs. Uniform in 1757: kalpak with dark blue bag, dark blue pelisse, dolman and breeches, yellow cuffs, lace and buttons, black fur trim to pelisse. Dark blue sash; dark blue sabretasche with yellow edging.

Husaren-Regiment von Nádasdy Nr 11

Raised on 10 December 1688. 1741 Ferenc Leopold Graf Nádasdy auf Forgaras; 1798 9th Hussars. Uniform in 1742: kalpak with light green bag, light green dolman, pelisse and shabraque, yellow cuffs and wolf's tooth edging to shabraque, yellow buttons and lace, light blue breeches, grey fur. Uniform in 1757: kalpak with red bag, dark blue pelisse and breeches, red dolman, yellow cuffs, buttons and lace. Sabretasche: red with yellow edging, black eagle and yellow crown.

Husaren-Regiment von Károly Nr 16

Raised on 13 January 1734. 1738 Ferenc Count Károly de Nagy-Károly; 1759 Rudolph Graff Pàlffy; 1798 6th Hussars. This was one of five new hussar regiments raised at this time to add to the existing three. The other four were: Graf Hávor (later 4th Hussars); Gabriel Splényi; Joseph Pestvármegyey; and Johann Ghillányi. Uniform in 1757: kalpak with light red bag, sky blue dolman with light red cuffs, sky blue pelisse and breeches, white buttons. Sabretasche: light red, sky blue edging, eagle and crown.

Husaren-Regiment von Kálnoky Nr 17

Raised on 17 April 1742 in Siebenburgen, from where it subsequently recruited. 1749 Anton Graf Kálnoky; 1798 2nd Hussars. Uniform in 1742: kalpak with red bag, light blue dolman, pelisse and breeches, yellow buttons and lace, dark blown fur, red shabraque with plain, wide, yellow edging and an elaborate yellow device in the rear corner, with a white, double eagle in the top. 1757: kalpak with red bag, sky blue pelisse and dolman with yellow lace and buttons, red breeches, yellow and sky blue sash. Red sabretasche with yellow 'K' within a wreath.

Husaren-Regiment Paul Anton Esterházy Nr 24

Raised on 17 January 1742, at ten companies, at his own expense, by Paul Anton Fürst Esterházy at Ödenburg. 1762 Gábor Freiherr von Lusinsky. In 1748 it took in part of the disbanded Husaren-Regiment Trips. Uniform in 1757: kalpak, light blue dolman and pelisse. Uniform in 1765: sea green dolman, pelisse and breeches, yellow buttons.

Husaren-Regiment von Baranyay Nr 30

Raised on 20 February 1696. Johann Freiherr Baranyay von Bodorfalva; 1798 8th Hussars. Uniform in 1720: brown fur cap with crimson bag, light green dolman, pelisse and shabraque, crimson cords, cuffs and breeches (with white tops) yellow buttons. Narrow crimson edging and ornate design to rear corner of the shabraque. Uniform in 1757: kalpak with red bag. The regulations ordered dark blue dolman, pelisse and breeches and yellow buttons and lace but the regiment retained the green dolman and pelisse, red and yellow sash and red breeches that it had worn since 1696.

Husaren-Regiment von Szechenyi Nr 32

Raised on 28 February 1702. 1742 Joseph Freiherr (Graf in 1749) Festetics de Tolna; 1757 Anton Graf Szechenyi; 1798 3rd Hussars. Four other hussar regiments (Czonka Beg (or Czungenberg), Esterhazy, Gombosz and Loósy) were raised at the same time, but disbanded in 1705. In 1748 the regiment took in part of the disbanded Husaren-Regiment Trips. Uniform in 1730: light brown fur cap with dark blue bag, dark blue dolman, pelisse and breeches, yellow buttons, red cords, red breeches with white tops, crimson shabraque with plain, wide yellow trim and an elaborate yellow device in the rear corner. Uniform in 1757: kalpak with dark blue bag, dark blue dolman and pelisse with red cuffs, dark blue breeches, yellow buttons. Sabretasche: red with yellow edging and yellow badge in the form of an 'S' within a wreath.

Husaren-Regiment von Dessewffy Nr 34

Raised on 5 November 1733. 1744 Joseph Freiherr Dessewffy; 1798 4th Hussars. Uniform in 1734: kalpak with red bag and cords, dark green dolman, pelisse and shabraque, red cuffs and cords, white buttons, grey fur, red breeches with dark green thigh decoration, The shabraque has a plain, wide red edge and a red double eagle device in the rear corner, with yellow claws and crown. Uniform in 1757: kalpak with red bag, sky blue dolman and pelisse, with red cuffs; red breeches, white buttons and lace. Sabretasche: sky blue with red edging, eagle and crown.

Husaren-Regiment von Morocz Nr 35

Raised on 8 December 1741. 1754 Emerich Freiherr von Morocz; 1759 Joseph Adam Graf Bethlen; 1798 10th Hussars. Uniform: red pelisses when raised. Uniform in 1757: kalpak with light red bag. light blue pelisse and dolman with light red cuffs and lace, yellow buttons; sky blue breeches. Sabretasche: details unknown.

Jazygier-Kumanier Nr 36 (Palatinal-Husaren-Regiment)

Raised under the leadership of the Palatin of Hungary, Graf Batthyányi in the Jazygiern and Kuman Districts and the Hayduck towns, at their own costs, with 1000 men, and taken into imperial service in 1756. Initially the regiment was called the Jazygier und Kumaneir Regiment or the Palatinal-Husaren-Regiment. In 1763 it was reduced to the strength of the other, regular hussar regiments. After the death of Graf Batthyányi in 1765, it received Inhabers, after which it was named. Uniform

Musicians of the artillery, 1762. Only the artillery had Bohemian bagpipers in their band. The silver-trimmed fox fur headgear is unique. (Knötel, XIV, 59)

in 1756: kalpak, dark blue dolman, pelisse and breeches, white buttons. Uniform in 1765: kalpak, light blue dolman, pelisse and breeches, white buttons. Under Török, officers wore gold cords to their peakless shakos, white fur to the pelisse, bright red breeches, silver lace, buttons and decoration.

Grenz-Husaren-Regiment Karlstädter Nr 40
Uniform in 1762: kalpak with red bag or black mirliton; dark blue dolman with yellow cuffs, dark blue pelisse and breeches, yellow lace and buttons, yellow and white sash. Sabretasche: dark blue with yellow edging, eagle and crown. Disbanded in 1780.

Grenz-Husaren-Regiment von Warasdiner Nr 41
Uniform in 1762: kalpak or mirliton, grass green dolman and pelisse, red cuffs, yellow lace and buttons, madder red breeches. Disbanded in 1780.

Grenz-Husaren-Regiment Banalisten Nr 42
Uniform in 1762: kalpak or mirliton, red dolman, grass green pelisse, madder red breeches. Disbanded in 1780.

Grenz-Husaren-Regiment Slavonier Nr 43
Uniform in 1762: kalpak with red bag, or black mirliton, grass green dolman and pelisse with yellow and white lace and yellow buttons. Red breeches and sash. Sabretasche: red with yellow edging and crown and a black eagle. Disbanded in 1780.

Grenz-Husaren-Regiment von Székler Nr 44

Uniform in 1762: kalpak or black mirliton, dark blue dolman, pelisse with yellow cuffs, white buttons and lace, dark blue breeches.

The following regiments were disbanded before 1769, and thus never received a number.

Husaren-Regiment von Splényi

Raised on 4 November 1733 by Oberst Gabriel Freiherr von Splényi. Splényi raised six companies at his own cost; the other four were paid for by the crown. In 1748 a company of the disbanded Husaren-Regiment Trips was incorporated. Disbanded in 1768. Uniform in 1757: kalpak with sky blue bag, sky blue dolman with yellow cuffs, lace and buttons, sky blue pelisse, red breeches. Yellow and sky blue sash. Sabretasche: red with yellow edging and 'E' within a wreath.

Husaren-Regiment von Hadik

Raised on 30 October 1734 by Oberst Johann Freiherr von Ghilányi, in Breisgau, with four companies, at his own cost. He was the first commander and Inhaber. 1753 Andreas von Hadik. In 1739 the regiment recruited in Slavonia, in 1748 in the Netherlands. In 1748 part of the disbanded Husaren-Regiment Trip was incorporated. In 1768 the regiment was split up between the regiments 1, 2, 3, 6, 8 and 10. Uniform in 1757: kalpak with red bag, dark blue dolman with red cuffs, yellow lace and white buttons, dark blue pelisse with red breeches, white buttons and lace. Sabretasche: red with a yellow edging. In the centre was a shield with a yellow and black rampant lion under a red crown. Uniform in 1760: the fur of the pelisse was grey, the collar of the dolman was black, piped yellow, the lace was

Austrian artillery and engineers, 1762. The artillery uniform was grey-brown at this time. The figure on the left holds a match stick. The Corps of Engineers was composed of officers only. (Knötel, VI 44)

yellow and black, the cuffs, breeches and shabraque were bright red with yellow decoration. In the rear corner of the shabraque was a black double eagle with yellow claws and crown. Sabretasche: crimson with a black rampant lion, holding a sabre, within gold leaves and under a gold crown.

Artillery
Earth grey coats, poppy red facings, yellow buttons.

Engineers (Ingenieurs)
Raised 1717: white coat, poppy red facings, yellow buttons.
Raised 1768: pike grey coat, pompadour facings, yellow buttons.

Miners (Mineurs)
Raised 1768; pike grey coat, pompadour facings, yellow buttons.

Sappers (Sappeurs)
Raised 1768: pike grey coat, pompadour facings, yellow buttons.

Pioneers (Pionniers)
Raised 1756: pike grey coat, grass green facings, yellow buttons.

5

THE HOLY ROMAN EMPIRE

In 1756 the Holy Roman Empire as it was also known, was presided over by Austria and consisted of that country, along with Bohemia, Carinthia, Moravia, the Austrian Netherlands (Belgium), Silesia, the United Provinces (Holland), Salzburg, the Tyrol, Trient, the Duchy of Württemberg, the Bishopric of Würzburg, the Landgravate of Baden and a host of mini- and micro-states, bishoprics, abbeys and principalities.

The states were organised into geographical 'Kreise' (districts or counties); these Kreise were the Austrian, Burgundian (the Low Countries), Lower Rhenish, Franconian, Bavarian, Swabian, Upper Rhenish, Westphalian, Upper Saxon and the Lower Saxon. Each Kreis was obliged to provide a contingent of troops or sums of money, to aid the empire's cause in time of war. During the Seven Years War, however, some of the smaller states of the empire sided with its enemies.

In 1757 the states were called upon by Austria to provide a 'Triplum' i.e. three times as many men as the basic military contribution, to serve alongside the Austrian Army against Prussia. The forces raised totalled 84,000 infantry and 36,000 cavalry, all of wildly varying quality and effectiveness. Of all the Kreise, only 42 were obliged to provide military contingents. They included six temporal princes (including the Landgraf of Hessen-Darmstadt and the Markgraf of Baden), five spiritual princes (the bishops of Basel, Fulda, Speyer, Strassburg and Worms), 24 counts, including those of Hanau, Leiningen, Rhein, Solms, Sayn-Wittgenstein, Stolberg, Waldeck, Wild and Ysenburg, five abbeys and the imperial cities of Frankfurt/Main, Friedberg (Hessen), Speyer, Wetzlar and Worms. These polyglot military units were organised into two corps, comprising together the 'Imperial Army' (die Reichsarmee), a convenient strategic holdall, invented to incorporate and make best use of these disparate martial units.

The nightmarish task of commanding this force was initially accepted by General-Feldmarschall the Prince Joseph Maria Friedrich Wilhelm von Hildburghausen; after the strain of trying to hold the ramshackle structure together until the end of 1757 (following the crushing defeat at Prussia's hands at Rossbach on 5 November) he requested to be allowed to resign. He was replaced by Feldmarschall Prinz Friedrich Michael von der Pfalz-Zweibrücken, who was to receive the Grand Cross of the Order of Maria Theresa for his successful efforts to rebuild the Imperial Army into something resembling a combat-ready military force. In 1761 he also resigned, to be replaced by Feldmarschall Johann Baptist von Serbelloni. The I Corps of this army was initially commanded by the Landgraf Joseph von Fürstenberg, the II Corps by the Markgraf Carl Friedrich von Baden-Durlach.

Each Kreis supplied one medium field gun and each infantry battalion had two light guns. Austria supplied the army command and staff structure, the medium and heavy field artillery, engineers and bridging train, as well as some infantry and cavalry units. Initially, the Imperial Army operated together with the French Army under Charles de Rohan, the Prince de Soubise, in western Germany.

The Austrian–Burgundian Kreis

The uniforms of those Austrian regiments attached to the Imperial Army are described in the Austrian section; we will only describe that of the mercenary Infanterie-Regiment Blau-Würzburg, which served with them.

Infanterie-Regiment Blau-Würzburg

This unit had two battalions, each of one grenadier and six musketeer companies and two 4-pounder guns. In 1760 the establishment was reduced to one battalion, and in 1761 it formed into a new regiment (together with Infanterie-Regiment Rot-Würzburg) of three battalions, three grenadier and 18 musketeer companies. In 1762 two companies of the 3rd Battalion were disbanded. The Inhaber was the Archbishop of Würzburg.

Uniform
Austrian style with blue facings, white hat edging, white small clothes, belts and brass buttons. The pouch had a brass badge. Grenadiers wore a fur, brass-fronted cap, with a blue bag. There were brass grenades on their pouches and brass match cases on their bandoliers; they bore sabres. NCOs had gold hat edging and braid to collar and cuffs; they carried a hazelnut stick and a grenadier sabre with brass hilt and black sheath. Sergeants bore halberds. The details of drummers' distinctions and of officers' sashes and sword straps are not known.

Colours
The regiment had one Leibfahne; it was white, the edges having flamed designs, white and red, white and blue, white and green are known to have existed, each with the white flame tips pointing inwards. The design was the same on both sides: imperial eagle under a bishop's mitre and on a crossed sword and crosier. On the eagle's breast was a gold-framed, quartered crest; upper left and lower right: yellow with black leopards, a silver bend across them, upper right and lower left: the red over white crest of Würzburg. The heart shield was the quartered personal crest of the Graf of Seinsheim; upper left and lower right: three white and three blue bars, upper right and lower left: on a yellow field a leaping, crowned black boar. The designs of the company colours are not known.

The Bavarian Kreis

Infanterie-Regiment Kurbayern (In II Corps)
Infantry Regiment Kurbayern consisted of three battalions (each of four companies of musketeers) and two companies of grenadiers and six 4-pounder guns. It was formed from two battalions of Infanterie-Regiment Pechmann – with its 1st Grenadier Company – and the 1st Battalion Infanterie-Regiment Holnstein, complete with grenadier company.

Uniform
Initially the contingents would have worn their old uniforms; from 1759 they both wore the following costume. It was of Austrian style, white hat edging, white and light blue cockade. Medium blue coat with red collar, lapels and cuffs, yellow lining, white buttons, black stock. White small clothes and belts. Only grenadiers and NCOs had sabres. Grenadiers wore fur caps with tin plates, red bag with white braid and tassel, brass match case to bandolier. NCOs had the usual silver braid to hats,

collars and cuffs and carried canes; sergeants had halberds. Officers had silver hat edging, silver waist sashes and sword knots, silver gorgets. Company officers had spontoons (short muskets if with the grenadier company).

Colours
There were two colours per battalion: one was a white Leibfahne with the Virgin, the other the white-blue diamonds. The finial was gilt, the staff probably light blue.

Infanterie-Regiment Salzburg
Initially this unit had one grenadier, eight musketeer companies and two 4-pounder guns. Later, it was joined by two companies of Kurpfalz infantry (as the Sulzbach contingent) and split into two battalions.

Uniform
Austrian style, no hat edging, white coat, red cuffs, lapels, waistcoat and turnbacks, brass buttons. Red aiguillette on the right shoulder. Nine buttons on each lapel, three beneath; three buttons on each cuff and pocket flap. They carried no sabre, only a bayonet in a brown sheath. The musket sling was red-brown. Grenadiers wore bearskin caps, with a brass grenade on the front and a red backing; they also carried sabres. Officers wore red and white hat cords and tassels, red and white sashes and sword knots. The gilt-hilted sword was carried in a brown sheath. There are no definite details about the colours carried.

There was no cavalry; the Bavarian cavalry was not mobilised in the Seven Years War, only the Upper Rhine *Kreiseskadron* (of 174 men, a kürassier unit) took the field (see the Upper Rhine section below).

Artillery
Yellow hat edging, pearl-grey coat, dark blue facings, brass buttons (eight on each lapel), buff small clothes, black gaiters, white belts.

Franconian Kreis

The following regiments each had two battalions each of a grenadier company, six fusilier companies and two 3-pounder guns. There were six colours per regiment, one of them a King's Colour (Leibfahne). The finials of those of Varell and Ferntheil were gilt; the staffs were black or black and white. The Leibfahne was white, left of the staff was 'FC' in gold; right of the staff was the black, crowned imperial double eagle, in the usual colours. The company colours (Ordinair-fahnen) had a central dark blue horizontal band, with top and bottom bands in the facing colours. The ciphers and double eagles were as for the Leibfahne.

Uniform
Dark blue Prussian style, belts and small clothes were white; facings were shown on collars, cuffs, lapels and skirt lining of the dark blue coats. Grenadiers had fur caps with brass plates, bags in the facing colour, braid and tassel in the button colour. Drummers wore waistcoats in the facing colour, with swallow's nests in white, edged in yellow. NCOs had button-colour edgings to the hat, to collars and cuffs; they carried canes. Initially they wore waistcoats in the facing colour. Sergeants had halberds. Officers wore hat edging in the button colour, silver gorgets with an oval gold insert, their aiguillettes (right shoulder), sashes and sword straps were in the silver and red colours of the Kreis. Fusilier officers carried spontoons, grenadier officers had short muskets. Officers' coat skirts were not turned back.

Infanterie-Regiment Anspach

In 1757 the Anspach contingent marched out in their old uniforms: white hat edging, pompons white, blue and the regimental facing colour. The grenadiers wore Prussian-style caps with red fronts, having a blue oval (edged yellow) containing a white badge, white and blue pompons, dark blue backing, white braid, red headband. Their coats were Prussian blue, facings (collar, lapels, cuffs and lining) were red. There were eight buttons in pairs on each lapel; under each lapel were three white lace loops, with red and blue lines. There were three such laces on the pockets, three on the cuff. Initially the waistcoats were in the facing colour, later white. They carried brass-hilted sabres in brown sheaths and had white belts and breeches. Officers had gold or silver hat edging and brooch, black cockade, silver and gold gorgets, white and blue sashes and sword straps.

The Leibfahne (King's Colour) had a white cloth; on the left of the staff, a green wreath with red berries and scroll, within the wreath the crowned golden cipher. To the right of the staff was the same wreath; inside the wreath was the red eagle, with the black and white quartered shield on its breast. The motto was in gold. The Ordinair-fahnen (regimental colours) were blue with three horizontal red stripes, bearing the same designs as on the Leibfahne. On the edges of each side was a golden grenade.

Infanterie-Regiment Cronegk (In I Corps)

Until mid-1757, this unit was known as 'vacant Gudenus'. White facings, brass buttons and Prussian grenadier caps with a blue oval holding a badge and motto; the backing was dark blue, the braid and headband white. The regiment had two battalions each of a grenadier company, six fusilier companies and two 3-pounder guns.

Infanterie-Regiment Ferntheil

From 14 May 1759, this became the Infantry Regiment Hohenlohe-Ingelfingen. Poppy red facings, brass buttons, Austrian grenadier caps. The regiment had two battalions each of a grenadier company, six fusilier companies and two 3-pounder guns.

Infanterie-Regiment Varell

Sulphur yellow facings, brass buttons and Prussian grenadier caps, red backing, yellow braid and headband. The regiment had two battalions each of a grenadier company, six fusilier companies and two 3-pounder guns.

Kürassier-Regiment Bayreuth (In II Corps)

This regiment had initially four, later five squadrons. Uniform in the Austrian style, yellow hat edging and loop, white coat (or buff yellow Kollet, without lapels) with poppy red collar, lapels, cuffs and turnbacks, brass buttons (six in pairs on the lapels, three on each cuff). Black stocks. The cuffs, turnbacks and the red waistcoat, were edged with white tape having three rows of red dicing. The shoulder strap was of the same braid. Buff breeches and gloves, black cuirass with black fittings, red waist sash, red, square shabraque with yellow edging. White belts, black harness with brass fittings, brass-hilted sword in black sheath, with white and red fit strap. Trumpeters: probably wore reversed colours and the red and white diced braid. Officers: gold hat edging, cuirass fittings and cuff edging; silver, red and black sash and sword strap. The contingents from Bamberg, Castell, Nuremberg, Schwarzenberg and Würzburg all wore items differing from the above mentioned scheme. There is no firm information about standards carried.

Dragoner-Regiment Anspach

The regiment had five squadrons, each of two companies; it was made up of contingents from several tiny states. The uniform was in the Austrian style: plain hat, black and white cockade, blue and white pompon, white coat with light blue collar, lapels, cuffs and turnbacks, white buttons (distributed as for the kürassier regiment), blue and white aiguillette on the right shoulder. Buff small clothes, white belts. Brass-hilted sword in black sheath with blue and white tassel. Square light blue shabraque with white edging, black harness. Trumpeters wore reversed colours, with diced blue and white braid. Officers wore silver buttons and lace. The contingent from Castell had black belts and white pouches; that of Würzburg had white pouches. Their officers had silver lace to their lapels and cuffs and wore red and silver sashes and sword straps. The contingents of Eichstätt and Schönborn had white pouches. The contingent of the *Deutschorden* (Teutonic Order) had three pairs of white laces to their lapels, a pair on the cuffs, white pouches, crossed bandoliers, a light blue wavy line in the white shabraque edging, white medallions in the corners and steel-hilted swords. There was one standard per company, but no details are known.

Artillery

There was a small corps of gunners, consisting of 3 officers, 1 quartermaster, 1 surgeon, 7 NCOs, 2 drummers and 67 armourers. Uniform: yellow hat edging and button, dark blue coat with poppy red facings to collar, lapels, cuffs, turnbacks, waistcoats and breeches, white belts, black gaiters. A red and blue twisted flask cord was worn over the right shoulder to left hip. There was a small black pouch on the front of the belt.

Rhine Electorate Kreis

There were no permanent *Kreis* units from this area, nor were there any command or staff elements. Only the four larger states (Archbishops of Köln, Mainz and Trier and the Prince Elector of the Palatinate) provided units from their own standing armies; all other smaller states paid money to the imperial treasury in lieu.

Regiments of the Holy Roman Empire. Left to right: grenadier of Kurmainz; Grenadier of Kurköln; Grenadier of Kurköln; Musketeer of Kurtrier. Knötel's basis for this plate was a series of rather naïve sketches, but they seem to have been fairly reliable. These regiments were present at the Battle of Rossbach. (Knötel, V 53)

Leib-Infanterie-Regiment Nothaft (Kurköln)

One battalion of a grenadier company (100 men) and six fusilier companies (120 men each), two 4-pounder guns.

Uniform

Austrian style: black stock, dark blue coat, red collar, cuffs, dark blue lapels (with 8 white buttons per side) and turnbacks. Tricorn with white edging and pompon, white waistcoat and breeches, black gaiters, white belts, brass buckles. Grenadiers: Austrian-style fur cap, brass plate with a black grenade, red backing, white tassel and braid trim. Drummers: blue and white braid trim to swallow's nests and sleeves; the drum major wore NCO badges and blue and silver braid decoration as for drummers. NCOs: silver lace to hat, collar and cuffs, and they carried a hazelnut stick; sergeants bore halberds. Officers: silver hat trim and wore gorgets; they were armed with a sword and spontoon.

Colours

The regiment had a Leibfahne; from 1761: on the face side: white ground with the Madonna in a golden sunburst, above her the motto:' MONSTRA TE ESSE MATREM', beneath her: 'F.W.G.Z.S.I.R.' On the other side: a sunburst holding the crest of Köln-Münster, with the badge of Königsegg in the centre. At the time of the reign of Clemens-August, his badge would have been worn here.

The Ordinair-fahnen (company flags) were horizontally divided into six wavy blue and white stripes, in the centre the quartered crest: upper left: white with a black cross (Köln); upper right: the leaping white horse of Lower Saxony on a red ground; lower left: three golden hearts on red (duchy of Engern); lower left: white-blue diamonds (Bavaria). In the centre the personal crest of the Elector: upper left and lower right: golden crowned lion on black (Pfalzgraf bei Rhein), upper right and lower left: white-blue diamonds (Bavaria). The heart shield bore the golden imperial orb on red. The crest was edged in gold, with gold laurel wreath, under an electoral cap and set upon crossed sceptre and, crosier.

Infanterie-Regiment Kurmainz

Four battalions, each of two grenadier companies (100 men) and four fusilier companies (120 men each), with eight 4-pounder guns

Uniform

Austrian-style with a white coat, black stock, green collar, cuffs with three brass buttons, lapels (with eight buttons per side) and turnbacks. Green waistcoat, white breeches, black gaiters. Grenadiers: an Austrian-style fur cap, brass plate with a silver grenade, green backing, yellow tassel and braid trim. Brass-hilted sabre, brass match case on white bandolier. Drummers: unknown, probably blue and yellow braid trim; the drum major wore NCO badges and blue and gold braid to sleeves. NCOs: gold lace to hat, collar and cuffs and carried a hazel-nut stick; sergeants carried halberds. Officers: gold hat trim, wore gilt gorgets and carried a sword and spontoon. The colours were as for Kurköln Infanterie-Regiment Nothafft.

Fusilier-Regiment Wildenstein (Kurköln)

This regiment had one battalion of grenadiers and six fusilier companies. It had two 4-pounder guns. In 1756 its Inhaber was Generalfeldwachtmeister Freiherr von Wildenstein, in1757 von Gudenus.

Uniform

Austrian-style with a dark blue coat, white collar, cuffs (with three brass buttons) and turnbacks; no lapels, white waistcoat and breeches, black gaiters. Fusiliers: tricorns with white edging and pompon; white belts with brass fittings. Grenadiers: Austrian-style fur cap, brass plate with a black grenade, white backing and tassel. Brass-hilted sabre in black sheath; a brass match case on bandolier; and a small black pouch at the front of the waist belt. Drummers: unknown, possibly decorated in blue and yellow braid trim to swallow's nests and sleeves; the drum major wore NCO badges and blue and gold braid. NCOs: gold lace to hat and coat and carried a hazel-nut stick; sergeants bore halberds. Officers: gold buttons, gilt gorget, sword and spontoon. There are no records of the appearance of the regimental colours. The battalion in Erfurt may have had red facings and white buttons.

Infanterie-Regiment Kurtrier (I Corps)

The regiment had two battalions each of four musketeer companies of 140 men and two 3-pounder guns. There were no grenadiers. The regiment was classed as 'bad' by Prince Soubise. This is not surprising, as they were all raw recruits. They fled the field at Rossbach and their later conduct was little better. The 2nd Battalion was used as escort for the artillery.

Uniform

Austrian style, white, scalloped hat edging, black cockade, red and blue pompon. White, collarless coat, with red lapels, cuffs and turnbacks; white buttons (five pairs on each lapel, three on each cuff). White belts and small clothes, black gaiters, no sabres.

Colours

The Leibfahne was white, with double yellow edging, having green leaves between them, gold rosettes on each corner. In the centre a crest under an electoral cap; the two small flags to either side were red over light blue. A light blue ribbon wound through the surrounding wreath and dangled onto the crest from under the cap. To the left was a crosier, to the right a sword. The crest was that of Archbishop Johann Philip Freiherr von Waldersdorff, who ruled from 1756 to 1768. It was quartered: top left and bottom right: red cross on a silver ground (Trier); top right and bottom left: red field, silver lamb with a red flag with a white cross (Prümm). The heart shield was also quartered: upper left and lower right: black ground bearing a lion (the top half red, the bottom silver) wearing a gold crown (Waldersdorff); upper right and lower left: silver, with two horizontal red bars (Niederisenburg). In the Arsenal in Berlin is a somewhat simpler flag which is white, in a light blue frame with a dark blue outer edge, on one side the cross of Trier in pink and crimson, green wreath, yellow plait, Electoral cap over the central crest and smaller versions in the corners, over the cipher 'EC'. On the reverse is the same Electoral cap, wreath and plait and the same Trier cross in pink and red, the pascal lamb etc. The heart shield is quartered: upper left and lower right: St George, upper right and lower left: the white Polish eagle on a red ground. There is then a further smaller, crowned heart shield, showing the black, yellow and green Saxon crest.

Infanterie-Regiment von Effern (Kurpfalz, in I Corps)

Two battalions each of two grenadier and four fusilier companies and two (four from 1758) 4-pounder guns. Its Inhaber was Johann Joseph Wilhelm Graf von Effern. The electorate also provided two companies of infantry to the Austrian Infantry Regiment Salzburg, as its contribution from the Bavarian Kreis.

Uniform

Prussian style, white hat edging in wolf's tooth style, black cockade, blue and white hat pompon. Dark blue coat, black stock, no collar, white cuffs (with three-button flaps), white lapels (with three pairs of brass buttons per side), one button under each lapel; white turnbacks. Four brass grenades to cartridge pouch; brown sheaths to sabre and bayonet. Belts white or buff. The grenadiers wore Austrian-style fur caps, with a brass plate, white backing, white tassel and braid trim. They also had an extra small black pouch to front of the waistbelt, with flaming grenade badge, and wore a brass match case to their bandolier. Grenadier officer: gilt gorgets, gold tassel and braid to their caps; small pouch to front of belt, with gold edging and lid; musket and bayonet. Drummers: information is uncertain, probably reversed colours, blue and white flame edging to drum hoops; drum major NCO badges, blue and silver braid. NCOs: gold lace to hat, hazelnut stick. Sergeants had gold lace to cuffs and carried halberds. Fusilier officers: gilt gorget, sword and spontoon, buff gloves, white sash (silver for field officers) with blue stripes, silver and blue sword strap. Silver spontoon blade.

Colours

Leibfahne: white with narrow silver edging, in the centre the two shields of the Pfalz-Neuburg crests on an ornate shield, above them the Order of St Hubertus and the chain of the Order of the Golden Fleece. Above the crest the Electoral cap with pearls and a ribbon. In the corners the interwoven silver cipher 'CPT' under the Electoral cap. Two silver cords and tassels. Ordinair-fahnen: blue cloth, with 'CPT', under a red Electoral cap, below it the cross of a military order. Large laurel wreath around the crest, touching the crowned ciphers in each corner. From 1760 the regiment had four colours, including a new Leibfahne: white cloth with wide edging of white and blue flames and yellow corner medallions, holding the cipher with Electoral cap. In the centre, the Virgin, with child and sceptre, standing on a snake. Above the Virgin a scroll with 'SUB TUUM PRAESIDIUM VIRGO GLORIOSA'. Ordinair-fahnen, 1st Pattern: red cloth with triple white-blue diamond pattern edging and the yellow corner badges with wreathed 'CPT' under a cap. In the centre the cipher, under a cap on clouds and in trophies of arms; two flags to the left, a lion and sword to the right; beneath the crest the Order of St Hubertus. Ordinair-fahnen, 2nd Pattern: yellow cloth, the other details as for the 1st Pattern, but no clouds around the central cipher.

Kurpfalz Garde zu Fuss (Foot Guards)

This unit was of one battalion of one grenadier company (100 men) and five musketeer companies (140 men each) with two 4-pounder guns. The Inhaber was Feldmarschalllieutenant Prinz Friedrich Michael, Pfalzgraf von Zweibrücken-Birkenfeld. Colours were as for the Regiment Effern.

Uniform

Prussian style, white and blue hat pompon, white edging, black cockade. Dark blue, collarless coat, gold aiguillette, red lapels, cuffs and turnbacks. White buttonholes to lapels and cuffs. Brass buttons, 8 on each lapel, 3 under each lapel, 3 on each cuff; blue cuff flap edged white. White small clothes, black gaiters. Buff belts, four brass grenades on the pouch lid. Black musket stock, buff leather sabre and bayonet sheaths. Grenadiers: Austrian-style bearskin caps with a brass front plate; until 1761 the bag was blue with white tape and tassel, from then it was red and white. They wore a small pouch with brass badge to front of waistbelt and a brass match case on bandolier. Drummers: not known; drum hoops were in white and blue flames. Corporals: gold hat edging, hazelnut stick. Sergeants: gold hat edging and edging to cuff; they bore halberds. Officers: gold hat edging, aiguillette, buttons and buttonholes to the lapels, buff gloves. Sash and sword strap, spontoon. Grenadier officers: equipment as for the previous regiment, white with blue.

Kürassier-Regiment Kurpfalz (In I Corps)

This regiment was formed from the 2nd and 3rd Squadrons of the Reiter-Regiment Prinz Friedrich Michael von Zweibrücken and the Upper Rhine Kreis Squadron, which had been formed in 1754 from three companies of the Kurpfälzischer Leibdragoner (Life Dragoon) Regiment.

Reiter-Regiment Prinz Friedrich Michael

Uniform

Austrian style, plain hat, white coat, black stock, bright red facings to cuffs and turnbacks, brass buttons, red and white aiguillette on the right shoulder, buff waistcoat and breeches. No cuirass was worn. White belts, yellow greatcoat. Brass-hilted sword in brown sheath, black pouch with brass badge, yellow saddle cloth with white edging. Officers had gold hat edging and small red collar patches. White leather straps with gold edging. Sash and sword strap as for the infantry.

Colours

The Leibstandarte was white. Blue cloth, fringed in the button colour. On the left face were embroidered pomegranate flowers and leaves; in the centre the princely crest in two cartouches, amid trophies of arms, under an electoral cap. The corner medallions had the cipher 'CPT' in palm fronds, inside the collar of the Order of St Hubertus instead of the crest, under the electoral cap, between two standards with the same cipher. On the right face was the same general design, but the central device was the cipher 'CPT', under a black scroll, with the motto: 'DOMINUS REGIT ME 1755'.

Kurpfalz Lieb-Dragoner Regiment

This unit had five squadrons each of two companies.

Uniform

Austrian style, plain hat, red coat, black stock, black lapels and cuffs, red lining, yellow buttons, buff waistcoat and breeches, white belts. Brass-hilted sword in brown leather sheath; white and blue tassel to fist strap. Officers had gold lace edging to the hat, otherwise as for infantry officers. Nothing is known of the standards carried.

Artillery

These men were provided by Kurtrier and Kurpfalz.

Uniform

Kurtrier: white hat edging, dark blue coat with red cuffs; red waistcoat and breeches. Kurpfalz: dark blue coat, turnbacks, waistcoat and breeches, crimson cuffs and lapels, brass buttons, white belts, infantry sabres. Feuerwerker: gold hat edging in wolfstooth pattern. Officers had gold hat edging.

Engineers

As for the artillery, but with black facings, gold lace buttonholes.

Apart from the *Kreis* troops listed above, there was also the Palatinate Auxiliary Contingent in French service 1757–1 January 1759. The contract was then terminated. The contingent consisted of the infantry regiments Prinz Karl, Birkenfeld, Osten, Baaden, and Preysing, ten battalions with a total force of some 6000 men. The grenadiers were usually formed into *ad hoc* combined battalions. The 2nd Battalion of Infantry Regiment Prinz Karl was taken prisoner at the surrender of Minden on 15 March 1758. Thereafter the Palatinate contingent counted only nine battalions. The remaining Palatinal troops did not participate in any of the Seven Years War campaigns, but remained within the Palatinate territories. Infanterie-Regiment von Isselbach served as the wartime garrison of the fortress of Düsseldorf on the Lower Rhine, while the 1st Nassau-Weilburg Battalion was in Jülich for the duration of the war. The smaller part of this force comprised the Palatinate's contingent to the Imperial Army. The Palatinate also provided two companies of infantry for the Infanterie-Regiment Salzburg as its contribution to the Bavarian Kreis. The non-mobilised regiment gave men and horses to bring the mobilised units up to strength.

The Swabian Kreis

Infanterie-Regiment Baden-Baden (II Corps)

This margravate was reigned over by Markgraf and Imperial Generalfeldzeugmeister Ludwig Georg Simpert von Baden-Baden, 1727–1761. This was a Kreis-Regiment, as provided by eleven mini-states of southwest Germany. It had two battalions, each of a grenadier and five musketeer companies. Each battalion had two 3-pounder regimental guns. The troops were organised, dressed and trained along Prussian lines.

Uniform

A tricorn edged white, dark blue coat, faced (collar, lapels, plain cuffs) and lined white, with yellow buttons and white small clothes, belts and gaiters. Black stock. NCOs: hats were edged in plain gold lace and they had gold lace to collar and plain, round cuffs. They carried canes. Sergeants carried halberds. Officers: carried spontoons and wore silver waist sashes (under the coat) and sword knots, with red-and-yellow lines. Officers' hats were edged in scalloped gold lace and they wore silvered gorgets. Belts were white. Grenadiers: brass-fronted mitre caps, with brown fur surround in the Austrian style, with blue backing, white braid and tassel. Hair was powdered, curled and worn in a plaited pigtail. It is not known what colours they carried.

Infanterie-Regiment Markgraf von Baden-Durlach (II Corps)

This margravate was reigned over by Markgraf Carl Friedrich IV of Baden-Durlach (born in 1728, reigned 1746–1811). In 1771, the ruling line of the house of Baden-Baden died out and both states came together under Carl Friedrich. There was one infantry regiment of two battalions, each with a grenadier and five musketeer companies. Each battalion had two 3-pounder regimental guns. The troops were organised, dressed and trained along Prussian lines.

Uniform

A dark blue coat, faced (collar, lapels, plain cuffs and shoulder straps) and lined red, with yellow buttons and white small clothes and gaiters. Black stocks, white belts. Officers: they carried spontoons and wore silver waist sashes (under the coat) and sword knots, with red-and-yellow lines. Hats were edged in scalloped gold lace and they wore silvered gorgets, bearing the crowned cipher 'CF'. NCOs: hats were edged in plain gold lace and they had gold lace to collar and plain, round cuffs. They carried canes; sergeants carried halberds. Grenadiers: brass-fronted mitre caps, bearing the cipher 'CF' under a ducal cap, with blue backing, red pompon, red headband with brass flaming grenades. Brass matchcase on the bandolier. Drummers: red and yellow braid to the sleeves and swallow's nests; drums were brass with red and yellow hoops. Hair was powdered, curled and worn in a plaited pigtail.

Colours

The Leibfahne was white, bearing the crowned, black, imperial double eagle, on its breast the quartered oval crest of Baden-Durlach. The Ordinair-fahnen were yellow. On one side they bore the crest as on the Leibfahne, on the other, was the great crest of the ruling house, held by two white griffons. The crests on the fields of these flags were on a pattern of red, yellow and black horizontal flames. The tips were gilt spear points, from which gold and black cords and tassels depended.

Kreis-Infanterie-Regiment Fürstenberg (II Corps)

The regiment had two battalions, each of a grenadier and five musketeer companies and two 3-pounder guns. One battalion was provided by Fürstenberg and the abbeys of Kempten and Weingarten; the other was made up of contingents from the city and Bishopric of Augsburg, the abbey of Ochsenhausen and 15 smaller states.

Uniform

Austrian style, white, faced (collar, lapels and plain cuffs) and lined red, white waistcoat, white breeches, and belts, brass buttons, black gaiters. Musketeers: tricorns edged white, with red-within-white pompons. Grenadiers: bearskin caps with brass plates, bearing the Fürstenberg crest, red bag, white braid and tassel. They had brass match cases to the bandolier and small black pouches to the front of the waist belt. NCOs: gold lace to the edge of the hat and to the edges of collar and cuffs; they carried canes. Sergeants had halberds. Officers: gilt gorgets on duty and silver waist sashes and sword knots.

Two grenadiers of Kreis-Infanterie-Regiment Fürstenberg, 1735. The uniform remained the same for the Seven Years War and was modelled on the Austrian fashion, with bearskin cap and brass match case on the bandolier. It is odd that the pouch badges are not also in the button colour. (Knötel, V 11)

Colours

The Leibfahne was white and bore, on both sides, the black, crowned, imperial double eagle, with the crest of Swabia (a white cross on a black ground over three black lions on a yellow ground) in an oval on its breast. Ordinair-fahnen were yellow; they bore on both sides the same crests as the sovereign's colour. Both sides of the company flag were decorated with horizontal red and white flames. The gilt flag staff finials were in the form of spear points bearing the Swabian crest.

Kreis-Infanterie-Regiment Württemberg

Raised in 1673 as the Herzögliches Regiment zu Fuss (Regiment of Foot) by Herzog Eberhard III; 1684 Schwäbisches Kreis-Regiment zu Fuss Baden-Durlach; 1701 Kreis-Infanterie-Regiment von Reischach; 1702 Kreis-Infanterie-Regiment Württemberg. The regiment consisted of one battalion of two grenadier companies (100 men each), ten fusilier companies of 149 men each, and two 3-pounder guns. The first Inhaber was was Herzog Carl Eugen von Württemberg (reigned 1737–1793); the second was General-Major Graf von Sayn-Wittgenstein.

Uniform

Prussian style, white hat edging, red and black pompon. Fusilier caps were worn in 1748 and 1781; it is not known if they were worn during the Seven Years War. Dark blue coat with black stock, yellow collar, lapels, cuffs, aiguillette (on the right shoulder) and buttons (eight on and two under each lapel). Red turnbacks, yellow small clothes, white breeches in summer. Belts, packs etc as in Prussia.

Grenadiers: Prussian-style grenadier caps with yellow bag, headband and braid, yellow and black pompon. Small pouch to front of waist belt, brass matchcase to bandolier. NCOs: gold hat edging, gold braid to collar and cuffs; canes and sabres were carried. Sergeants bore halberds. Officers: hats had scalloped gold lace edging, they wore gold waist sashes and sword straps, gilt gorgets when on duty. Fusilier company officers had spontoons, grenadier company officers had short muskets.

Colours

Leibfahne: white, on both sides the Württemberg crest; an oval shield within the red collar and eight blue jewels of an Order, the shield quartered: upper left: the yellow and black diamonds of Teck; lower left: two golden fish on red (Monbéliard); upper right: a yellow flag on a blue ground; lower right: a brown head wearing a red cap on a yellow ground (Heidenheim). The heart shield was yellow with three black antlers. The tip was gilt, the staff brown or striped black and yellow. Ordinair-fahnen: yellow ground; on one side were six horizontal double flames, top to bottom: black, black, white, light blue, black and black. On the flames a brown double eagle with golden crowns and halos, silver beak and talons; in the right talon a silver sword, in the left a gold and blue orb. On the breast of the eagle the crest of the Kreis: the top black with white cross, below this a yellow field with three black leopards, one above the other. The obverse of the flag bore six black double flames, on them the Württemberg crest as on the Leibfahne. The gilt tip bore the Kreis badge, the cross over three lions.

Kreis-Kürassier-Regiment Hohenzollern-Sigmaringen (II Corps)

This unit was made up of four squadrons, each of two companies, comprising men from 61 contingents.

Uniform

Austrian cut; a tricorn, edged white, with a black cockade, yellow loop and button, white tunic, red collar and plain cuffs, red turnbacks. The front of the tunic was edged with double yellow braid; there were no lapels or buttons. The waistcoat was red, the breeches buff. High, cuffed boots were worn. NCOs wore a white-over-black pompon and corner tassels to their hats, yellow or gold edging to collar and cuffs and black and white sword knots. The waist belt was white, the bandoliers red, with yellow edging. The brass-hilted sword had a brown sheath with brass trim. Officers had gold and black waist sashes and sword knots. It seems that cuirasses were not worn. Saddle furniture was red, edged white with two red stripes, with the arms of Württemberg on holster covers and in the rear, square, corners of the shabraque.

Colours

The Leibfahne was white, the three Ordinair-fahnen were yellow. All were fringed in gold, on both sides was the crest of Swabia within green palm fronds; the finials were spear points bearing the Swabian crest.

Kreis-Dragoner-Regiment Württemberg

Raised on 9 July 1683 from the Leibwache zu Pferde and the six Kreis-Kompagnien as the Schwäbisches Kreis Regiment zu Pferde von Höhnstett. 1731 Kreis-Dragoner-Regiment Herzog Carl Alexander von Württemberg with eight companies. 1737 Markgraf Carl Wilhelm von Baden-Durlach; 1738 'Württemberg'. This regiment initially had four squadrons, each of two companies, but was rapidly reduced to two squadrons.

Uniform

Prussian style, a tricorn with black cockade, yellow edging and button, black-within-yellow hat tassels. Initially a light blue tunic, but in 1759 it changed to dark blue, as the unit had been mistaken for Prussian dragoons. It had a black collar, lapels and plain cuffs, yellow turnbacks (red from 1759) and buttons, yellow shoulder strap, yellow aiguilette on the right shoulder. Lapels and cuffs were edged in white, yellow and blue braid. Waistcoat and breeches were buff and high, cuffed boots were worn. Belts were white, the brass-hilted straight sword was worn in a brown leather sheath. In 1759 the turnbacks became red. Officers: gold and black waist sashes and sword knots. Saddle furniture was dark blue, edged white, yellow and blue braid, with the arms of Württemberg on holster covers and in the rear, square, corners of the shabraque.

Colours

The Leibfahne was white, the squadron standard was yellow; both bore the Swabian crest, as did the gilt, spear point finial.

Swabian Kreis Artillery Company

Black tricorn, dark blue coat with red lapels, plain cuffs and lining, white buttons, red waistcoat and breeches, white belts, black gaiters.

Württemberg Artillery

Tricorn with yellow edging, dark blue coat, black collar, cuffs, lapels and lining, brass buttons. White small clothes and belts, black gaiters. There was also an artillery escort unit, with Austrian-style grenadier fur caps with brass plates instead of tricorns.

Upper Rhine Kreis

This area's contribution was supposed to be 8559 infantrymen and 1473 cavalrymen; they chose to reduce the cavalry considerably to a squadron of 174 men, attached to the Reiter-Regiment Prinz Friedrich to form the Kürassier-Regiment Kurpfalz (see the Rhine Electorate). The County of Waldeck was part of the Upper Rhine Kreis. This mini-state provided two companies of infantry, which formed part of Infanterie-Regiment Nassau.

Artillery

There is only data on the Hessen-Darmstadt artillery contingent: dark blue coat, black collar, lapels and cuffs, red lining, brass buttons, white small clothes, white belts, black gaiters. Officers' hats were edged in scalloped gold lace.

Infanterie-Regiment Hessen-Darmstadt

The Landgravate of Hessen-Darmstadt was ruled by Landgraf Ludwig VIII. It's Regiment Prinz George (named Infanterie-Regiment Hessen-Darmstadt when part of the Kreis) was the only unit from this state mobilised for war. The regiment had one grenadier and eight musketeer companies and two 3-pounder guns. The Inhaber was General Field Marshal Prinz Carl von Hessen-Darmstadt. By 1760, Hessen-Darmstadt also fielded four mortars and four 12-pounder cannon. Each piece carried up to 40 rounds in the limber, with a further 100 rounds on one or two ammunition carts or wagons in the artillery park, which also carried the cartridges for the infantry small arms. The artillery and park required at least 225 horses.

Uniform

White edging, pompon and button to hat, red neckstock. Dark blue, single-breasted coat of Prussian cut, with white aiguillette to the right shoulder, white shoulder strap on the left. White cuffs and turnbacks, twelve square-ended white lace loops to each side of the coat chest, two on each white-edged cuff flap, three on each pocket flap. White buttons. Brass plate to pouch, brass-hilted sabres in brown sheaths. Grenadiers: five brass grenades on pouches, silver plate to Prussian-style cap, with blue

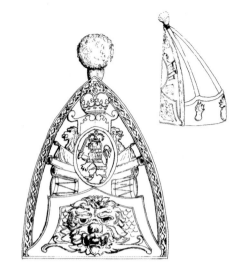

Above left: The infantry leibfahne of Hessen-Darmstadt.
Above right: Grenadier cap of Hessen-Darmstadt Infanterie-Regiment Erbprinz. White plate with blue field having the red and white striped Hessian lion, red, white and blue pompon, white backing (also shown as blue), white headband and braid, white metal grenades to headband.

field having the red and white striped Hessian lion, red, white and blue pompon, white backing (also shown as blue), white headband and braid, white metal grenades to headband. Brass match case to bandolier. Drummers: blue and white swallow's nests, white chevrons to each sleeve. The brass drum had red, white and blue flamed hoops. NCOs: silver collar and cuff edging, silver hat edging, canes were carried. Sergeants had halberds. Officers: silver, scalloped hat edging and red-white and blue hat cords. The shoulder aiguillette was also tricolour, as were the sash and sword strap. They had eight silver laces to the chest, two on the cuff flaps, three on the pocket flaps, two in the small of the back. The gorget was silver with the red and white Hessian lion on a blue ground. Buff gloves, gilt-hilted sword in brown sheath, silver spontoon with brown staff.

Colours
Liebfahne: white cloth, central Hessian crest with supporters, gilt tip with the reversed cipher 'L' (Ludwig), brown staff, tricolour cords and tassels. Ordinair-fahne: staff and tip as for the Leibfahne, tricolour flamed cloth, red, white and blue, with a central blue field, enclosed by a wreath and holding the Hessian lion.

Infanterie-Regiment Nassau-Weilburg (In I Corps)
Initially one then two battalions, each of one grenadier and five musketeer companies and two 3-pounder guns. This regiment included seven companies from the city of Frankfurt and two from Waldeck.

Uniform
Prussian style, hat edging white, pompon white or blue and white. Dark blue coat, black stock, white collar, lapels, round cuffs and turnbacks, two white lace loops under the lapels, 8 white buttons (in pairs) on the lapels, two on each cuff and pocket flaps, two in the small of the back. White belts and small clothes, black gaiters. Grenadiers: dark blue front plate to cap, with golden lion crest, white-blue pompon, white bag, headband and braid. Brass grenade badges to headband, brass match case on the

bandolier. Small black pouch with brass grenade badge to front of belt. Officers: silver hat edging. There are no details of drummers or colours.

Infanterie-Regiment Pfalz-Zweibrücken (In I Corps)

This regiment was possibly called 'Isenburg' from 1757. It initially had three then two battalions, each of five musketeer companies and two 3-pounder guns. The Inhaber until 1758 was Field Marshal Graf von Isenburg-Philipseich.

Uniform

Prussian style, a scalloped white hat edging, red and white pompon. Dark blue coat with black stock, red lapels, Brandenburg cuffs and turnbacks, brass buttons, six on each lapel, each with a white buttonhole, two white laces under each lapel, two buttons and laces on each cuff flap. White small clothes and belts. Officers: silver hat edging and red and white sashes and sword straps. There are no details of drummers or colours.

Upper Rhine Kreis Squadron

Uniform

Plain hat with white and light blue pompon, white coat, black stock, light blue cuffs and turnbacks, white buttons, black cuirass with brass fittings, white belts, buff waistcoat and breeches. Brass-hilted sword in brown leather sheath, with light blue and white strap tassel. Shabraque light blue with white and light blue edging. Officers: silver hat edging and silver edging to their bandoliers.

Colours

Light blue, with silver fringes and embroidery, gilt finial, silver cords and tassels. The Bavarian cavalry were not mobilised in the Seven Years War.

Upper Saxon Kreis

Coburg Contingent

White coat, with red facings and waistcoat; eight buttons and yellow laces to each lapel, two over the cuff.

Hildburghausen Contingent

Dark blue coats, faced yellow, brass buttons, white small clothes and belts.

Wiemar Contingent

Dark blue coats faced red, with brass buttons, white small clothes and belts. Drummers: red and white braid edging to collar, lapels, cuffs, swallow's nests and pocket flaps and down the sleeve seams, with Hungarian knots over the cuffs. The drums were brass, the hoops light blue with red stripes. Officers: white and red sashes and sword straps.

Dragoner-Regiment Sachsen-Gotha

This unit had two squadrons, each of two companies. The uniform was of Prussian style, white coat, red facings, brass buttons in pairs on the lapels. White waistcoat, buff breeches, white belts.

Ducal Saxon Infanterie-Regiment

The unit consisted of two battalions, each of five musketeer companies; the men came from the contingents of Coburg, Hildburghausen and Weimar. Uniform was of Prussian style.

Westphalian Kreis

Infanterie-Regiment Elverfeldt

This unit was provided by the Bishopric of Münster; it had one grenadier and seven musketeer companies and two 4-pounder guns. In peacetime it was the Münster Infanterie-Regiment Nr 2 of two battalions. The Inhaber was Generallieutenant Friedrich Christian Georg von Elverfeldt, who did not accompany the regiment on campaign.

Uniform

Prussian style, white hat edging, red and white pompon. Prussian blue coat, red facings, brass buttons; three on each cuff. White belts and small clothes; red stock. Brass-hilted sabre in brown sheath. Grenadiers: pierced, brass-fronted caps with a red lining, backing and headband and yellow braid. There was a small pouch to the front of the waistbelt and a brass match case on the bandolier. Drummers: rich braid decoration to their coats, possibly blue and white in this case. Brass drum with the princely crest, the hoops were white and light blue, either in stripes or flames. NCOs: gold hat edging, canes, blue and white pompon and maybe gold braid to the cuffs, buff gloves. Sergeants bore halberds. Officers: gold hat edging and blue and white pompon, silver and light blue sash and sword strap, gold gorget. Possibly gold lace to coat, buff gloves and a spontoon.

Colours

There were two colours, but little definite is known of them. One had the Bavarian white and blue diamonds, in the centre, with the cross of the Teutonic Order and a green wreath around the shield. Another pattern was white, with the central cipher 'MF' under an Electoral cap, all within a green wreath. Finials were gilt, the staffs in blue and white rings.

Infanterie-Regiment Mengersen

This unit was provided by the Bishopric of Paderborn; it had one grenadier, five musketeer companies and two 4-pounder guns. The Inhaber was Generallieutenant Freiherr Ferdinand Moritz von Mengersen, who did not accompany the regiment on campaign.

Uniform

Prussian style, hat edging and pompon white, Prussian blue coat with red lapels, cuffs and turnbacks, the first two edged white, white buttons, belts and small clothes. Seven buttons on each lapel, two beneath. There is no information available concerning the dress of officers, NCOs, drummers or as to the colours carried.

Infanterie-Regiment von Nagel

This unit was provided by the Bishopric of Münster; it had one grenadier, seven musketeer companies and two 4-pounder guns. In peacetime it was Münster Infanterie-Regiment Nr 5. The Inhaber was Oberst (later general) Joseph Marsil von Nagel zu Loburg. The uniform and colours were as for Infanterie-Regiment Elverfeldt, except that the hat pompon was different, but the difference is not known.

Artillery

Münster provided all artillery personnel; it consisted of a lieutenant, two ensigns, six NCOs and 27 gunners. Uniform: plain hat, dark blue coat, red facings, white buttons, small clothes and belts. There were 48 two-horse wagons and four pack horses.

6

THE DUCAL ELECTORATE OF BAVARIA AND THE PALATINATE

From 1745 to 1777, Bavaria was ruled by Maximilian Joseph of the House of Wittelsbach. These two states were combined in 1777, when the Bavarian branch of the family died out. There were the following Bavarian line infantry regiments in 1757, each with two battalions (except the Leibregiment, which had three), each consisting of a grenadier company and four musketeer companies. There was no light infantry and no cavalry was mobilised.

Uniform

Hair was powdered, curled and worn in a plaited pigtail. Cockades were light blue within white. Grenadiers wore Austrian-style bearskin caps with a bag in the facing colour, braid and tassel in the button colour. Coats were dark blue until 1760, when they changed to cornflower blue. Neck stocks were black for officers, red for the men. Facings were worn on collar, lapels, cuffs and lining. Belts were white, the long gaiters were black. Officers wore edging in the button colour to their tricorns, silver and light blue waist sashes and sword knots, wore silvered gorgets on duty; company officers carried spontoons.

Trooper, Bavarian Cavalry Regiment Prinz Maximilian. (David Morier (406839) from the Royal Collection)

Left to right: grenadiers of Bavarian infantry regiments Leibregiment, von Seckendorff and von Preysing, 1751. (David Morier (406829) from the Royal Collection)

The skirts of officers' coats were not turned back. NCOs had silver edging to collar and cuffs, carried canes and bore halberds. Drummers wore reversed colours up to 1760; after this they wore the normal regimental uniform, with swallow's nests at the shoulders, decorated with the yellow arms of Bavaria. The sleeves of their coats were edged with blue and white lace, which was also in chevrons on their sleeves and edged their cuffs. Drums were brass, with blue and white hoops. The artillery wore a blue-grey coat with dark blue facings.

Regiment	Facings	Buttons	Waistcoat	Breeches
Leibregiment	white★	white	white	white
Kurprinz	white	yellow	yellow	yellow
Herzog Clemens	orange	yellow	orange	dark blue
Minucci	yellow	white	yellow	yellow
Morawitzky	red	white	red	red
Preysing	red	white	yellow	yellow
Holnstein	pink	white	yellow	yellow
Pechmann	buff	yellow	buff	buff

★ these changed to black, decorated with white buttonhole laces during the war, but the exact date of the change is unclear.

7

THE DUCHY OF BRUNSWICK

The reigning duke was Carl I, who was born on 1 August 1713 in Braunschweig. He moved the ducal court there from Wolfenbüttel in 1753. The Duchy mobilised troops alongside the army of Frederick the Great.

Infantry

The uniforms, organisation, drill and tactics were modelled on those of Prussia. Each regiment had two battalions, each of one grenadier and five musketeer companies, each with 100 men. Musketeers wore tricorns with black cockades; grenadiers had metal-fronted mitre caps in the button colour, all in the Prussian style, bearing the crowned, reversed cipher 'C', over the springing white horse of Lower Saxony. The cap was topped with a pompon in the regimental colours. Coats were dark blue, with facings worn on the lying collar, round cuffs and lapels (if worn). Waistcoats, breeches and belts were white, unless otherwise mentioned. Some regiments had lace loops to the buttonholes. The long gaiters were black in winter, white in summer, and the neck stock was black. Hair was rolled, queued and powdered for parades. Corporals wore white or yellow lace edging to their cuffs and carried sticks, sergeants wore silver or gold lace (also to the hat) and those of musketeers carried halberds and canes. Grenadier NCOs carried short muskets and a small pouch on the front of the waistbelt. Drummers wore yellow coats, decorated with five bars of white lace on the sleeves and with swallows' nests in the facing colour at the shoulders. Officers wore silver gorgets, with red enamel inserts bearing the white horse on duty and silver and yellow sashes and sword straps. Company officers carried spontoons, with the crowned, reversed ducal cipher 'C'. The skirts of their coats were not turned back.

Brunswick grenadier cap, 1751.

Combined Grenadier Battalions

No 1
Leib-Regiment/Imhoff Grenadiers, independent as Battalion von Stammer in 1759, Warnstedt in 1761.

No 2
Behr/Zastrow Grenadiers, independent as battalion von Redecken in 1759, Imhoff in 1761.

No 3
Zastrow/Militia Grenadiers, formed of grenadiers contributed from von Zastrow and militia, raised in 1759 as Battalion von Wittdorf, Rothenburg in 1761, later Koppelow, Appelboom in 1762.

Füsilier-Battalion Von Völschen
Raised in July 1760 at four companies; it saw no action during the war.

Infanterie-Regiment von Stammer
Raised in 1688, 1756 von Behr; 1760 Mansberg. Red facings and lining; the lapels and round cuffs edged in white, white buttons; officers had gold lace to their hats. Yellow waistcoats. Hat pompon white within red. Grenadier cap: backing dark blue, headband white.

Infanterie-Regiment von Zastrow
Raised in 1683. Prinz Friedrich in 1761. Yellow facings, white buttons and cap plate, dark blue backing, white headband. Hat pompon white within dark blue.

Infanterie-Regiment von Imhoff
Raised in 1748. White facings, two white, bastion-ended lace loops under each lapel and in the small of the back. Brass buttons. The grenadier cap had a brass plate, dark blue backing, white headband. Hat pompon blue and white.

Left to right: grenadiers of the Brunswick infantry regiments von Weyhe, von Imhoff and von Kniestadt 1751. (David Morier, the Royal Collection)

Jäger Corps zu Fuss

Raised in 1759 as part of the Brunswick Jäger Corps, along with the Jäger Corps zu Pferd (see below). 1759 von Hoym; disbanded 1763. There were three foot brigades, in one of which the men supplied their own rifles. Dark green coat and waistcoat, red facings, white buttons and breeches, black belts.

Leib-Grenadiers

One battalion, raised in 1759; it did not take the field.

Leib-Regiment

Raised in 1666. Red facings and lining, no lapels. White, bastion-ended lace loops to front of coat and to the cuffs, brass buttons, scalloped white lace to the tricorn. Officers wore gold lace buttonholes and had gold lace to their hats. The grenadier cap had a brass plate, red backing, white headband. Red pompon with a white core. Their black cartridge pouch had a central, round brass plate and four corner grenades.

'Volontaires Auxiliaires' (Husaren-Eskadron der Volontaries Auxiliars de Bronswick)

Raised in 1762. 1759 von Rauch. It consisted of consisted of three companies of grenadiers (417 men) and 3 squadrons, one each of Turks, hussars and grenadiers à cheval (388 men). The mounted Turks wore white turbans wound around a red fez. Light blue, Turkish costume with a red sash, under a black kaftan, laced in white. The lance pennants were light blue over yellow, the sabre belts red, the scabbard was of steel, the harness black with brass fittings. In January 1763 the unit was taken into Prussian service. It was then disbanded and the men incorporated into the Magdeburg inspection infantry regiments.

Cavalry

Dragoner-Regiment Prinz Ludwig

This unit was converted into a regiment of carabiniers in 1759 (from 1760 onwards they were with the Allied army). Their uniform was initially red coats with green facings, waistcoat and lining, yellow buttons, buff breeches. In 1759 they were re-clothed in buff tunics, red collar, round cuffs and waistcoat, buff turnbacks edged red, buff breeches. There was also a red waist sash and waistcoat. The plain tricorn had a white over yellow plume and the cuirass was blackened, with the crowned ducal cipher in brass. The shoulder scales were brass. They also wore a red sabretasche, with a double white border and the white, crowned ducal cipher. Their brass-hilted straight swords had black scabbards on white slings.

Garde du Corps

One squadron of palace troops; they were not mobilised. Officers wore a dark blue coat, yellow cuffs, silver buttons and lace decoration, silver scalloped hat edging. The men wore yellow coats, faced and lined dark blue, dark blue waistcoats, silver buttons and hat edging.

Husaren-Regiment von Roth

Raised 1759; 1761 von Riedesel. Black mirliton, lined yellow; medium blue dolman, pelisse and breeches, black fur trim. The collar, pointed cuffs, buttons and lacing were yellow, the barrel sash red and yellow. They also had a yellow waistcoat and their boots were trimmed with yellow. Blue shabraque with yellow, wolf's tooth edging. The sabretsche was probably blue with yellow edging and crest. NCOs had silver lace edging to collar and cuffs.; officers' lace and buttons was gold.

Jäger Corps zu Pferd

Raised in 1759 as part of the Brunswick Jäger Corps. Dark green coats and waistcoats, buff facings.

Artillery

In 1746, the artillery had four companies. During the War of the Austrian Succession (1740–1748), one company was part of the contingent of Brunswick (4800 men) subsidised by England. In 1757, there were three companies with some 272 men, serving 14 pieces (six 3-pounder guns, two howitzers, six 2-pounder guns). In 1760 the unit was increased to 320 men. This regiment included the engineers. The uniform was a dark blue coat, red facings, lining and waistcoat, yellow buttons.

Colours

No colours or pictures of them from this era have survived. Each musketeer company carried a colour, the grenadiers carried none. They were probably of Prussian style, the red central disc having the springing white horse under the ducal crown, within laurel branches. The field bore an upright, wavy cross, with a grenade at the centre of each side. In each corner was the reversed, crowned ducal cipher 'C', within laurel branches. This motif was repeated in the gilt finial. The field of the Leibfahne was probably white, the cross blue, embroidery silver. The Ordinair-fahnen probably had a white upright cross and fields in the regimental facing colour.

Standards

The dragoons had swallow-tailed guidons, the cloth of the Leibstandarte was white, the others light blue. The heraldry was the same on all: on the one side the crowned crest of the duchy within golden laurel branches, tied with a blue ribbon. In each corner a golden rose. The other side was identical, except that the central motif was the springing white horse. There is no evidence of any standard carried by the carabiniers.

Left: Brunswick grenadier fifer, Leib-Regiment, full dress, 1756. He wears the Brunswick national colours of yellow and light blue. (Bayer-Pegau) Right: Brunswick grenadier NCO, Leib-Regiment, 1756. (Bayer-Pegau)

8

THE KINGDOM OF FRANCE

The monarch who reigned France and Navarre throughout this period was Louis XV, of the House of Bourbon. Born on 15 February 1710, he took the throne on 1 September 1715. Initially, Louis XV was a popular monarch, but the debauchery of his court, the return of the Austrian Netherlands (which had been gained following the Battle of Fontenoy on 11 May 1745) under the terms of the Treaty of Aix-la-Chapelle in 1748, the cession of New France (the vast tract of territory from northern Canada to the Gulf of Mexico and extending westwards to Lake Manitoba and Lake Winnipeg) to Britain and the loss of most of France's East and West Indian colonies at the conclusion of the Seven Years War in 1763, led Louis to become one of the most unpopular French kings.

Maison du Roi (Household Troops)

Units of this corps had richly ornamented ceremonial uniforms, which are not considered here. Badges of rank were as for the line. Officers wore gilt gorgets; the skirts of their coats were not turned back. Hair was powdered, curled and worn in a plaited pigtail.

Guards Infantry

Gardes Françaises
Raised on 1 August 1563. Six battalions each of one grenadier and five fusilier companies. Tricorn with white edging (also for the grenadiers), blue coat, red cuffs and lining, red waistcoat and breeches, no lapels, white buttons and pointed lace buttonholes (in groups of three) to coat, lapels, cuffs, pocket flaps and waistcoat, white edging to waistcoat. White fleur-de-lis to the turnbacks. Buff belts, edged white. In 1760, some battalions of this regiment fought in Germany under Prince Soubise.

Gardes Suisses
Raised in 1567. Four battalions each of six fusilier companies; the 16 best men of each company were grenadiers. Tricorn with white edging (also for the grenadiers), red coat, blue cuffs and lining, blue waistcoat and breeches, no lapels, white buttons and pointed lace buttonholes (in groups of three) to coat, cuffs, lapels, pocket flaps and waistcoat, white edging to waistcoat. Red fleur-de-lis to the turnbacks. Buff belts, edged white. In 1760, some battalions of this regiment fought in Germany under Prince Soubise.

Guards Cavalry

Garde du Corps (1st Company Écosse)
Raised in 1440. 1731 Duc de Ayen.

2nd Company (1st Française)
Raised on 4 September 1474. Duc de Mirepoix.

3rd Company (2nd Française)
Raised in 1479.

4th Company (3rd Française)
Raised on 1 March 1615.

All four companies wore blue, single-breasted coats, with red cuffs, lining, waistcoat and breeches, white edging to cuffs and waistcoat, white buttonhole loops to coat and waistcoat. The red saddle furniture was edged white. They were distinguished by the decoration on their silver bandoliers: 1st white squares; 2nd white and green squares; 3rd blue and silver squares; 4th yellow and silver squares.

Grenadiers Royaux
There were also eleven battalions of Grenadiers Royaux. These were militia named after their commanders. They wore the usuan tricorns edged in white Their facings were worn only on the coat collar, all buttons were white and they had horizontal pocket flaps with four buttons. They all carried a dark blue colour with a white upright cross, the latter sewn with gold fleur-de-lis. The finial was gilt, the cravat white. They are listed below for the name of their commander in 1756.

Grenadiers Royaux de Bergeret
(1759 de Narbonne), facings royal blue.

Grenadiers Royaux de Bruslan
(1759 d'Aulans), facings red.

Grenadiers Royaux de Chabrilland
(1762 Miromesnil), facings red edged white.

Grenadiers Royaux de Châtillon
(1759 de Longaunay; 1761 de Hoffelize), facings yellow.

Grenadiers Royaux de Chantilly
(1762 du Plessis d'Argentré), facings royal blue.

Grenadiers Royaux de Coincy
(1761 de Cambis), facings purple.

Grenadiers Royaux d'Aulans
(1759 le Camus; 1761 de Puységur; 1762 la Roche-Lambert), facings black.

Grenadiers Royaux de La Tresne
(1762 d'Aigremont), facings yellow edged white.

Grenadiers Royaux de Modène
(1761 le Camus), facings red edged green.

Grenadiers Royaux de Prugues
(1757 de Guyon; May 1757 d'Ally), facings dark green.

Grenadiers Royaux de Solar
(1759 Méhégan), facings red edged black.

Infantry

In 1749 each battalion of infantry consisted of one grenadier and twelve fusilier companies. Some regiments had a single battalion, others as many as four.

Uniform

In 1740 the French Army had the following regiments of line infantry: 99 (156 battalions) were French regiments and wore white coats. There were five German regiments (six battalions); they and the Scottish regiments wore dark blue coats. There were five Irish regiments of one battalion each and nine Swiss regiments (17 battalions). Both these latter nationalities wore red coats.

Tricorns were worn, laced in the button colour, with a black cockade. It was not until late in the war that grenadiers began to adopt the plain fur mitre cap. Coats, waistcoats, breeches, gaiters and belts were white, unless otherwise stated. Facings could be worn on collars, cuffs, lapels and turnbacks. No regiments had lapels unless specifically mentioned. All regiments had cuffs, and horizontal skirt pockets with three buttons, unless otherwise mentioned; many had double or triple pocket flaps, with up to three buttons to each buttonhole. Knötel gives buttons as 'yellow' or 'white'; some contemporary French sources state that the 'yellow' buttons were in fact made of copper.

Company officers carried a short fusil. Officers' coats were laced in silver or gold (the button colour) and they wore silver gorgets with the crowned, reversed royal cipher ('L'), when on duty. The skirts of their coats were not turned back. Sergeants had cuffs edged in silver or gold (the button colour) with three silver/gold loops on them. They carried halberds. Corporals had yellow/white cuff edging and loops; they also carried halberds. Hair was powdered, curled and worn in a plaited pigtail.

Drummers of French regiments wore the royal livery: dark blue coat, red collar, cuffs and lining, crimson and white chain-link pattern lace to the edges of lapels, cuffs, to the buttonholes, sleeve seams and to the edges of the buff drum bandolier. Drums were blue with yellow fleur-de-lis on the body; hoops were blue, cords white. Drummers of German regiments seem to have worn the royal livery; those of Irish regiments wore lace to the sleeves of their jackets. It is not known how the drummers of the Italian, Scottish and Swiss were dressed.

Nationality	Regimental Numbers
German	36, 46, 66, 101, 106, 108, 110, 111, 114, 115, 116, 118, 119
Irish	92, 93, 94, 98, 99, 109
Italian	48, 103
Liege	120, 121
Scottish	107, 113
Swedish	95
Swiss	49, 50, 51, 52, 55, 63, 90, 91, 102, 117

The dates of raising shown in the entries below are those dates on which the regiments were taken into the French standing army. Many of the older units had existed in private service for years prior to this date. Some of the regiments were named after royal figures or provinces; their titles did not change during the war. Other regiments had colonels-in-chief who were replaced during the conflict, thus their names changed.

Colours

Each company carried a colour. The senior company bore the King's or Colonel's colour, which was usually white and covered with gold fleur-de-lis. The other companies carried a colour '*d'ordonnance*', which had an upright white cross in the centre, often strewn with gold fleur-de-lis. The four fields were in various colours, most of which had no relation to the facings of the regiment.

The colours of the German regiments were often related to their regimental background, and much more colourful. Those of the Swiss regiments were most colourful, usually incorporating wavy, multi-coloured designs, emanating from the centre. Colours of Irish regiments incorporated the crown over the golden harp and the motto 'IN HOC SIGNO VINCES' ('victory with this sign'). They also reflected the colours of the regimental uniform. The colours of the Scottish regiments bore the St Andrew's cross, thistles and fleur-de-lis and the motto 'NEMO ME IMPUNE LACESSIT' ('none touch me with impunity'). The finial was a gilt spearpoint, from which a white cravatte hung to about half way down the colour.

The following entries are after Knötel, dated 1761. Details of the pockets and button distribution are taken from *Étrennes Militaires* of 1756 and 1758 and from *État Militair* of 1758, 1760 and 1761. There was obviously much changing of uniform detail during the war. The numbering system used here is based on regimental seniority in 1758 and was not used in practice.

Picardie Infanterie Nr 1

Raised in 1558. Four battalions. White collar, cuffs and lining, vertical pockets, red waistcoat, yellow buttons.

Champagne Infanterie Nr 2

Raised in 1588. Four battalions. White collar, cuffs and lining, double vertical pockets, red waistcoat, yellow buttons.

Navarre Infanterie Nr 3

Raised in 1588. Four battalions. White collar, cuffs and lining, red waistcoat, yellow buttons.

Piémont Infanterie Nr 4

Raised on 27 May 1569. Four battalions. White collar and lining, black cuffs, yellow buttons.

Normandie Infanterie Nr 5

Raised in 1616. Four battalions. Black collar and cuffs, white lining, white buttons.

La Marine Infanterie Nr 6

Raised on 26 September 1635. Four battalions. Black collar and cuffs, white lining, yellow loops red waistcoat, yellow buttons.

La Tour-du-Pin Infanterie Nr 7

Raised on 9 October 1595. Philippe Gabriel Marquis de. February 1761 René Gabriel, Comt de Boisgelin. Four battalions. Red collar, white cuffs and lining, yellow buttons.

Bourbonnois Infanterie Nr 8

Raised on 6 March 1597. Four battalions. Coat all white, no collar, double vertical pockets, each with six yellow buttons.

Auvergne Infanterie Nr 9

Raised in September 1635. Four battalions. White coat and buttons, no lapels until late in the war, violet cuffs and lapels.

Belzunce Infanterie Nr 10

Raised on 16 August 1597. Vicomte de Armand; February 1761 Gabrile François, Comte de Rouge. Four battalions. No collar, violet cuffs, yellow buttons. Violet lapels late in the war.

Mailly Infanterie Nr 11

Raised on 24 April 1610. Marquis de Louis; January 1758 César Marie, Marquis de Talaru; November 1761 Chevalier de Chatellux. Two battalions. All white coat, vertical pockets, yellow buttons, red waistcoat.

Du Roi Infanterie Nr 12

Raised on 2 January 1663. Four battalions. Blue cuffs, lining, waistcoat and breeches, yellow buttons. Three groups of orange buttonhole laces, with pointed ends, on the chest; the same lace loops to cuffs, pocket flaps and waistcoat, but singly on the latter garment.

Royal Infanterie Nr 13

Raised in 1660. Two battalions until December 1762, when it took in the disbanded Cambris Infanterie and had four. Light blue cuffs and waistcoat, white buttons, double vertical pockets.

Poitou Infanterie Nr 14

Raised on 16 September 1616. Two battalions until December 1762, when it took in the disbanded St Mauris Infanterie, thence four. Dark blue cuffs and waistcoat, yellow buttons, double, vertical pocket flaps, pointing outwards, each with six buttons.

Lyonnais Infanterie Nr 15

Raised in 1635. Two battalions until December 1762, when it took in the disbanded Nice Infanterie Nr 65, thence four. Red collar, cuffs and waistcoat, yellow buttons, double vertical pockets.

Dauphin Infanterie Nr 16

Raised on 15 June 1667. Two battalions until December 1762, when it took in the disbanded Guyenne Infanterie, thence four. No collar, yellow buttons, light blue cuffs with 19 small buttons along the top, double vertical pockets with nine large buttons on each flap, light blue waistcoat.

Vaubécourt Infanterie Nr 17

Raised on 7 July 1621. Two battalions until December 1762, when it took in the disbanded Lorraine Infanterie, thence four. At this point, the regiment's title became 'Aunis'. Black lapels, collar and cuffs, red waistcoat, yellow buttons, six on the pocket flap, five on the cuff.

Touraine Infanterie Nr 18

Raised on 29 April 1625. Two battalions. In December 1762, this unit took in the men of the disbanded Flandres Infanterie. Blue collar, cuffs and waistcoat, white lapels, double vertical pockets, facing outwards, with six white buttons on each.

Aquitaine Infanterie Nr 19

Raised on 17 January 1625. Two battalions until December 1762, when it took in the men of the disbanded Berry Infanterie, thence four. Dark blue collar, cuffs, lapels and waistcoat, yellow buttons, five on the pocket flap, four on the cuff.

D'Eu Infanterie Nr 20

Raised in March 1630. Two battalions. Dark blue collar cuffs and waistcoat, yellow buttons, three on the cuffs and the pocket flaps.

La Vieuville St Chaumont Infanterie Nr 21

Raised on 26 October 1629. Charles Louis Auguste de La Vieuville, Marquis de Saint-Chamond; May 1762 Eugène Octave Augustin Comte de Rosen. Two battalions. Carmine collar, cuffs and lapels, yellow buttons, three on the cuff, seven on the deep, square pocket flap.

Montmorin Infanterie Nr 22

Raised on 26 October 1629. 1745 Jean Baptiste Calixte, marquis de Montmorin de Saint-Herem; 1762 Comte de Crenolle. Two battalions. In December 1762 the regiment became Ile de France. Red collar, cuffs and waistcoat, double vertical pockets, yellow buttons, six on each pocket flap, four on each cuff.

Briqueville Infanterie Nr 23

Raised on 3 February 1630. N. de la Lucerne, Marquis de Briqueville. Two battalions. In December 1762 the regiment became Soissonnais. Red collar and cuffs, yellow buttons.

La Reine Infanterie Nr 24

Raised in 1659. Two battalions. Red collar, cuffs and lapels, dark blue waistcoat, white buttons, three on the cuff, eight on the deep, square pocket flap.

Limousin Infanterie Nr 25

Raised on 23 March 1684. Two battalions. Red cuffs and lapels, no collar, yellow buttons, two pairs on the cuff, two pairs on the pocket flaps.

Privates of Lyonnais Infanterie Nr 15. The two figures on the left show the uniform worn at least up to the end of 1762; that on the right is the simplified costume decreed to be adopted in 1763. The tunic has smaller skirts and reduced pockets and buttons. (Knötel, XVIII 39)

Royal-Vaisseaux Infanterie Nr 26
Raised on 20 September 1699. Two battalions. Blue collar and cuffs, yellow buttons.

Orléans Infanterie Nr 27
Raised 7 May 1642. Two battalions. Red collar, cuffs and waistcoat, yellow buttons.

La Couronne Infanterie Nr 28
Raised on 25 June 1643. Two battalions. Blue collar, cuffs and waistcoat, white buttons.

Bretagne Infanterie Nr 29
Raised on 4 February 1644. Two battalions. No collar, white cuffs, red lining and waistcoat, black lapels, yellow buttons.

Gardes Lorraines Infanterie Nr 30
Raised in April 1644 in Piemont, taken into French service in 1659. Two battalions. Blue coat, cuffs, skirts, breeches and waistcoats, no collar, white buttons and buttonhole lace loops.

Artois Infanterie Nr 31
Raised in 1610. Two battalions. Red waistcoat, yellow buttons, seven on each cuff, nine on each deep, square pocket flap.

Rohan-Montbazon Infanterie Nr 32
Raised in 1634 from Swedish recruits. 1745 Jules Hercules Mériadec Prince de Rohan and Duke de Montbazon; 1759 Florent Alexandre Melchior de La Baume, Comte de Montrevel. Two battalions. Red collar, cuffs and waistcoat, white buttons.

La Roche Aymon Infanterie Nr 33
Raised on 25 February 1651. 1745 Antoine Louis François, Marquis de la Roche-Aymon; 1760 Louis François Joseph, Comte de Montmorency Logny; 1761 Anne Charles Sigismond, Marquis de Royans. On 10 December 1762 the regiment took the name of the province of Hainaut. Two battalions. White collar, red cuffs and waistcoat, white buttons.

La Sarre Infanterie Nr 34
Raised on 20 May 1651. Two battalions. Blue collar and cuffs, red waistcoat, yellow buttons.

La Fère Infanterie Nr 35
Raised in October 1654. Two battalions. Red collar and cuffs, white buttons.

Alsace Infanterie Nr 36
A German regiment, raised for Swedish service, taken into French service in 1632. Three battalions until 18 January 1760, when it took in the men from Bergh Infanterie Nr 108 and had four battalions. Blue coat, red collar, cuffs, lapels and lining, white buttons.

Royal Roussillon Infanterie Nr 37
Raised on 25 May 1657. Two battalions. Blue collar, cuffs and waistcoat, yellow buttons, six on the cuff, three on the pocket flap.

Condé Infanterie Nr 38
Raised on 11 June 1644. Two battalions. Red collar, cuffs, lining and waistcoat, yellow buttons.

Bourbon Infanterie Nr 39

Raised on 8 July 1635. Two battalions. The title was retained until 1791. Red collar, cuffs and waistcoat, white buttons, five on the cuff, nine on each double, vertical pocket flap.

Grenadiers de France Nr 40

Raised on 15 February 1749 from 48 companies of grenadiers of disbanded units. Four brigades, each of twelve companies. Disbanded 4 August 1771. Blue coat and breeches, red collar edged white, blue cuffs with white lace buttonholes, red lapels and waistcoat, both with white lace buttonholes, white buttons. This unit wore a black bearskin with a red bag and tassel.

Beauvoisis Infanterie Nr 41

Raised on 12 July 1667. Two battalions. Red waistcoat, double vertical pockets, with six buttons on each flap, white buttons.

Rouergue Infanterie Nr 42

Raised on 20 November 1667. Two battalions. Red collar, cuffs and waistcoat, yellow buttons.

Bourgogne Infanterie Nr 43

Raised on 1 March 1668. Two battalions. White collar, red waistcoat, yellow buttons.

Royal Marine Infanterie Nr 44

Raised on 24 December 1669 for naval service; taken into the French Army in 1671. Two battalions. Blue collar, cuffs and waistcoat, white buttons.

Vermandois Infanterie Nr 45

Raised on 24 December 1699 for naval service; taken into the French Army: December 1671. Two battalions. Red collar and cuffs, blue waistcoat, yellow buttons, double vertical pocket flaps, six buttons on each flap.

Bentheim Infanterie Nr 46

A German regiment, raised in February 1668; it was taken into French service on 27 March 1670. Two battalions. 1759 Prinz von Anhalt-Köthen. On 18 January 1760 it took in men from the 1st Battalion of the disbanded Löwendahl Infanterie Nr 106, to have three battalions. Dark blue coat, buff collar, lapels, cuffs and lining, pinned back with two red hearts in the corners, white buttons. Some sources give double vertical pocket flaps.

Royal Artillerie Nr 47

Raised in 1671; Tricorn with yellow edging, dark blue coat, no lapels. Dark blue coat, red collar, cuffs, lining, waistcoat and breeches, brass buttons, buff belts.

Royal Italien Infanterie Nr 48

Raised on 27 April 1671. White, single-breasted coat, light blue collar, cuffs, lining, waistcoat and breeches, yellow buttons. Yellow lace buttonhole loops to coat and waistcoat.

Jenner Infanterie Nr 49

Raised in Berne on 17 February 1672; a Swiss regiment. Two battalions. Red coat and breeches, blue waistcoat, blue facings and turnbacks, white buttons. Blue lace buttonholes to the coat, white buttonholes and edging to the waistcoat.

Boccard Infanterie Nr 50
Raised on 17 February 1672; a Swiss regiment. Two battalions. Red coat, blue facings, waistcoat and breeches, white buttons. Blue buttonholes to the red lapels.

Reding Infanterie Nr 51
Raised on 16 February 1672; a Swiss regiment. Two battalions. Red coat, blue facings, turnbacks, waistcoat and breeches, white buttons. Blue buttonholes to the chest and pocket flaps.

Castellas Infanterie Nr 52
Raised on 5 December 1673; a Swiss regiment. 1757 Comte de Waldner. Two battalions. Red coat, lapels and breeches, blue collar, cuffs, turnbacks and waistcoat, white buttons. Blue buttonholes to the red lapels.

Languedoc Infanterie Nr 53
Raised on 20 March 1672. Two battalions. Blue collar, cuffs and lapels, yellow buttons.

Talaru Infanterie Nr 54
Raised on 30 October 1673. 1745 Marquis de Talaru; 1758 d'Aumont Duc de Mazarin; 1762 Comte de la Tour du Pin. Two battalions. All white, red waistcoat, yellow buttons, five each on the deep, square pocket flaps.

Wittmer Infanterie Nr 55
Raised 5 December 1673; a Swiss regiment. 1757 Comte de Waldner de Freudenstein. Red coat and lapels, blue collar, cuffs, lining, waistcoat and breeches, white buttons.

Médoc Infanterie Nr 56
Raised on 19 February 1674. Two battalions. Red collar, cuffs and waistcoat, white buttons.

Brissac Infanterie Nr 57
Raised on 1 March 1674. 1749: Cossé Duc de Brissac; 1759 Chevalier de Lemps; 1761 Vicomte de Puységur. Two battalions. Red collar, cuffs and waistcoat, no lapels, yellow buttons.

Vastan Infanterie Nr 58
Raised on 1 March 1674. 1748 Aubery Marquis de Vastan; 1761 François Claude Marquis de Bouillé du Chariol. From December 1762 the regiment was called Vexin. Two battalions. No collar, red cuffs and waistcoat, yellow buttons. Double vertical pocket flaps, each with six buttons.

Royal Comtois Infanterie Nr 59
Raised in 1685. 1757 Comte de Puységur; 1762 Comte de Noë. Two battalions. Blue collar and waistcoat, no lapels, yellow buttons. Double vertical pocket flaps, each with nine buttons.

Traisnel Infanterie Nr 60
Raised on 15 November 1674. 1742 Marquis de Traisnel. 1757 Comte de Brancas; 1758 Comte de Durfort. In December 1762 the regiment became the Beaujolais Infanterie. Two battalions. Crimson collar and lapels, blue cuffs, yellow buttons.

Provence Infanterie Nr 61
Raised on 4 December 1674. Two battalions. Red collar and waistcoat, white cuffs and lining, yellow buttons, nine small ones along the top of the cuff, four large ones on the pocket flap.

Cambis Infanterie Nr 62

Raised on 23 January 1676. Two battalions. Red collar, cuffs and waistcoat. A mixture of white and yellow buttons; white and yellow trim to the hat.

Planta Infanterie Nr 63

Raised on 28 January 1677; a Swiss regiment. Two battalions. Red coat, collar and cuffs, blue lining, waistcoat and breeches, white buttons; blue lace buttonholes to chest and pocket flaps.

Rohan-Rochefort Infanterie Nr 64

Raised on 22 February 1677. 1745 Prince de Rohan-Rochefort; 1761 Philibert-Yolandre de Saint-Mauris. In December 1762, this regiment was absorbed into the Poitou Infanterie Nr 14. Two battalions. Red collar, blue cuffs, with white lace buttonholes, yellow buttons.

Nice Infanterie Nr 65

Raised on 8 December 1678. Two battalions. Red cuffs and waistcoat, yellow buttons, vertical pocket flaps.

La Marck Infanterie Nr 66

Raised on 10 August 1680; a German regiment. Two battalions until 18 January 1760, when it took in the 2nd Battalion, Löwendahl Infanterie Nr 106. Blue coat, no collar, white cuffs and lining, buff lapels, white buttons. White lace buttonholes to coat.

Penthièvre Infanterie Nr 67

Raised on 20 February 1684. Blue collar and waistcoat, yellow cuffs, vertical pocket flaps, white buttons.

Guyenne Infanterie Nr 68

Raised on 21 February 1674. Two battalions. In 1762 this regiment was disbanded; the men went to Dauphin Infanterie Nr 16. Red collar and waistcoat, blue cuffs, yellow buttons.

Lorraine Infanterie Nr 69

Raised on 21 February 1684. Three battalions. Red cuffs and waistcoat, white collar, yellow buttons.

Flandres Infanterie Nr 70

Raised on 1 September 1684. Two battalions. On 10 December 1672 this regiment was disbanded; the men went to the Touraine Infanterie Nr 18. Blue collar and waistcoat, white and yellow buttons, two each along the top of the cuff, three yellow and two white on the deep, square pocket flap. White and yellow hat trim.

Berry Infanterie Nr 71

Raised on 2 September 1684. Three battalions. Red collar and waistcoat, blue cuffs, yellow buttons.

Béarn Infanterie Nr 72

Raised on 3 September 1684. Two battalions. Disbanded 25 November 1762; the men were dispersed to various regiments. Red collar, cuffs and waistcoat, yellow buttons.

Haynault Infanterie Nr 73

Raised on 4 September 1764. Two battalions. Disbanded 25 November 1762; the men were dispersed to various regiments. Red collar, cuffs and waistcoat, yellow buttons, nine on the deep square pocket flaps.

Boulonnois Infanterie Nr 74

Raised on 5 September 1684. One battalion. Blue collar and waistcoat, yellow buttons, four on each cuff, six on each deep, square pocket flap.

Angoumois Infanterie Nr 75

Raised on 6 September 1684. Two battalions. Blue collar, cuffs and waistcoat, white buttons.

Périgord Infanterie Nr 76

Raised on 7 September 1684. One battalion. Blue collar and cuffs, red waistcoat, white buttons.

Saintonge Infanterie Nr 77

Raised on 8 September 1684. One battalion. Blue collar, cuffs and waistcoat, yellow buttons.

Bigorre Infanterie Nr 78

Raised on 9 September 1684. One battalion. Blue collar, cuffs and waistcoat, yellow buttons.

Forez Infanterie Nr 79

Raised on 10 September 1684. One battalion. Red collar, cuffs and waistcoat, yellow buttons.

Cambrésis Infanterie Nr 80

Raised on 11 September 1684. One battalion. Red collar, cuffs and waistcoat, yellow buttons, nine on the horizontal pocket flap.

Tournaisis Infanterie Nr 81

Raised on 12 September 1684. One battalion. Red collar, cuffs and waistcoat, yellow buttons, five along the top of the cuff, five on the horizontal pocket flap.

Foix Infanterie Nr 82

Raised on 13 September 1684. One battalion. Red collar and cuffs, blue waistcoat, yellow buttons.

Bresse Infanterie Nr 83

Raised on 14 September 1684. One battalion. No collar, blue cuffs and waistcoat, yellow buttons, six on the cuff, six on the pocket flaps.

La Marche Infanterie Nr 84

Raised on 15 September 1684. One battalion. No collar, red cuffs, lapels and waistcoat, yellow buttons, nine on the pocket flap.

Quercy Infanterie Nr 85

Raised on 16 September 1684. One battalion. Red collar, cuffs and waistcoat, yellow buttons, five on the cuff, five on the pocket flap.

Comte de la Marche Infanterie Nr 86

Raised on 17 September 1684. One battalion. Blue collar, cuffs, lapels and waistcoat, white buttons.

Brie Infanterie Nr 87

Raised on 18 September 1684. One battalion. Disbanded 25 November 1762. Red collar, cuffs and waistcoat, yellow buttons, nine on the vertical pocket flap.

Soissonois Infanterie Nr 88

Raised on 19 September 1684. One battalion. Disbanded 25 November 1762. Blue collar, cuffs and waistcoat, yellow buttons, five on the cuff, five on the pocket flap.

Isle de France Infanterie Nr 89

Raised on 20 September 1684. One battalion. Disbanded 25 November 1762.

Diesbach Infanterie Nr 90

Raised on 1 January 1690; a Swiss regiment. Two battalions. Red coat, blue facings, waistcoat and breeches, white buttons.

Courten Infanterie Nr 91

Raised on 6 February 1690; a Swiss regiment. Two battalions. Red coat, collar and lapels, blue cuffs, lining, waistcoat and breeches, white buttons.

Bulkeley Infanterie Nr 92

Raised 18 June 1690 from Irishmen who had followed James II to France. One battalion. In 1762 it took in men from the disbanded Écosse Infanterie Nr 107. Red coat, collar and lining, dark green cuffs and waistcoat, white buttons.

Clare Infanterie Nr 93

Raised on 18 June 1690 from Irishmen who had followed James II to France. One battalion. On 21 December 1762 it took in the men of the disbanded Ogilby Infanterie. Red coat and waistcoat, yellow facings, white buttons.

Dillon Infanterie Nr 94

Raised on 18 June 1690 from Irishmen who had followed James II to France. One battalion. On 21 December 1762 it took in the men of the disbanded Lally Infanterie Nr 109. In 1775 the regiment was incorporated into the Bulkeley Infanterie Nr 92. Red coat and waistcoat, no collar, black cuffs, yellow buttons.

Royal Suédois Infanterie Nr 95

Raised on 1 August 1690 at Fleurus, from Swedish prisoners in Dutch service. Two battalions until 18 January 1760, when it was increased to three by men from the disbanded Pologne Infanterie Nr 116. Blue coat, buff facings, yellow buttons.

Chatres Infanterie Nr 96

Raised on 14 November 1691. Two battalions. Red collar, cuffs and waistcoat, yellow buttons, five on the deep, square pocket flaps.

Conty Infanterie Nr 97

Raised on 4 October 1692. Two battalions. Blue collar, cuffs and waistcoat, white buttons.

Roth Infanterie Nr 98

Raised on 27 February 1698 from men of King James II's guards; an Irish regiment. One battalion. Red coat, no collar, blue cuffs, lining, waistcoat and breeches, yellow buttons.

Berwick Infanterie Nr 99

Raised on 27 February 1698 from men of other Irish regiments. One battalion. Red coat and waistcoat, black collar and cuffs, white lining, double vertical pocket flaps, yellow buttons, six on each pocket flap.

Enghien Infanterie Nr 100

Raised on 1 February 1706. Two battalions. Red collar, cuffs and waistcoat, white buttons, five on each cuff and on each double, vertical pocket flap.

Royal Bavière Infanterie Nr 101

Raised on 1 January 1709; a German regiment. Two battalions until 1760, when it was increased to three by taking in men of the disbanded La Dauphine Infanterie Nr 115. Light blue coat and waistcoat, black collar, cuffs and lapels, white buttons, white lace buttonhole loops to lapels, waistcoat and pocket flap (four). Little red hearts at the joins of the turnbacks.

Salis Infanterie Nr 102

Raised on 1 June 1733 in the Swiss Canton of Grisons (Graubünden). Two battalions. Red coat, waistcoat and breeches, blue collar, cuffs and turnbacks, white buttons, four on each double, vertical pocket flap. Blue buttonhole loops to the f coat front.

Royal Corse Infanterie Nr 103

Raised on 10 August 1739. White coat and lining, no lapels, green collar and cuffs, red waistcoat, yellow buttons, four to each cuff and to each pocket flap.

Royal Lorraine Infanterie Nr 104

Raised on 30 January 1744. One battalion. White collar, cuffs and lining, black lapels, yellow buttons.

Royal Barrois Infanterie Nr 105

Raised on 1 November 1745. One battalion. Originally yellow collar and cuffs; black collar and lapels, white cuffs, yellow buttons in 1760.

Löwendahl Infanterie Nr 106

Raised on 1 September 1743; a German regiment. Two battalions. Disbanded in 18 January 1760; one battalion went to the Anhalt Infanterie Nr 46, the other to the La Marck Infanterie Nr 66.

Royal Écossais Infanterie Nr 107

A Scottish regiment, raised on 1 August 1744 by Lord Drummond of Perth in St Omer. Two battalions. On 21 December 1762 the regiment was disbanded, the men going to the Bulkeley Infanterie Nr 92. Blue coat, red collar, cuffs and waistcoat, white buttons and lace loops to coat, waistcoat and pocket flaps.

Bergh Infanterie Nr 108

A German regiment, raised on 12 August 1744 in the area of Jülich, near Cologne. One battalion. Disbanded on 18 January 1760; the men went to the Alsace Infanterie Nr 36. Blue coat, red facings, yellow buttons.

Lally Infanterie Nr 109

Raised on 1 October 1744 from Irish recruits. One battalion. Red coat, bright green collar, cuffs and waistcoat, yellow buttons.

Nassau-Usingen Infanterie Nr 110

Raised on 1 November 1745; a German regiment. Disbanded in 17 March 1758; the men went into Nassau Infanterie Nr 111. Dark blue coat, no collar, red cuffs, lapels and lining, white buttonhole loops to lapels, cuffs and pocket flaps.

Nassau (Prinz Louis) Infanterie Nr 111

A German regiment, raised on 1 November 1745 by Prinz Wilhelm Heinrich von Nassau-Saarbrücken. Two battalions until 20 March 1758, when it took a battalion of the disbanded Nassau-Usingen Infanterie Nr 110 and men of the Saint Germain Infanterie Nr 114. Blue coat, red collar, cuffs, lining, lapels, white buttons; three white loops on each pocket flap.

Royal Cantabres Infanterie Nr 112

Raised 15 December 1745 in the Basques country as Volontaires Cantabres (see Volontaires section). One battalion. Disbanded on 25 November 1762. Sky blue beret with white toorie, sky blue coat, red collar, cuffs, white lining, buttons and buttonhole loops.

Ogilvy Infanterie Nr 113

Raised on 28 February 1747 by David Lord O'Gilvy from Scottish survivors of the Battle of Culloden. One battalion. Disbanded on 21 December 1762. Red coat, no collar, blue cuffs, lining and waistcoat, yellow buttons.

Saint Germain Infanterie Nr 114

Raised on 1 July 1747; a German regiment of one battalion. Disbanded on 18 January 1760; the men went to Nassau (Prinz Louis) Infanterie Nr 111. Red coat, blue collar, cuffs, lining and waistcoat, the latter with white buttons, buttonhole loops and white edging.

La Dauphine Infanterie Nr 115

Raised on 1 July 1747; a German (Saxon) regiment of one battalion. It was disbanded on 18 January 1760, and the men went to the Royal Bavière Infanterie Nr 101. Dark blue coat, red collar, cuffs, lapels (the latter with white buttonhole loops) and lining, yellow buttons.

Royal Pologne Infanterie Nr 116

Raised 25 December 1747 Disbanded on 18 January 1760; the men went to the Royal Suedois Infanterie Nr 95. Blue coat, red facings, white buttons.

Lochman-Eptingen Infanterie Nr 117

Raised on 25 February 1758 from the area of Switzerland around Basle. Two battalions. Red coat, collar and lapels, blue cuffs, lining, waistcoat and breeches, white buttons.

Bouillon Infanterie Nr 118

Raised on 1 February 1757; a German regiment. It initially had two battalions, reduced to one on 21 December 1762. White coat, black collar, cuffs, lapels (the latter with white buttonhole loops), white lining and buttons.

Royal Deux-Ponts (Zweibrücken) Infanterie Nr 119

Raised on 1 April 1757; a German regiment. Initially two battalions, increased to three and then four in February 1758. Light blue coat, crimson collar and cuffs, white buttons, white buttonhole loops to collar and cuffs.

Vierzet Infanterie Nr 120

A Liege regiment. White coat, no collar, blue cuffs and lapels, yellow buttons.

Horion Infanterie Nr 121

A Liege regiment. Blue coat, no collar, red cuffs, lining, lapels and waistcoat, yellow buttons. Yellow buttonhole loops to coat, lapels and waistcoat, white lace loops to the coat.

Cavalry

These regiments were referred to as 'light cavalry' – even though they were in fact heavy cavalry – to distinguish them from the King's Household Cavalry and the Gendarmerie de France. Regiments had two squadrons each in 1756, except for Colonel-Général Cavalerie Nr 1, which had three. On 1 December 1761, the cavalry was ordered to be reorganised; many regiments were disbanded to be absorbed by the remainder, whose strength was increased to four squadrons each. In many cases, these amalgamations and disbandments did not take place until after the end of the war.

Uniform

The tricorn (with iron 'secret' skull cap in combat) was edged in the button colour, with a white cockade, collarless coat, usually with lapels, except for Royal-Allemand Cavalerie Nr 11. Facings were shown on epaulettes, cuffs and lapels, the turnbacks were often in a different colour from the facings. Buttons were worn in regimental pattern on lapels, cuffs and pocket flaps, usually eight on the lapels, three on the plain cuffs (Royal-Allemand had pointed cuffs) and horizontal pocket flaps. A buff leather waistcoat and breeches were worn. In action, a steel breastplate was meant to be worn under the coat; the exception to this rule was the Cuirassiers du Roy Nr 7, who wore the full cuirass over the coat. Saddle furniture was blue, with a regimental lace edging. Harness was black with steel fittings. The cavalry was armed with a heavy, straight-bladed sword in a black sheath, with a brass hilt and a pair of pistols. Belts were white.

Trumpeters and kettle drummers wore dark blue coats heavily decorated with the crimson and white Bourbon lace. Trumpet banners and kettle drum banners were coloured and embroidered much in the same style as the regimental standards.

Standards

Each company carried a small, square standard, heavily embroidered and fringed in gold or silver. The senior company bore the King's or Colonel's standard, usually white, showing the sun in gold, under the royal motto: NEC PLURIBUS IMPAR'. The regimental standards were embroidered with various heraldic devices, usually relating to the crest of their colonel-in-chief. The pike was in the form of a lance, with a gilt finial around which a white cravatte was knotted; it had golden fringed ends and hung down to just above the bottom of the standard. The pike was attached to a bandolier, usually in the regimental facing colour, edged and fringed in the button colour.

Colonel Général Cavalerie Nr 1

Raised in 1631, taken into the French Army on 26 October 1635. On 1 December 1761 the regiment took in a squadron of the disbanded Montcalm Cavalerie Nr 68. Red coat and lining, black lapels and cuffs, buff waistcoat, yellow buttons. Edging to the saddle furniture was a triple row of black and white checks.

Mestre de Camp Général Cavalerie Nr 2

Raised in 1635; taken into the French Army on 3 December 1665. On 1 December 1761 the regiment took in two squadron of the disbanded Saluces Cavalerie. Grey coat and lining, black lapels and cuffs, red waistcoat, yellow buttons, in pairs. Edging to the saddle furniture was (from the inside out) yellow, blue, black, red.

Commissaire Général Cavalerie Nr 3

Raised on 15 May 1635 On 1 December 1761 the regiment took in two squadrons of the disbanded Beauvilliers Cavalerie. Grey coat and lining, black lapels and cuffs, buff waistcoat, yellow buttons, in pairs. Edging to the saddle furniture was yellow; on it were two lines with a zig-zag between them, in black.

Royal Cavalerie Nr 4

Raised on 16 May 1635, taken into the French Army on 16 May 1643. On 1 December 1761 the regiment took in the two squadrons of the disbanded Vogue (ex-St Jal) Cavalerie. Blue coat and lining, red lapels, cuffs and waistcoat, white buttons, in pairs. Edging to the saddle furniture was yellow.

Du Roy Cavalerie Nr 5

Raised on 27 May 1635; taken into the French Army on 16 February 1646. On 1 December 1761 the regiment took in the two squadron of the disbanded Archiac Cavalerie. Blue coat, red lining, lapels, cuffs and waistcoat, white buttons, in pairs. Edging to the saddle furniture was crimson with a white lozenge pattern.

Royal-Étranger Cavalerie Nr 6

Raised on 26 February 1659. On 1 December 1761 the regiment took in the two squadron of the disbanded Charoste (ex-Egmont) Cavalerie. Blue coat, red pointed cuffs and lining, no lapels, buff waistcoat, white buttons, in pairs. Edging to the saddle furniture was yellow, with a red diamond pattern along it, the centres of the diamonds being white and yellow alternately.

Cuirassiers du Roy Nr 7

Raised on 24 January 1638. On 1 December 1761 the regiment took in squadron of the disbanded Ray (ex-Bussy-Lameth) Cavalerie. This regiment was the only one authorised to wear the full cuirass over the blue coat. Blue lining, red lapels, cuffs and waistcoat, white buttons, in pairs. Edging to the saddle furniture was diagonally striped yellow, white, yellow, red, yellow.

Royal-Cravates Cavalerie Nr 8

Raised on 13 August 1643. On 1 December 1761 the regiment took in the two squadrons of the disbanded Chabrillant Cavalerie. Blue coat and lining, red lapels, cuffs and waistcoat, white buttons, in pairs. Edging to the saddle furniture was yellow, with a double row of squares: white, red, blue, white.

Royal-Roussillon Cavalerie Nr 9

Raised on 13 October 1652. On 1 December 1761 the regiment took in the two squadrons of the disbanded Balincourt (ex Grammont) Cavalerie. Blue coat, red lining, lapels, cuffs and waistcoat, white buttons. Edging to the saddle furniture was yellow, with two blue zig-zags along it.

Royal-Piémont Cavalerie Nr 10

Raised in 1690; on 6 May 1690 it became Piémont. On 1 December 1761 the regiment took in squadron of the disbanded Talleyrand Cavalerie. Blue coat and lining, red lapels, cuffs and waistcoat, white buttons, in pairs. Edging to the saddle furniture was yellow, along it ran three sets of cubes; the outer two were yellow and blue, the centre was red and white, with the white between the two blue.

Royal-Allemand Cavalerie Nr 11

Raised on 10 August 1671. A new regiment formed in 1761 of the old Royal-Allemand, Nassau-Saarbruck and Württemberg. Bearskin caps with red backing, blue coat, red pointed cuffs and lining, no collar, no lapels (until 1761), red waistcoat, white buttons; white lace to coat and cuffs, red, white and blue buttonholes. Blue shabraque, edged wit orange lace decorated with red squares. This lace was also worm to lapels and cuffs from 1761.

Royal-Pologne Cavalerie Nr 12

Raised on 30 May 1653; it entered the French Army in September 1725. On 1 December 1761 the regiment took in the two squadron of the disbanded Marcieu Cavalerie. Blue coat, red lining, lapels, cuffs and waistcoat, white buttons. Edging to the saddle furniture was yellow, with a row of dark blue lozenges along it, each with a white central square.

Des Salles Cavalerie Nr 13

Raised on 1 July 1671. On 1 December 1761 the regiment became the Royal-Lorraine Cavalerie, consisting of four squadrons, and took in the men of the disbanded Lénoncourt Cavalerie. White coat, red lining, lapels and cuffs, buff waistcoat, white buttons. Edging to the blue saddle furniture was black braid with red chain link stitching.

Royal-Picardie Cavalerie Nr 14

Raised on 16 September 1652. 1749 Marquis de Fumel. A new regiment, formed in 1761 of the old Picardie and Bourbon-Busset. White coat, red lapels, cuffs and skirts, buff waistcoat.

Royal Champagne Cavalerie Nr 15

Raised on 1 October 1682 by the Duc de Tallard. 1743 Marquis de Laroche Foucauld. A new regiment, formed in 1761 of the Rochefoucauld-Langeac Cavalerie and Preyssac Cavalerie Nr 67. White coat, red lapels, cuffs and skirts, buff waistcoat.

Royal-Navarre Cavalerie Nr 16

Raised on 6 January 1647 by Ardenne d'Aragon. 1749 de Vienne. A new regiment formed in 1761 of the old Vienne and Moustiers Cavalerie. White coat, red lapels, cuffs and skirts, buff waistcoat, white buttons.

Royal-Normandie Cavalerie Nr 17

Raised on 8 July 1667. From 1749 until 1763 it was called the Comte de Poly St-Thiebault Cavalerie; on 31 March 1763 the regiment was amalgamated with the d'Escouloubre (ex Henrichmont) Cavalerie to form the new Royal-Normandie Cavalerie. White coat, red lining, lapels and cuffs, buff waistcoat, white buttons. Edging to the coat, lapels, cuffs, turnbacks, waistcoat and blue saddle furniture was black with yellow chain link pattern.

La Reine Cavalerie Nr 18

Raised on 4 July 1643. On 1 December 1761 the regiment took in the two squadrons of the disbanded St Aldegonde (ex La Viefville) Cavalerie. Red coat, blue lining, lapels and cuffs, red waistcoat, yellow buttons. Edging to the red saddle furniture was dark blue with a white lozenge pattern. A yellow fleur-de-lis was embroidered in the rear corners and on the holsters.

Dauphin Cavalerie Nr 19

Raised on 1 December 1661. On 1 December 1761 the regiment took in the two squadrons of the disbanded Dauphin-Étranger Cavalerie. Blue coat, red lining, lapels, cuffs and waistcoat, white buttons. Edging to the saddle furniture was yellow, with three rows of dark blue squares along it.

Bourgogne Cavalerie Nr 20

Raised in 1665. On 1 December 1761 the regiment took in the two squadrons of the disbanded Dampierre Cavalerie. Blue coat, red lining and cuffs, no lapels, buff waistcoat, white buttons. Edging to the saddle furniture was yellow, with three rows of white squares along it.

Berry Cavalerie Nr 21

Raised on 15 December 1677. On 1 December 1761 the regiment took in the two squadrons of the disbanded Lusignan Cavalerie. Blue coat, red lining, lapels and cuffs, buff waistcoat, white buttons. Edging to the blue saddle furniture was light blue, with a line of white squares along it.

Royal-Carabiniers Nr 22

Raised on 1 November 1693. This regiment had five brigades, each of two squadrons. On 1 December 1761 the regiment took the title Comte de Provence. Blue coat and lining, red lapels, cuffs and waistcoat, white buttons. White piping to cuffs, lapels and skirts. Edging to the saddle furniture was yellow with a broad white central stripe. This regiment was armed with rifled carbines.

Artois Cavalerie Nr 23

Raised in 1665. It was called Aquitaine Cavalerie, but on 1 December 1761 the regiment took in the two squadron of the disbanded Hericy (ex-Bezons) Cavalerie and became the Artois Cavalerie. Blue coat, red lining, lapels and cuffs, buff waistcoat, white buttons. Edging to the saddle furniture was yellow, with a blue zig-zag inside a red zig-zag, separated by a yellow zig-zag.

Orléans Cavalerie Nr 24

Raised in 1630 in Piémont, taken into French service on 16 May 1635. On 1 December 1761 the regiment took in the two squadrons of the disbanded Crussol Cavalerie. White coat, red lining, lapels and cuffs, buff waistcoat, white buttons. Edging to the saddle furniture was a blue and a white central line, between double rows of red and white checks.

Chartres Cavalerie Nr 25

Raised in 1761, formed of the old Trasseigny Cavalerie and Bellefonds Cavalerie. White coat and lining, red lapels and cuffs, buff waistcoat. Violet and white lace edging to facings and the blue saddle furniture.

Condé Cavalerie Nr 26

Raised on 7 December 1665. On 1 December 1761 the regiment took in the two squadrons of the disbanded Toulouse-Lautrec (ex Fleury) Cavalerie. White coat, red lining, lapels and cuffs, buff waistcoat, white buttons. Edging to facings and the saddle furniture was crimson velvet.

Bourbon Cavalerie Nr 27

Raised on 7 December 1665. On 1 December 1761 the regiment took in the two squadrons of the disbanded Noé (ex Clermont-Tonnere) Cavalerie. White coat, red lining, lapels and cuffs, buff waistcoat, white buttons. Edging to the saddle furniture was yellow with two rows of crimson along it, they having white squares along them.

Clermont Cavalerie Nr 28

Raised on 8 July 1667. White coat and lining, red lapels and cuffs, buff waistcoat all edged with crimson braid, white buttons. Edging to the blue saddle furniture was crimson wool.

Conti Cavalerie Nr 29

Raised on 24 September 1651. Grey coat, lining, lapels and cuffs, all edged in broad white braid, having a thin red and a thin blue sinusoidal line along it, forming ovals. Buff waistcoat, white buttons. Edging to the blue saddle furniture was as for the uniform. In the rear corner of the shabraque was a blue shield, edged red, with three yellow fleur-de-lis upon it.

Penthièvre Cavalerie Nr 30

Raised on 1 March 1674. On 1 December 1761 the regiment took in the two squadrons of the disbanded Des Cars Cavalerie. White coat, red lining, lapels and cuffs, all edged in the regimental lace (blue and yellow checks) buff waistcoat, white buttons. Edging to the blue saddle furniture was the regimental lace.

Noailles Cavalerie Nr 31

Raised on 20 December 1688 by Duc de Anne-Joules. White coat, red lapels, cuffs and lining, buff waistcoat, white buttons.

Regiments Disbanded in 1761

Archiac Cavalerie
Raised in 1665. On 1 December 1761 the regiment was disbanded; the men went into the Du Roy Cavalerie Nr 5. White coat and lining, red lapels and cuffs, buff waistcoat, white buttons. Edging to the coat, lapels, cuffs and saddle furniture was green with a yellow chain link design.

Beauvilliers Cavalerie
Raised on 5 August 1652. On 1 December 1761 the regiment was disbanded; the men went into the Commissaire Général Cavalerie Nr 3. White coat, red lining, lapels and cuffs, buff waistcoat, white buttons. Edging to the coat, lapels, cuffs, lining and the blue saddle furniture was dark buff with red chain link stitching.

Bellefonds Cavalerie
Raised on 3 March 1672. 1744 Marquis de Bellefonds; 1758 Chevalier de Durfort. On 1 December 1761 the regiment was disbanded; the men went into the new Chartres Cavalerie Nr 25, together with those of the Trasseigny Cavalerie. White coat, red lining, lapels and cuffs, buff waistcoat, white buttons. Edging to the coat, cuffs, lapels, turnbacks and to the blue saddle furniture was violet braid with yellow chain link stitching.

Bezons Cavalerie
Raised on 15 March 1749. 1749 Marquis de Bezons; 1758 Marquis d'Hericy. On 1 December 1761 the regiment was disbanded; the men went into the new Artois Cavalerie Nr 23, together with those of the Aquitaine Cavalerie. White coat, red lining, lapels and cuffs, buff waistcoat, white buttons (four to each cuff and to each pocket flap). Edging to the coat, cuffs, lapels, turnbacks and to the blue saddle furniture was two rows of black and yellow checks.

Bourbon-Busset Cavalerie
Raised on 1 March 1674. On 1 December 1761 the regiment was disbanded; the men went into the new Royal-Picardie Cavalerie Nr 14, together with those of the Fumel Cavalerie. White coat, red lining, lapels and cuffs, buff waistcoat, white buttons. Edging to the coat, cuffs, turnbacks and blue saddle furniture was blue with yellow chain link stitching.

Bussy-Lameth Cavalerie
Raised on 12 August 1694. 1752 Comte de Lameth; 1761 Chevalier de Ray. On 1 December 1761 the regiment was disbanded; the men went into the Cuirassiers du Roy Nr 7. White coat, red lining, lapels and cuffs, buff waistcoat, white buttons. Edging to the coat, cuffs, lapels, turnbacks and the blue saddle furniture was coffee with violet chain link stitching.

Chabrillan Cavalerie
Raised on 3 March 1672. On 1 December 1761 the regiment was disbanded; the men went into the Royal-Cravate Cavalerie Nr 8. White coat, red lining, lapels and cuffs, buff waistcoat, white buttons. Edging to the blue saddle furniture was white with black chain link stitching.

Clermont-Tonnerre Cavalerie
Raised on 21 February 1649. 1740 Comte de Clermont-Tonnerre; 1761 Marquis de Noë. On 1 December 1761 the regiment was disbanded; the men went into the Bourbon Cavalerie Nr 27. White coat and lining, red lapels and cuffs, buff waistcoat, white buttons. Edging to the blue saddle furniture was crimson.

Crussol Cavalerie
Raised on 3 February 1652. On 1 December 1761 the regiment was disbanded; the men went into the Orléans Cavalerie Nr 24. White coat, red lining, lapels and cuffs, buff waistcoat, white buttons. Edging to the coat, cuffs, lapels, turnbacks and to the blue saddle furniture was two rows of violet and white checks.

Dampierre Cavalerie
Raised on 16 December 1673. 1747 Comte de Dampierre; 1759 Marquis d'Espinchal. On 1 December 1761 the regiment was disbanded; the men went into the Bourgogne Cavalerie Nr 20. White coat, red lining, lapels and cuffs, waistcoat, buttons. Edging to the coat, cuffs, lapels, turnbacks and to the blue saddle furniture was white with green chain link stitching.

Dauphin-Étranger Cavalerie
Raised on 12 March 1674. 1742 Marquis de Soyecourt; 1759 Marquis de Vibraye. On 1 December 1761 the regiment was disbanded; the men went into the Dauphin Cavalerie Nr 19. Blue coat, red lining, lapels and cuffs, buff waistcoat, white buttons. Edging to the saddle furniture was yellow, with a tricolour zig-zag band red-blue-white, from inside to outside.

D'Egmont Cavalerie
Raised late in 1667. 1744 Comte d'Egmont; 1756 Duc de Charost. On 1 December 1761 the regiment was disbanded; the men went into the Royal-Étranger Cavalerie Nr 6. White coat, red lining, lapels and cuffs, buff waistcoat, white buttons. Edging to the blue saddle furniture was green with violet chain link stitching.

Descars Cavalerie
Raised on 15 March 1707. In 1761 the regiment was disbanded; the men went into the Penthievre Cavalerie Nr 30. White coat, red lining, lapels and cuffs, no collar, white buttons (two pairs on each cuff and on each horizontal pocket flap). Edging to the coat, cuffs, lapels, turnbacks and to the blue saddle furniture was two rows of light green and red checks.

De Vienne Cavalerie
Raised in 1646. 1749 Comte de Vienne; 1762 Marquis de Damas. On 1 December 1761 the regiment was disbanded; the men went into the new Royal-Navarre Cavalerie Nr 16, together with those of the Moustiers Cavalerie. White coat, red lining, lapels and cuffs, buff waistcoat, white buttons. Edging to the coat, cuffs, lapels, turnbacks and to the blue saddle furniture was white with red chain link stitching.

Fleury Cavalerie
Raised on 10 December 1673. 1749 Comte de Fleury; 1761 Comte de Toulouse-Lautrec. On 1 December 1761 the regiment was disbanded; the men went into the Condé Cavalerie Nr 26. White coat and lining, red lapels and cuffs, buff waistcoat, white buttons. Edging to the coat, cuffs, lapels, turnbacks and to the blue saddle furniture was a double row of red and blue checks.

Fumel Cavalerie
Raised on 16 September 1652. On 1 December 1761 the regiment was disbanded; the men went into the new Royal-Picardie Cavalerie Nr 14, together with those of the Bourbon-Busset Cavalerie. White coat, red lining, lapels and cuffs, buff waistcoat, white buttons. Edging to the coat, cuffs, lapels, turnbacks and the blue saddle furniture was red with yellow chain link stitching.

Harcourt Cavalerie

Raised on 1 January 1689. 1757 Comte de Harcourt; 1759 Comte de Preysac de Cadillac. On 1 December 1761 the regiment was disbanded; the men went into the new Royal Champagne Cavalerie Nr 15, together with those of the Rochefoucauld-Langeac Cavalerie. Red coat, blue lining, lapels and cuffs, buff waistcoat, no collar, white buttons (two pairs on each cuff and on each horizontal pocket flap). Edging to the coat, cuffs, lapels, turnbacks and to the blue saddle furniture was two rows of light green and yellow checks.

Nassau-Saarbruck Cavalerie

Raised on 16 October 1744; a German regiment. 1744 Guillaume Henri Prince de Nassau Saarbrück; 1758 Jean Adolphe comte de Nassau Ussingen. On 1 December 1761 the regiment was disbanded; the men went into the Royal-Allemand Cavalerie Nr 11. Bearskin with yellow bag and tassel, blue coat, yellow lining, lapels and cuffs, no collar, buff waistcoat with red edging, copper buttons. Edging to the coat, cuffs, lapels, turnbacks and to the blue saddle furniture was two rows of red and black squares. Trumpeters and kettle drummers wore a tricorn, orange tunic and breeches, red cuffs, lapels and lining, red waistcoat laced silver.

Wurtemberg Cavalerie

Raised on 18 October 1635; a German regiment incorporated into the French Army in 1635. On 1 December 1761 the regiment was disbanded; the men went into the Royal-Allemand Cavalerie Nr 11. White coat, red lining, lapels and cuffs, no collar, buff waistcoat, white buttons, four to each cuff and horizontal pocket flap. Edging to the coat, cuffs, lapels, turnbacks and to the blue saddle furniture was two rows of violet and blue squares. Trumpeters and kettle drummers wore yellow tunics with white lace which had a red, black and yellow pattern.

Grammont Cavalerie

Raised on 7 December 1665. 1745 Comte de Grammont; 1759 Marquis de Balincourt. On 1 December 1761 the regiment was disbanded; the men went into the Royal Roussillon Cavalerie Nr 9. White coat, red lining, lapels and cuffs, buff waistcoat, white buttons. Edging to the blue saddle furniture was dark buff with green chain link stitching

Henrichemont Cavalerie

Raised on 1 March 1674. 1749 Prince d'Henrichemont; 1759 Marquis d'Escouloubre. On 1 December 1761 the regiment was disbanded; the men went into the Royal-Normandie Cavalerie Nr 17. White coat, red lining, lapels and cuffs, buff waistcoat, white buttons. Edging to the coat, cuffs, lapels, turnbacks and to the blue saddle furniture was a double row of red and white checks.

Fitz-James Cavalerie

Raised in 1691 as 'Roi d'Angleterre', by ex-King James II from English exiles. Taken into the French Army in 1698. On 1 December 1761 the regiment was disbanded. Red coat, blue lining, lapels and cuffs, no collar, buff waistcoat, white buttons (two pairs on each cuff and on each horizontal cuff flap. Edging to the coat, cuffs, lapels, turnbacks and to the blue saddle furniture was twin rows of white and light green checks.

Lastic de St-Jal Cavalerie

Raised on 7 December 1665. 1744 François Comte de Lastic Saint-Jal; 1759 Marquis de Vogüe. On 1 December 1761 the regiment was disbanded; the men went into the Royal Cavalerie Nr 4. White coat, red lining, lapels and cuffs, buff waistcoat, white buttons. Edging to the coat, cuffs, lapels, turnbacks and the blue saddle furniture was red with dark green chain link stitching.

Lénoncourt Cavalerie

Raised on 6 January 1652. 1748 Marquis de Lénoncourt; 1758 Marquis de Toustain. On 1 December 1761 the regiment was disbanded; the men went into the Royal-Lorraine (Des Salles) Cavalerie Nr 13. White coat and lining, red lapels and cuffs, buff waistcoat, white buttons. Edging to the coat, cuffs, lapels, turnbacks and to the blue saddle furniture was two rows of blue and white checks.

Lusignan Cavalerie

Raised on 10 January 1668. On 1 December 1761 the regiment was disbanded; the men went into the Berry Cavalerie Nr 21. White coat and lining, red lapels and cuffs, buff waistcoat, white buttons. Edging to the facings and blue saddle furniture was blue and yellow checked lace.

Marcieux Cavalerie

Raised on 12 March 1652. On 1 December 1761 the regiment was disbanded; the men went into the Royal-Pologne Cavalerie Nr 12. White coat, red lining, lapels and cuffs, buff waistcoat, white buttons. Edging to coat, facings, waistcoat and to the blue saddle furniture was dark buff lace with turquoise chain link pattern.

Maugiron Cavalerie

Raised on 1 March 1674. 1740 comte de Maugiron; 1758 Comte de Trasseigny. On 1 December 1761 the regiment was disbanded; the men went into the new Chartres Cavalerie Nr 25, together with the men of the Bellefonds Cavalerie. White coat, red lining, lapels and cuffs, buff waistcoat, white buttons. Edging to the coat, cuffs, turnbacks and the blue saddle furniture was dark buff and violet double checks.

Montcalm Cavalerie

Raised on 15 March 1749. On 1 December 1761 the regiment was disbanded; the men of the 1st Squadron went into the Colonel Général Cavalerie Nr 1; the 2nd Squadron was disbanded. White coat, red lining, lapels and cuffs, buff waistcoat, white buttons (four to each cuff and to each pocket flap). Edging to the coat, cuffs, lapels, turnbacks and to the blue saddle furniture was a double row of red and yellow checks.

Moustiers Cavalerie

Raised on 10 December 1673. On 1 December 1761 the regiment was disbanded; the men went into the new Royal-Navarre Cavalerie Nr 16, together with those of the De Vienne Cavalerie. White coat, lining, lapels and cuffs, buff waistcoat, white buttons. Edging to the coat, cuffs, lapels, turnbacks and to the blue saddle furniture was white with violet chain link stitching.

Rochefoucauld-Langeac Cavalerie

Raised on 1 October 1682. On 1 December 1761 the regiment was disbanded; the men went into the new 15th Royal Champagne Cavalerie Nr 15, together with those of the Preyssac Cavalerie. White coat, red collar, lining, lapels and cuffs, buff waistcoat, white buttons. Edging to the coat, cuffs, lapels, turnbacks and the blue saddle furniture was coffee-coloured with black chain link stitching.

Saluces Cavalerie

Raised on 13 March 1672. 1745 Marquis de Saluces; 1759 Marquis de Seyssel. On 1 December 1761 the regiment was disbanded; the men went into the Mestre de Camp Général Cavalerie Nr 2. White coat and lining, red lapels and cuffs, buff waistcoat, white buttons. Edging to the coat, cuffs, lapels, turnbacks and to the blue saddle furniture was white, edged red and with red and black chain link stitching.

Volunteers of Marshal de Saxe Dragons, 1745. The uniform and helmet are very much the flavour of those adopted later for all the French dragoon regiments. Note the huge cuffs and the extensive array of buttons. (Knötel, IX 4)

Talleyrand Cavalerie

Raised on 9 August 1671. On 1 December 1761 the regiment was disbanded; the men went into the Royal-Piémont Cavalerie Nr 10. White coat, red lining, lapels and cuffs, buff waistcoat, white buttons. Edging to the blue saddle furniture was dark buff and dark green squares.

Viefville Cavalerie

Raised on 1 March 1674. 1743 Marquis de la Viefville; 1759 Marquis de Saint-Aldegonde. On 1 December 1761 the regiment was disbanded; the men went into the La Reine Cavalerie Nr 18. White coat, red lining, lapels (with white buttonhole loops) and cuffs, buff waistcoat, white buttons. Edging to the coat, cuffs, turnbacks and blue saddle furniture was white with blue chain link stitching.

Dragoons

By decrees of 18 August 1755 and 1 June 1756 each regiment of dragoons was organised in four squadrons each of four companies, each company of 40 mounted dragoons. The total strength of a regiment was 704 men excluding the regimental staff. They were armed with a sabre, musket and a pair of pistols; 64 men of each regiment were equipped with rifled muskets. Each squadron carried a guidon.

Uniform

Regiments wore the tricorn until about 1758, when it was gradually replaced by a brass helmet with a combe, having a black, horsehair crest flowing to the rear. This was worn with a turban. The uniform consisted of a single-breasted coat, with facings shown on the cuffs. The waistcoat was of a colour not always related to that of the cuffs. Fringed epaulettes were worn. Breeches were buff. Instead of riding boots, dragoons wore long, black leather gaiters, which buckled up the leg.

Drummers of Royal regiments wore the royal livery with crimson and white lace decoration; drummers of other regiments wore the livery of their colonels-in-chief. Trumpeters and kettle drummers wore dark blue coats heavily decorated with the crimson and white Bourbon lace. Trumpet banners and kettle drum banners were coloured and embroidered much in the same style as that of the regimental standards.

Guidons

Each company carried a small, swallow-tailed guidon, heavily embroidered and fringed in gold or silver. The senior company bore the King's, or Colonel's guidon, usually white, showing the sun in gold, under the royal motto: NEC PLURIBUS IMPAR' (possibly 'above all, like the sun'). The regimental guidon was embroidered with various heraldic devices, usually relating to the crest of their colonel-in-chief. The pike was in the form of a lance, with a gilt finial around which a white cravatte was knotted; it had golden fringed ends and hung down to just above the bottom of the guidon. The pike was attached to a bandolier, usually in the regimental facing colour, edged and fringed in the button colour.

Colonel Général Dragons Nr 1

Red coat, blue cuffs, waistcoat, lining, white epaulettes, buttons, buttonholes and edging to the waistcoat. Edging to the saddle furniture was red-white-red.

Mestre de Camp Général Dragons Nr 2

Red coat and waistcoat, white cuffs and lining, white buttons and lace buttonholes, buff breeches. Red-black red braid to saddle furniture.

Royal Dragons Nr 3

Blue coat, red cuffs, waistcoat, lining, red and white mixed epaulettes, white buttons, buttonholes and edging to the waistcoat. Edging to the saddle furniture was red, with a narrow white central stripe, flanked by narrow red, then dark blue stripes.

Du Roy Dragons Nr 4

Blue coat, white cuffs, blue waistcoat and lining, red and white mixed epaulettes with blue straps, white buttons (grouped in threes), buttonholes and edging to the waistcoat. Edging to the saddle furniture was red, with a yellow central band, flanked to each side by blue-red-white-red-blue stripes.

La Reine Dragons Nr 5

Red coat, blue cuffs, waistcoat, lining, red and white mixed epaulettes, white buttons, buttonholes and edging to the waistcoat. Edging to the saddle furniture and drummer's lace was red, with a blue central band having white chain link stitches along it.

Dauphin Dragons Nr 6

Blue coat, blue cuffs, waistcoat, lining, red and white mixed epaulettes with blue straps, white buttons (grouped in pairs), buttonholes; no edging to the waistcoat. Edging to the saddle furniture was red, with a white central band, having three rows of blue checks along it. Drummers wore blue-yellow-blue braid.

Orléans Dragons Nr 7

Red coat, blue cuffs, waistcoat, lining, white epaulettes, buttons, buttonholes and edging to the waistcoat. Edging to the saddle furniture was red-white-red.

Beauffremont Dragons Nr 8

Red coat, yellow cuffs, red waistcoat and lining, red and yellow mixed epaulettes, white buttons, buttonholes; no edging to the waistcoat. Edging to the saddle furniture was red-yellow-red.

Aubigné Dragons Nr 9

1745 Balthazar Urbain, chevalier d'Aubigné; 1761 Antoine Cléradius de Choiseul La Baume. Red coat, dark green cuffs, red waistcoat, lining, red and white mixed epaulettes, white buttons, buttonholes; no edging to the waistcoat. Edging to the saddle furniture was red, with a white central band having two red zig-zags along it.

Caraman Dragons Nr 10

1745 Marquis de Caraman; 1761 Marquis d'Autichamp. Red coat, light green cuffs, waistcoat, lining, white epaulettes, buttons, buttonholes and edging to the waistcoat. Edging to the saddle furniture was red-white-red.

La Ferronnaye Dragons Nr 11

1749 Comte de la Ferronnaye; 1762 Vicomte de Chabot. Red coat, blue cuffs, waistcoat, lining, white epaulettes, buttons, buttonholes and edging to the waistcoat. Edging to the saddle furniture was red-white-red.

Harcourt Dragons Nr 12

1748 Anne François d'Harcourt de Lillebonne, Marquis de Beuvron; 1758 Emmanuel François de Grossoles, Chevalier de Flammarens; 1762 Comte de Coigny. Red coat, black cuffs, red waistcoat and lining, yellow and black mixed epaulettes, white buttons, buttonholes; no edging to the waistcoat. Edging to the saddle furniture was red with a central row of black and yellow checks.

Apchon Dragons Nr 13

1748 Antoine Maurice, Comte d'Apchon; 1761 Armand Charles François, Marquis de Nicolaï d'Osny. Red coat, light blue cuffs, red waistcoat, lining, mixed blue and white epaulettes, white buttons, buttonholes; no edging to the waistcoat. Edging to the saddle furniture was red with a central row of yellow and blue checks.

Thianges Dragons Nr 14

1749 Amable Gaspard Vicomte de Thianges; 1761 Louis Jacques Chevalier de Chapt Rastignac. Red coat, yellow cuffs, red waistcoat and lining, mixed black and white epaulettes, white buttons, buttonholes; no edging to the waistcoat. Edging to the saddle furniture was red with a central row of black and white checks.

Marboeuf Dragons Nr 15

1755 Charles Louis René Marquis de Marboeuf; 1761 Jacques Aymard de Moreton Comte de Chabrillan; Red coat, red cuffs, waistcoat, lining, mixed blue and white epaulettes, white buttons (grouped in threes), buttonholes; no edging to the waistcoat. Edging to the saddle furniture was red with a central white band, having a purple stripe along its centre.

Languedoc Dragons Nr 16

Blue coat, red cuffs, blue waistcoat and lining, white epaulettes, buttons, buttonholes; no edging to the waistcoat. Edging to the saddle furniture is not known was.

Schomberg Dragons Nr 17

1755 Comte de Schomberg; 1762 Comte de Donnezan. Originally the Volontaires de Schomberg. Dragoon helmet with brass combe, flowing black horsehair crest, brown turban, with diamond-shaped pattern. Dark green coat, red collar, lapels, round cuffs and lining, yellow buttons. Buff waistcoat and breeches, red edging to waistcoat, red waist sash. Long black gaiters. They were armed with a brass-hilted sword and a carbine on white belts.

Hussars

Uniform

Trumpeters and kettle drummers wore dark blue coats heavily decorated with the crimson and white Bourbon lace. Trumpet banners and kettle drum banners were coloured and embroidered much in the same style as the regimental guidon. Like the dragoons, each company carried a small, swallow-tailed guidon, heavily embroidered and fringed in gold or silver. The senior company bore the King's or Colonel's guidon, usually white, showing the sun in gold, under the royal motto: NEC PLURIBUS IMPAR'. The regimental guidon was embroidered with various heraldic devices, usually relating to the crest of their colonel-in-chief. The pike was in the form of a lance, with a gilt finial around which a white cravatte was knotted; it had golden fringed ends and hung down to just above the bottom of the guidon. The pike was attached to a bandolier, usually in the regimental facing colour, edged and fringed in the button colour.

Bercheny Hussards

Raised 12 June 1720 by Comte Ladislaw-Ignace Bercsenyi, a Hungarian and a rebel against the Habsburg rulers of his homeland. This unit later became the 1st Hussars. Four squadrons. On 5 May 1758, the regiment took in two squadrons of the disbanded Polleresky Hussards. Uniform: red mirliton, black plume, red flame, edged white, white fleur-de-lis badge, white cords. Light blue dolman, pelisse and breeches, white buttons and lace, grey fur trim, red and white barrel sash, light blue sabretasche edged white with a white, crowned fleur-de-lis badge. Black boots, belts and harness, brass buckles. Leopard skin saddle cloth edged in light blue, brass-hilted sabre in brass sheath with black leather sections.

Polleresky Hussards

Raised on 1 August 1743 with two squadrons of the Bercheny Hussards. On 30 October 1756, it received two squadrons of the disbanded Ferrary Hussards, giving it four squadrons. On 5 May 1758, this regiment was disbanded for looting the German allied civilian population. Two squadrons went to the Bercheny Hussards and two to the Turpin Hussard, which then had six squadrons each. Uniform: black mirliton with white cockade and red fleur-de-lis, edging and lining to the wing. Light blue dolman, breeches and pelisse, black fur, white lace and buttons, red edging to pointed cuffs. Red and white barrel sash, red belts, bandolier and pouch, black boots. Red sabretasche and shabraque, edged white, with white fleur-de-lis badges.

Royale-Nassau Hussards

Raised on 10 November 1756 for Wilhem Heinrich, Prinz von Nassau-Saarbrücken. On 7 April 1758 the unit title became 'Volontaires Royaux de Nassau' and on 14 June 1758, it changed again to 'Royal-Nassau-Regiment', having four squadrons. Uniform: black mirliton with orange and white braid trim, white cockade, fleur-de-lis and short plume. Red pelisse, black fur and white braid and buttons. Royal blue dolman and breeches, white braid and buttons, buff collar and pointed cuffs, edged white. Orange and white barrel sash. White bandolier, yellow fittings, black pouch and boots. Red sabretasche, edged with white and orange braid, bearing a royal blue oval having a crowned rampant lion. Red shabraque, edged in white and orange braid, white fleur-de-lis badges in the four corners. Trumpeters wore orange tunics, faced red, with white buttons and buttonholes, usual hats, breeches.

Turpin Hussards

Raised on 25 January 1735 by the Comte de Esterhazy. 1748 Comte Turpin de Crissé; 1761 André-Claude Marquis Chamborant. Four squadrons. On 5 May 1758, the regiment took in two squadrons of the disbanded Polleresky Hussards. This unit later became the 2nd Hussars. Uniform: black mirliton with black flame, edged dark green, white cords and plume. Dark green dolman and pelisse, white buttons, lace and edging, black fur to pelisse, red breeches with white trim, black boots with white trim. Red and yellow barrel sash, white belts and sheepskin saddle cloth, the latter edged black. Brass-hilted sabre.

Volunteer Formations

There were the following volunteer organisations, many raised as early as the first War of the Austrian Succession. They functioned as light troops, on the model of the Austrian Croat infantry and hussars. Many of them were 'legions' containing infantry and cavalry units.

Arquebusiers de Grassin
In 1745 they wore red mirlitons, with round-topped brass plate, red flame edged black, white plume, red tassel. Dark blue frock coat, black cuffs all edged in grey fur, red collar and fringed epaulettes, red waistcoat, dark blue breeches, white gaiters, black belts with brass buckles. On 1 August 1749 they were amalgamated in the Volontaires de Flandre (see below).

Chasseurs-à-pied d'Origny
Raised on 4 January 1760 as Chasseurs d'Origny and was attached to the Turpin Hussards as foot jägers. Disbanded 4 April 1761. White hat edging, sky blue coat, black facings, red lining, white buttons, black buttonholes, red waistcoat and breeches, white belts, black gaiters.

Chasseurs-à-pied de Granpré
Raised on 4 January 1760 as Chasseurs de Sombreuil, the name being changed in 1761. Disbanded 4 April 1761. White hat edging, sky blue coat, red facings, lining and waistcoat, white buttons and buttonholes (in the shape of a clover leaf), white belts, red breeches, black gaiters.

Chasseurs de Cambefort
Raised on 12 December 1759, with one dragoon and one fusilier company. A cavalry unit. Black bearskin, with red bag and tassel, no plate. Dark blue coat and collar, red lapels, cuffs, waistcoat, lining and fringed epaulettes, white buttons, red breeches, dark blue saddle furniture edged red.

Chasseurs de Fischer
Raised on 1 November 1743 as Chasseurs. 1743 Johann Christian Fischer; 1761 Louis Gabriel d'Armentière, Marquis de Conflans. They were now Dragons-Chasseurs de Conflans. On 1 March 1763, the unit changed its name again, becoming the Légion de Conflans. In 1743 they wore black mirliton caps, with white cockade, plume and tassel, dark green dolman, red pelisse, breeches, sabre-tasche, saddle cloth and holster covers, the latter three embroidered with three yellow fishes under a crown and amid three fleur-de-lis. Steel-hilted sabre in black and steel sheath; black harness. In 1761 they wore black bearskin caps with brass front plate, red bag and white tassel, dark green coat, waistcoat and breeches, red half-lapels, round cuffs and fringed epaulettes, white buttons, long black gaiters, white belts, sabre and bayonet.

Chasseurs de Poncet
Raised on 7 March 1761. Disbanded on 10 December 1762. No data found as to the details of the uniforms worn. It was planned to consist of a company of foot Jägers, a squadron of mounted Jägers and a squadron of hussars.

Trooper of Fischer's Chasseurs à Cheval. Fischer was originally a servant, but he so distinguished himself at the Battle of Prague in 1742 that he became a favourite of the Marechal de Saxe, who gave him a commission in command of a company of chasseurs à cheval. They then became 500-strong and were expanded into a legion, including infantry, building a great reputation for themselves in the Seven Years War. All later Chasseur à Cheval regiments of the French Army stem from this unit. Note the canting heraldry on the horse furniture. (Knötel, V 59)

Chasseurs du Quartier Général

Raised on on 31 March 1761 as Chasseurs de Monet. March 1761 M. Monet; August 1761 M. de Bonn. Disbanded 20 November 1762. Both the horse and foot components wore a dark green mirliton, with white flame and the crowned, reversed cipher 'L', dark green, single-breasted coat, waistcoat and breeches, no facing colours, dark green lining, white buttons, buff belts with brass buckles. The mounted troops wore short, hussar boots and a dark green aiguillette on the right shoulder, white sheepskin saddle cloth edged dark green, whist sheepskin holster covers. Black harness with brass fittings. The foot wore long white gaiters and seem to have been armed with rifles and Hirschfänger sword-bayonets with brass hilts. Another plate shows the hussars in 1761 in white dolman and breeches, edged in dark green, white buttons, red barrel sash. The mirliton was dark green, with a white flame edged dark green and with a dark green tassel. The pelisse and saddle furniture as before.

Fusiliers de Montagnes

Raised on 12 February 1744 as Fusiliers du Roussillon. In 1751, the unit was renamed Fusiliers de Montagnes. Disbanded on 10 December 1762. Tricorn with white edging, loop and button, dark blue coat and breeches, red collar, lapels, round cuffs and lining, white edging and two buttonhole loops to the cuffs, white waistcoat. The neck of coat and shirt were worn open with a red and yellow neckerchief. The breeches fastened with red garters; socks were white, and the light blue thongs of the brown shoes were wound around the calves, forming diamond-shaped patterns. Belts were buff. At the waist front a square buff pouch with three brass fleur-de-lis on the lid. On the left hip a square pouch, edged in red, white and blue fringes. On its lid were two knives and a pistol, carried horizontally.

Royal Cantabres

Raised on 15 December 1745. On 8 July 1757 the unit was incorporated into the French regulars as the Royal-Cantabres Infanterie (see Infantry section).

Volontaires Corse

Raised on 1 December 1761. The infantry wore a black, dragoon-style helmet, with mock leopard skin turban, black peak and crest, the latter with flowing black horsehair mane. Light blue coat and breeches, white lining, black collar and cuffs, no lapels, white waistcoat, turnbacks and buttons. White belts, black gaiters. The cavalry had almost the same uniform, but with the following differences: buff waistcoat and breeches, white sheepskin saddle cloth with light blue, wolf tooth edging.

Volontaires du Dauphiné

Created on 1 March 1749 from the amalgamation of the Volontaires de Gantez, the Volontaires de Lancise, the Chasseurs de Sabattier and the Chasseurs de Colonne. In 1758 both horse and foot wore dark blue, single-breasted coats, with yellow collar and round cuffs, white buttons, yellow waistcoats, dark blue breeches, buff belts with brass buckles. The foot wore a tricorn with white cockade and trim and long white gaiters. The horse wore black bearskin caps, with dark blue front plate (bearing the reversed, crowned 'L'), dark blue bag, with white trim and tassel; they also had heavy cavalry boots. Dark blue saddle cloth and holster covers with white trim and crowned 'L' cipher.

Volontaires Étrangers

Raised on 1 June 1756. This unit became the Volontaires de Vignolles, then the Volontaires d'Austrasie from 1759–1762. Brass-combed dragoon helmet, with steel headpiece, leopard skin turban, dark blue coat, red half lapels, round cuffs and lining, white buttons, belts and breeches, brass buckles, dark blue waistcoat, high, cuffed boots, white aiguillette on the right shoulder, white fringed epaulette on the left. They were armed with brass-hilted sabres in brass sheaths.

Volontaires de Flandre

Created on 1 August 1749 by the amalgamation of the Arquebusiers de Grassin, the Fusiliers de la Morlière and the Volontaires Bretons. On 27 March 1757 the unit was divided into two, creating the Volontaires du Hainaut (see below). White hat edging, dark blue coat, faced red and lined dark blue, white buttons and buttonholes, dark blue waistcoat, white belts, breeches and gaiters.

Volontaires de Geschray

1747 Colonel de Geschray; 1757 Colonel de Beyerle. In 1758 they became the Volontaires d'Alsace. Disbanded 22 November 1759. In 1758 they are shown in plain tricorn, dark blue coat, red lapels, round cuffs, waistcoat and breeches, yellow buttons, yellow lace to lapels and waistcoat, red lace loops to the vertical pocket flaps. Buff belts, long white gaiters.

Volontaires de Nassau-Sarrebruck

Raised on 10 November 1756. They became the 'Volontaires Royaux de Nassau', before being integrated into the hussars (see Hussars section). Uniform: black mirliton with orange and white edging to black flame, white cockade and plume, white fleur-de-lis badge, dark blue dolman, with orange cuffs piped white, dark blue breeches, red pelisse with black fur, white buttons and lace to all garments. Red and yellow barrel sash. White belts, red sabretasche, edged in white and orange checks, with a crowned, white, rampant lion in the centre. Buff bandolier, red waist belt. White sheepskin saddle cloth and holster cover with orange trim. Brass-hilted sabre with steel and black leather scabbard. Black harness with brass fittings.

Volontaires de Schomberg

Raised on 30 March 1743. Later became the Schomberg Dragons Nr 17 (see Dragoon section). Dragoon helmet with brass combe, flowing black horsehair crest, brown turban, with diamond-shaped pattern. Dark green coat, red collar, lapels, round cuffs and lining, yellow buttons. Buff waistcoat and breeches, red edging to waistcoat, red waist sash. Long black gaiters. They were armed with a brass-hilted sword and a carbine on white belts.

Volontaires de Soubise

Raised on 20 February 1761. It was renamed the Légion de Soubise in 1766. Infantry: black bearskin, without plate, with white cords and plume to left side; dark blue, single-breasted coat, dark blue collar, white cuffs, lining, waistcoat, breeches, belts and buttons. Cavalry: mirliton with black flame and dark blue crown; white plume to left side, dark blue coat, lapels and waistcoat, white buttons and button-holes, white cuffs (with three buttons and buttonholes), white lining. White breeches, dark blue saddle cloth, edged white.

Volontaires de Wurmser

Raised on 11 January 1762. Disbanded in 1 March 1763. Hussar costume in 1762 for both horse and foot; black mirliton with black flame edged white, white plume. Dark green dolman and pelisse, black fur trim, white lace and buttons, red belts, dark grey breeches. The horse wore black hussar boots with white trim; the foot had black gaiters, also with white top trim. White sheepskin saddle cloth with dark green trim, black harness with brass fittings.

Volontaires du Hainaut

Created on 27 March 1757 when when the Volontaires de Flandre were subdivided into two units. It received half of the brigade originating from the former Volontaires Bretons and the entire brigade originating from the Arquebusiers de Grassin. In December 1762, the unit incorporated the Volontaires d'Austrasie. On 1 March 1763 it was renamed Légion du Hainaut. Uniform: Plain black bearskin cap, dark blue coat with black collar, pointed cuffs, lapels and lining, white buttons. Dark blue fringed epaulettes, dark blue breeches, long black gaiters, yellow waistcoat. Buff belts with brass buckles, brass-hilted sabres in black sheath.

Volontaires Étranger de Clermont-Prince

In 1758 they wore brass-combed dragoon helmets with a yellow turban, having red diamond shapes over it, white plume, issuing from a black cross with gold edging over the left ear. The horse wore a yellow, double-breasted coat with red collar, lapels, round cuffs and lining, white buttons and lace loops to lapels, cuffs and waistcoat, yellow breeches and high, cuffed boots. Harness was brown with brass fittings, dark blue saddle cloth and holster covers. Buff belts with brass fittings, brass-hilted

Troopers of Volontaires Liègois and Volontaires de Nassau-Saarbruck, 1757. A number of minor states bordering on France chose to raise volunteer corps to fight alongside her. These two light cavalry units fought in Thuringia. The latter unit wears the lion of Nassau and the lily of France. (Knötel, IX, 9)

swords in brown scabbards. The foot wore the same uniform, but the coat was single-breasted and they had white breeches and long gaiters. They were armed with musket, bayonet and the same sword as the horse.

Volontaires Liégeois (1756–1758)
Raised on 15 August 1758. Cavalry uniform: black fur cap without plate or visible decoration, dark blue coat with buff collar, half-lapels, round cuffs, lining and waistcoat, red waist sash. White edging to collar, white braid buttonholes to lapels (six), cuffs (two) and waistcoat. Long black gaiters, white belts, dark blue saddle cloth and holster covers, edged white.

Volontaires Royaux
Created on 15 August 1745 from several free companies. On 7 May 1758, the unit was renamed Légion Royale. Hats edged in silver, dark blue coat, red facings and lining, red waistcoat, white buttons, no buttonhole lace, white belts, breeches and gaiters.

Artillery

The 4-pound '*canons à la suédoise*' were used by the French Army as early as 1745, by which time a great number had been cast. The first castings in France were at Paris in 1740 by Jean Baptiste Sautray, Commissaire Général des Dontes de l'Artillerie de France. In this period the Prussian infantry of Frederick the Great was issued with three light artillery pieces per battalion. The Maréchal de Belle-Isle wrote to M. de Crémille (Directeur Général of the artillery) in 1756: 'It is not natural that our infantry must fight against the Prussian infantry with a disproportion of more half [in artillery pieces].' The French Royal Ordnance of 1757 was a law assigning one 4-pound *canon à la suédoise* to each French infantry battalion. By 1758 Capitaine d'Infanterie de Scionville has proposed the carriage be used in the French mountain artillery.

French artillery pieces available in 1756 included the M1757 Rostaing 1-pound amusette, pulled by one horse, and the 'Swedish' M1743 4-pounder battalion gun, which required a crew of eight gunners and eight infantrymen as assistants. This gun and carriage were of far more modern design than that of other French guns. It was lighter, had a shorter barrel of 16.5 calibres and weighed 325kg. The wood of the carriage was thinner than French gun carriages and was reinforced by metal strapping. It used a screw mechanism to adjust the angle of the barrel rather than the old wooden wedges. A gun carriage, barrel and limber weighed 730kg and each piece had to be pulled by three horses in tandem harness. M1743 ammunition was made up into cartridges containing the projectile and the propellant charge, which made for faster, safer loading. A well-trained crew could attain a rate of fire with this light piece of ten rounds per minute. An ammunition chest was carried on the carriage trails. This gun was modified by the French in 1757 and remained in service until 1798.

There were also Vallière-designed M1732 8-pounder cannon, 12-pounder cannon and the M1749 6.4 inch howitzer, throwing a 12.4kg shell. This weapon had been designed by the French Field Marshal Comte Hermann Moritz Graf 'Maréchal de Saxe'. The barrels of these Vallière guns were of antiquated design, overly long at 23.2 calibres and heavy, compared with the newer, lighter, shorter weapons of France's enemies. The French were still using larger charges than were really needed and this required the barrel to be much heavier that it should have been. This in turn made French gun carriages much heavier, making the pieces extremely difficult to move over bad roads and across country.

Vallière's 12-pounder's barrel weighed 1565kg; his 8-pounder barrel 1030kg and the Saxe howitzer barrel 320kg. Compare these weights with the Liechtenstein 6-pounder at 414kg, the 12-pounder at 812kg and 7-pounder howitzer at 280kg, to see just what weight advantages the Austrian artillery had over that of the French. For artillery uniform see Royal Artillerie Nr 47 in the Infantry section.

9

THE KINGDOM
OF GREAT BRITAIN

Infantry

There follows a table of regiments of the British Army as it was during the period 1756–1763. Many of the most junior regiments were disbanded in 1763, and the vacant numbers were re-allocated to new regiments, which were raised later. Thus it is impossible to compare this table with regiments which served in the Napoleonic Wars. Each regiment had one or two battalions, each with 9–13 companies, one of which was grenadiers. On campaign it was customary for the grenadier companies to be detached from their parent regiments and grouped together, in *ad hoc* elite battalions for special tasks.

Uniform
During the Seven Years War all regiments wore red coats unless otherwise specified. Musketeers wore tricorns and grenadiers wore cloth mitre caps bearing their regiment's special badge or the royal cipher, over a red label bearing the springing white horse of Hanover. The front part of the cap, and its backing, were in the regimental facing colour, as was the back headband. Facings were shown on the cuffs, lapels and turnbacks of the collarless coats. Waistcoats and breeches were red or dark blue; long white gaiters were worn. Belts were of buff leather. The coat and waistcoat of each regiment was decorated with its unique style of lace. The skirts of officers' coats were not turned back. They wore crimson silk waist sashes under the coat, gilt gorgets when on duty, and had gold and crimson sword straps. Hair was powdered, curled and worn in a plaited pigtail. No moustaches were worn. Musketeer company officers carried spontoons, grenadier company officers wore grenadier caps and carried short muskets; all officers (including those of the cavalry) wore their sashes from right shoulder to left hip. Grenadier NCOs and officers wore no wings. Sergeants wore crimson worsted waist sashes with a wide central stripe in the facing colour; they carried halberds. Corporals had a white cord knot with loose, tasselled ends hanging down about six inches, on the right shoulder.

 The details of the colours of many regiments are included below in the Royal Clothing Warrant of 1751.

The Foot Guards
The three regiments of footguards wore coats as for the line regiments, faced and lined dark blue and decorated with plain white lace and buttonholes. The buttonholes of the 1st Footguards were square-

ended, those of the 2nd and 3rd Regiments had pointed ends. All three regiments wore red waistcoats, dark blue breeches and long, white gaiters. The decoration of the grenadier caps was common for all three regiments, in that the dark blue front was decorated by the crowned star of the Order of the Garter and they all had white pompons with red centres. The grenadiers did not wear wings. The hats of the musketeers were edged with white binding.

1st Regiment of Foot Guards
Raised in Bruges in 1656 as part of exiled King Charles II's guards.

2nd or Coldstream Guards
Raised on 23 August 1650 by Oliver Cromwell as Monck's Regiment of Foot. On 14 February 1661 they were taken into the Royal Household troops.

3rd Scots Guards
Raised in 1642 by King Charles I of Scotland; taken into the English military establishment by King Charles II in 1664.

The Royal Clothing Warrant, 1751
Regulations for the Colours, Clothing, etc., of the Marching Regiments of Foot, and for the uniform Clothing of the Cavalry, their Standards, Guidons, Banners, etc.

Our Will and Pleasure is, That the following Regulations for the Colours, Clothing, etc. of Our Marching Regiments of Foot, and for the uniform Clothing of Our Cavalry, their Standards, Guidons, Banners, etc., be duly observed and put in execution, at such times as the particulars are, or shall be, furnished, viz., Regulation for the Colours, Clothing, etc., of the Marching Regiments of Foot.

No Colonel to put his Arms, Crest, Device, or Livery, on any part of the Appointments of the Regiment under his Command.

No part of the Clothing, or Ornaments of the Regiments to be altered after the following Regulations are put in execution but by Us, or Our Captain General's permission.

Colours
The King's, or first Colour of every Regiment, is to be the Great Union throughout.

The second Colour, to be the colour of the Facing of the Regiment with the Union in the upper Canton; except those Regiments which are faced with Red or White, whose Second Colour is to be the Red Cross of St George in a White Field, and the Union in the Upper Canton.

In the Centre of each Colour is to be painted, or embroidered, in Gold Roman Characters, the Number of the Rank of the Regiment, within the Wreath of Roses and Thistles, on the same Stalk; except those Regiments which are allowed to wear any Royal Devices, or ancient Badges, on whose Colours the Rank of the Regiment is to be painted towards the upper Corner.

The size of the Colours, and the length of the Pike, to be the same as those of the Royal Regiments of Foot Guards. The Cords and Tassels of all Colours to be crimson and gold mixed.

Drummers' Clothing
The Drummers of all the Royal Regiments are allowed to wear the Royal Livery, viz., Red. lined, faced, and lapelled on the breast with blue, and laced with Royal lace: The Drummers of all the other Regiments are to be clothed with the Colour of the Facing of their Regiments,

lined, faced, and lapelled on the Breast with Red, and laced in such manner as the Colonel shall think fit for distinction sake, the Lace, however, being of the Colours of that on the Soldiers' coats.

Grenadiers' Caps

The front of the Grenadiers' Caps to be the same Colour as the facing of the Regiment, with the King's Cypher embroidered, and Crown over it; the little Flap to be Red, with the White Horse and Motto over it, 'Nec aspera terrent'; the back part of the Cap to be Red; the turn-up to be the Colour of the Front; with the Number of the Regiment in the middle part behind. – The Royal Regiments, and the Six Old Corps, differ from the fore-going Rule as specified hereafter.

Drums

The Front or forepart of the Drums to be painted with the Colour of the facing of the Regiment, with the King's Cypher and Crown, and the Number of the Regiment under it.

Bells of Arms

The Bell of Arms to be painted in the same manner.

Camp Colours

The Camp Colours to be Square, and of the Colour of the facing of the Regiment, with the Number of the Regiment upon them.

Devices and Badges of the Royal Regiments and the Six Old Corps

1st Regiment or (Raised) The Royal Regiment

In the Centre of their Colours, the King's Cypher, within the Circle of St Andrew and Crown over it. – In the three corners of the Second Colour, the Thistle and Crown. – The Distinction of the Colours of the Second battalion is a flaming Ray of Gold descending from the upper corner of each Colour towards the centre. On the Grenadier Caps, the same Device, as in the centre of the Colours; White Horse and the King's Motto over it, on the little Flap. The Drums and Bells of Arms to have the same Device painted on them, with the Number or Rank of the Regiment under it.

2nd Regiment or (Raised) The Queen's Royal Regiment

In the centre of each Colour the Queen's Cypher on a Red Ground, within the Garter, and Crown over it. – In the three corners of the Second Colour, the Lamb, being the ancient Badge of the Regiment. On the Grenadier Caps, the Queen's Cypher and Crown, as in the Colours; White Horse and motto 'Nec asperra terrent' on the Flap. The Drums and Bells of Arms to have the Queen's Cypher painted on them in the same manner, and the Rank of the Regiment underneath.

3rd Regiment or The Buffs

In the centre of their Colours, the Dragon, being the ancient Badge, and the Rose and Crown in the Three corners of their Second Colour. On the Grenadier Caps the Dragon; White Horse and King's Motto on the Flap.
The same Badge of the Dragon to be painted on their Drums and Bells of Arms, with the Rank of the Regiment underneath.

4th Regiment, or The King's Own Royal Regiment
In the centre of their Colours the King's Cypher on a Red ground within the Garter, and Crown over it; In the three corners of their Second Colour the Lion of England, being their ancient Badge. On the Grenadier Caps the King's Cypher, as on the Colours, and Crown over it; White Horse and Motto on the Flap. The Drums and Bells of Arms to have the King's Cypher painted on them, in the same manner, and the Rank of the Regiment underneath.

5th Regiment
In the centre of their Colours, St George Killing the Dragon being their ancient Badge and in the three Corners of their Second Colour the Rose and Crown. On the Grenadier Caps, St George Killing the Dragon; the White Horse and Motto 'Nec aspera terrent' over it on the flap. The same Badge of St George and the Dragon to be painted on their Drums, and Bells of Arms, with the Rank of the Regiment underneath.

6th Regiment
In the centre of their Colours, the Antelope, being their ancient Badge, and in the three corners of their Second Colour, the Rose and Crown. On the Grenadier Caps the Antelope, as in the Colours, White Horse and Motto on the Flap. The same Badge of the Antelope to be painted on their Drums and Bells of Arms, with the Rank of the Regiment underneath.

7th Regiment or The Royal Fusiliers
In the centre of their Colours the Rose within the Garter, and Crown over it; the White Horse in the corners of the Second Colour. On the Grenadier Caps, the Rose within the Garter, and Crown, as in the Colours; White Horse and Motto over it 'Nec aspera terrent' on the Flap. The same Device of the Rose within the Garter and Crown on their Drums and Bells of Arms, Rank of the Regiment underneath.

8th Regiment or The King's Regiment
In the centre of their Colours the White Horse on a Red ground, within the Garter and Crown over it; In the three Corners of the Second Colour, the King's Cypher and Crown. On the Grenadier Caps, the White Horse as on the Colours – the White Horse and Motto 'Nec aspera terrent' on the Flap. The Same Device of the White Horse within the Garter, on the Drums and Bells of Arms; Rank of the Regiment underneath.

18th Regiment or The Royal Irish
In the centre of their Colours, the Harp on a Blue field, and the Crown over it, and in the three Corners of their Second Colour, the Lion of Nassau, King William the Third's Arms. On the Grenadier Caps the Harp and Crown as on the Colours, White Horse and Motto on the Flap. The Harp and Crown to be painted in the same manner, on the Drums and Bells of Arms, with the Rank of the Regiment underneath.

21st Regiment or The Royal North British Fusiliers
In the centre of their Colours, the Thistle within the Circle of St Andrew, and Crown over it, and in the three corners of the Second Colour, the King's Cypher and Crown. On the Grenadier Caps the Thistle, as on the Colours; White Horse and Motto over it 'Nec aspera terrent' on the Flap. On the Drums and Bells of Arms, the Thistle and Crown to be painted, as on the Colours, Rank of the Regiment underneath.

23rd Regiment or The Royal Welch Fusiliers

In the centre of their Colours, the Device of the Prince of Wales, viz., three Feathers issuing out of the Prince's Coronet; In the three Corners of the Second Colour, the Badges of Edward the Black Prince, viz., Rising Sun, Red Dragon, and the three Feathers in the Coronet, Motto 'Ich Dien.' On the Grenadier Caps the Feathers as in the Colours, White Horse and Motto 'Nec aspera terrent' on the Flap. The same Badge of the Three Feathers and Motto 'Ich Dien' on the Drums and Bells of Arms; Rank of the Regiment underneath.

27th Regiment or The Inniskilling Regiment

Allowed to wear in the centre of their Colours a Castle with three Turrets, St George's Colours flying in a Blue Field, and the Name Inniskilling over it. On the Grenadier Caps, the Castle and Name, as on the Colours; White Horse and King's Motto on the Flap. The same Badge of the Castle and Name on the Drums and Bells of Arms, Rank of the Regiment underneath.

41st Regiment or The Invalids

In the centre of their Colours, the Rose and Thistle, on a Red ground, within the Garter, and Crown over it; In the three Corners of the Second Colour, the King's Cypher and Crown. On the Grenadier Caps, Drums and Bells of Arms the same Device of the Rose and Thistle conjoined, within the Garter and Crown, as on the Colours.

Highland Regiment

The Grenadier of the Highland Regiment are allowed to wear Bearskin-Fur Caps, with the King's Cypher and Crown over it, on a Red ground in the Turn-up, or Flap.

Grenadiers of the British 1st, 2nd and 3rd Regiments of Foot, 1751. (David Morier (405578) from the Royal Collection)

Facings of the Regiments of Foot

Facing Colour	Regiment	Distinction	Pre-sent Colonel
Blue	1st or the Royal Regiment		Lieutenant-General St Clair
	4th or the King's Own Regiment		Colonel Rich
	7th or the Royal Fusiliers		Colonel Mostyn
	8th or the King's Regiment		Lieutenant-General Wolfe
	18th or the Royal Irish		Colonel Folliot
	21st or the Royal North British Fusiliers		Lieutenant-General Campbell
	23rd or the Royal Welch Fusiliers		Lieutenant-General Huske
	41st or the Invalids		Colonel Wardour
Green	2nd or the Queen's Royal Regiment	sea green	Major-General Fowke
	5th Regiment	goslin green	Lieutenant-General Irvine
	11th Regiment	full green	Colonel Botland
Green	19th Regiment	yellowish green	Colonel Lord George Beauclerk
	24 Regiment (lined with white)	willow green	Colonel Earl of Ancram
	36th Regiment	grass green	Colonel Lord Robert Manners
	39th Regiment		Brigadier Richbell
	45th Regiment	deep green	Colonel Warburton
	49th Regiment	full green	Colonel Trelawny
buff	3rd Regiment or The Buffs	pale buff	Colonel Howard
	14th Regiment		Colonel Herbert
	22nd Regiment		Brigadier O'Farrell
	27th or the Inniskilling Regiment		Lieutenant-General Blakeney
	31st Regiment		Colonel Holmes
	40th Regiment		Colonel Cornwallis
	42nd Regiment		Colonel Lord John Murray
	48th Regiment		Colonel Earl of Horne
white	17th Regiment	greyish white	Lieutenant-General Wynyard
	32nd Regiment		Colonel Leighton
	43rd Regiment		Colonel Kennedy
	47th Regiment		Colonel Lascelles
red	33rd Regiment (white lining)		Lieutenant-General Johnson
orange	35th Regiment		Lieutenant-General Otway

yellow	6th Regiment	deep yellow	Lieutenant-General Guise
	9th Regiment		Colonel Waldegrave
	10th Regiment	bright yellow	Colonel Pole
	12th Regiment		Lieutenant-General Skelton
	13th Regiment	philemot yellow	Lieutenant-General Pulteney
	15th Regiment		Colonel Jorden
	16th Regiment		Lieutenant-General Handasyde
	20th Regiment	pale yellow	Colonel Lord Viscount Bury
	25th Regiment	deep yellow	Colonel Earl of Panmure
	26th Regiment	pale yellow	Lieutenant-General Anstruther
yellow	28th Regiment	bright yellow	Lieutenant-General Bragg
	29th Regiment		Colonel Hopson
	30th Regiment	pale yellow	Colonel Earl of London.
	34th Regiment	bright yellow	Colonel Conway
	37th Regiment		Colonel Dejean
	38th Regiment		Colonel Duroure
	44th Regiment		Colonel Sir Peter Halket, Baronet
	46th Regiment		Colonel Murray
red with blue coats	Royal Regiment of Artillery		Colonel Belford

Abstract	
Facing Colour	**Number of Regiments**
blue	8
green	9
buff	8
white	4
red	1
orange	1
yellow	18
blue with red	1

Opposite above: Grenadiers of the 4th, 5th and 6th Regiments of Foot, 1751. (David Morier (405584) from the Royal Collection)

Opposite below: Grenadier, fifer and drummer, 49th Regiment of Foot, 1751. (David Morier (405596) from the Royal Collection)

Grenadier Caps of the Regiments of Foot

1st, 2nd (Coldstream) and 3rd Footguards, 1745

Dark blue front, silver star, dark blue garter with gold motto, red-within-white pompon, red and white small label, horse and motto. All three regiments wore plain white lace.

Drummers and Fifers, 1751

Dark blue front, gold crown with crimson cushions, brass drums, white lances. On the left, a white flag with a red 'G', on the right a red flag with a white 'R'; red and white small label, horse and motto.

1st Regiment of Foot

Dark blue front plate, gold crown with crimson cushions, dark blue Garter with gold motto, dark blue centre with gold 'GR', white embroidery, white edging and tuft, red lower label with white edging, motto and horse. White lace.

2nd Regiment of Foot

Green front gold crown with crimson cushions, embroidery, white edging and tuft, red lower label with white edging, motto and horse. Red, white and green tuft. White lace. Officer's cap, front: green front, gold crown with crimson cushions, dark blue Garter with gold motto, gold cipher on red ground. Rear: red backing, gold embroidery, dark blue band.

3rd Regiment of Foot

Buff plate, gold crown with crimson cushions, white embroidery, green dragon with red tongue, white edging, red, white and buff tuft, red lower label with white edging, motto and horse. White lace with yellow and red stripes. Officer's cap, front: buff front plate, dark green dragon with red tongue, silver embroidery, gold crown with crimson cushions, silver tuft. Rear: red backing, dark blue headband, silver embroidery.

4th Regiment of Foot

Dark blue plate, gold crown with crimson cushions, yellow embroidery, dark blue Garter with gold motto, red centre with gold 'GR', white edging, blue and white tuft, red lower label with white edging, motto and horse. White lace with blue zig-zag.

5th Regiment of Foot

Green plate, gold crown with crimson cushions, white embroidery, gold St George on a white horse, killing a green dragon, white edging and tuft, red lower label with white edging, motto and horse. White lace.

6th Regiment of Foot

Yellow plate, gold crown with crimson cushions, white embroidery with red leaves, white antelope with gold collar and chain, white edging, yellow and white tuft, red lower label with white edging, motto and horse. White lace with yellow diamonds and edging.

7th Regiment of Foot

Dark blue plate, Garter and centre, red rose with green leaves, gold crown with crimson cushions, white embroidery, white edging, blue and white tuft, red lower label with white edging, motto and horse. White lace with a blue stripe down one side.

8th Regiment of Foot

Dark blue plate, gold crown with crimson cushions, white embroidery, dark blue Garter, red centre, white horse on green earth, white edging, blue and white tuft, red lower label with white edging, motto and horse. White lace with yellow edging.

Grenadier's cap, 1st, 2nd (Coldstream) and 3rd Footguards, 1745. (Morier. 405597)

Cap of drummers and fifers of Footguards, 1751. (Morier 4745)

1st Regiment of Foot. (Morier 405578)

2nd Regiment of Foot. (Morier 405578)

2nd Regiment of Foot, officer's cap, front. (C.C.P. Lawson, Volume II)

2nd Regiment of Foot, officer's cap, rear. (C.C.P. Lawson, Volume II)

3rd Regiment of Foot, officer's cap, front. (C.C.P. Lawson, Volume II)

3rd Regiment of Foot, officer's cap, rear. (C.C.P. Lawson, Volume II)

3rd Regiment of Foot. (Morier 405578)

9th Regiment of Foot
Yellow plate, gold crown with crimson cushions, white embroidery, white edging, yellow and white tuft, red lower label with white edging, motto and horse. White lace with red stripes.

10th Regiment of Foot
Yellow plate, gold crown with crimson cushions, white embroidery, white edging, yellow and white tuft, red lower label with white edging, motto and horse. White lace with red edging and blue zig-zag.

11th Regiment of Foot
Green plate, gold crown with crimson cushions, white embroidery, white edging, green and white tuft, red lower label with white edging, motto and horse. White lace with red and green stripes.

12th Regiment of Foot
Yellow plate, gold crown with crimson cushions, white embroidery, white edging, yellow and white tuft, red lower label with white edging, motto and horse. White lace with a yellow stripe.

13th Regiment of Foot
Yellow plate, gold crown with crimson cushions, white embroidery, white edging, yellow and white tuft, red lower label with white edging, motto and horse. White lace with a red and a blue zig-zag.

14th Regiment of Foot
Yellow plate, gold crown with crimson cushions, white embroidery, white edging, red, white and buff tuft, red lower label with white edging, motto and horse. White lace with one edge red, the other blue and a blue zig-zag between them.

15th Regiment of Foot
Yellow plate, gold crown with crimson cushions, white embroidery, white edging and tuft, red lower label with white edging, motto and horse. White lace with black / yellow side stripes.

Grenadiers of the British 16th and 17th Regiments of Foot and a grenadier and drummer of the 18th Regiment of Foot, 1751. (David Morier (405583) from the Royal Collection)

4th Regiment of Foot.
(Morier 405579)

5th Regiment of Foot.
(Morier 405579)

6th Regiment of Foot.
(Morier 405579)

7th Regiment of Foot.
(Morier 405580)

8th Regiment of Foot.
(Morier 405580)

9th Regiment of Foot.
(Morier 405580)

10th Regiment of Foot.
(Morier 405581)

11th Regiment of Foot.
(Morier 405581)

12th Regiment of Foot.
(Morier 405581)

16th Regiment of Foot

Yellow plate, gold crown with crimson cushions, white embroidery, red 'GR', white edging, yellow and white tuft, red lower label with white edging, motto and horse. White lace with red stripes.

17th Regiment of Foot

Buff plate, gold crown with crimson cushions, green embroidery and 'GR', white edging, green and white tuft, red lower label with white edging, motto and horse. White lace with green side stripes and zig-zags.

18th Regiment of Foot

Dark blue plate, gold crown with crimson cushions, gold harp with white strings, white embroidery, white edging, blue ands white tuft, red lower label with white edging, motto and horse. White lace with a blue, wavy pattern.

19th Regiment of Foot

Green plate, gold crown with crimson cushions, white embroidery, white edging, green and white tuft, red lower label with white edging, motto and horse. White lace with red and blue side stripes.

20th Regiment of Foot

Yellow plate, gold crown with crimson cushions, white embroidery, white edging and tuft, red lower label with white edging, motto and horse. White lace with red and black edging.

21st Regiment of Foot

Dark blue plate, gold crown with crimson cushions, dark blue Garter with gold motto, dark blue centre with purple and green thistle, white embroidery, white edging, blue and white tuft, red lower label with white edging, motto and horse. White lace with yellow edging and blue zig-zag.

22nd Regiment of Foot

Yellow plate, gold crown with crimson cushions, white embroidery with bright yellow leaves, white edging and tuft, red lower label with white edging, motto and horse. White lace with red and blue side stripes.

23rd Regiment of Foot

Dark blue plate, gold crown with crimson cushions, white feathers, gold coronet, white embroidery, white edging and tuft, red lower label with white edging, motto and horse. White lace with yellow and blue side stripe and red diagonals along it.

24th Regiment of Foot

Green plate, gold crown with crimson cushions, white embroidery, white edging, green and white tuft, red lower label with white edging, motto and horse. White lace with a green stripe.

25th Regiment of Foot

Yellow plate, gold crown with crimson cushions, white embroidery, white edging and tuft, red lower label with white edging, motto and horse. White lace with blue/yellow/red side stripes.

26th Regiment of Foot

Yellow plate, gold crown with crimson cushions, white embroidery, white edging and tuft, red lower label with white edging, motto and horse. White lace with yellow side stripes.

13th Regiment of Foot.
(Morier 405582)

14th Regiment of Foot.
(Morier 405582)

15th Regiment of Foot.
(Morier 405582)

16th Regiment of Foot.
(Morier 405583)

17th Regiment of Foot.
(Morier 405583)

18th Regiment of Foot.
(Morier 405583)

19th Regiment of Foot.
(Morier 405584)

20th Regiment of Foot.
(Morier 405584)

21st Regiment of Foot.
(Morier 405584)

27th Regiment of Foot

Buff plate, gold crown with crimson cushions, dark blue disc with white castle badge, white embroidery, white edging and tuft, red lower label with white edging, motto and horse. White lace with two wavy yellow lines.

28th Regiment of Foot

Yellow plate, gold crown with crimson cushions, white embroidery, green 'GR', white edging, yellow and white tuft, red lower label with white edging, motto and horse. White lace with yellow side stripes and a black diamond pattern.

29th Regiment of Foot

Yellow plate, gold crown with crimson cushions, white embroidery, green 'GR', white edging, yellow and white tuft, red lower label with white edging, motto and horse. White lace with blue and yellow side stripes and a wavy blue pattern in the centre.

30th Regiment of Foot

Yellow plate, gold crown with crimson cushions, white embroidery, green 'GR', white edging, yellow and white tuft, red lower label with white edging, motto and horse. White lace with green side stripes. Drum major's cap: bright red front and small label (with brown drum, red hoops, black cords and sticks), white silk edging to label with gold edging and black motto; rose, thistle and shamrock in natural colours, gold crown with crimson cushions. The back of the cap is yellow, piped red (the pompon is missing); red headband, edged gold, green embroidery, drum as on the front, green foliage, red roses.

31st Regiment of Foot

Buff plate, gold crown with crimson cushions, white embroidery with orange leaves, white edging and tuft, red lower label with white edging, motto and horse. White lace with a green central stripe.

32nd Regiment of Foot

White plate, gold crown with crimson cushions, dark green embroidery with red roses, red 'GR', white edging, brown and white tuft, red lower label with white edging, motto and horse. White lace with black side stripes and a central black zig-zag.

33rd Regiment of Foot

Red plate, gold crown with crimson cushions, white embroidery, white edging, red and white tuft, red lower label with white edging, motto and horse. White lace.

34th Regiment of Foot

Yellow plate, gold crown with crimson cushions, white embroidery, green 'GR', white edging and tuft, red lower label with white edging, motto and horse. White lace with a yellow side stripe and a wavy blue pattern in the middle.

35th Regiment of Foot

Orange plate, gold crown with crimson cushions, white embroidery, white edging, orange and white tuft, red lower label with white edging, motto and horse. White lace with one red and one yellow side stripe and a yellow zig-zag.

36th Regiment of Foot

Grass green plate, gold crown with crimson cushions, white embroidery, white edging, green and white tuft, red lower label with white edging, motto and horse. White lace with a green central stripe.

22nd Regiment of Foot.
(Morier 405585)

23rd Regiment of Foot.
(Morier 405585)

24th Regiment of Foot.
(Morier 405585)

25th Regiment of Foot.
(Morier 405593)

26th Regiment of Foot.
(Morier 405593)

27th Regiment of Foot.
(Morier 405593)

28th Regiment of Foot.
(Morier 405594)

37th Regiment of Foot

Yellow plate, gold crown with crimson cushions, white embroidery, green 'GR', white edging, green, buff and white tuft, red lower label with white edging, motto and horse. White lace with one red zig-zag, one green zig-zag, two central yellow stripes.

38th Regiment of Foot

Yellow plate, gold crown with crimson cushions, white embroidery, light blue 'GR', white edging, green and white tuft, red lower label with white edging, motto and horse. White lace with green side stripes and a yellow central stripe.

39th Regiment of Foot

Dark green plate, gold crown with crimson cushions, white embroidery, white edging, green and white tuft, red lower label with white edging, motto and horse. White lace with a green central wavy pattern.

40th Regiment of Foot

Buff plate, gold crown with crimson cushions, white embroidery, dark green 'GR', white edging, black and white tuft, red lower label with white edging, motto and horse. White lace with a central black line, flanked by yellow lines.

41st Regiment of Foot or the Royal Invalids

This regiment had no grenadier company and no lace.

42nd Regiment of Foot

Red plate, silver edging, gold crown with crimson cushions, gold 'GR', black fur. White lace with a red central line.

43rd Regiment of Foot

White plate, gold crown with crimson cushions, white embroidery, green 'GR', white edging, blue and white tuft, red lower label with white edging, motto and horse. White lace with red side stripes and blue central stars.

44th Regiment of Foot

Yellow plate, gold crown with crimson cushions, white embroidery, green 'GR', white edging, yellow and white tuft, red lower label with white edging, motto and horse. White lace with a yellow central stripe, flanked by a black and a blue zig-zag.

45th Regiment of Foot

Dark blue plate, gold crown with crimson cushions, white embroidery, white edging, green and white tuft, red lower label with white edging, motto and horse. White lace with one green edging and green stars along it.

46th Regiment of Foot

Yellow plate, gold crown with crimson cushions, white embroidery, white edging, red, blue, yellow and white tuft, red lower label with white edging, motto and horse. White lace with one yellow edge and blue stars.

47th Regiment of Foot

White plate, gold crown with crimson cushions, green embroidery and 'GR', white edging, black and white tuft, red lower label with white edging, motto and horse. White lace with black outer and yellow inner zig-zags.

29th Regiment of Foot.
(Morier 405594)

30th Regiment of Foot.
(Morier 405594)

30th Regiment of Foot, drum major's cap. (C.C.P. Lawson, Volume II)

31st Regiment of Foot.
(Morier 405590)

32nd Regiment of Foot.
(Morier 405590)

33rd Regiment of Foot.
(Morier 405590)

34th Regiment of Foot.
(Morier 405591)

48th Regiment of Foot
Buff plate, gold crown with crimson cushions, white embroidery, green 'GR', white edging and tuft, red lower label with white edging, motto and horse. White lace with a blue side line and blue stars.

49th Regiment of Foot
Green plate, gold crown with crimson cushions, embroidery, white edging, green and white tuft, red lower label with white edging, motto and horse. White lace with a central yellow zig-zag.

50th Regiment of Foot
Assumed to be a black plate, gold crown with crimson cushions, white embroidery, white edging and tuft, red lower label with white edging, motto and horse. Lace not known.

52nd Regiment of Foot
Assumed to be a buff plate, gold crown with crimson cushions, white embroidery, white edging and tuft, red lower label with white edging, motto and horse. Lace not known.

53rd Regiment of Foot
Whitmore's 1759, Toovey's: yellow or red facings, lace.

54th Regiment of Foot
Campbell's 1757, Grey's 1760, Parslow's: white (or green) facings, white lace.

55th Regiment of Foot
Perry's 1757, Howe's 1758, Donaldson's 1758, Prideaux's 1760, Oughton's 1762, Gosnell's: deep yellow (dark green) facings, yellow lace with two green stripes.

56th Regiment of Foot
Manner's: dark green (or crimson) facings, white lace.

57th Regiment of Foot
Arabin's 1757, Cunynghame's: lemon yellow facings and lace.

58th Regiment of Foot
Anstruther's: white (black?) facings, white lace with a red central line.

59th Regiment of Foot
Montague's 1760, Owen's: buff facings (?), lace.

60th Regiment of Foot
Royal American: black (blue?) facings, no lace.

61st Regiment of Foot
Elliot's 1759, Gray's: buff facings, white lace with a blue stripe.

62nd Regiment of Foot
Strode's: buff facings, white lace with two black and two buff stripes.

63rd Regiment of Foot
Watson's 1760, Boothby's: dark green facings, white lace with green diagonal stripes.

35th Regiment of Foot.
(Morier 405591)

36th Regiment of Foot.
(Morier 405591)

37th Regiment of Foot.
(Morier 405588)

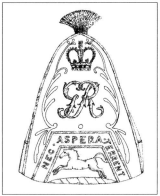

38th Regiment of Foot.
(Morier 405588)

39th Regiment of Foot.
(Morier 405588)

40th Regiment of Foot.
(Morier 405589)

42nd Regiment of Foot.
(Morier 405589)

43rd Regiment of Foot.
(Morier 405586)

64th Regiment of Foot
Barrington's 1759, Townshend's, Cary's: black facings, white lace with a yellow stripe.

65th Regiment of Foot
Armiger's: white facings, white lace with stripes of yellow, blue and red and a blue worm. Officer's cap, front: white plate, silver embroidery, red bottom label, white horse, edging and motto, green and yellow bottom stripe, silver tassel. Rear: red backing, white headband, silver embroidery and tassel.

66th Regiment of Foot
Sandford's 1758, Lafaussille's: lime green facings, white lace with two crimson stripes.

67th Regiment of Foot
Wolfe's 1759, Cavendish's 1760, Erskine's 1762, Hamilton-Lambert's: yellow facings, white lace with a lime green stripe.

68th Regiment of Foot
Lambton's: dark green facings, white lace with two yellow and one black stripe.

69th Regiment of Foot
Colville's: willow green facings, white lace with two yellow and two black stripes.

70th Regiment of Foot
Glasgow Lowland: deep grey facings, white lace with a blue stripe.

71st Regiment of Foot
Petitot's: white facings, white lace with two black and one red stripes.

72nd Regiment of Foot
Richmond's: red facings, white lace with two red and a black stripe.

73rd Regiment of Foot
Browne's: deep green facings, white lace with white, blue and yellow stripes.

74th Regiment of Foot
Talbot's: deep green facings, white lace with one yellow and two red stripes.

75th Regiment of Foot
Boscawen's 1762, Mariscoe's: red facings, white lace with two green and two yellow stripes.

76th Regiment of Foot
Forbes': facings and lace unknown.

77th Regiment of Foot
Montgomery's Highlanders: dark green facings, white lace; a kilted regiment.

78th Regiment of Foot
Fraser's Highlanders: buff facings, white lace; a kilted regiment.

79th Regiment of Foot
Drapers: light buff facings, white lace.

44th Regiment of Foot.
(Morier 405586)

45th Regiment of Foot.
(Morier 405586)

47th Regiment of Foot.
(Morier 405587)

48th Regiment of Foot.
(Morier 405587)

49th Regiment of Foot.
(Morier 405596)

65th Regiment of Foot, officer's cap,
front. (Victoria & Albert Museum)

65th Regiment of Foot, officer's cap,
rear. (Victoria & Albert Museum)

80th Regiment of Foot
Dark brown facings, no lace.

81st Regiment of Foot
Invalids: facings and lace unknown.

82nd Regiment of Foot
Invalids: facings and lace unknown.

83rd Regiment of Foot
Facings and lace unknown.

84th Regiment of Foot
Coote's: no details known.

85th Regiment of Foot
Crauford's: no details known.

86th Regiment of Foot
Worge's: no details known.

87th Regiment of Foot
Keith's Highlanders: green facings, white lace; a kilted regiment.

88th Regiment of Foot
Campbell's Highlanders: green facings, white lace; a kilted regiment.

89th Regiment of Foot
Morris's Highlanders: deep orange facings, white lace with a black stripe; a kilted regiment.

90th Regiment of Foot
Morgan's: no details known.

91st Regiment of Foot
Blaney's: no details known.

92nd Regiment of Foot
Gore's: no details known.

93rd Regiment of Foot
Bagshawe's: no details known.

94th Regiment of Foot
Vaughan's: no details known.

95th Regiment of Foot
Burton's: no details known.

Infantry Regiments Raised Before 1751

Regiment	Raised	Regiment	Raised
Foot Guards		23rd (Royal Welsh Fuzileers)	16 March 1689
1st	1656	24th	8 March 1689
2nd (Coldstream)	26 August 1650	25th (Edinburgh)	19 March 1689^
3rd	1642	26th	1688★
Line Infantry		27th (Inniskilling)	26 June 1689★
1st (Royal)	28 March 1625	28th	16 February 1694★
2nd (The Queen's Royal)	1 October 1661	29th	16 February 1694★
3rd (The Buffs)	1572	30th	12 February 1702★
4th (The King's Own)	13 July 1680	31st	23 April 1694★
5th	8 August 1674	32nd	1702★
6th	13 June 1667	33rd	1702★
7th (Royal Fuzileers)	11 June 1685	34th	12 February 1702★
8th (The King's)	19 June 1685	35th (The Prince of Orange's Own)	28 June 1701★
9th	19 June 1685	36th	10 May 1701★
10th	20 June 1685	37th	13 February 1702★
11th	13 June 1667	38th	13 February 1702★
12th	20 June 1685	39th	29 August 1702★
13th	20 June 1685	40th	25 August 1717★
14th	22 June 1685+	41st (Invalids)	11 March 1719★
15th	22 June 1685	42nd (Highland)	24 April 1725★
16th	1688+	43rd	1 March 1741★
17th	27 September 1688	44th	7 January 1741★
18th (Royal Irish)	1 April 1684	45th	11 January 1741★
19th	20 November 1688	46th	13 January 1741★
20th	20 November 1688	47th	15 January 1741★
21st (Royal North British Fuzileers)	23 September 1688	48th	31 January 1741★
22nd	8 March 1688	49th	25 December 1743★

^ disbanded 1782

★ disbanded 1881

+ disbanded 1809

Grenadiers and a fusilier of the 19th, 20th and 21st Regiments of Foot, 1751. (David Morier (405596) from the Royal Collection)

Infantry Regiments Raised After 1751

The following regiments were raised after publication of the 1751 Royal Clothing Warrant, taking the infantry from 49 to 124 regiments. On 15 June 1758, the 2nd battalions of fifteen regiments were renumbered as new regiments 61–75. In the list below, the number of the old regiment is shown in brackets beside the new numeric designation.

Regiment	Raised	Disbanded	Facings	Buttons	Lace
50th (The Queen's Own)	25 December 1755	1881	black	?	?
51st	25 December 1755	1881	white	?	?
52nd	25 December 1755	1881	black	?	?
53rd	20 December 1755	1881	scarlet	?	?
54th	20 December 1755	1881	white	?	?
55th	21 December 1755	1881	deep yellow	?	?

56th	23 December 1755	1881	deep green	?	?
57th	26 December 1765	1881	yellow	?	?
58th	28 December 1755	1881	white	?	?
59th	1757	1881	buff	?	?
60th (Royal American)	25 December 1755		black	?	?
61st (3rd)	21 April 1758	1881	buff	white	white, blue stripe
62nd (4th)	29 March 1742	1881	buff	white	white, 2 buff, 2 black stripes
63rd (8th)	1758	1881	dark green	white	white, green and white diagonal stripes
64th (11th)	21 April 1758	1881	black	white	white, yellow stripe
65th (12th)	21 April 1758	1881	white	white	white, yellow, blue, red stripes, blue worm
66th (19th)	21 April 1758	1881	lime green	white	white, two crimson stripes
67th (20th)	21 April 1758	1881	yellow	white	white, 1 lime green stripe
68th (23rd)	22 April 1758	1881	dark green	white	white, 2 yellow, 1 green stripe
69th (24th)	23 April 1758	1881	willow green	white	white, 2 yellow, 2 black stripes
70th (31st Glasgow Lowland)	28 April 1758	1782	dark grey	white	white, blue
71st (32nd)	28 April 1758	1763	white	white	white, 1 black, 2 red stripes
72nd (33rd)	28 April 1758	1763	red	white	white, 1 black, 2 red stripes
73rd (34th)	28 April 1758	1763	full green	white	white, blue and deep yellow stripes

74th (36th)	28 April 1758	1763	dark green	white	white, 1 yellow, 2 red stripes
75th (37th)	28 April 1758	1763	buff	white	white, 2 green, 2 yellow stripes
76th	22 November 1756	1763	?	?	?
77th (Montgomerie's Highlanders)	4 January 1757	1763	red, then green	government sett	?
78th (Fraser's Highlanders)	1745	1763	white	?	?
79th	2 November 1757	1763	blue	yellow	?
80th (Light Armed Foot; an American unit)	9 May 1758	1763	dark brown	black	?
81st (Invalids)	1757	1763	?	?	?
82nd (Invalids)	1757	1763	?	?	?
83rd	1757	1763	?	?	?
84th	25 December 1758	1763	?	?	?
85th (Royal Volunteers)	21 July 1759	1763	?	?	?
86th	24 August 1758	1763	deep orange	white	white, 1 black stripe
87th (Keith's Highlanders)	20 August 1759	1763	?	?	dark green, government sett
88th (Campbell's Highlanders)	1 January 1760	1763	?	?	green, government sett
89th (Morris's Highlanders)	13 October 1759	1763	?	?	buff, government sett
90th (Irish LI)	1759	1763	?	?	?
91st (Irish)	12 December 1759	1763	?	?	?
92nd (Donegal LI)	January 1760	1763	black	?	?
93rd	17 January 1760	1763	grey	?	?

94th (Royal Welch Volunteers)	12 January 1760	1763	blue	?	?
95th	May 1760	1763	?	?	?
96th	2 January 1760	1763	?	?	?
97th	20 August 1760	1763	?	?	?
98th	27 January 1761	1763	?	?	?
99th	8 January 1761	1763	?	?	?
100th (Campbell's Highlanders)	28 October 1760	1763	?	?	?
101st (Johnstone's Highlanders)	28 October 1760	1763	buff	?	?
102nd (Queen's Royal Volunteers)	28 October 1760				

Infantry Regiments Raised After 1751 (No Uniform Details Known)

Regiment	Raised	Regiment	Raised
103rd (Volunteer Hunters)	28 October 1760	115th (Royal Scottish Lowlanders)	26 October 1761
104th (King's Volunteers)	1 August 1761	116th (Invalids)	1 February 1762
105th (Queen's Own Royal Regiment of Highlanders)	15 October 1760	117th	1762 (disbanded same year)
106th (Black Musqueteers)	October 1761	117th (Invalids)	4 March 1762
107th (Queen's Own Royal Regiment of British Volunteers)	16 October 1761	118th	1761 (disbanded 1762)
108th	17 October 1761	118th (Invalids)	23 June 1762
109th	13 October 1761	119th	1761
110th (Queen's Royal Musqueteers)	14 October 1761	120th	3 August 1762
111th	16 October 1761	121st	13 February 1762
112th (King's Royal Musqueteers)	17 October 1761	122nd	13 February 1762
113th (Royal Highlanders)	17 October 1761	123rd	August 1762
114th (Royal Highland Volunteers)	18 October 1761	124th	3 August 1762

Service of Junior Regiments Disbanded in 1763

Regiment	Service	Regiment	Service
71st	UK	87th	with Prinz Ferdinand in Germany, Vellinghausen (16 July 1761), Grabenstein
72nd	Quiberon Bay 1758; Cuba 1762	88th	with Prinz Ferdinand in Germany, Vellinghausen (16 July 1761), Grabenstein
73rd	UK	89th	India
74th	Jamaica; 6 companies in Senegal 1759	90th	taking of the Moro, Havana 1762
75th	Jersey	91st	Martinique 1762
76th	Goree, Africa; S. Belleisle 1761; Martinique 1762	92nd	UK
77th	American War 1756–1763, Fort Duquesne, Cuba, Martinique 1762	93rd	UK
78th	Storm of Louisburg, Battle of Quebec	94th	America
79th	East Indies	95th	America
80th	America	96th	India
81st	garrison in Germany	97th	Germany, Vellinghausen 1760, siege of Belleisle
82nd	garrison in Germany	98th	siege of Belleisle, Cuba 1760
83rd	UK	99th	UK
84th	India	100th	Martinique 1762
85th	Portugal 1762	101st – 124th	UK
86th	Senegal		

Source: *United Services Magazine* 1863, Issue 3.

Cavalry

The Royal Clothing Warrant, 1751

Regulations for the Uniform Clothing of the Cavalry – Their Standards, Guidons, Banners, Housings, and Holsters, Caps, Drums, Bells of Arms and Camp Colours.

Standards and Guidons

The Standards and Guidons of the Dragoon Guards, and the Standards of the Regiments of Horse, to be of Damask, embroidered and fringed with Gold, or Silver; the Guidons of the Regiments of Dragoons to be of Silk, the tassels and cords of the whole to be of crimson silk and gold mixed; the size of the Guidons and Standards, and the Length of the Laces to be the same as those of the Horse and Horse Grenadier Guards.

The King's, or First Standards, or Guidon of each Regiment to be crimson with the Rose and Thistle conjoined, and crown over them; in the center His Majesty's Motto, 'Dieu et mon Droit' underneath; the White Horse in a compartment, in the first and fourth corner; and the rank of the Regiment, in gold or silver characters, on a ground of the same colour as the facing of the Regiment in a compartment in the second and third corners.

The Second and Third Standard, or Guidon of each Corps, to be of the Colour of the facing of the Regiment, with the Badge of the Regiment in the centre, or the Rank of the Regiment in Gold or Silver Roman Characters on a crimson ground, within a Wreath of Roses and Thistles on the same stalk, the Motto of the Regiment underneath; the White Horse on a Red ground to be in the first and fourth Compartments, and the Rose and Thistle conjoined upon a red Ground in the Second and Third compartments.

The Distinction of the Third Standard, or Guidon to be a figure 3 on a circular ground of Red, underneath the Motto.

Those Corps which have any particular Badge, are to carry it in the centre of their Second and Third Standard or Guidon, with the rank of the Regiment on a red ground, within a small wreath of Roses and Thistles, in the second and third corners.

Banners

The Banners of the Kettle Drums and Trumpets to be the colour of the facing of the regiment, with the badge of the Regiment, or its rank, in the centre of the banner of the Kettle Drums, as on the second Standard; the King's Cypher and Crown to be on the banners of the trumpets, with the rank of the regiment in figures underneath.

Drums

The Drums of the Dragoon Guards, and Dragoons to be of brass; the front, or forepart, to be painted with the colour of the facing of the regiment, upon which is to be the badge or rank of the regiment as in the second guidon.

Bells of Arms

The Bells of Arms to be painted in the same manner as the Drums.

Camp Colours

The camp Colours to be of the colour of the facing of the regiment, with the rank of the regiment in the centre – those of the Horse to be square, and those of the Dragoon Guards, or Dragoons, to be swallow-tailed.

Clothing of the Regiments; Distinction of the Serjeants and Corporals; Clothing of the Kettle Drummers, Trumpeters, Drummers, and Hautboys, Dummers' Caps

The Coats of the Dragoon Guards to be lapelled to the Waist with the colour of the regiment, and lined with the same colour; Slit sleeves, turned up with the colour of the lapell.

The Coats of the Horse to be lapelled to the bottom with the colour of the regiment and lined with the same colour (except the fourth regiment of Horse, whose facings are black, and the lining buff colour), small square Cuffs of the Colour of the lapell.

The Coats of the Dragoons to be without lapells, double breasted, slit sleeves, turned up with the colour of the facings of the regiment, the lining of the same colour.

The whole to have long Pockets, the buttonholes to be of a very narrow yellow or white lace, as hereafter specified, and set on two and two, or three and three, for distinction sake. The shoulder knots of the Dragoon Regiments to be yellow or white worsted, and worn on the right shoulder. The waistcoats and breeches to be of the colour of the facings, except those of the Fourth Regiment of Horse which are Buff colour.

The Serjeants of the Dragoon Guards and Dragoons to be distinguished by a narrow gold or silver lace on the lapells, turn up of the sleeves and pockets, and to have gold or silver shoulder knots. The Corporals of Horse by a narrow gold or silver lace on the lapells, cuffs, pockets and shoulder straps; the Corporals of Dragoon Guards and Dragoons by a narrow silver or gold lace on the turn up of the sleeves, and shoulder strap, and to have yellow, or white silk shoulder knots.

The Kettle Drummers', Trumpeters', Drummers' and Hautboys' Coats to be of the colour of the facing of the regiment, lined and turned up with red (except for Royal Regiment which are allowed to wear the Royal Livery, viz., red, lined, and turned up with blue – blue waistcoats and breeches) and laced with the same coloured lace, as that on the Housings and Holster Caps, red Waistcoats and Breeches. The Drummers and Hautboys of the Dragoon Guards, and the Kettle Drummers and Trumpeters of the Horse to have long hanging sleeves fastened at the waist.

The Caps of the Drummers to be such as those of the Infantry, with the Tassel hanging behind, the front to be of the colour of their facing with the particular badge of the regiment embroidered on it, or a trophy of guidons and drums, the little flap to be red, with the White Horse and Motto over it, 'Nec aspera terrent;' the back part of the Cap to be red likewise; the turn up to be the colour of the front, and in the middle part of it behind, a Drum, and the rank of the regiment.

Hats and Caps of the Cavalry

The Hats to be laced with gold or silver lace, and to have black cockades. The Royal North British Dragoons, only, to wear caps instead of Hats, which Caps are to be of the same form as those of the House Grenadier Guards; the front Blue with the same badge as on the Second Guidon of the Regiment; the flap red, with the White Horse and Motto over it, 'Nec apera terrent;' the back part to be red, and the turn up blue, with a Thistle embroidered, between the letters 'II. D.' being the rank of the Regiment. The Watering or Forage Caps of the cavalry to be red, turned up with the colour of the facing, and the rank of the regiment on the little flap.

Cloaks

The Cloaks to be red, lined as the Coats, and the Buttons set on at top, in the same manner, upon frogs, or loops of the same colours as the lace on the Housings, the capes to be the colour of the facings.

Housings and Holster Caps

The Housings and Holster Caps to be of the Colour of the facing of the Regiment (except the First Regiment, or the King's Dragoon Guards, and the Royal Dragoons, whose Housings are red, and the Fourth Regiment of Horse, whose Housings are buff colour), laced with one broad white or yellow worsted or mohair lace with a stripe in the middle of one third of the whole breath, as hereafter specified; the Rank of the Regiment to be embroidered on the Housings upon a red ground, within a wreath of Roses and Thistles, or the particular badge of the Regiment as on the Second Guidon or Standard; the King's Cypher, with the Crown over it, to be embroidered on the Holster Caps, and under the cypher the number or rank of the Regiment.

Uniforms of the Officers, etc

The Clothing or Uniform of the Officers, to be made up in the same manner as those of the Men, laced, lapelled, and turned up with the colour of the facing, and a narrow hold, or silver lace, or embroidery, to the binding and buttonholes, the buttons being set on in the same manner as on the Men's Coats; the Waistcoats and Breeches being likewise of the same colour as those of the Men.

The Housings and Holster Caps of the Officers to be of the colour of the facing of the Regiment, laced with one gold or silver lace, and a Stripe of velvet in the middle of the colour of that on the Men's.

The Standard belts to be the colour of the facing of the Regiment and laced as the housings.

Their sashes to be crimson silk, and worn over the left Shoulder.

Their Sword Knots to be crimson and gold in stripes, as those of the Infantry.

Quarter Masters

The Quarter Masters to wear crimson sashes round their waists.

Serjeants

The Serjeants to wear Pouches as the Men do, and a worsted sash about their waist, of the colour of the facing of the regiment, and of the stripes on the lace of the housings.

Horse Guards

1st or His Majesty's Horse Guards

Raised in 1658. 8 June 1788: absorbed 1st Troop, Horse Grenadier Guards; 25 June 1778: split into 1st and 2nd Regiments of Life Guards. Blue coat and breeches, red facings and waistcoat, yellow hat trim, red saddle furniture with white and yellow embroidery. 1st Troop with red aiguillette on the right shoulder, red and gold carbine bandolier. 2nd Troop with buff saddle furniture and aiguillette, white and gold carbine bandolier. 3rd Troop with yellow saddle furniture and aiguillette, yellow and gold carbine bandolier. 4th Troop (Scots) with blue saddle furniture and aiguillette, blue and gold carbine bandolier. Buff belts and gauntlets, basket-hilted, straight-bladed swords, heavy, cuffed boots. Devices on the saddle furniture for all four troops was the cipher 'GR' on red, within the blue Garter, gold embroidery under the crown.

1st Horse Grenadier Guards, 1st Troop

Raised in 1687 as 1st Troop of Grenadiers. Absorbed into 1st Troop Horse Guards on 8 June 1788 (see above). Red coats, no lapels, gold loops to the front of the chest, blue turnbacks. Blue flask cord attached to the carbine bandolier. Buff waistcoats, belts, gauntlets and breeches. Gilt basket hilts to swords. Red cap backing, blue tuft.

1st Horse Grenadier Guards, 2nd Troop

Raised in 1702 as Scots Troop of Grenadiers; 1709: 2nd Troop Horse Grenadier Guards; 8 June 1788: absorbed by 2nd Troop Horse Guards. Both troops wore cloth grenadier caps of a similar design to those of infantry regiments: front and headband in the facing colour, with the crowned, blue Garter enclosing 'GR', over a little red flap bearing the white horse and 'NEC ASPERA TERRENT' around the edge. As for the 1st but white laces, aiguilette and buttons. The cap was as for the 1st Troop, but with red tuft and probably a thistle in the little flap. Red flask cord. Both troops were absorbed into the Horse Guards on 8 June 1788.

Life Guards, 1st Troop

Raised in 1658 as The 1st or His Majesty's Own Troop of Horse Guards (see above). 8 June 1788: absorbed 1st Troop Horse Grenadier Guards; 25 June 1788: reorganised to form 1st Regiment of Life Guards. Blue coats, red facings, gold buttons and lace.

Life Guards, 2nd Troop

Raised in 1659 as Monck's Life Guards; 1660: 3rd or Duke of Albermarle's Troop of Horse Guards; 1661: 3rd or The Lord General's Troop of Horse Guards; 1670: 2nd or The Queen's Troop of Horse Guards. 8 June 1688: absorbed 2nd Troop of Horse Grenadier Guards; 25 June 1788: reorganised to form 2nd Regiment of Life Guards. Blue coats, red facings, gold buttons and lace.

Cavalry of the Line

The titles shown here are those used during the period 1756–1763. All coats were red, all belts buff, except for the Royal North British Dragoons, who wore white.

Regiments of Horse

1st Regiment of Horse

Raised on 28 July 1685 as the Earl of Arran's Regiment of Cuirassiers; later 6th Horse, later The Duke of Hamilton's Regiment of Cuirassiers. 1691: 5th Horse (upon disbandment of the old 5th); 25 December 1746: 1st (or Blue) Irish Horse; 1 April 1788: 4th Royal Irish Dragoon Guards. Pale blue facings, waistcoats and breeches, full lapels, white buttons and button-holes set in pairs, hat lace. Pale blue saddle furniture with white and red stripe and 'I H' badge. Drummers and trumpeters: pale blue coats eaced red, white lace with a red stripe. Pale blue regimental standards with gold and silver embroidery and fringes and 'I H' badge and the crest of England.

Trooper, Royal Horse Guards, 1751. (David Morier (406866) from the Royal Collection)

Cap of a trooper, 2nd or Scottish Troop of Horse Grenadiers, 1751. Dark blue front and Garter, the latter filled red with the golden cipher 'GR', gold crown, crimson cushions, red roses, purple thistles, green leaves. (C.C.P. Lawson, Volume II)

2nd Regiment of Horse

Raised on 29 July 1685 as the Duke of Shrewsbury's Regiment of Horse. 1690: 6th Horse; 25 December 1746: 2nd (or Green) Regiment of Irish Horse; 1751: 2nd Horse; 1 April 1788: 5th Regiment of Dragoon Guards. Dark green facings, waistcoats and breeches, full lapels, yellow buttons and buttonholes set in pairs, yellow/gold hat lace. Dark green saddle furniture With 'II H' badge. Drummers and trumpeters: dark green coats faced red, red waistcoats and breeches. Dark green regimental standards with gold embroidery and fringes and 'II H' badge and the motto: 'VESTIGIA NULLA RETRORSUM' ('we do not retreat').

3rd Regiment of Horse (Caribineers)

Raised on 31 July 1685 as The Queen Dowager's Regiment of Horse, or Lord Lumley's Horse. 1690: 8th Horse; 1692: The King's Regiment of Carabineers; 1794: 7th Horse; 1740: His Majesty's 1st Regiment of Carabineers; 25 December 1746: 3rd Irish Horse; 1 July 1751: 3rd Regiment of Horse. Pale yellow facings, waistcoats and breeches, full lapels, white buttons and buttonholes set in pairs, white/silver hat lace. Pale yellow saddle furniture with a white and red stripe and 'III H' badge. Pale yellow saddle furniture with white lace and a red stripe and 'III H' badge. Drummers and trumpeters: pale yellow coats faced red, red waistcoat and breeches, white lace with a red stripe. Pale yellow regimental standards with gold embroidery and fringes and 'III H' badge.

4th Regiment of Horse

Raised on 31 December 1688 as The Earl of Devonshire's Horse or 10th Horse. 1691: 9th Horse; 1691–1693: The Duke of Leinster's Regiment of Horse; 1694: 8th Horse; 25 December 1746: 4th (or Black) Irish Horse; 1 April 1788: 7th (The Princess Royal's) Dragoon Guards. Black facings, buff waistcoats and breeches, full lapels, yellow buttons and buttonholes set in pairs, yellow/gold hat lace. Buff saddle furniture with a white and black lace, 'IV H' badge. Drummers and trumpeters: buff coats, faced red, red waistcoats and breeches. Black regimental standards with gold embroidery and silver and gold fringes and 'IV H' badge.

Regiments of Dragoon Guards

1st Dragoon Guards

Raised on 6 June 1685 as the Queen's Regiment of Horse (2nd Horse). 1714: King's Own Regiment of Horse; 25 December 1746: The King's Dragoon Guards; 1 July 1751: 1st The (King's Dragoon) Guards. Dark blue facings, waistcoat and breeches, half lapels, yellow buttons and buttonholes, set in pairs, yellow/gold hat lace. Red saddle furniture, with the royal cipher within the crowned Garter, royal lace. Drummers and trumpeters: red coats faced blue, blue waistcoat and breeches, royal lace (yellow and blue). Blue regimental guidons with gold embroidery and fringes and King's cipher within the crowned Garter badge.

2nd Dragoon Guards

Raised on 20 June 1685 as the Earl of Peterborough's Regiment of Horse; 1715: The Princess of Wales's Own Regiment of Horse; 1727: the Queen's Own Regiment of Horse (when Princess

British 3rd Regiment of Horse, 1751. This regiment was raised in 1685 and originally bore the number 8, then 9. For courage at the Battle of the Boyne and in other actions in Ireland, it was awarded the title 'Carabiniers', or the 'King's Carabiniers'. In 1745 it became the 3rd Irish Horse and in 1788 it became the 6th Dragoon Guards (Carabiniers), which title it carried until 1920. (Knötel, XII 3)

Caroline became Queen); 25 December 1746: 2nd (The Queen's) Regiment of Dragoon Guards; 1767: 2nd Dragoon Guards (The Queen's Bays). Buff facings, waistcoats and breeches, half lapels, yellow buttons and buttonholes set in threes, yellow/gold hat lace. Buff saddle furniture with royal lace, the Queen's cipher within the Garter. Drummers and trumpeters: red coats with blue facings, blue waistcoats and breeches, royal lace, yellow and blue. Buff regimental guidons with gold embroidery and fringes and the Queen's cipher within the crowned Garter.

3rd Karabiniers (Prince of Wales') Dragoon Guards

Raised on 15 July 1685 as The Earl of Plymouth's Regiment of Horse. 25 December 1746: George Wade's Regiment of Dragoon Guards or 3rd Regiment of Dragoon Guards; 1 July 1751: 3rd Regiment of Dragoon Guards; 1765: 3rd (The Prince of Wales's) Dragoon Guards. White facings, waistcoats and breeches, half lapels, yellow buttons and buttonholes set in pairs, yellow/gold hat lace. White saddle furniture with a yellow and red stripe, with 'III. D. G.' badge. Drummers and trumpeters: white coats faced red, red waistcoats and breeches, yellow lace with a red stripe. White regimental guidons, with gold and silver embroidery and fringes and the 'III. D. G.' badge.

King's standard of the 4th Regiment of Horse. Crimson cloth, gold and silver fringes; red rose, purple thistle, green leaves. White scroll, black script, gold and silver crown with pearls and jewels, gold regimental designation (IV. H) on a black ground within a frame of green leaves with red and white roses, purple thistles and green shamrock leaves; white horse on a red ground, standing on a green field, within a gold frame. Iron spear point finial, gold and crimson cords and tassels)

Dragoons

1st or Royal Dragoons

Raised on 21 October 1661; later known as 'The Tangier Horse'. 1683: The King's Own Regiment of Dragoons; 1690: The Royal Regiment of Dragoons; 1 July 1751: 1st (Royal) Regiment of Dragoons. Dark blue facings, waistcoats and breeches, no lapels, yellow buttons and buttonholes set in pairs, yellow/gold hat lace. Red saddle furniture with royal lace and the crest of England within the crowned Garter. Drummers and trumpeters: red coats with blue facings, blue waistcoats and breeches, royal lace. Dark blue regimental guidons with gold embroidery and fringes and the crest of England within the crowned Garter badge.

2nd or Royal North British Dragoons (Scots Dragoons)

Raised on 25 November 1681 as the Royal Regiment of Scots Dragoons, or His Majesty's Regiment of Dragoons. 1 November 1688: 2nd Dragoons; 1702: Grey Dragoons or Scots Regiment of White Horse; 1737: Royal Regiment of North British Dragoons; 1 July 1751: 2nd (Royal North British) Regiment of Dragoons. Dark blue facings, waistcoats and breeches, no lapels, white buttons and buttonholes set in pairs, no hat lace. Dark blue saddle furniture with royal lace and a badge of the thistle within the circle of St Andrew. Drummers and trumpeters: red coats faced blue, blue waistcoats and breeches, royal lace. Dark blue regimental guidons with gold and silver embroidery and fringes and a badge of the thistle within the circle of St Andrew and the motto: 'NEMO ME IMPUNE LACESSIT' ('none touch me with impunity').

3rd (King's Own) Regiment of Dragoons

Raised on 2 August 1685 as The Queen Consort's Own Regiment of Dragoons. 1751: The 3rd (King's Own) Dragoons. Light blue facings, waistcoats and breeches, light blue full lapels, yellow buttons and buttonholes set in threes, yellow/gold hat lace. Light blue saddle furniture with royal lace and the white hose within the crowned Garter badge. Drummers and trumpeters: red coats with light blue facings, light blue waistcoats and breeches and royal lace. Light blue regimental guidons with gold embroidery and fringes and the white horse within the crowned Garter badge.

4th Regiment of Dragoons

Raised on 17 July 1685 as The Princess Anne of Denmark's Regiment of Dragoons. 1690: 4th Dragoons; 1 July 1751: 4th Regiment of Dragoons. Green facings, waistcoats and breeches, no lapels, white buttons and buttonholes set in pairs, white/silver hat lace. Green saddle furniture with white and blue stripe and 'IV. D.' badge. Drummers and trumpeters: green coats faced red, red waistcoats and breeches, white lace with a blue stripe. Green regimental guidonss with silver embroidery and fringes and 'IV. D.' badge.

5th (or Royal Irish) Dragoons

Raised on 20 June 1689 as James Wynne's Regiment of Dragoons, or 6th Dragoons. 1704: Royal Dragoons of Ireland; 7 July 1751: 5th Regiment of Dragoons; 1756: 5th (or Royal Irish)

Cap of a trooper, 2nd Royal North British Dragoons, 1751. Dark blue front, silver star, dark blue Garter with red cross on a white ground, red and white small label and motto, light blue tuft, red roses, purple thistles, green leaves. (Morier, 405603)

Regiment of Dragoons; 8 April 1799: disbanded. Blue facings, waistcoats and breeches, full lapels, white buttons and buttonholes set in threes, white/silver hat lace. Blue saddle furniture, royal lace and harp and crown badge. Drummers and trumpeters: red coats faced blue, blue waistcoats and breeches, royal lace. Blue regimental guidons with gold and silver embroidery and fringes and harp and crown badge.

6th or the Inniskilling Dragoons

Raised on 20 June 1689 as Sir Albert Cunningham's Regiment of Dragoons, from amalgamation of several regiments raised in Inniskilling in 1688. 1690: 7th Dragoons; 1691: 6th Dragoons; 1715: 6th (or Black) Dragoons; 1 July 1751: 6th (Inniskilling) Regiment of Dragoons. Full yellow facings, waistcoats and breeches, full lapels, white buttons and buttonholes set in pairs, white/silver hat lace. Full yellow saddle furniture, white lace with a blue stripe and the Inniskilling Castle within a wreath badge. Drummers and trumpeters: full yellow coats faced red, red waistcoats and breeches, white lace with a blue stripe. Full yellow regimental guidons with silver embroidery and silver and blue fringes and Inniskilling Castle badge.

7th or Queen's Regiment of Dragoons

Raised in May 1689 as The Queen's Own Regiment of Dragoons. 13 December 1690: The Queen's Own Regiment of Dragoons; 1691: 7th Dragoons; 15 February 1715: The Princess of Wales's Own Regiment of Dragoons; 1727: The Queen's Own Regiment of Dragoons; 1 July 1751: 7th (The Queen's Own) Regiment of Dragoons. White facings, waistcoats and breeches, no lapels, white buttons and buttonholes set in threes, white/silver hat lace. White saddle furniture, royal lace and the badge of the Queen's cipher within the crowned Garter. Drummers and trumpeters: red coats faced blue, blue waistcoats and breeches, royal lace (yellow and blue). White regimental standards with gold embroidery and fringes and the Queen's cipher within the crowned Garter badge.

8th Regiment of Dragoons

Raised on 1 February 1693 as Henry Conyngham's Regiment of Dragoons. 16 April 1714: disbanded; 22 July 1715: re-raised without loss of precedence as John Pepper's Regiment of Dragoons; February 1716: disbanded; 17 March 1719: re-raised without loss of precedence as Phineas Bowles's Regiment of Dragoons; 1 July 1751: 8th Regiment of Dragoons; 25 December 1775: 8th Regiment of Light Dragoons. Yellow facings, waistcoats and breeches, no lapels, white buttons and buttonholes set in threes, white/silver hat lace. Yellow saddle furniture, yellow and white stripe and 'VIII. D.' badge. Drummers and trumpeters: yellow coats faced red, white lace with a yellow stripe. Yellow regimental guidons with silver embroidery and silver and yellow fringes and 'VIII. D.' badge.

9th Regiment of Dragoons

Raised on 22 July 1715 as Owen Wynne's Regiment of Dragoons. 1719: 9th Regiment of Dragoons; 1783: 9th Regiment of Light Dragoons. Buff facings, waistcoats and breeches, no lapels, white buttons and buttonholes set in pairs, white/silver hat lace. Buff saddle furniture, white lace with a blue stripe and 'IX. D.' badge. Drummers and trumpeters: buff coats faced red, red waistcoats and breeches. Buff regimental guidons with silver embroidery and silver and blue fringes and 'IX. D.' badge.

10th Regiment of Dragoons

Raised on 22 July 1715 as Humphry Gore's Regiment of Dragoons. 7 January 1751: 10th Regiment of Dragoons; 29 September 1783: 10th (Prince of Wales's Own) Regiment of (Light) Dragoons. Deep yellow facings, waistcoats and breeches, no lapels, white buttons and buttonholes set in 3, 4 and 5, white/silver hat lace. Deep yellow saddle furniture, white lace with a green stripe and 'X. D.' badge. Drummers and trumpeters: deep yellow coats faced red, red waistcoats and breeches, white lace with a green stripe. Deep yellow regimental guidons with silver embroidery and silver and green fringes and 'X. D'. badge.

11th Regiment of Dragoons

Raised on 22 July 1715 as Philip Honeywood's Regiment of Dragoons. 1 July 1751: 11th Regiment of Dragoons; 1783: 11th Regiment of (Light) Dragoons. Buff facings, waistcoats and breeches, no lapels, white buttons and buttonholes set in 3 and 3, white/silver hat lace. Buff saddle furniture, white lace with a green stripe and 'XI. D.' badge. Drummers and trumpeters: buff coats faced red, red waistcoats and breeches, white lace with a green stripe. Buff regimental guidons with silver embroidery and silver and green fringes and 'XI. D.' badge.

12th Regiment of Dragoons

Raised on 22 July 1715 as Phineas Bowles's Regiment of Dragoons. 1 July 1751: 12th Regiment of Dragoons; 1768: 12th (The Prince of Wales's) Regiment of (Light) Dragoons. White facings, waistcoats and breeches, no lapels, white buttons and buttonholes set in pairs, white/silver hat lace. White saddle furniture, yellow lace with a green stripe, 'XII. D.' badge. Drummers and trumpeters: white coats faced red, red waistcoats and breeches, yellow lace with a green stripe. White regimental guidons with silver embroidery and silver and green fringes and 'XII. D.' badge.

13th Regiment of Dragoons

Raised on 22 July 1715 as Richard Munden's Regiment of Dragoons. 1 July 1751: 13th Regiment of Dragoons; 1783: 13th Regiment of (Light) Dragoons. Light green facings, waistcoats and breeches, no lapels, yellow buttons and buttonholes set in 3 and 3, yellow/gold hat lace. Light green saddle furniture, white lace with a yellow stripe and 'XIII. D.' badge. Drummers and trumpeters: light green coats faced red, red waistcoats and breeches. Light green regimental guidons with silver embroidery and silver and green fringes and 'XIII. D.' badge.

14th Regiment of Dragoons

Raised on 22 July 1715 as James Dormer's Regiment of Dragoons. 1 July 1751: 14th Regiment of Dragoons; 1776: 14th Regiment of (Light) Dragoons. Lemon yellow facings, waistcoats and breeches, no lapels, white buttons and buttonholes set in 3 and 3, white/silver hat lace. Lemon yellow saddle furniture, white, red and green striped lace and 'XIV. D.' badge. Drummers and trumpeters: lemon yellow coats faced red, red waistcoats and breeches. Lemon yellow regimental guidoss with silver embroidery and silver and red fringes and 'XIV. D.' badge.

British light troopers, 11th Dragoons, 1756. They wore the uniforms of their regiment, but with light boots and helmets, with a horsehair plume above the front plate. This plume had a red base, with the top part in the regimental facing colour. On the right front of the saddle a pistol was carried; on the front left side was a spade or an axe. On the holster covers, and in the rear corners of the shabraque, was a circular wreath, enclosing a red field with the regimental designation (here XI D). (Knötel, XVII 51)

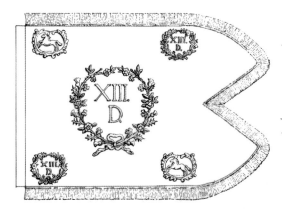

Regimental guidon of the 13th Dragoons. Light green cloth, green and silver fringes. Silver regimental designation (XIII. D) on a red ground within a frame of green leaves with red and white roses, purple thistles and green shamrock leaves. White horse on a red ground, standing on a green field, within a silver frame. Iron spear point finial, gold and crimson cords and tassels.

New Light Cavalry Regiments, 1759

In 1756 a troop of light cavalry was added to each existing cavalry regiment; these proved to be so useful that in 1759, entire regiments of such troops were formed. Their uniforms were of a new, lighter, shorter cut. Instead of hats, metal helmets with comb and crest were worn. Trumpeters wore reversed colours, saddle furniture and regimental guidons were in the facing colour. Their helmet front plates had the regimental designation (e.g. 'XX.' over 'LD') over a horizontal trumpet. Helmet turbans were in the facing colour, except for the 22nd Light Dragoons, who had red facings, but a yellow turban. Turban tassesl were in the button and lace colour. Waistcoats and breeches were white.

Farriers wore dark blue coats, black bearskin caps and carried axes, saws and spades. Their saddle furniture was in black bearskin, with white badges of horse-shoes on the holsters and crossed hammer and pincers in the rear corners of the saddle cloth. Their helmet front plates bore the regimental designation (e.g. 'XX' over 'LD') within an upturned horse-shoe and over crossed hammer and pincers.

In 1764 the drums were withdrawn from dragoon guard, dragoon and light dragoon regiments and each troop had a trumpeter, who was supposed to wear a bicorn instead of a helmet.

15th Regiment of (Light) Dragoons (Elliot's)

Raised on 17 March 1759. Dark green facings (changed to dark blue in 1766), white turnbacks, white waistcoats and breeches, dark green lapels, white buttons and buttonholes set in pairs, white woollen ringed epaulettes. Instead of hats they wore blackened copper helmets, with an upturned front flap bearing the crowned royal cipher (GR) between 'L' and 'D' in white on a black ground. The helmet had a turban in the facing colour, with tassels in the button colour and a fluted, white metal combe with a red horsehair crest. Belts were of light brown leather. Saddle furniture was dark green, with a white-red-white edging, the crowned cipher on the holsters and 'XV.' over 'L. D.' badge. Drummers and trumpeters: dark green coats faced white, with red buttonholes, epaulettes and helmet turban. Dark green regimental guidons with silver embroidery and fringes and 'XV. L. D.' badge. In reward for their actions at the Battle of Emsdorff on 14 July 1760, the regiment was granted new helmets bearing 'EMSDORF' and a list of their captures (five French battalions, their colous and 9 cannon) around the edge of the front flap. They also bore 'EMSDORF' on their guidons.

16th Regiment of (Light) Dragoons (or Burgoyne's Light Horse)

Raised on 4 August 1759. 1766: Queen's Light Dragoons. Red facings (changed to dark blue in 1766), white buttons and buttonholes. The facings had changed to dark blue by 1768, with royal lace. Holster covers bore the crowned cipher 'GR', with red lace having a black central stripe; in the saddle cloth rear corners a wreath of roses and thistles, having a red ground bearing: 'XVI. L. D', all under a scroll bearing: 'AUT CURSU AUT COMINUS ARMIS' ('either in the charge or hand to hand'). Red regimental guidons with silver painted devices, badges, motto and fringes.

Trooper, British 14th Dragoons, 1751. (David Morier (401506) from the Royal Collection)

Trooper, Duke of Cumberland's 15th Dragoons. (David Morier (404142) from the Royal Collection)

Trooper of the British 17th Light Dragoons, 1761. The regiment was raised on 7 November 1759 in Hertfordshire. In 1761 part of the regiment fought in Germany. When the War of American Independence broke out, the regiment was the first cavalry unit to be sent to that theatre. ((Knötel, XIV 19)

17th Regiment (or Corps) of Light Dragoons

Raised on 7 November 1759 as the 18th or Hale's Light Horse. 27 April 1763: 17th Regiment of Dragoons. Brass helmet, white horsehair crest, red cloth front flap with white bones, skull and motto, brown fur turban. White facings, buttons and buttonholes, white lace with a black edge. Red saddle furniture decorated with crossed bones over a skull, over a label bearing 'OR GLORY' and edged in broad white lace with two black stripes. Regimental guidons white with gold and silver painted designs, silver and red fringes, with skull and bones badge and the motto: 'OR GLORY'. Disbanded in 1763.

18th Regiment of (Light) Dragoons

Raised on 7 December 1759 as 19th Light Dragoons; renumbered 18th in 1763. White facings, buttons and buttonholes, red and white lace. Regimental standards were white with gold and silver painted designs, silver fringes and 'XVIII. L. D.' as on the saddle furniture. Disbanded in 1763.

19th Regiment of (Light) Dragoons

Raised on 7 December 1759; renumbered 19th in 1763. White facings, buttons and buttonholes. Presumably white saddle furniture and regimental standards with silver painted devices and fringes and 'XIX. L. D.' badge. Disbanded in 1763.

20th Regiment of (Light) Dragoons (or Inniskilling Light Dragoons)

Raised on 12 January 1760. Yellow facings, white buttons. Yellow saddle furniture and regimental standards with silver painted designs and fringes and 'XX. L. D.' badge. Disbanded in 1763.

21st Regiment of (Light) Dragoons (or Royal Forresters)

Raised on 5 April 1760. Black helmet with red horsehair crest, black front plate bearing the crowned royal cipher 'GR', between smaller 'R' and 'F' in white. Yellow facings, white buttons and buttonholes. Yellow saddle furniture and regimental standards with silver painted designs and fringes and 'XXI. L. D.' badge. Disbanded in 1763.

22nd Regiment of (Light) Dragoons

Raised in 1760. Red facings, French grey coat, white buttons and buttonholes. Red saddle furniture and regimental standards with silver painted designs and fringes and 'XXII. L. D.' badge. This regiment may have only existed on paper.

Trooper, British 17th Light Dragoons, 1760. (David Morier (406826) from the Royal Collection)

Trooper, 21st Light Dragoons, 1760. (David Morier (406843) from the Royal Collection)

Artillery

In 1716 the first permanent British artillery regiment had been established in Woolwich; prior to this, 'traynes' of artillery were raised when needed by Royal Warrant and disbanded again when the conflict was over. In 1722 the Artillery Regiment was grouped together with the artillery companies in Gibraltar and Minorca to become the Royal Regiment of Artillery. As the effective management of artillery involved a lot of scientific knowledge, the usual pool of recruitment for officers of infantry and cavalry (well connected young aristocrats who bought commissions) was of little use and officer candidates had to come from the more scholarly backgrounds and from the ranks of the professional gunners themselves.

While the cavalry and infantry regiments (apart from the Guards) were administered from Whitehall, the artillery was administered by the Board of Ordnance and promotion was purely by merit, not by purchase. The standard of training and organisation of the new arm was high and battlefield performance improved considerably as a result. After a few years, the establishment of each company was increased to permit the inclusion of Gentlemen Cadets, who would be trained before being commissioned. In 1740 an officer cadet school was opened at Woolwich and in 1764 this became the Royal Academy. Cadets were instructed in gunnery, ballistics, fortification, French, mathematics and algebra, to fit them for service in the combined artillery/engineer corps. Up to 1757 there were eighteen companies of artillery; in this year, they were reorganised into two battalions of twelve companies each. In 1760 this became three battalions, each of ten companies. The major personalities of the artillery of this period were General John Armstrong, Colonel Albert Borgand, John Müller and Benjamin Roberts. There was no horse artillery during this period.

Britain centred her artillery pieces on the 3-, 6-, 9- and 12-pounder cannon calibres, as did Austria, Denmark, Prussia and Russia. The most commonly-used battalion guns were the short 6-pounder (barrel length of 137cm, barrel weight of 241kg), usually drawn by two horses. In 1762, the British contingent operating in Germany had 34 such short 6-pounder guns. The light 12-pounder (barrel length of 152cm, barrel weight of 457kg) was the most commonly used field gun. It was usually drawn by five horses. Siege artillery consisted mainly of 24-pounder guns but iron 12-pounder guns were also used. The howitzers of the Royal Artillery were of 4.5 and 5.5 inch calibre. Of these pieces, the brass 9-pounder saw most service during the Seven Years War.

Uniform

Tricorn with yellow edging, dark blue coat, no collar, red lapels, cuffs and turnbacks. The lapels and cuffs were edged yellow; yellow buttons and lace. Dark blue waistcoat with yellow edging and buttonholes, dark blue breeches, black garters, white belts.

10

THE ELECTORATE OF HANOVER (BRAUNSCHWEIG-LÜNEBURG)

The Electorate of Hanover (Braunschweig-Lüneburg)
Hanover was geographically part of the Westphalian Kreis of the Holy Roman Empire, but allied to Britain by the personal union of the Elector George, who was also King George II of England. Generals wore the same uniforms as the British generals, but with yellow silk sashes and silver and gold sword straps.

Guards

Garde du Corps
Raised in 1642, initially of one squadron. Uniform: a tricorn with silver edge, red, single-breasted tunic with royal blue facings, silver lace and buttons, buff belts, waistcoat and breeches. They were armed with a straight sword in a black sheath. Saddle furniture was red, edged in silver, with the golden cipher 'GR' within the crowned Garter. The standard was square, white, heavily embroidered with the full English crest in gold and fringed. The kettle drum banners were of that same design.

Garde-Regiment
Raised in 1631; entitled *Fußgarde* (Foot Guards) with two battalions. Uniform: as for the line, red tunic, dark blue cuffs, lapels, waistcoat and turnbacks, yellow buttons. The front of the grenadier cap bore the crowned cipher within the silver star of the Order of the Garter. The bottom label was black with gold edging. Officers' gorgets were gilt with the royal crest and supporters of England.

Grenadiers à Cheval
Raised in 1742, one squadron. Uniform: red coat with black lapels and cuffs, red lining, gold buttons, gold and red aiguillette to the right shoulder. Light straw waistcoat and breeches, buff belts. The black-

Officer, grenadier and musketeer, Infanterie-Regiment von Ahlefeldt Nr 13A, 1760. The regiment was commanded by Oberstlieutenant von der Beck and was garrisoned in Ratzeburg and Hameln.

fronted grenadier cap bore the English crest in gold over the Saxon horse, also in gold; the backing was red, the black headband was edged gold. They were armed with a straight sword in a black sheath. The cartouche was black with two brass grenades in the lower corners of the lid and the crowned cipher 'GR' in the centre. Saddle furniture was red, square cut, with a yellow edging having black diamonds along it. In the rear corner and on the holster covers was the crowned cipher 'GR' in gold.

Infantry

Uniform

Based on the British style; the coat was red, collarless, with facings shown on lapels, Brandenburg cuffs (red with three buttons) and waistcoats. Turnbacks were white and the neck stock was black. There was lace to buttonholes, edging of lapels, cuffs, red cuff flaps, waistcoats, hat and grenadier cap in the button colour. Breeches and belts were buff, gaiters were white. Grenadier caps were initially metal, in the button colour; the backing was red, the headband in the facing colour with a yellow grenade at the rear. In the centre, on a red ground, was the crowned royal cipher 'GR' within the Order of the Garter, above a small flap bearing the white springing horse of Lower Saxony on a red ground, with a blue scroll bearing 'NEC ASPERA TERRENT'.

The caps of officers and NCOs were trimmed with gold or silver. Grenadiers wore brass match cases on their bandoliers. Officers of the line wore yellow silk waist sashes, from right shoulder to left hip, in the same style as in England, gorgets in the button colour, with the crowned royal cipher 'GR' when on duty. Their sword straps were in silver and yellow. Their lapels and cuffs were edged in gold braid. Musketeer officers bore spontoons, grenadier officers had short muskets; both wore tricorns. Sergeants wore waist sashes and had halberds. Officers and NCOs who were armed with short muskets, wore a white pouch with a large, central grenade and four small corner grenades on the lid, at the front of the waistbelt. Hair was powdered, curled and worn in a plaited pigtail. Initially the Battalion Sachsen-Gotha wore their old uniforms of white coats with red facings. When in the field, a small bunch of oak leaves was worn in the hat. At the start of the war, each grenadier battalion had one 3-pounder gun; later this was increased to two.

Organisation

In 1756, the Electorate of Hanover's infantry consisted of 23 line regiments, each with a single battalion. In 1757 a regiment raised in the Duchy of Sachsen-Gotha was taken into the pay of Hanover, and by 1759 it was taken onto the military establishment. In 1758, two so-called New Battalions No. 1 and No. 2 were raised (see numbers 10-B and 13-B below). Until 1759, the infantry's most junior regiment (13-A) was entitled Füsiliers.

Each battalion had seven companies of musketeers. The two new battalions, raised in 1758, were organised in five companies each. During the war, a number of *ad hoc* 'Combined Battalions' had been created, thus increasing the number of battalions, but reducing the strength of each.

Each battalion formed a small grenadier unit, comprising an officer and 64 men. During 1757 and 1758, there had been no regular organisation of grenadier battalions; they were thrown together as circumstances dictated and employed away from their parent regiments. In June 1759, three permanent grenadier battalions were created for the duration of the campaign. In 1762, the number of grenadiers nearly doubled as each battalion formed a complete company. There were hence six grenadier battalions, excluding the companies of the two new battalions, which remained with their parent units.

At the end of the war in 1763, the number of line infantry regiments was halved by combining two battalions into one. The regimental service numbers below were introduced only by 1783. The affix A or B serve to keep trace of the battalions origin within the new regiment.

Colours

Each battalion carried two colours. The Sovereign's colour was white; on one side it bore the crowned royal crest of England with supporters and the royal cipher 'GR' within the Garter. On the other side it bore the springing white horse of Lower Saxony within the Garter and the motto: 'NEC ASPERA TERRENT'. Battalion 10-B had no Sovereign's colour; instead it carried two identical battalion colours. The battalion colours were in a range of shades and bore a wide variety of allegorical scenes and figures.

Musketeer officer, Infanterie-Regiment Hardenberg and a Garde-Grenadiere, with French cavalrymen in the background. The scene is set at the Battle of Minden, 1 August 1759. The officer of Infanterie-Regiment von Hardenberg carries a spontoon and wears his sash over his right shoulder. The colour is that of the Garde and bears the same royal crest as that of England, as King George II of England was also Elector of Hanover. (Knötel, I 40)

Regiment	Raised	Facings	Buttons
1-A von Scheither	1665	dark green	yellow
1-B Alt-Zastrow; 1761 von Otten	1665	white	yellow
2-A von Spörken; 1760 von Meding	1665	buff	yellow
2-B von Fabrice; 1757 von Schele	1717	straw yellow	white
3-A von Knesebeck; 1758 von Reden	1665	black	white
3-B von Druchtleben; von der Schulenburg	1704	black	yellow
4-A von Ledebour; 1758 von Bock	1748	dark blue	white
4-B von Stolzenberg; 1759 von Marschalk; 1760 von Craushaar	1665	black	white
5-A von Grote; 1759 von Laffert; 1762 de la Motte	1648	yellow	white
5-B von Hodenberg; 1757 von Behr	1671	orange	yellow
6-A von Hardenberg	1648	orange	white
6-B von Zandreé; 1757 von Halberstadt; 1761 von Linsingen	1671	yellow	white
7-A von Wangenheim	1686	straw yellow	white
7-B von Hauss; 1758 von Linstow; 1759 von Plessen	1665	orange	yellow
8-A von Diepenbroick; 1759 1670von Rhöden; 17621751 Mecklenburg-Strelitz (Prinz Ernst von)	1692	white	white
8-B von Block	1670	white	white
9-A Sachsen-Gotha	1751	white	white
9-B Jung Zastrow	1665	dark green	white
10-A von Post; 1761 de Sancé; later Mecklenburg-Strelitz (Prinz Carl von)	1703	dark green	white
10-B 1st New Battalion von Marschalk; 1759 Monroy	1758	red	white
11-A de Cheusses; 1757 von Dreves; 1761 von Goldacker	1702	yellow	yellow
11-B von Oberg; 1756 de la Chevallerie	1648	yellow	yellow
12-A von Kielmannsegg	1741	mid green	white
12-B von Brunck; 1759 von Estorff	1745	mid green	white
13-A von Halberstadt; 1758 Fersen; 1760 von Ahlefeld. Till 1759 also called Fusiliers	1745	mid blue	white
13-B 2nd New Battalion von Wrede	1758	red	white

Grenadiers of Hanoverian infantry regiments von Oberg 11B, von Ledebour 4A and von Hardenberg 6A. (David Morier, the Royal Collection)

Grenadiers of Hanoverian infantry regiments Kielmannegg, Halberstadt and Münchow, 1751. (David Morier, the Royal Collection)

Cavalry

Each regiment had two squadrons, each with three companies. They are listed under the name of their chief in 1756.

Uniform

Tricorn edged in the button colour, a single-breasted white tunic with facings shown on cuffs, turn-backs and edging to the waistcoat turnbacks, light straw waistcoats, buff breeches and belts. The neck stock was black. They were armed with a pair of pistols, a straight, steel-hilted sword in a leather sheath and a carbine. Saddle furniture was in the facing colour, decorated with the crowned cipher 'GR' within the Garter, and a lace in the regimental pattern.

Colours

Each squadron bore a square standard, heavily embroidered and fringed in gold and silver. The 1st Squadron's standard was white, on both sides it bore the crowned English crest, with supporters; in the centre was the cipher 'GR' within the Garter and the motto 'DIEU ET MON DROIT' on a scroll below it. The colour of the others and the designs they bore varied widely. The lance finial was a gilt spear point, from which depended gold or silver cords and tassels.

Leib-Regiment Reuter (1 C-A)
Raised in 1682. Chiefs: 1756 von Breidenbach, von Pentz; 1758 von Spörken; 1761 von Jonquières. Yellow facings, white buttons. Lace to the saddle furniture was red, with a black pattern; within this were flowers and scroll work.

Zepelin Kavallerie (1 C-B)
Raised in 1745. Chiefs: 1756 von Zepelin; 1757 von Skölln; 1758 von Heise; 1761 von Estorff. Orange facings, yellow buttons; changed to black and white in 1760. Lace to the saddle furniture was a double strip of royal blue lace with a yellow zig-zag along it and edged in yellow piping, these divided by a narrower red strip. Instead of the 'GR' cipher, the crest in the Garter was the Saxon horse on a red ground.

Dachenhausen Kavallerie (2 C-A)
Raised in 1675. Chiefs: von Dachenhausen; 1758 Alt Bremer. Apple green facings, white buttons. Lace to the saddle furniture was vari-coloured leaf and flower work. Instead of the 'GR' cipher, the crest in the Garter was the Saxon horse on a red ground.

Hammerstein Kavallerie (2 C-B)
Raised in 1675. Chiefs: von Hammerstein; 1760 von Jüngermann; 1761 Alt Sprengel. Dark green facings, yellow buttons. Lace to the saddle furniture was an outer red braid, with alternate white and yellow oblongs in it; within this was leaf work in white, red and yellow.

Grothaus Kavallerie (3 C-A)
Raised in 1670. Chiefs: von Grothaus; 1761 Jung Bremer. Crimson facings, yellow buttons. Lace to the saddle furniture was red, edged yellow, with a white 'rolling' zig-zag along it. Instead of the 'GR' cipher, the crest in the Garter was the Saxon horse on a red ground.

Hodenberg Kavallerie (3 C-B)
Raised in 1689. Chiefs: 1756 von Schlütter; 1757 von Hodenberg. Red facings, white buttons. Lace to the saddle furniture was red with two white stripes along it.

Walthausen Kavallerie (4 C-A)

Raised in 1688. Chiefs: von Walthausen; 1757 von Reden; 1759 von Walthausen; 1761 Alt Behr. Dark blue facings, yellow buttons. Lace to the saddle furniture was striped yellow and white; within this was white, yellow and red leaf work. Instead of the 'GR' cipher, the crest in the Garter was the Saxon horse on a red ground.

Gilten Kavallerie (4 C-B)

Raised in 1701. Chiefs: von Gilten; 1758 von Breitenbach; 1759 von Veltheim; 1761 C.A. von Veltheim. Medium blue facings, white buttons. Lace to the saddle furniture was light blue with red and yellow arcs along both sides. The 'GR' cipher was large and without the Garter surround.

Dragoons

Uniform

Tricorn edged in the button colour, a double-breasted, collarless white tunic, with facings shown on lapels, cuffs and lining, an aiguillette in the button colour off the right shoulder, buff waistcoats, breeches and belts. The grenadier company wore a mitre cap, the front and headband in the facing colour, the backing red, the embroidery in the button colour. The crowned garter, enclosing 'GR', over a red label with the white horse. Straight-bladed swords in leather sheaths were carried. The men were also armed with muskets and pistols. The badge on the saddle furniture was the white horse on a red ground, within the crowned garter. The following regiments are listed under the name of their chief in 1756.

Drachenhausen Dragoner (5 C)

1759 Breidenbach; 1761 von Veltheim. Red facings, white buttons. Lace to the saddle furniture was white, red and black.

Breidenbach Dragoner (6 C)

1759 Reden; 1761 Walthausen. Liht blue facings, white buttons. Lace to the saddle furniture was lines of black, white and red.

Busche Dragoner (7 C)

1761 Müller. Facings dark blue, buttons yellow. Lace to the saddle furniture was red, white and yellow.

Bock Dragoner (8 C)

Crimson facings, yellow buttons. Lace to the saddle furniture was crimson, yellow, black and white.

Light Troops

These units were recruited during the war and paid off at the cessation of hostilities. They carried no colours or standards and had both cavalry and infantry troops.

Freytag's Jäger Corps

Raised in 1757; by the end of the war it had three mounted companies and three foot companies. Mounted troops wore a tricorn with white edging, dark green, single-breasted tunic, faced also in dark green, white buttons and buttonholes, dark green waistcoat, buff breeches, white belts. Dark green saddle furniture. Foot Jägers wore the same hats, coats and waistcoats, with white breeches and belts and knee boots. Grenadiers wore the Jäger uniform, but with a grenadier cap, all in dark green and white, with the English coat of arms.

Grothaus Kavallerie. The horses were supplied by the famous national stud farms. (Gmundener Prachtwerk)

Trooper, 4th Dragoon Squadron, Hanoverian Legion Britannique, 1761. Red coat and greatcoat, light blue facings and lining, white buttons and aiguilette, buff waistcoat, breeches and gauntlets, red saddle furniture with solid white edging, crown and 'GR II' cipher, brass-hilted sword in black sheath with brass fittings. (Das Gmundener Prachtwerk, Bomann Museum, Celle)

Légion Britannique

Raised in 1760, it was the most numerous of the auxiliary units. It was commanded by Major von Bülow, an Adjutant to Herzog Ferdinand von Braunschweig. The troops were mainly deserters and foreigners, with some Hanoverian troops and British officers. Originally the corps consisted of five infantry battalions, each with a squadron of dragoons. The five dragoon squadrons were amalgamated in 1762 to form a single regiment.

The uniforms were a plain tricorn with green cockade, a collarless, single-breasted tunic with facings shown only on the round cuffs, buff breeches and belts, high black gaiters. The neck stock was black. The infantry carried muskets, but no sabres. The dragoons wore the same uniform as their infantry companions, but with an aiguillette (supposedly) in the button colour from the right shoulder and high, black boots. Their saddle furniture was to be red, edged in the button colour, with the crowned 'GR II' in the square rear corner and on the holster covers. The plates of the Gmundener Prachtwerk show some variations from this scheme. They were armed with a steel-hilted, straight-bladed sword in a leather sheath, a pair of pistols and a musket.

Battalion	Commander	Coat	Buttons	Cuffs	Waistcoat
1st Battalion	Major von Stockhausen	light blue	brass	buff	buff
2nd Battalion	Major von Udam	royal blue	white	red (and turnbacks)	white
3rd Battalion	Major von Appelbom	white	white	orange (and turnbacks)	orange
4th Battalion	Captain de l'Ane	red	white	light blue (and turnbacks)	buff
5th Battalion	Major von Mauw	red	white	white	white
Combined Dragoon Regiment 1762	Major von Hattorf	The old uniforms were worn			

Luckner's Hussars

Raised in 1757 by Rittmeister Nikolaus Graf von Luckner with 54 hussars from Dutch service; by 1760 it had four squadrons, each of two companies. They wore typical hussar costume: black mirliton, dark green dolman and pelisse (the latter with black fur trim), yellow braid and buttons, red and white barrel sash, red breeches, black boots (yellow for officers), white belts. The steel-hilted sabre had a black and steel sheath. Saddle furniture was dark green with red edging. Knötel shows a completely different costume, with brown fur busby with red bag, red pelisse and saddle furniture, white dolman and breeches. The badges on the red saddle furniture and sabretasche were the white horse under a yellow crown; both had a wavy yellow edging.

Scheither's Corps

Raised in 1758, reaching a strength of four companies of mounted carabiniers. Uniform was a plan tricorn, with dark green cockade and hat cords, white, single-breasted tunic, belts and breeches, dark green shoulder straps, cuffs, waistcoat and braid to front of coat and to edgis of white turnbacks. Double wavy white braid to top and back of cuffs, white edging to dark green waistcoat. They were armed with carbines, pistols and a steel-hilted sabre in black and steel sheath. Dark green saddle furniture with wavy white edging and the white Saxon horse badge unde a white crown. The dark green sabretasche had a wavy white edging and bore the crowned 'GR' all in white.

Trooper, 5th Dragoon Squadron, Hanoverian Legion Britannique, 1761. Red coat and greatcoat, black facings, white lining and waistcoat, buff breeches, gauntlets and bandolier (the latter with a white central band), Brass-hilted sword in black sheath with brass fittings. Red saddle furniture with a solid white edging, white crown and 'GR II' cipher. Black and red harness, brass fittings. (Das Gmundener Prachtwerk, Bomann Museum, Celle)

Private, 1st Battalion, Hanoverian Legion Britannique, 1761. Light blue coat, brass buttons, white facings, lining and waistcoat, buff belts and breeches, brass-hilted sword in black sheath with brass fittings. (Das Gmundener Prachtwerk, Bomann Museum, Celle)

Stockhausen's Freikorps

Raised in 1759, it had one squadron. Uniform was a tricorn edged white, dark green, single-breasted tunic, also faced dark green, white buttons and buttonholes, dark green waistcoat, buff breeches, white belts. Dark green saddle furniture, edged white, with 'GR' cipher on a red ground within the crowned Garter. Foot Jägers wore the same hats, coats and waistcoats, white breeches and belts and knee boots. Grenadiers as for Jägers but with a grenadier cap, dark green and white with the English coat of arms.

Artillery

When they took the field in 1757, the Hanoverian guns were of old fashioned construction and relatively heavy. Most were loaded with loose powder rather than cartridges, and many of the gunners were untrained. These problems were tellingly displayed when a powder barrel exploded during an artillery duel during the Battle of Hastenbeck (26 July 1757) that caused chaos. As the war progressed, many of the original, cumbersome pieces were replaced by British or captured French guns. The gunners also improved in training and experience. In 1759 the Graf Wilhelm von Bückeburg, appointed grand master of the Allied Army's artillery, arranged for all guns to be equipped with a munitions box on the trails, carrying 20 rounds. From 1761 on, an additional 40 rounds was carried

Officer of the Hanoverian Luckner's Hussars. This shows the first uniform worn by the corps. In 1760 Luckner introduced his own uniform. The mirliton gave way to a brown fur colpack with short black plume, red bag and white cords. (Gmundener Prachtwerk)

on the guns limber, similar to the Prussian artillery. The introduction of lighter gun barrels in imitation of the celebrated Bückeburg 18-calibre 12-pounder failed to win over conservative opposition among the Hanoverian officers. Hanoverian cannon remained at a rather heavy barrel of 21 to 27 calibres length, instead of the proposed 20.

Uniform

Artillery uniform was the tricorn, edged in yellow, a light blue coat of infantry cut, with red cuffs, lapels, turnbacks and waistcoat, and brass buttons. Breeches and belts were buff, the pouch was white, with a brass grenade on the lid. Drivers of the artillery train wore plain hats, red coats with medium blue facings.

11

THE LANDGRAVATE OF HESSEN-KASSEL

In 1756, this state was ruled by Landgraf Wilhelm VIII (reigned 1751–1776). This principality was geographically part of the Upper Rhine Kreis, but allied with Britain and Prussia against Austria. The troops operated with the British, Brunswickers, Hanoverians and Prussians under the command of the Herzog von Braunschweig in the area of northwest Germany.

Infantry

The organisation, drill and tactics were modelled after those of Prussia; each regiment fielded only one battalion. It was not until 1760 that combined grenadier battalions were formed; they were composed as follows: Leib-Garde and Grenadier-Regiment; commander von Schlotheim. Haudring and Prinz Isenburg; commander von Papenheim. Fürstenberg and Prinz Carl; commander von Balcke. Leib-Regiment and Mannsbach; commander von Stirn. Erbprinz and Prinz von Anhalt; commander von Mirbach. Canitz and Hanau; commander von Rückersfeld.

Jäger Corps. Left to right: officer, NCO (note the stick), hornist, Jäger.

Uniform

Modelled after those of Prussia. Cockade white within red. Musketeers wore tricorns with plain white edging, grenadiers had metal-fronted mitre caps and headbands in the button colour, bearing the cipher 'WL' and the Hessian lion. The cap was topped with a pompon in the regimental colours; the backing was in the facing colour. Coats were dark blue, with plain round cuffs and with facings worn on the lying collar, cuffs and lapels. waistcoats, breeches and belts were white, unless otherwise mentioned. Some regiments had lace loops to the buttonholes. The long gaiters were black in winter, white in summer, the neck stock was white for officers, red for other ranks. Hair was rolled, queued and powdered for parades.

Corporals wore white or yellow lace edging to their cuffs and carried sticks, sergeants wore silver or gold lace and carried halberds and canes. Officers had silver or gold hat edging, they wore silver waist sashes with red stripes under their coats and their sword straps were silver and white. On duty they wore silver gorgets with a blue enamel oval showing the red-and-white striped Hessian lion. They wore silver silk waist sashes under their coats and gilt gorgets bearing the Hessian lion in the centre; they carried spontoons. Drummers wore the uniform of privates but with swallow's nests at the shoulder in the facing colour and white and red braid edging to these and to the sleeve seams, with seven chevrons, point up, on the sleeve. Drums were brass with red and white hoops.

Leib-Garde zu Fuss Nr 1

Raised in 1631; renamed '3. Garde' in 1760. Red facings, white buttons, white lace buttonholes with red stripes.

Infanterie-Regiment von Haudring Nr 2

Raised in 1683; 1757 Capellan; 1758 von Toll; 1760 Füsilier-Regiment von Bartheld. Orange facings, red turnbacks, white waistcoat, yellow buttons, no lace.

Infanterie-Regiment von Fürstenberg Nr 3

Raised in 1684; 1753 von Fürstenberg; 1759 von Gilsa. Red facings, buff waistcoats, white buttons, no lace.

Infanterie-Regiment Prinz Ysenburg Nr 4

Raised in 1687; 1759 von Bischhausen, 1762 von Wilke. No coallar, buff cuffs, lapels and waistcoats, red turnbacks, yellow buttons, white lace to edges of lapels, cuffs and cuff flap and two under the lapel.

Leib-Regiment Nr 5

Raised in 1688; 1760 von Wutginau. Red facings (no lapels), yellow waistcoat, buttons and lace.

Grenadier-Regiment Nr 6

Raised in 1702; renamed '2. Garde' in 1760. Red facings, white buttons, buttonhole lace and edging to lapels and cuffs.

Infanterie-Regiment Erbprinz Nr 7

Raised in 1700; renamed '4. Garde' and then 'Leib-Infanterie-Regiment' in 1760. Buff facings and waistcoat, white buttons and lace to buttonholes and lapel edges.

Infanterie-Regiment von Mansbach Nr 8

Raised in 1701. White facings and waistcoat, red turnbacks, yellow buttons and lace, two above the cuff, two under the lapels.

Infanterie-Regiment Prinz Karl Nr 9

Raised in 1702. No collar, red facings to edges of lapels and cuff flaps, white waistcoat, yellow buttons, no lace.

Infanterie-Regiment von Canitz Nr 10

Raised in 1702; 1759 von der Malsburg Canitz, dark yellow facings and waistcoat, white buttons, no lace.

Infanterie-Regiment Prinz von Anhalt Nr 11

Raised in 1745. No collar, red facings and turnbacks, white waistcoat and buttons, no lace.

Infanterie-Regiment von Hanau Nr 12

Raised in 1680; 1759 Prinz Wilhelm von Hessen (later Erbprinz). Crimson facings, white waistcoat, buttons and lace to buttonholes.

Regiment Garde Nr 13

Raised in 1760. Scalloped white edging to hat, dark blue coat, red collar and cuffs, yellow waistcoat and breeches, no lapels, white buttons and lace, white aiguillette on the right shoulder. Did not take the field.

Feldjägers

Raised in 1758; two companies. Dark green coats, crimson facings, yellow buttons.

Cavalry

Uniforms were a tricorn edged in the button colour, white, collarless, single-breasted coat with facings shown on cuffs, waistcoat and turnbacks, buff breeches and white belts. The saddle furniture (and the sabretasche) was in the facing colour, edged in the button colour and bore the crowned cipher 'WL'. Arms for kürassiers were a straight-bladed sword in a leather sheath and a pair of pistols. They wore no armour. Dragoons were also armed with a musket and wore an aiguillette in the button colour from the right shoulder. Their coats had lapels in the facing colour. Trumpeters wore reversed colours. NCOs and officers had gold or silver hat trim; officers' sashes and sword and sabre straps were in silver and red. The fifth regiment was the Garde du Corps and did not take the field.

Kürassier-Regiment Prinz Wilhem Nr 1

Raised in 1672. 1714 Prinz Maximilian; 1753 Prinz Wilhelm; 1760 Erbprinz. Light blue facings, yellow buttons. Kürassiers carried square standards, fringed in the button colour and heavily embroidered with the crest of Hessen-Kassel. The sovereign's standard was white, the other in the facing colour. Standard bandoliers were in the facing colour, decorated in the button colour.

Leib-Kürassier-Regiment Nr 2

Raised in 1684 as the Leibregiment zu Pferd; in 1760 became the Regiment Gendarmes. Red facings, yellow buttons.

Kürassier-Regiment von Miltitz Nr 3

Raised in 1704; 1759 von Oheim; 1760 von Einsiedel. Medium green facings, yellow buttons.

Kürassier-Regiment von Pruschenk Nr 4

Raised in 1704. 1740 Prinz Ysenburg; 1757 von Prüschenk; 1761 von Wolff. Facings sky blue, buttons white.

Artillerymen from Schaumburg-Lippe (left, bombardier) and Hessen-Hanau, 1763. (The Regimental History of the Hessen-Kassel Artillery)

Prinz Frederich Dragoner Nr 6

Raised in 1678. 1742 Sachsen-Gotha; 1757 Prinz Friedrich. Yellow facings, white buttons.

Leib-Dragoner Nr 7

Raised in 1688 as the Wartensleben Dragoons. Sky blue coat, red facings, yellow buttons. Dragoons bore swallow-tailed, fringed guidons, colours as for the cuirassiers.

Husaren-Korps

Raised in 1744. Brown fur busby, yellow dolman, light blue pelisse with black fur trim, white buttons and braid, yellow and white barrel sash, yellow breeches, white belts, steel-hilted sabre in black and steel sheath. Sabretasche and shabraque in light blue with white edging and crowned cipher 'WL'. It is unlikely that this regiment carried a standard.

Artillery

Raised in 1600; in 1741 the artillery corps received its first Inhaber, Oberst Dietrich Diede zu Fürstenstein. Field gun calibres were standardised and the foundry of the arsenal in Kassel began to design and cast gun barrels with the emphasis on improved lightness, to aid mobility. These guns were equipped with a screw sight. Up till 1759, Hessen-Kassel fielded battalion guns for only the 12 infantry regiments with the Allied army. There is fragmental record of some 6-pounders with the army in 1758.

The uniform was a tricorn edged white with crimson pompon, dark blue coat of infantry cut, wuth crimson collar, lapels, cuffs and turnbacks, white buttons, breeches and belts, yellow waistcoat, black gaiters. The distinctions of dress for officers, NCOs and drummers were as for the infantry.

12

THE COUNTY OF LIPPE-DETMOLD AND SCHAUMBURG-LIPPE

This county was geographically part of the Westphalian Kreis, but allied with Britain and Prussia against Austria. Graf (Count) Wilhelm zu Schaumburg-Lippe-Bückeburg (1724–1777) united the two German micro-states of Lippe-Detmold and Schaumburg-Lippe during his reign. His mother, Countess Margerete Gertrud von Oeyenhausen, was a daughter of King George I of England and his mistress, Ehrengard Melusine von der Schulenburg. Wilhelm had an overriding interest in the military and accompanied his father, General Graf Albrecht Wolfgang von Schaumburg-Lippe, on campaign in Dutch service during the War of the Austrian Succession (1740–1748). In 1747 Wilhelm's father resigned his command in Dutch service and died the next year, leaving his state heavily in debt.

Wilhelm had served in the Austrian Army as a volunteer in Italy and became a master gunner. He raised a corps of artillery (initially 109 men) in his principality in 1752, of which he was colonel-in-chief. No costs were spared on its training, equipment and weaponry; he even designed and cast cannon in a specially-built foundry. The famous Hanoverian (later Prussian) General Gerhard Johann David von Scharnhorst studied in Graf Wilhelm's artillery academy in Wilhelmstein.

At the outset of the Seven Years War, Graf Wilhelm was appointed Master General of Ordnance in the Hanoverian Army. He also raised a military contingent of an infantry regiment of a grenadier and seven musketeer companies, a company of dismounted Jägers (50 men), a squadron of mounted carabiniers (40 men), artillery and a staff of engineers. The corps fought at the battles of Minden and Wilhelmstal and was attached to the Hessen-Kassel brigade. At the beginning of the war, the corps took the field with 29 3-pounder battalion guns, four 8-, two 12-, three 18-pounder cannon, three howitzers and four heavy mortars. Eventually, there were about 350 artillery personnel. In 1762 Graf Wilhelm commanded the Anglo-Portuguese army (see Portugal chapter below), which which he conducted a brilliant defence of Portugal against the numerically far superior invading Spanish Army.

Hair was powdered, rolled and queued. Uniform cut was in the Prussian style, as were badges of rank. Officers wore a silver gorget when on duty with the troops; it had a gilt, crowned 'W' cipher. They wore waist sashes, but the colour details are not known. Apart from those of the Karabiniers, there is no data as to the design of the colours and standards carried by the Schaumburg-Lippe contingent.

Troops of Schaumburg-Lippe-Bückeburg, 1765. Left to right: jäger, grenadier, musketeer, bombardier, engineer. This plate is based on documents from the archives in Fortress Wilhelmsburg in Steinhudermeer Lake, given to Knötel by a military artist, Carl Henkel. A painting in the Bückeburg Heimatmuseum shows the jäger with a grey collar and cuffs; the grenadier has a brass headband and dark blue backing to his cap and two buttons on each cuff; the musketeer has plain white hat pompons. The black pouches at the fronts of the waists of the jäger and the bombardier were shown to be firmly attached to the waistbelt and not hanging below it. Both the bombardier and the engineer wore coats of the same shade of blue as the grenadier and the musketeer. (Knötel, I 34)

Schaumburg-Lippe-Bückeburg Karabiniers, 1753–1759. At first glance these uniforms seem hopelessly anachronistic, particularly when we consider that this unit was classified as light cavalry. They were initially raised at a strength of 75 mounted and 50 foot Jägers, and they soon earned a reputation as deadly fighters. The armour on the upper arms was dispensed with in 1758. The green label on the helmet bore the motto: 'PULCHRUM MORI SUCCURIT IN EXTREMIS' ('in danger lurks a fine death'). (Knötel, XV 36)

Schaumburg-Lippe-Bückeburg Infanterie

Plain tricorn with white pompon and hat cords. Dark blue, collarless, double-breasted coat, dark blue lapels, red, round cuffs, red turnbacks, brass buttons. White waistcoats, breeches and belts (with brass fittings), black gaiters. Grenadiers wore brass-fronted caps with a shield bearing the crowned 'W' cipher, brass headband, dark blue backing, white pompon. The lid of the black cartridge pouch also bore the crowned 'W' badge. The men were armed with a musket and brass-hilted sabre in a black sheath, worn on the waistbelt, under the coat. Drummers wore dark blue swallow's nests with white braid decoration and five white braid chevrons, point up, on each sleeve. The drums were brass, with red, white and blue striped hoops.

Schaumburg-Lippe-Bückeburg Jägers

Plain tricorn with yellow pompon and hat cords; dark green, single-breasted coat with grey collar and round cuffs, brass buttons, dark green turnbacks. Buff waistcoat, grey breeches, black boots and belts. They were armed with rifles and Hierchfänger (sword bayonets).

Schaumburg-Lippe-Bückeburg Karabiniers

Black steel helmets with brown bearskin turban, buff leather coat with red collar and cuffs, buff leather breeches and an elk hide tunic. They wore black steel cuirasses and armour on their upper arms. They had black leather cartridge pouches and sabretasche with crowned brass 'W' ciphers. Brass-hilted sabres in steel sheaths on black slings. Black sheepskin saddle cloth. Black harness with steel fittings. The black cartouch bandolier was worn over the buff carbine bandolier. The green greatcoat was carried over the holsters. The squadron was mounted on black Spanish stallions. The unit had one Leibstandarte and one regimental standard. The color of the regimental standard was red with a black border. It bore a crowned silver 'W' The cushions of the crown were of a darker red than the field of the standard. It is assumed that the Leibstandarte was white. The standard was fixed to the flagpole with silver nails. The flagpole was black with a silver finial.

Schaumburg-Lippe-Bückeburg Artillerie

Plain tricorn with yellow pompon and hat cords, dark blue, single-breasted, collarless coat with black round cuffs, red lining, white buttons. White waistcoat, dark blue breeches, black gaiters and belts. Short, straight artillery sword.

Engineers

These were all commissioned officers. Uniform was as for the artillery, but with a black collar to the coat and black boots.

13

THE KINGDOM OF PORTUGAL

Portugal began to establish a colonial empire early in the fifteenth century, and by 1756 she had acquired extensive colonies and trading outposts in Africa, the Far East and South America and had a monopoly on European trade in the Indian Ocean. Brazil was her most profitable overseas possession, and great wealth poured into Lisbon's treasury, with five per cent going to the ruling house. King Joseph loved the luxuries which he enjoyed due to this immense income – the arts and music, as well as a great deal of religious devotion – and so decided to turn over the distraction of actually ruling his kingdom to Count Sebastião José de Carvalho e Melo, future Marquis of Pombal.

Sebastião was an enlightened reformer, who wished to introduce English-style economic systems to Portugal. He also engaged in a bitter campaign to oust the Jesuits, whose presence stifled development. However, Sebatião's grasp of and interest in military matters was considerably less effective. Under his stewardship, the army atrophied. Enterprising young men of talent went into the navy, the merchant marine or to Brazil. By 1756 the infantry and cavalry regiments were neglected, badly administered, poorly trained and equipped and badly under strength. The artillery and the fortresses were no better. The command and staff structure was feeble, the generals aged and unequal to the tasks that faced them.

Thus, when Spain invaded Portugal in 1762, the nation's defences were in a parlous state. Britain was asked for and provided troops and materiel and Count Wilhelm of Schaumburg-Lippe was seconded to Portugal to overhaul all aspects of the creaking military machine and to command the defensive campaign against the Spanish invaders. He was so effective that the 1st Portuguese Infantry Regiment was named in his honour.

Infantry

The following list of infantry regiments takes into account the reorganisation carried out by the Count of Schaumburg-Lippe on 20 September 1762. However, various unit designations have been used by other authors.

In 1762 several infantry regiments were doubled in size (Braganza, Campo Mayor, Cascais, Castello de Vide, Chaves, Corte, Elvas, Faro, Lagos, Lisbon, Moncão, Moura, Olivença, Penamacor, Peniche, Porto, Setubal and Valença); most of these units had been reduced to single regiments by 1763.

Uniform

In 1750 Portuguese uniforms followed those of the catholic powers and were officially off-white, but there was no central procurement system and in 1762 the army was so ill-prepared for service that any available cloth was used to dress the hastily-recruited soldiers and some regiments appeared in brown, green or blue uniforms. The regiments used coloured facings for distinction, the colour chosen according to the colonel's personal taste. The position of buttons and pockets were also used for distinction. From 1754, the regiments were at peace establishment, some with only 360 men; war establishment was 1200 men in two battalions, a strength never reached by any Portuguese regiments during the war.

The cockade was red within a blue ring. Officers' collar and cuffs were edged with gold embroidery. Breeches were white and short riding boots were worn. Status was shown by a crimson waist sash with gold fringes. Musketeers wore tricorns, trimmed in the button colour; grenadiers used fur caps similar to French and Spanish design, with red bags, although some sources say mitre caps. White belts and long black gaiters were worn. Hair was powdered, curled and worn in a plaited pigtail.

Officers had gold or silver hat trim, buttons and lace; they had gold sword knots and carried canes with gold knobs, cords and tassels. Gilt gorgets were worn on duty; company officers carried spontoons, sergeants carried halberds. Belts were buff. Musicians' coats were liberally covered in yellow lace. Generals wore tricorns with gold trim and black feather edging, dark blue coats, with dark blue collars and cuffs and white turnbacks.

Colours

Very little definite information has been found. Infantry regiments used two colours: one sovereign's and one regimental. The latter was designed by the colonel; no identifiable examples seem to have survived. The sovereign's colour bore the crowned arms of Portugal in the centre, within a baroque frame, on a geometrical design in the form of a union jack in two colours. The staff bore a spear point tip, with cravats and cords, probably in the regimental button colour.

Regiment	Raised	Coat	Cuffs	Turnbacks	Waistcoat	Breeches	Buttons
Algarve (Faro Battalion)	1641	white	yellow	white	white	white	?
Algarve (Faro Battalion)	1641	white	blue	white	white	white	?
Bragança	1641	dark blue	red	red	dark blue	dark blue	white
Campo Major	1641	?	?	?	?	?	?
Cascais	1641	?	?	?	?	?	?
Castello de Vide	1641	?	?	?	?	?	?
Chaves	1643	blue	red	blue	white	blue	?
Corte	1659	light blue, light blue facings			white	?	white
Faro	1657	?	?	?	?	?	?
Lagos	1693	?	?	?	?	?	?
Lisboa	1659	light blue, light blue facings			white	white	?
Monção	1641	white	red	red	white	white	white
Moura	1641	?	?	?	?	?	?
Olivença	1641	?	?	?	?	?	?
Porto	1659	blue	red	red	red	red	yellow
Penamacor	1643	?	?	?	?	?	?
Peniche	1659	white	red	white	white	white	?
Setubal	1668	?	?	?	?	?	?
Valença	1657	blue	red	red	blue	blue	white
Marine Infantry Regiments (da Armada)							
1st Regiment (officers)	1641	green	red	red	green	green	yellow/golden
2nd Regiment (officers)	1641	green	red	red	green	green	white/silver (and lace)

Cavalry

Cavalry regiments had ten companies in five squadrons. Uniform consisted of a tricorn, trimmed in the button colour, a dark blue coat with facings on the cuffs and turnbacks, white waistcoats, buff leather breeches and below-knee boots. Officers had silver buttonhole lace to the cuffs and wore crimson waist sashes with silver tassels. In 1762 another cavalry regiment was raised, titled 'Mecklenburg', aka 'Corte'; it had dark blue coats, light blue facings and brass buttons. The cavalry wore tricorns edged in white, white waistcoats, buff leather breeches and high boots. White fringed epaulettes were worn. Saddle furniture was in the coat colour, edged in the facing colour. Belts were buff. All heavy cavalry and dragoon regiments were under strength.

Standards

Cavalry regiments used four square standards, one per squadron. That of the 1st Squadron was red, 2nd – yellow, 3rd – white, 4th – blue. All bore the crowned royal arms in the centre, within a baroque frame.

Regiment	Raised	Coat	Facings	Buttons
Alcantara	1707	white	red	?
Almeida	1707	green	red	?
Cais	1707	white	?	?
Bragança	1715	?	?	?
Elvas	1715	?	?	?
Moura	1715	dark blue	yellow	yellow

Little is known of the dragoon uniforms; it is likely that they wore white coats, but there is no information available as to facings and buttons. Their uniforms were of infantry cut; they carried swords, muskets and had drummers.

Regiment	Raised	Coat	Facings	Buttons
Penamacor	1707	?	?	?
Chaves	1715	?	?	?
Evora	1715	?	?	?
Olivença	1715	white	?	?

Artillery

The uniforms were of infantry cut, belts were buff.

Regiment	Coat	Cuffs	Turnbacks	Waistcoat	Breeches	Buttons
Beira	white	green	white	white	white	white
Algarve	green	red	green	green	green	white
Alentejo	green	red	green	red	green	white

Privates of Austrian infantry regiments, 1762. Left to right: Karl von Lothringen (standing), Lascy, de Ligne, Sachsen-Gotha (background), Wied (foreground) and Arhemberg. (Knötel, VI, 12)

Privates of Hungarian infantry regiments, 1762. Left to right: Simbschen Nr 53, Gyulai Nr 51, Adam Batthyany Nr 34, Josef Esterhàzy Nr 36 (standing), Erzherzog Ferdinand Nr 2 (seated) and Haller Nr 31. Despite the introduction of white tunics, there was still plenty of national character to these uniforms. (Knötel, VI 13)

Austrian junior officer and trooper, unidentified Kürassier-Regiment, 1740–1769. Note the gilt peak at the top-front of the officer's cuirass. (Rudolf von Ottenfeld)

Left to right: trooper of Trenck's Pandurs, and a Carlstädter-Sluiner Croat infantryman, 1756. Both uniforms reflect the national costumes of the border regions of that time. (Rudolf von Ottenfeld)

Austrian artillery officer and private of the Artillery Corps, 1762. (Rudolf von Ottenfeld)

Austrian border sharp-shooter and infantryman, 1740–1798. The regiments are unidentified. (Rudolf von Ottenfeld)

Left to right: grenadiers from Austrian infantry regiments Haller, Bethlen and an unidentified regiment. (David Morier, the Royal Collection)

Left to right: grenadiers of Austrian infantry regiments Los Rios Nr 9, von Waldeck Nr 35 and von Wurmbrandt Nr 50, 1750. (David Morier (406861), the Royal Collection)

Trooper, Austrian Kürassier-Regiment von Diemar Nr 15. (David Morier (404295) from the Royal Collection)

Trooper, Austrian Husaren-Regiment von Károly, 1751. (David Morier (406840) from the Royal Collection)

Troopers of Austrian dragoon regiments, 1756–1762. This plate shows the wide variety of uniforms worn by these soldiers. Left to right: Batthyanyi (Nr 7); Hessen-Darmstadt (Nr 19); Sachsen-Gotha (Nr 28); Althann (background); Daun/Löwenstein-Wertheim/St Ignon (Nr 31, seated); Prinz Eugen von Savoy (Nr 9). (Knötel, V 10)

Austrian hussar troopers, 1762. Left to right: Splenyi, Kaiser (Nr 1), Baranyay (Nr 30), Bethlen (Nr 35, background), Esterházy (foreground), Haddik. Note the various designs on the lids of the sabretasches (decoration was left to the regimental Chefs) and the fact that the sabres were worn inside the slings of the sabretasche. (Knötel, V 51)

Trooper, Austrian Kürassier-Regiment Hohenzollern-Hechingen Nr 1. (David Morier (404242) from the Royal Collection)

Brunswick company officer, Leib-Regiment, full dress uniform, 1756. (Bayer-Pegau)

Brunswick officer, Infanterie-Regiment von Imhoff, 1756. Note the extremely large silver gorget. (Bayer-Pegau)

Left to right: trooper of Horse Life Guards (mounted), trooper and mounted drummer, Dragoons of the Guard, Hessen-Darmstadt, 1750. The figures are shown in parade uniforms; the daily dress had no silver braid. Officers of the Horse Life Guards had parade dress of red tunics with blue collars and cuffs, with no lapels and richly decorated with gold braid. Their daily uniform had no gold braid, instead wearing a gold aiguilette on the right shoulder.

Left to right: officer and grenadier of the Hessen-Darmstadt Leib-Grenadiers, and a grenadier of the Leib-Grenadier-Garde, 1750. The uniform of the Leib-Grenadiers was based on the Austrian model and the officers carried short muskets. Drummers and musicians were clothed in the house colours: blue tunics, red small clothes and white buttons and braids. (Knötel, XIII 8)

EXPLICATIONS POUR LES TYPES.

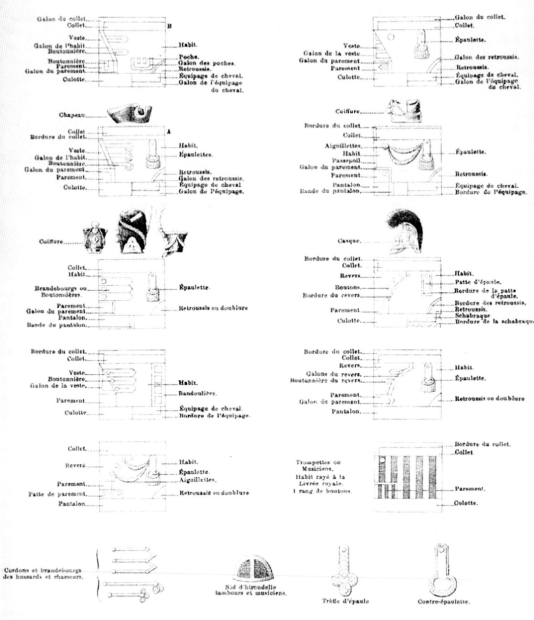

The key for the French uniform plates published by Lienhart and Humbert in Les Uniformes de l'Armée Française, 1690–1894, published in Leipzig by M. Ruhl in various editions from 1897–1906.

Aiguelette: aiguillette (an ornate lanyard), Bandes: a wide stripe, Boutonnière: button hole lace, Brandenbourgs: braids across the chest, Conte-epaulette: contre epaulette (an epaulette without fringes), Cordons: cords to the headgear, Casque: helmet, Coiffure: headgear, Collet: collar, Culotte: breeches, Doublure: facings, Epaulette: epaulette (a fringed shoulder strap), Equipage de cheval: saddle furniture, Gallon: wide edging, Habit: tunic, coat, Nid d'hirondelle: swallow's nest, worn at the shoulder by drummers and musicians, Parement: cuff, Passepoil: piping, Retroussis: turnbacks of the coat skirt, Revers: lapels, Trèfle: trefoil, Veste: waistcoat.

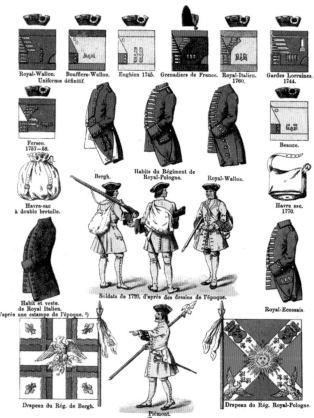

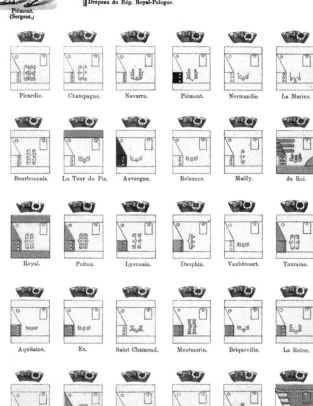

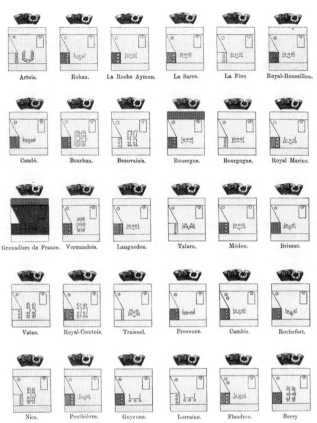

French line infantry continued. (Lienhart and Humbert, in Les Uniformes de l'Armée Française, 1690–1894, Volume III)

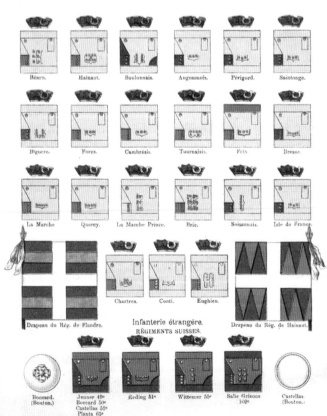

French line infantry and Swiss line infantry in French service. (Lienhart and Humbert, Les Uniformes de l'Armée Française, 1690–1894, Volume III)

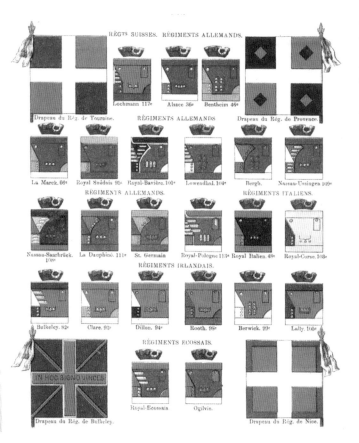

Swiss, German, Italian, Irish and Scottish line infantry regiments in French service. (Lienhart and Humbert, Les Uniformes de l'Armée Française, 1690–1894, Volume III)

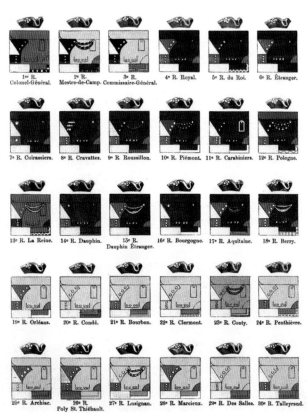

French line cavalry regiments, 1757. (Lienhart and Humbert, Les Uniformes de l'Armée Française, 1690–1894, Volume II)

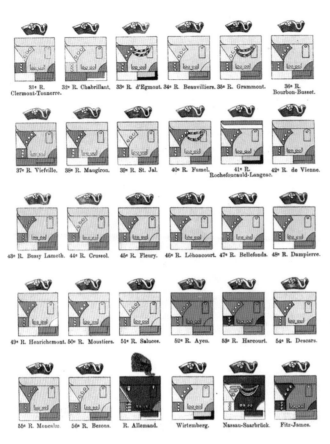

French line cavalry continued. (Lienhart and Humbert, Les Uniformes de l'Armée Française, 1690–1894, Volume II)

31ᵉ R. Clermont-Tonnerre. 32ᵉ R. Chabrillant. 33ᵉ R. d'Egmont. 34ᵉ R. Beauvilliers. 35ᵉ R. Grammont. 36ᵉ R. Bourbon-Busset.

37ᵉ R. Viefville. 38ᵉ R. Maugiron. 39ᵉ R. St. Jal. 40ᵉ R. Fumel. 41ᵉ R. Rochefoucauld-Langeac. 42ᵉ R. de Vienne.

43ᵉ R. Bussy Lameth. 44ᵉ R. Crussol. 45ᵉ R. Fleury. 46ᵉ R. Léhoncourt. 47ᵉ R. Bellefonds. 48ᵉ R. Dampierre.

49ᵉ R. Henrichemont. 50ᵉ R. Moustiers. 51ᵉ R. Saluces. 52ᵉ R. Ayen. 53ᵉ R. Harcourt. 54ᵉ R. Descars.

55ᵉ R. Moncalm. 56ᵉ R. Bezons. R. Allemand. Wirtemberg. Nassau-Saarbrück. Fitz-James.

French line cavalry, 21 December 1762. (Lienhart and Humbert, Les Uniformes de l'Armée Française, 1690–1894, Volume II)

1ᵉʳ R. Colonel-Général. 2ᵉ R. Mestre-de-Camp. 3ᵉ R. Commissaire-Général. 4ᵉ R. Royal. 5ᵉ R. du Roi. 6ᵉ R. Étranger.

7ᵉ R. Cuirassiers. 8ᵉ R. Cravattes. 9ᵉ Roussillon. 10ᵉ R. Piémont. 12ᵉ R. Pologne. 13ᵉ R. Lorraine.

14ᵉ R. Picardie. 15ᵉ R. Champagne. 16ᵉ R. Navarre. 17ᵉ R. Normandie. 18ᵉ R. La Reine. 19ᵉ R. Dauphin.

20ᵉ R. Bourgogne. 21ᵉ R. Berry. 22ᵉ R. Carabiniers. 23ᵉ R. d'Artois. 24ᵉ R. Orléans. 25ᵉ R. Chartres.

26ᵉ R. Condé. 27ᵉ R. Bourbon. 28ᵉ R. Clermont. 29ᵉ R. Conty. 30ᵉ R. Penthièvre. 31ᵉ R. Noailles.

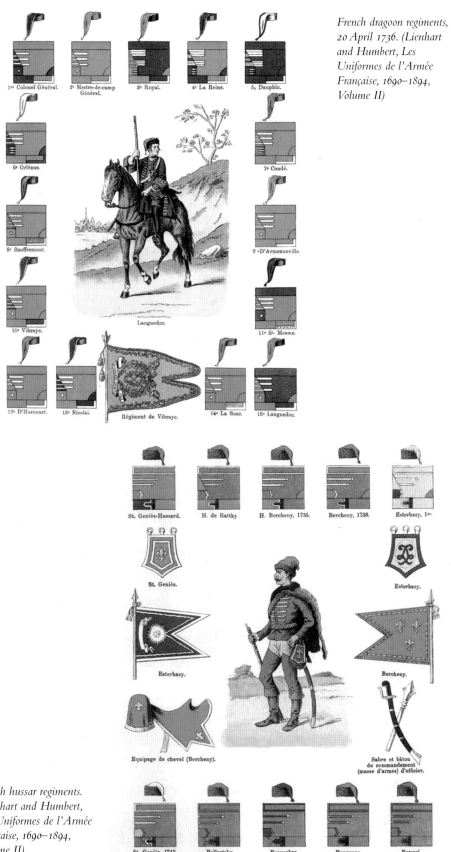

French dragoon regiments, 20 April 1736. (Lienhart and Humbert, Les Uniformes de l'Armée Française, 1690–1894, Volume II)

1er Colonel Général. 2e Mestre-de-camp Général. 3e Royal. 4e La Reine. 5e Dauphin.

6e Orléans. 7e Condé.

8e Bauffremont. 9 «D'Armenonville.

Languedoc.

10e Vibraye. 11e St. Mesme.

12e D'Harcourt. 13e Nicolai. Régiment de Vibraye. 14e La Suze. 15e Languedoc.

St. Geniès-Hussard. H. de Rattky. H. Bercheny, 1735. Bercheny, 1738. Esterhazy, 1er.

St. Geniès. Esterhazy.

Esterhazy. Bercheny.

Equipage de cheval (Bercheny). Sabre et bâton de commandement (masse d'armes) d'officier.

French hussar regiments. (Lienhart and Humbert, Les Uniformes de l'Armée Française, 1690–1894, Volume II)

St. Geniès, 1743. Pollertzky. Beausobre. Raugrave. Ferrari.

Grenadiers of the British 7th, 8th and 9th Regiments of Foot, 1751. (David Morier (405580) from the Royal Collection)

Grenadiers of the British 10th, 11th and 12th Regiments of Foot, 1751. (David Morier (405579) from the Royal Collection)

Grenadiers of the British 16th, 17th and 18th Regiments of Foot, 1751. (David Morier (405583) from the Royal Collection)

Grenadier, 40th Regiment of Foot, private, Invalids Regiment and grenadier, 42nd Highland Regiment, 1751. (David Morier (405589) from the Royal Collection)

Trooper, British Royal Horse Guards, 1751. (David Morier (401505) from the Royal Collection)

Trooper, British 2nd Royal North British Dragoons, 1751. (David Morier (405603) from the Royal Collection)

Drummer and trooper, 15th Light Dragoons, 1760. This regiment is the oldest light cavalry regiment in the British Army. The uniform was originally red tunics with green facings; drummers wore green with red and white decorations. The drum banners bore the regimental badge of a hart, chased by a hound. (Knötel, XI 58)

Dragoon of the 16th Light Dragoons, 1760. In 1816 the regiment was converted to lancers; since then their title has been the 16th (Queen's) Lancers. The double-breasted waistcoat with the black, shawl collar is a singular piece of clothing. The black helmet was decorated with a sprig of oak leaves. (Knötel, XI 59)

Hanoverian von Freytag's Freikorps, 1760. Left to right: mounted Jäger, Jäger, grenadier. Hanoverian troops wore a sprig of oak leaves in their hats on campaign, in the Austrian style. This Freikorps was raised in 1756 and rose to have six mounted and six foot companies, including one of grenadiers. It had an impressive combat record. (Knötel, V 42)

Freikorps von Scheither (left) and von Luckner (right), 1762. This corps was raised in 1757 by von Hauptmann Georg Albrecht Heinrich Scheither; it consisted of four companies of mounted carabineers, a company of grenadiers and one of Jägers. (Knötel, IV 24)

Grenadiers of Hanoverian infantry regiments de Cheusses and von Spörke, 1751. (David Morier, the Royal Collection)

Grenadiers from Hanoverian infantry regiments von Borch and von Brunck. (David Morier, the Royal Collection)

Trooper, British 7th Queen's Dragoons, 1751. (David Morier (401507) from the Royal Collection)

Trooper, Hanoverian Wrede Kavallerie. (David Morier, the Royal Collection)

Hanoverian Hammerstein Kavallerie, 1756. The orange facings and yellow buttons changed to black and white respectively in 1760. The continental armies did not dock the tails of their horses as the British did at this time. (Gmundener Prachtwerk)

Grenadiers à Cheval. The very singular, black-fronted grenadier cap bore the British crest with supporters over the springing Saxon horse, all in gold. The saddle furniture was also very ornate. (Gmundener Prachtwerk)

Prussian Freibataillon le Noble, 1756–1763. In the foreground a Jäger, in the typical green uniform; in the background, musketiers. The officer has the silver edging to his hat. The corps had two battalions and a detachment of Jägers. The musketiers of all Freikorps wore dark blue coats with light blue facings, waistcoats and breeches; they were differentiated by their headgear and the cut of their tunics. (Knötel, II 38)

Prussian Infanterie-Regiment von Forcade, 1756. In 1806 this regiment had the number 23. The grenadier cap is a reconstruction, based on Lehmann (Forschungen und Urkunden zur Grschichte der Preussischen Armee) as no example has survived. Normally a grenadier had a central brass plate and four brass corner grenades on his cartridge pouch. (Knötel, X 36)

Prussian trooper, Dragoner-Regiment von Baireuth, 1756. All Prussian dragoon regiments wore light blue coats. Although the regiment is shown with plain red saddle furniture, it must be assumed that the usual crowned royal ciphers would have been worn. (Knötel, I 41)

Prussian Infanterie-Regiment Prinz Heinrich von Preussen Nr 35, 1757. Frederick the Great raised this regiment for his brother in 1740, from the Lieb-Kompagnie of IR Nr 6; as fusiliers, they wore the particular cap. The grenadier company wore the same metal plate and yellow headband and backing, but with a red-white-red pompon and red and white braid decoration. The white flag with the blue central disc is that of the Leib-Kompagnie. Note the uniform of the medical orderly. As a fusilier regiment, the officers wore no lace on their coats. (Knötel, I 6)

Prussian Kürassier-Regiment von Seydlitz, 1757. Left to right: mounted troopers, trooper, mounted junior officer. The uniform shown was worn throughout the Seven Years' War. In 1762 the hats lost their white edging and white plumes were adopted. Those of officers had black bases; those of the NCOs had black tips. From 1757 to 1774 the regiment was regarded as a model cavalry unit under the command of its famous Chef, von Seydlitz. (Knötel, I 22)

Prussian Husaren-Regiment von Werner, 1758, Regiment's Chef and trooper. This regiment was Nr 6 in 1806, in which year it was destroyed. This plate is based on a portrait of Major General von Werner in the undress hussar officer's uniform, with the tricorn, complete with the white feather trim of a general officer. Note the yellow leather boots, which were indicative of senior officers. It is very rare to see the pelisse worn buttoned up. (Knötel, XI 23)

Prussian drummer, Dragoner-Regiment von Krockow (Nr 2 in 1806), 1760. Each squadron of dragoons had three drummers, for transmitting the commander's signals. In 1760, these were replaced by two trumpeters and only one drummer was retained. The drum hoops were in different colours for each regiment. As a drummer, he wears swallows' nests decorated in the special red and white musicians' lace. The regiment was destroyed in 1806. (Knötel, XVII 21)

Prussian Freikorps Mayer. Left to right: jäger 1760, hussar 1758. The Freikorps was raised in September 1756 in Saxony, at one battalion, with a detachment of Jägers. Mayer died in 1759 and was succeeded by von Collognon, then in 1760 by von Courbiere. In 1761 a second battalion was raised, and a detachment of hussars. The infantry wore the dark blue coats with light blue facings, waistcoats and breeches. The costume of the hussar is based on notes in Rabe's collection. (Knötel, XVIII 37)

Prussian officer and trooper, Corps Bosniaken, 1760. Initially this regiment had no uniforms; these appear to have been the first adopted. This regiment came into Prussian service from Albania; it later became the 'Corps Towarczys'. (Knötel, VI 31)

Prussian Freikorps von Kleist, 1760. Left to right: troopers, dragoons, private, Croats, officer Croats. This corps was raised in Berlin, Saxony and Mecklenburg in 1760. It consisted of a battalion of Croats, 300 Jägers and eight squadrons of dragoons (horse grenadiers). There were also five squadrons of hussars, which operated together with the 1st Hussars. The corps had an excellent combat record and was disbanded at the end of the war. (Knötel, I 7)

Prussian Freikorps von Gschray, 1761. Left to right: trooper of dragoons, infantry private, infantry officer. The corps was raised in Minden and Nordhausen, but never reached its allotted strength of six companies and six squadrons. Gschray was ambushed and captured on 23 August 1761; the corps was disbanded at the end of the war. It should be noted that this plate differs in many details from Menzel's version of these uniforms. (Knötel, V 6)

Members of the junior staff of various Prussian regiments, 1761. Left to right: infantry, regimental quartermaster, auditor or regimental surgeon; Kürassier regimental quartermaster, auditor of dragoons and regimental surgeon of the Green (1st) Hussars. (Knötel, XVII 46)

Prussian Dragoner-Regiment von Pomeiske, 1762 (Nr 9 in 1806, in which year it was destroyed). We see saddle furniture without decoration here, as no picture of any ciphers has been found. It is most likely that ciphers were worn. Climbing into the saddle with all the campaign gear behind it must have been very difficult. Note the aiguillette in the button colour behind the right shoulder. (Knötel, IX 13)

Prussian Infanterie-Regiment von Kanitz, 1762. This battalion was composed of the four grenadier companies of Infanterie-Regiments Nrs 2 and 7. The pompons on top of the grenadier mitre caps were the same as those worn in the tricorns of the musketeers of the same regiment. (Knötel, II 1)

Russian infantry 1756–1762. Left to right: grenadier, musketeer private, field officer, subaltern officer. Since being placed on a permanent footing by Peter the Great in 1700, Russian infantry were organised on the Prussian model. (Knötel, III 27)

Russian infantry, 1742–1763. Background: sergeant and two musketeers, Preobrazensky Leib-Guard, Semenovsky Leib-Guard and Izmailovsky Leib-Guard, 1742–1762. Grenadier, Novomirgorod Garrison, 1760–1763. Foreground: musketeer and grenadier, Pandur Regiment 1752–1763; officer, grenadiers of the Footguards 1742–1762. (Knötel, III 34)

Russian infantry in their 1762 Prussian-style uniforms, which were probably never introduced. Their regiments are named for their colonel; during the war they had geographical names but there is little information as to the specific title changes. Left to right: grenadier, Regiment Essen (foreground); grenadier officer and grenadier, Battalion Wiess (background); grenadier, Regiment Kettenburg (lying); grenadier, Regiment Zöge von Manteuffel; grenadier, Regiment Prinz Wilhelm; grenadier, Regiment Prinz August (sitting); musketeer, Regiment Prinz Wilhelm (background). (Knötel, VIII 54)

Russian artillery, 1757–1758. Left to right: officer of bombardiers, drummer of bombardiers, gunner, artillery fusilier. The Bombardier Corps wore a type of grenadier cap. This consisted of a front plate, headpiece, neck shield and a brass comb, which extended from the top of the headpiece to the rear. Artillerymen were armed with short muskets. In winter they acted as infantry; in summer, they moved out into camps and practiced gun drill, shooting and laboratory work. (Knötel, XI 44)

Russian hussars, 1741–1764. Left to right: trooper, Vengersky; trooper, Moldavsky; officer and trooper, Gruzinsky; trooper, Serbsky. It was unusual for the uniforms of the officer and trooper of Gruzinsky to be so different from one another. The cipher is that of Tzarina Elizaveta Petrovna. (Knötel, VI 46)

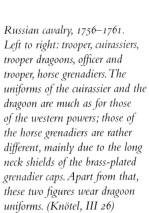

Russian cavalry, 1756–1761. Left to right: trooper, cuirassiers, trooper dragoons, officer and trooper, horse grenadiers. The uniforms of the cuirassier and the dragoon are much as for those of the western powers; those of the horse grenadiers are rather different, mainly due to the long neck shields of the brass-plated grenadier caps. Apart from that, these two figures wear dragoon uniforms. (Knötel, III 26)

Russian 2nd Hussars in their 1762 Prussian-style uniforms, which were probably never introduced. Their names reflect the title changes of that year. Left to right: officer, Zobeltitz Hussars; trooper, 2nd Hussars; officer, 2nd Hussars. Note the reversed imperial cipher on the sabretasche. The uniform resembles that of the Prussian Yellow Hussars. (Knötel, IX 2)

Russian Leib Dragoons (Vladimirsky during the war), 1756–1762. Left to right: grenadier trooper, dragoon, kettle drummer. Note the blue and white decoration to the dragoon's bandolier. The custom of employing negro bandsmen was widespread at this time. (Knötel, IX 23)

14

THE KINGDOM OF PRUSSIA

Infantry

Each regiment had its own distinctive facing colour, buttons and – in most cases – elaborate embroidered lace buttonholes, which might be worn on any number of buttons, according to the regiment. Officers had one system, NCOs another, the rank and file their own, or they wore none at all. The drummers and fifers also had their own systems, which included swallow's nests in the facing colour, edged in their lace and lace down the back and front sleeve seams with nine chevrons of lace, point up, on the sleeve. In some regiments, these chevrons were replaced by horizontal bars. The same lace edged the drum bandolier. Drums were brass, with the crowned royal cipher within an oval. Drum hoops were striped diagonally, red and the button colour. They had white cords. Officers wore silver and black silk waist sashes, worn under the coat, and silver and black sword straps. Their hats were edged in gold or silver lace and, when on duty, they wore gilt gorgets with a central, light blue oval bearing the Prussian eagle with the royal cipher 'FR'.

Company officers were armed with spontoons. Exceptionally, grenadier company officers were dressed and armed as musketeer officers. Senior NCOs wore quartered black and white hat pompons, had silver or gold edging to their hats, cuffs and cuff flaps and silver and black sabre knots; they bore halberds and carried canes. Corporals had white or yellow hat edging and black and white hat pompons and sabre knots; they carried sticks. Hair was powdered, curled and worn in a plaited pigtail. Officers wore black neckstocks; those of the NCOs and men were red unless otherwise noted. The grenadier companies wore metal-fronted mitre

Line infantry colour with upright, wavy piles. This pattern was carried by infantry regiments 4, 5, 8, 9, 11, 16, 21, 22, 23, 24, 26, 27, 52, 54 and 55.

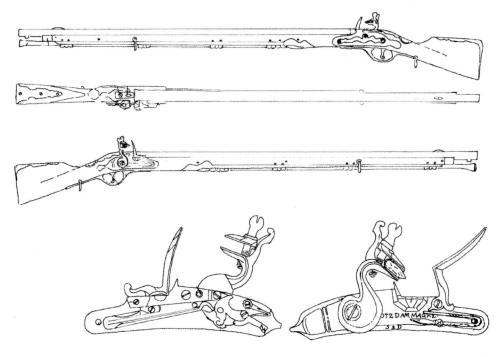

PRUSSIAN M1723/40

caps, in the button colour, with coloured headbands, cap backing, braid trim and pompons. They also had metal side and rear emblems on the headbands; in a few cases, the entire headband was metal. Each regiment had its own, unique design of front plates and headband fittings.

Regiments numbered 33 and 35–49 were fusilier regiments. They had the same establishment as musketeer regiments, but wore special, metal-fronted caps in the button colour, with the low crown and headband, usually in the facing colour. These crowns were topped by a small round dome with a grenade flame; this dome was held up by four metal straps. The front plates, side and rear headband ornaments were the same designs as for the grenadier companies. They also had plain round cuffs, without flaps and their officers had no buttonhole embroidery.

Colours

It seems that by the outbreak of the war, all infantry regiments had been issued with new pattern colours, bearing the cipher 'FR'. The fields of all Leibfahnen (King's Colours) were white; the fields of Ordinair-fahnen (regimental colours) were usually in the colour of the central disc of the Leibfahne, with central discs and any crosses also in this colour. A regiment's Leibfahne was carried by the senior musketeer company of the regiment; all other musketeer companies carried an Ordinair-fahne.

The two grenadier companies were detached from their parent regiments in the field and were concentrated into four-company combined grenadier battalions. They did not carry colours.

Colours were decorated with black and silver cords and tassels, reaching down to about two-thirds of the height of the cloth. The gilt finials were pierced to show the cipher 'FR'. The colour of the pikestaff varied with regiment. In the central disc was (usually) a black eagle in flight to the right, under a scroll (usually white, always edged in gold or silver) bearing 'PRO GLORIA ET PATRIA' (in gold or silver), all within a gold/silver laurel wreath. If the central disc was black, the eagle was gold. There were flaming gold/silver grenades in the centre of each side of the colour and in each corner

Line infantry colour with straight corner piles. This pattern was carried by infantry regiments 7, 12, 13, 17, 25, 28, 29, 30, 31, 39, 42, 45, 48, 50, 51 and 53.

Line infantry colour with wavy corner piles. This pattern was carried by infantry regiments 18, 46 and 47.

Line infantry colour with a Maltese cross. This pattern was carried by infantry regiment 19. Colours carried by infantry regiments 19 and 32 had narrow, eight-pointed, straight-sided crosses on the regimental colours and upright, narrow crosses on the king's colours.

Colour carried by garrison regiments 1, 2, 3 and 4.

was a crowned gold/silver wreath enclosing the cipher 'FR'. This is known as the 'plain' pattern. Except in the cases regiments Nrs 19 and 34, the designs of a regiment's Leibfahne and Ordinair-fahne patterns and decorations were identical; only the colours differed.

Colour Pattern	Design
1	plain
2	plain, plus an upright, narrow wavy cross
3	plain, plus narrow, straight corner piles
4	plain, plus narrow, wavy corner piles
5	plain, plus narrow, wavy upright cross and straight corner piles
6	plain, plus an upright Maltese cross

Infanterie-Regiment von Winterfeldt Nr 1

Raised in 1619. 1758 von Lattorf; 1760 von Zeuner. Disbanded in 1806. Facings poppy red. Lace: officers silver lace edging to lapels and cuffs, two embroidered silver loops under each lapel, on each pocket flap and in the small of the back; NCOs silver edging to lapels, cuffs and cuff flaps; men white, oblong buttonholes to and under the lapels, on the pocket flaps, cuff flaps and in the small of the back; drummers white with a wavy red pattern. Grenadier cap: tin plate, white headband, blue backing, white braid and pompon. Leibfahne: Pattern Nr 1, orange centre, silver decoration. Ordinair-fahne: white centre, orange field, silver decoration.

Infanterie-Regiment von Kanitz Nr 2

Raised in 1619. This regiment became the new Infanterie-Regiment Nr 1 after 1806. Facings light brick red. Lace: officers gold embroidered edging to lapels, cuffs and cuff flaps; NCOs gold, pointed, with a golden tassel, two below the lapels and two in the small of the back; men crimson, pointed, with a white tassel; drummers red with a black and white design. Grenadier cap: brass plate, red headband, buff backing, white braid, red-within-black pompon. Leibfahne: Pattern Nr 1, black centre, gold decoration. Ordinair-fahne: white centre, black field, gold decoration.

Infanterie-Regiment Anhalt-Dessau Nr 3

Raised in 1665. 1758 von Kahlden (killed at Zorndorf); 1759 Prinz von Anhalt-Bernburg. Disbanded in 1806. Facings (no lapels) poppy red. Lace: officers gold (12 buttons to each side of the chest); NCOs (7 buttons each side of the coat) two black and silver buttonholes, each with a tassel, under each lapel; men black and white woven lace, with black and white tassels, two under each lapel, two in the small of the back; drummers white oblong. Grenadier cap: tin plate, white headband, white backing, yellow and black braid, white pompon with black dots. Leibfahne: Pattern Nr 1, yellow centre, silver decoration. Ordinair-fahne: white centre, yellow field, silver decoration.

Infanterie-Regiment von Kalnein Nr 4

Raised in 1671. 1757 von Rautern; 1758 von Kleist (Georg Friedrich). Disbanded in 1806. Facings orange (no lapels). Lace: officers gold; two buttons under each lapel, two in the small of the back, three on each cuff flap, three on each pocket flap; NCOs gold, pointed, with a tassel; men white, pointed, with white tassels, six to each side of the coat; drummers white with red and blue semicircular edging. Grenadier cap: brass plate, red headband, buff backing, blue-red-blue

Infanterie-Regiment von Kalnein grenadier cap. (The Wehrgeschichtliches Museum, Rastatt)

Infanterie-Regiment von Winterfeldt Nr 1

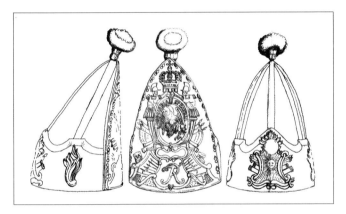

Infanterie-Regiment von Kanitz Nr 2

Infanterie-Regiment Anhalt-Dessau Nr 3

Infanterie-Regiment von Kalnein Nr 4

Infanterie-Regiment Herzog Ferdinand von Braunschweig, 1757. The golden embroidery on the lapels of the officer's coat was abandoned in 1766. The musketeer has two yellow braid buttonholes with white tassels under each lapel; NCOs wore two in gold, without tassels. The company officer wears the gorget, silver and black silk waist sash and silver and black sword knot. (Knötel, XVIII 53)

braid, royal blue pompon with a red ring, three brass grenades on the headband. Leibfahne: Pattern Nr 2, red centre, yellow wavy cross, gold decoration. Ordinair-fahne: white centre, red field, yellow wavy cross, gold decoration.

Infanterie-Regiment Herzog Ferdinand von Braunschweig Nr 5

Raised in 1672. Disbanded in 1806. Facings pale buff. Lace: officers gold embroidered buttonholes, with tassels, two under each lapel, two on each pocket flap and two in the small of the back; NCOs gold, oblong; men orange, pointed, with white tassels; drummers white with two yellow and light blue diamond chains along the length. Grenadier cap: brass plate, blue headband, buff backing, red-white-red braid, red-within-white-within yellow pompon. Leibfahne: Pattern Nr 2, yellow centre, orange wavy cross, gold decoration. Ordinair-fahne: white centre, orange wavy cross, gold decoration.

Grenadier Garde Nr 6

Raised in 1673. 1756 von Retzow; 1759 von Saldern. Disbanded in 1806. Facings scarlet (no lapels). Lace: officers gold; eight to each side of the coat, four to each cuff, two on each pocket flap, four in the small of the back; NCOs white neck stock, knotted gold lace, as for the officers, but only six on the sides of the chest; men as for NCOs, plain gold, pointed; drummers gold with double stripes (red, yellow, red) along the length. Pale buff waistcoat and breeches. Grenadier cap: brass plate and headband, red backing, yellow braid, red-within-white pompon. They were taller than for other regiments. Leibfahne: Pattern Nr 1, white centre, light blue scroll, silver decoration. Ordinair-fahne: light blue centre, white scroll and filed, silver decoration.

Grenadier Garde grenadier cap. (The Wehrgeschichtliches Museum, Rastatt)

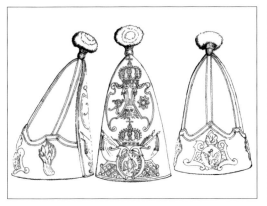

*Infanterie-Regiment Herzog Ferdinand von
Braunschweig Nr 5*

Grenadier Garde Nr 6

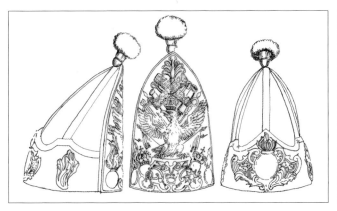

Infanterie-Regiment von Braunschweig-Bevern Nr 7

*Infanterie-Regiment von
Amstell Nr 8*

Infanterie-Regiment Quadt Von Wikeradt Nr 9

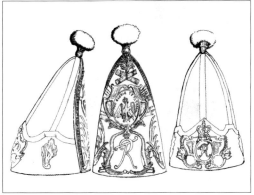

Infanterie-Regiment von Knobloch Nr 10

Infanterie-Regiment von Braunschweig-Bevern Nr 7

Raised in 1676. 1757 Herzog von Alt-Bevern. Disbanded in 1806. Facings pink. Lace: officers silver, eight on each lapel; NCOs silver, oblong; men squared white laces; drummers not known. Grenadier cap: tin plate, white headband and braid, crimson backing and pompon. Leibfahne: Pattern Nr 3, dark blue centre, white scroll, red corner piles, silver decoration. Ordinair-fahne: white centre, dark blue scroll and field, red corner piles, silver decoration.

Infanterie-Regiment von Amstell Nr 8

Raised in 1677. 1757 von den Hagen, aka Geist (killed at Hochkirch); 1759 von Queis. This regiment became the new Infanterie-Regiment Nr 2 after 1806. Facings scarlet. Lace: officers gold, eight on and two under each lapel, three on each cuff, two in the small of the back; NCOs gold oblong; men white, pointed, with two light blue stripes; drummers white with green and red lateral bars. Grenadier cap: brass plate, red headband, dark blue backing, red-within-white-within yellow braid and pompon. Leibfahne: Pattern Nr 2, black centre and wavy cross, white scroll, gold decoration. Ordinair-fahne: white centre, scroll and cross, gold decoration.

Infanterie-Regiment Quadt Von Wikeradt Nr 9

Raised in 1677. 1756 von Kleist (Friedrich Ludwig 'Jung-Kleist'); 1758 von Oldenburg; 1758 von Puttkammer; 1759 von Schenckendorff. Disbanded in 1806. Facings scarlet. Lace: officers gold lace edging to lapels and cuffs; NCOs narrow gold oblong; men narrow white, square ended, six on each lapel, two on the cuff flap, two in the small of the back; drummers white with two red stripes having black rings along them. Grenadier cap: brass plate, red headband and backing, red-within-yellow braid and pompon. Leibfahne: Pattern Nr 2, dark green centre, white scroll, red cross, gold decoration. Ordinair-fahne: white centre, dark green scroll and field, red cross, gold decoration.

Infanterie-Regiment von Knobloch Nr 10

Raised in 1683. 1757 von Pannewitz; 1759 von Mosel. Disbanded in 1806. Cuffs, waistcoat and breeches lemon yellow; no collar or lapels. Lace: officers silver, with tassels, two under each lapel, three on each cuff flap, two in the small of the back; NCOs silver, knotted; men white, pointed, with white tassels; drummers white with red and white diagonal stripes. Grenadier cap: tin plate, yellow headband, backing and pompon, grey braid. Leibfahne: Pattern Nr 1, light green centre, white scroll, gold decoration. Ordinair-fahne: white centre, light green scroll and field, gold decoration.

Infanterie-Regiment von Below, 1757. The drummer's uniform is based on a contemporary description; his lace is white with a blue stripe. The company officer carries a spontoon. (Knötel, XIV 26)

Infanterie-Regiment von Below Nr 11

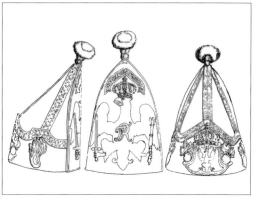

*Infanterie-Regiment Erbprinz von Hessen-
Darmstadt Nr 12*

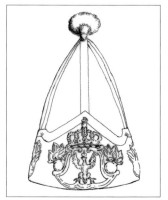

*Infanterie-Regiment von
Itzenblitz Nr 13*

Infanterie-Regiment von Lehwaldt Nr 14

Garde du Corps Nr 15

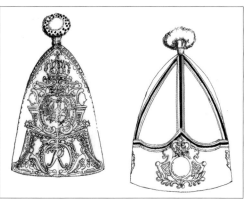

Infanterie-Regiment Graf zu Dohna Nr 16

Infanterie-Regiment Erbprinz von Hessen-Darmstadt Nr 12 grenadier cap. (The Wehrgeschichtliches Museum, Rastatt)

Infanterie-Regiment von Below Nr 11

Raised in 1685. 1758 von Rebentisch. This regiment became the new Infanterie-Regiment Nr 3 after 1806. Facings crimson. Lace: officers gold, two under each lapel, three on each cuff flap, two in the small of the back; NCOs gold, oblong; men narrow, white, square-ended; drummers white with two light blue stripes along it. Grenadier cap: tin plate with light blue oval disc bearing the black Prussian eagle and gold motto, tin headband, white backing, red braid and pompon. Leibfahne: Pattern Nr 2, crimson centre and cross, white scroll, gold decoration. Ordinair-fahne: white centre and cross, crimson scroll and field, gold decoration.

Infanterie-Regiment Erbprinz von Hessen-Darmstadt Nr 12

Raised in 1685 from Infanterie-Regiments Nrs 1, 3, 4, 5, 6 and 7. 1757 von Finck. Disbanded in 1806. Facings light brick red. Lace: officers gold embroidered, six on and two under each lapel, three on each cuff, two on each cuff flap, two in the small of the back; NCOs gold, pointed, with a tassel; men white, pointed, with white tassels; drummers white with three light red stripes along it. Grenadier cap: brass plate with black eagle, royal blue-within-light red pompon, light red headband, royal blue backing, brass 'braid'. On the back of the headband was a black Prussian eagle on a brass cartouche; a brass grenade to each side of the headband. Leibfahne: Pattern Nr 3, light green centre and cross, white scroll, gold decoration. Ordinair-fahne: white centre and cross, light green scroll and field, gold decoration.

Infanterie-Regiment von Itzenblitz Nr 13

Raised in 1687. 1759 von Syburg. Disbanded in 1806. Facings white, buff waistcoat and breeches. Lace: officers silver, two embroidered loops under each lapel, two on the pocket flaps, two in the small of the back; NCOs silver, knotted, with a silver tassel; men white, pointed, with white tassels; drummers red with two white diamond–shaped chains along it. Grenadier cap: tin plate, buff headband, dark blue backing, white braid, buff pompon. Leibfahne: Pattern Nr 3, black centre, white scroll, red cross, silver decoration. Ordinair-fahne: white centre, black scroll and field, silver decoration.

Infanterie-Regiment von Lehwaldt Nr 14

Raised in 1688. This regiment became the new Infanterie-Regiment Nr 4 after 1806. Facings light brick red. Lace: officers gold; two under each lapel, two in the small of the back. NCOs narrow, gold oblong; men have six narrow white lace buttonholes, in the shape of a horizontal figure 8, with two red stripes on each lapel and two on each cuff flap; drummers white with a red central stripe. Grenadier cap: brass plate, white headband and backing, orange braid and pompon. Leibfahne: Pattern Nr 1, red centre, white scroll, gold decoration. Ordinair-fahne: white centre, red scroll and field, gold decoration.

Garde du Corps Nr 15

Raised in 1688 by Carl Philipp Baron von Wylich zu Lottum. Made up of I. Leibgarde Bataillon, II. Garde Bataillon and III. Bataillon. This regiment became the new Infanterie-Regiment Garde Nr 8 after 1806. Facings poppy red collar and cuffs, buff waistcoat and breeches. Lace: (1st Battalion) officers embroidered silver, with tassels; NCOs silver buttonholes and edging to lapels and cuffs; men silver, pointed with a tassel. (2nd and 3rd Battalions): officers silver; NCOs and men silver, pointed;

Infanterie-Regiment von Manteuffel Nr 17

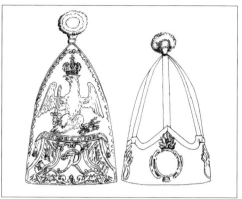

Infanterie-Regiment Prinz von Preussen Nr 18

Infanterie-Regiment Markgraf Carl Nr 19

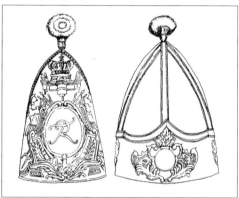

Infanterie-Regiment von Zastrow Nr 20

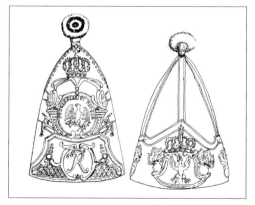

Infanterie-Regiment von Hülsen Nr 21

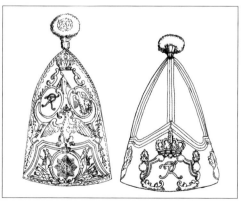

Infanterie-Regiment Prinz Mortiz von Anhalt Nr 22

Garde du Corps, 1763. Left to right: officer, standard bearer, troopers. Two battalions of Garde du Corps existed under Friedrich I. Frederick the Great re-raised a battalion on his accession to the throne and in 1756 this was increased to three battalions. Note the polished steel cuirass. (Knötel, III 46)

drummers (both battalions) silver with two red stripes along it. 1st Battalion Grenadier cap: tin plate and headband, red backing, silver braid, red-within-white pompon. Leibfahne: Pattern Nr 1, white centre, silver decoration. The cloth showed alternate, narrow, vertical stripes of white and silver. Ordinair-fahne: light blue centre, white scroll, silver decoration. Same pattern cloth as for the Leibfahne. These pattern colours were carried by all three battalions.

Infanterie-Regiment Graf zu Dohna Nr 16

Raised in 1689 from a battalion of Infanterie-Regiment Nr 10. 1752 von Syburg. This regiment became the new Infantry Regiment Nr 5 after 1806. Facings light red. Lace: officers gold embroidered buttonholes; nine (in three sets of three) on each lapel, two under each lapel, four over each cuff, two on each pocket flap and two in the small of the back. NCOs and men had the same distribution; NCOs narrow, gold oblong; men white pointed, with two red and one, central black stripe, white, red and black tassel; drummers white with three red and two black stripes along it. Grenadier cap: brass plate, red headband, buff backing, black-within-white-within-red braid, red-within-white pompon, the outer ring having black spots. Leibfahne: Pattern Nr 2, light orange centre and cross, white scroll, gold decoration. Ordinair-fahne: white centre and cross, light orange scroll and field, gold decoration.

Infanterie-Regiment von Manteuffel Nr 17

Raised in 1693 from one battalion of Infanterie-Regiment Nr 15. Disbanded in 1806. Facings white. Lace: officers embroidered gold buttonholes, six (in pairs) on and two under each lapel, two above each cuff, two on the pocket flap and two in the small of the back. NCOs and men had the same scheme. NCOs: gold, pointed with a golden tassel; men white, pointed, with six narrow red stripes and a similar tassel; drummers white, with yellow diamond along it, each with a light blue cross, having a black central diamond. Grenadier cap: brass plate, white headband and backing, white braid with red pattern, white-within-red-within-green pompon.. Leibfahne: Pattern Nr 3, crimson centre and cross, white scroll, gold decoration. Ordinair-fahne: white centre and cross, crimson scroll and field, gold decoration.

Infanterie-Regiment Prinz von Preussen Nr 18

Raised in 1698 from a battalion of Infanterie-Regiment Nr 1. 1758 vacant. Disbanded in 1806. Facings pink. Lace: officers silver, embroidered lace buttonholes, with tassels, in pairs, on each lapel, two under each lapel, two over each cuff, two in the small of the back. NCOs and men had the same scheme. NCOs: silver, pointed with a silver tassel; men white, pointed, with white tassels; drummers

Infanterie-Regiment von Forcade de Biaix Nr 23

Infanterie-Regiment von Schwerin Nr 24

Infanterie-Regiment von Kalckstein Nr 25

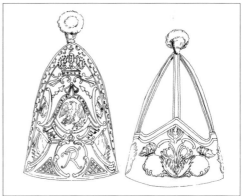

Infanterie-Regiment von Meyerinck Nr 26

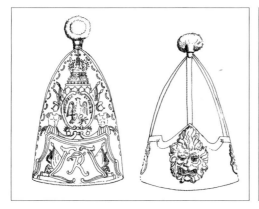

Infanterie-Regiment von Kleist Nr 27

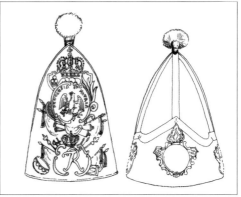

Infanterie-Regiment Herault de Hautcharmoy Nr 28

Infanterie-Regiment Prinz von Preussen grenadier cap. (The Wehrgeschichtliches Museum, Rastatt)

silver or white, with a wide, wavy pink line along it. Grenadier cap: tin plate, black-within-yellow-within red pompon, pink headband and backing, white braid. On the headband were three tin grenades.. Leibfahne: Pattern Nr 2, blue centre, white scroll, silver decoration. Ordinair-fahne: white centre, blue scroll and field, red cross, silver decoration.

Infanterie-Regiment Markgraf Carl Nr 19

Raised in 1702, from Infantry Regiment Nrs 4, 6, 7, 11 and 12. Disbanded in 1806. Facings orange collar and cuffs, no lapels, buff waistcoats and breeches. Lace: officers silver embroidered loops, with tassels, distributed as for Infantry Regiment Nr 10; NCOs gold; men white, pointed, with four orange stripes and two orange zig-zags along it and white and orange tassel; drummers orange with white edges and white Maltese crosses along it. Grenadier cap: brass plate, red headband, buff backing, white braid with buff pattern, white pompon, with a buff centre, having red spots.. Leibfahne: Pattern Nr 6, crimson centre and cross, white scroll, gold decoration. Ordinair-fahne: white centre and cross, crimson scroll and field, gold decoration.

Infanterie-Regiment von Zastrow Nr 20

Raised in 1688 from men of Infanterie-Regiments Nrs 7 and 9. 1756 von Zastrow (killed at Aussig); 1757 von Bornstedt; 1759 von Stutterheim. Disbanded in 1806. Facings scarlet. Lace: officers golden woven buttonholes, with tassels; eight on each lapel, two under each lapel, two over each cuff, two on each pocket, two in the small of the back; NCOs gold lace to cuff, two, pointed, gold buttonholes over each cuff; men lapels, cuffs and cuff flaps of men's coats were edged with white braid, having three blue stripes; drummers white with a central red, white and blue stripe. Grenadier cap: brass plate, crimson headband, dark blue backing, red-within-green-within-white braid, pompon with red centre, white ring, green ring and red outer.. Leibfahne: Pattern Nr 1, dark green centre, white scroll, gold decoration. Ordinair-fahne: white centre, dark green scroll and field, gold decoration.

Infanterie-Regiment von Hülsen Nr 21

Raised in 1713 from men of Infanterie-Regiments Nrs 8, 9, 10, 13 and 17, which had just returned from Dutch service. Disbanded in 1806. Facings scarlet; no lapels. Lace: officers silver embroidered buttonholes with tassels: eight to each side of the coat, three over each cuff and on each pocket flap, two in the small of the back; NCOs gold, pointed with a gold tassel; men white and red, with tassels; drummers silver with two narrow red stripes. Grenadier cap: brass plate, red headband, buff backing, black-within-white braid, black-within-white-within-black-within-red pompon.. Leibfahne: Pattern Nr 2, crimson centre, white scroll, black cross, gold decoration. Ordinair-fahne: white centre, crimson scroll and field, black cross, gold decoration.

Infanterie-Regiment von Hülsen grenadier cap. (The Wehrgeschichtliches Museum, Rastatt)

Infanterie-Regiment von Schultze Nr 29

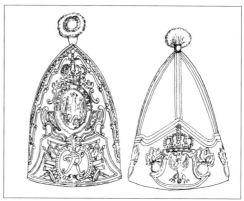

Infanterie-Regiment von Pritz Nr 30

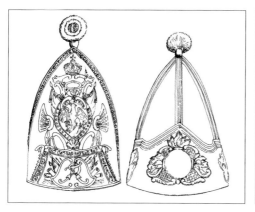

Infanterie-Regiment von Lestwitz Nr 31

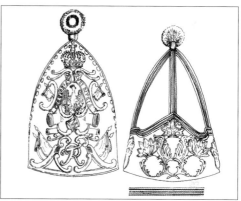

Infanterie-Regiment von Tresckow Nr 32

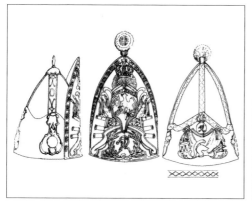

Infanterie-Regiment Baron de la Motte Fouqué Nr 33

Infanterie-Regiment Prinz Ferdinand von Preussen Nr 34

Infanterie-Regiment Prinz Mortiz von Anhalt Nr 22

Raised in 1713, from a battalion of Infanterie-Regiment Nr 6. 1756 1760 von Schenkendorf. Parts of this regiment became the new Infantry Regiment Nr 9 after 1806Facings poppy red, buff waistcoats and breeches. Lace: officers gold, six (in pairs) on and two under each lapel, two over the cuff, two on the pocket, two in the small of the back. NCOs gold, pointed; men: no buttonhole lace on the lapels; cuffs and cuff flaps edged in red and white striped braid; drummers silver. Grenadier cap: brass plate, red headband, dark blue backing, dark blue-within-white braid, pompon with a red centre, dotted blue, within a white ring. Leibfahne: Pattern Nr 2, dark blue centre, white scroll, red cross, gold decoration. Ordinair-fahne: white centre, dark blue scroll and field, red cross, gold decoration.

Infanterie-Regiment von Forcade de Biaix Nr 23

Raised in 1713, from men of Infanterie-Regiments Nrs 1 and 13. 1756 von Puttkammer. Disbanded in 1806. Facings pink. Lace: officers silver; NCOs silver, pointed; men white with six narrow light blue stripes; drummers white, with narrow side stripes and a light blue central line of diamonds, each having a white central square. Grenadier cap: tin plate, white headband, dark blue backing, crimson braid, crimson and white pompon. Leibfahne: Pattern Nr 1, white centre, light blue scroll and corner medallions, silver decoration. Ordinair-fahne: light blue centre and corner medallions, white scroll, silver decoration.

Infanterie-Regiment von Schwerin Nr 24

Raised in 1715. 1756 von Schwerin (killed at Prag); 1757 Freiherr von der Goltz. Disbanded in 1806. Facings poppy red. Lace: officers gold; NCOs gold, knotted; men red and white striped; drummers white with a yellow, black and red pattern. Grenadier cap: brass plate, red headband, blue backing, white braid with red zig-zag, yellow pompon with red centre within white and black rings. Leibfahne: Pattern Nr 2, dark green centre and cross, white scroll, gold decoration. Ordinair-fahne: white centre and cross, dark green scroll and field, gold decoration.

Infanterie-Regiment von Kalckstein Nr 25

Raised in 1713. 1756 von Kalckstein; 1760 von Ramm. Disbanded in 1806. Facings scarlet. Lace: officers gold; men pointed, white with six narrow light blue stripes, with blue and white tassel; drummers crimson with a white and dark blue pattern. Grenadier cap: brass plate, white headband, red backing, white braid with three black lines along it, white pompon with a red centre inside a yellow ring. Leibfahne: Pattern Nr 3, dark green centre, white scroll, lemon yellow cross, gold decoration. Ordinair-fahne: white centre, dark green scroll and field, lemon yellow cross, gold decoration.

Infanterie-Regiment von Schwerin, 1757. The white gaiters were worn in summer only; in winter they were black. Note the officer's complex hairstyle and the company flags. (Knötel, I 18)

Infanterie-Regiment Prinz Heinrich von Preussen Nr 35

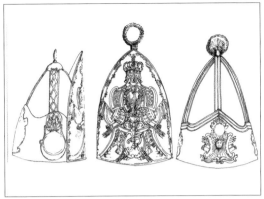

Infanterie-Regiment von Münchow Nr 36

Infanterie-Regiment von Kurssell Nr 37

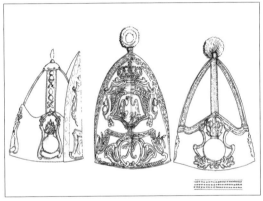

Infanterie-Regiment von Brandes Nr 38

Infanterie-Regiment Jung Braunschweig Nr 39

Infanterie-Regiment von Kreytzen Nr 40

Infanterie-Regiment von Meyerinck Nr 26

Raised in 1714. 1758 von Wedel; 1761 von Linden. Disbanded in 1806. Facings brick red. Lace: officers gold; NCOs gold, pointed; men orange and white with tassels. Grenadier cap: brass plate, white headband and backing, white braid with red edges, white pompon with red centre. Leibfahne: Pattern Nr 2, lemon yellow centre and cross, white scroll, silver decoration. Ordinair-fahne: white centre and cross, lemon yellow scroll and field, silver decoration.

Infanterie-Regiment von Kleist Nr 27

Raised in 1715. 1756 von Kleist (Friedrich Ulrich 'Alt-Kleist') 1757 von der Auffenberg; 1759 von Lindstedt. Disbanded in 1806. Facings poppy red. Lace: officers gold; NCOs narrow gold, oblong; men narrow silver, oblong; drummers silver. Grenadier cap: brass plate, white headband, red backing, white braid, red pompon with yellow centre. Leibfahne: Pattern Nr 2, dark blue centre, white scroll, the vertical arms of the cross are yellow, the horizontal arms red, gold decoration. Ordinair-fahne: white centre, dark blue scroll and field, same cross as on the Leibfahne, gold decoration.

Infanterie-Regiment Herault de Hautcharmoy Nr 28

Raised in 1723. 1758 von Münchow; 1758 von Kreytzen; 1759 von Ramin; 1760 von Thiele. Disbanded in 1806. Facings buff. Lace: officers silver; NCOs silver; men none; drummers white with two yellow zig-zags along it. Grenadier cap: tin plate, blue headband, red backing, white braid, orange pompon. Leibfahne: Pattern Nr 3, black centre, white scroll, light blue cross, gold decoration. Ordinair-fahne: white centre, light blue scroll and cross, gold decoration.

Infanterie-Regiment von Schultze Nr 29

Raised in 1725. 1756 von Borck; 1757 von Schultz; 1758 von Wedel; 1758 von Knoblauch. Disbanded in 1806. Facings crimson. Lace: officers gold; NCOs narrow gold; men white with narrow red edges; drummers white with two red stripes outside two blue stripes, with a narrow central white stripe. Grenadier cap: brass plate, light red headband, white backing, white braid with dark blue central stripe edged in red, white pompon with dark blue centre in a light red ring. Leibfahne: Pattern Nr 3, dark blue centre white scroll, yellow cross, gold decoration. Ordinair-fahne: white centre, dark blue scroll and field, yellow cross, gold decoration.

Infanterie-Regiment von Pritz Nr 30

Raised in 1728. 1757 von Kannacher; 1759 von Stutterheim. The 3rd Battalion became the new Infanterie-Regiment Nr 10 after 1806. Facings buff, no lapels or collar. Lace: officers silver embroidered, 8 (in pairs) to each side of the chest, two above each cuff, two in the small of the back; NCOs silver; men white; drummers white, with two blue lines down the sides and a red central line. Grenadier cap: brass plate, light red headband, white backing, white braid edged dark blue, white pompon with red centre in a dark blue ring. Leibfahne: Pattern Nr 3, dark green centre, white scroll, black cross, gold decoration. Ordinair-fahne: white centre, dark green scroll and field, black cross, gold decoration.

Infanterie-Regiment von Lestwitz Nr 31

Raised on 1 February 1729 from men of the Infanterie-Regiments 9, 10, 28, 29. The 3rd Battalion of this regiment became the new Infantry Regiment Nr 11 after 1806. Facings pink, no lapels. Lace: officers scalloped gold (to the hat only, no buttonholes); NCOs gold; to hat, cuffs and cuff flaps only: men none; drummers pink with two narrow white lines enclosing a row of white diamonds. Grenadier cap: brass plate, pink headband and backing, white braid with pink central stripe edged yellow, white pompon with pink centre in a yellow ring. Leibfahne: Pattern Nr 3, light blue centre and cross, white scroll, gold decoration. Ordinair-fahne: white centre and cross, light blue field, gold decoration.

Infanterie-Regiment Graf von Wied zu Neuwied Nr 41

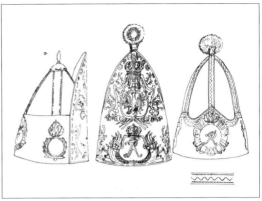

Infanterie-Regiment Markgraf von Brandenburg Nr 42

Infanterie-Regiment von Kalsow Nr 43

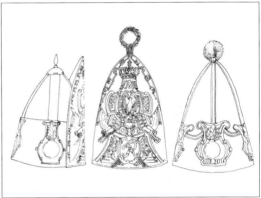

Infanterie-Regiment von Jungkenn Müntzer Nr 44

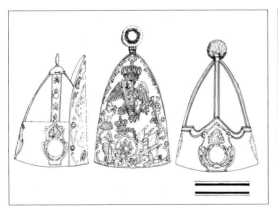

Infanterie-Regiment von Dossow Nr 45

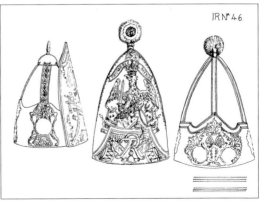

Infanterie-Regiment Duke von Württemberg Nr 46

Infanterie-Regiment Baron de la Motte Fouqué grenadier cap. (The Wehrgeschichtliches Museum, Rastatt)

Infanterie-Regiment von Tresckow Nr 32

Raised in 1743, from two garrison battalions (Geldern and Lippstadt). Disbanded in 1806. Facings buff; buttons brass. Lace: officers gold scalloped lace to the hat only; no buttonholes; NCOs gold to cuff and cuff flaps only; men none; drummers yellow edges, blue central band with white and red lozenges and diamonds. Grenadier cap: brass plate, buff headband, red backing, yellow braid with red central stripe, flanked by white, then blue stripes, red pompon with yellow centre within dark blue then white rings. Leibfahne: Pattern Nr 5, blue centre, white scroll, black upright cross, red saltire, gold decoration. Ordinair-fahne: white centre, blue scroll and field, crosses as for Leibfahne, gold decoration.

Infanterie-Regiment Baron de la Motte Fouqué Nr 33

Raised in 1734. Taken into the Prussian Army in 1736; converted to a fusilier regiment in 1740. The 3rd Battalion of this regiment became the new Infantry Regiment Nr 12 after 1806. Facings white, buttons brass. Lace: officers scalloped gold edging to the hat, no buttonholes; NCOs gold to top and back of cuffs: men none; drummers white with three blue stripes. Fusilier cap: brass plate, yellow headband and top. Grenadier cap: brass plate, orange headband and backing, white braid with orange, open diamond pattern along it, white pompon with red centre in an orange ring. Leibfahne: Pattern Nr 1, blue centre, white scroll, silver decoration. Ordinair-fahne: white centre, blue scroll and filed, silver decoration.

Infanterie-Regiment Prinz Ferdinand von Preussen Nr 34

Raised in 1740, from the 2nd Battalion of Infantry Regiment Nr 15. Disbanded in 1806. Facings poppy red, buttons white, buff waistcoat and breeches. Lace: officers scalloped silver edging to the hat, no buttonholes; NCOs silver, to top and back of cuffs: men none; drummers a dark blue central stripe, flanked by yellow then red stripes, narrow white edges. Fusilier cap: tin plate and headband, dark blue backing. Grenadier cap: as for fusiliers plus white braid and dark blue pompon with red centre in a white ring. This regiment is unique, in that the Leib- and Ordinair-fahnen were of different designs. Leibfahne: Pattern Nr 1, white centre, scroll and field, bearing a very narrow, light blue, upright cross, silver decoration. Ordinair-fahne: light blue centre, narrow, upright cross and narrow saltire, white scroll, silver decoration.

Infanterie-Regiment Prinz Heinrich von Preussen Nr 35

Raised in 1740 from part of Infanterie-Regiment Nr 6. Disbanded in 1806. Facings, waistcoat and breeches sulphur yellow, buttons white. Lace: officers silver scalloped hat edging, no buttonholes; NCOs silver to top and back of cuff; men none; drummers two rows of light blue and yellow checks. Fusilier cap: tin plate, red-white-red pompon, lemon yellow headband and backing, white braid with red side stripes and hatching. On the

Infanterie-Regiment Prinz Heinrich von Preussen grenadier cap. (The Wehrgeschichtliches Museum, Rastatt)

Infanterie-Regiment von Wietersheim Nr 47

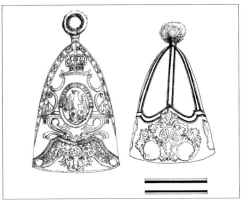

Infanterie-Regiment Erbprinz von Hessen-Kassel Nr 48

Infanterie-Regiment von Seers Nr 49

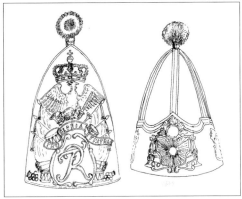

Infanterie-Regiment von Weitersheim Nr 50

Infanterie-Regiment von Wylich Nr 51

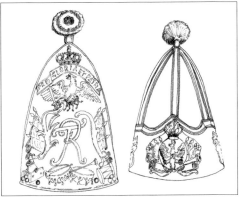

Infanterie-Regiment von Blanckensee Nr 52

rear of the headband was an eagle on crossed cannon barrels and trophies in tin; tin flames to each side of the headband. Grenadier cap: as for fusiliers, but with red and white braid, red pompon with red centre within a white ring. Leibfahne: Pattern Nr 1, light blue centre, white scroll, silver decoration. Ordinair-fahne: white centre and scroll, light blue field, silver decoration.

Infanterie-Regiment von Münchow Nr 36

Raised in June 1740. Disbanded in 1806. Facings white (no lapels) buttons yellow. Lace: officers gold scalloped edging to the hat; NCOs gold to top and back of the cuffs; men none; drummers white with blue side stripes. Fusilier cap: brass plate, white headband and backing, white and light blue braid, white-within-light blue pompon. Grenadier cap: as for fusiliers, plus white braid with light blue edging and central stripe, light blue pompon with a white centre. Leibfahne: Pattern Nr 1, light, purple-brown centre, white scroll, gold decoration. Ordinair-fahne: white centre, light purple-brown scroll and field, gold decoration.

Infanterie-Regiment von Kurssell Nr 37

Raised in 1740. 1758 von Braun. Disbanded in 1806. Facings crimson (no lapels), buttons yellow. Lace: officers gold scalloped hat edging; NCOs gold to top and back of cuff; men none; drummers white with two red stripes, each having a dark blue central line. Fusilier cap: brass plate, scarlet top and headband. Grenadier cap: as for fusiliers plus white braid with a scarlet central stripe, scarlet pompon with a white centre. Leibfahne: Pattern Nr 1, light green centre, white scroll, gold decoration. Ordinair-fahne: white centre, light green scroll and field, gold decoration.

Infanterie-Regiment von Brandes Nr 38

Raised in 1740. 1756 von Zastrow. Disbanded in 1806. Facings scarlet, buttons yellow. Lace: officers scalloped golden hat edging; NCOs gold to top and back of cuffs; men none; drummers white with three scarlet stripes. Fusilier cap: brass plate, light blue top and headband. Grenadier cap: as for fusiliers, plus light yellow braid with two white stripes, light yellow pompon with light yellow centre in a white ring. Leibfahne: Pattern Nr 1, crimson centre, white scroll, gold decoration. Ordinair-fahne: white centre, crimson scroll and field, gold decoration.

Infanterie-Regiment Jung Braunschweig Nr 39

Raised in 1740. 1758 vacant. Disbanded in 1806. Often known as Jung Braunschweig. Facings, waistcoat and breeches lemon yellow (no lapels), white buttons. Lace: officers scalloped silver hat edging; NCOs silver to top and back of cuffs; men none; drummers white with yellow open diamonds flanked by yellow triangles, points outwards, between the diamonds. Fusilier cap: tin plate, lemon yellow top and headband. Grenadier cap: as for fusiliers, plus white braid and a white pompon. Leibfahne: Pattern Nr 3, dark lemon yellow centre and cross, white scroll, silver decoration. Ordinair-fahne: white centre and cross, dark lemon yellow scroll and field, silver decoration.

Infanterie-Regiment von Kreytzen Nr 40

Raised in 1732 by the Prinz von Sachsen-Eisenach, taken into Prussian service in 1740. 1759 von Gabelenz. Disbanded in 1806. Facings, waistcoats and breeches raspberry pink, buttons white. Lace: officers scalloped silver hat edging, three silver buttonholes on and two under each lapel, two on the cuff, on the pocket flap and in the small of the back; NCOs silver to top and back of cuffs; men none; drummers pink with white side stripes and a white zig-zag along the centre. Fusilier cap: tin plate, raspberry pink top and headband. Grenadier cap: as for fusiliers plus white braid with raspberry pink pattern, raspberry pink pompon, with similar centre in a white ring. Leibfahne: Pattern Nr 1, but the usual central laurel wreath is replaced on both flags by the collar of the Order of the Black Eagle, outside a ring of golden oak leaves. Pink centre, white scroll, gold decoration. Ordinair-fahne: white centre, pink scroll and field, gold decoration.

Infanterie-Regiment Graf von Wied zu Neuwied Nr 41

Raised in 1716. Taken into Prussian service from Württemberg in 1741. Disbanded in 1806. Facings light crimson, buttons yellow. Lace: officers scalloped gold hat edging and two buttonholes under the lapels, two in the small of the back; NCOs gold to top and back of cuffs; men yellow; drummers yellow. Fusilier cap: brass plate, light crimson top and headband. Grenadier cap: as for fusiliers, plus white braid with light crimson central stripe, light crimson pompon, with similar centre in a white ring. Leibfahne: Pattern Nr 1, buff centre, white scroll, silver decoration. Ordinair-fahne: white centre, buff scroll and field, silver decoration.

Infanterie-Regiment Markgraf von Brandenburg Nr 42

Raised in 1741, mainly from Austrians captured at the fall of Brieg in that year. 1756 von Schenkendorf, 1760 von Kliest. Disbanded in 1806. Facings orange, buttons yellow. Lace: officers scalloped gold hat edging; NCOs gold to top and back of cuffs; men none; drummers white with two rows of orange zig-zags. Fusilier cap: brass-fronted with black top and headband. Grenadier cap: brass plate, orange headband and backing, white braid with this orange side lines and a central orange zig-zag, white pompon, with a white centre in an orange ring. Leibfahne: Pattern Nr 3, orange centre and cross, white scroll, gold decoration. Ordinair-fahne: orange centre and field, white scroll and cross, gold decoration.

Infanterie-Regiment von Kalsow Nr 43

Raised on 10 August 1741 from the garrison of Breslau. 1756 von Kalsow, 1757 von Kalkreuth, 1758 von Bredow, 1760 von Ziethen. Disbanded in 1806. Facings light orange (no lapels), buttons yellow. Lace: officers scalloped gold hat edging; NCOs gold to top and back of cuffs; men none; drummers white with two orange side stripes and a central row of open, orange diamonds. Fusilier cap: brass-fronted, light orange headband, white top. Grenadier cap: as for fusiliers, plus white braid edged yellow, orange pompon with a white centre. Leibfahne: Pattern Nr 1, white centre and field, light green scroll, gold decoration. Ordinair-fahne: light green centre and field, white scroll, gold decoration.

Infanterie-Regiment von Jungkenn Müntzer Nr 44

Raised in January 1742, with men of Infanterie-Regiment Nr 28 as the cadre. 1759 von Hofmann; 1760 von Grant. Disbanded in 1806. Facings red, no lapels. Lace: officers plain gold hat edging; eight embroidered gold buttonholes to each side on the chest, two on and two over each cuff, two in the small of the back; NCOs gold to top and back of cuffs; men red, with white tassels; drummers yellow, with two red side stripes and black, pointed crosses in the centre. Fusilier cap: brass-fronted, with black top and headband. Grenadier cap: brass plate, light red headband, buff backing, light blue braid edged black, black pompon with light blue centre. Leibfahne: Pattern Nr 3, light blue centre, white scroll and field, red cross, gold decoration. Ordinair-fahne: white centre, light blue scroll and field, red cross, gold decoration.

Infanterie-Regiment von Dossow Nr 45

Raised in August 1743 from men of Infantry Regiment Nr 31. 1757 Hessen-Kassel. Disbanded in 1806. Facings scarlet, buttons yellow. Lace: officers narrow gold hat edging, plain gold buttonholes (two under each lapel,

Infanterie-Regiment von Dossow fusilier cap. Brass plate, black headband, headpiece and backing, brass 'braid'; on the headband were three brass grenades.

two in the small of the back); NCOs gold to top and back of cuffs; men white with red and white tassels; drummers white, with two red side stripes and a row of dark blue, diagonal bars across the centre. Fusilier cap: brass-fronted, with black headband and top. Grenadier cap: brass plate, royal blue headband, white backing, mustard yellow braid with black, then pink side stripes, pink pompon with mustard yellow centre in a black ring. Leibfahne: Pattern Nr 3, dark blue centre, white scroll, orange cross, gold decoration. Ordinair-fahne: white centre, light blue scroll, orange cross, gold decoration.

Infanterie-Regiment Duke von Württemberg (nominal) Nr 46

Raised in 1743. 1756 von Schöning; 1757 von Bülow. Disbanded in 1806. Facings black with yellow buttons; buff waistcoat and breeches. Lace: officers none; NCOs gold; men none; drummers yellow with red side stripes and a row of black and red central designs. Fusilier cap: brass-fronted, with black headband and buff top. Grenadier cap: brass plate, black headband, buff backing, red-edged braid, with a black central stripe, edged yellow, red pompon with a black centre in a yellow ring. Leibfahne: Pattern Nr 2, buff centre, white scroll, black cross, gold decoration. Ordinair-fahne: white centre, buff scroll and field, black cross, gold decoration.

Infanterie-Regiment von Wietersheim Nr 47

Raised in 1743. 1757 von Rohr; 1759 von Grabow. Disbanded in 1806. Facings lemon yellow, buttons yellow. Lace: officers scalloped gold hat edging, no buttonholes; NCOs gold; men none; drummers yellow, with red side stripes and the same central design as for Infanterie-Regiment Nr 46, but in light blue and red. Fusilier cap: brass-fronted with lemon yellow top and headband. Grenadier cap: brass plate, lemon yellow headband and backing, lemon yellow braid with a red central stripe, lemon yellow pompon with a red centre. Leibfahne: Pattern Nr 2, lemon yellow centre, white scroll and field, light blue cross, gold decoration. Ordinair-fahne: white centre, lemon yellow scroll and field, light blue cross, gold decoration.

Infanterie-Regiment Erbprinz von Hessen-Kassel Nr 48

Raised in 1743 as a garrison battalion; converted to a fusilier regiment in 1756. Disbanded in 1806. Facings poppy red, buttons yellow. Lace: officers narrow plain gold hat edging, six embroidered gold buttonholes on and two under each lapel, two over each cuff and in the small of the back, three on each pocket flap; NCOs gold; men white with orange tassels; drummers red edges with white diamonds along them, having orange centres; white central stripe with white and orange bars along it. Fusilier cap: brass-fronted, with blue top and headband. Grenadier cap: brass plate, buff headband, light red backing, light blue braid having an orange central stripe. Flanked with black lines, light blue pompon with an orange centre in a black ring. Leibfahne: Pattern Nr 3, crimson centre, white scroll, light blue cross, silver decoration. Ordinair-fahne: white centre, crimson scroll and field, light blue cross, silver decoration.

Infanterie-Regiment von Seers Nr 49

Raised in 1742, in Neisse, as a regiment of pioneers and miners; converted to a fusilier regiment in 1758. 1758 von Diericke. Disbanded in 1806. Facings dark blue (no lapels), white buttons, dark orange waistcoat and buttons. Lace: officers scalloped silver hat edging, eight embroidered silver buttonholes to each side of the chest, two on each cuff and in the small of the back, three on each pocket flap; NCOs silver; men none; drummers white outer edges, dark blue inner stripes flanking an orange central stripe with a dark blue worm. Fusilier cap: white-fronted with blue top and dark orange headband. Grenadier cap: tin plate, dark orange headband, blue backing, braid and pompon unknown. Leibfahne 1756–1758: unique pattern, white centre, scroll and field, central black eagle superimposed on an orange, upright cross, limited to within the central filed and surrounded by silver leaves and six groups of entrenching tools, flaming grenades in each corner replaced the corner medallions, no grenades in the centres of each side, silver decoration. Ordinair-fahne: same design; orange centre, scroll and field, white cross, silver decoration. Leibfahne from 1758: Pattern Nr 1; light brown centre, white scroll and field, silver decoration. Ordinair-fahne: white centre, light brown scroll and field, silver decoration.

Garrison Regiments

These regiments served in the field as needed. Their uniforms were very plain, without lace buttonholes, collars or lapels. There were two rows of six buttons, in pairs, on the chest, two on each cuff flap or the cuff, two on the horizontal pocket flap, one on the shoulder strap and one at the join of the turnbacks. Waistcoat and breeches were dark blue, turnbacks were red, gaiters black, belts white. Facings were shown only on the cuff. If the cuff were in the Swedish (plain round) style, the buttons would be on the cuff. For those units with Prussian cuffs, the two buttons would be on the dark blue, red-edged, square flap above the cuff. Officers wore a narrow hat edging in the button colour, the usual sashes, silver and gold gorgets, carried canes and wore buff gloves. NCO distinctions were as for the line regiments. Drummers wore dark blue swallow's nests with four vertical stripes in the button colour.

Until 1763, all garrison infantry regiments bore colours of the following designs. The Leibfahne was all white, in the centre was the crowned cipher 'FR' within a laurel wreath; in the centre of each side was a small, flaming grenade; in each corner was a long, flaming grenade. As with the line, the flames pointed towards the centre. Finial, cords and tassels were as for the line. Regiments Nrs 1 to 4 also had narrow, straight black corner piles. The Ordinair-fahne had the same design as before but the cloths were coloured according to the regiment involved.

Infanterie-Regiment von Luck Nr 1

Raised in 1718. 1757 von Puttkamer. Disbanded in 1788. Dark blue facings, white buttons, Prussian cuff. Grenadier cap: tin plate, red headband, blue backing, white braid with a yellow central zig-zag, flanked by two red zig-zags, green pompon with red centre. Leibfahne: gold embroidery, black corner piles. Ordinair-fahne: dark blue field, black corner piles, gold embroidery.

Infanterie-Regiment Alt-Sydow Nr 2

Raised in 1717. Disbanded in 1788. White facings and buttons, Prussian cuff. Grenadier cap: tin plate, red headband, blue backing, white braid with a central blue zig-zag and flanking red zig-zags, green pompon. Leibfahne: black corner piles, gold embroidery. Ordinair-fahne: dark blue field, black corner piles, gold embroidery.

Infanterie-Regiment von Grolman Nr 3

Raised in 1718. Disbanded in 1788. Dark blue facings, brass buttons, Prussian cuff. Grenadier cap: brass plate, white headband and backing, white braid with black edging, white pompon with black centre and narrow black lines down the sides. Leibfahne: gold embroidery, black corner piles. Ordinair-fahne: dark blue field, black corner piles, gold embroidery.

Infanterie-Regiment von Grape Nr 4

Raised in 1740. 1759 von Mohrenstamm; 1760 von Lettow. Disbanded in 1788. Dark blue facings, brass buttons, Prussian cuff. Grenadier cap: brass plate and headband, red backing, white braid, red within white pompon. Leibfahne: gold embroidery, black corner piles. Ordinair-fahne: dark blue field, gold embroidery black corner piles.

Infanterie-Regiment von Mütschefahl Nr 5

Raised in 1741. 1759 Jung-Sydow. Disbanded in 1788. Black facings, brass buttons, Prussian cuff. Grenadier cap: pompon. Leibfahne: gold embroidery. Ordinair-fahne: black field, gold embroidery.

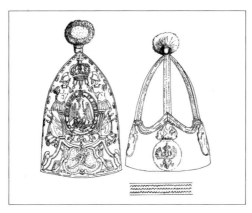

*Infanterie-Regiment von Luck Nr 1
(Garrison Regiment)*

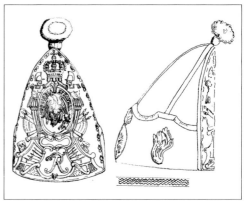

*Infanterie-Regiment Alt-Sydow Nr 2 (Garrison
Regiment)*

Infanterie-Regiment von Mütschefahl Nr 5 (Garrison Regiment)

*Infanterie-Regiment von Lattorf Nr 6
(Garrison Regiment)*

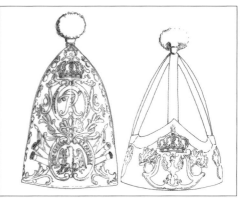

*Infanterie-Regiment von Lange Nr 7
(Garrison Regiment)*

THE KINGDOM OF PRUSSIA

Infanterie-Regiment von Lattorf Nr 6

Raised in 1741. Disbanded in 1788. Orange facings, white buttons, Prussian cuff. Grenadier cap: tin plate, bright orange headband and backing, white braid with orange side lines and central hashes, white pompon with white centre in an orange ring. Leibfahne: silver embroidery. Ordinair-fahne: turquoise field, silver embroidery.

Infanterie-Regiment von Lange Nr 7

Raised in 1741. Disbanded in 1788. Crimson facings, brass buttons, Prussian cuff. Grenadier cap: brass plate, crimson headband and backing, royal blue braid, white pompon. Leibfahne: gold embroidery. Ordinair-fahne: red field, gold embroidery.

Infanterie-Regiment von Nettelhorst Nr 8

Raised in 1741. 1757 von Wickeradt. Disbanded in 1788. Black facings, white buttons, Prussian cuff. Grenadier cap: tin plate, black headband and backing, white braid, raspberry pink pompon. Leibfahne: silver embroidery. Ordinair-fahne: dark blue field, silver embroidery.

Infanterie-Regiment de la Motte Nr 9

Raised in 1743. 1759 von Bonin. Disbanded in 1788. Black facings, brass buttons, Swedish cuff. Grenadier cap: brass plate, buff headband, light red backing, light blue braid having an orange central stripe, flanked with black lines, light blue pompon with an orange centre in a black ring. Leibfahne: gold embroidery. Ordinair-fahne: orange field, gold embroidery.

Infanterie-Regiment von Blanckensee Nr 10

Raised in 1743 in Bohemia. Disbanded in 1788. Black facings, white buttons, Swedish cuff. Grenadier cap: tin plate, black headband and backing, deep yellow braid and pompon. Leibfahne: silver embroidery. Ordinair-fahne: light blue field, silver embroidery.

Infanterie-Regiment von Manteuffel Nr 11

Raised in 1743. 1760 von Ingerslaben. Disbanded in 1788. Crimson facings, white buttons, Prussian cuff. Grenadier cap: tin plate, deep crimson headband and backing, white braid, deep crimson pompon. Leibfahne: silver embroidery. Ordinair-fahne: crimson field, silver embroidery.

Infanterie-Regiment von Kalckreuth Nr 12

Raised in 1744. Disbanded in 1788. Black facings, brass buttons, Swedish cuff. Grenadier cap: brass plate and headband, bright red backing, yellow braid, white pompon with bright red centre. Leibfahne: gold embroidery. Ordinair-fahne: light blue field, gold embroidery.

Infanterie-Regiment von Salmuth Nr 13

Raised in 1743. Disbanded in 1788. Black facings, brass buttons, Swedish cuff. Grenadier cap: plate, headband, backing, braid, pompon. Leibfahne: gold embroidery. Ordinair-fahne: orange field, gold embroidery.

New Regiment

Raised 1742. No Chef. Disbanded in 1763. This unit was formed from men unfit for field service. Originally the cuffs were red, Prussian; they later changed to black, Swedish style with white buttons. No colours were presented.

Feld-Jägers

These were first raised in 1740. All uniform details were as for the fusiliers of line infantry except as noted below. Dark green tunic and turnbacks, red collar, shoulder straps, Swedish cuffs and piping to turnbacks, yellow buttons. Grey breeches, short, black gaiters, black leatherwork.

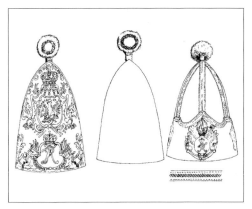

*Infanterie-Regiment von Nettelhorst Nr 8
(Garrison Regiment)*

*Infanterie-Regiment von Blanckensee Nr 10 (Garrison
Regiment)*

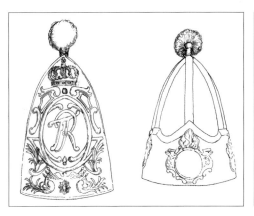

*Infanterie-Regiment von Manteuffel Nr 11
(Garrison Regiment)*

*Infanterie-Regiment von Kalckreuth Nr 12
(Garrison Regiment)*

*Infanterie-Regiment von Weitersheim Nr 17 grenadier
cap. (The Wehrgeschichtliches Museum, Rastatt)*

*Infanterie-Regiment von Hauss Nr 55 grenadier cap.
(The Wehrgeschichtliches Museum, Rastatt)*

Feld-Jäger-Corps zu Pferde

Raised 1740. Canary green coat, buff leather breeches, boots; white waistcoat, poppy red cuffs and collar, gold aiguillette. Officers wore eight embroidered gold loops to each lapel, two on each cuff, two on the pocket flap; four in the small of the back. A wide scalloped gold hat edging. Jägers' plain hats had plumes, white over black; green and silver hat cords and fist straps.

Saxon Regiments

These regiments were taken into the Prussian Army in October 1756. They were clothed in fusilier uniforms (dark blue coats, no collars or lapels, plain round cuffs) and the waistcoats and breeches were in the facing colour. All badges of rank were as for the Prussian Army. It seems that they all wore tricorns instead of fusilier caps. Desertion was rife; most of these units melted away very quickly; see the details below. As with the Prussian regiments, the *Leibfahne* was white, with coloured corner flames. The details of the regimental colours give first the background, second the corner flames.

Regiment			Disbanded	Facings	Buttons	Colours
50	von Wietersheim	ex-von Rochow	30 July 1757	buff	white	pink, green
51	von Wylich	ex-Graf Bruhl	31 July 1757	white	yellow	crimson, dark blue
52	von Blanckensee	ex-Garde zu Fuss	2 August 1757	buff	white	dark blue, crimson
53	von Manstein	ex-Minkwitz	6 May 1757	buff	white	black, red
54	von Saldern	ex-Prinz Gotha	captured 1760 at Wittenberg	white	yellow	red, green
55	von Hauss	ex-Fürst Lubomirsky	1763	white	yellow	white, light blue
56	von Lön	ex-Prinz Friedrich August	28 March 1757	buff	yellow	black, yellow
57	Jung-Braunschweig	ex-Prinz Xaver	1st Battalion 30 March 1757; 2nd Battalion 25 November 1757	buff	yellow	light blue, yellow
58	von Flemming	ex-Prinz Clemens	August 1757	white	white	green, red
59	Prinz Friedrich Wilhelm	ex-Prinz Max	3 August 1756	white	white	red, yellow

Cavalry

Kürassiers

From early times (1688) the coat worn by these regiments of heavy horse was usually a buff leather 'Kollet', which had excellent protective properties against sword cuts and was relatively light and flexible. Facings were worn on the collar, the Swedish cuffs and on the narrow shoulder straps. The short turnbacks were in the coat colour. Apart from the colour of the facings and buttons, each regiment was distinguished by a braid edging to the front of the coat, the cuffs, turnbacks, waistcoats and carbine bandoliers. The skirts of officers' tunics were to the knee; those of the men were cut short so that they just covered the buttocks. The breeches were in buff leather; white gauntlets and knee cuffs were worn, as were stiff high-jacked boots.

Headgear was a large bicorn with national cockade, black loop and regimental button. Under the bicorn an iron skull cap was worn when in action. White plumes were worn for parades from 1762 onwards. For NCOs the plume tip was black, for officers the base was black. From about 1735 onwards, the leather tunics were replaced with white cloth items; only Kürassier-Regiment Nr 2 retained the yellow colour and were then known as 'the yellow riders'. Waistcoats were originally in the coat colour, but in 1735 they were changed to be in the regimental facing colour. Only the Gens d'Armes retained them in blue as before. After the First Silesian War (1741–1742) the facings of some regiments changed; they then remained the same until 1806. From about 1720 a two-piece metal cuirass was worn, but from 1735 the back plate was discarded and the front plate held in place by straps. The cuirass (breastplate) was polished for the Garde du Corps, blackened for the other regiments. These breastplates were abandoned under Frederick the Great. The cuirasses of officers were edged in gilt metal and their shoulder straps were covered in gilt plates. On the top centre of the breastplate they wore the crowned Prussian crest in trophies of arms, all gilt. A waist sash in the facing colour was worn over the tunic.

Leatherwork was white. Weapons were a brace of pistols and a heavy, straight-bladed sword. A pouch (very much like the sabretasche of the hussars) was carried from the waist belt and sat high up on the left hip. It was in the facing colour, edged with the regimental lace and bore various designs. Harnesses were black with steel fittings. Holster covers and the square shabraques were in either the facing colour or the colour of the coat and were edged in the regimental lace. The designs on the holster covers and in the rear corners of the shabraque varied from regiment to regiment.

Apart from the daily uniform, officers also had a white state uniform with lapels, Swedish cuffs and collar in the colour of their waistcoats. On each lapel were six embroidered lace loops, two under them, two on the cuff, two on each pocket flap and four in the small of the back. The small clothes were buff.

The lids of officers' cartouches were in the facing colour, edged in the regimental braid, usually enclosing trophies of arms and the crowned royal cipher. Officers' cartouche lids of Kürassier-Regiments Nr 7, 8, 9, 11 and 12 bore the crowned black Prussian eagle on trophies of arms. Officers of each regiment wore gold or silver lace decorations to their buttonholes that were unique to their regiment; they also wore the usual waist sashes. Those of NCOs were in the facing colour, edged in braid in the button colour, bearing a crowned round plate showing the royal cipher. The badges of rank for NCOs varied from regiment to regiment, but they all wore the black and white quartered pompons and black and white sword straps. Troopers had black pouch lids with a round

Old style Prussian cavalry standard with FWR cypher.

brass plate bearing the Prussian eagle. NCOs cuffs were decorated with gold or silver lace, the pattern varying from regiment to regiment. Standard bearers had standard bandoliers in the facing colour, edged and fringed in the button colour. The finial of the pike was in the form of a lance. Standards were decorated with black and silver cords and tassels, reaching down to about two-thirds of the height of the cloth.

The old pattern standards (presented under King Friedrich Wilhelm) were square and made of damask, fringed in the button colour. The Leibstandarte had a central disc in the colour of the Eskadrons-Standarte; the field was entirely white. In the central disc was a black eagle, over low hills, climbing towards a sun on the right; to the left of the eagle was a white scroll bearing 'NON SOLI CEDIT'. The disc was crowned and surrounded by green laurel leaves, tied with red ribbon. In each corner were crowned green laurel leaves enclosing the cipher 'FWR', also tied with red ribbons. Decoration was in the button colour.

The central disc in the new style standards (presented by Frederick the Great) had a black eagle under a scroll bearing 'PRO GLORIA ET PATRIA'; the crowned, green central and corner wreaths enclosed the cipher 'FR'. Some new pattern standards had plain fields, others had wide corner rays. If the central disc were black, the eagle would be gold.

The following regiments had five squadrons each, except the Garde du Corps which had three. Their regimental names are per their Chefs in 1756, their numbers those assigned in 1806.

Kürassier-Regiment von Buddenbrock Nr 1

Raised on 10 June 1666. 1757 von Krockow (Alt-Krockow); 1759 von Schlabberndorf. Disbanded in 1806. Buff tunic and breeches, poppy red collar, cuffs, sash and waistcoat. The regimental lace was white with three red stripes; the officers' lace was silver. Holster covers and the shabraque bore the crowned royal cipher within a braid edging. All five standards were lost at the capitulation of Pasewalk on 29 October 1806. Leibstandarte: old pattern, yellow centre, white field, green wreaths, gold embroidery. Eskadrons-Standarte: white centre and corner medallions, yellow field, green wreaths, gold embroidery.

Kürassier-Regiment Prinz von Preussen Nr 2

Raised in 1655. 1730 Prinz August Wilhem von Preussen; 1758 Prinz Heinrich von Preussen. Disbanded in 1806. Lemon yellow tunics, white breeches, crimson facings and braid (the latter was white on the waistcoat). Officers' lace was silver. Sabretasche, holster covers and the shabraque were red and bore the crowned royal cipher within braid edging. Leibstandarte: new pattern, red centre, white field and corner medallions, yellow corner piles, silver embroidery. Eskadrons-Standarte: white centre and corner medallions, red field, yellow corner piles, silver embroidery. All five standards were lost at the capitulation of Ratkau on 7 November 1806.

Leibregiment zu Pferde von Katte Nr 3

Raised in 1672. 1747 von Katte; 1758 von Lentulus. Disbanded in 1806. Buff tunic and breeches, dark blue facings, dark blue velvet braid with a wide central white stripe; officers' lace gold. Sabretasche, holster covers and the shabraque were dark blue and bore the crowned royal cipher within braid edging. Leibstandarte: old pattern, all white, gold embroidery. Eskadrons-Standarte: as for the Leibstandarte. All five standards were lost at the capitulation of Prenzlau on 28 October 1806.

Kürassier-Regiment von Gessler Nr 4

Raised in 1674. 1733 von Gessler, 1757 von Schmettau. Became the new Kürassier-Regiment Nr 1 in 1807. Buff tunic and breeches, black facings, white braid with three lines of dark blue squares; officers' lace gold. The sabretasche was black with the crowned royal cipher and regimental lace. Holster covers and the shabraque were white and bore a crowned shield bearing the crowned Prussian eagle within braid edging. Leibstandarte: old pattern, red centre, white field, gold embroidery. Eskadrons-Standarte: white centre and corner medallions, red field, gold embroidery.

Kürassier-Regiment Markgraf Friedrich von Brandenburg Nr 5

Raised in 1683. 1756 von Krosigk (killed at Kollin); 1757 von Zieten (killed at Zorndorf); 1758 von Aschersleben; 1761 von Löllhöfel. Became the new Dragoner-Regiment Nr 5 in 1807. Buff tunic and breeches, sky blue facings, white and sky blue diced braid, officers' lace gold. The sabretasche was sky blue and bore the crowned royal cipher. Holster covers and the shabraque were sky blue and bore a crowned white shield bearing the crowned black Prussian eagle within braid edging. Leibstandarte: new pattern, light blue centre and corner piles, white field and corner medallions, gold embroidery. Eskadrons-Standarte: white centre, corner piles and corner medallions, light blue field, gold embroidery. One standard was lost in the clash at Steckenitz on 6 November 1806; the others were destroyed by their bearers prior to the capitulation of Erfurt.

Kürassier-Regiment Baron von Schönaich Nr 6

Raised in 1688. 1759 von Vasold. Disbanded in 1806. Buff tunic and breeches, light brick red facings, white braid with a light brick red pattern; officers' lace gold. Sabretasche, holster covers and the shabraque were light brick red and bore the crowned royal cipher within braid edging. Leibstandarte: new pattern, dark blue centre, field and corner medallions, gold embroidery. Eskadrons-Standarte: white centre and corner medallions, dark blue field, gold embroidery. Three standards were lost at the capitulation of Anklam on 1 November 1806; two were saved.

Kürassier-Regiment von Driesen Nr 7

Raised in 1688. von Driessen; 1758 von Horn; 1762 von Manstein. Disbanded in 1806. Buff tunic and breeches, lemon yellow facings; white braid with three lemon yellow stripes, officers' lace silver. Sabretasche, holster covers and the shabraque were lemon yellow and bore the crowned royal cipher within braid edging. Leibstandarte: new pattern, red centre, white field and corner medallions, gold embroidery. Eskadrons-Standarte: white centre, red field and corner medallions, gold embroidery. All five standards were lost at the capitulation of Magdeburg on 11 November 1806.

Kürassier-Regiment von Rochow Nr 8

Raised in 1690. 1757 von Seydlitz. Disbanded in 1806. Buff tunic and breeches, dark blue facings, white braid with two wide, dark blue stripes and narrow dark blue edge piping, officers lace silver. The sabretasche was dark blue with the crowned royal cipher and braid edging. Holster covers and the shabraque were white and bore the crowned Prussian eagle within braid edging. Leibstandarte: old pattern, black centre, white field and corner medallions, gold embroidery. Eskadrons-Standarte: white centre, black field and corner medallions, gold embroidery. All five standards were lost at the capitulation of Pasewalk on 29 October 1806.

Kürassier-Regiment Prinz von Schönaich-Carolath Nr 9

Raised in 1691. 1758 von Bredow. Disbanded in 1806. White tunic and breeches, crimson facings, white braid with three crimson stripes, officers' lace gold. The sabretasche was crimson with the crowned royal cipher and braid edging. Holster covers and the shabraque were crimson and bore a crowned white shield bearing the crowned Prussian eagle within braid edging. Disbanded in 1806. Leibstandarte: new pattern, light green centre, white field and corner medallions embroidery.

New style Prussian dragoon guidon with FR cypher.

Eskadrons-Standarte: white centre, light green field, scroll and corner medallions, gold embroidery. All five standards were lost at the capitulation of Pasewalk on 29 October 1806.

Gens d'Armes Nr 10

Raised in 1691. 1747 von Katzler; 1761 von Schwerin. Disbanded in 1806. Buff tunic and breeches, red facings, red braid with a golden stripe, officers' lace gold. The sabretasche was red with the crowned royal cipher. Dark blue holster covers and the shabraque bore a crowned, eight-pointed star, as did their cartouche lids within braid edging. Prior to 1803, troopers' cartouche lids were white, edged in regimental braid and in\ the centre the round brass plate bearing the crowned royal cipher. After this date they became plain black with the same plate. Leibstandarte: old pattern, yellow centre, white field and corner medallions, gold embroidery. Eskadrons-Standarte: white centre and corner medallions, yellow field, gold embroidery. Four standards were lost in the clash at Wichmannsdorf on 27 October 1806, the fifth in the capitulation of Anklam on 1 November 1806.

Leib-Karabiniers Nr 11

Raised in 1692. 1751 von Pennevaire; 1759 von Bandemer. Disbanded in 1806. Buff tunic and breeches, light blue facings, white braid with a light blue central, open diamond pattern between two light blue stripes; officers' lace silver. Sabretasche, holster covers and the shabraque were light blue and bore the crowned royal cipher within braid edging. Leibstandarte: old pattern, light blue centre, white field and corner medallions, gold embroidery. Eskadrons-Standarte: white centre, light blue field, corner medallions and scroll, gold embroidery. All five standards were lost at the capitulation of Pasewalk on 29 October 1806.

Kürassier-Regiment Baron von Kyau Nr 12

Raised in 1695. 1759 von Span; 1762 von Dallwigk. Disbanded in 1806. Buff tunic and breeches, dark orange facings, white braid with two wide orange stripes; officers' lace gold. Orange sabretasche with the crowned royal cipher and braid edging. Holster covers and the shabraque were orange and bore a crowned white shield bearing the crowned Prussian eagle within braid edging. Leibstandarte: old pattern, buff centre, white field and corner medallions, gold embroidery. Eskadrons-Standarte: white centre, buff field and corner medallions, gold embroidery. All five standards were lost at Pasewalk.

Garde du Corps Nr 13

Raised in 1740 with the King as Chef. 1747 von Blumenthal; 1758 von Wackenitz; 1760 von Schaetzel. This regiment became the new Kürassier-Regiment Nr 3 in 1807. Buff tunic and breeches, red facings, red braid with silver stripes; blue waistcoats; officers' lace silver. The sabretasche was red with the crowned royal cipher and braid edging. Holster covers and the shabraque were orange and probably bore a crowned, eight-pointed star, as did their cartouche lids within braid edging. From 1803 this star was also worn on troopers' cartouche lids, which had been white up to that point. Leibstandarte: In 1741, the Garde du Corps was presented with a new pattern silver damask vexillum, as a Leibstandarte. It was 50cm², fringed in silver. The five laurel wreaths were gold, tied with red ribbons. The finial of the white pike staff was a silver Prussian eagle. The cloth hung on a gilt rod, held by silver chains in the eagle's beak. The four other standards had orange central and corner medallions.

Dragoons

Originally the dragoons wore the same bicorns, breeches, boots, gauntlets, waistcoats and buff leather tunics as the kürassiers; their cuffs were usually light blue. Under Friedrich Wilhelm I, red facings were also to be seen, and light blue woollen coats of infantry style were introduced; all cuffs were of Swedish style, and there was an aiguillette on the right shoulder strap in the button colour. Facings were worn on the collar, Swedish cuffs, lapels and turnbacks. Officers' parade uniform coats were decorated with embroidered lace loops in the button colour, six on and two under each lapel, two on the cuff, two on each pocket flap and four in the small of the back. Leatherwork was white and the cartridge pouch was worn on the carbine bandolier. The brass-hilted 'Pallasch' (the long, straight sword) was carried in a brown leather sheath. It had a basket pattern guard and an eagle's head for the pommel. Harness was black, heavy-cavalry style with steel fittings. The holster covers and shabraques were usually in the facing colour and bore lace edging and ciphers or eagles, as with the kürassiers. Some regiments had square ended shabraques, others had rounded ends. Dragoon regiments had drummers instead of trumpeters, and were made up of five squadrons.

The dragoons bore swallow-tailed guidons instead of the square cavalry standards of the kürassiers. Standard bearers had standard bandoliers in the facing colour, edged and fringed in the button colour. The finial of the pike was in the form of a lance. Standards were decorated with black and silver cords and tassels, reaching down to about two-thirds of the height of the cloth. The old pattern standards were swallow-tailed on the fly side and made of damask, fringed in the button colour. The Leibstandarte had a central disc in the colour of the Eskadrons-Standarte; the field was entirely white. In the central disc was a black eagle, over low hills, climbing towards a sun on the right; to the left of the eagle was a white scroll bearing 'NON SOLI CEDIT'. The disc was crowned and surrounded by green laurel leaves, tied with red ribbon. In each corner were crowned laurel leaves enclosing the cipher 'FWR', also tied with red ribbons. Decoration was in the button colour. The central disc in the new style standards had a black eagle under a scroll bearing 'PRO GLORIA ET PATRIA'; the crowned corner wreaths enclosed the cipher 'FR'. Some new pattern standards had plain fields, others had wide corner rays. If the central disc were black, the eagle would be gold.

The following regiments are named for their Inhabers in 1756. The regimental numbers are those introduced in 1784, and officially designated in 1806.

Dragoner-Regiment von Normann Nr 1

Raised in 1689. 1761 von Zastrow. Disbanded in 1806. Black facings, yellow buttons. Shabraque and holster covers were light blue, edged in yellow regimental braid, with a crowned white shield bearing the crowned Prussian eagle. Leibstandarte: old pattern, yellow centre, plain white field, gold embroidery. Eskadrons-Standarte: white centre, plain yellow field, gold embroidery. One standard was lost in the clash of Hansfeld on 6 November 1806, the others in the capitulation of Boitzenburg on 12 November.

Dragoner-Regiment von Blanckensee Nr 2

Raised on 13 August 1725. 1757 von Krockow. Disbanded in 1806. White facings, yellow buttons. Shabraque and holster covers were white with the crowned royal cipher in light blue, edged in light blue braid with two white lines along it. Leibstandarte: old pattern, yellow centre, white field, straight red corner piles, gold embroidery. Eskadrons-Standarte: white centre, yellow field, straight red corner piles, gold embroidery. All five standards were lost at the capitulation of Prenzlau on 28 October 1806.

Dragoner-Regiment Truchsess Graf zu Waldburg Nr 3

Raised on 30 December 1704. March 1757 von Meinicke; April 1761 von Franss. Disbanded in 1806. Pink facings, white buttons. Shabraque and holster covers were pink, edged in pink lace having two white lines along it. It is not known what badges they bore. Leibstandarte and Eskadrons-Standarte: Old pattern, white centre and field, gold embroidery. Four standards were lost at the capitulation of Erfurt on 16 October 1806, the other was saved.

Dragoner-Regiment von Oertzen Nr 4

Raised on 3 January 1705. 4 October 1756 von Katte; 17 October 1757 von Czettritz. Disbanded in 1806. Buff facings, white buttons. Shabraque and holster covers were red, edged in white lace having three light blue lines along it. It is not known what badges they bore. Leibstandarte: old pattern, all white, gold embroidery. Eskadrons-Standarte: light blue centre, all white field, gold embroidery. Two standards were lost at the capitulation of Ratkau on 7 November 1806.

Dragoner-Regiment Markgraf Friedrich von Bayreuth Nr 5

Raised on 2 April 1717. Became the new Dragoner-Regiment Nr 1 in 1807. Crimson facings, white buttons. Shabraque and holster covers were red, edged in white lace having three red lines along it. It is not known what badges they bore. Leibstandarte: new pattern, black centre, plain white field, gold embroidery. Eskadrons-Standarte: white centre, plain black field, gold embroidery. One standard was lost in the clash at Zehdenick on 26 October, another in the capitulation of Ratkau.

Dragoner-Regiment von Schorlemmer Nr 6

These were the famous 'Porcelain Dragoons', taken into Prussian service from Saxony in May 1716. 9 November 1760 von Meier. Became the new Dragoner-Regiment Nr 2 in 1807. White facings and buttons. Shabraque and holster covers were light blue, edged in white lace having two red lines along it. It is not known what badges they bore. Leibstandarte: new pattern, dark blue centre, white field, yellow, wavy corner piles, gold embroidery. Eskadrons-Standarte: white centre, dark blue field, yellow, wavy corner piles, gold embroidery.

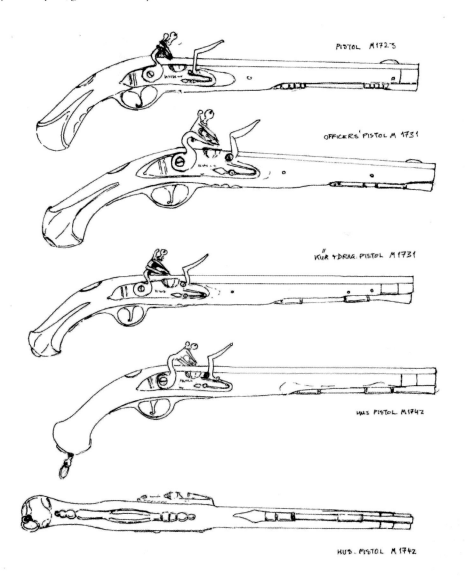

PISTOL M1723

OFFICERS' PISTOL M1731

KÜR + DRAG. PISTOL M1731

HUS PISTOL M1742

HUS. PISTOL M1742

Dragoner-Regiment von Plettenburg Nr 7

Raised on 15 June 1757. June 1761 vacant. Became the new Dragoner-Regiment Nr 3 in 1807. Red facings, yellow buttons. Shabraque and holster covers were pink, edged in pink and yellow regimental lace. It is not known what badges they bore. Leibstandarte: old pattern, black centre, white field, red, wavy corner piles, gold embroidery. Eskadrons-Standarte: white centre, black field, red, wavy corner piles, gold embroidery.

Dragoner-Regiment von Langermann Nr 8

Raised in 1744 from Dragoner-Regiment von Plettenberg. 4 March 1757 Dubislav Friedrich von Platen (Alt-Platen). Became the new Dragoner-Regiment Nr 4 in 1807. Scarlet facings, white buttons. Shabraque and holster covers were scarlet, edged in white lace having two blue lines along it. It is not known what badges they bore. Leibstandarte: new pattern, black centre, white field, red, wavy corner piles, gold embroidery. Eskadrons-Standarte: white centre, black field, red, wavy corner piles, gold embroidery.

Dragoner-Regiment Herzog von Holstein–Gottorp Nr 9

Raised in 1 December 1743 from Dragoner-Regiment Nr 1. 9 April 1761 von Pomeiske. Disbanded in 1806. Light blue facings, no lapels, white buttons and buttonhole laces. Shabraque and holster covers were light blue, edged in white lace having two red lines along it. It is not known what badges they bore. Leibstandarte: new pattern, yellow centre, white field, red, wavy corner piles, silver embroidery. Eskadrons-Standarte: white centre, yellow field, red, wavy corner piles, silver embroidery. All five standards were lost at the capitulation of Ratkau on 7 November 1806.

Dragoner-Regiment Graf Finck von Finckenstein Nr 10

Raised on 1 December 1743 from Dragoner-Regiment Nr 1. Disbanded in 1806. Orange facings, white buttons. Shabraque and holster covers were orange edged in white lace having orange edging. It is not known what badges they bore. Leibstandarte: new pattern, orange centre, red, wavy corner cross, white field, silver embroidery. Eskadrons-Standarte: white centre, red, wavy corner cross, orange field, silver embroidery. All five standards were lost at the capitulation of Ratkau on 7 November 1806.

Dragoner-Regiment von Stechow Nr 11

Raised on 18 December 1740, mainly from Saxon prisoners of war. 6 March 1758 Leopold Johann von Platen (Jung-Platen). Disbanded in 1806. Lemon yellow facings, white buttons. Shabraque and holster covers were lemon yellow, edged in white lace having lemon yellow edging. It is not known what badges they bore. Leibstandarte: new pattern; yellow centre; white field, white diagonal cross, silver embroidery. Eskadrons-Standarte: white centre and diagonal cross, yellow field, silver embroidery. All five standards were lost at the capitulation of Prenzau on 28 October 1806.

Dragoner-Regiment Herzog von Württemberg Nr 12

Raised in 1734 as part of the army of Württemberg; taken into Prussian service on 28 September 1741. Disbanded in 1806. Black facings, white buttons. Shabraque and holster covers were red, edged in white lace having red edging. It is not known what badges they bore. Leibstandarte: new pattern; centre red; field white; embroidery silver. Eskadrons-Standarte: Centre white; field red; embroidery silver. One standard was lost at Schwartau on 6 November, the other standards were lost at the capitulation of Ratkau on 7 November 1806.

Hussars

Hussars wore the traditional Hungarian costume of a richly laced dolman and pelisse, coloured barrel sash, leather breeches and short boots with the top front cut out in a 'V' shape with a tassel. The pelisse was lined with fur in the regimental colour and this was worn slung over the left shoulder. NCOs and trumpeters often wore fox fur edging. The original headgear was the fur trimmed cap; in 1756 this had given way to the mirliton, or winged cap and by 1786 the brown fur colpack was being worn.

Prussian hussar uniforms were singular, in that on top of the buff breeches they wore 'Scharivari', over-trousers extending from the calf up to the top of the thigh, usually in the dolman colour, edged in the button colour. Boots were below-knee length, with a 'V' cut out at the front, edged in the button colour, with a tassel at the front centre. In earlier times, troopers wore black boots; NCOs wore red and officers wore yellow.

They were armed with a carbine, curved sabre in a steel sheath and a pair of pistols. Harnesses were black, Hungarian-style with steel fittings. They used the Hungarian-style 'Bock' saddle made on a birch wood frame. The sabretasches of the NCOs and troopers bore the crowned cipher 'FR' within a wide edging in the button colour. Officer's sabretasches bore the crowned Prussian eagle amid trophies of arms. Prussian hussar regiments carried no standards during the Seven Years War, and had ten squadrons each. The following regiments are named for their Inhabers in 1756. The regimental numbers are those introduced in 1784, and officially designated in 1806.

Husaren-Regiment von Szekely Nr 1

Raised in 1721. 1758 Friedrich Wilhelm Gottfried Arend von Kleist. Disbanded in 1806. Brown fur colpack with dark green bag and white cords. Dark green pelisse with white fur trim, white lace and buttons. Light green dolman, red collar and cuffs edged white, white lace and buttons. Red and white barrel sash, buff leather breeches with light green Scharivari. Light green sabretasche with white crowned royal cipher and edging. Dark green shabraque with light green wolf's tooth edging and white piping. The regiment surrendered at Anklam on 1 November 1806.

Husaren-Regiment von Zieten Nr 2

Raised in 1730 from men of Husaren-Regiment Nr 1. They were titled the 'Leibhusaren' or Zieten-Husaren, after their commander, Oberst Hans Joachim von Zieten. Disbanded in 1806. They wore a dark blue pelisse, scarlet dolman with dark blue collar and cuffs, white buttons and lace, dark blue and white barrel sash. Dark blue Scharivari. Scarlet sabretasche with white crowned cipher and white edging. Dark blue shabraque with scarlet wolf's tooth edging and white piping, dark blue, round portmanteau edged scarlet. The regiment surrendered at Ratkau on 7 November 1806.

Husaren-Regiment von Wartenberg Nr 3

Raised in 1740. May 1757: von Warnery; 1758 von Möhring. Disbanded in 1806. In 1756 this regiment wore a brown fur busby with white bag, white dolman, with yellow collar and cuffs, yellow buttons and braid, dark blue pelisse and Scharivari, yellow and white barrel sash. The fur trim for troopers was white, fox fur for NCOs. They bore a yellow sabretasche with white, crowned royal cipher and edging. They had a dark blue shabraque with white wolf's tooth edging and yellow piping; round, dark blue portmanteau with white piping. The regiment surrendered at Ratkau on 7 November 1806.

Husaren-Regiment von Puttkamer Nr 4

Raised in 1741. December 1759 August Lavin von Dingelstädt; November 1762 Balthazar Ernst von Bohlen. Their uniform was a black mirliton, light blue dolman, light blue collar, cuffs and Scharivari, white pelisse, collar and cuffs, white buttons, silver lace for officers, blue and white lace for other ranks. Red and white barrel sash. The pelisse fur was white for officers and men, red fox for NCOs. Officers had silver lace. White shabraque and round portmanteau with light blue wolf's tooth edging, white piping; white sabretasche with light blue crowned royal cipher and edging. The regiment became the new 1st Husaren-Regiment in 1807, the 4th Husaren-Regiment in 1816.

*Trooper, Husaren-
Regiment von Vippach,
1752 (Nr 4 in 1806). The
regiment was raised as a
lancer (Ulan) regiment
in 1740, but converted to
hussars two years later. The
black felt winged cap, or
mirliton, was worn through
the Seven Years War. Due
to their white pelisses, this
regiment was nicknamed
'the Baa Lambs'. (Knötel,
VIII 55)*

Husaren-Regiment von Reusch Nr 5

Raised in 1741. They wore a black dolman, pelisse, Scharivari and sabretasche. White fur trim was
worn by officers, black for the men. The dolman had scarlet collar and cuffs, white buttons and lace,
red and white barrel sash, white breeches. The black mirliton, or winged cap, was originally decorated
on the front with a white skeleton; by 1791 this had been reduced to a skull and crossed bones. Black
shabraque with red wolf's tooth edging and white piping; round portmanteau, piped red. The regiment became the new 1st Leib-Husaren Regiment after 1806, then split in 1808 to form the 1st and
2nd Leib-Husaren Regiment.

Husaren-Regiment von Wechmar Nr 6

Raised in 1741. 1746 Ludwig Anton Baron von Wechmar; 1757 Johann Paul von Werner. The regiment was destroyed in 1806. They wore a dark brown dolman with yellow collar, cuffs, buttons and
lace, yellow and white barrel sash, dark brown pelisse and Scharivari. Privates had white fur trim to
the pelisse, NCOs had black, officers' were edged with the white fur of foxes' throats. Originally they
wore white breeches; by 1806 these were light blue. The shabraque and sabretasche were brown with
yellow edging, cipher and decoration. The regiment was destroyed in 1806.

Husaren-Regiment von Seydlitz Nr 7

Raised in 1743. This regiment was captured at Maxen on 20 November 1759 and not re-raised. The
uniform was a black mirliton with white cords, red dolman, pelisse and Scharivari. The red shabraque
had red wolf's tooth edging, piped white, the red sabretasche had white edging and crowned cipher,
white buttons and lace.

Trooper, Husaren-Regiment von Belling, 1758 (Nr 8 in 1806). This regiment became the famous Blücher Hussars Nr 5 after 1806. The man wears summer field service dress. Due to their badge of a reclining skeleton on the mirliton, the regiment was known as 'Der Ganze Tod' ('The Whole Death'). In 1764 the uniform became black, with crimson facings and white lace and buttons. (Knötel, I 2)

Husaren-Regiment von Malachowski Nr 8

Raised in 1743. They wore a black mirliton with white cords, lemon yellow dolman with light blue collar and cuffs, a light blue pelisse with black fur, white buttons and lace, light blue and white barrel sash, light blue Scharivari. White breeches were worn later on; saddle furniture was a light blue shabraque, with lemon yellow, wolf's tooth edging and white piping. The sabretasche was light blue with white edging and crowned cipher. The regiment was destroyed in 1806.

Husaren-Regiment von Belling Nr 9

Raised in 1758. The regiment surrendered at Ratkau on 7 November 1806, but almost every member escaped and made their way to East Prussia to rejoin the rump of the Prussian Army. This regiment wore a black dolman and pelisse, black collar and cuffs, brass buttons and green lace, black fur, red and white barrel sash. Black sabretasche. On the front of the mirliton was a reclining skeleton. The regiment became Blücher Husaren-Regiment Nr 5 after 1806.

Bosniaken

Raised in 1745 as the 'Corps Bosniaken' with ten squadrons; renamed 'Corps Towarczys' in 1799, with fifteen squadrons. 1745 Joseph Theodor von Ruesch; 1759 von Beust; 1762 Daniel Friedrich von Lossow. Initially they had no uniforms; later they wore black, long-skirted coats and breeches, red tunics piped in white. Half of the regiment carried lances, sabres and pistols, the other half had carbines, sabres and pistols. The regiment became the 1st and 2nd Ulan Regiments in 1808.

Freikorps

Prussia raised many units of light troops during the war to fill a tactical gap; their value had been demonstrated well by the Austrians. However, many Freikorps never reached their contracted strength and were disbanded before taking the field. Musketeers of almost all Freikorps wore dark blue uniforms faced light blue, with light blue waistcoats and breeches and white buttons. Badges of rank were as in the Prussian Army. Unit distinctions are shown below. Unless otherwise stated, all units wore dark blue coats with light blue facings, waistcoats and breeches.

Frei-Infanterie

Freibataillon le Noble Nr 1

Raised in 1756. Dark green coat, yellow collar, cuffs, waistcoat and breeches (some sources show light green facings, waistcoat and breeches), buff belts, buttons and buttonhole laces. Austrian-style black cap (Czakelhaube) with front flap bearing the crowned 'FR' in white; dark blue coat, light blue facings, white buttons, tall black gaiters. At least some of the men were armed with rifles.

Freibataillon von Mayr Nr 2

Raised in 1756. 1759 Collignon; 1760 Courbiere. A 2nd Battalion was raised in 1760. They were captured by the Russians in 1761, exchanged and fought at Freiberg on 29 October 1762.

Freibataillon von Kalben Nr 3

Raised in 1756, 1758 Salenmon. Captured at Maxen, exchanged and fought at Torgau in November 1760; fought at Freiberg on 29 October 1762. Coat and facings dark blue, light blue waistcoat and breeches.

Freibataillon d'Angelelli Nr 4

Raised in 1756. 1760 Collignon. Captured at Landshut, exchanged and a 2nd Battalion raised, very heavy losses against the French at Nordhausen on 27 March 1761. Tricorn, dark blue coat, light blue collar, cuffs, lapels, waistcoat, breeches, yellow buttons.

Freibataillon de Chossignon Nr 5

Raised in 1757. 1758 Montjou. Absorbed into Frei-Infanterie Nr 7 in 1759. Tricorn, dark blue coat, light blue facings and small clothes, yellow buttons.

Freibataillon von Rapin Nr 6

Raised in 1757 from French prisoners of war taken at Rossbach. 1759 von Luederitz. The 2nd Battalion was raised in 1760; the unit fought at Freiberg on 29 October 1762. Tricorn, dark blue coat with light blue round cuffs, dark blue collar with red tabs to the ends, each with a small yellow button. No lapels, but two rows each of six yellow buttons; red turnbacks. Light blue waistcoat and breeches, long black gaiters.

Freibataillon von Wunsch Nr 7

Raised in 1758. Absorbed Frei-Infanterie Nr 5 in 1759. Dark green coat, waistcoat and breeches, red collar, lapels, cuffs and turnbacks, natural brown leather belts, tricorns. The Jägers wore dark green coats and waistcoats, red collars, lapels and cuffs, yellow buttons and were armed with rifles.

Freibataillon du Verger Nr 8

Raised in 1758. 1759 Quintus Icilius. The 2nd Battalion was raised in 1760 and the 3rd in 1761. Tricorn with light blue pompons; dark blue coat, light blue facings, waistcoat and breeches, yellow buttons and buttonhole lace, red turnbacks. White belts, high black gaiters. The Jäger company had dark green coats.

Trooper of Prussian hussars, Freikorps von Kleist, 1760. This unit operated together with the 1st (Green) Hussars, whose Chef (Colonel-in-Chief) was von Friedrich Wilhelm Gottfried Arnd von Kleist. (Knötel, VI 43)

Prussian Freikorps von Schony, 1761. Left to right: hussar, grenadier, infantry officer. Major Carl Ludwig von Schony (a disaffected Hungarian) entered Prussian service in 1761 and raised his Freikorps in Breslau. It included grenadiers, musketiers and hussars; all uniforms had a strong Hungarian flavour. The hussars wore dark blue pelisses with black fur trim and yellow lace and buttons. (Knötel, IV 11)

Freibataillon Graf von Hordt Nr 9

Raised in 1758. A drummer is shown wearing a tricorn edged white and with light blue pompons, dark blue coat with light blue collar, lapels, round cuffs all edged white; white buttons and buttonhole lace, dark blue swallow's nests edged and decorated in white; red turnbacks. White belts, brass drum with red and white striped hoops, black gaiters.

Freibataillon von Trümbach Nr 10

Raised in 1759. It was also known as *Volontaires de Prusse*. It had a squadron of dragoons attached, which later became hussars. In January 1761, these hussars were transferred to Major von Bawr's hussar regiment (Freikorps Nr 21). The first uniform of the infantry was green and red, as for the Prussian Jägers. In 1761 a new uniform was introduced for all but the Jägers: dark blue coat, red facings, white small clothes, white buttons. Grenadiers and pioneers wore bearskins. The hussars wores white dolman and breeches, dark blue pelisse, brown fur busbies.

Freihusaren Jung-Kleist (Friedrich Ludwig) Nr 11a

Raised in late 1759. Brown fur busby with red bag and red and white plume, red dolmans and breeches, green pelisses, white buttons and braid, yellow boots.

Freikorps von Kleist (Joachim Friedrich) Nr 11b

Raised in February 1760 by General Friedrich Ludwig von Kleist. Leichte Dragoner (light dragoons), eventually of ten squadrons. Dark green coats, cuffs and lapels, white buttons and buttonholes, white aiguillette, dark green waistcoats, bearskins with a white metal plate bearing the black, Prussian eagle. Officers wore tricorns. The regiment bore black guidons.

Von Kleist'sches Freikorps Nr 12a

Raised in 1761 by General Friedrich Ludwig von Kleist of a battalion of 'Grüner Kroaten' (Green Croats). The Croats were later expanded from a battalion into the 'Ungarisches Infanterie-Regiment von Kleist'. Black felt chako, green Hungarian jackets with red braiding (later white), red waist barrel-sashes, green breeches.

Freibataillon von Kleist (Friedrich Ludwig) Nr 12b

Raised in spring 1761; title Kleist (Friedrich Ludwig) Jägerkorps of three companies, commanded by Kapitain Kümpel. Green coats and waistcoats, red facings, white buttons.

Freikorps von Kleist Dragoons' grenadier cap: tin plate, black fur, dark green headpiece and backing.

Frei-Dragoner-Regiment von Glasenapp Nr 13

Raised in 1760. Tricorns, light blue tunics and cuffs, yellow lining and waistcoat, white aiguillette and white buttons.

Freibataillon Jeney Nr 14

Raised in 1760. Also known as *Volontaires d'Ostfriese*. It had a squadron of dragoons attached, who later became hussars. In January 1761, these hussars were transferred to Husaren-Regiment von Bawr. The uniform for the infantry was green and red, as for the Prussian Jägers. In 1761 a new uniform was introduced for all but the Jägers: dark blue coat, red facings, white small clothes, white buttons. Grenadiers and pioneers wore bearskins. The hussars wores white dolman and breeches, dark blue pelisse, brown fur busbies.

Freibataillon von Schack Nr 15

Raised in 1760. Bearskin bonnets, dark blue coats, light blue facings and small clothes, yellow buttons and aiguillette.

Freibataillon von Heer Nr 16

Raised in 1761. Also known as *Schweizer-Bataillon*. Grenadier caps, light blue coats, dark blue facings, white buttons and lace.

Freibataillon de Bequignolles Nr 17

Raised in 1761. Tricorn, dark blue coat, light blue facings and small clothes, white buttons and white aiguillette.

Freibataillon de la Badie Nr 18

Raised in 1761. Also known as *Volontaires Etranger*. This unit was disbanded due to high desertion rates. Tricorn, dark blue coats, light blue collar patches, pointed cuffs and small clothes, white buttons and lace.

Freikorps von Schony Nr 19

Raised in 1760. It consisted of a battalion of Hungarian grenadiers and a squadron of hussars. Grenadiers: Austrian-style grenadier cap with brass front plate, bearing the black Prussian eagle, black fur trim and headband, red bag with yellow piping and light blue tassel. Dark blue coat, light blue collar and cuffs, red turnbacks; yellow edging to collar, yellow frogging to the chest (seven bars), yellow 'bear's claws to the pointed cuffs. Light blue waistcoat and breeches trimmed yellow, red waist sash, short boots, white belts. The hussars had light blue dolmans and dark blue pelisses.

Freikorps von Gschray Nr 20

Raised in 1761. Consisted of a *Freibataillon* and a *Freidragoner-Eskadron*. Dragoons: light blue coat, black lapels and cuffs, yellow buttons, buttonhole lace, waistcoat and breeches, white belts. Bicorns with yellow pompons, white gauntlets, high, cuffed boots. Infantry: tricorns with yellow pompons, dark blue coats with dark blue facings, yellow buttons and buttonhole lace, red turnbacks. A yellow fringed shoulder strap was worn on the left shoulder. Yellow waistcoat and breeches, white belts, high black gaiters.

A Prussian artillery bombardier cap, showing burning grenades. (The Wehrgeschichtliches Museum, Rastatt)

Prussian artillery summer uniform, 1750. Left to right: bombardier, gunner, officer. Bombardiers wore fusilier-style caps with brass plates and black, oilskin headpieces from 1731 to 1750, when they were withdrawn. He wears two long pickers on his powder flask bandolier, for cleaning out the vent holes on the guns. Gunners carried straight-bladed swords; the officers wore the infantry sword. (Knötel, IV 21)

Prussian miners, 1758. The Prussians were far more advanced than the British in the development of technical troops. Even during the Peninsular War, Wellington's sieges suffered due to a lack of qualified engineers and miners. (Knötel, VIII 45)

Von Bawr Husaren Freikorps Nr 21
Raised in 1760. Black felt cap (mirliton), dark blue dolman and pelisse, white buttons and lace.

Légion Britannique Freikorps Nr 22
At the end of 1762, Frederick the Great agreed to take over the *Légion Britannique*, which until then had been in Hanoverian service. The war then ended, so nothing practical came of this; the men transferred into Prussian service, but the units were then disbanded. For uniform details see Chapter 10.

Volontaires Auxiliaires Freikorps Nr 23
In early 1763, the Duke of Brun-swick agreed to transfer this unit into Prussian service. It consisted of three companies of grenadiers, three squadrons of Turks (or Spahis), and a squadron each of hussars and horse grenadiers. The men transferred into Prussian service, but the units were then disbanded. For uniform details see Chapter 7.

Artillery

In 1756 the Field Artillery Regiment comprised 1st Batallion von Möller and 2nd Batallion von Dieskau. Foot artillery wore dark blue uniforms of infantry cut, with black facings and brass buttons. The tricorn was worn, except by bombardiers, who wore low-crowned, black leather caps like those of the fusiliers, with brass front plate and fittings. The horse artillery wore uniforms of the same colour as the foot artillery, but of dragoon style. In 1759, the three Prussian armies fielded a total of 536 pieces, including 238 battalion guns. The heavier pieces were distributed as follows:

Ordnance	Frederick Silesia	Genereal Fouqué Silesia	Prince Henry Saxony	General Dohna Pomerania	Total
24-pdr cannon	–	–	–	1	1
Heavy 12-pdr 'Brummer'	30	–	20	–	50
Medium 12-pdr 'Austrian'	50	10	28	19	107
Light 12-pdr cannon	20	20	6	10	64
7-pdr howitzer	24	–	5	15	44
10-pdr howitzer	12	6	4	1	23
18-pdr howitzer	–	–	–	2	2
25-pdr mortar	7	–	–	–	7
	143	36	63	56	298

Prussian artillery bombardier cap: brass plate and trimmings, black headband and cap, no pompon.

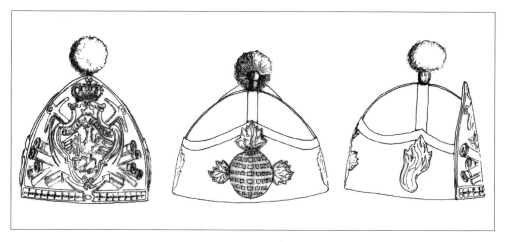

Miner cap: tin plate, pink headband and cap, white pompon.

Pontonniers

Raised in 1715; they wore foot artillery uniform.

Miners

Raised from the Pontonniers (Infanterie-Regiment von Seers Nr 49) in 1758. Dark blue uniform of infantry cut, no lapels or collar, dark blue cuffs (later black velvet), white buttons, pink lining, waistcoat and breeches, long black gaiters, white belts. Other ranks' headgear was a tin plate fronted, low-crowned cap with pink headband and headpiece.

Ingenieurs

Dark blue uniform of infantry style, black velvet lapels and cuffs, white buttons, silver hat edging, white small clothes.

15

THE EMPIRE OF
ALL THE RUSSIAS

This vast, underdeveloped empire was rule by Tsarina Elizabeth Petrovna from 1741 to 25 December 1761 (5 January 1762 in western calendars). She was the sworn enemy of Frederick the Great and sided with Austria during the Seven Years War. Just when military affairs seemed to be heralding the Prussian king's defeat, Elizabeth died, to be succeeded by her nephew, Peter III. Peter was an ardent admirer of Frederick the Great and at once declared peace and withdrew his forces. This was deeply unpopular in Russia and Peter was deposed on 9 July 1762. Eight days later he was murdered, to be succeeded by his widow, Ekaterina Alekseyevna. It is most likely that his scheme to dress his army in Prussian-style uniforms never left the drawing board.

In 1756, officers wore black and gold waist sashes; dismounted officers bore fusils in the field and wore silvered gorgets when on duty. Off duty, they carried canes with gilt knobs. NCOs carried canes. Rank was shown by gold hat edging and gold lace to the collar and the cuffs. On the latter, one gold stripe inside the edging meant corporal, two was a sergeant, three a sergeant major. Drummers and trumpeters wore swallow's nests in the facing colour, edged in regimental lace, at the shoulders and had four bars of lace across the sleeve; musicians had just the lace bars. Drums were brass with hoops painted in white and dark green triangles. Hair was powdered, curled and worn plaited into a pigtail. All dates are in the old Russian style.

Foot Guards

Dark green coat, red cuffs and turnbacks, red waistcoat and breeches, gilt buttons. The brass-fronted grenadier mitre caps had a red plume, musketeers wore white edged tricorns. The regiments were differentiated by the colour of their collars, as shown below. They used the normal gold lace badges of rank on collars and cuffs. Musketeer officers wore their waist sashes under the coat. Grenadier company officers wore their sashes from right shoulder to left hip and their pouch bandoliers were in the facing colour, edged and embroidered in the button colour. The skirts of officers' coats were not turned back. When on duty, all officers wore large silver gorgets with the imperial cipher within trophies of arms and under the crown, or with the regimental badge under a crown.

Grenadier officer, Infanterie-Regiment Manteuffel, 1756–1762. The cap plate and the embroidery on the bandolier were in the button colour, the sash was silver with black and orange stripes. (Viskovatov)

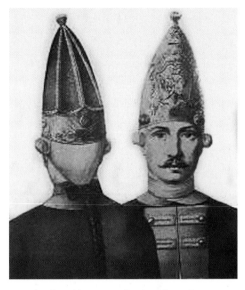

Details of a soldier's grenadier cap plate of Infanterie-Regiment Manteuffel, 1756–1762. (Viskovatov)

The flags were the same for all three Leib-Guard regiments: sovereigns' flags were white, fringed in gold and extremely ornate. On both sides was the crowned imperial eagle, on its breast a red circular disc, holding the crowned imperial cipher (EP). In the corners were the crowned imperial ciphers within wreaths and under the imperial eagle. Company flags had the same designs on an orange ground.

Izmailovsky Leib-Guard

Raised on 22 September 1730. Dark green collars. Three battalions, each of a grenadier and four musketeer companies, an artillery company and eight 3-pounder guns.

Preobrazensky Leib-Guard

Raised in 1683. Red collars. Four battalions, each of six companies, two of them grenadiers, a company of bombardiers and twelve 3-pounder guns.

Semenovsky Leib-Guard

Raised in 1683. Light blue collars. Three battalions each of a grenadier and four musketeer companies, an artillery company and eight 3-pounder guns.

Guards Artillery Company

Raised on 30 April 1695.

Lifeguard Horse Regiment

Raised on 7 March 1721. Five squadrons each of two companies. Service uniform was a tricorn edged in gold and having a white cockade, a buff tunic, with buff collar, cuffs and turnbacks, all edged red, buff gauntlets and breeches. The tunic hooked together on the chest. This regiment took no part in the war.

Chevalier Guards Regiment

Raised on 31 March 1724. One squadron of two companies.

Detail of an officer's grenadier cap, Infanterie-Regiment Manteuffel, 1756–1762. (Viskovatov)

Grenadier and pioneer, Infanterie-Regiment Manteuffel, 1756–1762. (Viskovatov)

Infantry

The following musketeer regiments had three fusilier battalions (of four companies each), a grenadier company and an artillery company with four 3-pounder guns; this increased during the war. From 1757 each regiment had only two fusilier battalions. Most Russian line infantry regiments wore the same uniforms. These consisted of a dark green, single-breasted tunic with red collar, cuffs and turnbacks and brass buttons, red waistcoat and breeches, black gaiters in winter, white in summer. Musketeers wore tricorns, edged white, with a white cockade and brass button. Grenadiers (and grenadier company officers) wore brass-fronted mitre caps, bearing the crowned double eagle over another cartouche, bearing the crest of the colonel-in-chief of the regiment, or of the city in the regiment's title. The headpiece and the long neck shield were of black leather. Belts were buff. The sovereign's colour was white, bearing the crowned imperial eagle, with a shield on its breast, having the arms of the colonel-in-chief (or city of its title) on it. The regimental colours were in various colours and bore the crowned crest of the colonel-in-chief (or city of its title).

1st Grenadiers
Raised in 1756 with two battalions of five companies each. Regimental flags in red with white corner flames.

2nd Grenadiers
Raised in 1756 with two battalions of five companies each. Regimental flags in red with white corner flames.

3rd Grenadiers
Raised in 1756 with two battalions of five companies each. Regimental flags in red with white corner flames.

4th Grenadiers

Raised in 1756 with two battalions of five companies each. Regimental flags in red with white corner flames.

Apsheronsky

Raised on 9 July 1724. Part of the old Nisowsky Corps; brought into the regular army in 1745. Regimental flags in light blue with yellow corner flames.

Arkhangelogorodsky

Raised on 25 June 1700. Regimental flags in dark green with red corner flames.

Astrakhansky

Raised on 25 June 1700. Regimental flags in red with yellow corner flames.

Azovsky

Raised on 25 June 1700. Regimental flags in red with yellow corner flames.

Bjelosersky

Raised in 1708. Regimental flags in orange with green corner flames.

Butyrsky

Raised in 1624. Regimental flags in dark green with crimson corner flames.

Ingermannlandsky

Raised on 25 June 1700 as Infantry Regiment Roman Bruce. Regimental flags in dark green with red corner flames.

Kabardasky

Raised on 15 December 1726. Part of the old Nisowsky Corps; brought into the regular army in 1745. Regimental flags in light blue with crimson corner flames.

Kazansky

Raised on 25 June 1700. Regimental flags in dark green with red corner flames.

Kegsgolmsky

Raised in 1710. Regimental flags in yellow with red corner flames.

Kievsky

Raised on 25 June 1700. Regimental flags in red with yellow corner flames.

Koporsky

Raised in 1703. Regimental flags in dark green with red corner flames.

Kurinsky

Raised on 26 February 1726. part of the old Nisowsky Corps; brought into the regular army in 1745. Regimental flags in crimson with yellow corner flames.

Ladogasky

Raised 29 July 1708. Regimental flags in dark green with red corner flames.

Moscowsky (1st)

Raised in 1700. In 1727 Lefort's Infantry Regiment became 1st Moscow. Regimental flags in dark blue with yellow corner flames.

Moscowsky (2nd)

Raised on 25 June 1700. Regimental flags in dark blue with yellow corner flames.

Muromsky

Raised in 1708. Regimental flags in dark green with red corner flames.

Narvsky

Raised on 6 December 1703. Regimental flags in light blue with red corner flames.

Navaginsky

Raised in 1726. Part of the old Nisowsky Corps; brought into the regular army in 1745. Regimental flags in orange with dark green corner flames.

Nevasky

Raised on 21 July 1706. Regimental flags in dark green with red corner flames.

Nizhegorodsky

Raised on 25 June 1700. Regimental flags in light blue with red corner flames.

Nizovsky

Raised on 9 May 1726. Part of the old Nisowsky Corps; brought into the regular army in 1745. Regimental flags in dark green with crimson corner flames.

Novgorodsky

Raised on 25 June 1700. Regimental flags in orange with dark green corner flames.

Permsky

Raised on 25 June 1700. Regimental flags in dark green with red corner flames.

Pskovsky

Raised on 25 June 1700. Regimental flags in orange with dark green corner flames.

Riazansky

Raised on 6 December 1703. Regimental flags in dark blue with yellow corner flames.

Rostovsky

Raised on 25 June 1700. Regimental flags in orange with red corner flames.

Sankt-Peterburgsky

Raised in 1703. Regimental flags in dark green with red corner flames.

Schlüsselburgsky

Raised on 25 June 1700. Regimental flags in red with yellow corner flames.

Sibyrsky

Raised on 25 June 1700. Regimental flags in dark green with red corner flames.

Smolensky

Raised on 25 June 1700. Regimental flags in dark blue with yellow corner flames.

Suzdalsky

Raised on 21 July 1707. Regimental flags in dark green with red corner flames.

Tchernigovsky

Raised 25 July 1725. Regimental flags in yellow with red corner flames.

Tenginsky

Raised on 26 February 1726. Part of the old Nisowsky Corps; brought into the regular army in 1745. Regimental flags in yellow with crimson corner flames.

Tobolsky

Raised on 6 December 1703. Regimental flags in dark green with red corner flames.

Troitsky

Raised on 25 June 1700. Regimental flags in dark green with red corner flames.

Uglitshky

Raised on 1 October 1708. Regimental flags in light blue with red corner flames.

Velikolutsky

Raised on 25 June 1700. Regimental flags in light blue with red corner flames.

Viatsky

Raised on 25 June 1700. Regimental flags in dark blue with yellow corner flames.

Vladimirsky

Raised on 25 June 1700. Regimental flags in dark green with red corner flames.

Vologdasky

Raised in 1700. Regimental flags in dark blue with yellow corner flames.

Voronezhky

Raised on 25 June 1700. Regimental flags in light blue with red corner flames.

Vyborgsky

Raised on 25 June 1700. Regimental flags in dark green with red corner flames.

Yaroslavlsky

Raised on 25 June 1700. Regimental flags in light blue with red corner flames.

Grenadier officer's cap plate, pouch and bandolier and those of the soldiers. (Viskovatov)

Observation Corps

The Observation Corps was raised in October 1756 as an autonomous corps. It was raised by the Tsarina on the advice of Count Shuvalov, who also commanded it. Theoretically it was supposed to consist of 30,000 men, but only 12,000 were recruited. It took the field in 1758. The grenadier regiment had two battalions and each of the five musketeer regiment had three; they wore infantry uniform. The corps was disbanded in early 1760, the men being transferred into the artillery as fusiliers.

Cavalry

Cuirassiers

Each regiment had five squadrons, each of two companies. They wore buff leather tunics (fabric for officers), with red collar, cuffs, turnbacks and waistcoats; buff gauntlets and breeches. Only a breastplate was worn; it was black, edged in red, with metal shoulder scales. For officers, the breastplate was edged silver, with the crowned imperial cipher in the upper central part; the shoulder scales were silvered. Officers' hats were edged silver, as were their cuffs and turnbacks.

Bevernsky

Raised in 1702; became the Yaroslavsky Dragoons in 1708; converted to cuirassiers in 1733. Squadron standard unknown.

Kazansky

Raised in July 1701 as a dragoon regiment; converted to cuirassiers on 30 March 1756. Squadron standard in dark green.

Kievsky

Raised on 20 August 1668 as a dragoon regiment; converted to cuirassiers in 1756. Squadron standard in red.

Leib Cuirassiers of Her Majesty

Raised in 1704 as the Portessasky Dragoons; renamed the Nievski Dragoons in 1708; converted to Leib Cuirassiers in 1733. Squadron standard in dark green.

Minichovsky

Raised on 27 January 1709 as a dragoon-grenadier regiment von der Roppa; converted in 1727 the Vyborgsky Dragoons; converted in 1731 to the Minichovsky Curassiers. Squadron standard unknown.

Novotroitsky

Raised in May 1708 as a dragoon regiment; converted to cuirassiers in 1756. Squadron standard in dark green.

Prince Fedorovitch or Altesse Impériale

Raised in 1702. The 1st (Leib) squadron bore a white standard, fringed in gold; on the face side was the crowned imperial eagle in the centre and a crowned laurel wreath enclosing the imperial cipher in each corner. On the other side the corner decorations were as on the face side and the central emblem was the crowned imperial cipher within a gold laurel wreath. The four other squadrons each bore a coloured, royal blue, standard (not a guidon) bearing the crowned imperial cipher in the centre of both sides, on a white disc, within golden palm and laurel wreaths. All ranks wore the tricorn with white binding.

Horse Grenadiers

These regiments were raised in 1756 when six dragoon regiments were converted to horse grenadiers. A regiment consisted of five squadrons, each of two companies. Regiments had a kettle drummer and each company had two drummers. Each regiment was accompanied by two 3-pounder cannon. In 1762, when Tsar Paul ascended the throne, these regiments were converted to cuirassiers. All ranks wore the grenadier cap. The 1st (Leib) squadron bore a white standard, fringed in gold, with the crowned imperial eagle in the centre and a crowned laurel wreath enclosing the imperial cipher in each corner. The four other squadrons each bore a coloured standard (not a guidon) bearing the regimental crest.

Astrakhansky

Raised in July 1701 as the Prince of Lvov Dragoons; renamed Astrakhansky Dragoons in 1706; converted to horse grenadiers in 1756. Squadron standards in red.

Kargopolsky

Raised in September 1706 as the Misina-Puschkinsky Dragoons; re-named Kargopolsky Dragoons in May 1707; converted to horse grenadiers in 1756. Squadron standards in dark green.

Narvsky

Raised in 1705 as the Pestov Dragoons; renamed Narvsky Dragoons on 10 March 1708; converted to horse grenadiers in 1756. Squadron standards in light blue.

Rizhsky

Raised on 27 January 1709 as a dragoon regiment; converted to horse grenadiers in 1756. Squadron standards in yellow.

Ryazansky

Raised on 24 May 1705 as a dragoon regiment; converted to horse grenadiers in 1756. Squadron standards in dark blue.

Sankt-Peterburgsky

Raised on 7 January 1707 as the Zhibinsky Dragoons (later Leib-Dragoons); converted to horse grenadiers in 1756. Squadron standards in dark green.

Russian cavalry 1756–1762. Those from 1762 bear the name of their regimental colonel, rather than the geographical names used during the war. Left to right: grenadier, Prinz Georg Ludwig Dragoons; officer, Leib Cuirassiers of Her Majesty; grenadier officer, Leib Dragoons (previously Vladimirsky); trooper and officer, Lomza Cuirassiers (previously Rizhsky); trooper, Slobotzky Hussars. The style of the hussar's mirliton is unique to Russia. (Knötel, III 21)

Dragoons

Each regiment consisted of five squadrons, each of two companies and was accompanied by two 3-pounder cannon. It seems that all dragoon regiments wore the same uniform of a light blue coat with red collar, cuffs and turnbacks, brass buttons, white trimming to hat, buff waistcoat with light blue collar and cuffs, buff breeches light blue, plain saddle furniture. The 1st (Leib) squadron bore a white standard, fringed in gold, with the crowned imperial eagle in the centre and a crowned laurel wreath enclosing the imperial cipher in each corner. The four other squadrons each bore a coloured standard (not a guidon) bearing the regimental crest. One company was of grenadiers who wore the brass-fronted mitre cap, bearing the regimental badge, surmounted by the imperial eagle.

Arkhangelogorodsky
Squadron standards in dark green.

Azovsky
Squadron standards in red.

Ingermannlandsky
Raised in July 1704 as the Menschikova Dragoons; renamed Ingermannlandsy Dragoons on 13 November 1727. Squadron standards in dark green.

Kiev
Squadron standards in light blue.

Lutsky
Squadron standards in light blue.

Moscowsky
Raised in February 1700 as the Preobrazhensky Dragoons; renamed Moscowsky Dragoons in October 1706. Squadron standards in dark blue.

Nizegorodsky
Raised on 7 November 1702 as the Bodevia Dragoons; renamed Nizhegorodsky Dragoons in October 1706. Squadron standards in light blue.

Novgorodsky
Squadron standards in orange.

Olonetsky
Squadron standards in red.

Permsky
Squadron standards in dark green.

Pskovsky
Raised in July 1701 as the Novikov Dragoons; renamed Pskovsky Dragoons in 1706. Squadron standards in orange.

Revelsky
Squadron standards in dark green.

Rostovsky
Raised in August 1706 as the Streschniev Dragoons; renamed Rostovsky Dragoons in 1707. Squadron standards in yellow.

Sibyrsky
Squadron standards in dark green.

Tobolsky
Squadron standards in dark green.

Troitsky
Squadron standards in dark green.

Tversky
Squadron standards in light blue.

Viatsky
Squadron standards in royal blue.

Vladimirsky
Raised in July 1701 as Zhdanov Dragoons; renamed Vladimirsky Dragoons in October 1706. Squadron standards in dark green.

Vologdasky
Squadron standards in royal blue.

Yamburgsky
Raised in 1707 as the Ustyuzhki Dragoons; renamed Yamburgsky Dragoons in November 1712. Squadron standards in red.

Hussars
The following regiments were later disbanded. Establishment was for five squadrons; no standards. Each regiment had a kettle drummer and each squadron had a trumpeter. Officers wore the same uniform as that of their men, but with gold cords and buttons, yellow boots and grey fur trim to the pelisse.

Bolgarsky (Bulgarian)
Raised on 10 May 1759 at five squadrons. Uniform was reportedly identical to that of the Zelty Hussars, but this is unconfirmed.

Gruzinsky (Georgian)
Entered Russian service between 1736 and 1739; it became a regular regiment on 14 October 1741. Troopers wore black colpacks with red bag and cords, yellow dolman, pelisse and sabretasche, with red cords, brass buttons, black fur, yellow and black sash, red breeches and shabraque, the latter with black, wolf's tooth edging. Black belts. Yellow sabretasche with red edging and crowned 'EP' cipher. Knötel shows that troopers wore red dolman and breeches, blue pelisse, black boots.

Makedonsky (Macedonian)
Raised on 10 May 1759 at five squadrons. Red mirliton and breeches, light blue dolman, pelisse and breeches, light blue shabraque and sabretasche with red edging and crowned cipher, black and sash, black belts and boots, black fur, yellow cords and buttons.

Moldavsky (Moldavian)

Entered Russian service between 1736 and 1739; it became a regular regiment on 14 October 1741. Red bag and cords to the colpack, red dolman and breeches, red and black sash, royal blue pelisse, brass buttons. Royal blue shabraque and sabretasche, with red cords, wolf's tooth edging and crowned cipher, royal blue cords and trim to the dolman and breeches.

Serbsky (Serbian)

Entered Russian service in 1723. It had ten companies in five squadrons. Light blue dolman, pelisse, breeches, sabretasche and shabraque, all with black braiding, fur, edging and cipher. Black busby with light blue bag, black and light blue sash. Brass buttons.

Slobodsky (Slovakian)

Raised on 27 September 1756, with ten squadrons. White mirliton, pelisse, shabraque (with light blue, wolf's tooth edging) and sabretasche, white and black sash, light blue dolman and breeches, black fur, cords, edging and crowned cipher. Black belts.

Vengersky (Hungarian)

Entered Russian service between 1736 and 1739; it became a regular regiment on 14 October 1741. The uniform was entirely red, with black fur, cords, trim and brass buttons, black and red sash.

Zeltiy (Yellow)

Raised on 11 December 1760, at five squadrons. The uniform was all yellow, with black cords, fur, crowned cipher and trim, brass buttons. The shabraque was black with yellow wolf's tooth trim.

Light Horse

These three regiments were converted to hussars on 3 May 1765. They wore Cossack costume in dark blue, with fur busbies.

Achtyrsky Free Cherkassian Kazak Regiment

Raised on 17 June 1651 from the Free Ukranian Host.

Isumsky Free Cherkassian Kazak Regiment

Raised on 17 June 1651 from the Free Ukranian Host.

Sumskoi Free Cherkassian Kazak Regiment

Raised on 17 June 1651 from the Free Ukranian Host.

Cossacks

1st Chuguyevsky Kazak Regiment

Raised 25 July 1749.

2nd Chuguyevsky Kazak Regiment

Raised 25 July 1749.

Artillery

The great reformer of the Russian artillery in this era was Count Peter Ivanovitch Schuvalov (1710–1762). Although he had little formal academic ballistic knowledge, he was very successful in pushing forward improvements to weapons and equipment. He took control at just the right moment, for Peter the Great had neglected his artillery and many infantry regiments were without their guns. Schuvalov was supported by Mikhail Vasilievich Danilov (1722–1790) and Peter Alexandrovich Rumyantsev (1725–1796). On 11 January 1757, Schuvalov revised the artillery corps' establishment, so that it consisted of two artillery regiments each of two battalions, each battalion of four companies of gunners and one of bombardiers, a total of 3089 officers and men. There was also a Secret Howitzer Corps of four companies. The companies were organised as for the infantry and were capable of acting in the field or in fortresses.

The artillery pieces of the Russian Army were heavier (calibre for calibre) that those of western European powers. Each piece was accompanied by two small ammunition wagons, holding 120 solid shot and 30 canister rounds. In 1757 Russian field artillery had 164 guns: 4 2-Pud mortars (1 Pud = 32.8kg), 12 1-Pud howitzers, 12 1/2-Pud howitzers, 20 12-pounder cannon, 16 8-pounder cannon, 28 6-pounder cannon, 24 3-pounder cannon and 48 6-pounder Coehorn mortars. There were also heavy mortars of 2 1/2 and 9-Pud for siege work. It also used a ballistic oddity: the 'Unicorn', a cross between a cannon and a howitzer, with a bore length of ten calibres and a conical chamber for the charge. It was lighter than cannon of the same calibre and easier to move on the battlefield, but the reduced charge used meant that its range was relatively limited.

Two 3-pounder cannon were attached to each infantry battalion, as were two 6-pounder bronze 'Coehorn' mortars. In 1758, light Unicorns (1/2-Pud) were formed into batteries of four guns, which were attached to cavalry brigades. In 1759, 181 of Schuvalov's 'secret' howitzers (oval-bored pieces, firing grape) were issued to the infantry regiments in place of their 3-pounders. After one year, however, they were withdrawn again and concentrated into batteries within the field artillery. Some of these weapons were captured by the Prussians, others were given to the Austrians; neither nation found them to be effective enough to be adopted into their armouries.

Uniform was a red coat, waistcoat and breeches, black collar, cuffs and turnbacks, brass buttons. A black tricorn with white edging was worn by all but the bombardiers, who wore a brass-fronted mitre cap with black crown and neck shield and a white plume. The front plate was decorated with trophies of arms. This cap was not worn in the field.

Apart from this, there was the engineer and pontoon regiment; they wore artillery uniform with white metal buttons.

16

THE ELECTORATE
OF SAXONY

From 1735 to 1763, Saxony was ruled by Prince Elector Friedrich August II, who was also King August III of Poland and Grand Duke of Lithuania. Frederick the Great invaded neutral Saxony on 6 September 1756; the Saxon Army – which was completely unprepared – had been withdrawn into a geographically strong position just southeast of Pirna, on the right bank of the river Elbe, on 3 September. Their few supplies soon ran out and the numerically superior Prussians surrounded them, to starve them into submission. Friedrich Augustus had entered a defensive alliance with Russia and Austria and appealed for help. Austria sent an army under Field Marshal Maximilian Graf von Browne, to rescue the Saxon troops. Frederick headed off this thrust with his victory over the Austrians at Lobositz on 1 October 1756. The 18,000 starving Saxons, under Field Marshal Graf Friedrich August von Rutowski, surrendered to the Prussians on 14 October.

Frederick the Great at once tried to force the Saxon troops into his service, but all but 53 Saxon officers refused and were dismissed. Three of the Saxon infantry units (Leibgrenadier-Garde, Königin and the grenadier battalion Kurprinzessin) flatly refused to swear allegance to Prussia; their men were distributed among various Prussian regiments. The other ten Saxon infantry regiments were sworn in, organised on Prussian lines, issued with Prussian uniforms, presented with Prussian colours and given new, Prussian colonels-in-chief and officers (see Prussian chapter).

The Saxon cavalry regiments Karabiniergarde, three regiments of Chevauxlegers (Prinz Albrecht, Graf Brühl and Prinz Karl) and the two Ulan regiments were taken into Austrian pay and joined the army in 1757, participating in all campaigns till 1763. The Saxons forced into Prussian service deserted in droves and made their way south into Austrian territory and later Hungary. By October 1757 over 7000 men had been assembled there; they were formed into new regiments. On 11 March 1758, the new Saxon Army was taken into French service. To avoid contact with the Prussians, who would have shot any prisoners taken as deserters, they marched westwards through southern Germany and arrived in Strassburg in July 1758. In September, they were attached to Contades' French Army in Westphalia. The regiments formed part of Chevert's and Fitzjames' divisions, reinforcing Soubise's army in Hessen. These Saxons first saw action at the Battle of Lutterberg (10 October 1758), where their determined attacks decided the day for the French Army.

Uniform

Until 1766 Saxon generals wore white coats with red facings, lining, waistcoat and breeches. Rank was shown by the amount of gold embroidery on the coat and waistcoat. The hat had scalloped gold lace edging and white, cut feather trim; a white plume was worn. The silver and crimson waist sash was worn under the coat; the sword strap was also silver and crimson. Hair was powdered, curled and worn plaited into a pigtail.

Dismounted officers wore silver and crimson waist sashes and sword straps, silvered gorgets on duty and carried canes with gilt knobs. Infantry subalterns had plain, narrow gold hat edging, captains had scalloped hat edging and field officers' hats had the scalloped edging and a white feather edging. The cockade was white. Musketeer company officers carried spontoons, grenadier company officers carried fusils. NCOs wore narrow gold hat edging and their rank was shown by gold braid to the collar and to the cuffs as follows: corporal a single braid, sergeant two braids, sergeant major three. NCOs had white and crimson hat tassels, carried canes and bore sabres, the sergeants also had spontoons. Grenadiers had sabres; musketeers only bayonets. Drums were brass, bore the full arms of Saxony-Poland and had hoops painted white and the facing colour.

Each infantry battalion had two guns attached to it, entitled *Geschwindstücke* (swift guns) mostly 6-pounders, but also a few 3-pounders. Each piece was served by eight gunners and had a four-horse team. Each infantry regiment was accompanied by 29 wagons and 140 horses; each cavalry regiment had 33 wagons and 150 draught horses.

Guards

Colours

Theoretically, each company carried a colour; that of the *Leibkompagnie* was white, the others were to be in the regimental facing colour. In practice, this was almost never achieved, but new flags were issued in 1752, which followed the scheme. The design was common for all; the face side bore the Saxon/Polish/Lithuanian crest and the royal cipher (FA), on a crowned ermine coat, the obverse bore the crowned royal cipher, on a pedestal, within palm fronds. The edges of the colours were richly decorated. In 1756 all colours and standards were laid up in Königstein fortress until 1763.

Leibgrenadiergarde
Two battalions of grenadiers, each of seven companies. The uniform was a red coat, with yellow lapels, plain round cuffs and turnbacks, white buttons, yellow waistcoat and breeches, white belts, white gaiters in summer, black in winter. Headgear was a brass-fronted Prussian-style grenadier cap, with brass headband, yellow backing and pompon, white braid. Colours: poppy red, averse: Polish crest, reverse: crowned cipher.

Garde zu Fuss
White coat, red facings, yellow buttons. Brass-fronted mitre caps, yellow headband, red backing.

Garde du Corps
Red coat, light blue facings, yellow buttons.

Karabiniergarde
Raised in 1713. Buff coat, red facings, yellow buttons, red and black striped braid with a yellow central stripe.

Line Infantry

Each regiment had ten musketeer companies and two grenadier companies in two battalions. At time of mobilisation, the grenadier companies were grouped in pairs, to form four-battalion grenadier battalions. Up to 1761 the grenadiers wore Prussian-style grenadier caps, with the plates and braid in the button colour, backed in the facing colour; in this year, Austrian-style, bearskin-fronted caps were adopted. Officers' caps had gilt front plates with the Electoral crest; to the rear hung gold cords and tassels. The caps of NCOs and men had brass plates and white cords and tassels. All regiments wore white coats, with facings shown on the lying collar, plain round cuffs, turnbacks and waistcoat. Musketeers wore tricorns with white cockade and edging and three pompons in the regimental facing colour within a white rim. Belts and breeches were white; gaiters were white in summer, black in winter.

Regiment	Facings	Buttons
Königin (Prinz Joseph from 1756)	crimson	yellow
Kurprinzessin	pale blue	yellow
Prinz Friedrich August	yellow	yellow
Prinz Maximilian	green	yellow
Prinz Xavier	pale blue	yellow
Prinz Clemens	dark blue	yellow
Graf Brühl	red	yellow
Fürst Lubomirsky	yellow	white
Minckwitz	dark blue	white
Sachsen-Gotha	pale blue	white
Friesen	green	yellow
Rochow	red	yellow

When these regiments were re-raised again to fight alongside the French and Austrians, they seem to have re-adopted their old uniforms, with white coats and their old facings and buttons. Ten companies of grenadiers were raised from men of the kürassier regiments. They would have worn the fur-trimmed grenadier caps of Austrian style.

Cavalry

Kürassiers

These regiments had four squadrons, each of two companies. They wore plain tricorns, buff coats, buff breeches, black breastplates and white belts. Officers wore the gilt, crowned royal cipher on the upper central part of the breastplate and their shoulder scales were gilt; their harness leather was crimson. Facings (which were worn on collar, cuffs and turnbacks) and buttons are shown below. The front of the tunic was hooked together; it was edged on both sides with a special regimental braid for other ranks, which also edged the collar, cuffs and skirt turnbacks. This regimental braid edged the saddle furniture, which was in the facing colour and bore the crowned royal cipher in the button colour. Officers had gold or silver lace, in the button colour, to hats and tunics. NCOs had gold or yellow hat edging. The standard bandolier was in the facing colour, edged and fringed in the button colour. Kettle drums were silvered and had banners in the facing colour, embroidered in the button colour. From 1765–1763, the kürassier regiments deserted to join their infantry colleagues in French service, where they were formed into grenadier battalions. Standards were square, the Leibstandarte was white, the others in the facing colour, embroidered and fringed in the button colour.

Regiment	Raised	Facings	Buttons	Lace
Leibregiment	1680	red	yellow	yellow with red edging
Kronprinz	1702	dark blue	white	dark blue with white edging
von Arnim	1703	crimson	white	red with a white ladder pattern
Anhalt-Dessau	1698	yellow	white	yellow with black and white edging
von Vitzthum	1702	dark blue	yellow	dark blue with white ladder pattern
von Plötz	1704	green	yellow	yellow with a green ladder pattern★

Kürassier-Regiment Von Plötz was captured by the Prussians in 1756 and attached to their Dragoner-Regiment Württemberg. Within a year, most of the men had deserted and made their way to Austria, where they were distributed amongst the three light horse regiments and some became grenadiers in the cavalry grenadier battalions. In 1761, all twelve regiments were organised to have one grenadier and four musketeer companies. The grenadiers were formed into a battalion of Leibgrenadiergarde and two of Feld-Grenadier-bataillons.

Dragoons and Chevauxlegers

From 1695 dragoons wore red coats, and from 1730 each regiment had a company of grenadiers, who wore grenadier caps, with the front plate in the facing colour, edged in regimental lace, bearing the crowned royal cipher, also in that lace. The headband was in the coat colour, the backing in the facing colour. Dragoons wore an aiguillette in the button colour on the right shoulder. Drummers and trumpeters wore reversed colour, had swallow's nests in the regimental lace to the shoulders, seven chevrons of lace, point up, on each sleeve and an edging of that lace to front and back of the sleeve. Belts were white, breeches were buff. Facings were worn on collar, lapels, cuffs, turnbacks and waistcoats.

Chevauxlegers wore green coats until 1765, when they also adopted red tunics. Saddle furniture was in the facing colour, edged in the regimental braid. It bore the crowned cipher. Belts were white, breeches were buff.

Dragoner-Regiment Graf Rutowsky

Raised in 1741. Red coat, black collar, lapels and cuffs, buff waistcoats, gold buttons.

Graf Brühl Chevauxlegers

Raised in 1735. Green tunic, light blue facings, brass buttons.

Prinz Albrecht Chevauxlegers

Raised in 1745. White tunic, yellow facings.

Prinz Karl Chevauxlegers

Raised in 1734. 1758 Herzog von Kurland. Green coat, red facings, brass buttons. Lace to green saddle furniture: yellow with two red stripes.

Uhlanen (Tartars)

These wore national costume of a Cossack-style fur trimmed cap, white caftan, with slit sleeves, with frogging on the chest in the regimental colour. Officers wore full beards and were armed with pistols and scimitars. They seem to have worn small sabretasches, high up on the right hip, in the facing colour, decorated with the crowned cipher in crimson and silver cord. The front rank soldiers carried lances, with pennants in white and the regimental colour, pistols and sabres; the rear rank carried carbines, pistols and sabres. Belts were buff. Other ranks wore moustaches only. They rode on Hungarian saddles on sheepskin shabraques. Officers had embroidered, square shabraques. Trumpeters wore red, fez-like caps, with fur turbans.

Graf Renard

Red lining to the caftan, red shirt, waistcoat and baggy breeches, officers wore crimson and silver 'Passgürtel' or waist belt, gold buttons. Frogging on the chest was one loop at the top, then a pair, then three loops.

Graf Rudnicki

Dark blue lining to the caftan, dark blue shirt, waistcoat and baggy breeches, officers wore crimson and silver 'Passgürtel' or waist belt, silver buttons. Frogging on the chest was in four pairs.

Artillery

Uniform was a tricorn, green tunic of infantry cut, red facings, brass buttons, buff waistcoat and breeches. The artillery corps consisted of the Haus-Kompagnie (one company at the Dresden Arsenal and fortress personnel), the Field Artillery Battalion (four companies), the all-officer Engineer Corps (Ingenieurkorps), a section of miners (mineurs, 9 men), a platoon of bridge builders (Pontoniers, 28 men), the artisans (Handwerker) and the draught horse party (Rosspartei, 223 men and 627 horses) This organisation was responsible for requisitioning sufficient horses for the artillery equipment at time of mobilisation.

The five artillery companies totalled some 600 men. By 1756, the heavy artillery *parc* of Saxony consisted of twelve 24-pounder guns, each with a 10-horse team, 27 x 12-pounders, each with a ten or twelve-horse team, four 6-pounders and four 24-pounder howitzers, each with a ten-horse team. These all fell into Prussian hands.

Junior officer of Saxon Kürassier-Regiment von Vitzthum and farrier, Leibregiment, stable dress.

17

THE KINGDOM OF SPAIN

At this time, Spain was ruled by the Bourbon monarch, Philip V until 1759, when his son, Charles III assumed the throne until 1788. Spain was allied with France and the Holy Roman Empire against Prussia and her allies.

Infantry

Generals wore dark blue coats with red collars, cuffs lining and waistcoat. Rank was indicated by up to three lines of gold embroidery to collars, cuffs, and waistcoats. The cockade was red.

Spanish infantry regiments consisted of two battalions of approximately 600 men each, organised in one grenadier and eight fusilier companies. Spanish uniforms were similar in cut and appearance to French infantry uniforms at the time, mostly white in colour. Breeches and gaiters were white. Grenadiers wore fur caps with cloth bags in the facing colour, with trim and tassel in the button colour, and brass match cases on their bandoliers. Musketeers wore tricorns with an edging in the button colour. On the lid of the cartridge pouch was the royal arms (the cross of Burgundy) in brass. Hair was powdered, curled and worn plaited into a pigtail. Belts were white.

Drummers wore the uniform of their regiment, but all facings were edged in crimson and white Bourbon lace, as was the front of the coat and the waistcoat. Colonels-in-chief sometimes dressed their drummers in their family livery. Drums were of brass, with red rims. Sergeants bore halberds, musketeer company officers had spontoons, those of the grenadier companies had short muskets. Officers wore red silk waist sashes and gold and red sword straps. When on duty, officers wore gilt gorgets.

All flags were white; the king's colour bore the crowned great crest of Spain, with the collar of the Order of the Golden Fleece, on the red cross of Burgundy. At each end of the cross was the crowned crest of the title of the regiment. The company flags had just the Burgundian cross and the corner crests. The spearhead finials were gilt and red silk cravats hung to halfway down the flag.

Regiment	Raised	Coat	Waistcoat	Collar	Cuffs and Turnbacks	Buttons
Africa	1535	white	blue	–	blue	silver
Aragón	?	white	red	white	red	gold
Asturias	?	white	light blue	–	light blue	silver
Burgos	?	white	white	–	red	gold
Cantabria	1703	white	white	–	blue	silver
Castilla (Rey in 1766)	?	white	white	–	violet	silver
Córdoba	1566	white	red	red	red	gold
Corona	1566	white	blue	–	blue	silver
España	?	white	white	–	light green	gold
Fijo de Badajoz	?	white	white	yellow	yellow	silver
Fijo de Ceuta	?	white	red	red	red	silver
Fijo de Oran	?	white	green	green	green	silver
Galicia	1566	white	red	red	red	silver
Granada	?	white	white	–	green	gold
Guadalajara	?	white	red	–	red	silver
la Princesa	?	white	white	carmine	carmine	gold
León	?	white	red	red	red	silver
Lisboa	1580	white	red	–	red	gold
Lombardia	1534	white	white	–	red	silver
Mallorca	?	white	red	–	red	gold
Murcia	?	white	white	blue	blue	silver
Navarra	1705	white	red	red	red	gold
Príncipe	?	white	white	carmine	carmine	silver
Real America	?	blue	yellow	yellow	yellow	silver
Reina	?	blue	red	–	red	silver
Saboya	1633	white	blue	blue	blue	silver
Sevilla	?	white	blue	blue	blue	silver
Soria	1580	white	red	red	red	silver
Toledo	?	white	blue	–	blue	gold
Vitoria	1658	white	red	–	red	silver
Zamora	1580	white	red	–	red	silver
Foreign Regiments						
Antiguo de Reding (Swiss)	1742	blue	yellow	-	yellow	silver

Brabante (Wallon)	?	white	blue	blue	blue	gold
Bruselas (Wallon)	?	white	white	–	white	silver
Buch (Swiss)	1734	blue	red	–	blue	silver
Dunant (Swiss)	1742	blue	red	–	red	silver
Flándes (Wallon)	?	white	blue	blue	blue	silver
Hibernia (Irish)	1709	red	green	green	green	gold
Irlanda (Irish)	?	red	blue	blue	blue	gold
Milán (Italian)	1678	white	blue	–	blue	silver
Nápoles (Italian)	1572	white	red	–	red	silver
Nuevo de Reding (Swiss)	1742	blue	red	–	red	silver
Ultonia (Irish)	1709	red	black	black	black	gold

Light Infantry

Uniform as for the line except that the tunic was dark blue.

Regiment	Collar	Cuffs and Flap	Lapels	Buttons
1st Aragon	red	red	red	white
2nd Aragon	dark blue	red	red	yellow
Barbastro	red	red	dark blue	white
1st Barcelona	yellow	yellow	dark blue	white
2nd Barcelona	dark blue	yellow	yellow	white
Campo Mayor	dark blue	crimson	crimson	white
1st Cataluña	yellow	yellow	yellow	yellow
2nd Cataluña	dark blue	yellow	yellow	yellow
Gerona	yellow	yellow	yellow	white
Navarra	crimson	crimson	dark blue	white
Taragona	yellow	yellow	dark blue	yellow
Valencia	crimson	crimson	crimson	white

Light Cavalry

Uniform

Tricorn hats were laced in the button colour and bore the red cockade; the coats were single-breasted, without collars. Facings were shown on the cuffs, waistcoats, breeches and saddle furniture, which was edged in the button colour, but bore no ciphers. Belts were buff. Long, cuffed boots were worn. Horse regiments were armed with heavy, straight-bladed swords and pistols.

Standards

The sovereign's standard was white and square, fringed in the button colour and bearing the great crest of Spain, complete with the collars. Gold embroidery edged the cloth. The spearhead finial was gold and gold cords and yellow-red-yellow cravats, with gold tasselled ends, hung down to the length of the cloth of the standard. The other three standards were in the regimental facing colour.

Regiment	Coat	Cuffs	Lapels	Buttons	Breeches
Alcantara	white	red	red	white	red
Algarve	white	light blue	none	white	light blue
Andalucia	white	light blue	none	yellow	light blue
Barcelona	white	light blue	light blue	yellow	light blue
Borbón	dark blue	red	red	white	red
Brabante	white	light blue	light blue	white	light blue
Calatrava	white	red	none	white	red
Costa de Granada	dark blue	yellow	none	white	yellow
Extremadura	white	red	red	yellow	red
Farnesio	dark blue	red	none	yellow	red
Flandes	white	light blue	none	white	light blue
Granada	white	crimson	none	yellow	crimson
Malta	white	light blue	white	white	light blue
Milán	white	red	none	white	red
Montesa	white	light blue	none	white	light blue
Ordenes	dark blue	red	none	white	red
Reina	red	dark blue	none	white	dark blue
Santiago	dark blue	red	none	white	dark blue
Sevilla	white	light blue	none	yellow	light blue

Dragoons

All regiments wore yellow coats of infantry cut, except for Reina, who wore red. All regiments wore aiguillettes on the right shoulder in the button colour. Waistcoats were in the facing colour, except for Lusitania, who wore yellow. Facings were shown on collars, cuffs, turnbacks, waistcoats, breeches and saddle furniture, except as noted below. Instead of riding boots, dragoons wore black leather gaiters, with buckles and straps up the sides. They were armed with infantry muskets and had drummers. Saddle furniture was yellow, edged in the button colour, without ciphers. Dragoons carried guidons, with the same colour scheme and designs as the standards of the heavy cavalry.

Regiment	Facings	Buttons
Batavia	light blue, edged white, white laces to the cuff buttons	white
Bélgica	red with white laces and tassles	white
Edimburgo	light blue (no lapels)	white
Frisia	red	yellow
Lusitania	black (no lapels, white buttonholes)	white
Merida	light blue (no lapels)	white
Numancia	light blue (no lapels)	white
Pavia	red	white in pairs
Reina	light blue	white
Sagunto	black (no lapels)	white

Artillery

Tricorns laced in yellow, dark blue coats, collar and breeches, red cuffs, waistcoats, turnbacks and breeches, brass buttons, white gaiters and belts.

Engineers

A small, all officer corps. The uniform was dark blue, with silver lace and buttons, red cuffs and waistcoats, dark blue breeches and white stockings. The hat, cuffs and waistcoat were edged in silver lace, as were the buttonholes and pocket flaps.

18

THE KINGDOM OF SWEDEN

Sweden was ruled by King Adolf Fredrik, of the house of Schleswig-Holstein-Gottorp from 1751 to 1771.

A peculiarity of the Swedish infantry was that, due to pressing economic reasons, it consisted of two types of regiments: *varvade* and *indelta*. The six *varvade* regiments were raised by conventional recruitment, regularly paid, kept up to strength and accommodated in barracks. *Indelta* regiments – the bulk of the army and the earliest formations to have been raised – were conscripted from the general populace at a rate of so many men for an area, who were gathered each spring to undergo 28 days of drill and arms training, then dispersed back to their homes until called out in an emergency. For these regiments, only a command and maintenance cadre of officers, NCOs and men were retained on full pay, to guard and maintain the regimental weapons and stores.

The usual conventions of current military dress applied to the Swedish Army. Uniforms were extremely simple, with many regiments having identical costumes. Officers wore gold edging to the hat, a silver gorget when on duty, their skirts were not turned back, their breeches were in the coat colour. They did not wear gold waist sashes. Company officers carried spontoons, grenadier officers wore grenadier caps and bore short muskets. Privates wore waistcoats and breeches often in the facing colour. Grenadiers wore metal-fronted mitre caps of Prussian style, in the button colour, mostly in black wax covers. NCOs wore white small clothes, had silver edging to the hat and bore halberds, but no canes. Drummers wore the same uniforms as privates, but with white and gold braid on the sleeves and the swallow's nests. Drums were brass, with the provincial coat of arms and blue and yellow hoops. Hair was powdered, curled and worn plaited in a pigtail.

The Guard

Foot Guards

Kungl Livgardet (Royal Life Guards)
Raised in 1617. In 1756 it had 18 companies, ten of which went to Pomerania in August 1757. Uniform was a tricorn with white edging, dark blue, singe-breasted coat with yellow facings, waistcoat and breeches, white buttons and gaiters, white belts with brass fittings. Grenadiers had mitre caps with tin front plates. *Liffana*: white field sown with gold crowns; the central device consisted of the crowned golden cipher 'AR' flanked by two golden lions. *Kompanifana*: white field bearing the crowned royal cipher 'AR'; a small crown in each corner. This regiment did not take the field during the war.

Drottningens Livregemente (Queen's Life Guards)

Raised in 1703. It had 12 companies, mainly consisting of Germans. In 1757 four campanies were sent to Stralsund. Uniform was as for the Livgardet, but with brass buttons and cap plate, white facings, waistcoat and breeches. *Liffana*: white field, the central device probably consisting of the golden crowned cipher 'AR'; a gold crown in each corner. *Kompanifana*: blue field; same devices as for the *Liffana*. This regiment did not take the field during the war.

Kronprinsens (Crown Prince's Regiment)

Raised in 1719 as 'Horn's Regiment', renamed Kronprinsens in 1747. It had two battalions each of four companies. In August 1757 four companies were sent to Pomerania. Uniform was dark blue, with yellow facings, waistcoat and breeches, white buttons. *Liffana*: white field; the central device is unknown. *Kompanifana*: dark blue field; the central device consisted of golden rays with a gold star and three white crowns in the middle; a golden crown in each corner.

Horse Guards

There was a palace unit called the 'Adelsfanan' (Noble Guard), but it did not take to the field and is not considered here.

Upplands Livregemente

Raised in 1623. Ten companies of the regiment went to Pomerania. Uniform was a plain tricorn with brass button, dark blue, single-breasted tunic, white facings buff breeches and belts, blue saddle furniture with wide yellow edging and three yellow crowns on holster covers and in the rear, square corner.

Livdragoner

Raised in 1536. Four companies of the regiment went to Pomerania in 1761. Uniform as for the Liv Regiment.

Line Infantry

Line infantry regiments consisted of two musketeer battalions (eight companies in all) and a platoon of about 50 grenadiers. Each musketeer battalion had two 3-pounder guns. In 1758, all the grenadiers with the Swedish Army in Pomerania were concentrated into two battalions. In 1756 the entire strength of the Swedish Army was about 35,000 men. Most units were at half their established strength and the supply system for food and forage left much to be desired, particularly in the conscript regiments. Regular regiments are identified with the letter 'R', conscript regiments with a 'C'.

Colours

There seem to have been two types, one for the conscript regiments and another for the regulars. For the conscript regiments, the colonel's battalion carried the sovereign's colour (*Liffana*) and a company colour (*Kompanifana*). The lieutenant-colonel's battalion carried two *Kompanifanor*. The sovereign's colour was white, with the crowned royal arms of Sweden flanked by two crowned golden lion supporters. The corner of the first canton bore the provincial badge. The company colour was in the provincial colour and bore the provincial badge, within a green laurel wreath, tied with a golden ribbon.

For the regular regiments the sovereign's colour was white, the device was the crowned royal cipher in gold, within green palm branches, tied with a golden ribbon. The company colours varied for each regiment and are described in the regimental sections. The pikes used as staffs to carry the colours were yellow. That of the sovereign's colour had a gilt finial; that of the company colours had a steel tip, bearing the royal cipher.

Åboläns Regemente C

A Finnish regiment raised in 1620 when the Finnish Grand Regiment was divided into smaller units. It became a conscript regiment in 1694. Facings yellow, buttons white.

Älvsborgs Regemente C

Raised in 1613 as the Västergötlands Grand Regiment. Facings yellow, buttons white.

Björneborgs Regemente C

A Finnish regiment raised in February 1626 when the Finnish Grand Regiment was divided into smaller units. Facings yellow, buttons yellow.

Cronhjelmska Regemente R

Raised in 1722 in Sveaborg. Facings white, buttons white, blue breeches. *Kompanifana*: a quartered field with an upper triangle of light blue and yellow diagonal stripes, a lower light blue triangle and yellow left and right triangles, the central device being a golden crown; the crowned golden cipher 'F' in each corner.

Dalarnas Regemente C

Raised in 1617 as the Upplands Grand Regiment. Facings yellow, buttons white.

Elimas Regemente C

Raised in 1620 as the Vyborg Finnish Regiment; in 1721, Russia annexed part of this region and the regiment was reduced to a single battalion. In 1744, after Russia annexed more of these territories, the battalion was reduced to a single company. Facings yellow, buttons white.

Hälsinge Regemente C

Raised in 1615 as the Norrland Grand Regiment. Facings yellow, buttons white.

Hamiltonska Regemente R

Raised in 1741 at Helsingfors (now Helsinki). Facings and buttons white, blue breeches. *Kompanifana*: a dark blue field with three diagonal white stripes, from upper fly to lower hoist corner; the central device was a crowned lilac-coloured globe, within the central white flame, containing the three gold Swedish crowns.

Hessensteinska Regemente R

Raised before 1719, as a training unit in Västgöta. Facings yellow, buttons white, yellow breeches. *Kompanifana*: a yellow field, the central device was a blue circle with three diagonal wavy stripes (running from top left) and charged with a crowned gold lion; each corner carried a crowned golden royal ciphers.

Jämtlands Regemente C

Raised in 1648. In 1680, it was renamed Jämtlands Dragonregemente, but it was never mounted. Facings yellow, buttons white.

Jönköpings Regemente C

Raised in 1618 as the Östergötland Grand Regiment. Facings yellow, buttons white.

Kalmar Regemente C

Raised in 1616 as part of the Småland Grand Regiment. Facings yellow, buttons white.

Kronobergs Regemente C
Raised in 1616 as part of the Småland Grand Regiment. Facings yellow, buttons white.

Löwenfelska Regemente R
Raised in 1721 with troops originating from the Västraskånska and Östraskånska regiments. Facings and buttons white, blue breeches. Company colour: a dark blue field bearing the crowned royal cipher in gold.

Närke-Värmlands Regemente C
Raised in 1614 as the Södermanlands Grand Regiment. Facings red, buttons white.

Nylands Regemente C
Raised in 1626. It became a conscript regiment in 1696; a Finnish regiment. Facings yellow, buttons yellow.

Österbottens Regemente C
Raised in 1620. It became a conscript regiment in 1733; a Finnish regiment. Facings yellow, buttons yellow.

Östgöta Infanteriregemente C
Raised in 1618 as the Östergötland Grand Regiment. Facings yellow, buttons white.

Posseska Regemente R
Raised in 1743 at Stralsund. Facings white, buttons, waistcoats and breeches yellow. Company colour: as for the sovereign's colour, but with a dark blue ground.

Savolax Regemente C
Raised in 1626 as the Savolax and Myslotts Land Regiment. It became a conscript regiment in 1695; a Finnish regiment. Facings yellow, buttons white.

Skaraborgs Regemente C
Raised in 1613 as the Västergötlands Grand Regiment. Facings yellow, buttons white.

Södermanlands Regemente C
Raised in 1614 as the Södermanlands Grand Regiment. Facings yellow, buttons yellow.

Spenska Regemente R
Raised in 1749 at Stralsund. Facings red, buttons yellow, waistcoats and breeches white. Company colour: red field, with a central device of a crowned lilac-coloured circle, charged with the three Swedish gold crowns, within golden palm fronds.

Tavastehus Regemente C
Raised in 1626 when the Finnish Grand Regiment was divided into smaller units. It became an *indelta* regiment in 1696; a Finnish regiment. Facings yellow, buttons white.

Upplands Regemente C
Raised in 1617, as the Upplands Grand Regiment. Facings yellow, buttons white.

Västerbottens Regemente C
Raised in 1615 as the Norrland Grand Regiment. Facings white, buttons white.

Västgöta-Dals Regemente C
Raised in 1613 as the Västergötlands Grand Regiment. Facings yellow, buttons yellow.

Västmanlands Regemente C
Raised in 1617 as the Upplands Grand Regiment. Facings yellow, buttons white.

Temporary Combined Tactical Units
These wore the uniforms of their parent regiments.

Fabritius Bataljon
Raised in August 1759 by Major Fabritius from men unfit for field service from various regiments, for garrison duty in Stralsund.

Finnish Grenadiers
Raised in November 1761 from the Finnish regiments in Pomerania.

I. German Grenadiers
Raised on 18 July 1758, from the grenadiers of the four German (Pomeranian) regiments serving in Pomerania.

II. German Grenadiers
Raised in July 1761, from the grenadiers of the four German (Pomeranian) regiments serving in Pomerania.

I. Swedish Grenadiers
Raised in July 1758, from the grenadiers of the Swedish conscript regiments serving in Pomerania.

II. Swedish Grenadiers
Raised in August 1761, from grenadiers of the Swedish conscript regiments serving in Pomerania along with 120 grenadiers of the Kronprinsens Regiment and 40 grenadiers of the combined battalion.

Cavalry

Cuirassiers
Each regiment had eight companies. Uniform was a plain tricorn, a blue, single-breasted coat, with facings shown on collar, plain cuffs, turnbacks and waistcoat. Breeches were buff leather, belts were buff. Saddle furniture was blue, edged yellow. They wore polished steel breastplates under their coats and buff gauntlets. They were armed with a straight-bladed sword, two pistols and a carbine. Trumpeters had yellow swallow's nests, edged in white.

Each cuirassier squadron bore a square, fringed standard, heavily embroidered in gold and silver, on a lance, with a gilt finial bearing the royal cipher. *Lifstandar*: white field, the central device was the crowned royal arms of Sweden flanked by two crowned golden lions; the upper inner quarter bore the provincial crest. *Kompanistandar*: Obverse: the provincial crest. Reverse: yellow field; central device was the crowned, golden royal cipher 'AF', within a golden laurel wreath beneath tied with a red ribbon.

Jämtlands
Raised in 1670. Facings blue, buttons yellow. *Kompanistandar* had a blue field.

Swedish infantry private, trooper of the Bla Husarenregiment (foreground), trooper of dragoons, trooper of the Gula Husarenregiment. Due to a chronic lack of funds, Swedish uniforms were very simple. The death's head badge on the busby (or colpack) of the yellow hussar has Prussian overtones. (Knötel, V 59)

Norra Skånska
Raised in 1658 and was named Norra Skånska Horse Regiment in 1676. Facings buff, buttons yellow. *Kompanistandar* had a yellow field.

Östgöta
Raised in 1636. Facings red, buttons yellow. *Kompanistandar* had a red field.

Smålands
Raised in 1543. In 1684 it became the Smålands Cavalry Regiment. *Kompanistandar* had a yellow field.

Södra Skånska
Raised in 1676. Facings buff, buttons yellow. *Kompanistandar* had a yellow field.

Västgöta
Raised in 1628. Facings yellow, buttons yellow. *Kompanistandar* had a light blue field.

Dragoons
Each regiment had eight companies. Uniform and saddle furniture was as for the cuirassiers, without the breastplate. Dragoon guidons were cut out in a 'V'shape on the fly side.

Nylands Dragonregemente
Raised in southern Finland in 1632 as the Nylands and Tavastehus Cavalry Regiment. Blue coat, facings yellow, buttons yellow. *Kompanistandar* had a red field.

Bohusläns Dragonregemente
Raised in Bohuslän in 1660 for colonel Rutger von Ascheberg. Green coat, facings yellow, buttons yellow. *Kompanistandar* had a green field.

Karelska Dragonregemente
Raised in 1632 in eastern Finland as the Vyborgsläns Cavalry Regiment. This unit had only two and a half companies. Blue coat, facings red, buttons yellow. *Kompanistandar*, had a red field.

Hussars

Each regiment had six squadrons. Uniform was typical hussar dress, with mirliton, dolman, pelisse, barrel sash, sabretasche bearing the crowned cipher 'AF'. Saddle furniture was in the dolman colour, edged yellow. They were armed with light sabres in black sheaths, pistols and a carbine. Belts were yellow. Hussars bore no standards at this time.

Bla Husarenregiment

Raised on 19 December 1757. Cornflower blue dolman, with yellow collar and cuffs, cornflower blue pelisse and over-breeches. Black mirliton with yellow crown, cords and frontal rosette. Yellow barrel sash, buttons and lace, black boots, topped yellow. Officers wore gold lace and buttons, gold sabre straps.

Gula Husarenregiment

Raised on 20 October 1761. Brown fur busby with yellow bag, white cords and white skull and bone badge to the front. Black dolman, saddle furniture and over-breeches, white buttons and lace. Yellow collars and cuffs to the dolman, yellow barrel sash. Officers wore silver lace and buttons, gold sabre straps.

Light Troops

Hästjägare (Mounted Rifles)

Raised in the autumn of 1757. It had two squadrons. Uniform not known.

Husarskyttekår Company

Raised by order of 14 March 1758. These were foot riflemen, wearing hussar-style costume. Initially they were attached to the Bla Hussars, but in 1761, they became an independent unit, known as the Rosenquist Foot Jäger Company. Uniform not known.

Köhler's Company

Raised on 2 November 1761. It saw no action. Uniform was all Russian green, yellow collars, cuffs and buttons.

Böhnens Fribataljon

Raised on 30 April 1758 from deserters. Uniform blue with yellow facings.

Schwarter's Company

Raised on 2 November 1761. Uniform Russian green with yellow. It is unlikely that this unit saw action.

Artillery

At the beginning of the Seven Years War, the Swedish artillery counted about 3000 men in 38 companies. By the end of August 1757, 935 artillerymen of the regiment had been transported across the Baltic towards Swedish-Pomerania. The regiment was equipped with twelve 12-pounder guns, twelve 6-pounders, 36 3-pounder battalion guns, two 16 pounder howitzers and eight 8-pounder howitzers. Carriages and limbers were painted light blue with unpainted brass fittings. In 1761, the Swedish Army suffered from a shortage of horses and was forced to leave all its field guns in the town of Grimen. Only the battalion guns took the field. The uniform was of infantry style, all dark blue, yellow buttons, buff belts, black gaiters.

THE DUCHY OF WÜRTTEMBERG

The Duchy was ruled over by Herzog Carl Eugen (1728–1793), who had been educated in Prussia. The army of Württemberg was dressed almost exactly as that of Prussia, as well as being organised and drilled in the same manner. Although the small state took the field against Prussia in this war, and her costs were paid by France, there was so much anti-French feeling amongst the Protestant members of the army, that it had to be arranged for the contingent to be placed under Austrian command until 1758.

The army then joined the French Army in Hessen, but the high desertion rates were symptomatic of the low morale which pervaded the little army. By 1760, they were back under Austrian control. Württemberg was part of the Swabian Kreis and provided a regiment each of cavalry and infantry for that force, in addition to the troops shown here.

The Garde zu Fuss regiment had a battalion of grenadiers and two of musketeers, each of four companies. The other regiments had only two battalions, each of a grenadier and five musketeer companies. In the field, the grenadier companies were taken from their parent regiments from 1759 and formed into six combined grenadier battalions, known by the names of their commanders. Each battalion initially had one 3-pound gun. In 1758 they were issued with French-manufactured 4-pounders.

Infantry

Uniform

Uniforms, badges of rank, and other outward features of soldiers, officers, NCOs, drummers and pioneers were all as in Prussia. Hair was powdered, curled and worn plaited into a pigtail. Tricorns were edged in the button colour; the hat pompon was black over yellow. Traditionally Württemberg's infantry had worn pale coloured coats, but in 1752, dark blue was adopted. The facings were shown on the lying collar, lapels, plain round cuffs, shoulder straps and turnbacks. The skirts of officers' coats were not turned back.

Officers wore gorgets in the button colour and wore gold waist sashes with black stripes under the coat and gold and black sword straps. Buttons were worn, six on each lapel, two under each lapel, three on each plain cuff, three on each pocket flap, two in the small of the back and one at the join of the skirt turnbacks.

An aiguillette in the button colour was worn on the right shoulder. Grenadier cap: plates were in the button colour and bore the reversed cipher 'C', under a star and the ducal crown. The headband was also in metal, the backing in the facing colour, the braid in the button colour. Breeches and belts white and the long black gaiters were black, with regimental buttons.

Füsilier-Regiment von Truchsess
1759 vacant; 1762 Prinz Friedrich Wilhelm. Black facings, yellow buttons, white waistcoat.

Kreis-Infanterie-Regiment Württemberg
Raised in 1673 as the Herzögliches Regiment zu Fuss by Herzog Eberhard III; 1684 Schwäbisches Kreis-Regiment zu Fuss Baden-Durlach; 1701 Kreis-Infanterie-Regiment von Reischach; 1702 Kreis-Infanterie-Regiment Württemberg.

Leib-Grenadier-Regiment
Raised in 1758 from the Garde zu Fuß. Crimson facings, white buttons, black-over-yellow hat pompon, yellow waistcoat. This unit had white buttonhole laces and tassels, as for the Leib-Infanterie-Regiment. All companies wore brass-fronted grenadier caps with brass headband, crimson backing and yellow braid.

Leib-Infanterie-Regiment von Werneck
Garde zu Fuß in 1758. This unit had six white buttonhole laces, with white tassels, on each lapel, two under each lapel, three on each plain cuff. Facings were crimson, yellow waistcoat; the hat pompon was yellow over black.

Infanterie-Regiment Prinz Friedrich Wilhelm
Raised in 1759. 1761 von Roman; 1763 von Stain. White facings and waistcoat, yellow buttons, light blue hat pompons.

Infanterie-Regiment Prinz Louis
Raised in 1744. Red facings, white buttons, white waistcoat, yellow-over-red hat pompons, blue headband to grenadier cap.

Infanterie-Regiment von Roeder
1759 von Wolff. Pink facings, white buttons, white hat pompons, white waistcoat.

Infanterie-Regiment von Werneck
Raised in 1758 from the Leib-Infanterie-Regiment. Crimson facings, white buttons, black-over-yellow hat pompon, yellow waistcoat. This unit had white buttonhole laces and tassels, as for the Leib-Infanterie-Regiment.

Infanterie-Regiment von Spiznass
Raised on 8 March 1716. 1758 von Roman; 1761 Prinz Friedrich Wilhelm; 1762 von der Gabelenz. In 1752 they wore red facings, yellow buttons, white waistcoat. By 1762 the facings had changed to red; the hat pompon was light blue over red, as was the grenadier cap headband.

Grenadier Battalions
In the field, the grenadier companies were taken from their parent regiments from 1759 and formed into six combined grenadier battalions, known by the names of their commanders.

Grenadier Bataillon von Lengenfeld

Formed from Infanterie-Regiment Prinz Louis and Infanterie-Regiment von Spitznas. 1759 von Witzleben.

Grenadier Bataillon von Plessen

Formed from Leib-Infanterie-Regiment von Werneck. 1758 von Plessen; 1759 von Bode; 1762 von Plessen (again).

Grenadier Bataillon von Bouwinghausen-Walmerode

Formed from Füsilier-Regiment von Truchsess and Infanterie-Regiment von Roeder in 1758. 1759 von Reischach; 1760 von Altenstein; 1762 von Reischach (again).

Feld-Grenadier-Bataillon von Heimburg

Raised in 1761 and disbanded in 1767.

Grenadier Bataillon Herzog

Raised in 1762 from the Leib-Grenadier-Regiment. In June 1763, when another battalion was created with the name of Hausgrenadierbataillon, it had to be renamed and was designated as the Herzogsgrenadierbataillon (Duke's Grenadier Battalion). 1762 von Altenstein. Disbanded in 1765. Did not see active service during the war.

Cavalry

Each cavalry regiment had four escadrons each of two companies.

Kürassier-Regiment General-Major Ludwig Wilhelm August von Phull

Raised on 10 May 1758 with four squadrons; in March 1761 it was converted to a dragoon regiment. The regiment was disbanded in 1766.

The uniform was a tricorn with scalloped yellow edging, black cockade, yellow loop and button, buff tunic, red collar, lapels, plain red cuffs, turnbacks and waistcoat, all edged in red lace, having two yellow stripes along it. Buff gauntlets and breeches, white belts. Troops were armed with a steel-hilted, straight-bladed sword in a black sheath with steel fittings. They also carried a pair of pistols. A black cuirass, with brass edging and fittings and red and yellow cuffs was worn. Saddle furniture was red, square-cut, edged in the regimental lace and bearing the cipher of a reversed 'C', in black. After the conversion to dragoons, the armour was discarded, a yellow aiguillette was added to the right shoulder and the troops were armed with muskets.

The form of the sovereign's standard is not known, but it was almost certainly white, embroidered and fringed in the button colour. The squadron standards seem to have been red, square, fringed in gold. Both sides bore the same basic layout: corner ciphers of the reversed 'C'; a central surround of a circular 'wreath' made up of trophies of arms. Within this on the obverse was the great crest of Württemberg. On the reverse was an allegorical scene of two goddesses under a scroll bearing: '17 PROVIDE ET CONSTANTER 58', in silver and gold. The gilt, spearpoint finial was pierced to show the reversed 'C' cipher; gold cords and tassels hung down to the bottom of the standard. The standard bandolier was red, edged and decorated in gold. The brown wooden staff was decorated with red ribbon, held with gold nails.

Dragoner-Regiment von Degenfeld

Raised in 1758. 1759 von Röder; 1762 von Rothkirch. Uniform was a tricorn edged in yellow scalloped lace, with a black cockade and yellow button; an off-white tunic with black collar, lapels, plain round cuffs and turnbacks, yellow buttons, yellow waistcoat and aiguillette off the left shoulder, buff gauntlets and waistcoat, white breeches, and saddle furniture, the latter presumably edged black and with the cipher of the crowned, reversed 'C'. Harness was of black leather with steel fittings. There is no information as to standards carried.

Leib-Grenadiers à Cheval
Raised on 11 October 1758, with four squadrons. Chef was the Duke of Württemberg. Uniform was a plain brown bearskin, without plate, with a red bag and yellow braid ans tassel. The tunic was red, with black collar, lapels, plain round cuffs and turnbacks, yellow buttons and aiguillette off the right shoulder, white waistcoat, breeches and belts, buff gauntlets. Saddle furniture was red, edged in red braid, having black edges and a wavy white line along it. It was decorated with the reversed 'C'. Arms were a steel-hilted, straight-bladed sword in a black sheath with steel fittings, a musket and a pair of pistols. Some sources state that they wore a black steel cuirass under the coat, but this is unlikely. There is no information on standards.

Kreis-Regiment
Raised on 9 July 1683 from the Leibwache zu Pferde and the six Kreis-Kompagnien as the Schwäbisches Kreisregiment zu Pferde von Höhnstett. 1731 Kreis-Dragoner-Regiment Herzog Carl Alexander von Württemberg with eight companies. 1737 Markgraf Carl Wilhelm von Baden-Durlach; 1738 Württemberg.

Light Troops
Gorcy Husaren
Raised in 1735 with one squadron, increased to four in 1758. Chef was Jean-Baptiste Gorcy de la Mariniere. Uniform was a brown busby with red bag, yellow braid and tassel and a black plume, dark green dolman and pelisse, red breeches, yellow braid and buttons, brown fur trim to the pelisse, black collar and cuffs to the dolman, red and yellow barrel sash, buff bandolier. The curved, brass-hilted sabre had a black sheath with brass fittings. The saddle furniture and sabretasche were red, with yellow edging and yellow, reversed 'C' cipher. As light troops, it is unlikely that they carried standards.

Feldjäger zu Fuss
Raised 1759 at one company, from the foresters of the duchy. Uniform was a tricorn with plain yellow edging and yellow button, dark green tunic and waistcoat, with red collar, lapels, plain round cuffs and turnbacks, yellow buttons and yellow aiguillette from the right shoulder, white breeches, black gaiters, brown belts. They were armed with rifles and a *Hirschfänger* or sword bayonet with a brass hilt in a brown scabbard.

Feldjäger zu Pferd
Raised in 1759 with two squadrons. Uniform was as for the Feldjägers, but with buff breeches and long, black riding boots, Saddle furniture was dark green, edged in yellow and having the crowned, reversed 'C' cipher.

Freihusaren von Glasenapp
Raised in 1759 with two squadrons. Uniform was a brown busby, red pelisse with brown fur trim and white braid and buttons. The dolman was light blue with red collar and cuffs, white braid and buttons. The barrel sash was red and white. Breeches were buff, with light blue *Scharawaden* edged white. Belts were white, boots black. Saddle furniture and sabretasche were light blue edged white with the white, reversed 'C' cipher.

Artillery

There was one company in 1757; in 1758 it was increased to a battalion of five companies. In 1760 it was again increased to 600 men in order to serve the 20 heavy guns, that had been acquired. Uniform in 1756 was a tricorn, edged yellow and having a yellow-over-black pompon, dark blue tunic of infantry cut, with black collar, lapels, plain round cuffs and turnbacks, yellow buttons, white waistcoat, breeches and belts. They were armed with a brass-hilted, straight-bladed sword in a black sheath with brass fittings. Later in the war, the tunic became light blue. Officers' hats had scalloped gold lace edging.

20

THE BISHOPRIC OF WÜRZBURG

Würzburg was geographically part of the Franconian Kreis of the Holy Roman Empire. It maintained three infantry regiments (Drachsdorff, Kolb and Hutten), a regiment of dismounted dragoons, some artillery and a militia regiment. As its contribution to the Imperial war effort, Würzburg formed two infantry regiments from the existing three, which were known by the colour of their facings as 'Rot' and Blau' Würzburg. Blau served with the Austrian-Burgundian Kreis of the Imperial Army, while Rot served directly as part of the Austrian Army.

Both regiments were organised on Austrian lines and wore Austrian-style uniforms, differing from one another only in their facings and the colour of the flames around the borders of their colours. Both regiments had two battalions, each of one grenadier and six musketeer companies and two 4-pounder guns. In 1760 the establishment was reduced to one battalion and in 1761, the combined regiment had three battalions, totalling three grenadier and 18 musketeer companies. In 1762 two companies of the 3rd Battalion were disbanded. The Inhaber was the Archbishop of Würzburg.

The uniform was of Austrian style, with red/blue facings, white hat edging, white small clothes, belts and brass buttons. The pouch had a brass badge. Grenadiers wore a fur, brass-fronted cap, with a red/blue bag. There were brass grenades on their pouches and brass match cases on their bandoliers; they bore sabres. NCOs had gold hat edging and braid to collar and cuffs; hazelnut stick, grenadier sabre with brass hilt and black sheath. Sergeants bore halberds. The details of drummers' distinctions and of officers' waist sashes and sword straps are not known; probably they were gold.

The regiment had one Leibfahne; it was white, the edges having flamed designs; white and red, white and blue, white and green are known to have existed, each with the white flame tips pointing inwards. The design was the same on both sides: imperial eagle, under a bishop's mitre and on crossed sword and crosier. On the eagle's breast was a gold-framed, quartered crest: upper left and lower right: yellow with black leopards, a silver bend across them; upper right and lower left: the red over white crest of Würzburg. The heart shield was the quartered personal crest of the Graf of Seinsheim: upper left and lower right: three white and three blue bars; upper right and lower left: on a yellow field a leaping, crowned black boar. The designs of the company colours are unknown.

Infanterie-Regiment Rot-Würzburg

Raised in 1756 from the old Infantry Regiments Drachsdorff and Hutten, plus some men from Kolb, and served with the Austrian Army until 1759, when it was transferred to the Imperial Army.

Infanterie-Regiment Blau-Würzburg

Raised in 1757 from 500 men of the old Infantry Regiment Kolb and new recruits; it joined the Imperial Army that summer, as part of the Austrian–Burgundian Kreis contingent. It suffered heavy casualties at Rossbach. In 1761 it was incorporated into Infanterie-Regiment Rot-Würzburg.

APPENDIX 1

KEY BATTLES

These actions have been selected not because of their magnitude, but because of the impact that they had on subsequent events. Thus, Plassey, Quebec and Wandewash, which were at best relatively minor tactical events, are included because of their historical importance, which was much greater than that of other battles involving tens of thousands of men.

This war took place in several theatres in Europe, North America, India and on the high seas. Each action entry includes the date, nature and location of the action, with a brief description of the significant geographical surroundings to aid location on a map, the names of the rival commanders involved, the rough numbers of combatants, the outcome of that action and details of the previous and subsequent actions in that theatre.

As many place names have changed in the intervening years, the old name and the new names are included. In the case of naval ships, the number of guns carried is provided in brackets after the name. Sometimes details of numbers of engaged battalions/squadrons from a particular regiment are not available; absence of the information does not imply that the entire regiment was present. Similarly details of brigade commanders has often been lost, in which case regiments belonging to an unnamed brigade are just listed under 'Brigade:'.

Battle of Minorca, 20 May 1756

Location
Off the eastern end of the island of Minorca, in the western Mediterranean Sea.

In March 1756, the Admiralty, panic-stricken by the news that the French were preparing to invade British-held Minorca, ordered Admiral Byng in Gibraltar to prepare to do battle with the French force. The main fortress of Minorca, Fort St Philip, was chronically undermanned after years of inactivity, and the naval force in the harbour inadequate to fend off any serious enemy naval threat. Although his ships were very limited in number and many were in unseaworthy condition and undermanned, Admiral Byng was not allowed to draw on any of the resources available to repair, refit and reinforce his command before the action. Rear Admiral Temple West was appointed as Byng's second-in-command.

On 10 April the French squadron (twelve ships of the line and five frigates) left Toulon escorting 198 transports carrying 16,000 men with regimental artillery and 36 field guns under the Duc de

Richelieu. On 18 April, the French began to disembark, unopposed, at Ciutadella on Minorca and in two days the operation was completed. On 23 April, Commodore Edgcumbe's small squadron of *Princess Louisa* (60), *Portland* (50), the frigates *Chesterfield* (44), *Dolphin* (24) and the sloop *Porcupine* (16), escaped from Port Mahon and sailed for Gibraltar.

The battle between the fleets took place on 20 May and was inconclusive, but the state of Byng's ships was cause for concern. He held a council of war on *Ramillies* on 24 May; the unanimous decision was taken to return to Gibraltar. Byng sent off his report to the Admiralty. The failure to hold Fort St Philip and Minorca caused public outrage amongst Byng's fellow officers and the country at large. Byng was ordered to return to England. Upon landing on 19 August, Byng was sent to Greenwich. Here, he remained in confinement until 23 December, when he was transferred to Portsmouth. On 27 December 1756, Byng's trial began on board the *St George* (96) in the harbour; it continued until 27 January 1757, when he was pronounced guilty of a breach of the Articles of War, which had recently been revised to mandate capital punishment for officers who did not do their utmost against the enemy, either in battle or pursuit. The Admiral was transferred to the *Monarch* (74), also in the harbour. On 14 March 1757, Byng was executed at Portsmouth, aboard that ship. The loss of Minorca gave control of the Mediterranean to France until 1763.

British Order of Battle
Admiral John Byng with eleven ships of the line and seven frigates.

In order of their place in the line of battle: *Defiance* (60), *Portland* (50), *Lancaster* (66), *Buckingham* (68/70), *Captain* (64), *Intrepid* (64), *Revenge* (64), *Princess Louisa* (60), *Trident* (64), *Ramillies* (90) (flagship), *Culloden* (74), *Kingston* (60), *Deptford* (48), *Phoenix* (24), *Fortune* (14), *Experiment* (24) and *Dolphin* (22)

Losses: 43 killed, 68 wounded

French Order of Battle
Marquis de la Galissonière with twelve ships of the line and five frigates.

In order of their place in the line of battle: *Orphée* (64), *Hippopotame* (50), *Redoutable* (74), *Sage* (64), *Guerrier* (74), *Fier* (50), *Foudroyant* (80, flagship), *Téméraire* (74), *Content* (64), *Lion* (64), *Couronne* (74), *Triton* (64), *Junon* (42), *Rose* (30), *Gracieuse* (24), *Topaze* (24) and *Nymphe* (20)

Losses: 38 killed, 115 wounded

Battle of Lobositz, 1 October 1756

Location
Lovosice, Czech Republic, on the left bank of the upper Elbe (now the Labe), opposite Litomerice, midway between Dresden and Prague and on Route 30/E 55.

Frederick the Great had opened the war by invading Saxony, whose army was not mobilised, much of it being concentrated on the river Elbe, near Pirna. His aim was to eliminate Saxony, militarily, from the coalition of his enemies and even to integrate the Saxon regiments into his own army. On 18 September, he had succeeded in surrounding that part of the Saxon Army at Pirna. He knew that Austrian Field Marshal Maxilmilian Ulysses Graf von Browne was advancing north from Prague in Bohemia, to rescue the Saxon troops; leaving a blocking force to hold the Saxons – now out of food and starving – he set off south to head off von Browne.

Frederick had 29,000 men; Field Marshal von Browne had 34,500. The two armies met on 30 September just west of the town of Lobositz. The road on to Pirna passed between two hills just 1.5km west of the town, the Loboschberg to the north and the Homolkaberg (Wowcinberg) to the south. The Prussians seized the pass in this 200m-wide saddle and camped there overnight. The Austrian right wing under Lascy, also climbed the Lobosch and dug in opposite them.

Next morning, a thick mist lay over the field, reducing vision to less than 100m. The Prussian Army was drawn up along the heights facing the town to the east. All that Frederick could see of the Austrians were Grenz-Infanterie behind vineyard walls in the valley of the Morellenbach (Modla) stream, behind the village of Sullowitz (Sulejovice), to his southern flank and cavalry in front of Lobositz, with heavy artillery in front of the right centre of their line. In fact, the Austrian line extended from Sullowitz north to the village of Welhotta, on the Elbe, a length of over 4km. The Prussians were deployed with their infantry on the forward faces of the two hills, their cavalry across the road in the centre, behind them. As the action began, Prussian cavalry charged in the centre and were overthrown twice. Frederick had given the battle up as lost at 1300 hours and had handed command over to Field Marshal von Keith. Keith organised an infantry assault on Lobositz, to try to stabilise the action.

On the northern wing, the Herzog (Duke) von Brauschweig-Bevern's Prussian infantry, after three hours' fighting, finally managed to push the Austrians back against the Elbe and Lobositz, part of them escaping north, down the Elbe. The Prussians pressed on to the town, which by now was ablaze, and managed to throw the Austrians out. By 1500 hours, firing finally ceased. The Austrians fell back south to Budin (Budyine), south of Prague, in good order and von Browne even managed to slip a corps of troops past Frederick, in an attempt to relieve the Saxons. But it was too late, that small, starving army had surrendered on 16 October, before help could arrive.

Losses were about 3000 killed, wounded and missing on each side, the Austrians also losing three guns and two standards. This elimination of Saxony from the ranks of Prussia's enemies and of the Austrian threat from the south, gave Frederick a breathing space, which he used to secure his southern conquest and prepare for the continuation of the war in 1757.

Austrian Order of Battle

Commander Field Marshal Maximilian Ulysses Graf von Browne

Advance Guard
General-Major von Haddik

Karabiniers (8 companies)
Grenadiere zu Pferde (8 companies)
combined grenadiers (35 companies)
detachment from Banal and Karlstädter Grenz-Infanterie-Regiments (1 company)
Husaren-Regiment Haddik (5 squadrons)
Husaren-Regiment Baranyay (4 squadrons)

First Line
General von Lucchesi, Lieutenant-General E. von Kollowrat

Right Wing Cavalry (deployed in the centre of the line)
Lieutenant-General von Radicati, assisted by Major-General O'Donnell

Kürassier-Regiment Anspach (6 squadrons)
Kürassier-Regiment Cordova (6 squadrons)
Dragoner-Regiment Erzherzog Joseph (6 squadrons)

Centre Infantry
General C. von Kollowrat, Field Marshal-Lieutenant W. von Starhemberg

Brigadier-General von Wied's Brigade:
Infanterie-Regiment Kaiser
Infanterie-Regiment Jung-Braunschweig-Wolfenbüttel

Infanterie-Regiment Harsch (2 battalions each)

Brigadier-General von Perony's Brigade:
Infanterie-Regiment Baden-Durlach
(2 battalions)
Infanterie-Regiment Alt Braunschweig-
Wolfenbüttel (2 battalions)

Brigadier-General von Macquire's Brigade:
Infanterie-Regiment Wallis (2 battalions)
Infanterie-Regiment Harrach (2 battalions)

Left Wing Cavalry
Major-General von Löwenstein

Kürassier-Regiment Trautmannsdorff
(6 squadrons)
Kürassier-Regiment Serbelloni (6 squadrons)
Dragoner-Regiment Liechtenstein (6 squadrons)

Second Line

Right Wing Cavalry
Brigadier-General von Lobkowitz

Erzherzog Ferdinand Kürassier-Regiment (6
squadrons)
Stampach Kürassier-Regiment (6 squadrons)

Centre Infantry
Brigadier-General von Krottendorf's Brigade:
Infanterie-Regiment Sachsen-Hildburghausen
(2 battalions)
Infanterie-Regiment Kollowrat-Krakowski
(2 battalions)
Infanterie-Regiment Nikolaus Esterhazy
(2 battalions)
Infanterie-Regiment Joseph Esterhazy
(2 battalions)

Brigadier-General von Wolffersdorff's Brigade:
Infanterie-Regiment Keuhl (2 battalions)
Infanterie-Regiment Waldeck (2 battalions)

Left Wing Cavalry
Brigadier-General von Hedwiger

Kürassier-Regiment Brettlach (6 squadrons)
Kürassier-Regiment Carl Palffy (6 squadrons)

Reserve
Brigadier-General von Draskowitz

Grenz-Infanterie-Regiment Banal (2 battalions)
Grenz-Infanterie-Regiment Karlstädter
(2 battalions)

Detached to Leitmeritz and Schreckstein on the Elbe
General Graf von Lacy

Combined Grenadiere zu Pferde:
Dragoner-Regiment Batthyanyi (1 company)
Dragoner-Regiment Erzherzog Joseph
(1 company)
Dragoner-Regiment Kollowrat-Krakowsky
(1 company)
Dragoner-Regiment Liechtenstein (1 company)

Infantry:
Grenz-Infanterie-Regiment Karlstädter
(400 men)
Infanterie-Regiment Alt Colloredo-Waldsee
(2 battalions)
Infanterie-Regiment von Browne (2 battalions)

Artillery
General Feuerstein
70 3-pounder battalion guns
twelve 6-pounders
six 12-pounders
six howitzers
Pontoon train

Total: 34,500 men and 94 guns

Prussian Order of Battle

King Friedrich II, Field Marshal von Keith

Infantry Division under General Prinz von Preussen

Lieutenant-General Prinz von Bevern's Brigade (Major-General von Quadt von Wickeradt assisting):
Combined grenadiers (Regiments 5 and 20)
Infanterie-Regiment Hülsen (2nd Battalion)
Infanterie-Regiment Manteuffel (2 battalions)
Infanterie-Regiment Blankensee (2 battalions)
Infanterie-Regiment Braunschweig-Bevern
(2 battalions)

Lieutenant-General Ferdinand Prinz von Braunschweig-Wolfenbüttel's Brigade (Major-General von Hülsen assisting):
Infanterie-Regiment Alt-Anhalt (3 battalions)
Infanterie-Regiment Alt-Braunschweig
(2 battalions)
Infanterie-Regiment Quadt von Wickeradt
(2 battalions)
Infanterie-Regiment Hülsen (1st Battalion)

Unbrigaded Regiments:
Grenadier Bataillon 3/6 Kleist
Grenadier Bataillon 24/34 Grumbkow

Infantry Division under Lieutenant-General von Kleist

Major-General von Zastrow's Brigade:
Infanterie-Regiment Kleist (2 battalions)
Infanterie-Regiment Münchow (2 battalions)

Major-General von Itzenplitz's Brigade:
Infanterie-Regiment Itzenplitz (2 battalions)
Infanterie-Regiment Zastrow (1st Battalion)
Grenadier Battalion 17/22 Puttkamer (1 battalion)

Cavalry under Field Marshal von Gessler

Lieutenant-General von Katzler
Major-General von Luderitz's Brigade:
Kürassier-Regiment Markgraf Friedrich
(5 squadrons)
Leibregiment zu Pferde (5 squadrons)

Major-General von Driesen's Brigade:
Kürassier-Regiment Schöneich (5 squadrons)
Kürassier-Regiment Driesen (5 squadrons)

Lieutenant-General von Kyau
Major-General von Schöneich's Brigade:
Leibkarabiniers (5 squadrons)
Kürassier-Regiment Rochow (5 squadrons)

Major-General von Pennevaire's Brigade:
Gardes du Corps (1 squadron)
Gens d'Armes (5 squadrons)
Kürassier-Regiment Prinz von Preussen
(5 squadrons)

Lieutenant-General von Schwerin
Major-General von Örtzen's Brigade:
Dragoner-Regiment Örtzen (5 squadrons)
Dragoner-Regiment Truchsess (5 squadrons)

Lieutenant-General von Katte (Major-General Thruchsess assisting)
Dragoner-Regiment Bayreuth (10 squadrons)

Unbrigaded Regiment:
Husaren-Regiment Szeckely (3 squadrons)

Artillery
Four 24-pounders
30 12-pounders
four 50-pound mortars
eight 10-pounder howitzers
52 battalion pieces

Total: 18,249 infantry, 10,500 cavalry, 98 guns

Battle of Kolin, 18 June 1757

Location
A small town in the Czech Republic, about 80km east of Prague, on Route 12 and on the left bank of the upper river Elbe.

The Prussian Army (34,000 men) advanced east from Prague, which they had laid siege to. Austrian Field Marshal Leopold Joseph Graf Daun had placed his army of 60,000 men to the south of that road, on some hills (the Kamhajek ridge), just to the south of the modern villages of Brezan, Bristwi and Krechor, thus adopting a flanking position, west of Kolin itself. Frederick the Great, full of confidence, deployed along the road and advanced south, hoping to turn the Austrian eastern flank. Due to a misunderstanding of the Prussian King's orders however, it was von Daun who seized the chance the resultant disorder presented, turning the Prussian left wing and rolling up their army.

Austrian losses were 8144 killed, wounded and missing. The Prussians lost 13,773, of whom some 5380 were captured. They also lost 45 guns and 22 colours and standards. Kolin was Frederick's first defeat; his over-confidence cost him dearly. It forced him to lift the siege of Prague, to abandon Bohemia and to retreat north, into Saxony. He also called back a small force of Prussians operating in Hanover, with his allies; this was to cost them dearly, at the Battle of Hastenbeck, on 26 July.

An Austrian force under General Graf Maquire, using light troops and classic guerrilla warfare tactics, were similarly able to harass and scatter a superior corps of 30,000 Prussians under Prinz August Wilhelm of Prussia and to destroy huge quantities of their supplies in the magazines at Zittau on 19 July.

Austrian Order of Battle

Field Marshal Graf Leopold Joseph von Daun

First Line

Extreme Right Wing

Division under Lieutenant-General von Nádasdy
Grenz-Infanterie-Regiment Banal (2 battalions)
Grenz-Infanterie-Regiment Karlstädter-Szluiner (2 battalions)
Grenz-Infanterie-Regiment Warasdiener-Kreuzer (1 battalion)

Division under Field Marshal von Morocz
Brigadier-General von Schröder's Brigade:
Husaren-Regiment Morocz (6 squadrons)
Husaren-Regiment Festétics (6 squadrons)
Husaren-Regiment Dessewffy (1 squadron)

Brigadier-General von Erdödy's Brigade:
Husaren-Regiment Kaiser (6 squadrons)
Husaren-Regiment Karlstädter (2 squadrons)

Major-General von Nostitz's Saxon Brigade:

Chevauxlegers Prinz Karl (4 squadrons)
Chevauxlegers Prinz Albrecht (3 squadrons)
Chevauxlegers Graf von Brühl (4 squadrons)

Division under Field Marshal von Haddik
Brigadier-General von Sczechény's Brigade:
Husaren-Regiment Banal (3 squadrons)
Husaren-Regiment Warasdiner (1 squadron)
Husaren-Regiment Splényi (2 squadrons)

Brigadier-General von Palffy's Brigade:
Husaren-Regiment Esterházy (2 squadrons)
Husaren-Regiment Jazygier-Kumanier (5 squadrons)
Husaren-Regiment Baranyay (2 squadrons)

Brigadier-General von Babocsay's Brigade:
Husaren-Regiment Haddik (2 squadrons)
Husaren-Regiment Kálnoky (6 squadrons)
Husaren-Regiment Nádasdy (5 squadrons)

Brigadier-General von Starhemberg's Brigade:
combined cavalry regiment (1000 kürassiers and dragoons from various regiments)

Grenadier Reserve
10 companies

Right Wing Cavalry
Lieutenant-General Graf Serbelloni (Benedikt Daun assisting)

Dragoner-Regiment Savoy
Dragoner-Regiment Kollowrat-Krakowski
Dragoner-Regiment Kalkreuth

The Centre
Lieutenant-General Baron von Marschall (Lieutenant-General Graf von Colloredo assisting)

Division under Field Marshal von Andlau
Brigadier-General von Esterházy's Brigade:
Infanterie-Regiment Erzherzog Carl
(2 battalions)
Infanterie-Regiment von Moltke (3 battalions)

Brigadier-General von Mayern's Brigade:
Infanterie-Regiment von Puebla (3 battalions)
Infanterie-Regiment von Mercy-Argentau (1 battalion)

Division under Field Marshal von Puebla
Brigadier-General von Gemmingen's Brigade:
Infanterie-Regiment von Arenburg
(3 battalions)
Infanterie-Regiment von Türheim (3 battalions)

Brigadier-General von Angern's Brigade:
Infanterie-Regiment Leopold von Daun
(3 battalions)
Infanterie-Regiment J. von Harrach
(2 battalions)

Left Wing Cavalry
General Graf von Stampach (Field Marshal Graf von Kollowrat assisting)

Kürassier-Regiment von Serbelloni
Dragoner-Regiment von Porporati
Dragoner-Regiment von Hessen-Darmstadt

Left Flank Guard
Brigadier-General von Beck's Brigade:
Grenz-Infanterie-Regiment Slavonisch-

Gradiscaner (2 battalions)
Grenz-Infanterie-Regiment Slavonisch-Brooder
(2 battalions)
combined volunteer battalion of line infantry

Second Line

Right Wing Cavalry
Lieutenant-General Graf Serbelloni (Benedikt Daun assisting)

Division under Lieutenant-General O'Donell
Kürassier-Regiment Infant von Portugal
Kürassier-Regiment Schmerzing
Dragoner-Regiment De Ligne

The Centre
Lieutenant-General Baron von Marschall (Lieutenant-General Graf von Colloredo assisting)

Division under Field Marshal von Starhemberg
Brigadier-General von Kottendorf's Brigade:
Infanterie-Regiment von Neipperg
(3 battalions)
Infanterie-Regiment von Gaisruck (3 battalions)

Brigadier-General von Wulffen's Brigade:
Infanterie-Regiment Haller von Hallerstein
(2 battalions)

Division under Field Marshal von Sincere
Brigadier-General von Plonquet's Brigade:
Infanterie-Regiment Hoch und Deutschmeister
(2 battalions)
Infanterie-Regiment von Baden-Baden
(2 battalions)
Infanterie-Regiment von Botta Danorno
(3 battalions)

Left Wing Cavalry
General Graf von Stampach (Field Marshal Graf von Kollowrat assisting)

Division under Field Marshal von Wöllwarth
Kürassier-Regiment von Gelhay
Kürassier-Regiment von Alt-Modena
Dragoner-Regiment von Sachsen-Gotha

Reserve
General Graf Colloredo

Division under Field Marshal von Wied
Brigadier-General von Reichlin's Brigade:
Infanterie-Regiment von Los Rios (1 battalion)
Infanterie-Regiment von Salm-Salm
(2 battalions)
Infanterie-Regiment von Platz
Infanterie-Regiment E. von Starhemberg

Brigadier-General von Müffling's Brigade:
Infanterie-Regiment von Arberg (1 battalion)
Infanterie-Regiment von Sachsen-Gotha
(1 battalion)
Infanterie-Regiment von Mercy-Argentau
(1 battalion)

Infanterie-Regiment von De Ligne (1 battalion)

Division under Field Marshal von Lützow
Brigadier-General von Castiglione's Brigade:
Kürassier-Regiment von O'Donell
Kürassier-Regiment von Birkenfeld

Brigadier-General von Köbel's Brigade:
Dragoner-Regiment Jung-Modena
Dragoner-Regiment von Württemberg
Saxon Karabiniergarde (4 squadrons)

Total: 54,000 men in 51 battalions, 43 grenadier companies, 171 squadrons, with 60 heavy guns

Prussian Order of Battle

King Friedrich II

Vanguard

Cavalry Vanguard
Lieutenant-General von Ziethen

Division under Lieutenant-General von Ziethen
Husaren-Regiment von Puttkammer
(10 squadrons)
Husaren-Regiment von Werner (10 squadrons)
Husaren-Regiment von Seydlitz (5 squadrons)

Division under Major-General von Katte
Husaren-Regiment von Ziethen (10 squadrons)
Husaren-Regiment von Wartenberg
(10 squadrons
Husaren-Regiment von Székely (5 squadrons)

Infantry Vanguard
Lieutenant-General von Hülsen

Grenadier Bataillon von Finck (13/26, 1 battalion)
Grenadier Bataillon von Waldau (12/39, 1 battalion)
Grenadier Bataillon von Nimschöfsky (33/42,
1 battalion)
Grenadier Bataillon von Wangenheim
(47/Garrison Regiment 7, 1 battalion)

Grenadier Bataillon von Möllendorf (9/10,
1 battalion)
Grenadier Bataillon von Kahlden (Garrison
Regiments 3, 4 and New Garrison Regiment, 1
battalion)
Infanterie-Regiment von Schultze (2 battalions)
Infanterie-Regiment von Münchow (2 battalions)
Dragoner-Regiment von Stechow (5 squadrons)

First Line

Right Wing Infantry
Lieutenant-General Prinz von Anhalt-Dessau

Infanterie-Regiment von Bornstedt (2 battalions)
Infanterie-Regiment von Manteuffel (2 battalions)
Infanterie-Regiment von Anhalt (2 battalions)
Infanterie-Regiment von Kalckstein (2 battalions)

Right Wing Cavalry
Lieutenant-General Prinz von Schöneich

Dragoner-Regiment von Meinike (5 squadrons)
Kürassier-Regiment von Schöneich (5 squadrons)
Kürassier-Regiment von Driesen (5 squadrons)
Garde du Corps (3 squadrons)

Left Wing Infantry
Lieutenant-General von Treskow

Infanterie-Regiment Braunschweig-Bevern
(2 battalions)
Infanterie-Regiment Prinz von Preussen
(2 battalions)
Infanterie-Regiment von Hülsen (2 battalions)
Infanterie-Regiment Anhalt-Dessau (3 battalions)

Left Wing Cavalry
Lieutenant-General von Penavaire

Leibregiment zu Pferde (5 squadrons)
Leibkarabiniers (5 squadrons)
Kürassier-Regiment von Kyau (5 squadrons)
Kürassier-Regiment von Krockow (5 squadrons)

Second Line

Right Wing Infantry
Prinz von Bevern

Infanterie-Regiment von Kreytzen (2 battalions)
Grenadier Bataillon von Gemmingen (41/44, 1
battalion)

Left Wing Infantry
Lieutenant-General von Tresckow

Füsilier-Regiment von Wied (2 battalions)
Füsilier-Regiment Prinz Heinrich von Preussen

Left Wing Cavalry
Lieutenant-General Penavaire

Dragoner-Regiment von Katte (5 squadrons)
Dragoner-Regiment von Blanckensee
(5 squadrons)

Reserve
Major-General von Krosigk

Kürassier-Regiment Prinz von Preussen
(5 squadrons)
Kürassier-Regiment von Rochow (5 squadrons)
Dragoner-Regiment von Normann (5 squadrons)

Artillery
Two batteries

**Total, 32 battalions (each with two battalion
guns), 116 squadrons, 28 heavy guns, c.3,000
men**

Battle of Plassey, 23 June 1757

Location

A small town on Route 34, between Kolkata (Calcutta) in the south and Rajshahi on the river Ganges, in West Bengal Province, India. The town of Palashi lies near the river Bhagarathi, about 240km north of Kolkata.

Vice Admiral Watson and Colonel Robert Clive had attacked and taken the French fort at Chandernagore on 24 March 1757. This arrogant action had aroused the anger of Siraj ud Dowlah, the Nabob of Bengal, who began to mobilise his army. On 13 June, Clive left Chandernagore and advanced up the river Bhagirathi, with a tiny, mixed force of European and native troops, to engage Siraj ud Dowlah's army, having previously arranged to act together with Mir Jafar Ali Khan, the commander of Siraj's army, against the Nabob; Khan intended to take the throne for himself.

At 0100 hours on 23 June, Clive's little force had disembarked on the eastern bank of the river, about 2 miles to the north of the town of Plassey. Clive took post with his left flank resting on one of the Nabob's walled hunting lodges on the river bank. Immediately behind his line of infantry was a large, walled, rectangular mango grove, into which he sent his baggage; some 200m to his front was a small hill, on top of which St Frais (the French artillery commander working for the Nabob) had set up his four guns. About 2km to the north of this hill were the entrenchments of the Indian army, running from the river, out to the east. The ground was largely flat, open and covered with scrub.

At dawn, Siraj's force filed south out of the camp and formed an arc to the east of Clive's tiny group, with the main body to the north, expecting to sweep their enemy into the river. Clive's infantry was in three groups, in a line facing northeast, the 1st Battalion of the 39th Regiment of Foot in the centre. Three 6-pounder guns were on each end of the line. At 0800 hours the French guns opened up what quickly became a general barrage. Although Clive's guns gave an excellent account of themselves, there could be only one outcome if this fire-fight was maintained for long. He commanded his force to withdraw southwards into the mango grove, where they were ordered to lie down. The subsequent Indian artillery fire was ineffective, while Clive's guns, firing through makeshift embrasures on the grove walls, took a heavy toll of their enemies. At 1100 hours, Clive called a council of war, in which it was decided to hold fast until nightfall and then to attack the enemy camp at midnight.

A heavy monsoon downpour interrupted the action; the British gunners had protected their ammunition from the rain but the Indian gunners had not and thus Siraj was suddenly deprived of his artillery. Mir Mudin ordered his advanced guard division to advance south on the grove, but his command was ripped apart by well-aimed grape discharges at close range and withdrew in confusion. Mir Mudin was mortally wounded.

This reverse shook Siraj ud Dowlah, who summoned Mir Jafar and ordered him to destroy Clive. Mir Jafar pretended to obey, but secretly sent a note to Clive, urging him to attack. Before this could occur, Siraj ud Dowlah sought advice from another of his commanders, who also happened to be a conspirator of Clive's. This general advised Siraj to leave the field and return to Moorshedabad, leaving the management of the battle to his commanders. This Siraj did, taking an escort of 2000 cavalry with him.

At 1400 hours, the Indian firing ceased, they harnessed up their artillery and pulled off north, back into their camp, leaving St Frais and his guns alone. Clive went off to get some sleep before the night's raid. He was raised by a messenger to be told that Major Kilpatrick was aiming to attack St Frais. Clive rushed up to forbid the attack, but, seeing the tactical situation, he took command of two companies and set off, leaving Kilpatrick to follow with the rest of his 'army'. At the noise of the resultant combat, the Nabob's army began to issue forth again from their trenches.

Clive decided to attack. The Indian soldiers were now effectively leaderless and uncoordinated; they were easy meat for Clive's guns and the troops of the conspirators hung back and watched. By 1700 hours Siraj's loyal men had had enough and streamed away to the north. St Frais abandoned his four guns and joined them, leaving Clive and Mir Jafar to contemplate their impending takeover of Siraj's state and fortunes.

Clive's losses were 7 Europeans and 16 sepoys killed, 13 Europeans and 36 sepoys wounded. Siraj ud Dowlah lost about 500 killed and wounded and 40 of his guns. A few days later, on 29 June, he was assassinated by one of Mir Jafar's sons, Miran. Mir Jafar Ali Khan was installed as Nabob of Bengal, Bihar and Orissa by Clive in Moorshedabad on 29 June 1757; in reality, he was the puppet of the Honourable East India Company, and the rich provinces of Bengal, Bihar and Orissa fell under their control. Thus guile had achieved what militarily never should have been.

British Order of Battle

Advanced Posts
two 6-pounder guns
two howitzers

Centre
1/39th Regiment of Foot (Major Eyre Coote)
Bombay European Infantry Regiment (2 companies, Captain George Gaupp)
Bengal European Infantry Regiment (5 companies, Captain Alexander Grant)
Madres European Infantry Regiment (5 companies, Major James Kilpatrick)

Left Wing
1st Bengal Native Infantry (1050 men)

Artillery
Lieutenant Hater RN

six 6-pounder guns
9th Battery, 12th Artillery Regiment RA
sailors from HMS *Tiger* (57 men)
eight 6-pounders, two howitzers, circa 3230 men.

Indian Order of Battle

Advanced Guard
Mir Mudin

5000 cavalry
7000 infantry

Right Wing
Rai Durlabh Ram

unknown strength

Centre
Yar Lutuf Khan

unknown strength

Left Wing
Mir Jafar Ali Khan
10,000 Pathan cavalry

Artillery
Four light French guns with 45 men
50 Indian guns (18-, 24- and 32-pounders)

Battle of Hastenbeck, 26 July 1757

Location

A small town to the east of the river Weser in northern central Germany, just southeast of the fortress town of Hameln, southwest of Hanover and north of Kassel.

At the beginning of July 1757, the French Army of the Lower Rhine, under Field Marshal Louis-Charles d'Estrees, with 50,000 infantry, 10,000 cavalry and 76 field guns, pushed eastwards from the Rhine and, on 16 July, crossed the river Weser at Höxter, about 60km south of Hameln. They then turned north, following the river towards Hameln and Hanover.

The French were opposed by a smaller allied Army of Observation (Brunswickers, Bückeburgers, Hanoverians and Hessen-Kasselers) under General William Augustus, the Duke of Cumberland, son of King George II of England. It consisted of 30,000 infantry, 5000 cavalry, 28 field guns (and 62 battalion guns). Six battalions of Prussian infantry had been withdrawn from Cumberland's command by Frederick the Great just prior to this action, following Frederick's defeat at the Battle of Kolin (18 June) by the Austrians.

Cumberland's task was to defend the Electorate of Hanover and he selected a good defensive site, in the hills just south of Hameln and north of the village of Hastenbeck and behind a swampy stream, which stretched west of the village. His front was about 5km long. Misreading the terrain however, he left his eastern flank, the wooded Obensberg ridge, very under-protected. The entire terrain was close and unsuitable for cavalry.

D'Estrees reconnoitred the Allied position and considered it too strong to assault frontally. As the western flank was firmly anchored on the river, he aimed to concentrate his assault on the centre (a holding attack) and east of Cumberland's line, overlapping the Obensberg – an oblique attack. This outflanking task he gave to General de Chevert's division. The plan involved a night march through wooded country, which caused considerable confusion amongst the French troops, but by 0200 hours on 26 July, de Chevert's troops were on the unoccupied ridge, east of Cumberland's flank.

The morning was misty; the combat began at 0530 hours, but de Chevert's advance was held up until the Comte de Lorge's Brigade arrived. At 0900 hours, de Chevert began his assault, giving the signal for d'Estrees' main body to advance as well.

By 1000 hours, the French artillery in the centre had achieved domination of that part of the line. By now, Cumberland became aware of the threat to his left wing and transferred troops there from the western part of his line. Von Hardenberg's Hanoverian Brigade struck de Lorge's Brigade on de Chevert's division in the flank and rolled it up, causing heavy losses. He used captured French guns to fire at the rest of de Chevert's force, which was now advancing into the Allied rear and sent some squadrons of cavalry into the gap created by the defeat of de Lorge's Brigade.

At this point, French General de Maillebois reported to d'Estrees (falsely as it transpired) that some 10,000 Allied troops were about to turn the French right flank. D'Estrees ordered counter measures, which disrupted his planned attack by some two hours. By this time, Cumberland had had enough but was able to begin a timely withdrawal from the field, abandoning and burning his camp. He fell back northwest, past Hameln fortress.

French losses were 1500 killed, wounded and missing. The Allies lost 300 killed, 900 wounded, 220 captured and 11 guns. This relatively minor victory allowed the French to force the Duke of Cumberland back north, to Stade on the southern side of the lower Elbe, near Hamburg. Cornered, he had to agree to disband his army and allow them to occupy the Electorate of Hanover, terms which they dictated at the Convention of Klosterzeven. The Duke of Cumberland fell into disfavour for agreeing this treaty, which was promptly repudiated by the British government and Herzog Ferdinand of Brunswick was given command of the Allied army.

Allied Order of Battle

General William Augustus, the Duke of
Cumberland

First Line

Right Wing Infantry
Lieutenant-General von Zastrow

Brigadier-General von Block's Hanoverian Brigade:
Infanterie-Regiment von Druchtleben (3B)
(1 battalion)
Infanterie-Regiment von Knesebeck (3A)
(1 battalion)
Infanterie-Regiment von Scheither (1A)
(1 battalion)
Bückeburg Batallion
Infanterie-Regiment von Sachsen-Gotha (9A)
(1 battalion)
Infanterie-Regiment von Stolzenberg (4B)
(1 battalion)
Infanterie-Regiment von Post (10A) (1 battalion)
Artillery Batteries 1A and 1B

*Brigadier-General von Sporcken's Hanoverian
Brigade:*
Infanterie-Regiment Jung-Zastrow (9B)
(1 battalion)
Infanterie-Regiment von Diepenbroick (8A)
(1 battalion)

Scouts on the Right Wing
Hanoverian Jäger zu Pferde (1 squadron)

The Centre
Lieutenant-General von Wutginau (Hessen-Kassel)

Brigadier-General Prinz von Anhalt's Brigade:
Leib-Regiment (1 battalion)
Infantry Regiment Prinz Karl (1 battalion)
Infantry Regiment Prinz von Anhalt
(1 battalion)
Infantry Regiment von Fürstenberg (1 battalion)

Brigadier-General von Gilsa's Brigade:
Infanterie-Regiment von Kanitz (1 battalion)
Infanterie-Regiment Hanau (1 battalion)
Infanterie-Regiment von Haudring (1 battalion)
Artillery Battery Nr 2

Brigadier-General von Fürstenberg's Brigade:
Infanterie-Regiment Prinz Ysenburg
(1 battalion)
Infanterie-Regiment von Mannsbach
(1 battalion)
Infanterie-Regiment Erbprinz (1 battalion)
Grenadier-Regiment (1 battalion)

Left Wing Infantry
Lieutenant-General von Imhoff

*Brigadier-General Erbprinz von Braunschweig's
(Brunswick) Brigade:*
Infanterie-Regiment von Behr (2 battalions)
Leib-Infanterie-Regiment Regiment
(2 battalions)

*Brigadier-General von Behr's (Brunswickers and
Hanoverians) Brigade:*
Infanterie-Regiment von Zastrow (1 battalion)
Infanterie-Regiment von Imhoff (2 battalions)
Infanterie-Regiment von Brunck (12B)
(1 battalion)
Infanterie-Regiment von Block (8B)
(1 battalion)

Advanced Guard on the Left Wing
Brigadier-General von Hardenberg's Brigade:
Hanoverian grenadiers (2 battalions)
Hessian grenadiers (1 battalion)
Brunswicker grenadiers (1 battalion)
Artillery Battery Nr 3

Brigadier-General von Schulenburg's Brigade:
Hanoverian grenadiers (1 battalion
Brunswicker grenadiers (1 battalion)
Hessian grenadiers (von Stockhausen, 1 battal-
ion)

Hanoverian Detachment on the Weser
Dragoner-Regiment von Bock (4 squadrons)
Husaren-Regiment (1 squadron)
Bückeburg Karabiniers (1 squadron)

Hanoverian Detachment on the
Obensberg
Major von Freytag
Fussjäger (3 companies)

Second Line

Right Wing Cavalry
Brigadier-General von Dachenhausen's Hanoverian Brigade:
Dragoner-Regiment von Busche (7C)
(4 squadrons)
Dragoner-Regiment von Breidenbach (6C)
(2 squadrons)
Grenadiere-zu-Pferde (C-B) (1 squadron)
Dragoner-Regiment von Dachenhausen (5C)
(2 squadrons)
Leibgade-zu-Pferde (C-A) (1 squadron)

Brigadier-General von Zeppelin's Hanoverian Brigade:
Hammerstein Kavallerie (2C-B) (2 squadrons)
Schollen Kavallerie (1C-B) (2 squadrons)
Reden Kavallerie (4C-A) (2 squadrons)
Gilten Kavallerie (4C-B) (2 squadrons)

The Centre
Brigadier-General von Einsiedel's Hessian Brigade:
Leib-Regiment (2 squadrons)
Kürassier-Regiment von Miltitz (1 squadron)
Kürassier-Regiment Prinz Ysenburg
(2 squadrons)

Brigadier-General von Urff's Brigade:
Prinz Wilhelm (2 squadrons)
Leib-Dragoner (4 squadrons)

Left Wing Infantry
Brigadier-General von Kielmannsegg's Brigade:
Infanterie-Regiment von Kielmannsegg (12A)
(1 battalion)
Infanterie-Regiment von Oberg (11B)
(1 battalion)
Grenadier Garde (2 battalions)

Brigadier-General von Hodenberg's Brigade:
Infanterie-Regiment von Wagenheim (7A)
(1 battalion)
Infanterie-Regiment von Hodenberg (5B)
(1 battalion)

Detachments

Detachment at Afferde
Brigadier-General von Ledebur

Dragoner-Regiment von Dachenhausen (5C)
(2 squadrons)
Leib-Regiment (1 C) (2 squadrons)
Infanterie-Regiment von Ledebur (4A)
(1 battalion)
Infanterie-Regiment von Fabrice (4C)
(1 battalion)

Detachment East of Afferde
Colonel von Dachenhausen

Dragoner-Regiment von Dachenhausen (2C)
(2 squadrons)

Detachment between Afferde and Diedersen
General-Major von Breidenbach

Dragoner-Regiment von Breidenbach (6C)
(2 squadrons)
Infanterie-Regiment von Sporcken (2A)
(1 battalion)
Infanterie-Regiment von Hardenberg (6A)
(1 battalion)
Infanterie-Regiment von Zandre de Caraffa
(6B) (1 battalion)

Total: 30,000 infantry, 5000 cavalry, 28 guns

Saxon cavalrymen, 1756. Left to right: corporal, Prinz Karl Chevauxlegers; trooper, Graf Brühl Chevauxlegers; officer, Dragoner-Regiment Graf Rutowsky. (Knötel, IV 31)

Saxon infantrymen, 1745–1750. Left to right: officer, Grenadier Battalion Bellegarde; drummer, Infanterie-Regiment Königin; grenadier, Leibgrenadiergarde; fusilier, Infanterie-Regiment von Rochow, 1750. These would have been the uniforms worn in 1756, before the Saxon Army was captured by the Prussians. (Knötel, V 26)

Von Schill's Hussar Squadron, 1761. This unit was raised under Austrian auspices, then transferred to Saxon service. The figure in the background is an NCO; he has a red bag to his fur busby and fox fur to his pelisse. (Knötel, XII 56)

Drummer of the Spanish Murcia Regimiento de Infantería, 1759. (Conde de Clonard, Álbum de la Infantería Española, by permission of the Asociación Cultural de Modelismo Histórico Alabarda and the Kronoskaf Seven Years' War website)

King's colour of the Spanish Murcia Regimiento de Infantería. (Kronoskaf Seven Years' War website)

Colonel's colour of a Swiss infantry regiment in Spanish service. (Kronoskaf Seven Years' War website)

Regimental colour of the Spanish Granada Regimiento de Infantería. (Kronoskaf Seven Years' War website)

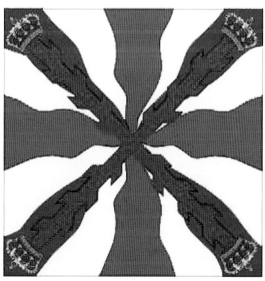

Regimental colour of the Swiss Nuevo de Reding Regimiento de Infantería in Spanish service. (Kronoskaf Seven Years' War website)

Württemberg trooper, Kürassier-Regiment von Phull; private, Jäger Corps; trooper, Husaren-Regiment von Gorcy. The Jäger Corps was a small organisation, used for headquarters dispatch duties.(Knötel, II 41)

Württemberg Leib-Grenadiers à Cheval. Left to right: officer, trooper, NCO (dismounted), NCO (mounted). With their cuirasses and very showy uniforms, this unit gives the impression of having been a regiment close to the duke's heart. (Knötel, New Series, 36)

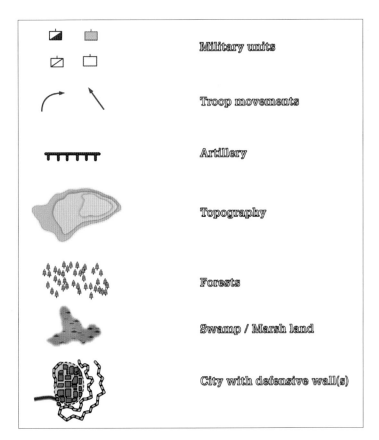

Military units

Troop movements

Artillery

Topography

Forests

Swamp / Marsh land

City with defensive wall(s)

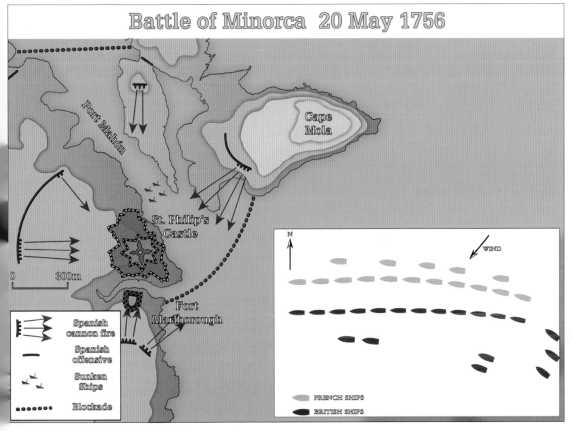

Battle of Minorca 20 May 1756

Port Mahón

Cape Mola

St. Philip's Castle

Fort Marlborough

0   300m

Spanish cannon fire

Spanish offensive

Sunken Ships

Blockade

N

WIND

FRENCH SHIPS

BRITISH SHIPS

BATTLE OF LOBOSITZ 1 OCTOBER 1756

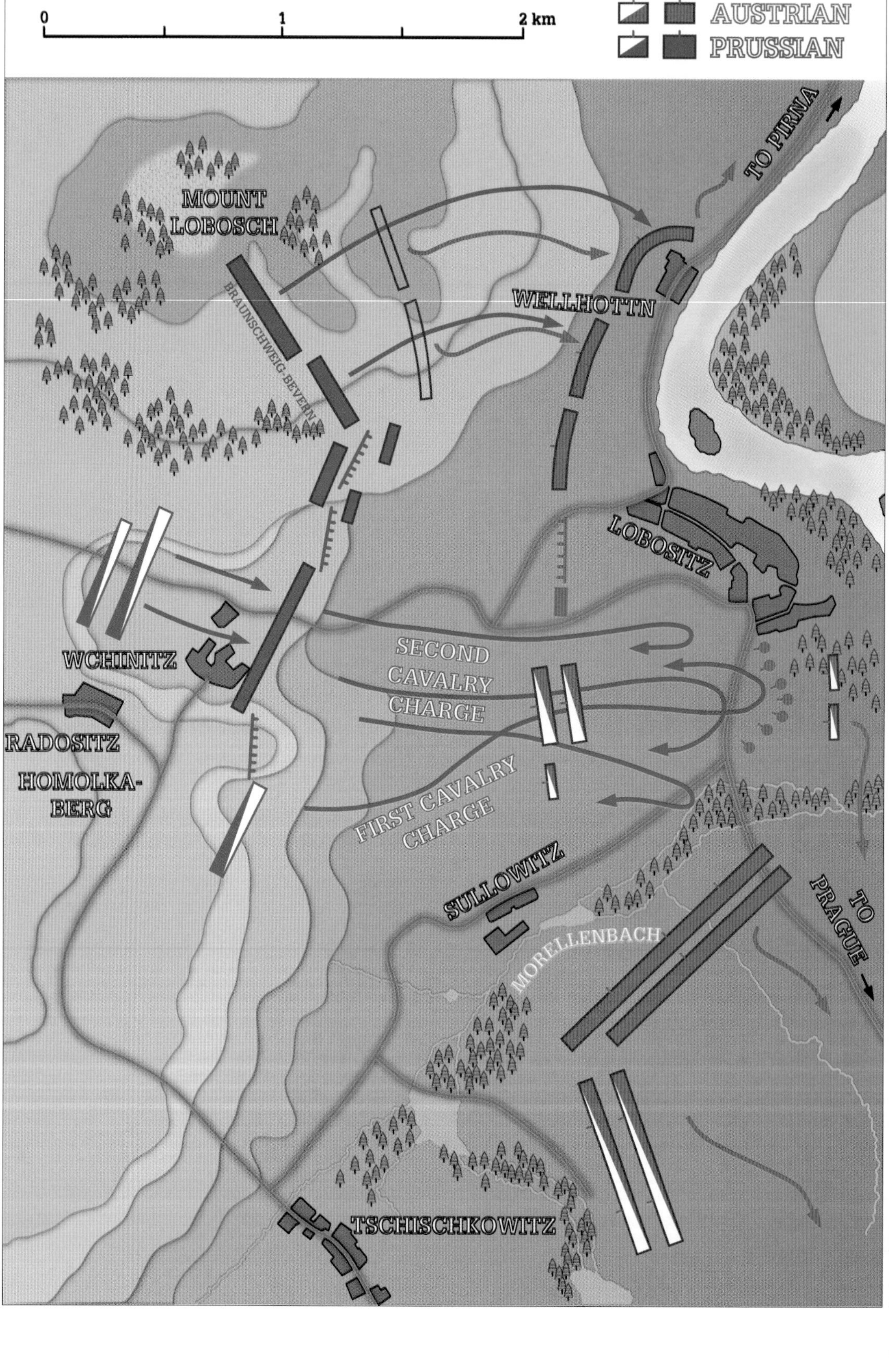

0 — 1 — 2 km

AUSTRIAN
PRUSSIAN

MOUNT LOBOSCH

TO PIRNA

BRAUNSCHWEIG-BEVERN

WELLHOTTN

LOBOSITZ

WCHINITZ

SECOND CAVALRY CHARGE

RADOSITZ

HOMOLKA-BERG

FIRST CAVALRY CHARGE

SULLOWITZ

MORELLENBACH

TO PRAGUE

TSCHISCHKOWITZ

THE BATTLE OF KOLIN 18 JUNE 1757

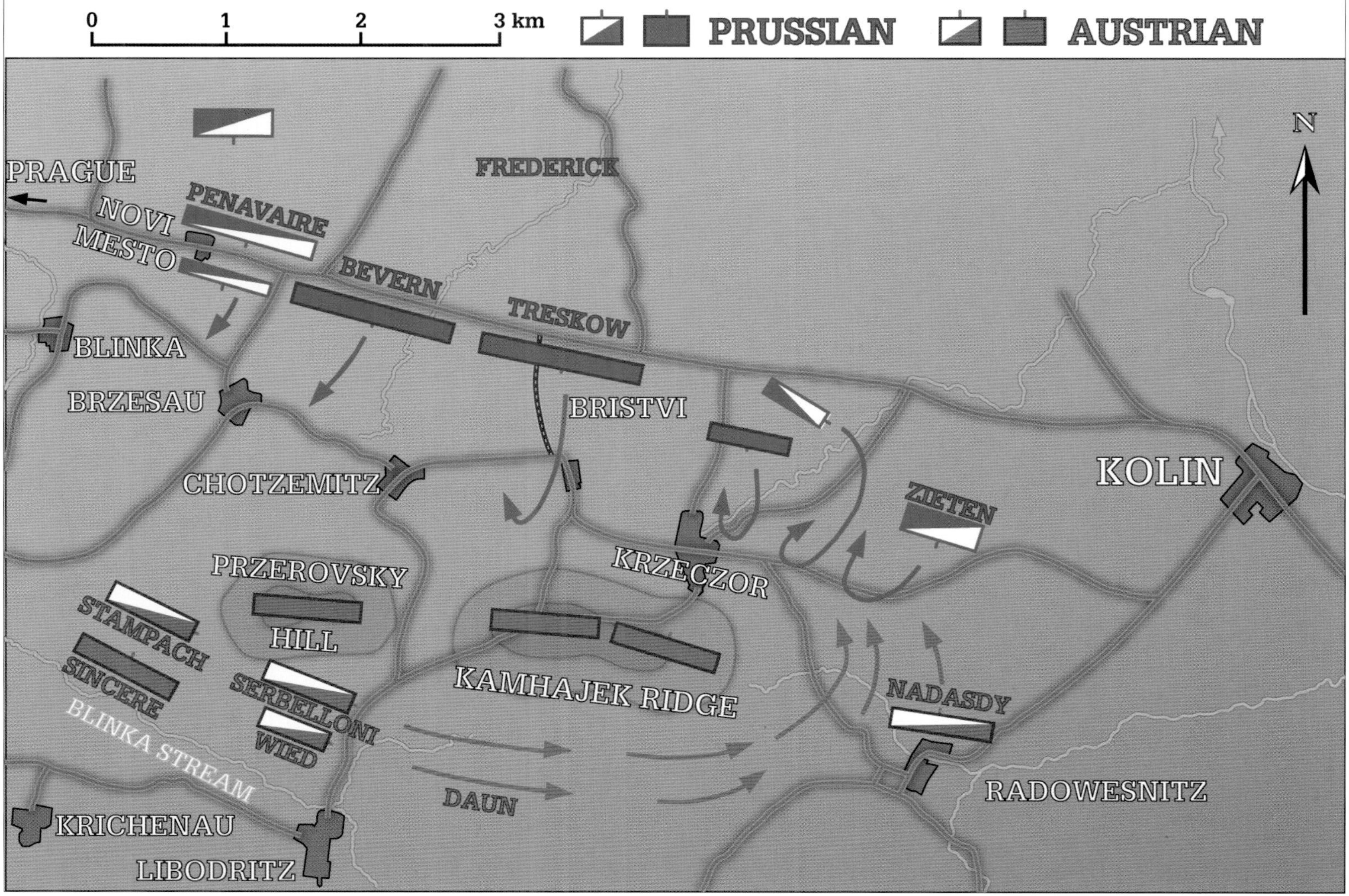

PRUSSIAN AUSTRIAN

N

0 1 2 3 km

PRAGUE

FREDERICK

NOVI MESTO

PENAVAIRE

BEVERN

TRESKOW

BRISTVI

ZIETEN

KOLIN

BLINKA

BRZESAU

CHOTZEMITZ

KRZECZOR

NADASDY

RADOWESNITZ

PRZEROVSKY HILL

STAMPACH

SINCIERE

SERBELLONI

WIED

KAMHAJEK RIDGE

DAUN

BLINKA STREAM

KRICHENAU

LIBODRITZ

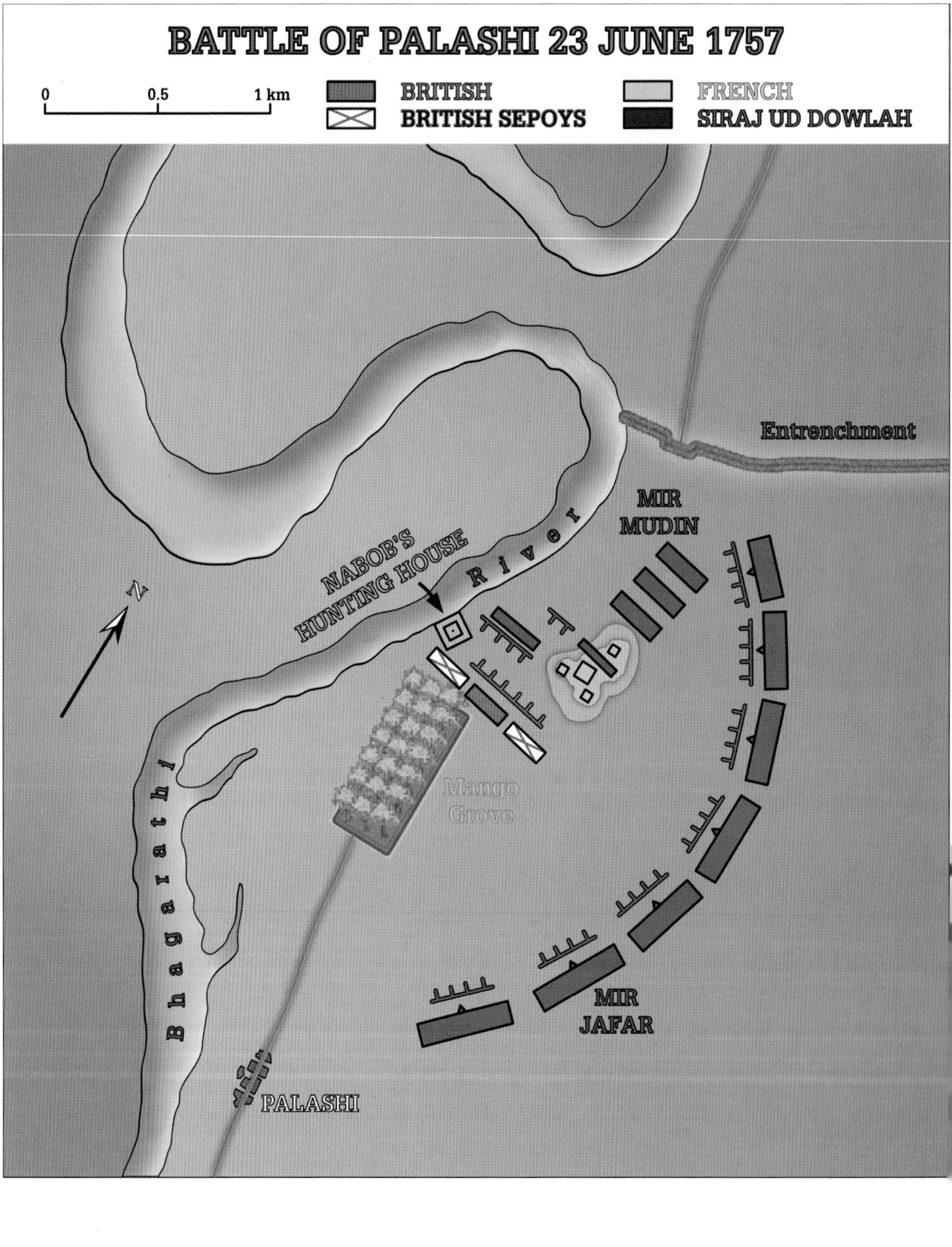

BATTLE OF PALASHI 23 JUNE 1757

0   0.5   1 km   BRITISH   FRENCH
BRITISH SEPOYS   SIRAJ UD DOWLAH

Entrenchment

MIR MUDIN

NABOB'S HUNTING HOUSE   River

N

Bhagarathi

Mango Grove

MIR JAFAR

PALASHI

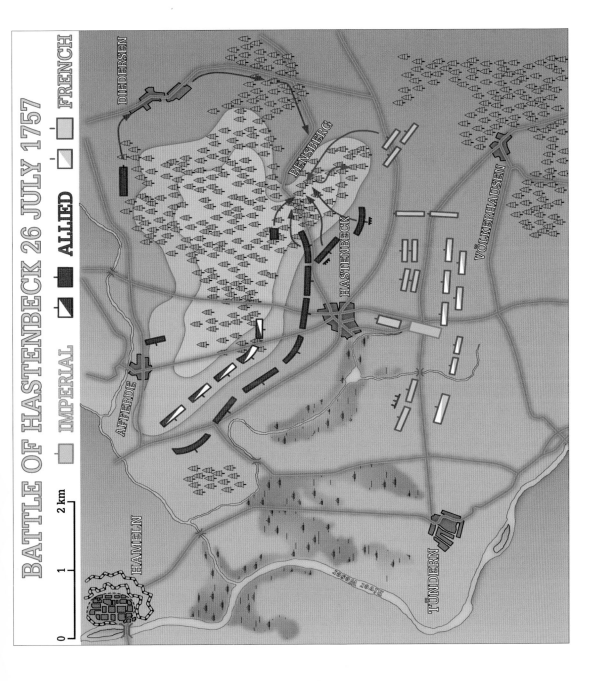

BATTLE OF HASTENBECK 26 JULY 1757

IMPERIAL ▨ | **ALLIED** ■ | **FRENCH** ▥

0 | 1 | 2 km

HAMELN

DIEDERSEN

AFFERDE

BENSBERG

HASTENBECK

VÖLKERHAUSEN

TÜNDERN

RIVER WESER

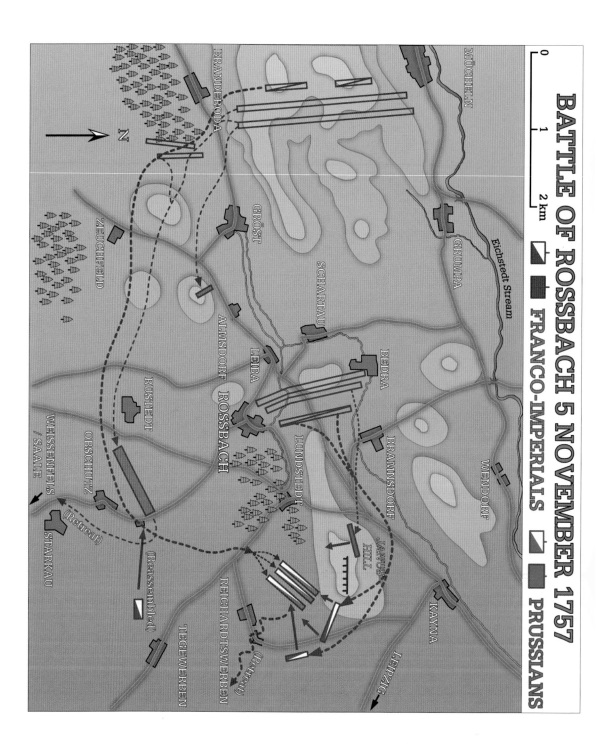

BATTLE OF ROSSBACH 5 NOVEMBER 1757

FRANCO-IMPERIALS PRUSSIANS

0   1   2 km

N

MÜCHELN

BRANDERODA

GRÖST

GRUMPA

Eichstedt Stream

SCHARTAU

ZEUCHFELD

BEDRA

ALMSDORF

LEIBA

WENDORF

RÜSTEDT

ROSSBACH

LUNDSTEDT

BRAMNSDORF

OBSCHÜTZ

WEISSENFELS / SAALE

(Retreat)

(Reassembled)

JANUS

HILL

STARKAU

REICHARDTSWERBEN

KAYNA

(Retreat)

LEIPZIG

TEGEWERBEN

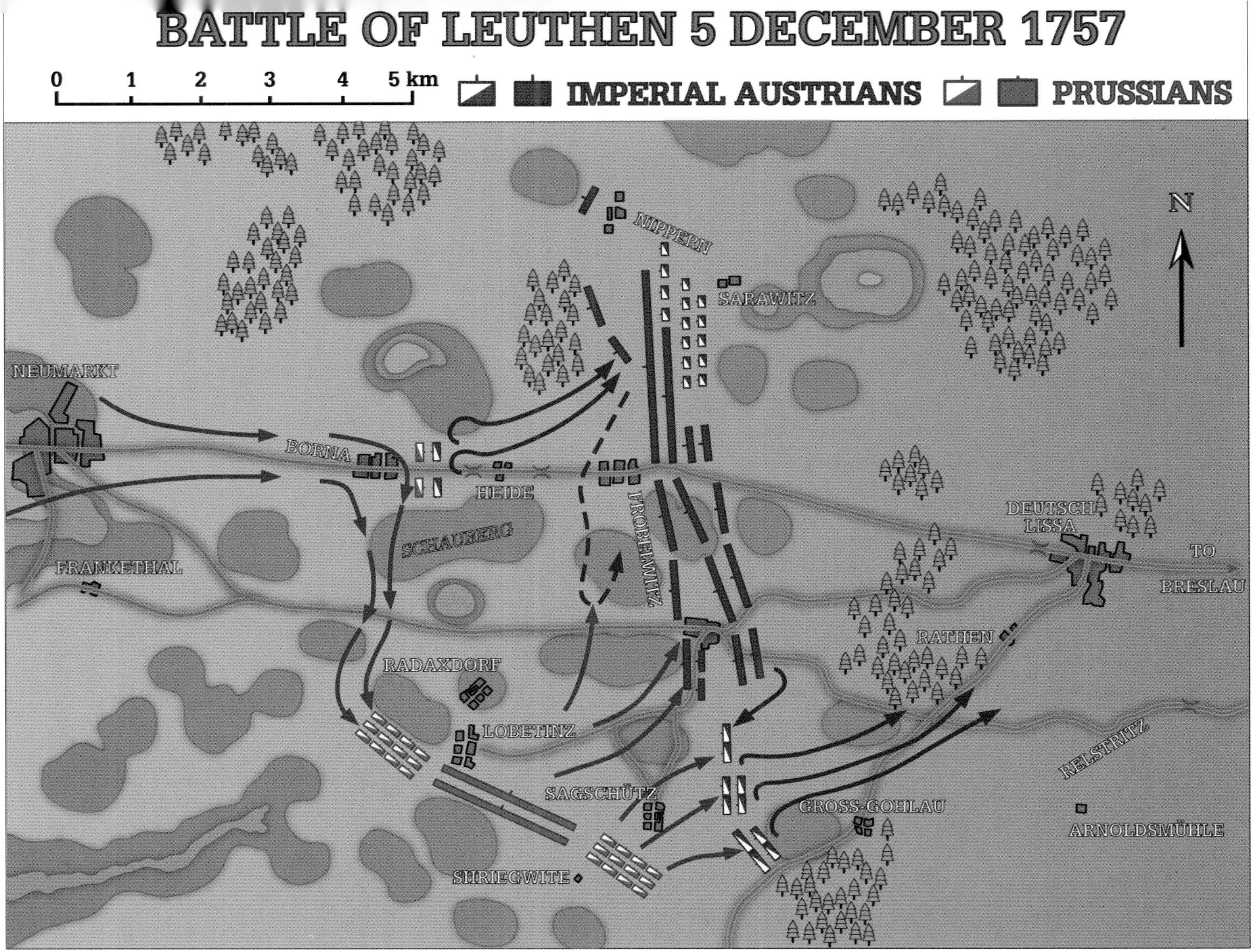

BATTLE OF LEUTHEN 5 DECEMBER 1757

IMPERIAL AUSTRIANS   PRUSSIANS

0 1 2 3 4 5 km

N

NEUMARKT

FRANKENTHAL

BORNA

SCHAUBERG

HEIDE

RADAXDORF

LOBETINZ

SAGSCHÜTZ

SCHRIEGWITZ

NIPPERN

SARAWITZ

FROBELWITZ

RATHEN

GROSS-GOHLAU

DEUTSCH-LISSA

ARNOLDSMÜHLE

WEISTRITZ

TO BRESLAU

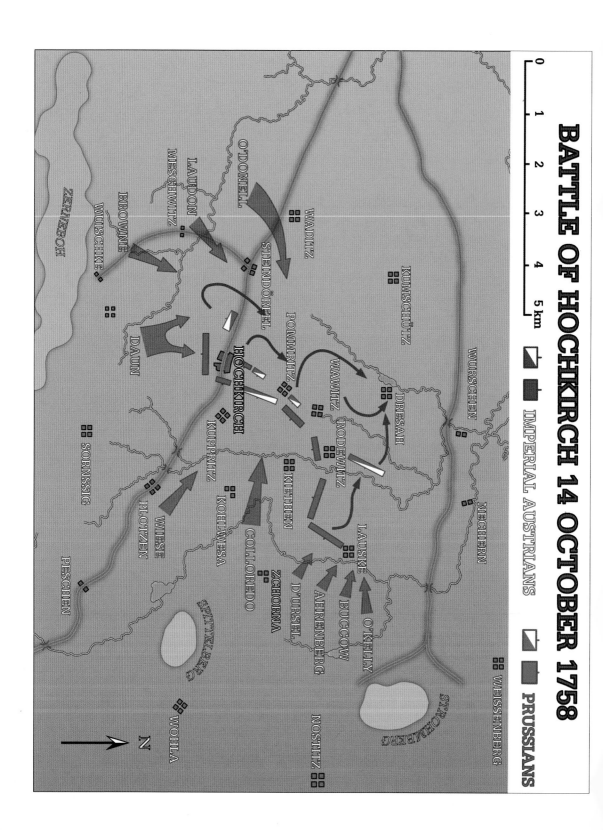

BATTLE OF HOCHKIRCH 14 OCTOBER 1758

IMPERIAL AUSTRIANS

PRUSSIANS

N

0 1 2 3 4 5 km

ZERNEBOH

O'DONELL
WADITZ
KUMSCHÜTZ
WURSCHEN
NECHERN
WEISSENBERG

MESCHWITZ
LAUDON
STEINDÖRFEL
POMMRITZ
WAWITZ
DRESAH

BROWNE
WUISCHKE
DAUN
HOCHKIRCH
RODEWITZ
LAUSKE
O'KELLY
BUCCOW
SCHOMBERG

SORNSSIG
KUPPRITZ
KIETHEN
D'URSEL
AHRENBERG

PLOTZEN
WIESE
KOHLWESA
ZCHORNA
NOSTITZ

PESCHEN
COLLOREDO
SPITTELBERG
WOHLA

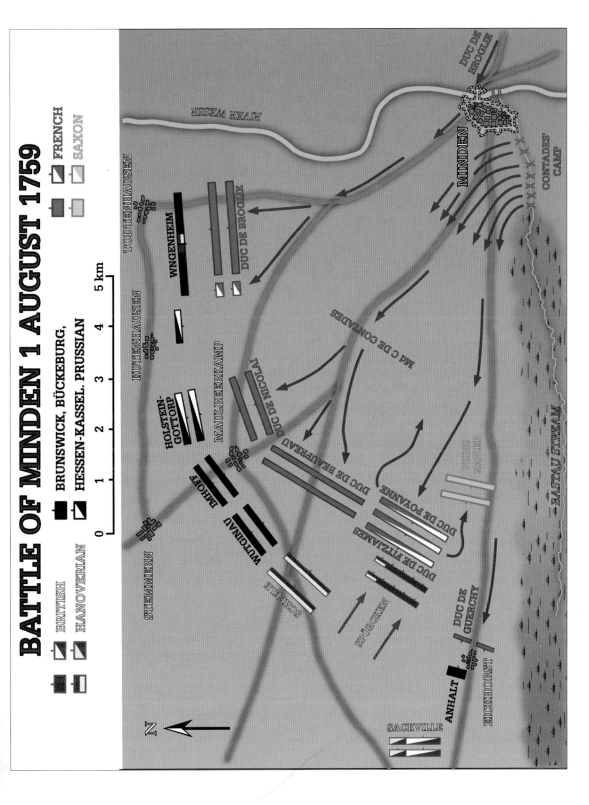

BATTLE OF MINDEN 1 AUGUST 1759

BRITISH

BRUNSWICK, BÜCKEBURG,

HANOVERIAN

HESSEN-KASSEL, PRUSSIAN

FRENCH

SAXON

N

5 km
0 1 2 3 4

RIVER WESSER

TODTENHAUSEN

KUTENHAUSEN

STEMMERN

MINDEN

DUC DE BROGLIE

WINGENHEIM

DUC DE BROGLIE

CONTADES' CAMP

Mal DE CONTADES

MAULBEERKAMP

HOLSTEIN-GOTTORP

DUC DE NICOLAI

INHOFF

WUTGINAU

DUC DE BEAUPREAU

DUC DE POYANNE

PRINZ XAVIER

SCHEELE

DUC DE FITZJAMES

SPÖRCKEN

BASTAU STREAM

ANHALT

DUC DE GUERCHY

HICKHORST

SACKVILLE

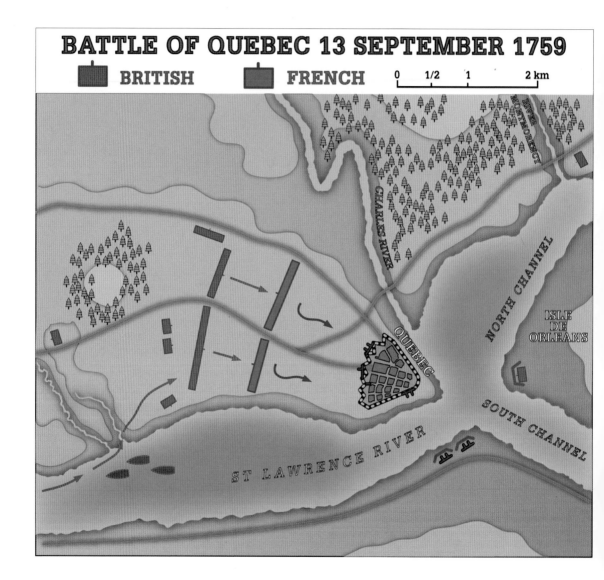

BATTLE OF QUEBEC 13 SEPTEMBER 1759

BRITISH   FRENCH

0   1/2   1   2 km

RIVER MONTMORENCY

CHARLES RIVER

QUEBEC

NORTH CHANNEL

ISLE DE ORLEANS

SOUTH CHANNEL

ST LAWRENCE RIVER

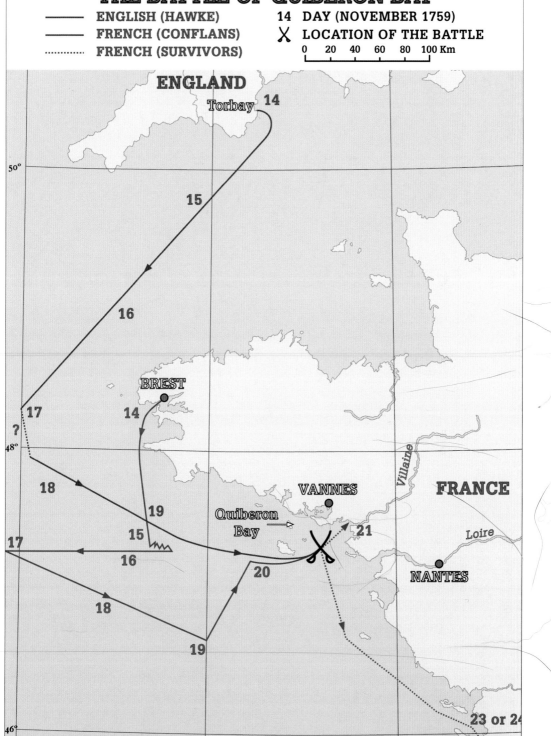

TRACKS OF ENGLISH AND FRENCH FLEETS BEFORE AND AFTER THE BATTLE OF QUIBERON BAY

——— ENGLISH (HAWKE)
——— FRENCH (CONFLANS)
·········· FRENCH (SURVIVORS)

14 DAY (NOVEMBER 1759)
✗ LOCATION OF THE BATTLE

0   20   40   60   80   100 Km

ENGLAND

Torbay **14**

50°

15

16

BREST   **14**

17
?
48°

18

19

17

15
16

18

19

VANNES

Quiberon
Bay

21

20

FRANCE

Villaine

Loire

NANTES

23 or 24

46°

ROCHEFORT

6°   4°   2°

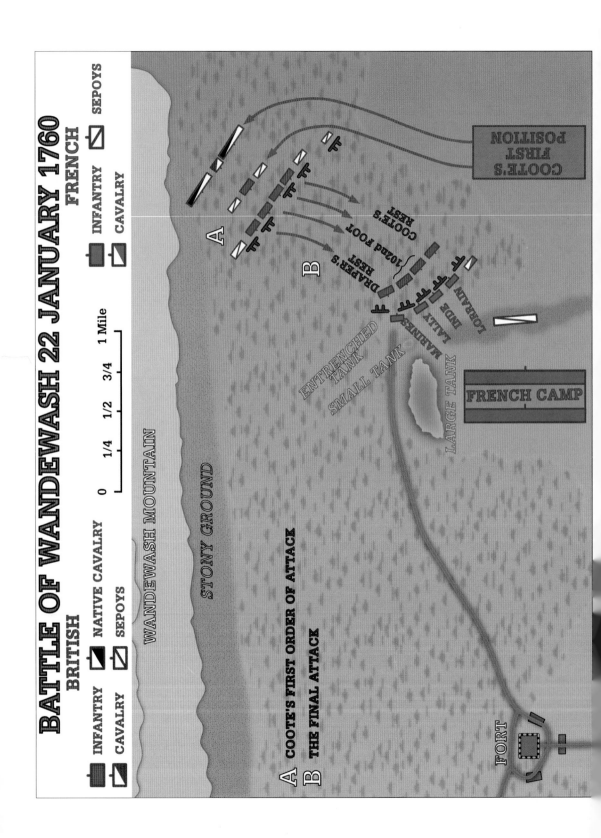

BATTLE OF WANDEWASH 22 JANUARY 1760

BRITISH

- ▮ INFANTRY
- ◪ NATIVE CAVALRY
- ◹ SEPOYS
- ◹ CAVALRY

0   1/4   1/2   3/4   1 Mile

FRENCH

- ◹ SEPOYS
- ▮ INFANTRY
- ◻ CAVALRY

WANDEWASH MOUNTAIN

STONY GROUND

A COOTE'S FIRST ORDER OF ATTACK

B THE FINAL ATTACK

COOTE'S FIRST POSITION

COOTE'S REST

102nd FOOT

DRAPER'S REST

ENTRENCHED TANK

SMALL TANK

MARINES

LALLY

INDE

LORRAIN

LARGE TANK

FRENCH CAMP

FORT

French Order of Battle

Field Marshal Louis-Charles-César d'Estrees commanding; Charles, Prince de Soubisse, second-in-command.

First Line

Right Flank

Division under Field Marshal de Chevert (Maréchal de Camp de Vougé and Maréchal de Camp de Maupeau assisting)
Light troops:
Volontaires de Hainault (1 battalion)
Volontaires de Flandres (1 battalion)
Volontaires d'Armee (2 squadrons)
Combined grenadiers (12 companies)
Picardie Infanterie (4 battalions)
Navarre Infanterie (4 battalions)
La Marine Infanterie (4 battalions)

Eu Brigade (Comte de Lorge):
Eu Infanterie (2 battalions)
d'Enghien Infanterie (2 battalions)

Right Wing Infantry
Marquis d'Armentières

Austrian Brigade:
Infanterie-Regiment de Ligne
Infanterie-Regiment Sachsen-Gotha

Belzunce Brigade:
Belzunce Infanterie (4 battalions)

La Couronne Brigade:
La Couronne Infanterie (2 battalions)
Conty Infanterie (2 battalions)

Alsace Brigade:
Alsace Infanterie (3 battalions)
St-Germain Infanterie (1 battalion)

Dragoon Brigade:
Colonel-General Cavalerie (4 dismounted squadrons)
Mestre de Camp Cavalerie (4 dismounted squadrons)
Orléans Cavalerie (4 dismounted squadrons)

Infantry of the Centre
Marquis de Contades

Mailly Brigade:
Mailly Infanterie (4 battalions)

Brigade Lyonnais:
Lyonnais Infanterie (2 battalions)
La Roche-Aymon Infanterie (2 battalions)

Brigade Vaubecourt:
Vaubécourt Infanterie (2 battalions)
Condé Infanterie (2 battalions)

Orléans Brigade:
Orléans Infanterie (2 battalions)
Chatres Infanterie (2 battalions)

Left Wing Infantry
Duc de Broglie

M. de Guerchy's Brigade du Roi:
Du Roi Infanterie (4 battalions)

M. de St-Perm's Grenadier Brigade:
Grenadiers Royaux de Solar (2 battalions)
Grenadiers de France (4 battalions)

Left Wing Cavalry
Duc de Brissac

Royal Cravate Brigade:
Royal Cravate Cavalerie (2 squadrons)
Noailles Cavalerie (2 squadrons)
Charost Cavalerie (2 squadrons)

Mestre de Camp Général Brigade:
Mestre de Camp Général Cavalerie (2 squadrons)
2 unidentified regiments (4 squadrons)

Second Line

Right Wing Cavalry (Behind Infantry of the Centre)
Duc D'Orléans

Colonel-General Brigade:
Colonel-General Cavalerie (3 squadrons)
Clermont-Tonnerre Cavalerie (2 squadrons)

Dauphine Brigade:
Dauphin Cavalerie (2 squadrons)
Moustiere Cavalerie (2 squadrons)
Talleyrand Cavalerie (2 squadrons)

Cuirassiers du Roy Brigade:
Cuirassier Regiment Du Roy (2 squadrons)
2 unidentified regiments (4 squadrons)

Left Wing Infantry
Duc de Broglie

Division under de Souvrie and von Isselbach
1st Palatinate Brigade:
Infanterie-Regiment von Osten (2 battalions)
Infanterie-Regiment Prinz Karl (2 battalions)
Infanterie-Regiment von Preysing (2 battalions)

2nd Palatinate Brigade:
Infanterie-Regiment von Baaden (2 battalions)
Infanterie-Regiment Prinz von Birkenfeld (2 battalions)

Poitöu Brigade:
Poitou Infanterie (2 battalions)
Provence Infanterie (2 battalions)

Royal Suédois Brigade:
Royal Suédois Infanterie (2 battalions)
Baviere Infanterie (2 battalions)

Left Wing Cavalry
Duc de Broglie

Royal-Pologne Brigade:
Royal-Pologne Cavalerie (2 squadrons)
Harcourt Cavalerie (2 squadrons)
Henrichemont Cavalerie (2 squadrons)

Du Roy Brigade:
Du Roy Cavalerie (2 squadrons)

Rochefoucauld-Langeac Cavalerie (2 squadrons)
Condé Cavalerie (2 squadrons)

The Reserve

Infantry
Champagne Brigade:
Champagne Infanterie (4 battalions)

Division Coming up from Imbeck:
Reding Infanterie (2 battalions)
Salis de Mayenfeld Infanterie (2 battalions)

Cavalry
Commissaire Général Brigade:
Commissaire Général Cavalerie (2 squadrons)
Bellefonds Cavalerie (2 squadrons)
Aquitaine Cavalerie (2 squadrons)

Bourgogne Brigade:
Bourgogne Cavalerie (2 squadrons)
Bourbon-Busset Cavalerie (2 squadrons)

Royal Roussilon Brigade:
Royal Roussilon Cavalerie (2 squadrons)
Saluces Cavalerie (2 squadrons)
Fumel Cavalerie (2 squadrons)

Royal-Carabiniers (6 squadrons)
Bercheny Hussards (4 squadrons)
Polleresky Hussards (4 squadrons)

Artillery
M. de la Vallière

Corps Royal de l'Artillerie:
Lamotte Batallion
Menouville Batallion
68 guns
8 howitzers

Total: 84 battalions (50,000 infantry), 83 squadrons (10,000 cavalry), 84 battalion guns, 68 heavy field guns, 8 howitzers

Battle of Rossbach, 5 November 1757

Location

A village in north-eastern Germany, about 30km west-south-west of Leipzig, in the centre of a triangle formed by the towns of Freyburg, Merseburg and Weissenfels.

Frederick the Great, with 22,000 men and 79 guns, marched from Dresden on 31 August to confront the Franco-Imperial Army, which was his most immediate threat, advancing eastwards through Thuringia in Saxony. The main bodies of the Austrians to his south and the Russians to his east were quiescent, giving him an excellent opportunity to exploit his interior lines for this purpose. The two forces closed up in an area to the west of Leipzig and southwest of Merseburg on the river Unstrut and proceeded to manoeuvre for some days, each looking for an opening to strike. The Austrian commander of the joint Franco-Imperial Army was Field Marshal Joseph Friedrich Wilhelm, Duke of Sachsen-Hildburghausen; he was assisted by the French Lieutenant-General Charles de Rohan, Prince de Soubise. Together they had 42,000 men but only 45 field guns. Soubise was the more cautious of the two Allied commanders, but on the morning of 5 November, he agreed to undertake an offensive against the Prussians, despite the fact that many of his troops were dispersed around the area, foraging.

At this point, the Franco-Imperial Army was encamped on high ground, on a north-south axis from the village of Mücheln in the north, to Branderoda in the south, facing eastwards. Their Prussian foes were about 5km to the east, between the villages of Bedra in the north, to Rossbach, facing west. Behind the Prussian position was a low ridge, the Janushügel, running east to west, which was to play a crucial role in the coming battle.

The Allied plan was to undertake a very wide right hook, to assault the Prussian left wing. They moved off just before 1100 hours, in two distinct sections, first the cavalry under General de Broglie, behind them the infantry. A flank guard under French General Count St Germain, consisting of eight battalions and twelve squadrons, was positioned between these columns and the Prussian left wing.

Frederick had been observing this motion all morning and initially thought that the Allies were commencing a general withdrawal to their magazines in Freyburg an der Unstrut, a few kilometres to the south, and that St Germain's corps was a rearguard. But one of his officers, Captain von Gaudi, observed that the enemy had turned to the east, obviously attempting to turn the King's southern flank. As soon as the sceptical Frederick had convinced himself of what was actually happening, he decided to take his chance and to accept the battle that he had been working and hoping for. At about 1430 hours, Frederick ordered his cavalry, under the command of Major General von Seydlitz (a junior, but very competent commander), to march east, along the dead ground behind the Janushügel and then to sweep south, to take the head of the Allied column in flank. He also set up a battery of 18 field guns on the Janushügel and deployed hussars to occupy the crest of the ridge, to deny the enemy's patrols any view of what he was doing.

The Allies' plan had a weakness; their columns had to cover about 12km to reach their target point behind the Prussian left wing. The Prussians had only about a third of that distance to cover to achieve their aim. During the march over open ground, the Franco-Imperial forces became strung out, with the 33 squadrons of the Austro-Imperial cavalry in the lead, now far ahead of the leading French infantry column of 32 battalions. Behind the infantry came twelve squadrons of French cavalry. The French reserve column of eight battalions and ten squadrons, under General de Broglie, became tangled up with eleven German battalions and the Imperial Army's reserve artillery.

Just after 1400 hours, just south of the village of Pettstädt, the Allied commanders called a halt and discussed whether the attack ought not to be postponed until the next day, but Sachsen-Hildburghausen insisted that the advance continue. At 1430 hours, French observers saw the Prussian Army begin to strike their tents and file off eastwards, behind the Janushügel. Assuming that they were making for Merseburg – in order to escape across the river Ustrut over the bridge there –

Sachsen-Hildburghausen ordered the speed of march to be increased, eager to catch his enemy while they were impeded by the crossing.

Frederick's 18 guns on the Janushügel now opened up on the Allied columns to the south. Eight French guns were deployed to oppose them, but their uphill fire was ineffective. Seydlitz, who had been keeping eyes on the enemy columns, passed the eastern end of the Janushügel with the 4000 men of his 38 Prussian squadrons, and wheeled them south, in two lines. The 7000 Austro-German Imperial cavalry were taken completely by surprise as the enemy poured over the low ridge before them. They tried to form line of battle as best they might, but only the two Austrian cuirassier regiments (Brettlach and Trautmannsdorff) managed to do it in time, but they were overwhelmed within ten minutes. The disorganised, outnumbered Imperial cavalry stood no chance at all. At 1600 hours, barely 30 minutes after the first Prussian cavalry charge, they were in full flight to the southeast, around the village of Reichartswerben and away from their unfortunate infantry. Letting them go, von Seydlitz rallied his cavalry south of the battlefield, between the villages of Obschutz and Tagewerben. The fleeing Austro-Imperial cavalry overran a relief force of French cavalry under Prince Soubise and de Broglie and fled away towards the river Unstrut.

At this point, the Franco-Imperial infantry column was just north of Obschutz and in some disorder. The 24 Prussian infantry battalions were advancing south from the Janushügel and the Prussian battery on the ridge had been pounding the enemy infantry as they hurried along; now they moved south, to just northwest of Reichardtswerben, to better engage the disorganised mass of the enemy infantry.

The well-drilled Prussian infantry line closed to within about 50m of their disorganised foes, who were still partially in columns, halted and began to fire into their wavering targets. The Prussian rate of fire was high (3–4 rounds per minute) and telling. It continued for about 15 minutes and then von Seydlitz and his victorious cavalry crashed into the exposed enemy right wing. That settled the battle; the Franco-Imperial infantry broke and poured off to the southwest, a panic having broken out in the Franconian infantry regiments Ferntheil, Kronegg and Varel and Kurtrier. The regimental guns were abandoned in the rush to get away. Only the regiments Darmstadt and Blau-Würzburg kept their heads and their spirits; they and St Germain's corps formed the rearguard.

It was now 1730 hours; Frederick let the fleeing troops go. It transpired that only seven Prussian infantry battalions had come close enough to the enemy infantry to use their muskets and in only two of those did the expenditure of cartridges reach 12–15 per man. The Franco-Imperials lost 800 killed, 2200 wounded and 5000 captured, including eight generals and 300 officers. They also lost 72 guns (both field and battalion pieces), 21 standards (two from Fitz-James Cavalerie, one each from Penthièvre Cavalerie, Saluces Cavalerie, Bussy-Lameth Cavalerie and Descars Cavalerie), three pairs of kettle drums, many infantry colours and most of the baggage. The Prussians lost 169 killed and 379 wounded, including von Seydlitz, who was promoted to Lieutenant-General on the field.

In the following days, Frederick followed his beaten foe only as far west as Eckartsberga, north of Jena; patrols went further, as far as Erfurt, gathering up stragglers and abandoned guns and equipment. The Imperial Army poured away to the west, as did the French. Prince Soubise reported to his king: 'the ruin of your army is complete'.

Relieved of any immediate credible enemy threat to the west, east and north, Frederick turned his attention to his favourite project: the re-conquest of Silesia. By 10 November, he and his army were in and around Leipzig. On 5 December, he soundly defeated the Austrian Army of Prince Carl von Lothringen and Field Marshal von Daun at Leuthen; by the end of December, Silesia was his again.

Prussian Order of Battle

King Friedrich II commanding, Field Marshal James von Keith second-in-command

First Line

Flank Guard

Husaren-Regiment Szekely (5 squadrons)

Right Wing Infantry

Lieutenant-General Ferdinand von Braunschweig

Major-General von Itzenplitz's Brigade:
Grenadier Battalion 17/22 Kremzow
Grenadier Battalion 19/25 Ramin
Infanterie-Regiment Markgraf Karl
(2 battalions)
Grenadier Battalion 1/23

Major-General von Retzow's Brigade:
Infanterie-Regiment von Meyerinck
(2 battalions)
Grenadier Garde (2nd and 3rd Battalions)

Right Wing Cavalry

Major-General von Seydlitz

Major-General von Seydlitz's Brigade:
Dragoner-Regiment von Meinicke
(5 squadrons)
Dragoner-Regiment von Czettritz (5 squadrons)
Leibregiment Kürassiers (5 squadrons)

Left Wing Infantry

Lieutenant-General Heinrich Prinz von Preussen

Major-General von Geist's Brigade:
Infanterie-Regiment von Itzenplitz (2 battalions)
Infanterie-Regiment von Forcadre (2 battalions)
Grenadier-Garde (1 battalion)

Major-General von Oldenburg's Brigade:
Infanterie-Regiment von Kleist (2 battalions)
Infanterie-Regiment Alt Braunschweig (2 battalions)
Grenadier Battalion 5/20 Jung-Billerbeck
Grenadier Battalion 7/30 Lubath

Second Line

Right Wing Cavalry

Major-General von Seydlitz

Brigadier-General von Schöneich's Brigade:
Kürassier-Regiment Garde du Corps (3 squadrons)
Kürassier-Regiment Gens d'armes (5 squadrons)
Kürassier-Regiment von Rochow (5 squadrons)
Kürassier-Regiment von Driesen (5 squadrons)

Infantry of the Centre

Lieutenant-General von Forcade

Major-General von Asseburg's Brigade:
Infanterie-Regiment von Winterfeldt (2 battalions)
Infanterie-Regiment von der Goltz (2 battalions)

Major-General von Grabow's Brigade:
Infanterie-Regiment von Hülsen (1st Battalion)
Grenadier Battalion 13/26 Finck (1 battalion)

Total: 27 battalions (16,600 men) with, 45 squadrons (5400 men), 56 battalion guns 18 heavy guns, for a total of approximately 22,000 men

Franco–Austrian Order of Battle

Field Marshal Joseph Friedrich Wilhelm, Duke of Sachsen-Hildburghausen commanding

First Line

Right Wing Cavalry (Austrian and Imperial)

General-Major von Brettlach's Brigade:
Kürassier-Regiment von Brettlach (7 squadrons)

Prinz von Hohenzollern's Imperial Brigade:
Kürassier-Regiment von Hatzfeld (3 squadrons)
Kürassier-Regiment von Hohenzollern (4 squadrons)
Dragoner-Regiment Württemberg (2 squadrons)

Infantry of the Centre (French)
Comte de Montboisier and Chevalier de Nicolaï

M. de Crillon's Piémont Brigade:
Piémont Infanterie (4 battalions)

M. de Custine's La Viefville Saint-Chamond Brigade:
St-Chaumond Infanterie (2 battalions)
Cossé Brissac Infanterie (2 battalions)

Royal-Roussilon Brigade:
Royal Deux-Ponts Infanterie (2 battalions)
Royal-Roussilon Infanterie (2nd Battalion)

M. de Planta's Swiss Brigade:
Reding Infanterie (2 battalions)
de Planta Infanterie (2 battalions)

Left Wing Cavalry (French)
Lieutenant-General Comte de Mailly (M. de Raugrave assisting)

La Reine Brigade:
La Reine Cavalerie (2 squadrons)
Bourbon-Busset Cavalerie (2 squadrons)
Fitz-James Cavalerie (2 squadrons)

Bourbon Brigade:
Beauvilliers Cavalerie (2 squadrons)
Volontaires Liégeois (2 squadrons)
Bourbon Cavalerie (2 squadrons)

Second Line

Right Wing Cavalry (Austrian and Imperial)
Kürassier-Regiment von Trautmannsdorf (7 squadrons)

Prince von Hohenzollern's Imperial Cavalry Brigade:
Kürassier-Regiment Bayreuth (4 squadrons)
Dragoner-Regiment Ansbach (4 squadrons)

Infantry of the Centre (French)
Comte de Lorges (Comte de Vaux and the Marquis de Rougé assisting)

Mailly Brigade:
Mailly Infanterie (4 battalions)

La Marck German Brigade:
La Marck Infanterie (2 battalions)
Royal-Pologne Infanterie (1 battalion)
St-Germain Infanterie (1 battalion)

De Castellas Swiss Brigade:
De Castellas Infanterie (2 battalions)
Salis de Mayenfeld Infanterie (2 battalions)

Wittmer's Swiss Brigade:
Wittmer Infanterie (2 battalions)
Diesbach Infanterie (2 battalions)

The Reserve

Right Wing Cavalry (French)
Marquis de Poulpry (Chevalier d'Ailly assisting)

Penthièvre Brigade:
Penthierve Cavalerie (2 squadrons)
Saluces Cavalerie (2 squadrons)
Bussy-Lameth Cavalerie (2 squadrons)

Infantry of the Centre (French)
Duc de Broglie

Comte de Orlick's Poitou Brigade:
Poitou Infanterie (2 battalions)
Provence Infanterie (2 battalions)

Prince Camille's Rohan-Montbazon Brigade:
Rohan Montbazon Infanterie (2 battalions)
Beauvoisis Infanterie (2 battalions)

Left Wing Cavalry (French)
Marquis de Chetardie (Marquis de Castries assisting)

Lusignan Brigade:
Lusignan Cavalerie (2 squadrons)
Descars Cavalerie (2 squadrons)

Other Units

Corps St Germain
Condé Cavalry Brigade:
Condé Cavalerie (2 squadrons)
Bezons Cavalerie (2 squadrons)
Lastic de St Jal Cavalerie (2 squadrons)

Touraine Brigade:
Condé Infanterie (2 battalions)
Touraine Infanterie (2 battalions)

La Marine Brigade:
La Marine Infanterie (4 battalions)

Poly Brigade:
Grammont Cavalerie (2 squadrons)
Montcalm Cavalerie (2 squadrons)

Poly St-Thiebault Cavalerie (2 squadrons)

Graf von Loudon's Austrian Brigade:
unidentified border infantry regiment (3 battalions)
unidentified hussar regiment (perhaps Haddik) (3 squadrons)

Imperial Infantry
Prinz von Hessen-Darmstadt (Baron von Drachsdorff assisting)

Count Holstein's Brigade:
Infanterie-Regiment Blau-Würzburg (2 battalions)
Infanterie-Regiment Hessen-Darmstadt Kreis (1 battalion)

Infanterie-Regiment Varell (2 battalions)

Brigadier-General von Ferntheil's Brigade:
Infanterie-Regiment Kur-Trier (2 battalions)
Infanterie-Regiment von Cronegk (2 battalions)
Infanterie-Regiment von Ferntheil (2 battalions)

Artillery
Aumale Battalion (French), 33 pieces
Imperial Artillery, 12 pieces

Total: 62 battalions, 82 squadrons, 45 field guns; approximately 41,000 men.

Battle of Leuthen, 5 December 1757

Location
A village (now Lutynia) in Poland, about 20km west of the city of Breslau (now Wroclaw, on the river Oder).

While Frederick the Great had been defeating the Franco-Austrians at Rossbach on 5 November, another Austrian army under Field Marshal Prinz Carl von Lothringen and Field Marshal Graf von Daun, pushed northwards from Bohemia into Silesia. On 14 November Austrian General von Nádasdy occupied the city of Schweidnitz (Swidnica) some 43km southwest of Breslau, and on 22 November von Lothringen defeated a Prussian corps under the Herzog August Wilhelm von Braunschweig-Wolfenbüttel-Bevern, on the south-western side of Breslau. The Prussian corps withdrew, leaving Silesia's first city in Austrian hands.

After a brief period of reorganisation and replenishment, Frederick and his army left Dresden and marched eastwards, to reclaim his treasured province. Marching via Görlitz, he passed through Parchwitz (now Prochowice), just northeast of Liegnitz (now Legnica) very early on 4 December. That night, he camped at Neumarkt (now Sroda Slaska) some 22km towards Breslau and about 10km from the intervening village of Leuthen.

What makes Frederick's victory at Leuthen an exceptional achievement is that he knew that the enemy heavily outnumbered his own force. After a 12km march next morning, the Prussian vanguard (12 battalions, 50 squadrons and ten guns under Lieutenant-General the Prinz von Württemberg) bumped into, surprised and overthrew the Austrian General von Nostitz, with three Saxon and two Austrian hussar regiments (18 squadrons), which fell back to the east and onto the Austrian right wing, just to the east of the village of Nippern, which was surrounded by peat bogs. From here, the Austrian line ran south for almost 10km through Frobelwitz, to the village of Leuthen, which was packed with the least reliable infantry of the Imperial Army *Kreis* regiments. Carl von Lothringen commanded about 70,000 men (84 battalions, 144 squadrons) and 210 field guns, which were deployed in well-selected defensive positions, the only fault being that he had left some hills close to his front unoccupied, meaning that there was a lot of dead ground, which he could neither see nor command with artillery fire.

Frederick had just 28,600 men (47.5 battalions, 133 squadrons) and 78 field guns but the Prussians knew this ground well; as the day brightened, Frederick scouted out the enemy positions for three hours and made an audacious plan. Recognising the strength of the Austrian right and not having the force to batter his way through their centre, he planned to employ his oblique attack to turn their southern flank at Leuthen, using the dead ground to cover his move. Leaving a force of cavalry to hold the high ground, he ordered his main body to turn south and march for two hours to a point between Leuthen and Schreigwitz; for this entire march, they would be out of the Austrians' sight. Once here, deployed on an east-west line, they would be sitting directly on the end of the Austrian line, ideally placed to roll it up.

Amazingly, Carl von Lothringen and Graf von Daun elected to sit and allow this movement to take place, making no serious effort at any counter-measures at all. The Prussian advanced guard were left visible on the heights at Borne, opposite Nippern, and General von Lucchesi, commanding the Austrian right wing, feared that he was about to be attacked by them and requested large cavalry reinforcements. Initially, von Lothringen refused, but at the third, urgent request, he relented and ordered von Daun to move all of his reserve cavalry and some other units from the south of his line to the north.

Just after 1200 hours, on the southern Austrian wing, General von Nádasdy, the local commander, saw the Prussian main body moving into the area of Lobetinz and Kertschütz, about 1.5km away from his position and knew that he was in great peril. By this daring move of his army, across the front of the enemy line and into position across the Austrian southern flank, Frederick achieved tactical surprise and local superiority of numbers at his chosen point of attack. Nádasdy sent for reinforcements, and they were dispatched, but time was on the Prussians' side. Nádasdy also launched a spoiling attack against the advancing Prussians and initially overthrew von Zieten's cavalry before the accompanying Prussian infantry drove the Austrian horse back. From the mill in Lobetinz, Frederick could now overlook the whole of the Austrian left wing, extended back through Sagschütz to the east.

Fürst Moritz von Anhalt-Dessau commanded the attack against the Austrian left wing for the King; he had ordered his infantry to advance north, in oblique formation, the right flank leading, with four battalions in column on the right wing. His cavalry of the advanced guard extended to the right and clashed with Nádasdy's cavalry, eventually routing them and driving them off to the northeast towards Rathen, on the river Weistritz.

The Prussian infantry advanced and pushed the Württembergers and Bavarians back north on Leuthen. Austrian forces were now streaming south to prop up the southern end of their line and a grim struggle developed for control of Leuthen. The Austrian divisions of Angern, Esterhazy and Maquire hurried up, but were overolled by their retreating comrades and the pursuing enemy and could achieve nothing, except to form a magnificent target for the Prussian artillery, drawn up on the heights north of Sagschütz and Lobetinz.

General Graf von Lucchese brought his cavalry down south, past Frobelwitz to help his infantry, but they were taken in the right flank by General von Driesen, with the Prussian cavalry of the left wing, which had been held concealed behind the hills at Radaxdorf, and by fire from Oberst von Angelelli's three Frei-Battalions in Gross-Heidau, west of Frobelwitz. The Austrian cavalry fell back to the east, riding down their own infantry; a general panic gripped the Austrians, who fled eastwards to the river Weistritz. In the gathering gloom and a snowstorm, the battle ended as the Prussians cleared Lissa of Grenz (border) infantry.

This amazing victory yielded amazing fruits; the Prussians took 55 colours and standards, 131 guns and over 12,000 prisoners. Fürst Moriz von Anhalt-Dessau was promoted to field marshal on the spot. Prussian losses were 223 officers and 6159 men killed, wounded and missing.

Austrian losses were about 6500 killed and wounded in the battle; in the days after the battle the total of their captives reached 21,500. The Austrian Army fled back to Breslau and then further, in the next days, to Austrian territory in Bohemia. Fredrick laid siege to Breslau, which surrendered on 19 December, together with 18,000 prisoners. Frederick was master of Silesia again; Prinz Carl von Lothringen resigned in disgrace, having lost about three-quarters of his army within a few hours.

Prussian Order of Battle

King Friedrich II commanding

Vanguard
Generallieutenant Friedrich Eugen, Prinz von Württemberg

Cavalry
General-Major von Stechow

Husaren-Regiment von Ziethen (10 squadrons)
Husaren-Regiment von Werner (10 squadrons)
Husaren-Regiment von Warnery (6 squadrons)
Husaren-Regiment von Seydlitz (4 squadrons)
Dragoner-Regiment von Württemberg (5 squadrons)

Husaren-Regiment von Szekely (5 squadrons)
Husaren-Regiment von Puttkammer (10 squadrons)

Infantry
Generallieutenant Prinz von Bevern

Brigadier-General von Kalkreuth's Brigade:
Grenadier Bataillon 37/40 Manteuffel (1 battalion)
Grenadier Bataillon 1/23 Wedell (1 battalion)

Brigadier-General von der Goltz's Brigade:
Grenadier Bataillon 19/25 Ramin (1 battalion)

Brigadier-General von Lattorf's Brigade:
Infanterie-Regiment von Bornstedt (1 battalion)

Infanterie-Regiment von Asseburg
(1st Battalion)

Brigadier-General von Wedel's Brigade:
Infanterie-Regiment von Itzenplitz (2 battalions)
Infanterie-Regiment von Mayerinck (2 battalions)

Light Troops
Marquis d'Angelelli

Freibataillon le Noble (1 battalion)
Freibataillon d'Angelelli (1 battalion)
Freibataillon von Kalben (1 battalion)
Jäger zu Fuss (1 company)

Artillery
Ten 12-pounder guns

First Line

Right Wing Cavalry
Generallieutenant von Ziethen

General-Major von Lentulus's Brigade:
Gardes du Corps (3 squadrons)
Gens d'Armes (5 squadrons)

General-Major von Schmettau's Brigade:
Kürassier-Regiment von Seydlitz (5 squadrons)
Kürassier-Regiment Markgraf Friedrich (5 squadrons)

General-Major Baron von Schöneich's Brigade:
Kürassier-Regiment von Schöneich (5 squadrons)

Infantry of the Centre
Generallieutenant Prinz Moritz von Anhalt-Dessau

Refused Right Flank Guard
General-Major von Rohr

Grenadier Bataillon 4/16 Kleist (1 battalion)
Grenadier Bataillon 45 Unruh (1 battalion)

Right Division
Ferdinand Prinz von Preussen

General-Major Prinz Franz von Braunschweig's Brigade:

Grenadier Bataillon 17/22 Kremzow (1 battalion)
Infanterie-Regiment Markgraf Karl (2 battalions)
Grenadier Garde (2nd and 3rd Battalions)

General-Major von Kahlden's Brigade:
Grenadier-Garde Retzow (1 battalion)
Infanterie-Regiment von Kannacher (2 battalions)
Infanterie-Regiment von Pannwitz (2 battalions)

Left Division
Generallieutenant von Retzow

General-Major von Münchow's Brigade:
Infantcric-Rcgimcnt von Gcist (2 battalions)
Infanterie-Regiment von Winterfeldt (2 battalions)

Major-General von Geist's Brigade:
Infanterie-Regiment von Forcade (2 battalions)
Infanterie-Regiment Alt-Braunschweig (2 battalions)
Grenadier Bataillon 3/6 Hacke (1 battalion)
Grenadier Bataillon 35/36 Schenkendorff (1 battalion)

Left Flank Refused Wing
General-Major von Bornstedt

Grenadier Bataillon 21/27 Dieringshofen (1 battalion)
Füsilier-Regiment von Kursell (1st Battalion)

Left Wing Cavalry
Generallieutenant von Driesen

General-Major von Krockow (Senior)'s Brigade:
Kürassier-Regiment von Krockow (5 squadrons)
Leib-Karabiniers (5 squadrons)

General-Major von Normann's Brigade:
Kürassier-Regiment von Driesen (5 squadrons)

General-Major von Meier's Brigade:
Dragoner-Regiment von Bayreuth (5 squadrons)
Kürassier-Regiment von Kyau (5 squadrons)

Second Line

Right Wing Cavalry
Generallieutenant von Ziethen

General-Major von Czettritz's Brigade:
Dragoner-Regiment von Normann (5 squadrons)
Dragoner-Regiment von Czettritz (5 squadrons)

General-Major von Krockow (Jung)'s Brigade:
Dragoner-Regiment Jung-Krockow (5 squadrons)
Dragoner-Regiment von Stechow (5 squadrons)

Infantry of the Centre
Generallieutenant von Forcade

General-Major von Bülow's Brigade:
Infanterie-Regiment Prinz von Preussen
(1st Battalion)
Füsilier-Regiment von Münchow (1st Battalion)
Füsilier-Regiment Jung Braunschweig
(1st Battalion
Füsilier-Regiment Alt Württemberg
(1st Battalion)
Grenadier Bataillon 29/31 Östenreich (1 battalion)
Grenadier Bataillon G-VI/G-VIII von Plötz
(1 battalion)

General-Major von Oldenburg's Brigade:

Infanterie-Regiment Prinz Ferdinand
(1st Battalion)
Grenadier Bataillon GNG/GIII/G-IV von
Kahlden (1 battalion)
Füsilier-Regiment Prinz Heinrich (1st Battalion)
Infanterie-Regiment von Kalckstein (2 battalions)

Left Wing Cavalry
Generallieutenant von Driesen

Kürassier-Regiment Baron von Kyau (5 squadrons)

General-Major von Bredow's Brigade:
Kürassier-Regiment von Schöneich (5 squadrons)
Kürassier-Regiment von Gessler (5 squadrons)

Total: 47 1/2 battalions, 133 squadrons and 78 heavy gun (14 x 24-pounder guns, ten heavy 12-pounder 'Brummer' brought from the walls of Glogau fortress, 39 x light 12-pounder field guns, 94 battalion guns, eight howitzers and 7 mortars); approximately 28,600 men

Austrian Order of Battle

Commander-in-chief: Prinz Carl von
Lothringen commanding; Field Marshal Graf
von Daun second-in-command

The army was split into the main body and the
corps of General Nádasdy.

MAIN ARMY

Vanguard
unidentified border infantry unit (3 battalions)
Husaren-Regiment Paul Anton Esterhàzy
Hussaren-Regiment Szechényi

Cavalry
Field Marshal von Nostitz

Saxon Brigade:
Chevauxlegers Prinz Karl (4 squadrons)
Chevauxlegers Graf von Bruhl (4 squadrons)
Chevauxlegers Prinz Albrecht (4 squadrons)

Austrian Brigade:
Husaren-Regiment von Nádasdy (5 squadrons)
Husaren-Regiment von Dessewffy (5 squadrons)

First Line

Right Flank Guard
Major-General von Luzinsky (Duke von
Arenberg assisting)

Infanterie-Regiment Sachsen-Gotha
Infanterie-Regiment Königsegg (1 battalion)
Infanterie-Regiment Los Rios (1 battalion)

Right Wing Infantry
Feldzeugmeister Graf von Kheul

**Division under Field Marshal von
Macquire**
Infantry Regiment von Aremberg (1 battalion)
Infanterie-Regiment von Puebla (2 battalions)
Infanterie-Regiment von Daun (2 battalions)

Division under Field Marshal von Andlau

Infanterie-Regiment von Neipperg (2 battalions)

Infanterie-Regiment von Botta d'Ardorno
(2 battalions)

Infanterie-Regiment Kaiser (2 battalions)

Right Wing Cavalry

General der Kavallerie von Lucchesi

Division under General Lucchesi

Spada Brigade:

Kreis-Kürassier-Regiment Hohenzollern
(5 squadrons)

Kürassier-Regiment von Lucchesi (5 squadrons)

Dragoner-Regiment Erzherzog Joseph
(5 squadrons)

Woellwurth Brigade:

Kürassier-Regiment von Stampach (5 squadrons)

Kürassier-Regiment von Löwenstein (5 squadrons)

Left Wing Infantry

Felzeugmeister Colloredo

Brigadier-General von Puebla's Brigade:

Infanterie-Regiment Erzherzog Carl (2 battalions)

Infanterie-Regiment von Sachsen-
Hildburghausen (2 battalions)

Infanterie-Regiment von Moltke (1 battalion)

Brigadier-General von D'Arberg's Brigade:

Infanterie-Regiment Piccolomini (1 battalion)

Infanterie-Regiment von Kheul (2 battalions)

Infanterie-Regiment Nikolaus Esterházy
(2 battalions)

Général de Brigade von Angern's Brigade:

Infanterie-Regiment Joseph von Esterházy
(2 battalions)

Infanterie-Regiment Alt Braunschweig-
Wolfenbüttel (2 battalions)

Left Wing Cavalry

General der Kavallerie von Serbelloni

Brigadier-General von Hohenzollern's Brigade:

Kürassier-Regiment von Kalckreuth
(5 squadrons)

Kürassier-Regiment von Gelhay (5 squadrons)

Kürassier-Regiment von Ansbach (5 squadrons)

Brigadier-General von Buccow's Brigade:

Kürassier-Regiment Erzherzog Ferdinand
(5 squadrons)

Dragoner-Regiment von Hessen-Darmstadt
(6 squadrons)

Second Line

Right Flank Guard

Major-General von Luzinsky (Duke von
Arenberg assisting)

Infanterie-Regiment Mercy-Argentau
(1 battalion)

Infanterie-Regiment Andlau (1 battalion)

Infanterie-Regiment Haller von Hallerstein
(1 battalion)

Infanterie-Regiment Arberg (1 battalion)

Right Wing Infantry

Feldzeugmeister Graf von Kheul

**Division under Field Marshal von
Starhemberg**

Infanterie-Regiment von Kollowrath-
Krakowsky (2 battalions)

Infanterie-Regiment Baden-Durlach (1 battalion)

Infanterie-Regiment von Wallis (1 battalion)

Infanterie-Regiment von Pallavicini (1 battalion)

Infanterie-Regiment Carl von Lothringen
(1 battalion)

Infanterie-Regiment von Waldeck (1 battalion)

Right Wing Cavalry

Division of Field Marshal von Esterhazy

Brigadier-General von Daun's Brigade:

Dragoner-Regiment von Daun (5 squadrons)

Dragoner-Regiment von Württemberg
(5 squadrons)

Brigadier-General von Trauttmannsdorff's Brigade:

Kürassier-Regiment von Serbelloni
(5 squadrons)

Kürassier-Regiment von Anhalt-Zerbst
(5 squadrons)

Left Wing Infantry

Feldzeugmeister Colloredo

Brigadier-General von Wied's Brigade:
Infanterie-Regiment von Harrach (2 battalions)
Infanterie-Regiment Jung Braunschweig-
Wulfenbüttel (2 battalions)
Infanterie-Regiment von Baden-Baden
(1 battalion)
Infanterie-Regiment von Gaisrück (1 battalion)

Brigadier-General von Haller's Brigade:
Infanterie-Regiment von Harsch (2 battalions)
Infanterie-Regiment von Bethlen (1 battalion)
Infanterie-Regiment Hoch und Deutschmeister
(1 battalion)
Infanterie-Regiment von Browne (1 battalion)
Infanterie-Regiment Rot-Würzburg (1 battalion)

Left Wing Cavalry

General der Kavallerie von Serbelloni

Division under Field Marshal von Stampach

Brigadier-General von Starhemberg's Brigade:
Kürassier-Regiment von O'Donell (5 squadrons)
Kürassier-Regiment von Schmerzing (5 squadrons)

Brigadier-General von Kolowrath-Krakowski's Brigade:
Dragoner-Regiment von Kolowrath-Krakowski
(6 squadrons)
Kürassier-Regiment von Birkenfeld (5 squadrons)

Third Line

Right Flank Guard

Major-General von Luzinsky (Duke von
Arenberg assisting)

Infanterie-Regiment De Ligne (1 battalion)

NÁDASDY'S CORPS

First Line

Left Wing Reserve

Field Marshal von Forgách

Infanterie-Regiment Heinrich von Daun
(2 battalions)
Infanterie-Regiment Leopold von Pálffy
(1 battalion)

Infanterie-Regiment Haller von Hallerstein
(1 battalion)

Far Left Bavarian Contingent

Lieutenant-General Graf von Aix

Infanterie-Regiment Kurprinz (1st Battalion)
Infanterie-Regiment von Preysing
(1st Battalion)
Infanterie-Regiment Herzog Clements
(2 battalions)
Leib-Regiment (2 battalions)

Extreme Left Württemberg Contingent

Field Marshal von Spiznass

Brigadier-General von Romann's Brigade:
3rd Grenadier Batallion von Plessen
2nd Grenadier Batallion von Georgi
1st Grenadier Batallion von Rettenberg

Brigadier-General von Röder's Brigade:
Füsilier-Regiment von Truchsess (2 battalions)
Infanterie-Regiment von Röder (2 battalions)
Infanterie-Regiment Prinz Louis (2 battalions)
Infanterie-Regiment Garde zu Fuss (2 battalions)

Left Wing Cavalry Reserve

Field Marshal O'Donell

Brigadier-General von Cleres's Brigade:
Dragoner-Regiment Jung-Modena
(6 squadrons)

Brigadier-General von Castiglione's Brigade:
Dragoner-Regiment von Batthyányi (6 squadrons)
Dragoner-Regiment von Zweibrücken-
Birkenfeld (5 squadrons)

Second Line

Left Wing Reserve

Field Marshal von Forgách

Infanterie-Regiment von Waldeck (1 battalion)
Infanterie-Regiment von Luzan (1 battalion)
Infanterie-Regiment von Forgách (1 battalion)
Infanterie-Regiment von Clerici (1 battalion)
Infanterie-Regiment von Batthyányi
(1 battalion)

Infanterie-Regiment Johann von Pálffy
(1 battalion)

Far Left Bavarian Contingent
Lieutenant-General Graf von Aix

Infanterie-Regiment von Morawitzky
(2 battalions)
Infanterie-Regiment vn Minucci (2 battalions)

Extreme Left Württemberg Contingent
Field Marshal von Spiznass

Infanterie-Regiment von Spiznass (2 battalions)

Left Wing Cavalry Reserve
Field Marshal o'Donell

Brigadier-General von Cleres' Brigade:
Dragoner-Regiment von Sachsen-Gotha (5
squadrons)

**Total: 84 battalions, 144 squadrons and 210
guns; approximately 70,000 men**

Battle of Hochkirch, 14 October 1758

Location

A village in Saxony, eastern Germany, on Route E40/B6, between Bautzen in the west and Löbau in the east and about 15km north of the border with the Czech Republic.

Frederick the Great had initially invaded Moravia (now Slovakia), but had been forced to abandon that project to counter Russian threats to his eastern border. Austria and Russia had aimed to coordinate the efforts of their armies against Prussia, but this came to nothing. Despite this, the main Austrian army in Bohemia, under Field Marshal Graf von Daun, entered Saxony and was at Bautzen on 28 August, hoping to cooperate with the Imperial Army under Field Marshal Prinz Friedrich Michael von Pfalz-Zweibrücken, which had advanced northeast from Bamberg in Franconia to Teplitz, in northern Bohemia. This placed him about 80km southwest of Daun. On 27 August, Pfalz-Zweibrücken's army stood at Pirna on the northern bank of the river Elbe, about 10km upstream from Dresden.

Prinz Heinrich von Preussen's small Prussian army stood on the defensive at Struppen, on the southern bank of the river Elbe, about 6km upstream from Pirna. On 1 September, Field Marshal Graf Daun's army reached the area just northeast of Meissen, intending to throw a bridge over the Elbe there to cross to the southern bank, advance southeast around Dresden, and crush Prinz Heinrich's army against the river and the Imperial Army.

Then came news of Frederick's main army advancing south from Frankfurt/Oder; Daun – ever cautious – abandoned his plan and withdrew eastwards, to a strongly fortified camp at Stolpen, by the river Wessnitz, between Dresden and Bautzen. This post was close to his lines of communication, back to Austria through Zittau, on the border of Bohemia.

On 11 September, Frederick the Great arrived in Reichenberg – just northwest of Dresden – with his main army and took up command of Prinz Heinrich's force. He now aimed to manoeuvre eastwards, towards Bautzen, to threaten von Daun's lines of communication. If von Daun withdrew, Frederick then hoped to invade Silesia again and relieve his besieged garrison in Neisse in the south. This ploy succeeded and von Daun abandoned his camp at Stolpen and moved east, to Kittlitz, just north of Löbau. The Austrian corps of the Markgraf von Baden-Durlach took post at Reichenbach (between Löbau and Görlitz, on von Daun's right flank).

To provoke the Austrians either to withdraw or to risk a battle, on 10 October Frederick advanced southeast to Hochkirch, with von Retzow's advanced guard ordered to keep pace with him to his east, by occupying the dominant Stromberg, 1.5km south of Wurschen. The king's main force advanced in thick mist, but von Retzow delayed his march and the Austrians changed the position of their line and took the Stromberg before he came up. Frederick was furious and had von Retzow placed under arrest and demanded his sword. The King now ordered the Prussian Army to set up camp, in a line from north and east of Rodewitz, south, through and including Hochkirch, only about 3km west of the strongly-placed enemy lines. Frederick's generals were aghast at his choice; his Chief of Staff, General von der Marwitz, refused to mark out the lines and was placed under arrest until 13 October. If the site of the Prussian lines was tactically bizarre, the manning of it was also most eccentric. Instead of the infantry occupying the centre, with the cavalry on or behind the flanks, a considerable stretch of the centre of the line – from Hochkirch north to the village of Pommritz (some 1500m) – was 'held' by four regiments of cuirassiers.

Field Marshal James Francis Edward Keith, one of Frederick's most experienced commanders, now rejoined the Prussian Army, having recovered from a recent illness. When he saw the position of the camp, he exclaimed to Frederick: 'That Austrians deserve to be hanged if they do not attack us here!' The King replied: 'We must assume that they fear us more than they do the gallows.' In fact, Frederick had finally – and grudgingly – recognised the great risk he was taking and decided to evacuate the camp and move to a new position via Weissenberg, northeast of Glossen, behind Daun's right flank.

Fatefully however, he delayed this move until the evening of 14 October, by which time the army received a consignment of bread from the bakery in Bautzen.

In the Austrian camp however, the entire army was spoiling for a fight, eager to attack the insolent, extremely vulnerable Prussians who lay tantalisingly within their grasp. Their scouting patrols could see everything that went on in the Prussian lines, as they were overlooked from many points. Even the normally ultra-cautious Graf von Daun could no longer resist the chance that Frederick's rash arrogance had presented him with. Together with the Markgraf of Baden-Durlach's corps, he had 78,000 men, twice as many as Frederick.

Daun planned a wide left hook (an oblique approach), aimed to land, driving northwards, in the Prussian rear area to the west of Hochkirch, which village was strongly held. At the time when this blow in the south was to be landed (0500 hours on 14 October), Austrian holding attacks were to be launched at the Prussian centre and northern flank. The northern flank assaulting force under the Herzog von Arenberg was covered to the north by Baden-Durlach's corps, which was to keep Frederick's advanced guard at Weissenberg out of the action.

Daun's plan worked faultlessly; the three outflanking columns under generals O'Donell, Laudon and Browne, bypassed Hochkirch in the thick mist and struck into the rear, aiming at Pommritz. General Sincere's column assaulted Hochkirch from the south. The Prussian outposts, the Freikorps, were completely surprised and thrown back onto their own infantry, as these struggled to respond to the sudden threat. A frantic struggle for the possession of Hochkirch raged; the village was soon ablaze, but the fighting continued. Laudon's columns forced their way northwards into the Prussian lines, his artillery pounding the enemy. On the Prussian side, orders were sent to von Retzow to rejoin Frederick as quickly as possible; the baggage trains were ordered off to the west, through the defile of the village of Dresah.

Meanwhile, at Hochkirch the Prussian heavy artillery battery south of the village had been taken and was used against them to devastating effect. Fighting swayed to and fro; a Prussian counterattack threw some of O'Donell's cavalry back, but the Austrian plan won the day. They overpowered the Prussians, whose position was not helped when several of their regiments began to run out of ammunition. The Prussians abandoned Hochkirch and at 0900 hours there was a lull in the combat.

On the northern flank, the Austrian attack had also been successful; the Prussians east of Rodewitz had been forced back, abandoning their heavy artillery in front of the bridge over the Löbauer Wasser stream. The Prussian Army was being crushed from both flanks in on its centre.

Von Retzow's advanced guard at last appeared, but pursued by Baden-Durlach's corps; von Retzow managed to take post at Belgern, on the northern edge of the battlefield, in time to see his army withdrawing through Dresah, towards Bautzen. The Austrians contented themselves with bombarding the retreating Prussians with artillery; there was no immediate pursuit.

Prussian losses amounted to 246 officers and 8851 men (30 per cent of their strength), 101 cannon, including 66 heavy pieces and 30 colours and standards. Losses among senior commanders were heavy: Field Marshal Keith, Generals Freiherr von Hagen, Geist, Friedrich Franz von Braunschweig and von Krockow had been killed outright or mortally wounded. It would take several months to repair the damage that Frederick's arrogance had caused his army.

The Austrians lost 325 officers, 7262 men and four standards. Field Marshal von Daun did not pursue Frederick until 17 October and then advanced only as far as Würschen, 10km east of Bautzen; he thus failed to reap any strategic spoils from his brilliant but bloody victory.

Prussian Order of Battle

King Friedrich II commanding; Field Marshal
von Keith second-in-command

Advanced Guard near Weissenberg
Generallieutenant von Retzow

Infanterie-Regiment von Pannewitz (2 battalions)
Infanterie-Regiment von Manteuffel (2 battalions)
Infanterie-Regiment Prinz Ferdinand von
Preussen (2 battalions)
Infanterie-Regiment von Kalckstein (2 battalions)
Infanterie-Regiment von Rebentisch (2 battalions)
Füsilier-Regiment Jung-Braunschweig
(1 battalion)
Grenadier Bataillon 9/10 Bähr (1 battalion)
Grenadier Bataillon 33/42 Nimschöfsky
(1 battalion)
Freibataillon le Nobel (1 battalion)
Husaren-Regiment von Werner (5 squadrons)
Husaren-Regiment von Puttkammer (5 squadrons)
Dragoner-Regiment von Bayreuth (10 squad-
rons)
Dragoner-Regiment Jung-Platen (5 squadrons)

Extreme Right Wing
Generallieutenant von Kanitz

Freikorps von Angelelli (1 battalion)
Freikorps Du Verger (1 battalion)

Generallieutenant von Bieberstein:
Infanterie-Regiment von Forcade (2 battalions)
Kürassier-Regiment von Schöneich (5 squadrons)
Husaren-Regiment von Ziethen (10 squadrons)
Dragoner-Regiment von Czettritz (5 squadrons)

Infantry Right Wing
Generallieutenant von Kanitz
Infanterie-Regiment Markgraf Carl (2 battalions)
Infanterie-Regiment von Geist (2 battalions)
Infanterie-Regiment von Kannacher (2 battalions)
Grenadier Bataillon 41/44 Beneckendorff
(1 battalion)
Grenadier Bataillon 21/27 Diringshofen
(1 battalion)
Grenadier Bataillon 3/6 Plotho (1 battalion)
Grenadier Bataillon 12/39 Pieverlingk (1 battalion)

Infantry of the Centre
Generallieutenant Prinz Karl von Brandenburg

Infanterie-Regiment von Itzenplitz (2 battalions)
Infanterie-Regiment Prinz von Preussen
(2 battalions)
Infanterie-Regiment vacant Wedell (2 battalions)
Infanterie-Regiment von Wedell (2 battalions)
Infanterie-Regiment Garde
(2nd and 3rd Battalions)
Infanterie-Regiment von Bornstedt (2 battalions)
Grenadier-Garde (1 battalion)
Grenadier Bataillon 37/40 Manteuffel (1 battalion)

Cavalry of the Centre
Generallieutenant von Ziethen

Brigadier-General von Bredow's Brigade:
Gardes du Corps (3 squadrons)
Gens d'Armes (5 squadrons)

Général de Brigade von Krockow's Brigade:
Leib-Karabiniers (5 squadrons)
Kürassier-Regiment von Bredow (5 squadrons)
Husaren-Regiment von Puttkammer (5 squadrons)
Dragoner-Regiment von Normann (5 squadrons)

Left Wing Cavalry
Generallieutenant von Seydlitz

Kürassier-Regiment von Krockow (5 squadrons)
Kürassier-Regiment von Kyau (5 squadrons)
Kürassier-Regiment von Schmettau (5 squadrons)
Kürassier-Regiment von Seydlitz (5 squadrons)
Dragoner-Regiment von Krockow (5 squadrons)

Vanguard
Generallieutenant von Manteuffel

Infanterie-Regiment Alt-Braunschweig
(2 battalions)
Grenadier Bataillon 1/23 Rathenow (1 bat-
talion)
Grenadier Bataillon 19/25 Heyden (1 battalion)
Grenadier Bataillon G-NG/G-III/G-IV
Wangenheim (1 battalion)
Grenadier Bataillon 8/46 Alt Billerbeck
(1 battalion)

Grenadier Bataillon G-VI/G-VIII Rohr (1 battalion)
Grenadier Bataillon 15/18 Kleist (1 battalion)
Feldjäger zu Fuss (2 companies)

Austrian Order of Battle

Field Marshal Graf von Daun commanding

The Right Flank (on the Stromberg)
General-Major Graf O'Kelly

Infanterie-Regiment Heinrich Daun (1 battalion)
Infanterie-Regiment von Königsegg (1 battalion)
Infanterie-Regiment von Thürheim (2 battalions)

Right Wing Cavalry
Generallieutenant von Buccow

Major-General Graf von Argenteau:
Dragoner-Regiment von Batthyányi 95 squadrons)
Kürassier-Regiment von O'Donell (5 squadrons)

Husaren-Regiment Kaiser (6 squadrons)
Husaren-Regiment Paul Antony von Esterházy
(6 squadrons)
Kürassier-Regiment Erzherzog Leopold
(5 squadrons)
Kürassier-Regiment von Stampach (5 squadrons)
Kürassier-Regiment von Ahalt-Zerbst
(5 squadrons)

Right Wing Infantry
Generallieutenant von Ahrenberg

Right Column under General-Major Graf d'Arberg
Infanterie-Regiment Kaiser (2 battalions)
Infanterie-Regiment Sachsen-Hildburghausen
(2 battalions)
Infanterie-Regiment von Botta d'Adorno
(2 battalions)
Infanterie-Regiment von Angern (2 battalions)
Infanterie-Regiment von Arenberg (2 battalions)
Infanterie-Regiment von Forgách (2 battalions)

Left Column under General-Major Herzog d'Ursel
Infanterie-Regiment von Lothringen (2 battalions)
Infanterie-Regiment von Waldeck (1 battalion)

Infanterie-Regiment von Gaisruck (2 battalions)
Infanterie-Regiment Roth Würzburg (1 battalion)
Infanterie-Regiment von Sachsen-Gotha
(2 battalions)

Field Marshal Graf von Colloredo's Column
Brigadier-General von Bülow's Brigade:
Infanterie-Regiment von Neipperg (2 battalions)
Infanterie-Regiment von Puebla (2 battalions)
Infanterie-Regiment von Andlau (1 battalion)
Kreis-Infanterie-Regiment Mainz (1 battalion)

Kürassier-Regiment von Serbelloni (5 squadrons)

General-Major von Wiese's Column
unidentified border infantry units (600 men)
Kommiandierte Infanterie (600 men)
Dragoner-Regiment Erzherzog Joseph
(5 squadrons)
Dragoner-Regiment von Württemberg
(5 squadrons)

The Main Body
Generallieutenant von Sincère

Right Column under Generallieutenant Marquis von d'Aysne
Vanguard
Infanterie-Regiment Joseph Esterházy
(2 battalions)
Infanterie-Regiment Nikolaus Esterházy
(2 battalions)

First Line
combined grenadiers under Browne (4 battalions)
Infanterie-Regiment von Harsch (2 battalions)
Infanterie-Regiment von Clerici (1 battalion)

Second Line
Infanterie-Regiment Alt-Colloredo (1 battalion)
Infanterie-Regiment von Starhemberg
(1 battalion)

Infanterie-Regiment von Batthyányi (2 battalions)
Infanterie-Regiment von Wallis (1 battalion)

Left Column under General-Major von Forgách
Vanguard
unidentified border infantry units
Infanterie-Regiment Erzherzog Carl (2 battalions)

First Line under Graf Herberstein
combined grenadiers under Siskovitch
(4 battalions)
Infanterie-Regiment von Los Rios (2 battalions)
Infanterie-Regiment L. von Daun (2 battalions)

Second Line under Los Rios
Infanterie-Regiment von Harrach (2 battalions)
Infanterie-Regiment Jung-Braunschweig-
Wolfenbüttel (2 battalions)
Infanterie-Regiment von Wallis (1 battalion)

Generallieutenant Graf von Laudon's Column
unidentified border infantry units
Infanterie-Regiment von Arberg (2 battalions)
Infanterie-Regiment von Kollowrat-Krakowski
(1 battalion)
Infanterie-Regiment Haller von Hallerstein (2
battalions)

Kürassier-Regiment von Gelhay (5 squadrons)
Kürassier-Regiment von Schmerzing (5 squadrons)
Husaren-Regiment von Nádasdy
Husaren-Regiment von Károly
Husaren-Regiment von Dessewffy
Dragoner-Regiment von Zweibrücken-
Birkenfeld (5 squadrons)
Dragoner-Regiment von Löwenstein

Generallieutenant von O'Donell's Column
Vanguard under Major-General Graf von Browne
Infanterie-Regiment von Browne (2 battalions)
Infanterie-Regiment de Ligne (2 battalions)

*Cavalry under Generallieutenant Graf von
Aspremont*
Brigadier-General von Martigny's Brigade:
Dragoner-Regiment von Hessen-Darmstadt
(5 squadrons)
Kürassier-Regiment Erzherzog Ferdinand
(5 squadrons)

Brigadier-General von St-Ignon's Brigade:
Kürassier-Regiment von Anspach (5 squadrons)
Kürassier-Regiment von Buccow (5 squadrons)

combined carabiniers and horse grenadiers
(16 squadrons)

Battle of Minden, 1 August 1759

Location

On the left bank of the river Weser in northern Germany, west of Hanover, south of Bremen and just north of the Wiehengebirge – Wesergebirge ridges and the famous Minden Gap.

The Franco-Allied army of the Maréchal de Contades, including the corps of General Victor-François, Duc de Broglie, had occupied western Germany, from Cologne upstream as far as Frankfurt/Main and were pushing eastwards towards the Electorate of Hanover. Their aim was to sieze this state, which was closely allied to England, to ravage and loot it to the benefit of the French treasury and then to use it as a bargaining chip to force England to evacuate the French colonies in north America, which she had taken.

Early on 8 July, a small French force, aided by a German traitor, captured the Allied-held fortress of Minden, together with its stragetic river Weser bridge, by a *coup de main* from the west. De Contades was now able to threaten the city of Hanover. Together with de Broglie's corps, he commanded 57,000 men and 162 guns (including the regimental pieces) and was under great pressure from the French court to achieve a signal victory. His army lay in a very strong defensive position, west of the Weser, south of the marshy river Bastau, which ran along the north of the great ridges, into the Weser, through the fortress of Minden. De Broglie's corps was on the eastern side of the Weser. Commander of the Allied forces was Ferdinand, Herzog von Braunschweig. His army was made up of British, Brunswick, Bückeburg, Hessian and some Prussian regiments. They totalled 41,000 men and 170 guns. He deployed his army on the western bank of the Weser, in an arc to the north and west of Minden, through the villages of Hahlen (now just north of the Mittellandkanal), Maulbeerkamp (Minderheide) and Stemmer, with a detachment under General von Wangenheim in Todtenhausen, close to the Weser itself.

On 31 July de Contades ordered an attack for the following day. As the existing bridges over the Bastau were totally inadequate to permit his army to cross rapidly, he had several new ones built. This activity alerted the Allies to his intent and they prepared for battle. Due to the properties of the ground over which they were to advance, Contades placed the main body of his cavalry to the left centre of his battle line. De Broglie's corps was to cross to the left bank of the river through Minden itself and advance north, to attack von Wangenheim's detached corps at Todtenhausen.

Ferdinand von Braunschweig deployed his army for battle. The British infantry were in Hanoverian General von Spörken's division, towards the right of his line. To their right was the Prinz von Anhalt's division; behind them were Lieutenant-General Lord Sackville's Anglo-Hanoverian cavalry. At 0500 hours on 1 August, the Allied Army advanced from its lines towards the enemy, who were already over the Bastau. The opposing lines closed up to one another, in an arc, about 400–500m from the walls of the fortress of Minden. Some time after 0800 hours, legend has it that von Braunschweig sent orders to von Spörken that his infantry were to advance with drums beating, *when given the order*. As it was then quite normal for the drums to beat during an advance on the battlefield, this tale must be suspect. Be that as it may, the Anglo-Hanoverian infantry (six British and two Hanoverian battalions) deployed in two three-deep lines, as was normal, and set off against the French cavalry to their front, which was highly unusual. They were supported on their right by a British artillery battery. As was to be expected, Contades sent 24 squadrons of his cavalry to charge through this tactical aberration; however, the cavalry were decimated by a volley from the infantry, discharged at very close range and by supporting fire from the British artillery battery accompanying them.

While the battle raged in more conventional style all along the line, the Anglo-Hanoverian infantry continued its lone advance. Von Braunschweig sent repeated orders to Lord Sackville to advance his cavalry to support the success of the infantry, but nothing could move that commander from his post in the rear.

Contades now sent 25 more squadrons of cavalry at von Spörken's infantry; they too were blown away by well-aimed musketry fire at close range. French infantry, just east of the village of Hahlen tried to take von Spörken's division in its right flank, but were forced back by British and Hanoverian artillery fire. In desperation, Contades sent in the last of his cavalry, 16 squadrons (2000 men) against the front and right flank of von Spörken's division; they broke through his first line, but the second held firm and the French cavalry were sent reeling back again. French Lieutenant General Comte de Guerchy, falling back from the fighting in Hahlen, directed eight of his infantry battalions to assault the right flank of Spörcken's line. By now, Hessian General von Wutginau's Hanoverian and Hessian infantry had come up on von Spörken's left, adding their fire to the defeat of the cavalry and disrupted de Guerchy's plan. Contades' badly battered left wing began to crumble under these hammer blows, even though half of Sackville's cavalry were still firmly anchored to their start positions, west of Hahlen. His subordinate commander, Lieutenant-General John Marquis of Granby, had eventually taken matters into his own hands and joined in the battle with his second line cavalry of the right wing.

On the eastern flank, de Broglie's attempted surprise assault on von Wangenheim's post south of Todtenhausen had been beaten off; a local stalemate resulted. De Contades saw that he was being crushed against the Bastau; his cavalry was spent, his infantry wavering. He ordered a withdrawal, which was accompanied by a heavy artillery fire fight, in which the better Allied gunners soon achieved the upper hand.

At about this time, the Erbprinz von Braunschweig's column, on the far western flank, crossed the river Werra near Gohfeld, northeast of Herford, threatening to cut off de Contades' army. The French force in that area disintegrated, some fleeing south over the Werra, some going northwest towards Lübbecke.

French casualties were 480 officers and 7686 men killed, wounded and missing, 43 guns, 10 pairs of colours and 7 standards and two pairs of silver kettle drums. General Prince de Camille had been killed while the Comte de Lutzelburg and the Marquis de Monti had been taken prisoner. The Allies lost 150 officers and 2660 men, half of these from the six British battalions who, from 78 officers and 4434 men, lost 1252. They were the 12th, 20th, 23rd, 25th, 37th and 51st Foot. Also engaged in this amazing feat were two battalions of the Hanoverian Garde zu Fuss, and one of the Infanterie-Regiment von Hardenberg.

During the following night, Maréchal de Contades abandoned his communications with Paderborn, crossed to the right bank of the Weser, breaking down the bridge of Minden, burned his bridges of boats over that river and retired south to Kassel. His army was not only beaten but very demoralised; he was subsequently relieved of his command and replaced by Victor-François, Duc de Broglie.

The Allied Army advanced after him into the Hessian region, recapturing Kassel and Marburg. They also recovered the city of Münster, north of Dortmund and all territories previously lost during this campaign.

For his amazing conduct during the battle, Lord Sackville was disgraced; in order to clear his name, he requested a court martial. The evidence presented against him was damning and the court martial declared him 'unfit to serve His Majesty in any capacity whatsoever.'

Allied Order of Battle

Field Marshal Ferdinand Herzog von
Braunschweig-Lüneburg

First Column

Right Wing Cavalry
Lieutenant General Sir George Sackville

First Line
Lieutenant General Sir George Sackville

Colonel John Mostyn's British Brigade:
Royal Horse Guards (3 squadrons)
1st King's Dragoon Guards (3 squadrons)
6th Inniskilling Dragoon Guards (3 squadrons)

Oberst Karl von Breitenbach's Hanoverian Brigade:
Grenadier zu Pferde (2 squadrons)
Dragoner-Regiment von Breitenbach
(4 squadrons)
Garde du Corps (1 squadron)

Bremer Kavallerie (2 C-A) (2 squadrons)
Veltheim Kavallerie (4 C-B) (2 squadrons)

Second Line
Lieutenant-General Marquis of Granby

Colonel Elliot's British Brigade:
3rd Dragoon Guards (2 squadrons)
10th Dragoon Regiment (2 squadrons)
2nd Royal North British Dragoon Regiment
(2 squadrons)

Second Column
Major Haase

Hanoverian Artillery Brigade:
sixteen 12-pounder guns
four 3-pounder guns
two 30-pound howitzers

British Heavy Artillery Brigade:
six 12-pounder guns

Artillery Protection Unit:
Infanterie-Regiment von Sachsen-Gotha
(1 battalion)

Third Column
Hanoverian Generallieutenant von Spörken

First Line
Major-General Waldegrave's British Brigade:
12th Regiment of Foot (1 battalion)

British Light Artillery Brigade:
nine guns

37th Regiment of Foot (1 battalion)
Hanoverian Garde zu Fuss (2 battalions)

Second Line
Major-General Kingsley's British Brigade:
20th Regiment of Foot (1 battalion)
51st Regiment of Foot (1 battalion)
25th Regiment of Foot (1 battalion)

Fourth Column, Prinz von Anhalt's Division
General-Major von Scheele

First Line
General-Major von Scheele's Hanoverian Brigade:
Infanterie-Regiment von Hardenberg
(1 battalion)
Infanterie-Regiment von Reden (1 battalion)
Infanterie-Regiment von Scheele (1 battalion)

Second Line
General-Major von Wissembach's Hanoverian Brigade:
Infanterie-Regiment von Stolzenberg (1 battalion)
Infanterie-Regiment von Estorff (1 battalion)
Infanterie-Regiment Erbprinz Friedrich
(Hessian) (1 battalion)

Fifth Column
Colonel Braun

Hanoverian Heavy Artillery Brigade
two captured French 8-pounder guns
twelve 6-pounders
two 3-pounder guns
three 16-pound howitzers

Sixth Column
Generallieutenant von Wutginau

First Line
General-Major von Toll's Hanoverian Brigade:
Infantry Regiment Wangenheim (1 battalion)
Hessian Leib-Garde zu Fuss (1 battalion)
Bückeburg Light Artillery Brigade (eight
6-pounder guns)
Hessian Infanterie-Regiment von Toll (1 battalion)

Second Line
General-Major von Bischhausen's Hessian Brigade:
Infanterie-Regiment Prinz von Anhalt
(1 battalion)
Infanterie-Regiment von Bischhausen
(1 battalion)
Infanterie-Regiment von Mannsbach (1 battalion)

Seventh Column
Generallieutenant von Imhoff (Braunschweig)

First Line
General-Major von Einsiedel's Brigade:
Hessian Infanterie-Regiment von Gilsa
(1 battalion)
Hessian Infanterie-Regiment von Prinz
Wilhelm (1 battalion)
Hessian Leib-Grenadier-Regiment (1 battalion)
British Light Artillery Brigade under Captain
Foy (nine guns)
Branschweig Infanterie-Regiment von Behr
(2nd Battalion)

Second Line
General-Major von Behr's Brigade:
Hessian Leib-Infanterie-Regiment (1 battalion)
Braunschwieg Infanterie-Regiment von Imhoff
(2 battalions)

Eighth Column

Left Wing Cavalry
Generallieutenant Herzog von Holstein-
Gottorp

First Line
Holstein's Brigade:
Hanoverian Hammerstein Kavallerie
(2 squadrons)

Hessian Leib-Kavallerie (2 squadrons)
Hessian Prinz Wilhem Erbprinz Kavallerie
(2 squadrons)
Prussian Dragoner-Regiment von Holstein-
Gottorp (5 squadrons)

Second Line
Generallieutenant von Urff's Brigade:
Hessian Miltitz Kavallerie (2 squadrons)
Hessian Pruschenk Kavallerie (2 squadrons)
Prussian Dragoner-Regiment von Finkenstein
(5 squadrons)

General-Major von Reinecke's Detachment
Near Hille, guarding the Eickhorst causeway
crossing the peat bog: Braunschweig Infantry
Regiment von Imhoff (1 battalion); two
12-pounder guns, two 6-pounder guns.

Wangenheim Corps
Generallieutenant von Wangenheim

Right Wing Cavalry

First Line
General-Major von Reden's Hessian Brigade:
Leib-Dragoon Regiment (2 squadrons)
Prinz Friedrich Dragoner-Regiment (4 squadrons)

Second Line
General-Major von Hanstein's Hanoverian Brigade:
Leib-Regiment Reuter (2 squadrons)

*General-Major von Grothausen's Hanoverian
Brigade:*
Reden Kavallerie (2 squadrons)
Heise Kavallerie (2 squadrons)
Hodenberg Kavallerie (2 squadrons)
Grothaus Kavallerie (2 squadrons)

Third Line
Prussian Husaren-Regiment von Ruesch
(1 squadron)

Infantry of the Centre
Hanoverian Brigade:
Infanterie-Regiment von Kielmannsegg
(1 battalion)
Infanterie-Regiment von Spörken (1 battalion)

Infanterie-Regiment Jung-Zastrow (1 battalion)
Infanterie-Regiment von Halberstadt (1 battalion)
Infanterie-Regiment von Schulenburg
(1 battalion)
Infanterie-Regiment von Oberg (1 battalion)
Infanterie-Regiment von Laffert (1 battalion)
Infanterie-Regiment von Scheither (1 battalion)

Artillery:
six 6-pounders

Brigade:
combined Hanoverian grenadiers (1 battalion)
combined British grenadiers (1 battalion)
combined Hessian grenadiers (2 battalions)
combined Brunswick grenadiers (2 battalions)

Hessian Artillery:
sixteen 12-pounder guns
four 6-pounders
two 3-pounders
two 20-pound howitzers

Schaumburg-Lippe-Bückeburg Artillery:
six 6-pounders
ten 3-pounders

Artillery Protection Unit:
Infanterie-Regiment Schaumburg-Lippe-
Bückeburg (1 battalion)

**Total: 42,000 men in 48 battalions, 65
squadrons and 105 artillery pieces**

Franco-Saxon Order of Battle

Maréchal de Camp Louis, Marquis de Contades
(Lieutenant-General Comte de Noailles and
Maréchal de Camp de Raugrave assisting)

The army was split into the main body and the
corps of Maréchal de Camp Victor-François
Duc de Broglie.

Broglie Corps

First Line
Artillery (deployed in front of the infantry):
six 12-pounders
four howitzers
twelve other pieces

Second Line
M. de St-Pern's Grenadiers de France Brigade:
Grenadiers de France (4 battalions)
Grenadiers Royaux de Modène (2 battalions)
Grenadiers Royaux de Chantilly (2 battalions)

Piémont Brigade:
Piémont Infanterie (4 battalions)
Dauphin Infanterie (2 battalions)

Royal Deux Ponts Brigade:
Royal Deux Ponts Infanterie (2 battalions)
Royal Bavière Infanterie (2 battalions)

Waldner Brigade:
Waldner Infanterie (2 battalions)
Planta Infanterie (2 battalions)

Third Line
Maréchal de Camp Prince Camille

Commissaire Général Brigade:
Commissaire Général Cavalerie (2 squadrons)
Lameth Cavalerie (2 squadrons)
Des Salles Cavalerie (2 squadrons)

Penthièvre Brigade:
Penthièvre Cavalerie (2 squadrons)
Toustain Cavalerie (2 squadrons)

Prinz von Holstein's Brigade:
Royal-Allemand Cavalerie (2 squadrons)
Nassau-Sarrebruck Cavalerie (2 squadrons)
Württemberg Cavalerie (2 squadrons)

Light Troops
Apchon Dragons (4 squadrons)
Volontaires de Schomberg (3 squadrons)
Royal Nassau Hussards (4 squadrons)

Main Army

Right Wing Infantry

First Line
Maréchal de Camp Chevalier de Nicolaï's Division
(Lieutenant-General Beaupréau assisting)

Picardie Brigade:
Picardie Infanterie (4 battalions)
La Marche Infanterie (1 battalion)

Belzunce Brigade:
Belzunce Infanterie (4 battalions)

Touraine Brigade:
Touraine Infanterie (2 battalions)
d'Aumont Infanterie (2 battalions)

Rouerge Brigade:
Rouergue Infanterie (2 battalions)
La Marche Infanterie (1 battalion)
Tournaisis Infanterie (1 battalion)

Artillery:
34 guns

Second Line
Lieutenant-General Comte de St-Germaine's
Division (Maréchal de Camp Leyde and
Maréchal de Camp Glaubitz assisting)

Anhalt Brigade:
Anhalt-Köthen Infanterie (2 battalions)
St-Germaine Infanterie (1 battalion)
Bergh Infanterie (1 battalion)

Auvergne Brigade:
Auvergne Infanterie (4 battalions)

Cavalry of the Centre

First Line
Maréchal de Camp Duc de Fitzjames' Division
(Lieutenant-General de Vougé and Lieutenant-
General de Castries assisting)

Colonel Général Brigade:
Colonel Général Cavalerie (3 squadrons)
Marcieux Cavalerie (2 squadrons)

Vougé Cavalerie (2 squadrons)
Condé Cavalerie (2 squadrons)

Royale-Cravate Brigade:
Royale-Cravate Cavalerie (2 squadrons)
Rochefoucauld Cavalerie (2 squadrons)
Talleyrand Cavalerie (2 squadrons)

Mestre de Camp Brigade:
Mestre de Camp Cavalerie (2 squadrons)
Fumel Cavalerie (2 squadrons)
d'Espinchal Cavalerie (2 squadrons)
Poly Cavalerie (2 squadrons)

Second Line
Maréchal de Camp du Mesnil's Division
(Lieutenant-General Andlau and Lieutenant-
General d'Orlick assisting)

du Roy Brigade:
du Roy Cavalerie (2 squadrons)
Henrichemont Cavalerie (2 squadrons)
Moustieres Cavalerie (2 squadrons)
Noé Cavalerie (2 squadrons)

Bourgogne Brigade:
Bourgogne Cavalerie (2 squadrons)
Liégoise Cavalerie (2 squadrons)
Archiac Cavalerie (2 squadrons)

Royal-Étranger Brigade:
Royal-Étranger Cavalerie (2 squadrons)
Crusson Cavalerie (2 squadrons)
Noailles Cavalerie (2 squadrons)
Balincourt Cavalerie (2 squadrons)

Third Line
Maréchal de Camp Marquis de Poyanne's
Division (Maréchal de Camp Bellefonds and
Maréchal de Camp Bissy assisting)

Gendarmerie de France:
Gendarmes Écossais and Gendarmes de
Bourgogne (1 squadron)
Gendarmes Anglais and Chevau-légers de
Bourgogne (1 squadron)
Gendarmes Bourguignons and Gendarmes
d'Aquitaine (1 squadron)
Gendarmes de Flandres and Chevau-légers
d'Aquitaine (1 squadron)

Gendarmes de la Reine and Gendarmes de Berry (1 squadron)
Chevau-légers de la Reine and Chevau-légers de Berry (1 squadron)
Gendarmes du Dauphin and Gendarmes d'Orléans (1 squadron)
Chevau-légers du Dauphin and Chevau-légers d'Orléans (1 squadron)

Corps des Carabiniers de Monsieur le Comte Provence (10 squadrons)

Left Wing Infantry

First Line
Maréchal de Camp Guerchy's Division (Maréchal de Camp Laval and Maréchal de Camp Maugiron assisting)

Condé Brigade:
Condé Infanterie (2 battalions)
D'Enghien Infanterie (2 battalions)

Aquitaine Brigade:
Aquitaine Infanterie (2 battalions)
Vastan Infanterie (2 battalions)

Du Roi Brigade:
Du Roi Infanterie (4 battalions)

Champagne Brigade:
Champagne Infanterie (4 battalions)

Artillery:
30 pieces

Second Line
Maréchal de Camp Lucase's Saxon Division (Graf von Solms assisting)

First Saxon Brigade:
Infanterie-Regiment Fürst Lubomirsky (1 battalion)
Infanterie-Regiment Prinz Clemens (1 battalion)
Infanterie-Regiment Prinz Joseph (1 battalion)
Infanterie-Regiment Prinz Friedrich August (2 battalions)
Infanterie-Regiment Prinz Xaver (2 battalions)
Infanterie-Regiment Prinz Karl (1 battalion)
Second Saxon Brigade:
Infanterie-Regiment Kurprinzessin (2 battalions)
Infanterie-Regiment Sachsen-Gotha (1 battalion)
Infanterie-Regiment Prinz Anton (1 battalion)
Infanterie-Regiment Graf Brühl (1 battalion)
Füsilier-Regiment von Rochow (1 battalion)

Maréchal de Camp Duc d'Havré Corps
In an advanced post at Eichhorst, on the left wing, opposing von Reinecke at Hill

Regiment Navarre Infanterie (4 battalions)
Volontaires du Dauphiné (1 battalion)
Volontaires Liégeois (1 battalion)
Volontaires de Muret (2 companies)
four 8-pounder guns

Garrison of Minden
Maréchal de Camp de Bisson

Lowendahl Infanterie (2 battalions)
Bouillon Infanterie (2 battalions)

Total: 57,000 men in 84 battalions, 85 squadrons and 90 artillery pieces

Battle of Quebec, 13 September 1759

Location
On the west bank of the lower St Lawrence River in eastern Canada, at the junction of Routes 40 and 73.

The failed British assault on Ticonderoga (Carillon) on 8 July 1758, had saved French Canada from British invasion in that year. King Louis XIV was obsessed with taking revenge on Frederick the Great for insulting his mistress, Madame de Pompadour, which led to French military resources being concentrated in central Europe, while French Canada was left to wither. In November 1758, the French-held fort Duquesne (now Pittsburgh) was abandoned, due to the French inability to maintain the garrison there.

On 6 June 1759, a British amphibious force under the command of Vice-Admiral Charles Saunders and Major-General Wolfe sailed from Louisburg, on the northeastern corner of Nova Scotia, to take Quebec. Louisburg had been taken from the French in July 1758. On 21 June, the expedition approached the town from the northeast, having successfully navigated the difficult channel of the lower St Lawrence. The troops were disembarked on the right bank of the St Lawrence River, at Levis Point, opposite Quebec. The natural defences of the town were very strong and General Louis-Joseph de St Véran, Marquis de Montcalm and his staff (Major-General François de Gaston, Chevalier de Lévis, Colonel Louis Antoine de Bougainville and Lieutenant-Colonel de Sennezergue), distributed some 12,000 troops in a 9km collection of fortified redoubts and batteries from the Saint-Charles River to the Montmorency Falls, along the shallows of the river in areas that had previously been targeted by British attempts to land. Montcalm had drawn up his army in an entrenched camp, downstream of the town, on the heights on the left bank.

Quebec was a strong tactical nut to crack and for weeks, General Wolfe had no effective answer to the problem that faced him. On 24 July, French-held Fort Niagara surrendered to the British, effectively cutting off all French settlements in western America from their Canadian base. A British thrust northwards on Montreal, upstream of Quebec was soon launched. The French abandoned Fort Ticonderoga on 26 July, but that was as far as the British advance went before winter set in. The morale effects of news of these developments on the foes at Quebec were, however, considerable. General Wolfe and Admiral Holmes were galvanised into fresh efforts. On 31 July they attempted to assault the French riverside fortifications, but were bloodily repulsed. A re-think was needed.

From 7–11 September, the British boats, loaded with soldiers, passed up the river on flood tide and down again on the ebb, as if seeking landing places; they also sent boats to Beauport, 10km downstream from Quebec. This ploy aroused the French garrison and caused much marching and counter-marching and part of the French force was detached to Beauport. Bougainville and 3000 men were sent to Cape Rouge, 13km upstream of the town, on 3 September.

On Wednesday 12 September, Wolfe's luck turned. Two deserters came in from Bougainville's camp, Montcalm's aide-de-camp, with news that at next ebb tide a convoy of French boats with provisions would pass down the river from Montreal to Quebec. Wolfe saw at once that, if his own boats went down in advance of the convoy, he could turn the intelligence of the deserters to good account. He sent orders to the British troops at Saint-Nicolas to embark and made his disposition for a landing at Anse-au-Foulon. The naval ships were thus sent upstream to Cape Rouge, where they held Bougainville's entire attention.

During the night of 12/13 September, Saunders' fleet made a feint on the shoals of Beauport, some 10km downstream from Quebec, while Holmes' squadron prepared for the real landing above the town. At 0200 hours Holmes gave the signal for the troop transport boats to cast off, and two hours later they landed undetected at Anse-des-Mères, a little downstream from the intended spot. As quietly as possible, the leading group of volunteers climbed the wooded slopes. At dawn, they reached the top; they surprised and routed a French guard post and the rest of the force was soon up with them.

About 1.5km to their east was a grassy plain, the Heights of Abraham. Wolfe deployed his force of 4500 men but only one battalion gun, facing Quebec's walls and about 1000m from them. At 0600 hours, Montcalm rode out of the town to see what was going on and saw the British line. He at once issued orders for his available troops (5000 men with three field guns) to turn out.

Just before 1000 hours, the French advanced out of the town; at 1035 hours they were shattered by a full volley of British musketry. The French never recovered; another volley swept them away towards the town. Bougainville now appeared from the west, but was quickly repulsed.

At the moment of victory, General Wolfe was hit three times and mortally wounded; his second-in-command, General Monckton, was also wounded. By strange chance, Montcalm was also mortally wounded, as was his second-in-command. British losses were 10 officers killed and 37 wounded, 48 men killed and 535 wounded. French losses were given by the British as about 1500 killed, wounded and captured; the French reported about 640. The French field force fled away towards Montreal, leaving the garrison of Quebec helpless. They surrendered on 17 September and control of Canada was wrested from France.

At Montreal that September, Lévis and 2000 troops confronted 17,000 British and American troops. The French capitulated on 8 September 1760, and the British took possession of Montreal. The Treaty of Paris was signed in 1763 to end the war and gave possession of parts of New France to Great Britain, including Canada and the eastern half of French Louisiana.

British Order of Battle

Major-General James Wolfe

Royal Artillery (15 men)
15th Regiment of Foot (1 company)
28th Regiment of Foot (1 company)
35th Regiment of Foot (1 company)
40th Regiment of Foot (1 company)
43rd Regiment of Foot (1 company)
47th Regiment of Foot (1 company)
48th Regiment of Foot (1 company)

58th Regiment of Foot (1 company)
60th Regiment of Foot (3rd Battalion and one company of the 4th Battalion)
Fraser's Highlanders (2 companies)
Roger's Rangers (51 men)
Royal Marines (30 men)
Louisburg Grenadiers (3 companies)

Total: approximately 4400 men and one battalion gun

French Order of Battle

Louis Joseph de Saint Véran, Marquis de Montcalm

Right Wing
Major-General Dumas
two field guns
Montreal and Quebec militia (1 bn)
La Sarre Infanterie (2nd Battalion)

Centre
Marquis de Montcalm

Languedoc Infanterie (2nd battalion)
Béarn Infanterie (2nd Battalion)

Left Wing
Major-General Senezergues

Guyenne Infanterie (2nd Battalion)
Royal Roussillon Infanterie (1st Battalion)
Montreal and Trois-Rivières militia
two field guns

François-Xavier de Saint-Ours:
Light Infantry (1/2 battalion)

Total: 1900 regulars, 1500 militia and Indians and 4 guns

Battle of Quiberon Bay, 20 November 1759

Location

Between the island of Belle Ile and the mouth of the river Vilaine in northwestern France, south of the town of Vannes, in the northeastern sector of the Bay of Biscay.

During 1759, the Royal Navy, under Sir Edward Hawke, maintained a close blockade on the French coast in the vicinity of Brest. In that year the French had made plans to invade England and Ireland, and had assembled transports and troops around the Loire estuary. The defeat of the French Mediterranean fleet at the Battle of Lagos in August, had frustrated the invasion plan, but L.G. Étienne-Françoise, Duc de Choiseul, French Foreign and Defence Minister, still contemplated a descent on the Irish coast. He ordered the French fleet to escape the blockade and collect the troops assembled in the Gulf of Morbihan, just south of the town of Vannes. These were 17,000 men under the Duc d'Aiguillon.

On 9 November a westerly gale came up and, after three days, the ships of Admiral Edward Hawke's blockade were forced to run for Torbay on the south coast of England. Robert Duff was left behind in Quiberon Bay, with a squadron of five 50-gun ships and nine frigates to keep an eye on the transports. In the meantime, a small squadron from the West Indies joined Admiral Hubert de Brienne, Comte de Conflans in Brest and, when an easterly wind came on the 14th, Conflans slipped out. He was sighted by HMS *Actaeon* which had remained on station off Brest despite the storms but failed to rendezvous with Hawke, and by HMS *Juno and Swallow* who tried to warn Duff but were chased off by the French. Duff however, managed to escape and join up with Hawke. Once given the news of the emergence of the French fleet, Admiral Hawke sailed for Quiberon and into a gale, blowing from the south-southeast.

Shortly after dawn on 20 November, Conflans sighted part of Duff's squadron, 30km off Belle Isle. Realising that this was not the main British fleet, he gave chase. Duff split his ships to the north and south, with the French vanguard and centre in pursuit, whilst their rearguard held off to windward to watch some unidentified sails appearing from the west. They transpired to be Hawke's fleet. The French abandoned the chase of Duff and were in some confusion as the British fleet closed in. At 0830 hours, Hawke hoisted the signal for his ships to form a line abreast.

Conflans had a choice: to fight in his current disadvantageous position in high seas and a very strong, squally wind from the west-northwest, or to run into Quiberon Bay and dare Hawke to follow him into its labyrinth of shoals and reefs. He quite sensibly chose the latter. At about 0900 hours Hawke, in *Royal George*, gave the signal for general chase, along with a new signal for his first seven ships to form in line ahead and, despite the weather and the dangerous waters, set full sail. At 1400 hours, the rearmost French ships opened fire on the closing British fleet. By 1430 hours, Conflans, in *Soleil Royal*, rounded Les Grandes Cardinaux, the rocks at the end of the Quiberon peninsula that give the battle its French name. At this point, the first shots were fired by *Warspite*, possibly without the orders of her captain. Now the British fleet was starting to overtake the rear of the French fleet even as their vanguard and centre made it to the safety of the bay. The battle was on. At 1430 hours, when *Warspite* and *Dorsetshire* were close up with the enemy's rear, Hawke made the signal to engage. The British fleet was then to the south of Belle Isle. A little later *Revenge, Magnanime, Torbay, Montagu, Resolution, Swiftsure* and *Defiance* also came into action, and hotly engaged the French rear. *Magnifique* sustained the first attacks and fought for an hour before being forced to disengage.

The French *Formidable*, carrying the flag of Rear-Admiral du Verger, was attacked by *Resolution* and, in addition, received a broadside or two from every other British ship that passed her. The French *Superbe*, who had opened her lower deck ports in the very heavy weather, had taken on water and foundered at about the same time.

At about 1530 hours, de Conflans, who had for an hour continued to retire towards the far end of the bay with the vanguard, finally turned around.

Thirty minutes later, the *Formidable*, having been severely damaged, struck her colours. The losses amongst her crew were severe: du Verger and over of 200 others being killed. Formidable was taken possession of by *Resolution*. At this point, Hawke rounded les Cardineaux. Meanwhile *Thésée*, who had been battling with HMS *Torbay*, foundered. *Superbe* capsized, and the badly damaged *Héros* struck her flag to Lord Howe, in *Magnanime*, but was later able to run aground on the Four Shoals, and all her crew escaped to shore that night.

The wind had now shifted to the northwest, further confusing Conflans' half-formed line. He tried desperately to resolve the chaos, but finally decided to put to sea again. His flagship headed for the entrance to the bay just as Hawke was coming in. Hawke had a chance to rake the *Soleil Royal*, but *Intrépide* got in the way and took the salvo. Meanwhile, Conflans' flagship had fallen to leeward and was forced to anchor off Croisic, away from the rest of the French fleet. By now it was about 1700 hours and darkness was gathering, so Hawke gave the signal to anchor.

During the night, eight French ships managed to navigate their way through the shoals to the safety of the open sea, and escape south, to La Rochforte. Seven other French ships and frigates were still in the Vilaine estuary. Due to the violent weather, Admiral Hawke could not mount an attack. The French in the estuary then jettisoned their guns and rode on the rising tide and northwesterly winds, to move over the sandbar at the mouth of the river, upstream to safety. Four of their ships-of-the-line broke their backs on the mud. The badly damaged French *Juste* was lost with all hands as she made for the Loire, and HMS *Resolution* grounded on the Four Shoals during the night.

On 21 and 22 November, by taking advantage of the flood tide and wind, the French ships *Glorieux*, *Robuste*, *Dragon*, *Éveillé*, *Brillant*, *Inflexible*, *Sphynx*, *Vestale*, *Aigrette*, *Calypso* and *Prince Noir*, which were near the mouth of the Vilaine, managed to move up into the river, but several of the largest could never be brought out again and were effectively written off.

Soleil Royal had unknowingly anchored in the midst of the British ships; as soon as this was realised, she slipped her cable and tried to escape to the safety of the batteries at Croisic. HMS *Essex* pursued her with the result that both vessels were wrecked on the Four Shoals. The gale at last moderated on 22 November, and three of Duff's squadron were sent to destroy the beached ships. Conflans set fire to *Soleil Royal* while the British burnt *Héros*. Hawke now tried to attack the ships in the Vilaine with fireboats, but to no effect.

The power of the French fleet was broken; it would not recover before the war was over; Quiberon Bay was the Trafalgar of the Seven Years War. Britain controlled the seas and the flow of European colonial commerce and military movements. France was unable to reinforce her colonies in America or to exploit her victory at the Battle of St Foy, Quebec, on 28 April 1760.

French losses in this action were seven ships of the line sunk or burned; several others were lost up the Vilaine. 2500 sailors were killed, wounded or missing. Royal Navy losses were two ships of the line wrecked and fewer than 50 men killed and 250 wounded.

Royal Navy Order of Battle

Ship	Guns	Commander	Men	Notes
Royal George	100	Captain Campbell	880	Flagship of Sir Edward Hawke
Union	90	Captain J. Evans	770	Flagship of Sir Charles Hardy
Duke	80	Captain Samuel Graves	800	
Namur	90	Matthew Buckle	780	
Resolution	74	Henry Speke	600	Wrecked on the Le Four shoal
Hero	74	George Edgcumbe	600	
Warspite	74	Sir John Bentley	600	

Hercules	74	W. Fortescue	600	
Torbay	70	Augustus Keppel	520	
Magnanime	70	Viscount Howe	520	
Mars	70	Commodore James Young	520	
Swiftsure	70	Sir Thomas Stanhope	520	
Dorsetshire	70	Peter Denis	520	
Burford	70	G. Gambier	520	
Chichester	70	W.S. Willet	520	
Temple	70	Honorable W. Shirley	520	
Essex	64	Lucius O'Brien	480	Wrecked on the Le Four shoal
Revenge	64	J. Storr	480	
Montague	60	Joshua Rowley	400	
Kingston	60	Thomas Shirley	400	
Intrepid	60	J. Maplesden	400	
Dunkirk	60	R. Digby	420	
Defiance	60	P. Baird	420	
Chatham	50	J. Lockhart	350	
Minerva	32	A. Hood	220	
Venus	36	T. Harrison	240	
Vengeance	28	F. Burslem	200	
Coventry	28	D. Digges	200	
Sapphire	32	J. Strachan	220	

French Navy Order of Battle

Ship	Guns	Commander	Men	Notes
First Division				
Soleil Royal	80	Captain B. de Chasac	950	Flagship of Marquis de Conflans – ran aground and burnt
Orient	80	Captain N. de la Filière	750	Flagship of Chevalier de Guébridant Budes – escaped to Rochforte
Glorieux	74	Villars de la Brosse	650	Escaped up the Vilaine
Robuste	74	Fragnier de Vienne	650	Escaped up the Vilaine
Dauphin Royal	70	Chevalier d'Uturbie Fragosse	630	Escaped to Rochforte
Dragon	64	Vassor de la Touche	450	Escaped up the Vilaine
Solitaire	64	Vicomte de Langle	450	Escaped to Rochforte
Second Division				

Tonnant	80	Captain St Victoret	800	Flagship of Chevalier de Beauffremont – escaped to Rochefort
Intrépide	74	Chastologer	650	Escaped to Rochforte
Thésée	74	Kersaint de Coetnempren	650	Foundered
Northumberland	70	Belingant de Kerbabut	630	Escaped to Rochforte
Superbe	70	Montalais	630	Sunk by *Royal George*
Eveillé	64	Prévalais de la Roche	450	Escaped up the Vilaine
Brillant	64	Keremar Boischateau	450	Escaped up the Vilaine
Third Division				
Formidable	80	Captain St André	800	Flagship of De Saint André du Vergé – taken by *Resolution*
Magnifique	74	Bigot de Morogues	650	Escaped to Rochforte
Héros	74	Vicomte de Sanzay	650	Surrendered, but ran aground next day during heavy weather; burnt
Juste	70	François de Saint Aloüarn	630	Wrecked in the Loire
Inflexible	64	Tancrede	540	Lost at the entrance to the Vilaine
Sphinx	64	Goyon	450	
Bizarre	64	Prince de Montbazon	450	Escaped to Rochforte
Frigates and corvettes				
Hébé	40		300	Returned to Brest
Vestale			254	Escaped up the Vilaine
Aigrette				Escaped up the Vilaine
Calypso				Escaped up the Vilaine
Prince Noir/ Noire				Escaped up the Vilaine
Vengeance	?			

Battle of Wandewash, 22 January 1760

Location

Now Vandivasi, near the southeast coast of India, about 100km southwest of the port of Chennai (once Madras), at the junction of State Highways 5, 115 and 116. This area was known as the Carnatic in 1760.

Due to the fixation of the French King Louis XV on concentrating all available forces against Frederick the Great in Europe, and to the British naval victory at Quiberon Bay, on 20 November 1759, supplies of reinforcements to French forces overseas had ceased. In central southern India, the French commander, General Thomas-Arthur Tollendal Comte de Lally, was based in Pondicherry, some 120km south of Madras (now Chennai).

On 14 January, taking 500 Europeans, 1000 Sepoys, and 650 French and the Mahratta Horse, Lally left Trivatore and marched on the British-held fort of Wandewash, determined to recapture it. Lieutenant-Colonel Sir Eyre Coote, local commander of the forces of the Honourable East India Company, received intelligence of his departure in Madras and set out to thwart him.

De Lally's force attacked Wandewash on 15 January and drove the small British garrison inside. Wandewash fort lay in an open plain, about 3km south of the Wandewash mountain ridge and 2km west of a large pond, with two small, artificial reservoirs to its east. A ridge ran south from the reservoirs. The French camped south of the large pond, parallel to and west of the ridge. Lally set about building a siege battery, which opened fire on 20 January. At 0700 hours on 22 January, Coote's advanced guard bumped into some 3000 Mahratta cavalry, allies of the French, and dispersed them with some well-aimed discharges of grape. This cavalry took no further part on the action.

Coote advanced northwards, east of the ridge and onwards to the foot of the mountain ridge, before de Lally became aware of him. The Frenchman left the fort and deployed his troops in a line, the northern flank anchored on the eastern reservoir, extending over 1000m south-southeast, in front of the ridge. 900 Sepoys were set along the ridge itself.

Lally sent his European cavalry in a right hook around Coote's southern flank, which chased off his native cavalry. British artillery grape drove off the French assault. Coote then closed to within effective range of the French and began to bombard them with artillery. Lally ordered his line forward; when close to the British, he formed infantry columns. Musketry from the British line shattered this column and the French fell back through their own Sepoys. Then a French ammunition wagon in the entrenched reservoir exploded, killing and injuring over 80 of the men there. The French force was ripped apart by artillery and musketry and both flanks fell back.

This defeat was the death blow to the French presence in India; on 5 April 1761, their last post on the sub-continent surrendered. De Lally returned to France in 1763, where he was accused of high treason, found guilty and beheaded on 9 May 1766.

Losses were 200 French killed, 200 wounded and 160 captured, including General Bussy and Chevalier Godeville. Casualties amongst the French Indian allies are not known. The French lost 22 guns and all their baggage. Coote's losses were 63 killed and 141 wounded; 6 Sepoys were killed and 15 wounded, and the Indian cavalry lost 17 killed and 32 wounded.

British Order of Battle

79th Regiment of Foot (1 battalion)
84th Regiment of Foot (1 battalion)
102nd Regiment of Foot (2 battalions)
Madras European Dragoons (1 squadron)
Indian cavalry (2 regiments)
2000 Sepoys
16 guns

150 European and 300 Indian infantry in the fort

French Order of Battle

Lorraine Infanterie (1 battalion)
Lally Infanterie (1 battalion)
Bataillon des Indes (1 battalion)
Indian infantry (1600 men)
European cavalry (150 men)
17 guns

APPENDIX 2

KEY PLACES

German	Polish	Location
Allenstein	Olsztyn	100km south of Kaliningrad on Route 51
Bartenstein	Bartoszyce	50km south of Kaliningrad, on Route 51
Bautzen	Budesin	east of Dresden, on Route 6
Braunsburg	Braniewc	between Stralsund and Magdeburg
Breslau/Oder	Wroclow/Odra	east of Legnica, north-east of Swidnica, south of Poznan
Bromberg/Vistula	Bydgoszec/Visla	south of Gdansk, west-north-west of Warsaw, west of Torun on the E 261
Bruck	Gdynia	on the Baltic, 20km north of Danzig
Bunzlau	Boleslawiec	between Dresden and Wroclaw, just south of the E 40
Colberg	Kolobrzeg	Baltic coast, 100km north-east of Szczecin
Danzig	Gdansk	Baltic coast, 100km west of Kaliningrad
Demmin	Demmin	80km east of Rostock, 50km south of Stralsund
Dirschau	Tczew	30km south-south-east of Danzig
Elbing	Elblag	80km south-east of Danzig on Route E 77
Friedland	Pravdinsk	50km south-east of Kaliningrad
Geiersberg	Sepow	180km east of Dresden, 100km west of Wroclaw
Glogau/Oder	Glogow/Odra	260km south-south-west of Poznan, 110km north-west of Wroclaw
Goldberg	Zlotoryja	midway between Görlitz on the Polish/German Grenz-and Wroclaw/Odra
Grodno/Niemen	Grodno/Neman	
Guttstedt	Dobre Miasto	

Haynau	Chojnow	20km south of Warsaw, west of the Wisla
Heilsberg	Lidzbark Warminski	south of Kaliningrad, east of Elblag
Hermsdorf	Jermanice-Zdroj	
Hochkirch	Hochkirch	On B6, east of Bautzen
Hoyerswerda	Wojerecy	near Bautzen
Insterburg	Cernjahhovsk	80km east of Kalingrad on Route A299
Jauer	Jower	
Kay/Paltzig	Kije/Palck	two small villages between Zullichau and Crossen on the Oder, north-west of Glogau and west-south-west of Posen
Koslin	Koszalin	200km north-east of Szczecin on Route E28
Kowno/Niemen	Kaunus/Neman	
Krakow/Vistula	Krakow/Vistla	south Poland, east of Katowicze
Küstrin/Oder and Wartha	Kostrzyn/Odra and Warta	north of Frankfurt/Oder
Leuthen	Lutynia	20km west of Breslau
Liegnitz	Legnica	east of Görlitz
Lublin	Bystrzyca	160km south-east of Warsaw on Route 17/E372
Marienwerder/Vistula	Grudziadz/Vistla	south of Danzig
Maxen		12km south-south-east of Dresden
Moys	Görlitz	a suburb of Zgorzelec, east of the Oder/Odra
Olmütz	Olomouc	north-east of Brno
Parchwitz	Prochowiece	between Wroclaw and Lubin, west of the Odra
Peenemünde		Baltic coast, north of Wolgast
Pillau	Baltijsk	Baltic coast, west of Kaliningrad
Posen/Wartha	Poznan/Warta	east of Berlin, south-west of Bromberg/Bydgoszcz
Prag	Praha (Sterboholy)	south of Dresden
Pr. Eylau	Bagrationovsk	south of Kaliningrad
Reichenberg	Liberec	east-south-east of Dresden
Schneidemuhle	Pila	180km east of Szczecin at the junction of Routes 10 and 11
Schweidnitz	Swidnica	30km south-west of Breslau, on the river Weistritz (Strzegomka)
Stargard	Starogard Gdanski	50km east of Gdansk on Route 22
Stettin	Szczecin	Baltic coast, up the Odra estuary
Swinemünde	Swinoujscie	Baltic coast, on Odra mouth
Thorn/Vistula	Torun/Visla	east of Bromberg/Bydgoszcz
Warsaw	Warszawa/Visla	Polish capital on the Vistula/Wisla
Zamosk	Zamosc	in southeast Poland on Route E372
Zorndorf	Sarbinowo	10km north of Kostrzyn/Oder

APPENDIX 3

KEY PEOPLE

Austria

Joseph Freiherr von Alvintzy de Berberek

Born on 1 February 1735 in Alvinc (now Vintu de Jos, southwest of Alba Julia, Romania), then in Hungary. In 1750, he joined the hussars. During the Seven Years War he was a captain of grenadiers. He was distinguished in the Battle of Torgau (3 November 1760), the capture of Schweidnitz (1 October 1761) and the clash at Teplitz in 1762. He was badly wounded at Torgau and Teplitz. He was again distinguished in the raid on Habelschwert (today Bystrzyca, in Poland) in the War of the Bavarian Succession and was promoted in 1789 from Oberst to General-Major. He also fought in the wars against the Turks from 1788–1790. In 1786 he had been appointed Chef of Infantry Regiment Nr 19, a post he held until 1810. He was promoted to Feldmarschalllieutenant on 21 May 1794, under Clerfait in Luxemburg and commanded a division in the Reserve at the victorious Battle of Neerwinden on 18 March. He was made ADC to the Prince of Orange for the Austro-Dutch victory at Charleroi on 3 June 1794. For his services during the campaigns in the Netherlands he received the Maria-Theresien-Orden and Commander's Cross on 28 May 1793. In May 1796, at the age of 61, he took command of the defeated Austrian Army in Italy from Beaulieu, coming out of Lombardy, and revitalised it. On 7 July 1794, he was awarded the Maria-Theresien-Orden Grand Cross. In 1796 he was defeated by Napoleon and was relieved of command in Italy. He was appointed General Officer Commanding of Hungary in 1808 and died in Ofen in 1810.

Karl Maria Raimund Leopold Herzog von Arenberg, Arschot und Croy

Born on 1 April 1721 in Schloß Enghien. His father was Leopold Philipp Karl Joseph, a Feldmarschall und Generalissimus of the Austrian troops in the Netherlands. In 1743 young Arenberg took part in his first campaign as Oberstleutnant (lieutenant-colonel) in Infanterie-Regiment d'Arberg (Nr 55) and was also promoted to Oberst (colonel) and became Chef of the 2nd Walloon Infanterie-Regiment, which he raised. He led this regiment on the campaigns of 1744 and 1745. In 1746 he became Chef of Infanterie-Regiment Nr 12. In 1748 he was distinguished in the defence of Maastricht and was promoted to General-Major. After the resignation of his father in 1749, he became lieutenant of Hennegau and Mons. In 1754 he became Chef of Infanterie-Regiment Nr 21, a post he held until his death. In 1755 he was promoted Field Marshal; he fought at the Battle of Prague, at Gabel, was distinguished at Moys and at the siege of Schweidnitz. In 1758 he was promoted to Feldzeugmeister. At the

Battle of Hochkirch he commanded the Austrian right wing. On 4 December 1758 he was awarded the Maria-Theresien-Orden Grand Cross. In the campaign of 1759 he was defeated by Prussian General von Wunsch on 29 October near Dresden. In 1760 he fought in the Battle of Torgau, commanding the right wing until he was badly wounded. Maria Theresa appointed him privy councillor in 1765, and in 1770 he was promoted to Field Marshal. He died on 17 August 1778.

Adam Freiherr Bajalich von Bajahaz

Born in 1734 in Szegedin, Hungary. In 1750 he entered the Infanterie-Regiment Erzhog Ferdinand, but left the army four years later. In 1758, he entered the Warasdiner Grenz-Infanterie-Regiment as a lawyer. In 1760 he became a Leutnant and fought in the Seven Years War. In 1768 he was promoted to Kapitän-Leutnant; 1773 to Hauptmann and after the War of the Bavarian Succession, to major. In 1783, he was Oberstleutnant (lieutenant-colonel) in the Szluiner Grenz-Infanterie-Regiment. In the war against the Turks (1787–1792) he was several times distinguished: in 1790 he was promoted to Oberst and created Freiherr. In 1793 he was promoted to General-Major and commanded a brigade on the Upper Rhine under General der Kavallerie Graf Wurmser. On 24 September 1795, he was again distinguished in the victory at Handschuhsheim, for which he earned the Maria-Theresien-Orden Knight's Cross. On 30 May 1796, he was ordered to take his brigade via Bregenz into the Tyrol to make the attempt to try to relieve Wurmser in Mantua; in this he failed. He was promoted Feldmarschalllieutenant on 1 February 1797 and commanded a division at Rivoli on 14/15 January of that year.

In the retreat out of Italy in March 1797, he was part of the right wing together with Feldmarschalllieutenant Contreuil. They went via Udine, Cividale and Caporetto, up the valley of the Isonzo to Tarvis. Erzherzog Carl, with the divisions of Hohenzollern and Reuss, took the eastern route via Gradiska and Görz to Laibach.

On 21 March, Massena's Avantgarde had pushed General-Major Ocskay out of Tarvis and blocked the Austrian escape route. The Austrian General Contreuil attacked and pushed the French back to Saifnitz, but next day he was assaulted by Massena, defeated with heavy losses and thrown back through Tarvis, towards Villach. Bajalich and Köblös were still on the wrong side of Tarvis. On 23 March with the divisions of Massena, Guyeux and Serrurier closing them in, both were forced to surrender with 4000 men, 25 guns and 500 wagons. On 31 March, in St Vieth, Napoleon opened negotiations for peace as he was now dangerously over-extended and the French armies on the Rhine could not come into action to aid him. Bajalich retired in 1797 and died on 5 June 1800 in Carlstadt (Karlovac), Croatia.

Maximilian Ulysses Browne, Reichsgraf Baron de Camus und Mountany

Born on 23 October 1705 in Basel, Browne was descended from an old Irish family; his father, Ulysses was a supporter of the English King James II. In 1716, his father and his uncle, George, were ennobled by the Austrian Emperor.

In 1732, young Maximilian was appointed Oberst (colonel) and commander of his uncle's Infanterie-Regiment Nr 57; he took part in the campaign of 1734 in Italy, where he distinguished himself. In 1735 he was promoted to General Feldwachmeister (a rank used until about 1750, when it was replaced by General-Major).

In 1737 he became Chef of Infanterie-Regiment Nr 37 and fought against the Turks until 1739, in which year, he was promoted to Feldmarschalllieutenant. In 1740 he commanded the inadequate Austrian forces in Silesia; he was forced to withdraw to Moravia. Now under command of Graf Neipperg, he successfully commanded the right wing at Mollwitz.

In the following years he fought on various fronts and was sent on several diplomatic missions. In 1745 he was promoted to Feldzeugmeister and in the next year he was sent to Italy, where he played a part in the successful campaign in 1747, such as in the victory of Piacenza and the capture of Genoa. He conducted peace negotiations in Italy following the Peace of Aachen. In 1749 he was appointed to command in Siebenbürgen and in 1751 to command in Bohemia. Here, he threw himself into the task of training his troops in the new 'Daun Tactical System' of 1749. In 1753 he was promoted to Field Marshal. In 1756, he opposed the initial Prussian attack and led the attempt to rescue the Saxon Army at Pirna, during which he fought the Battle of Lobositz. Although he left the battlefield, he was by no means beaten, a fact which FredericK the Great acknowledged.

In 1757, supreme command was given to Prinz Carl von Lothringen, which was a bitter blow for Browne. Despite this, he offered to serve under the Prince. Browne was caught by surprise by the Prussian invasion of Bohemia in this year. He commanded the Austrian right wing in the Battle of Prague and beat off all Prussian attacks. He was wounded while leading his grenadiers in a charge and died some weeks later on 26 June 1757 in Prague as a Field Marshal. He was a very competent, decisive commander, who often bridled at being subordinate to less competent superiors.

Joseph Franz, Graf von Canto d'Yrlès

Born on29 March 1726, of Scottish descent. In 1745, he entered Infanterie-Regiment Pallavicini (Nr 15) as a Fähnrich (in 1763 the five most senior Freikorporale of a regiment were distinguished by being given commissions as 'Fähnriche' or 'Fahnenjunker' and wore the officers' sword knot on their NCO sabre). He fought in the Seven Years War, at the Battle of Prague (6 May 1757), and at Breslau on 22 November, that same year. In 1762, he was distinguished in action at Teplitz. In 1758, he was promoted to captain, 1768 to major, in 1773 to Oberstleutnant (lieutenant-colonel) and appointed commander of a grenadier battalion. In the War of the Bavarian Succession (1778–1779) he was promoted to Oberst. He fought with his regiment in the wars with the Turks (1787–1792) and was distinguished in action at the pass of Rogatyn, in the Ukraine (April 1788). On 10 March 1789, he was promoted to General-Major during the siege of Cochim, in Poland. In August 1794 he was in Italy in Feldmarschalllieutenant Baron Wenkheim's division. On 9 March 1795 he was promoted to Feldmarschalllieutenant. In 1796 he was commandant of Mantua fortress, during which, on 10 August 1796, he was awarded the Maria-Theresien-Orden Commander's Cross. When Wurmser made his first attempt to lift the siege of the fortress in August, Napoleon was forced to break off the operation for some days and abandoned his siege train in the batteries and trenches. Canto d'Yrlès destroyed the siege works and took the siege train into Mantua. He also used the chance to gather in supplies and forage. The siege of the place was resumed and lasted until early 2 February 1797, when it surrendered to the French. D'Yrles' health was now ruined; he died on 11 April 1797, in Warasdin on the river Drau, Croatia.

Franz Sebastian Karl Joseph de Croix, Graf von Clerfait

Born on 14 October 1733 in Bruille castle, Hennegau, in Belgium. In 1753 he joined the Austrian Army; he fought with repeated distinction during the Seven Years War, particularly at the Battle of Prague (6 May 1757), Hochkirch (14 October 1758) and Liegnitz (15 August 1760). At the end of the war he was a colonel at only 30 years of age. At the end of the War of the Bavarian Succession, in 1779, he was promoted to General-Major. In 1775, he had been appointed Chef of Infanterie-Regiment Nr 9, an office he held until his death. When Belgian separatists rose up in 1787–1788, he resisted their repeated calls to join the rebellion, remaining true to the Kaiser. On 14 April 1783 he was promoted to Feldmarschallieutenant and fought in the wars against the Turks (1787–1792). On 10 November 1788 he was promoted to Feldzeugmeister, in recognition of his victories at Mehadia and on 27 July 1788, at Calafat on the Danube, on the Romanian/Bulgarian border. On 9 October 1789 he was awarded the Maria-Theresien-Orden Knight's Cross and on 19 December 1790, the Maria-Theresien-Orden Grand Cross.

On 22 April 1795, Clerfait was promoted to Field Marshal and installed as a Knight in the Order of the Golden Fleece. In this year, he commanded the Austrian Army on the Middle and Upper Rhine against General Jourdan, and beat Schaal in the Battle of Mainz on 29 October.

On 21 December 1795, he concluded an armistice with the French and returned to Vienna. Here, he fell foul of intrigues; his conclusion of the armistice was heavily criticised and he was removed from command. He died on 28 July 1798 in Vienna.

Josef Maria, Graf von Colloredo-Mels und Waldsee

Born in 1735 in Regensburg, Josef he entered Austrian military service in the artillery and fought in the Seven Years War, during which he was several times distinguished in action. On 6 October 1763, he was promoted to General Feldwachmeister. On 19 January 1771, he was promoted Feldmarschalllieutenant and charged with command of the border areas with Turkey. In 1769, he was appointed Chef of Infanterie-Regiment Nr 57. In the war with the Turks in 1778/9 he commanded the artillery at the siege of Belgrade. In 1779, he was appointed Director of the Artillery; he raised the corps of bombardiers and did much to improve the technical efficiency of this arm. On 6 February 1785, he was promoted to Feldzeugmeister and on 12 October 1789 to Field Marshal. He became an active member of the Hofkriegsrat and was responsible for the abolition of infantry regimental guns and the formation of field batteries on the French model. He died in Vienna in 1818.

Leopold Joseph Graf von Daun (or Dhaun)

Born in Vienna on 24 September 1705, son of Graf Wirich Philipp von Daun. He was intended for the church, but his natural inclination for the army, in which his father and grandfather had been distinguished generals, proved irresistible. In 1718 he served in the campaign in Sicily, in his father's regiment. He had already risen to the rank of Oberst (Colonel) when he saw further active service in Italy and on the Rhine in the War of the Polish Succession (1734–1735). He continued to add to his distinctions in the war against the Ottoman Empire (1737–1739), in which he attained the rank of Feldmarschalllieutenant. In the War of the Austrian Succession (1740–1748), Daun distinguished himself by the careful leadership which was his greatest military quality.

He was present at the battles of Chotusitz and Prague, and led the advanced guard of Khevenhüller's army in the victorious Danube campaign of 1743. Field Marshal Count Traun, who succeeded Khevenhüller in 1744, thought highly of Daun, and entrusted him with the rearguard of the Austrian Army. He held important commands in the battles of Hohenfriedberg (where he was defeated) and Soor, and in the same year (1745) was promoted to the rank of Feldzeugmeister. After this he served in the Low Countries, and was present at the Battle of Val.

He was highly valued by Empress Maria Theresa, who made him commandant of Vienna and a Knight of the Golden Fleece, and in 1754 he was elevated to the rank of Field Marshal. During the interval of peace that preceded the Seven Years War he was engaged in carrying out an elaborate scheme for the reorganisation of the Austrian Army, and it was chiefly through his efforts that the Theresian Military Academy was established at Wiener-Neustadt in 1751. He was not actively employed in the first campaigns of the war, but in 1757 he was placed at the head of the army which was raised to relieve Prague. On 18 June 1757 Daun defeated Frederick the Great for the first time in his career in the desperately fought Battle of Kolin. In commemoration Maria Theresa instituted a military order bearing her name, and Daun was awarded the first Grand Cross of that order. The union of the relieving army with the forces of Prinz Carl von Lothringen at Prague reduced Daun to the position of second-in-command, and in that capacity he took part in the pursuit of the Prussians and the victory of Breslau.

Frederick now reappeared and won his most brilliant victory at Leuthen. Daun was present on that field, but was not held accountable for the disaster, and when Prinz Carl resigned his command, Daun was appointed in his place. With the campaign of 1758 began the war of manoeuvre in which Daun, though he missed, through over-caution, many opportunities of crushing the Prussians, at least maintained a steady and cool resistance to the fiery strategy of Frederick. In 1758 Major-General von Laudon, acting under Daun's instructions, forced the Prussian king to raise the siege of Olmütz (the Battle of Domašov), and later in the same year Daun himself surprised Frederick at the Battle of Hochkirch and inflicted a severe defeat upon him.

On 20 and 21 November 1759 he surrounded the entire corps of General Finck at Maxen, forcing the Prussians to surrender. These successes were counterbalanced in the following year by the defeat of Loudon at Liegnitz, which was attributed to Daun's inactivity. This was followed by Daun's own defeat at the Battle of Torgau. In this engagement Daun was so severely wounded that he had to return to Vienna to recuperate. He continued to command until the end of the war, and afterwards worked at the reorganisation of the imperial forces. In 1762 he had been appointed president of the Hofkriegsrath. By order of Maria Theresa a monument to his memory was erected by Balthasar Ferdinand Moll in the church of the Augustinians, with an inscription describing him as the 'saviour of her states'. In 1888 the 56th Regiment of Austrian Infantry was named after him. Graf von Daun was perhaps over cautious and has been criticised for failing to exploit a victory. He died on 5 February 1766.

Empress Maria Theresa Walburga Amalia Christina

Maria Theresa was born on 13 May 1717. She was the only female ruler of the Habsburg dominions and the last of the House of Habsburg. She was the sovereign of Austria, Hungary, Croatia, Bohemia, Moravia, Mantua, Milan, Lodomeritz and Galicia, the Austrian Netherlands (now Belgium), and Parma. By marriage she was Duchess of Lorraine, Grand Duchess of Tuscany, German Queen and Holy Roman Empress.

She married Franz Stephan von Lothringen (Lorraine) and bore him sixteen children, including Queen Marie Antoinette of France, Queen Maria Carolina of Naples, Duchess Maria Amalia of Parma and two Holy Roman Emperors, Joseph II and Leopold II. Franz died in August 1765 and was succeeded as co-ruler of the Holy Roman Empire by Joseph II, Maria Theresa's fourth child and first son. As might be expected, his mother disapproved of many of her son's decisions.

Maria Theresa was an absolute sovereign who ruled by the counsel of her advisers, including Graf Friedrich Wilhelm von Haugwitz and Gottfried van Swieten, a Dutchman, born in Leiden. Maria Theresa was a relatively popular, conservative monarch. She introduced financial and educational reforms, promoted commerce and the development of agriculture and reorganised Austria's ramshackle military, all of which strengthened Austria's international standing. However, she refused to allow religious tolerance in her catholic realm. She retained her throne despite the string of defeats during the three wars. She died on 29 November 1780.

Wenzel Freiherr von Hynogek Kleefeld

Born in 1710 or 1711 in Kaurzim in Bohemia, Wenzel joined the Austrian Army as a volunteer in 1731 and fought in the War of the Austrian Succession. By 1750 he had been promoted to Oberst (colonel) and was ennobled in 1754. In 1757 he was commander of the Szluiner Grenz-Infanterie-Regiment and fought at the Battle of Kolin, where he defended the village of Chotzemitz, before the Austrian main line. He was wounded in this action. By 1759 he had been promoted to General-Major and fought in all actions in Saxony, being distinguished at Maxen on 20 November. In the spring of 1760, he was able to capture the notorious Prussian partisan, Hauptmann Friodeville. In the clash at Freiberg, on 15 October, he commanded the advance guard; they met two Prussian battalions and took or killed most of them, taking three flags and two guns. In 1763 Kleefeld was promoted to Feldmarschalllieutenant, and on 21 November of that same year, was presented with the Maria-Theresien-Orden Knight's Cross. In 1778 he was promoted to Feldzeugmeister; he retired in 1777 and died in 1799, in Marburg in Steiermark.

Ernst Gideon, Freiherr Laudon (or Loudon)

Born on 2 February 1717 in Tooten, Livonia. His father was Otto Gerhard von Laudon, a Swedish officer. In 1732, he entered the Russian army as a cadet; he later fought in the War of the Polish Succession under Field Marshal Münnich and in the Balkans against the Turks. He resigned in 1742 as Oberleutnant and tried, without success, to enter Prussian service. Thanks to his connections to Oberst (colonel) Franz von der Trenck, he succeeded in obtaining an appointment as a captain in his notorious Corps of Pandurs. He fought with this unit in 1744/45 in Alsace, Silesia and Bohemia, before resigning in disgust at the conduct of his commander. He then went to Vienna and obtained a post in the Infanterie-Regiment Karlstädter, where he proved to be a capable administrator.

In 1753 he was promoted to Oberstleutnant (lieutenant-colonel) and so pleased his general (Ulysses von Browne) with his Croats, that at the beginning of the 1757 campaign, he was promoted to Oberst. Following further successful guerrilla-type operations against the Prussian withdrawal from Bohemia, he was promoted again, to General Feldwachmeister in August 1757. In 1758 he was presented with the Maria-Theresien-Orden Knight's Cross and the Maria-Theresien-Orden Grand Cross. On 30 June 1758, he achieved the destruction of a vital 4000-wagon strong Prussian supply convoy at Domstadtl in Moravia. This forced Frederick the Great to abandon the siege of Olmütz. Three days later, he was promoted to Feldmarschalllieutenant. In March 1759, he was made an Austrian Freiherr. In the campaign of 1759, he commanded his own corps, with which he invaded the Prussian province of Neumark and joined up with the Russian army under General Saltykov, to defeat the Prussians at Kunersdorf on 12 August 1759. He was unable to convince the Russians to join him in pursuing and destroying the Prussians.

In the campaign of 1760, Laudon achieved a complete victory over the corps of Prussian General Fouqué at Landeshut. On 15 August 1760, abandoned by Daun and Lacy, Laudon suffered a sever defeat at Liegnitz. In 1761, he was unable to convince the Russians to attack the Prussian camp at Bunzelwitz, but he was able to take the fortress of Schweidnitz by a coup de main on 1 October 1761.

From 1766–1769 he was appointed Inspector General of Infantry, then General Officer Commanding Moravia. He was promoted to Field Marshal on 27 February 1778 and commanded a secondary army on the Saxon border. In 1769 he was sent with a corps to fight the Turks in the Balkans, together with a Russian army. After great success he was appointed Commander-in-Chief and his crowning achievement was the recapture of Belgrade on 8 October 1769, which led to a peace treaty at Schwichtow. In March 1790, Laudon assumed command of the army of observation on the Moravian border with Prussia, where he died on 14 July. Immensely popular with the nation and the soldiers, Laudon lacked any sense of diplomacy with the higher echelons, thus great military advancement eluded him.

Prince Charles Alexander Lorraine (or Lothringen)

Born on 12 December 1712 in Luneville. He was the son of Duke Leopold Joseph of Lorraine and Elisabeth Charlotte d'Orleans. His eldest brother, Franz Stephan married the Archduchess Maria Theresa, daughter of the Austrian Emperor Charles VI. She later became Empress of Austria.

On 7 January 1744, he married Maria Theresa's only sister, Archduchess Maria Anna and the couple were made joint governors of the Austrian Netherlands.

Charles Alexander entered Austrian military service in 1737. He was one of the senior Austrian commanders during the War of the Austrian Succession (1740–1748) and was defeated by Marshal Maurice de Saxe at the Battle of Rocoux (11 October 1746), leading an Anglo-Hanoverian-Dutch-Austrian Army of 97,000 against 120,000 French. This led to the Austrians losing control of their sector of the Netherlands.

During the First Silesian War (1740–1742) and the 2nd (1744–1745) he was defeated by Frederick the Great at the Battle of Chotusitz (17 May 1742) losing 19,000 casualties and 18 guns. In the Second War he was again defeated by Frederick at the Battle of Hohenfriedberg (4 June 1745) losing 13,730 casualties to the Prussians' 4800.

In the Seven Years War, (1756–1763) he commanded the Austrian Army at the battles of Prague (6 May 1757), Breslau (22 November 1757) and Leuthen (5 December 1757), being defeated in all three engagements. Following his defeat in the Battle of Prague, the Prince was besieged in that city until breaking out and joining up with von Daun's army on 26 June. He was then replaced by Leopold Joseph Graf Daun and returned to the administration of the Netherlands until his death on 4 July 1780 in Tervuren.

Johann Sigismund Maquire, Graf von Inniskilling

He was born in Ireland and entered Austrian military service as a subaltern at an early age, serving in various infantry regiments. He distinguished himself on campaign under General von Browne as colonel of the Warasdiner-Kreuzer Grenz-Infanterie-Regiment at the storming of the Bocchetta post in Italy. In 1747 he was promoted to General-Major and appointed Chef of Grenz-Infanterie-Regiment Nr 5. By the outbreak of the Seven Years War he was already a Feldmarschalllieutenant. In 1759 he commanded the siege of Dresden, which surrendered on 4 September. In 1760 he was awarded the Maria-Theresien-Orden Grand Cross and successfully defended Dresden against a Prussian siege. In 1763 he became Chef of Infanterie-Regiment Nr 35. He was later commandant of the fortress of Olmütz; he died on 12 January 1767 in Troppau (Opava).

Franz Leopold von Nádasdy auf Fogaras

A member of an old Hungaro-Siebenburgen aristocratic family, he was born on 30 September 1708 in Radkersburg/Steiermark. His parents were Graf Franz and Rosa, Gräfin Schrattenbach. In 1727 he joined Husaren-Regiment Csáky (later Nr 9) as a trooper and quickly became an NCO. Due to continued distinguished conduct in campaigns in Corsica, Italy and on the Rhine, he became Oberst (colonel) and commander of Husaren-Regiment Czungenberg (later Nr 8) in 1734. In 1739 he became commander of his old regiment (Nr 9); in 1741 he then became Chef of the regiment, which post he held until his death. In 1888 it was decreed that this regiment should bear his name '*auf ewige Zeiten*' (for all time). In 1744 Franz was promoted to General-Major and shortly after to Feldmarschalllieutenant; in 1745 he was again promoted and appointed commandant of the fortress of Ofen. In 1758 he was appointed Banus von Kroatien (steward of Croatia).

Nádasdy proved himself to be a careful, competent commander, who knew just how to exploit the talents of the light troops under his command. He was distinguished in 1745 by his raid through Prussian-occupied Silesia, especially in the Battle of Traunenau (Soor) on 30 September, where he captured Frederick the Great's war chest and field baggage. Next year, in Italy, he took the town of Piacenza, together with over 7000 prisoners and played major roles in the taking of Roddofreddo, Novi, Genua, and the Bocchetta pass.

As Ban of Croatia, he organised the raising of new troop formations in the lands along the lower Danube and in 1757 led them to join von Daun's army. After he had spent some time in Moravia and Silesia, von Daun recalled him to his main army in Bohemia, where, in the Battle of Kolin (18 June 1757) Nádasdy's charge into the flank of the Prussian Army sealed the Austrian victory and caused Frederick the Great to break off the siege of Prague. Following this battle, von Daun was the first to be awarded the Maria-Theresien-Orden Grand Cross and Nádasdy was the second. Nádasdy was also instrumental in the Austrian victories of Landeshut and Moys. He also took the fortress of Schweidnitz on 13 November 1757, thirteen days after the destruction of three of the peripheral forts. He took large stocks of supplies, weapons, munitions, as well as a chest of 335,000 Gulden, four generals and 6000 men. The last large battle at which he was actively involved was that of Leuthen on 5 December 1757. Nádasdy had advised his commander, Lothringen, not to leave his safe position there, but was ignored and Austria suffered its worst defeat of the war, which cost them 6000 dead, 20,000 captured and 200 cannon. After this disaster, Nádasdy returned to the Banat, where he concentrated on improving the border infantry regiments to such a degree that they were no longer regarded as low-quality militia units. He died on 22 March 1783 in Karlstadt.

Graf Karl O'Donnell

A descendant of an old Irish aristocratic family of Tyrconnell, he was born in 1715. Following the defeat at the Battle of Blackwater, the family had to leave Ireland; part of the clan went to Spain, and the brothers Charles, John and Henry entered Austrian military service.

Karl entered Kürassier-Regiment Bernes as a cornet, and was promoted to Rittmeister for service during the war against the Turks, having been wounded in the clash at Grocka on 22 July 1739. He was soon promoted to major, then to Oberstleutnant (lieutenant-colonel) in Dragoner-Regiment D'Ollone.

On 8 December 1742 he was promoted to Oberst (colonel) in Dragoner-Regiment Balloyra Nr 2. He was repeatedly decorated for bravery, especially at Piacenza on 16 June 1746, after which he was chosen by Fürst Joseph Liechtenstein to carry the captured standards to Vienna. During the raid into Provence, Karl commanded his own corps and took part in all actions in that campaign in 1748.

At Lobositz in 1756 his conduct won him promotion to Feldmarschalllieutenant and the appointment as Chef of Kürassier-Regiment Cordova (later Dragoner-Regiment Nr 5). At the Battle of Kolin Karl contributed much to von Daun's victory over the Prussians. Karl was wounded and captured in the Battle of Leuthen on 15 December 1757. Following his release, he at once returned to the army and fought at Hochkirch, commanding the cavalry of the left wing. In the campaign of 1759, he skilfully commanded the rearguard after the clash of Düben and kept the Prussians at bay. His greatest achievement was at the Battle of Torgau on 3 November 1760, commanding the cavalry on the left wing, with which he charged the Prussian cavalry, which was threatening the Austrian right wing, capturing Prussian General von Finkenstein in the process and giving the Austrian infantry time to reform. The battle ended in a Prussian victory. Von Daun had been wounded, so O'Donnell took command of the army and led it safely back to Dresden. For this, he was awarded the Maria-Theresien-Orden Grand Cross.

O'Donnell retained army command until autumn 1762, but was defeated by the Herzog von Braunschweig-Bevern on 16 August at Reichenbach. On 8 December O'Donnell was appointed General Officer Commanding of the Netherlands; in 1764 he became a privy councillor and in 1765 was appointed Inspector General of Cavalry. In 1768 he became Governor of Siebenburgen until his resignation at the end of 1770. He fell ill in Vienna and died on 26 March 1771.

Christian Karl Prinz zu Stolberg-Gedern

Born on 14 July 1725 in Gedern, between Frankfurt/Main and Fulda in central Germany, in 1742 he received command of a company of infantry in Dutch service thanks to the patronage of General Fürst Karl von Waldeck. In 1745 he was given command of a regiment of infantry (probably one of the two regiments of Waldeck) in Dutch service, which he then commanded in the following campaign of the War of the Austrian Succession against the French. He was wounded in a skirmish at Asche on 12 August 1745. In 1746 he was taken prisoner at the fall of Brussels, but quickly exchanged. In 1747 he was distinguished (and again wounded) at the defence of Bergen op Zoom. His regiment was paid off after the Peace of Aachen (18. October 1748) and three years later, he transferred into Austrian service in the Infanterie-Regiment Graf Wartensleben Nr 28.

On 21 January 1758 he was granted the rank of Generalfeldmarschalllieutenant in the Imperial Army, which he took up that winter in Franconia. The Commander-in-Chief was Prinz Christian von Pfalz-Zweibrücken and in this year Stolberg-Gedern took part in the campaign in Saxony. During the subsequent winter, he exercised command of that army in Culmbach.

In 1759 he was again in Saxony under Pfalz-Zweibrücken. In August he was sent to aid General Wenzel Freiherr Kleefeld, who was besieging Torgau and on 18 August, he signed the capitulation of that place with the commander, the Prussian General von Wolffersdorf.

He fought in the clash at Dresden on 5 September and that at Colditz on 21 September. On 19 November he accepted the surrender of General von Fink's corps at Maxen. In 1760 he was again in Saxony under Pfalz-Zweibrücken and was distinguished on 18 August in the clash at Strehla. In 1761 he replaced Pfalz Zweibrücken as commander of the Imperial Army and on 9 May he was promoted to Generalfeldzeugmeister. In that November he was appointed governor of the imperial fortress of Philippsburg, north of Karlsruhe, on the east side of the Rhine. The imperial Commander-in-Chief, Serbelloni, was inactive and there was very little martial activity. In the spring of 1762, Stolberg-Gedern again commanded the imperial troops; in May, he led them from Thuringia against Saxony, but, as he was unable to link up with the Austrian Army, he had to fall back into Franconia. At the end of August, he came under the command of General der Kavallerie Andreas Graf Hadik von Futak, who had taken over from Serbelloni. Hadik ordered him to bring his force eastwards to Bohemia;

they joined up at Dresden on 6 September and operated against Prinz Heinrich von Preussen in a series of actions, the most important of which was that on 15 September at Freiberg on the Mulde River, southwest of Desden. Stolberg-Gedern had constructed a defensive position, west of the town and Hadik had fallen back to Dresden.

Stolberg-Gedern commanded 30,000 men (Austrians and imperials) in 49 battalions and 68 squadrons. Early on 29 October, in the last significant action of the Seven Years War, he was attacked by the Prussians; after a brief defence, he was thrown out of his lines. Due to the lack of energetic pursuit, he was able to withdraw in good order, south through Bohemia, then west, into Franconia, setting up his headquarters in Nürnberg. Hostilities ended on 27 November 1762. Stolberg-Gedern went to Vienna and resigned his command, then returned to Gedern, where he died on 21 July 1764.

Britain

Robert Clive

Robert Clive was born in 1725 at Styche, the family estate, in Shropshire. His father was a lawyer and MP for Montgomeryshire. His mother was a daughter of Nathaniel Gaskell of Manchester. Robert was their eldest son, they also had five daughters and another son.

In 1743 or 1744, Clive was sent out to Madras (now Chennai) as a 'writer' in the service of the Honourable East India Company (HEIC). On the voyage to India, his ship was detained for nine months in Brazil and Clive seized this opportunity to learn Portuguese.

In 1746, Madras capitulated to Bertrand-François Mahé de La Bourdonnais (comte de La Bourdonnais), who was a French naval officer and administrator, in the service of the French East India Company and Clive was among those captured. However, the subsequent breach of that capitulation by Joseph-François, Marquis Dupleix, Governor General of the French establishment in India, led Clive to escape from Madras and to take refuge at Fort St David, some 32km south. There, Clive obtained a commission of ensign. However, in 1748, the peace of Aix-la-Chapelle forced him to return to his civil duties.

In 1751, Clive was appointed commissary for the supply of provisions for the HEIC's troops, with the rank of captain. He also seems to have exercised command over the troops, for he headed a force of 200 Europeans and 300 native infantry sepoys, with which to seize the town of Arcot, capital of Chanda Sahib, the Nawab of the Carnatic, who was allied to the French in India. This action was to force Chanda Sahib to lift his siege of Trichinopoly (now Tiruchirapalli) held by a weak British battalion. Chanda Sahib sent a large army, including French troops, under his son Raja Sahib, who entered Arcot and besieged Clive in the citadel for 50 days. The small British garrison had been greatly reduced by casualties. The siege was lifted by Muhammad Ali, ally of the HEIC and pretender to the throne of Arcot, with 3000 Mahratta soldiers.

From 1753 to 1756 Clive was in England; when he returned to India, it was as a lieutenant-colonel in the British Army and governor of Fort St David. This fortress was near the town of Cuddalore, 160km south of Madras on the Coromandel Coast of India. Muhammed Ali was now Nawab of the Carnatic. On his way to Fort St David, Clive had captured Bombay (now Mumbai) and Gheria (now Vijaydurg), a stronghold of the Mahrattas. Clive assumed command at Fort St David on 20 June 1756, the day on which the Nawab of Bengal, Siraj Ud Daulah, captured Calcutta (now Kolkata). Together with Admiral Watson, Clive went to retake the city. Clive disembarked his troops some miles below Calcutta, marched through the jungles and invested Fort William, near the town and on the banks of the river Hoogly. He captured this fort on 2 January 1757. However on 4 February, he was defeated by the Bengali relief army in the combat of Calcutta and forced to retire within the walls of the fort. After a few days, the Nawab was forced to come to terms with Clive because he had to leave to face an invasion from Afghanistan. On 9 February, a treaty was concluded between the British and the Nawab. It was agreed that all British property taken at Calcutta would be restored and that the British would recover all privileges formerly granted to them. On 11 February, the treaty was expanded into an offensive and defensive alliance.

In March 1757, Clive sent the fleet upriver against Chandernagore (now Chandannagar), while he besieged it by land. The capture of this French settlement on 23 March gave the combined forces prize to the value of £130,000. When the Nawab of Bengal realised that Clive had ignored his instructions and attacked Chandernagore, he decided to break the treaty that he had signed with the British. He made overtures to the French Governor General of their colony of Pondicherry, Charles Joseph Patissier, Marquis de Bussy-Castelnau. Clive, not sure of the reaction of the Nawab, decided to keep his entire force in Bengal. Meanwhile, overtures were made to the authorities at Calcutta by a group of Indian conspirators led by Mir Jafar, the commander-in-chief of the Nawab's army. Together with Admiral Watson, Governor Drake and Mr Watts of the HEIC, Clive made a treaty in which it was agreed to give the office of viceroy of Bengal, Behar and Orissa to Jafar, who was to pay a million sterling to the HEIC for its losses in Calcutta and the cost of its troops, half a million to the British inhabitants of Calcutta, £200,000 to the native inhabitants, and £70,000 to its Armenian merchants. On 13 June 1757, Clive left Chandernagore with his force consisting of 900 Europeans, 200 Portuguese, 2100 Sepoys, and 10 guns. He marched upstream of the Hooghly towards Murshidabad, the capital of the Mogul viceroys of Bengal. On 21 June, he arrived on the river bank opposite Plassey (now Pâl shi), a village 20km from Murshidabad. Two days later, 50,000 Bengalis and allies closed up to Clive's 2800 men in their defensive position at Plassey. But several of the Bengali leaders had rallied to Mir Jafar before the battle and they now defected from Siraj ud-Daulah, who fled to Murshidabad. The British 'won the day'. On 24 June, Mir Jafar was saluted by Clive as Nawab of Bengal, Orissa, and Bihar. Clive then hastened with his troops to Murshidabad, reaching the city on the same evening. Siraj ud-Daulah had fled before his arrival, but parties were sent out at once in search of him, and a few days later he was brought back and assassinated. On 29 June, Clive entered the city and formally installed Mir Jafar on the throne. He then spent the succeeding months in dividing the spoils of the victory, of which the troops received no small share. Clive also took care that the HEIC should be the true power in Bengal and that Mir Jafar was its puppet. For this victory, Clive was given a peerage as Baron Clive of Plassey. He appointed the 25-year-old Warren Hastings as his agent to reside at the Court of Mir Jafar.

In 1760, after reorganising the native sepoys units and refortifying Calcutta, Clive returned to England because of health problems. He had accumulated a fortune of at least £300,000 and an annuity of £27,000 a year. He remained in England for three years, reforming the British offices of the HEIC. The treaty of Paris in 1763 formally confirmed Muhammad Ali in the position of Nawab of the Carnatic, won for him by Clive.

In 1764, things were not going well in India and the court of proprietors of the HEIC hurried out Lord Clive to Bengal once again, in the dual capacity of Governor and Commander-in-Chief. Jafar Ali Khan had died and had been succeeded by his son-in-law, Mir Kasim. The latter induced not only the viceroy of Oudh, but the Emperor of Delhi himself, to invade Bihar. Major Munro suppressed the first mutiny in the Bengal Army and then scattered the united hostile armies in the Battle of Buxar in October. The emperor, Shah Alam II, detached himself from the league, while the Viceroy of Oudh threw himself on the mercy of the British.

On 3 May 1765, Clive landed at Calcutta. He consolidated the British hold on Bengal, making it the base from which the future British India could expand. He then returned to the Viceroy of Oudh all his territory save the provinces of Allahabad and Kora, which he made over to the weak emperor, Shah Alam II. From the latter he secured the most important document in the whole of British history in India up to that time, granting the rule of Bengal, Bihar and Orissa to the HEIC. By this deed the Company became the sovereign rulers of 30 million people, yielding an annual revenue of £4 million. Clive also obtained control of the Deccan itself. He then reorganised the civil services of the new territories. He raised the salaries which had tempted its members to be corrupt, forbade the acceptance of gifts from natives and exacted covenants under which participation of civil servants in the inland trade was stopped. No less important were his military reforms. With his usual tact and nerve he put down a mutiny of the English officers at a time when two Mahratta armies were marching on Bengal. He divided the whole army into three brigades, so as to make each a complete force, in itself equal to any single native army that could be brought against it.

Clive left India for the last time in February 1767. From 1772, he had to defend his past actions in India against his numerous and vocal critics in Great Britain. Cross-examined by a Parliament suspicious of his vast wealth, he claimed to have taken relatively limited advantage of the opportunities presented to him: 'By God … I stand astonished at my own moderation'. Clive committed suicide in his home in Berkeley Square, London, on 22 November 1744.

William Augustus, Duke of Cumberland

Born on 15 April 1721 in London, William Augustus was the third son of King George II of England and Caroline of Ansbach. In 1726, William Augustus was created Duke of Cumberland. In 1740, Cumberland sailed as a volunteer in the fleet under the command of Sir John Norris, to get to know the navy, the service the King had decided he should enter. Naval life did not appeal to the Duke and he entered the Army early in 1742, being appointed Major-General in December. Next year, he saw action in the Battle of Dettingen, Germany, where he was wounded. He was promoted to Lieutenant-General after that battle and soon became captain general.

In 1745, Cumberland returned to Flanders as Commander-in-Chief of the Allied Army consisting of British, Hanoverian, Austrian and Dutch troops. On 11 May, while trying to relieve Tournai, besieged by the French under Marshal Saxe, Cumberland was defeated at the Battle of Fontenoy. During this battle, he personally led a British column which penetrated the French centre but was finally repulsed. He then coolly conducted an orderly retreat. Later that year, he was recalled from Flanders to serve under General Jean-Louis Ligonier in the British force sent against Prince Charles Edward Stuart who had invaded northern England. As the British advanced on Derby, the rebels retreated northwards. Cumberland followed them to Penrith. However, his vanguard was repulsed at Clifton Moor. Cumberland pushed on and after the capture of Carlisle, he retired to London.

In 1746, after the defeat of General Hawley at Falkirk, Cumberland was appointed commander of the British forces in Scotland. On 30 January he arrived in Edinburgh; he then advanced on Aberdeen, where time was spent improving the tactical training of his troops. On 8 April Cumberland set out from Aberdeen towards Inverness. Eight days later, he fought and won the decisive Battle of Culloden. At the end of the battle he ordered his troops to give no quarter. During the ensuing pursuit, his troops completely destroyed the forces of the Young Pretender. Cumberland remained in Scotland for another three months, hunting down the rebel remnants and stamping out the embers of revolt. For this ruthless operation, he earned the nickname 'Butcher'. In 1747 Cumberland was back in Flanders at the head of the Allied Army, but on 2 July he was once more heavily defeated by Maréchal de Saxe at Lauffeld.

For the next ten years of peace, Cumberland play-acted his role as captain-general of the British Army which he left totally unprepared for the upcoming war. When it broke out he was offered command of the Allied Army in Hanover, and he demanded the dismissal of Prime Minister William Pitt as a condition of his acceptance. Pitt's government fell in April and Cumberland duly assumed his command. His prime aim was to protect the Electorate of Hanover from French invasion. On 26 July, he was defeated by the French at the Battle of Hastenbeck, near Hameln on the river Weser. On 8 September, after a long retreat northwards towards the sea, he finally capitulated to the French at Klosterzeven. The terms of capitulation specified that he would disband his army and evacuate Hanover. When he returned to Great Britain, his disgrace was complete but George II refused to be bound by the terms of the capitulation. Cumberland resigned his public offices and retired into private life, first at Windsor then in London. In the summer of 1765 he became ill, dying on 31 October.

George Augustus, King of England and Elector of Hanover

Born on 30 October 1683, he was King of Great Britain and Ireland, Duke of Brunswick-Lüneburg (Hanover) and Prince Elector of the Holy Roman Empire from 11 June 1727 until his death. He was son of King George I of England and Sophia Dorothea of Celle. He was the last British monarch to have been born outside Great Britain (in Hanover), and was famous for his numerous family rows with his father and his son. As king, he exercised little control over policy in his early reign, the government instead being controlled by Parliament. He was also the last British monarch to lead an army in battle, at Dettingen, on 27 June 1743.

George II entered the War of the Austrian Succession, supporting Maria Theresa's claim to the imperial throne and British troops were involved in that war for years, a fact which much of the British public disapproved of, as they felt that the expense was more for the benefit of Hanover than for England.

William Pitt the Elder, a prominent parliamentarian, had opposed England's involvement in the War of the Austrian Succession and was thus in disfavour with the King. At the outbreak of the Seven Year's War in 1756, Austria sided with Russia and France; the British reaction was to treat all nations of that coalition as enemies. Fearing for his old ancestral home of Hanover, George II allied himself with Prussia. The war spilled over into the British and French colonies in America, India, Africa and other parts of the world. George II died suddenly on 25 October 1760 of an aortic aneurism.

George Washington

Born on 22 February 1732, in Bridges Creek, Virginia, Washington had a rudimentary education, leaving school in the autumn of 1747. He then lived in Mount Vernon with his half-brother Lawrence, who was also his guardian.

In 1748, Washington, then only sixteen, was appointed surveyor of the Fairfax property; soon afterwards he became a public surveyor, mostly on the frontier for the next three years. In 1751, he accompanied Lawrence, who was stricken with consumption, to the West Indies, where he had an attack of smallpox which left him marked for life. In 1752, Lawrence Washington died, making George executor under the will and heir to Mount Vernon.

In October 1753, Washington was chosen by Governor Robert Dinwiddie as the agent to warn the French away from their new posts on the Ohio. Shortly after his return, he was appointed lieutenant-colonel of a Virginia militia infantry regiment, under Colonel Joshua Fry.

In April 1754, Washington was sent to the Ohio River with two companies of infantry. On 28 May, he defeated a force of French and Indians at Great Meadows, Fayette County, Pennsylvania, but at the beginning of that summer, he was forced to capitulate to the French at Fort Necessity.

In February 1755, General Edward Braddock arrived in Virginia; Washington was soon made a member of Braddock's staff, with the rank of colonel. He then took part to the disastrous expedition against Fort Duquesne, at the junction of the Allegheny and Monongahela rivers, where they become the Ohio River, where Braddock's force was ambushed and utterly defeated on the Monongahela. During this combat, Washington distinguished himself and probably saved the expedition from total annihilation. In August 1755 Washington, now 23, was commissioned commander of the Virginia forces.

In 1756 and 1757, Washington was sent to defend a frontier of more than 500km with just 700 men. The task was very difficult due to the insubordination and irregular service of his soldiers. From April to November 1758, Washington took part in another expedition against Fort Duquesne under the command of General Forbes. On 24 November the French blew up the fortifications of the fort and retreated up the Allegheny River to Fort Venango. Forbes occupied the ruins of the Fort Duquesne on 28 November. By the end of the year, the war was over and Washington resigned his commission.

In January 1759, Washington married Martha Dandridge, widow of Daniel Parke Custis. His marriage brought him a large increase in his property, making him one of the richest men in the colonies. He dedicated himself to running the family estate of Mount Vernon for the next fifteen years. Like many rich planters, Washington in Virginia, he was repeatedly elected to the House of Burgesses.

In 1765, as a member of the House of Burgesses, Washington opposed the Stamp Act and in May 1770, when the House of Burgesses was dissolved, Washington was among the members who met at the Raleigh tavern and adopted a non-importation agreement, boycotting English goods. On 5

August 1774, the Virginia convention appointed George Washington as one of seven delegates to the first Continental Congress, which met at Philadelphia on 5 September. When Congress adjourned, he returned to Virginia where he continued to be active in the House of Burgesses, urging on the organisation, equipment and training of local troops for home defence.

In March 1775, Washington was appointed a delegate from Virginia to the second Continental Congress, where he served on committees for fortifying New York, procuring ammunition, raising funds and formulating army regulations. The war began in Massachusetts, troops from New England flocking to the neighbourhood of Boston. But the resistance, if it was to be effective, had to have the support of the colonies to the southward. Washington, as the Virginia colonel who was serving on all the military committees of Congress and as an experienced military officer from the Seven Years War, was the obvious choice. When Congress, after the clashes at Lexington and Concord, resolved that the colonies ought to be put in a position of defence, the first practical step was the unanimous selection on 15 June of George Washington as commander-in-chief of the armed forces of the United Colonies. He accepted the nomination, but refused to take a salary and asked only that his expenses should be repaid. On 17 June 1775, Washington was installed in office. He set out at once for Cambridge, Massachusetts, where, on 3 July he took command of the levies there assembled for action against the British garrison in Boston.

His tasks were daunting; he had to create a military organisation and instil discipline in new officers and soldiers, to organise supplies of stores, clothing, weapons, ammunition and transport, to maintain correspondence with Congress and to plan and execute military operations in far-flung reaches of the country. His first aim was to expel the British from Boston. He then planned the expeditions against Canada under Richard Montgomery and Benedict Arnold, and sent out privateers to harass British mercantile commerce.

Washington remained in command of the colonial forces until 23 December 1783. General Charles Cornwallis surrendered the British forces in Yorktown in October 1781, but peace negotiations with Britain dragged on until September 1783. There being no more major engagements in North America, Washington resigned his commission and retired to Mount Vernon. In May 1787 the Federal Convention met in Philadelphia; Washington was present as the delegate from Virginia and was unanimously elected as the presiding officer; in this capacity he signed the constitution which was drawn up and was unanimously elected as the first President of the United States. He was re-elected for a second term in 1792.

In 1797, Washington retired from the presidency and returned to Mount Vernon. In 1798 he was again appointed to command the army, which had been assembled in face of a war with France. Whilst in office, he suddenly became ill and died at Mount Vernon on 14 December 1799.

James Wolfe

Born on 2 January 1727 in Westerham, Kent, he was the son of Edward Wolfe an army officer and veteran of Marlborough's campaigns; his mother was Henrietta Thompson. In 1741, James Wolfe accompanied his father, colonel in the 12th Marine Regiment (Durourel's), on the unsuccessful expedition against Carthagena de Indias, now Cartagena in Colombia. In November 1741, he was commissioned into his father's regiment.

In April 1742, Wolfe embarked for Flanders where he participated with the 12th Regiment of Foot in the Rhine Campaign in the War of the Austrian Succession. On 27 June 1743, at the Battle of Dettingen, Wolfe distinguished himself and was promoted to lieutenant. In 1744, he was promoted to captain of a company in the Barrel's 4th Regiment of Foot. In 1745, a detachment of the 4th Regiment of Foot was sent to Scotland to deal with the Highland rebellion led by Charles Edward Stuart. Wolfe was employed as a brigade-major.

On 17 January 1746, Wolfe was present at General Henry Hawley's defeat by the Scots at the Battle of Falkirk, their last significant success. On 16 April, he was present at Cumberland's victory at Culloden where he acted as ADC to General Hawley. Following this, Wolfe was employed with his regiment in Scotland, laying waste to the country. He then returned to the continent, serving with his old regiment, the 12th Regiment of Foot; on 2 July 1747, he took part in the Battle of Lauffeld, where he was wounded. His conduct in that action won him the commendation of the Duke of Cumberland. In 1749, Wolfe was promoted to major of the 20th Regiment of Foot stationed at Stirling and on 20 March 1750, he was promoted to lieutenant-colonel.

In 1757, Wolfe served on the staff in the unsuccessful Rochefort Expedition but his prospects were not affected by the failure. Indeed, he was brought to the attention of William Pitt, the Prime Minister. On 23 January 1758, Wolfe was promoted to Brigadier-General for the planned expedition against the French port of Louisbourg, Newfoundland, under Generals Amherst and Boscawen. The landing near Louisbourg was carried out in the face of strenuous opposition, Wolfe leading the foremost troops. During the siege Wolfe had charge of a most important section of the attack and the fiercest fighting took place on his lines. On 27 July, after a stout defence, Louisbourg surrendered. Soon afterwards, Wolfe returned to England to recover his health but on learning that Pitt desired him to continue in America he at once offered to return.

In 1759, Wolfe was appointed to command the expedition against Quebec by William Pitt, with the rank of Major-General. At the beginning of June, the Quebec expeditionary force sailed from Louisbourg, landing near the city on the St Lawrence River at the end of June. Wolfe did not get on well with the naval commanders on the expedition and this hampered successful operations, as the Royal Navy's ships were vital to his operations.

After many frustrations and suffering from illness, Wolfe's patience was rewarded with his decisive victory on the Plains of Abraham on 13 September. Although wounded early in the battle, he refused to leave the field; a second bullet, passing through his lungs inflicted the mortal injury. While he was lying on the field, semi-conscious, someone nearby exclaimed: 'They run; see how they run!' 'Who run?' asked Wolfe. 'The enemy!' came the answer, 'They give way everywhere!' Wolfe rallied briefly and gave a last order that the French retreat should be cut off. He then murmured: 'Now God be praised, I will die in peace,' and expired. Quebec capitulated five days later.

France

King Louis XV

Born on 15 February 1710, he ruled as King of France and Navarre from 1 September 1715 until his death. He succeeded to the throne at the age of five, at the death of his great-grandfather, Louis XIV. Louis was nicknamed 'the Well-Beloved', but the military and economic losses which France suffered during his reign brought about the crisis that brought on the French Revolution. His first cousin twice removed, Philippe II, Duke of Orléans, served as Regent until Louis's majority in 1723. Louis' former tutor, Cardinal Andre-Hercule de Fleury was his chief minister from 1726 until his death in 1743, at which time the young king took over control of the French state. Louis took only a sporadic interest in government. He was heavily influenced by a series of favourites, particularly his mistresses Madame de Pompadour and, after Pompadour's death in 1764, the Comtesse du Barry.

In 1725, Louis married Maria Leczczynska, the daughter of the King of Poland. In 1733, France became involved in the War of the Polish Succession, in an attempt to restore the queen's father to the Polish throne. The attempt failed, but France gained the Duchy of Lorraine. In 1740, in the War of the Austrian Succession, France allied with Prussia against Britain and Austria. The French won a series of military victories and occupied the Austrian Netherlands (now Belgium and Luxemburg). However, Louis subsequently returned the territory to Austria, for which he was lauded abroad but heavily criticised in France.

During the Seven Years War alliances were reversed, and the French became allied with their long-standing enemy Austria against Britain and Prussia. Enmity between Frederick the Great of Prussia and Louis was personal as well as political. Frederick had developed a strong dislike for Louis' mistress, Madame Pompadour, about whom he wrote and circulated scathing verses.

The French military defeats in Canada, India and Europe resulted in the loss of most her colonies to Britain, marking a low point in French prestige and costing the French treasury dearly. Louis XV maintained an extremely extravagant court, despite the reduced national circumstances, and he became one of the most unpopular monarchs in French history. He died at Versailles on 10 May 1774 and was succeeded by his grandson who became the unfortunate Louis XVI.

Victor François, Duc de Broglie

Born in Paris on 19 October 1718, he initially served with his father, François-Marie, 1st Duc de Broglie, at Parma and Guastalla. In 1734, during the War of the Polish Succession, de Broglie fought in Italy as captain in a cavalry regiment. He took part to the battles of Parma and Guastalla. He soon obtained the colonelcy of the Luxembourg Infanterie in that same year, which he retained until 1736.

In 1741, at the beginning of the War of the Austrian Succession, de Broglie took part in the campaign in Bohemia under Maréchal de Saxe. On 1 March, he was promoted aide-major général of the infantry. On 26 November, he took part in the storming of Prague. De Broglie was promoted to brigadier on 26 April 1742, and on 1 April 1743, after having been twice wounded in action, he was promoted to Major-General; he served in Bavaria and Alsace. In 1744 and 1745, he saw further service on the Rhine. He was present at the battles of Rocoux, Lauffeld and Maastricht, under the Marshal de Saxe. On 1 May 1745, de Broglie was promoted to Maréchal de Camp and on his father's death that year, he succeeded him as the second Duc de Broglie. On 10 May 1748 he was promoted to Lieutenant-General.

In 1757, de Broglie served under Maréchal d'Estrées; he was present at the Battle of Hastenbeck (26 July), when Cumberland's allied army was defeated. He was then detached to the army of Prince de Soubise and was present at the disastrous defeat at Prussian hands of Rossbach on 7 November, but managed to keep his units intact and led them back to Hanover.

In 1758, Broglie commanded the vanguard of Soubise's army in Hessen. The hostility of the Maréchal de Belle-Isle prevented him from assuming command of the army. On 23 July, de Broglie, at the head of Soubise's vanguard, defeated Prince Ysenburg at the clash of Sandershausen.

In 1759, de Broglie served in Germany under the Marquis de Contades. On 13 April, de Broglie won a victory over Ferdinand of Brunswick in the Battle of Bergen. On 1 August, the French Army of the Lower Rhine under Contades was heavily defeated at the Battle of Minden by the Anglo-Hanoverians and de Broglie replaced Contades as commander of the French Army. On 16 December, de Broglie was promoted to Marshal of France; he also received the title of Prince of the Holy Roman Empire from Kaiser Franz I of Austria.

On 10 July 1760, de Broglie won the clash of Korbach against the Allied Army, but, on 16 July 1761, he lost the Battle of Vellinghausen by his premature attack and fell into disgrace. During the 1770s, de Broglie was first governor of the Trois-Évêchés and then of Alsace. In 1778, Broglie returned to active service to assume command of the troops assembled to operate against Great Britain. In 1789, at the beginning of the French Revolution, de Broglie commanded the troops assembled around Versailles by Louis XVI. On 11 July, the King appointed him Secretary of State to War, but de Broglie emigrated. In 1792, Broglie commanded the 'army of the princes' who operated in Champagne during the Austro-Prussian invasion. His eldest son, Charles-Louis-Victor, Prince de Broglie, died during the Terror. In 1797, Broglie went to Russia and then to Riga in 1798. He died at Münster in 1804, refusing to return to France.

Louis Comte de Clermont-en-Argonne Bourbon-Condé (or Conti)

Born on 13 August 1717, he was the youngest son of Louis III de Bourbon-Condé and Mademoiselle de Nantes. He was destined for a religious career, but in 1733 he received permission from Pope Clement XII to enter the army. During the War of the Polish Succession, Louis de Bourbon-Condé was promoted lieutenant-general and took part to the campaign in the Netherlands. During the War of the Austrian Succession, he fought with distinction in the Battle of Dettingen on 27 June

1743. Louis became a friend of Madame de Pompadour and carried her cockade when preparing for combat. In 1753, he became a member of the Académie Française.

During the Seven Years War, due to the influence of Madame de Pompadour, Louis assumed command of the French Army of the Rhine in 1758. On 14 February, he arrived in Hanover to supersede Richelieu as commander of the French Army. Richelieu had been gone for a week and Louis had to assume the command with no help from the man he was relieving. The tactical situation was bad, Louis reporting to the King: 'I found your Majesty's army divided into three parts. The part which is above the ground is composed of pillagers and marauders, the second part is underground, and the third is in hospital. Should I retire with the first or wait until I join one of the others?'

An Allied offensive soon drove his army back to the Rhine. At the beginning of June, the Allies crossed the Rhine and forced Condé back west to Rheinberg, then to Neuss. On 23 June, he was defeated at the Battle of Krefeld by Ferdinand of Brunswick. After this battle, Condé was immediately dismissed and replaced by Contades. After the war, Condé took part to the efforts to reorganisation the French Army. In 1765, he secretly married Elisabeth-Claire Leduc, a dancer of the Opéra, with whom he lived at the castle of Berny near Fresnes. He died on 2 August 1776.

Louis Georges Érasme, Marquis de Contades

Born on 19 October 1704 near Beaufort, Anjou, he was the son of Gaspard de Contades and of Jeanne-Marie Crespin de La Chabosselaye. He entered the army in 1720 and married Marie-Françoise Magon, daughter of François Magon, in October 1724. On 10 March 1734, Contades became colonel of the Flandres Infanterie and on 18 October he was promoted to Général de Brigade. On 1 January 1740, Contades was promoted to Maréchal de Camp and on 1 May, a new promotion made him Lieutenant-General.

In 1756, Contades served under Field Marshal d'Estrées in the French Army which invaded Hanover; on 26 July, at the Battle of Hastenbeck, Contades commanded the first line of the infantry of the centre. In January 1758, he was named governor of Fort-Louis on the Rhine. In July, after the defeat of Clermont at the Battle of Krefeld, he replaced him as commander-in-chief of the French Army of the Rhine. In August, Contades crossed the Rhine and proceeded eastwards to invade the Prussian provinces there, whilst simultaneously supporting Soubise's offensive in Hessen. On 24 August, he was promoted to Field Marshal, but the campaign did not go well for him. In mid-November his army re-crossed the Rhine and went into winter quarters on the west bank of the river.

In January 1759, Soubise seized the city of Frankfurt-am-Main. In June, Contades crossed the Rhine again and invaded Hessen-Kassel. By mid-July, he had captured Minden, but on 1 August, he was severely defeated by Duke Ferdinand of Brunswick at the Battle of Minden. Soon after this battle, Contades ceded command of the French Army to d'Estrées. In 1763, Contades was commander-in-chief in Alsace and in 1788, he became Governor of Lorraine. He died on 19 January 1795, in Livry.

Thomas Arthur Comte de Lally, Baron de Tollendal

He was born in January 1702 at Romans, Dauphiné, the son of Sir Gerard O'Lally, an Irish Jacobite who married a French aristocrat. In 1721, he entered the French Army and in 1734, during the War of the Polish Succession, he served against Austria. In 1743, he fought at the Battle of Dettingen. In May 1745, at the Battle of Fontenoy, Lally was commander of his own regiment in the famous Irish Brigade. He was made a Général de Brigade on the field by Louis XV. The same year, Lally accompanied Charles Edward Stuart to Scotland, and in January 1746 he served as ADC to the Prince at the Battle of Falkirk. After the defeat of the Young Pretender at Culloden, Lally managed to escape to France where he served under Maréchal de Saxe in the Low Countries.

In 1748, after the capture of Maastricht, Lally was promoted to Maréchal de Camp. In 1756, when war broke out with Great Britain, Lally was given the command of a French expedition to India. This expedition took a certain time to organise and finally left Brest in May of the next year and took almost twelve months to reach India.

On 7 April 1758, Lally arrived at Pondicherry with his staff. Even though he was still waiting for some troops to arrive, he ordered General d'Estaing to attack the British in Madras. He also took extreme measures to replenish the hitherto empty treasury, levying contributions from the local rulers, from the French Compagnie des Indes and from members of his own staff. In May, his troops captured Cuddalore. On 2 June it was the turn of British-held Fort Saint-David to surrender to the French. The British forces in Madras then began to prepare to retake the place, but Lally decided to evacuate it and to return to Pondicherry. Later the same month, he conducted another punitive expedition to raise funds from various Indian districts in the region of Tanjore. During this raid, he looted temples and executed priests, thus alienating the locals. Lacking supplies, he then retired to Pondicherry. In December, Lally laid siege to Fort Saint-George in Madras state. A French fleet under d'Aché failed to blockade Madras, allowing the British Navy to relieve the fort and to reinforce it with Draper's 79th Regiment of Foot. Lally raised the siege on 17 February 1759 and fell back to Pondicherry.

On 22 January 1760, Lally was defeated by Sir Eyre Coote at the Battle of Wandiwash. He once more retired to Pondicherry where he was besieged. On 3 September, a sortie conducted by Lally failed and on 16 January 1761, he was forced to surrender the place. The fortress was destroyed and Lally was sent back to England as a prisoner of war. Whilst in captivity in London, he received news that he had been accused of treason in France. In 1763, he returned to France, only to be arrested and imprisoned in the Bastille. On 6 May 1766, he was found guilty and beheaded three days later.

François-Gaston Chevalier de Lévis

Born on 23 August 1720, in the chateau of Ajac near Limoux, in the Languedoc. He came from one of the oldest family of the French nobility and was the second son of Jean-Gaston, Baron d'Ajac.

In 1735 he was promoted lieutenant in the La Marine Infanterie. During the War of the Polish Succession, he took part in the campaign on the Rhine where he was promoted captain on 1 June 1737. From 1741, during the War of the Austrian Succession, he fought in the campaign in Bohemia and was at the capture of Prague in 1742. In 1743, he took part in the campaign in Germany where he fought at the Battle of Dettingen on 27 June. In 1747, he was promoted aide-major in the Armée d'Italie. Next year, he was promoted to colonel and appointed chevalier, in the Order of Saint-Louis.

In 1756, Lévis was selected by the Comte d'Argenson to accompany Montcalm to Canada as Général de Brigade. On 6 April, he sailed from Brest aboard the frigate *La Sauvage* and arrived in Quebec on 31 May. During early June, he organised the newly arrived battalions of the regiments of La Sarre and Royal-Roussillon and marched them to Montreal. On 27 June, Montcalm and Lévis left Montreal for Fort Carillon (Ticonderoga), where Lévis remained as commander. Throughout the summer, Lévis sent war parties to harass and to disrupt the British forces assembling on Lake George to the south.

In July and August 1757, Lévis took part to the French expedition against Fort William Henry led by Montcalm. In 1758, he was preparing a raid on the Mohawk and Hudson rivers when he was hastily recalled to reinforce Montcalm on Lake Champlain. Lévis joined Montcalm's force on the eve of the Battle of Carillon, fought on 8 July, in which the French were victorious. Following this battle, Lévis was promoted to General-Major. At the end of October, he withdrew to winter quarters in Montreal.

On 31 July 1759, Lévis assumed command of the French left wing and successfully defended the shore of Beauport, when the British sent a powerful expedition against Quebec. A few days later, on 9 August, he was sent to Montreal to prepare the defence of the Upper Saint-Laurent River against another British force under General Amherst. When he heard of Montcalm's defeat at the Battle of Quebec on 13 September, Lévis rushed to the rescue of the defeated French Army which he joined at Jacques-Cartier on 17 September. He took command of the demoralised troops, rallied them and marched on Quebec to learn that the town had capitulated on 18 September. He then went into winter quarters, using the time to prepare for a counter-attack on the city.

On 20 April 1760, Lévis set out from Montreal with 7000 men and marched on Quebec. He defeated General Murray at Sainte-Foy on 28 April and laid siege to the city. On 9 May, a British frigate arrived at Quebec, soon followed by further vessels carrying troops and Lévis was obliged to raise the siege and fall back south to Montreal. A British assault on Montreal forced the French Army to capitulate in front of an overwhelmingly superior force on 8 September. On 18 October Lévis sailed from Quebec, arriving at La Rochelle in France on 27 November. On 18 February 1762, Lévis was promoted to General-Leutnant and took part in the campaign in Germany, under the command of the Prince de Condé. On 30 August, at the Battle of Nauheim, he led the French vanguard to victory. In 1765, Lévis became Governor of Artois; in 1771 and he was appointed captain of the guards of the Comte de Provence, the future Louis XVIII. In 1776, Lévis received the title of Chevalier des Ordres du Roi and on 13 June 1783, he was promoted to Field Marshal. On 24 April 1784, Lévis succeeded to the family title; he died on 26 November 1787, in Arras.

Louis Joseph de Saint Véran, Marquis de Montcalm

Born on 29 February 1712 at Château de Candiac, Nîmes, Montcalm joined the French Army, at the age of nine; in 1727, he became an ensign in the Hainaut Infanterie and in 1729 his father bought him a captaincy. In 1733, he saw active service under Berwick on the Rhine and was first under fire at the sieges of Kehl, on the upper Rhine, in 1733 and at Philipsbourg the next year.

In 1735, Montcalm's father died, leaving him heir to a considerable but heavily indebted estate. In 1736 the Marquis de la Fare, a friend of the family, arranged an advantageous marriage to Angélique Louise Talon du Boulay to strengthen his position and increase his prospects of promotion. The union brought him influential alliances and some property., as well as ten children, though only two sons and four daughters survived to 1752.

In 1741, Montcalm took part in the Bohemian campaign against Austria, where he served as ADC to the Marquis de la Fare. He returned to France the following year. On 7 March 1743, Montcalm was made colonel of the Auxerrois Infanterie and on 12 April, he was installed a chevalier of the Ordre de Saint-Louis.

In 1745, Montcalm fought in Italy under Maréchal de Maillebois and in 1746, during the disastrous action under the walls of Piacenza, Montcalm twice rallied his regiment. He was wounded and captured during the action. He returned to France on parole in 1747, where he was promoted to the rank of Général de Brigade. He was soon after exchanged and rejoined the army in Italy where he took part in the Battle of Assiette in July. The same year he was severely wounded by a musket ball during the disastrous action of Exilles. In 1749 he received the colonelcy of a cavalry regiment.

On 25 January 1756, Montcalm received a letter sent from Versailles by D'Argenson, Minister of Defence, informing him that he had been selected to command the French troops in Canada with promotion to General-Major. Général de Brigade Chevalier de Lévis was to be his second in command, with the rank of brigadier. On 3 April he sailed from Brest on the frigate *Licorne*. The fleet accompanying him also brought two battalions to reinforce the French Army in Canada: La Sarre and Royal-Roussillon. Montcalm disembarked at Quebec on 11 May. He immediately put Canada in a state of defence by dispatching troops to Fort Carillon (Ticonderoga), Fort Frontenac and Fort Niagara. He then organised the attack on Fort Oswego on Lake Ontario. After a brief siege from 10–14 August, the fort surrendered. Montcalm destroyed the fortifications there, as well as those at Fort Ontario and Fort George. Leaving the area on 21 August, he returned to Montreal.

In the spring of 1757, Montcalm concentrated most of his army at Fort Carillon. On 29 July, he started to advance in two columns upon Fort William Henry which stood near the shores of Lake Saint-Sacrement (Lake George). From 4–9 August, he besieged the fort, which then surrendered; the British garrison was authorised to withdraw into New England, but it was ambushed and largely massacred by Indians. The captured fort was then destroyed and Montcalm withdrew to Carillon.

Next spring, Montcalm expected a British attack on Fort Carillon. He thus reinforced the place with the Berry and Languedoc battalions on 25 June. He supervised the construction of a huge earthwork about 1km in front of the fort. On 6 July a British army under Abercomby landed on the north shore of Lake St Sacrement and marched on Carillon in four columns. After a skirmish where Lord Howe was killed, the British returned to their landing place, but attacked again on 8 July. Abercromby assaulted the entrenchments and, after several repulses, the British retired leaving some 2000 men on the field. Carillon was Montcalm's greatest victory.

By 1759, the strategic situation had seriously deteriorated for the French in Canada. They had lost the port of Louisbourg in Newfoundland, as well as several forts on the western frontier. The British now organised an amphibious expedition against Quebec in the heart of Nouvelle-France, commanded by General Wolfe. He unsuccessfully besieged the city, defended by Montcalm, from July to mid September. Wolfe ordered his troops to burn the French villages along the St Lawrence River, hoping to lure the French out of their entrenched positions around the city. Finally, during the night of 12/13 September, Wolfe landed at a small cove at the foot of the cliffs protecting Quebec. In a matter of hours, his army was drawn up on the Plains of Abraham west of the city fortifications. Montcalm soon appeared at the head of his army, to offer battle. He rode along the ranks encouraging his men and then ordered a general advance. The ensuing battle soon turned to the advantage of the British troops. Montcalm was mortally wounded while trying to rally his men. He died early in the morning of 14 September and was buried in the convent of the Ursulines in the city.

Charles de Rohan, Prince de Soubise

Born on 16 July 1715, in Versailles, Charles de Rohan was the son of Jules François Louis de Rohan, Prince de Soubise, captain-lieutenant of the Gendarmes de la Garde, and Anne-Julie-Adélaïde de Melun. He was also the grandson of the Princesse de Soubise, who is known to history as Madame Pompadour, one of the mistresses of Louis XV. In 1724, Soubise's parents both died from smallpox at Paris. His maternal grandfather Hercule then took charge of him and he was raised at the court where he became the companion of the young Louis XV, who was the same age.

In 1732, Soubise joined the 1st company of the Mousquetaires de la Garde de la Maison du Roi, thus beginning a military career where his close relation with the King and the protection of Madame de Pompadour guaranteed him rapid promotion. In 1733 Soubise was promoted to captain, in 1740 to Général de Brigade and in 1743 to Maréchal de Camp.

Soubise took part to the Battle of Fontenoy in 1745, where he accompanied Louis XV. In 1748 he was appointed lieutenant-general and in 1749, he inherited the estates of Roberval, Rhuis and Saint-Germain. In 1751, Louis XV appointed him Governor General of Flanders and Hainaut and Governor of Lille. In 1755, he was made a Minister of State.

In 1757, soon after the beginning of the Seven Years War, Soubise was placed in command of a corps of 24,000 men which operated together with the Austrian Reichsarmee in Germany. On 5 November, this combined army sustained the crushing defeat of Rossbach at the hands of Frederick the Great. During this battle Soubise was unable to coordinate the action of his troops.

On 23 July 1758, the vanguard of Soubise's army under the Duc de Broglie defeated a Hessian force at Sandershausen. On 10 October, Soubise won the Battle of Lutterberg against an Allied army. For these victories, Soubise was showered with honours and awards, obtained the title of Maréchal de France and being made a peer of the realm. In 1761, Soubise commanded the Army of the Rhine of 110,000 men. The next year he defeated Ferdinand of Brunswick at the Battle of Nauheim, but there were no strategic ramifications.

After the Seven Years War, Soubise lived the life of a courtier in Paris, protected by Madame du Barry and other favourites of the King. In 1774, at the death of Louis XV, his successor Louis XVI confirmed Soubise in his charge of Minister of State. In 1784, after the bankruptcy of his son-in-law and the *collier de la reine* scandals, Soubise retired from public affairs. He died on 4 July 1787.

Hanover

Friedrich Wilhelm Ernst Graf zu Schaumburg-Lippe-Bückeburg

Born on 24 January 1724 in London, the son of Albrecht Wolfgang, Count of Schaumburg-Lippe and his first wife Countess Margarete Gertrud of Oeynhausen (1701–1726), a daughter of King George I and his mistress Ehrengard Melusine von der Schulenburg. Wilhelm accompanied his father in Dutch service during the War of Austrian Succession, and was present at the Battle of Dettingen in 1743. He then fought in Austrian service in their Italian campaign. He succeeded his father as Graf on 25 October 1748 and reformed many aspects of his mini-state; he raised a military force including 300 gunners and introduced general military service liability for young men.

Wilhelm sided with Prussia during the Seven Years War and was appointed a Feldzeugmeister in the Hanoverian Army and fought at Krefeld, Minden (where he was distinguished by his management of the allied artillery), Lutterberg, Wellinghausen, the siege of Münster, Kassel, Wesel and Marburg. In 1762, at the request of the Marquis of Pombal, he took command of the allied troops in Portugal against the Spanish invasion. William conducted a brilliant defensive campaign of marches and counter-marches, so that the enemy, although superior in numbers by a factor of three-to-one, were always confronted by well-placed defenders and never dared an all-out attack. At the request of Pombal, Lippe stayed on for a year after the peace agreement to rebuild and train the Portuguese Army to a more professional standard.

Wilhelm married the Gräfin Marie Barbara Eleonore von Lippe-Biesterfeld (1744–1776) on 12 November 1765. She bore him two children: Emilie (1771–1774) and an unnamed son, who died shortly after his birth in 1772.

Wilhelm was a recognised military theorist and advocated purely defensive warfare. One of his best-known citations is: '*Kein anderer als der Defensivkrieg ist rechtmäßig!*' 'Only defensive warfare is justified!' He built an artillery foundry in Bückeburg and cast cannon for England and Portugal. He also built a small fortress 'Wilhelmstein' which contained an artillery school, at which David von Scharnhorst later studied. Wilhelm died on 10 September 1777 at Wölpinghausen, just west of Steinhudermeer and was succeeded by his cousin, Graf Philipp II, Ernst von Lippe-Alverdissen.

Prussia

Leopold I, Fürst von Anhalt-Dessau

Born 3 July 1676 in Dessau, between Berlin and Leipzig, to Johann Georg II and Henriette Katherina von Oranien. Known as 'Der Alte Dessauer' (the old Dessauer), he was the first important reformer of the Prussian Army and sovereign prince of the House of Anhalt-Dessau. He was also the most popular Prussian general. In 1693, at the age of seventeen, he was made Chef of Infanterie-Regiment Nr 3 and succeeded to the throne of his principality.

It was as a reformer of the musket drill and tactical performance of the Prussian infantry that he was to become famous. He introduced cadenced marching and, in 1718, he replaced the wooden ramrods of the muskets with iron. However, his obsession with the infantry meant that similar tactical improvements in the cavalry and artillery did not take place.

From 2 July–1 September 1695 he took part in the successful Anglo-Austro-Dutch siege of the French-held city of Namur. In 1698, against his parents' wishes, he married the commoner daughter of an apothecary, Anna Luise Föhse. In 1701 the Emperor ennobled her; she acted as Regent of Anhalt-Dessau whenever her husband was away on campaign.

From 1701–1704 he commanded the Prussian troops in the War of the Spanish Succession and was distinguished against the French in the sieges of Kaiserswerth on the lower Rhine (1702), Venlo (April–June 1702), Bonn (1703) and Huy (1703). In that year he was promoted to Generalleutnant and on 20 September he fought at the Battle of Höchstädt. On 13 August 1704, he fought at the Battle of Blindheim (Blenheim). In 1705 he led a Prussian corps down to Italy, where he took part at the Battle of Cassano and of Turin (7 September 1706) under Prince Eugene of Savoy. In 1708 he accompanied Prince Eugene to the Netherlands and in 1709 he fought at the siege of Tournai and the Battle of Malplaquet. In 1710 he was given command of the whole Prussian field army.

In 1712 he again commanded the Prussian field army and was promoted to General Field Marshal after having taken the fortress of Moers without firing a shot. He became a close companion of King Friedrich Wilhelm I and, although a non-smoker – a member of the Tabakcollegium (Tobacco Society), the King's smoking club. In the Great Northern War, Prussia declared against Sweden in 1715; Leopold commanded 40,000 men, and on 16 November he defeated a smaller Swedish force, under King Charles XII on the island of Rügen in the Baltic.

In the subsequent 20 years of peace, Leopold concentrated on perfecting the combat effectiveness of the Prussian infantry, making it the most efficient fighting machine in Europe. Prussian infantry achieved the fastest rates of musketry fire of all European armies, five shots per minute on some occasions. He also interceded on behalf of Crown Prince Friedrich (later Friedrich II/Frederick the Great, who had been condemned to death by his father, King Friedrich Wilhelm for desertion), to have him reinstated in the army. During the war of the Polish Succession (1733–1735), in his capacity of Imperial Field Marshal, he fought on the Rhine, again under Prince Eugene. In 1740 he commanded the Prussian troops which invaded the Austrian province of Upper Silesia in the first Silesian war.

After the death of Eugene of Savoy (24 April 1736) Prince Leopold was considered as the best general in Europe. He served under Frederick the Great in the Second Silesian War (1744–1745). On 14 December 1745, at the age of 68, he won a decisive victory over the Saxons at the Battle of Kesselsdorf.

However, Moritz's fortunes underwent a great negative change. At the Battle of Kolin (18 June 1757) he commanded the infantry of the centre, which, through a misunderstanding with the King, was prematurely drawn into action and failed. In the disastrous days which followed, Moritz was under the cloud of Frederick's displeasure. In October 1757, Prinz Moritz was left with very inadequate forces to defend Berlin against the daring raid of the Austrian General Graf Hadik auf Futak. He was only rehabilitated by his victory at Leuthen (5 December 1757). At the close of the day, Frederick rode down the lines and called out to General Prince Moritz, 'I congratulate you, Herr Feldmarschall!' At Zorndorf (25 August 1758) he again distinguished himself, but at Hochkirch (14 October 1758) he was wounded and captured by the Austrians. Moritz died of blood poisoning soon after his release. At the news of his death, Frederick the Great just said: '*der Alte Dessauer ist verrecket*,' ('the Old Dessauer is dead').

Carl II Wilhelm Ferdinand Braunschweig-Wolfenbüttel

Carl was born on 9 October 1735 in Wolfenbüttel, eldest son of Herzog Carl I. He succeeded to the throne of the duchy in 1780 and had entered the Prussian Army some time before this point and quickly rose to the rank of general. From 1773 he was Chef of Infanterie-Regiment Nr 21 and in 1787, he was appointed Field Marshal. His uncle, Herzog Ferdinand von Braunschweig-Lüneburg (1721–1792), was also a Prussian field marshal. During the Seven Years War, Carl had his baptism of fire when he fought under the Duke of Cumberland in 1757; he led the charge of a brigade at the Battle of Hastenbeck.

On 16 January 1764 he married Princess Augusta, the eldest sister of King George III. In the summer of 1787 he took a force of 26,000 Prussian troops to the fortress of Wesel on the Rhine, and in September he entered the United Provinces to oust the Patriots, avert a civil war and return the governor, William V of Orange, to power. The Patriots fled to Amsterdam, and the city surrendered on 10 October.

During the War of the First Coalition, he received the command of the Prussian and Austrian troops on the river Rhine. His allied invasion of France, aiming to take Paris and rescue the French royal family, failed with the cannonade of Valmy on 20 September 1792. In 1794 he left the Office of the Commander-in-Chief of the Allied Army. During the War of the Fourth Coalition in 1806, he was again appointed Commander-in-Chief of the Prussian Army. For some he was regarded as the reincarnation of Frederick the Great, while others criticised his age and growing indecision. During the Battle of Auerstedt, near Hassenhausen on 14 October 1806, a ball shattered his eyes. He was taken to Ottensen, then in neutral Danish territory, where he died on 10 November. Napoleon dispossessed the duchy and incorporated it into the Kingdom of Westphalia.

August Wilhelm, Herzog von Braunschweig-Wolfenbüttel-Bevern

Born on 10 October 1715 in Braunschweig, August Wilhelm was the son of Herzog Ernst Ferdinand von Braunschweig-Wolfenbüttel-Bevern. August Wilhelm was the founder of the younger Bevern line. He was commissioned into Prussian military service in 1731, and in 1734 he took part in the War of the Polish Succession under King Friedrich Wilhelm I on the Rhine. In 1739 he was promoted to Oberst (colonel) and appointed to command Infanterie-Regiment von Kalkstein Nr 25. In 1740, he took part in the First Silesian War under Frederick the Great, at the sieges of Brieg (now Brzeg) on the upper river Oder and Neisse (now Nysa, north of the Czech border). By this time he had been appointed Chef of Infanterie-Regiment Nr 7 in 1741, and was was wounded at the Battle of Mollwitz on 10 April. In the Second Silesian War, he fought at Hohenfriedberg as General-Major, having been promoted in 1743. In 1746 he was appointed Commandant of Stettin, and in 1750, he was promoted to General-Leutnant.

At the start of the Seven Years War, he commanded a brigade on the Prussian left wing at the Battle of Lobositz on 1 October 1756; when his men ran out of ammunition, he ordered a bayonet charge, which decided the battle. He also fought at Reichenberg on 21 April 1757, where he commanded and defeated the Austrian General Graf von Königsegg. He also fought at Prague on 6 May, where he commanded part of the right wing. At the Prussian defeat at the Battle of Kolin, on 18 June 1757, he again commanded the right wing.

He was accused by General-Major von Retzow (commander of Grenadiergardebtaillon Nr 6) of having wilfully failed to go to the aid of Generalleutnant von Winterfeldt, when the latter was defeated and mortally wounded in the clash at Moys on 7 September 1757, but the charge was considered baseless. He was then appointed Commander-in-Chief in Silesia, but was twice defeated by the Austrians under Herzog Karl von Lothringen at the Battle of Breslau (22 November) and was captured the next day. In May 1758 he returned from captivity and was appointed governor of Stettin. Next year, he was promoted to General. In August 1762, he conducted another siege of Schweidnitz; Austrian Field Marshal von Daun attempted to relieve it on 16 August, but was driven off by von Bevern at the Battle of Reichenbach about 18km southeast of the fortress. The place fell on 9 October. The Herzog died on 2 August 1781 as Governor of Stettin (now Szczecin).

Ferdinand, Herzog von Brunswick-Lüneburg

Ferdinand was born on 12 January 1721 in Wolfenbüttel. The fourth son of Ferdinand Albert II, Duke of Brunswick-Lüneburg, Ferdinand joined the Prussian Army as a colonel in 1740. He was present at the battles of Mollwitz and Chotusitz, and after Markgraf Wilhelm von Brandenburg was killed in 1744, Ferdinand became Chef of Frederick the Great's Leibgarde, Infantry Regiment Nr 15. At the Battle of Soor (30 September 1745) he distinguished himself greatly, especially in the assault of a steep hill, incidentally defended by his older brother Duke Ludwig Ernst of Brunswick-Lüneburg, who was in Austrian service, commanding the Infanterie-Regiment Alt-Wolfenbüttel. Ferdinand fought in the Second Silesian War before leading part of the invasion of Saxony and Bohemia in 1756 during the Seven Years War. He participated at the Battle of Rossbach, and then became commander of the Allied Hanoverian Army.

In the first campaign of the Seven Years War, Ferdinand, now a lieutenant-general, commanded one of the Prussian columns which converged upon Dresden, and in the operations which led up to the surrender of the Saxon Army at Pirna (1756). At the Battle of Lobositz he led the right wing of the Prussian infantry. In 1757, he distinguished himself at Prague, and also served in the Rossbach campaign.

Shortly after this, he took command of the German Army of Observation from the Duke of Cumberland, who had failed to prevent the French invasion of Hanover. Ferdinand accepted the appointment on the condition that he would have direct access to King George II. His new commission placed him in Hanoverian service, but, despite this, Frederick the Great continued to communicate with him as though he were under his direct command.

He found the army dejected by a reverse and a capitulation, yet within a week of his taking up the command, he assumed the offensive, and thus began a victorious career. By the spring of 1758 he had driven the French out of Hanover and back across the Rhine, which made his reputation in Britain, and helped boost support for British involvement in the war. From June 1758, following the capture of the port of Emden on the river Ems, British troops arrived on the continent and were placed under Ferdinand's command. In the War of the Austrian Succession, he fought at the battles of Mollwitz, Chotusitz and Soor.

In promoting him to Field Marshal in November 1758, Frederick the Great acknowledged his debt in the words, '*Je n'ai fait que ce que je dois, mon cher Ferdinand*.' After Minden, King George II of Great Britain appointed him to the Order of the Garter, and the thanks of the British Parliament were voted on the same occasion. Later in the war, he fought at Rheinberg, Krefeld, Minden, Kloster Kamp, Vellinghausen, Wilhelmstal, Warburg, the Second Battle of Lutterberg and at the siege of Kassel. After the war, he was honoured by other sovereigns, and he received the rank of field marshal and a regiment from the Austrians.

The estrangement of Frederick the Great and Ferdinand in 1766 led to the Duke's retirement from Prussian service, but there was no open breach between the old friends. Ferdinand retired to Brunswick and his castle of Vechelde, where he occupied himself in building and other improvements. He became a patron of art and education, and a great benefactor of the poor. He died on 3 July 1792.

Field Marshal James Francis Edward Keith

Born on 11 June 1696 in the castle of Inverugie, near Peterhead, the second son of William, 9th Earl Marischal of Scotland. His elder brother (the last Earl Marischal, the friend of Frederick the Great), had exclusive rights to the family honours. Of fervent Jacobite stock, both he and his brother took the wrong side in the rebellion of 1715 and were forced to flee Scotland. Initially James entered Spanish service, but, being a Protestant, his prospects were extremely limited. He then decided to try his luck in Russia and was fortunate enough to gain a recommendation to Tsar Peter II, who granted him a commission.

Keith arrived in Moscow in 1729, and at once gained the favour of the young sovereign (partly taught in military matters by the Scot, Captain Bruce), who gave him a lieutenant-colonel's commission in a newly-raised regiment of guards of which Count Lowenwolde was Colonel. He rose rapidly, because he always did his military duty and refused to get involved in court politics.

He was soon in the field against Sweden in the Great Northern War, where he was active in the reduction of the fortress of Willmannstrand. The war went on until the capture of Helsingfors and the Åland Islands forced the cession of Karelia to Russia in 1721. It was in Wilmannstrand that he met an orphan prisoner, Eva Merthens, who became his mistress. On his death he left all his money to her and their children.

The Tsar died in 1730 and Keith took the oath of allegiance to the new Tsarina, Anna Ivanovna, Duchess of Courland (niece of Peter the Great), who came from Mittau, near Riga in Latvia, to assume the Russian throne. Keith was made lieutenant-colonel of her bodyguard, a pivotal position. When the Polish war came in 1733, he found himself serving under the Irish Catholic, General de Lacy. The Russians besieged Danzig in 1734; after its fall, Keith was promoted to Lieutenant-General, but Keith did not like the work of pacifying Poland, a task he thought 'not a very honourable one.' He next fought in the war against Prussia, and then against the Turks in the Ukraine. Keith was wounded in the knee at Otchakoff on 2 July 1737. 'I had sooner,' said the Tsarina Anna, 'lose ten thousand of my best soldiers than Keith.' Although this latter war was successful, culminating in the capture of Jassy in 1739, Keith protested against his commander, General von Münnich's waste of human life. On his return to Russia, he was appointed Governor of the Ukraine; his humane rule made him judged to be one of the best governors that unfortunate country had ever had.

On the death of the Tsarina Anna on 28 October 1740, her grandnephew, the minor, Ivan Antonovitch (of Brunswick) was declared Tsar. For 22 days Anna's favourite, Johann Ernst Biron, Duke of Courland, acted as Regent, but a palace revolution gave the position to the Tsar's mother, Anna Leopoldovna. Her rule was weak and brief, ending suddenly on 25 November 1741, when her mother's cousin, Elizabeth (younger daughter of Peter the Great) put herself at the head of her Guards, assumed the title of Tsarina, and sent the deposed royal family into permanent exile.

Foreign officers in Russian service enjoyed less success under Elizabeth than they had under Anna, and Generals Douglas, Keith, Lieven and Lowendahl, soon all tendered their resignations. To encourage him to stay, Elizabeth offered Keith the command in chief in the war against the Persians and the Order of St Andrew, Keith stayed, took the Order, but did not accept the command.

During the War of the Austrian Succession Keith was very successful, later appointed commander-in-chief of the army on that front and Minister Plenipotentiary to Sweden, receiving ceremonial swords and honours. Keith also fought in the Prussian campaign (1741–1743), but his star was now on the wane, his commands removed one by one. It was said that the amorous Empress wished to marry him, and he feared Siberia if he refused.

Keith had tired of Russian service; in 1747 he was allowed to resign his commission. He promptly entered the service of Frederick the Great as a field marshal. Two years later, he was appointed Governor of Berlin. In 1756, at the outbreak of the Seven Years War, he commanded the troops covering the siege of the Saxon Army at Pirna, and distinguished himself at the Battle of Lobositz. In 1757, he commanded at the siege of Prague and later in this same campaign he defended Leipzig against a greatly superior force. Keith was present at the great Prussian victory of Rossbach, and, while the King was fighting the campaign of Leuthen, he conducted a raid into Bohemia.

In 1758 he was again in the field, only to die, leading a desperate attempt to turn the tide in the Prussian defeat at the Battle of Hochkirch. He was buried on the field with military honours by the Austrian Marshal Daun and General Lacy (the son of his old commander in Russia). Soon afterwards, Frederick transferred Keith's body to the garrison church of Berlin.

August Wilhelm, Prinz von Preussen

Born on 9 August 1714, August Wilhelm (known as Wilhelm) was the brother of Frederick the Great and eleventh son of King Friedrich Wilhelm I of Prussia. In 1744 he received the title 'Prinz von Preussen' and was Crown Prince to his brother. He entered the army at an early age, as was the custom, and in 1741 was promoted to General-Major in the cavalry. In 1745 he was promoted to General-Leutnant and two years later to General der Infanterie. He was a benevolent and very popular officer.

Following his defeat by the Austrians under Field Marshal Graf von Daun at the Battle of Kollin (18 June 1757), Frederick the Great was forced to raise the siege of Prague; he then divided his army. That part on the right bank of the river Elbe (52 battalions and 80 squadrons), he gave command of to Prince Moritz von Anhalt-Dessau, a man of proven courage, an excellent subordinate commander but unsuited for independent command. Moritz proposed to withdraw north to Zittau in Saxony, east of Dresden, but the King forbade this. Frederick gave command of the other half of the army (30,000 strong) to his brother, Wilhelm, with generals von Winterfeld and von Schmettau as close advisers. At this point, Frederick's part of the army was around Leitmeritz, midway between Prague and Dresden; that of Prince Wilhelm was at Jungbunzlau on the river Iser almost 100km off to the east. The aim was for the army to reunite at Bautzen, northeast of Dresden.

When Prince Wilhelm took command, he was given orders to stay at Leitmeritz on the Elbe for as long as possible and to maintain a ten-day supply of bread at all times. This was so that he would be able to advance east to the defence of the fortress of Schweidnitz if the Austrians invaded Silesia. He was also to raise reinforcements in Silesia and use them to escort convoys of flour to the army at Zittau and to scout out and report on all possible routes in the area.

On 1 July von Daun crossed the Elbe and pushed a force under General von Nadasdy to within 7km of Jungbunzlau. Prince Wilhelm withdrew two marches to Neuschloss, where he left the direct route to Gabel and Zittau and went north to Böhmisch-Leypa about 70km south of Bautzen and 50km northwest of Gabel. This was halfway between the King and Zittau. Frederick approved both withdrawals in retrospect, but wrote: 'If you withdraw any further, you will soon have your back to the gates of Berlin.'

On 7 July, von Daun reached Münchengrätz, about 35km east of the Prince's position in Böhmisch-Leypa. To avoid a battle, Wilhelm sought permission to withdraw to Gabel, south of Zittau, to which the King agreed on 5 July, but added that the Prince should then fortify his position, concentrate all possible forces in Silesia with him and advance south again to Neuschloss, as that would be the best way to force von Lothringen to abandon any further offensive moves. Prince Wilhelm had held a council of war on 14 July, where it was decided to march northeast to the main magazine at Zittau (away from the King) via Kaunitz and Rumburg, as one officer had said that 'The roads were good and there was an Austrian corps on the better road through Georgenthal.' This, it transpired, was the worst possible decision, as the information was incorrect.

The Austrians under General Graf Maquire von Inniskiling, took Gabel and the magazines in the town on 15 July. The Prussian garrison of 2000 men of Infanterie-Regiments Nr 43 and 46, under General-Major Nikolaus Lorenz von Puttkammer were mostly captured.

On 17 July Prussian General von Schmettau was sent off to reinforce the garrison of Zittau, but he arrived only on 19 July. Prince Wilhem followed; the mountain roads were narrow and led through forests from which Austrian light troops (Grenzers, hussars and Croats) mounted a series of crippling ambushes, causing traffic jams and splitting up the columns. The weather was awful, the drivers fled, some 2000 soldiers deserted and the ammunition wagons, rations and pontoons were abandoned.

Meanwhile, the Austrians, under Maquire, had fallen upon Zittau on 19 July and bombarded the place, setting fire to the rations for 40,000 men for three weeks. On 23 July Zittau surrendered, while Prince Wilhelm, with a force superior to that of the Austrians, was stuck in the woods about 10km away. The Prussian garrison (Infanterie-Regiments Nr 37, 49 and the grenadiers of Infantry Regiment Nr 42 under Oberst von Diericke) surrendered. Following this disaster, Prince Wilhelm withdrew northwest for five days to Bautzen; he was not pursued, but his army dissolved behind him.

King Frederick arrived at Bautzen on 29 July; the atmosphere between the royal brothers was icy. As the Prince sought to hand over his report, the king wheeled his horse and rode off. With the exception of von Winterfeld (his ADC and favourite), the King was extremely critical of the generals who had been with the Prince. The debacle had forced the King to abandon Bohemia and the whole army was demoralised. The magazines at Zittau and Gabel, the towns themselves and the entire supply train had been lost, all due to Prince Wilhelm and his advisors. The King ordered General-Leutnant von Winterfeld to convey his displeasure to the Crown Prince and the rest of his generals: 'You all deserve to be court-martialled for your conduct; you deserve to lose your heads, but the King does not wish to push this matter so far, as he cannot forget that one general is also his brother.'

Prinz Wilhelm's command was given to the Herzog von Braunschweig-Bevern. Shortly after this, Wilhelm left the army and returned to his castle at Oranienburg, where he died on 12 June 1758.

Friedrich Heinrich Ludwig, Prinz von Preussen

Friedrich Heinrich was born on 18 January 1726 in Berlin. He was the thirteenth child of King Friedrich Wilhelm I of Prussia and his wife, Queen Sophie Dorothea (von Hannover). He was known as 'Prinz Heinrich von Preussen'.

In 1740, at the age of 14, he was made Chef (Colonel-in-Chief) of Füsilier-Regiment Nr 35, a post he held until his death. His military training was overseen by Oberst von Stille, whom he accompanied as adjutant in the First Silesian War (1740–1742), fighting at the Battle of Chotusitz on 17 May 1742. From May 1744 he received permission to drill his regiment himself. In the Second Silesian War (1744–1745) he again took the field and was almost taken prisoner on one occasion. He earned his spurs at the Prussian victory at the Battle of Hohenfriedberg on 4 June 1753. On 15 July he was promoted to General-Major. He also distinguished himself in the clash of Trautenau on the subsequent retreat. He then fell ill with smallpox and had to leave the field. Over several campaigns, he proved himself to be a much more careful general than his brother, husbanding his men well and taking fewer casualties. Although he was ever in his elder brother's shadow, he knew his generalship well enough to criticise some aspects of Frederick the Great's martial skills and foreign policy in a pamphlet published in 1753 under the nom-de-plume of 'Maréchal Gessler'.

At the outbreak of the Seven Years War in 1756, Heinrich commanded an infantry Brigade during the invasion of Saxony. On 16 February 1757 he was promoted to Generallleutnant. At the Battle of Prague (6 May 1757) he commanded the Prussian left wing (Generals von Schwerin with the infantry and von Zieten with the cavalry), which rolled up the Austrian right wing and secured the Prussian victory.

Following the Prussian defeat at Kolin which led to the abandonment of Bohemia by Frederick the Great, he commanded the rearguard under Feldmarschall Keith as they fell back into Saxony and was distinguished in the clash at Lietmeritz. In the legendary Prussian victory of Rossbach (5 November 1757), Heinrich commanded the right wing. He was wounded and forced to return to Leipzig until the spring of 1758.

He was then given command of an independent force, covering the line of the river Elbe against Franco-Imperial incursions. He also managed to recover the Duchy of Brunswick from French control. In 1759 he went on the offensive and advanced southwards to the river Main. After the devastating Prussian defeat by the Austro-Russians at the Battle of Kunersdorf on the lower River Oder (12 August 1759) his royal brother fell into a state of depression for four days, during which time, Heinrich assumed command of the army. On 25 September, after slipping away from under Austrian Field Marshal von Daun's nose at Görlitz, on the upper River Neisse two days earlier, he defeated an Austrian corps of 3000 men under General von Wehla at Hoyerswerda, northeast of Dresden, and pushed the French-Imperialist army back west to Bautzen. This minor victory at Hoyerswerda caused the ultra-cautious Austrian commander-in-chief, General Graf Leopold Joseph von Daun, to abandon further operations against Prussia for this year. On 29 October, Prinz Heinrich defeated another minor Austrian corps at Pretsch.

Heinrich was appointed Commander-in-Chief in Silesia in 1760; he relieved Breslau and prevented the union of the Austrian and Russian armies. In 1761 he was given the Saxon theatre to command and was again successful. On 29 October 1762, with 22,000 men, he defeated an Austrian force of 30,000 under Field Marshal Prinz Christian Karl von Stolberg-Gedern at Freiberg, between Dresden and Chemnitz, causing them some 7400 casualties. This was the last major action of the war.

After 1763, Heinrich embarked on a diplomatic career, visiting Stockholm and St Petersburg, preparing the ground for the First Partition of Poland in August 1772. He was an active Freemason, and was popular with the upper ranks of European society. He was offered the crown of Poland, much to his royal brother's annoyance. The partition of Poland took place, Prussia, Russia and Austria each slicing off chunks of the hapless state.

In 1778 he again commanded an army in the War of the Bavarian Succession, a low-key affair, but showed little energy or activity, which earned him much criticism from the King. On several occasions he was aided by Generalfeldmarschall von Kalckreuth on his staff. Following the death of Frederick the Great in 1786, Heinrich hoped to have great influence over his successor, Friedrich Wilhelm II, but this was not to be.

In the grounds of his palace in Rheinsberg, Heinrich built an obelisk, on which were the names of all those Prussian generals who had fallen foul of his royal brother. He died on 3 August 1802.

King Friedrich II (Frederick the Great)

Frederick was born on 24 January 1712. He was of the Hohenzollern dynasty and in his role as a prince-elector of the Holy Roman Empire, he was Friedrich IV of Brandenburg. He was also the Prince of Neuchatel through marriage.

His father was Friedrich Wilhelm I, the Soldier King, who spent a fortune collecting tall men from all over Europe to serve in his Grenadier-Garde-Bataillon. The two had a difficult relationship. In 1730 Frederick tried to flee to England, together with his friend, Hans Hermann von Katte, a lieutenant of cuirassiers. They were caught and imprisoned in Küstrin fortress, and the King had them court-martialled and condemned to death for desertion. Frederick was pardoned, but von Katte was beheaded on 30 November 1730, while the Crown Prince was forced to watch.

On 12 June 1733, Frederick entered an arranged marriage with Elisabeth Christine of Brunswick-Bevern, a Protestant relative of the Austrian Habsburgs. He wrote to his sister Wilelmina that, 'There can be neither love nor friendship between us' and he considered suicide, but agreed to the match. He had little in common with his bride and resented the political marriage as an example of the Austrian interference which had plagued Prussia since 1701. Once Frederick secured the throne in 1740, he prevented Elisabeth from visiting his court in Potsdam, granting her instead Schönhausen Palace and apartments at the Berliner Stadtschloss; despite this, his wife remained devoted to him.

Frederick was what modern historians would term an enlightened absolutist monarch. He had a close if turbulent friendship with Voltaire and the two corresponded for years. He modernised the Prussian bureaucracy and civil service and promoted religious tolerance throughout his realm. He patronised the arts and philosophers, and he himself wrote and played music for the flute.

Shortly after becoming king, he attacked Austria in the First Silesian War (1740–1742) and wrested that province from her. He justifiably won much military acclaim for himself and his Prussian Army, the infantry of which were then the best in Europe. Often a brilliant general and master of the exploitation of his interior lines against the enemies who almost always surrounded him, Frederick was occasionally prone to committing resounding military blunders, such as at the Battle Hochkirch on 14 October 1758. He was again at war with Austria – and much of the rest of Europe – in the Second Silesian War and the Seven Years War, up to 1763. By that time Prussia had become a powerful nation.

Near the end of his life, Frederick united most of his disconnected realm through the First Partition of Poland on 22 September 1772. He died on 17 August 1786 and was buried at his favourite residence, Sanssouci in Potsdam, just outside Berlin. Because he died childless, Frederick was succeeded by his nephew, Friedrich Wilhelm II of Prussia, son of his brother, Prince August Wilhelm.

Kurt Christoph, Graf von Schwerin

Born on 26 October 1684 in Löwitz, Pomerania, in 1700, Schwerin joined the Schwerin regiment of his uncle, the lieutenant-general Dettlof von Schwerin, in the company of his brother, Oberstleutnant Bernd Detlof von Schwerin. In 1701, at the beginning of the War of the Spanish Succession, the regiment was transferred to Holland. In 1703, he was commissioned as Leutnant, and on 2 July 1704, he fought at the Battle of Schellenberg (Donauwörth) and at Blindheim (Blenheim) on 13 August. In 1705 he was promoted to Kapitän and Kiech, and in 1707 to Oberstleutnant (lieutenant-colonel). He fought at the battles of Ramillies (23 May 1706), Malplaquet (11 September 1709) and Gadebusch (9 December 1712), under the Swedish commander General Magnus Stenbock.

He then accompanied the Swedish Army on their invasion of Russia in 1707, was promoted to Oberst in 1708, and fought at the Battle of Poltava, in the central Ukraine, on 8 July 1709. The Swedish King Karl XII had been wounded prior to the battle, and Swedish Field Marshal Carl Gustaf Rehnskiöld commanded the army. Peter the Great commanded a superior Russian army, which had been reformed and retrained since previous battlefield debacles, and the outcome was a crushing Swedish defeat. The King and the survivors (including Schwerin) fled into the Turkish-controlled city-fortress of Bender, in Moldova, on the river Dniestr. The Turks tolerated (and paid for) the Swedes for four years, but then turned against King Karl and attacked him on 1 February 1713; Schwerin was captured at the 'Kalabalik' (crowd or mob) of Bender, together with the King Karl.

On 3 September 1713 he was promoted to General-Major by Herzog Friedrich Wilhelm von Mecklenburg-Schwerin. In 1719, he conducted a brilliant action on 6 March at Walsmühlen, in Mecklenburg, against the invading Hanoverian Army. As a reward, he was promoted to General-Leutnant two days later. The Great Northern War ended very soon after the death of Karl XII on 11 December 1718; in the subsequent Treaty of Stockholm of 1720 (between Sweden on the one side and Prussia and Hanover on the other), part of Mecklenburg-Strelitz fell to Prussia. Schwerin thus transferred into Prussian service, as General-Major, under King Friedrich Wilhelm I. Initially, he was employed on diplomatic missions for his new ruler, but, in 1722, he was appointed Chef of Infanterie-Regiment Nr 24. In 1730 he was a member of the court-martial which tried the future Frederick the Great and his friend, Hans Hermann von Katte, and condemned von Katte to death. That same year, he was appointed governor of Peitz, a town in eastern Brandenburg, near the confluence of the rivers Spree and Neisse. In 1731 he was promoted to General-Leutnant and on 8 March 1733, he was awarded the High Order of the Black Eagle. In 1739, he was promoted General of Infantry, and on 30 June 1740 to General Field Marshal; he was ennobled Graf a month later. On 10 April 1741, during the War of the Austrian Succession, he won the Battle of Mollwitz against the Austrians, which secured Prussia's grip on Silesia.

In 1742, after the conclusion of the First Silesian War, Schwerin was governor of the important fortresses of Brieg on the Oder and Neisse, on the river of the same name. In the Second Silesian War (1744–1745), Schwerin commanded part of the Prussian Army which, marching from Glatz, met Frederick the Great's section of the army under the walls of Prague and took the Ziskaberg fortress. Schwerin then played an important role in the siege and capture of Prague (16 September 1744). When Frederick II was compelled to retreat from Bohemia, Schwerin again distinguished himself. He then retired to his estate during the years of peace.

In 1757, Schwerin led the Prussian columns that invaded Bohemia, operating successfully against the superior Austrian Army. He then joined King Frederick, who was laying siege to Prague. On 6 May, leading an assault on the left wing, with the colour of an infantry regiment in his hands, he was killed by a musket ball.

Friedrich Wilhelm Freiherr von Seydlitz

Born on 3 February 1721 in Kalkar, in the Duchy of Cleve on the lower Rhine in western Germany, Friedrich Wilhelm was the son of Luise von Tugendreich and Daniel Florian Freiherr von Seydlitz, a captain in the Prussian Dragoner-Regiment von Sonsfeld Nr 2, stationed at Kalkar. The family came from the Swedish state of Mecklenburg-Schwedt.

Friedrich's father died in 1728; his widow moved to Freienwalde-an-der-Oder, northeast of Berlin, where Seydlitz was brought up in straitened circumstances. In 1735, at the age of fourteen, he went as a page to the court of Markgraf Friedrich Wilhelm von Brandenburg-Schwedt (his father's old colonel). Here he acquired mastery of horsemanship as well as a love of tobacco, alcohol and women. In 1740, Seydlitz was commissioned Kornett in the Markgraf Friedrich von Brandenburg-Schwedt's Kürassier-Regiment Nr 5. During the First Silesian War, he served as a subaltern under Oberst von Rochow.

On 20 May 1742, the regiment was camped in Kranowitz near Ratibor, on the northern border of the modern Czech Republic. Oberst von Rochow, learning that some 6000 Hungarian irregulars were approaching the town, sent Seydlitz with 30 men to hold a village in front of his position. The Hungarians attacked and Seydlitz was captured after putting up a brave fight. He was imprisoned in the fortress of Raab, in western Hungary. When King Frederick II heard of his gallant conduct, he offered to exchange an Austrian captain for him. This was done on 11 June. In 1743, von Seydlitz was promoted to captain in the Husaren-Regiment von Natzmer Nr 4.

At the end of the First Silesian War his regiment was cantoned in Trebnitz, east of Berlin; at the renewed outbreak of hostilities in 1744, the regiment was assigned to the vanguard of General-Leutnant von Nassau. On 22 May 1745, the regiment attacked an Austrian unit near the town of Katholisch-Hennersdorf near Landeshut, but were defeated. On 4 June at the Battle of Hohenfriedberg, they were on the Prussian right wing. During the battle, Seydlitz captured the Saxon General von Schlichting; for this, he was promoted to major. On 30 September that same year, at the Battle of Soor, Seydlitz was wounded by a musket ball in the left arm during this hard-fought action, which was a costly Prussian victory. Later in 1745, Seydlitz was again in action against the Austrian rearguard under General Graf von Burghausen near Zittau in south-east Saxony and routed them.

In 1752, von Seydlitz was promoted to Oberstleutnant. He had forged a reputation for being an exemplary cavalry officer and was transferred to Dragoner-Regiment Nr 2 (Prinz Ludwig von Württemberg), tasked with bringing it up to standard. In 1753 he was transferred again, taking command of Kürassier-Regiment von Rochow Nr 8 which soon became another model cavalry unit. In 1755, he was promoted to Oberst.

In 1756, at the beginning of the Seven Years War, Seydlitz's regiment took part to the invasion of Saxony, in Ferdinand of Brunswick's column, which advanced upon Pirna via Leipzig and Dresden. The unprepared Saxon Army was concentrated at Pirna southeast of Dresden and was quickly surrounded and blockaded by the Prussians. Seydlitz's regiment advanced up the river Elbe with the army of Frederick the Great, to intercept an Austrian relief force led by Field Marshal Maximilian von Browne. The armies clashed at Lobositz on 1 October. Seydlitz's regiment took part in the second Prussian charge which, after initial success, was broken up and he was almost captured. The Prussians were finally victorious and the Saxon Army surrendered, due to lack of food. In 1757, Seydlitz was attached to the advanced guard of the column of Prince Moritz von Anhalt-Dessau, but did not take part in the Battle of Prague on 6 May, as it was on the opposite side of the river Moldau.

Following the Prussian victory at Prague, Seydlitz's Kürassier-Regiment Nr 8 accompanied the King, who moved east to intercept the Austrian relief army of Field Marshal Graf Leopold von Daun. On 18 June, at the Battle of Kolin, General-Major von Krosigk's cavalry brigade (Kürassier-Regiment Nr 2, Kürassier-Regiment Nr 8 and Dragoner-Regiment Nr 1) was ordered to support the faltering Prussian line. Krosigk was killed in this action and Seydlitz assumed command. He counterattacked the Austrian cavalry with Dragoner-Regiment Württemberg and the Saxon Karabiniers, who were pursuing the defeated units of General-Major von Pennavaire's brigade. Seydlitz's charge broke the enemy cavalry and overthrew Infanterie-Regiment Haller Nr 31. But the battle was lost and the Prussians withdrew after dark, the cavalry regiments of Seydlitz and Ziethen providing the rearguard. On 20 June, von Seydlitz was promoted to General-Major and awarded the Pour le Merite (one of the highest Prussian military and civil orders, awarded for valuable services to the state).

In September 1757, Frederick's army was back in Saxony to oppose the advance of a Franco-Imperial Army under the joint commands of the French Prince Charles de Soubise and General-Leutnant Prinz Joseph Friedrich von Sachsen-Hildburghausen. On 19 September, Seydlitz with some 1800 men surprised a superior force of 6000 infantry and 4000 cavalry in Gotha, west of Erfurt. On the morning of 5 November, before the Battle of Rossbach, Frederick placed Seydlitz in command of his entire cavalry (38 squadrons), thus superseding two more senior generals. The role of Seydlitz in the ensuing battle was decisive. The Franco-Imperial cavalry managed to resist the charge of his first line of 15 squadrons, but Seydlitz immediately launched his second line (18 squadrons) routing the enemy. He then quickly rallied his squadrons north of Reichardtswerben, advanced south to Tagewerben and launched a decisive assault on the enemy infantry to the west, routing it completely. Seydlitz was wounded in an arm during this battle. He left the army to recuperate which took some time, as he was already suffering from syphilis, acquired several years previously. On 20 November, he was awarded the High Order of the Black Eagle and was promoted to General-Leutnant.

In 1758 he fought at Hochkirch (14 October) and Zorndorf (24 August). In the latter action, he was given command of the cavalry on the left wing. He refused to obey the initial orders given to him by Frederick and awaited what he considered to be the proper moment to launch a cavalry charge against the advancing Russians. He quickly routed the enemy cavalry; he then rallied and charged the Russian infantry, but failed to break it. He rallied his cavalry behind Zorndorf, waiting for a better moment to attack. Just when all seemed lost for the Prussians, Seydlitz led 61 squadrons against the Russian cavalry, pushing it back into the marshes by the village of Quartschen. He then returned to rescue the Prussian infantry, forcing the Russians to fall back.

On 12 August 1759, at Kunersdorf about 5km east of Frankfurt/Oder, the Prussian Army faced an Austro-Russian army. Seydlitz and the Prince von Württemberg tried to outflank the enemy left wing around the ponds near the village, but they quickly realised that the area was swampy and not good for cavalry and halted. Frederick repeatedly ordered Seydlitz to charge, whatever the state of the ground. He finally obeyed and was wounded during the charge, which was beaten off. The Prussians were badly beaten, but the Austro-Russians did not follow up their victory. After the battle, Seydlitz was taken to Berlin to recover. On 18 April 1760, during his convalescence, he married Susanna Albertina, Gräfin von Hacke.

In May 1760, although not fully recovered, Seydlitz rejoined the King at Meissen, but seeing his condition, Frederick sent him back to Berlin to recover. In early October of that year, a small Russian corps under General von Todleben crossed the river Oder and threatened Berlin. Seydlitz (though still sick) opposed any withdrawal; at the head of an improvised force, he routed some Cossacks near Köpenick, just southeast of the capital. However, the arrival of Russian reinforcements obliged the Prussians to abandon Berlin and to withdraw west, to Spandau. The arrival of Prussian reinforcements caused the Russians to withdraw.

On 20 May 1761, Seydlitz reported for duty to Prinz Heinrich in Saxony. He was given an independent command composed of troops of all arms. It was the first time that he had other arms than cavalry under his command and many doubted his ability to handle them. On 25 August, Seydlitz, led his command (15,000 horse and several infantry battalions) to Nauendorf, north of Halle/Saale. He brushed with the Austrians on 26 August and on 2 and 4 September. In October, he commanded a force to head off a French advance on Magdeburg.

In 1762, Seydlitz commanded a division of Prinz Heinrich's army in Saxony. On 12 May, he took part to the crossing of the Mulda in southern Saxony. From 27–29 September, Prince Heinrich stopped several Austrian counter-attacks along the river. On 14 and 15 October the Austrians concentrated their attacks on the Prussian right wing. Seydlitz was forced to retire after losing 2000 men and 10 guns. On 16 October, Prince Henry had to retire to Reichenbach, between Döbeln and Mittweida. Then on 29 October, Prince Heinrich counter-attacked the Austrians at Freiberg on the river Freiberger Mulde, between Chemnitz and Dresden. The Allies were entrenched to the southwest of Freiberg. Seydlitz commanded the right wing. He led a decisive bayonet charge at the head of two of his grenadier battalions against the Dreikreuzer Heights. Soon the Imperial Army was retreating across the Mulda, southeast to Frauenstein, later east to Pirna, on the left bank of the river Elbe, upstream from Dresden. This was the last battle of the war.

After the Peace of Hubertusburg, Seydlitz was made Inspector-General of the Cavalry in Silesia. The most promising cavalry officers were systematically sent to him to have their tactical skills polished and honed. In 1767, Seydlitz was promoted to General der Kavallerie. His later years were clouded by domestic difficulties and he fell out badly with the King, although during his last illness, Frederick visited him a last time. Seydlitz died at Ohlau on 27 August 1773.

Hans Karl von Winterfeldt

Winterfeldt was born on 4 April 1707, in Vanselow, Pomerania, south of Greifswald on the Baltic coast. In 1720 he entered Kürassier-Regiment Nr 12, of which his uncle, Major-General von Winterfeldt, was Chef. In 1722, he was commissioned cornet. His tall stature and soldierly bearing attracted the attention of King Friedrich Wilhelm I, who had him transferred him to his Grenadier-Garde-Bataillon (Infanterie-Regiment Nr 6), the 'Giant Grenadiers' as a lieutenant. He was soon ADC to the King. In 1732, Winterfeldt was sent with a party of selected non-commissioned officers to St Petersburg, to assist in the organisation of the Russian Army of Tsar Peter II. While the guest of Field Marshal Count Burkhard Christoph von Münnich (a native of Oldenburg in Germany), he fell in love with and married his own cousin, Julie von Maltzahn, who was the Marshal's stepdaughter and a maid-of-honour to the Grand Duchess Elizabeth.

In 1734, Winterfeldt became friendly with the Crown Prince (later Fredrick the Great) whom he accompanied on the Rhine campaign. This complicated his relationship with the King, who was at odds with his son. However, Winterfeldt remained Frederick's friend. In 1740 Frederick II succeeded to the throne; Winterfeldt was promoted major and appointed his ADC. On 16 December of that year, following the death of the Holy Roman Emperor, Charles VI of Austria, Frederick II invaded the Austrian province of Silesia and the First Silesian War broke out. Winterfeldt was sent on a mission to St Petersburg, to gain the support of the Tsar, but was unsuccessful.

On 10 April 1741, at the Battle of Mollwitz, Winterfeldt commanded a grenadier battalion with great distinction. On 17 May, Winterfeldt won further glory in the celebrated minor clash of

Rothschloss, where the Prussian hussars defeated the Austrians. In June 1741, Winterfeldt was promoted to Oberst. The First Silesian War ended in 1742; it was quickly followed by the Second, which broke out in 1744 and lasted until 21 December 1745, when it was ended by the Treaty of Dresden. Silesia remained firmly in Prussia's grip.

In 1745, Winterfeldt was promoted to General-Major, his commission back-dated to January 1743. After the Prussian victory of Hohenfriedberg (4 June 1745), Frederick gave Winterfeldt the estate of Tatiau for his service. On 24 November, at Katholisch-Hennersdorf, where the sudden and unexpected invasion of the Austro-Saxons was checked by the vigour of General von Zieten, Winterfeldt arrived on the field in time to take a decisive part in the victory. During the ten years' peace that followed, Winterfeldt was in constant attendance upon the King, except when employed on confidential missions. In 1756, Winterfeldt was promoted to General-Leutnant and awarded the High Order of the Black Eagle; he was also sent to England, to negotiate the Convention of Westminster (16 January 1756) by which each party agreed to combine to protect the Electorate of Hanover from foreign invasion. Frederick opened the Seven Years War with a pre-emptive strike against Saxony; Winterfeldt advised him against absorbing the Saxon troops into his own army, but was ignored.

Winterfeldt's close relationship with the King earned him many enemies among the rest of the royal entourage. In 1757, von Winterfeldt fought at Prague (6 May) and was entrusted with the command of the retreat after the Battle of Kolin on 18 June. During these operations, Winterfeldt was obliged to work in close contact with the King's brother, Prinz Wilhelm, Herzog Wilhelm von Braunschweig-Bevern, General von Zieten and others of his enemies. Prinz Wilhelm's corps of the army was badly mauled by the Austrian light troops and, faced with the wrath of Frederick the Great, he resigned from the army and died soon afterwards. The King continued to favour Winterfeldt, who became more unpopular. On 7 September 1757, Winterfeldt was mortally wounded in the clash at Moys, southeast of Görlitz on the river Neisse. He died the next day.

Hans Joachim von Zieten

Born on 24 May 1699 in Wustrau near Ruppin in Brandenburg, Zieten was the son of a landowner. He began his military career as a volunteer in Infanterie-Regiment von Schwendy (Nr 24) in 1715. He served for ten years without promotion and thought that his height (1.6m) was working against him, so resigned in 1724. In 1726, he obtained a commission as a lieutenant in the Prussian Dragoner-Regiment von Wuthenau (Nr 6), but soon fell out with his squadron commander, whom he challenged to a duel. For this, Zieten was sentenced to fortress imprisonment for one year. As soon as he was released, he promptly challenged his superior officer to another duel and was as promptly cashiered.

In 1730, Zieten tried his military luck again and managed to be reinstated as an officer in the newly formed Husaren-Regiment von Beneckendorff (Nr 2). His talents as a light cavalry officer soon shone through. In 1735, during the War of the Polish Succession, he served as Eskadron Chef under the Austrian General von Baronay on the Rhine, against France. This gave him the opportunity to learn light cavalry work from the only army who really mastered the art during this period.

In 1736, he was promoted to major. In 1741, Zieten was promoted Oberstleutnant (lieutenant-colonel) at the outbreak of the First Silesian War. On 17 May he met his old mentor-turned enemy von Baronay, in a clash near the castle of Roth, near Mollwitz. Zieten charged 1400 Austrian cavalrymen at the head of 600 hussars, and broke and scattered them. Some days later, Baronay sent him a complimentary letter. General von Winterfeld, who commanded at Roth, reported well upon Zieten's conduct and for this action he was awarded the Pour le Merite. In that same year, he was promoted to Oberst (colonel) and became Chef of his Husaren-Regiment Nr 2.

In February 1742, Zieten led a reconnaissance through Moravia and up to within 4km of Vienna, bringing back considerable booty and intelligence. During the retreat to Silesia in that year, Zieten and his regiment were part of the rearguard. In the short peace between the First and Second Silesian Wars, Prussian light cavalry regiments were tactically re-trained, to become recognised as the best in Europe, combining discipline with daring. In 1744, at the outbreak of the Second Silesian War, Zieten was promoted to General-Major. Soon after, he fought the brilliant action of Moldaustein.

In 1745, Zieten, at the head of 500 hussars, led the now legendary Zietenritt, a 22-hours ride behind enemy lines with the object of delivering the King's order to General Markgraf von Schwedt at Jägerndorf in Upper-Silesia. Falling in behind a regiment of Austrian dragoons on the way, Zieten pretended to be an Austrian unit. By the time the truth was discovered, they were able to slip away to the Prussian force in Jägerndorf, taking only very light casualties. Following the orders brought in by Zieten, von Schwedt's force was able to join the King in time for the victorious Battle of Hohenfriedberg on 4 June 1745. Zieten distinguish himself in this action, at Striegau, on the eastern flank of the field. He was again distinguished at the clash of Katholisch-Hennersdorf on 23 November 1745.

Following the end of the war, Frederick the Great tasked Zieten and Winterfeld with training the hussar regiments to be battlefield cavalry, fighting in close order. In August 1756, von Zieten was promoted to General-Leutnant. Next year, he played vital roles during the battles of Reichenberg and Prague. On 18 June at Kolin, he led the left wing of cavalry; in this disastrous Prussian defeat, his wing was the only part of the army to hold its own. On 5 December at the Battle of Leuthen Zieten's cavalry opened the action and ended the battle with its decisive charges on the Austrians' open flank.

At the Battle of Liegnitz on 15 August 1760, Zieten contained the main body of the Austrian Army. On 3 November, at the Battle of Torgau, he committed perhaps the only tactical error of his career, when he misdirected a frontal assault on the Austrian positions. He redeemed himself later that same day by his dashing charge on the Siptitz heights, which turned the action in Prussia's favour. In 1763, after the Peace of Hubertusburg ended the Seven Years War, Zieten went into retirement in Wustrau, outside Berlin. His health did not allow him to assume active service during the campaign of 1778; he died on 27 January 1786 in Berlin.

Russia

Field Marshal Count Stepan Fiodorovitch Apraxin (Apraksin)

Born on 10 August 1702, Count Apraxin served in the war against the Turks (1736–1739) under the command of General Münnich. He was rapidly promoted to general. He was present at the capture of Ochakov in 1737 and brought to the Russian capital news about the capture of Khotin in 1739. Several years later, he led a Russian diplomatic mission to Persia. At the court of St Petersburg, Apraxin was one of the fiercest opponents of the pro-Prussian party.

At the beginning of the Seven Years War in May 1757, Field Marshal Apraxin was given command of the Russian Army, which was to invade East Prussia. On 30 August he fought the victorious Battle of Gross-Jägersdorf against the Prussian general von Dohna. Apraxin then advanced to Allenburg. Although East Prussia lay defenceless before his army, Apraxin did nothing, not even attempt to take the port city of Königsberg. It has been rumoured that Apraxin was bribed by the British into inactivity. On 13 September Apraxin began his withdrawal eastwards through Lithuania, back into Russia. On 28 October 1757 he was removed from command and General Villim Vilimovich Fermor took over. The Tsarina, Elizabeth Petrovna, was extremely displeased at this apparently pointless retreat of her army, and ordered an enquiry into Apraxin's conduct. During the inquiry in Narva, it came out that Apraxin had acted upon instructions from the Russian Foreign Minister, Chancellor Bestuzhev. The Chancellor was immediately disgraced and Apraxin was charged with taking bribes from Frederick II. During his trial, Apraxin fell ill and died on 17 August 1758.

General Count Villim Vilimovich Fermor

Fermor entered Russian military service in 1720. In 1734, during the War of the Polish Succession, Fermor, now a major, distinguished himself at the siege of Danzig. From 1736 to 1739, he served under the command of Field Marshal Munnich in the war against the Turks. In 1740, he became commandant of the fortress of Vyborg; from 1741 to 1743, he took part in all the operations against the Swedes in Finland.

In 1746, Fermor was promoted to lieutenant-general. He was also chairman of the Imperial Public Works Department and oversaw the construction of the Imperial Palace in Saint-Petersburg. He was appointed general commander of St Petersburg, Finland and government of Novgorod in 1751.

In 1756, at the beginning of the Seven Years War, Fermor was placed at the head of a support corps in Apraxin's army and on 30 August 1757, he fought under Apraxin at the Battle of Gross-Jägersdorf, commanding the 1st Division. On 28 October, when Apraxin was removed from command, Fermor was promoted commander-in-chief of the Russian Army.

In March 1758, after the capturing Elbing and Thorn, Fermor was designated as Governor-General of East Prussia. In July, his army advanced into Brandenburg, and in August it laid siege to Cüstrin. Frederick II relieved the fortress and on 25 August, fought the bloody and inconclusive Battle of Zorndorf against Fermor's army. The Tsarina awarded Fermor the title of Count, in recognition of this achievement. After this battle, Fermor progressively retired towards Poland and East Prussia. For the campaign of 1759 however, Fermor was demoted to the rank of general for hesitance and irresolution, ceding overall command of the Russian Army to Count Piotr Semionovitch Saltykov. On 27 July Fermor took part at the Battle of Paltzig where he led the first line of infantry of the centre. On 12 August of that year, at the Battle of Kunersdorf, Fermor commanded the 1st Divison in the centre of the Russian line.

In 1760, when Saltykov was removed from command, Fermor briefly assumed the role of Commander-in-Chief before being replaced by Alexander Borissovitch Buturlin. After the death of Tsarina Elizabeth Petrovna in 1762, Fermor was named Governor-General of Smolensk and in 1764 he was appointed a member of the senate by Tsarina Catherine II. Fermor died on 8 February 1771.

Count Piotr Semionovich Saltykov

Born in 1700, Saltykov was a distant relative of Tsarina Anna Ivanovna. In 1714, on Tsar Peter the Great's instructions, Saltykov left Russia to undergo naval training in France where he spent most of his life until 1733. In that year he was granted the hereditary title of Count and promoted to lieutenant-general. In 1759, Saltykov was appointed Commander-in-Chief of the Russian Army in Prussia and on 23 July, defeated the Prussian general Wedel at the Battle of Paltzig. A few weeks later, on 12 August, assisted by an Austrian corps under Loudon, he won the bloody Battle of Kunersdorf against Frederick the Great. On 18 August he was promoted to Field Marshal.

In 1763 he became Governor-General of Moscow and was placed in charge of the Moscow Senate Office. During Saltykov's term of office, a number of new post offices were established, and the Golovinsky and Kolomensky Palaces and a number of the city gates were restored. Many of the bridges across the Moscow river were in rickety condition and Saltykov had them rebuilt. He also continued dismantling the walls of the White City (a belt of fortifications around Moscow) in order to provide building material for the construction of the state orphanage, which had been ordered by Catherine the Great. The city arsenal was also restored. To maintain the supply of bread to the city's inhabitants, Saltykov arranged wholesale purchases of bread from the landowners on Moscow's periphery. He also secured regular wine deliveries to Moscow. In 1765, he took part in the public burning of books 'harmful to society' at the order of the Tsarina.

During the plague outbreak in 1771, which caused mass departure of landowners, city officials and rich merchants from Moscow, Saltykov asked Catherine the Great for permission to leave the city, but left for his Marfino estate in the outskirts of Moscow, without waiting to receive her reply. The Tsarina dismissed him on 13 November 1771, as serious rioting had broken out in the capital in his absence. Saltykov died on 15 December 1772.

Tsarina Elizabeth Petrovna

Elizabeth was born on 18 December 1709, the daughter of Peter I the Great and Catherine I. She was born before the official marriage of her parents and this fact was used against her in the power struggles which pervaded the Russian court. Even as a child she had a reputation for extraordinary beauty and vivacity, and Peter the Great considered marrying her to the young French king Louis XV. However, the French court rejected this possibility. Other marriages were considered but rejected by Elizabeth. In May 1727, at the death of her mother, Elizabeth was eighteen and practically independent. She took advantage of her freedom to take a lover, Alexius Shubin, a sergeant in the Semenovsky Guards.

During the period when Menshikov assumed real power in the court, Elizabeth was treated with great respect by the government of Peter II. However, when the Dolgorukis took control of the state, she was practically banished from court. Non-Russians (many of them Germans) were invited into the government, a practice which Elizabeth deplored.

Her cousin Anna Ivanovna reigned from 1730 to 1740. During her reign, Elizabeth was very discreet. Nevertheless, Anna felt the need to banish Shubin, Elizabeth's lover, to Siberia after having his tongue cut out. Elizabeth soon found a new lover, a handsome young Cossack named Alexius Razumovski who probably became her husband. During the regency of Anna Leopoldovna, after the death of her cousin Anna Ivanovna, Elizabeth was supposed to take the veil. Only the intervention of the Prince of Holstein (later Peter III) saved her. At this point, Elizabeth began considering overthrowing the government; La Chetardie, the French ambassador, was probably the first to suggest this to her, his motive being lessening Austrian influence in Russian politics.

At midnight on 6 December 1741, Elizabeth along with her physician, Armand Lestocq, her chamberlain, Michael Ilarionvich Vorontsov, her future husband, Alexius Razumovski, and Alexander and Peter Shuvalov, two of the gentlemen of her household, drove to the barracks of the Preobrazhensky Guards. She managed to convince this regiment to support her claim to the throne. All the ministers were arrested and Anna Leopoldovna and her children were captured in their beds in the Winter Palace. The coup was a complete success.

Elizabeth Petrovna was crowned in the Dormition Cathedral of the Moscow Kremlin on 25 April 1742. No sooner had Elizabeth assumed power that she abolished the cabinet council system and reconstituted the senate. She also quickly evicted the foreigners from the management of many departments of the government, replacing them with Russians.

Most of the great powers of Europe had been involved in the War of the Austrian Succession since 1740, but Elizabeth's first concern was to resolve her dispute with Sweden. Direct negotiations wee opened on 23 January 1743 in Abo. For Russia, these negotiations were led by the new Vice Chancellor, Alexius Bestuzhev-Ryumin. On 7 August 1743, Sweden ceded to Russia all the southern part of Finland east of the river Kymmene, which thus became the boundary between the two states, including the fortresses of Villmanstrand and Fredrikshamn. Concerning the ongoing conflict in Europe, Bestuzhev-Ryumin was not in favour of alliances with France or Prussia, seeking instead to build relations with Austria and Britain.

In 1748, Russia finally sent an auxiliary corps of 30,000 men to the Rhine to assist Austria. As it happened, this force never fought, as peace was signed between the warring states at Aix-la-Chapelle on 18 October that same year.

On 16 January 1756, Britain and Prussia signed the Treaty of Westminster whereby the two countries would unite their forces against any foreign power entering Germany or traversing it. Elizabeth considered this treaty subversive and decided that Prussia represented a danger to the Russian Empire. Accordingly, she joined the Franco-Austrian alliance, determined to limit Prussia's power.

On 17 May 1757, she sent the Russian Army, 85,000 strong, against East Prussia. Two years later, on 12 August 1759, Frederick II of Prussia suffered a crushing defeat at Kunersdorf at the hands of the Russians. An Austrian corps hurried to join the Russians, to deliver the final blow. Only the total absence of coordination between the Russian and Austrian commanders saved Frederick.

A new treaty was signed between Russia and Austria on 21 May 1760; it included a secret clause, guaranteeing East Prussia to Russia as an indemnity for war expenses. The campaigns of 1760 were far from successful for both France and Russia. Louis XV began to consider making peace.

On 22 January 1761, the French ambassador announced to the court of St Petersburg that Louis XV desired peace. On 23 January, the Austrian ambassador, Esterhazy, presented a similar despatch. On 12 February, Elizabeth replied to the French and Austrian ambassadors that she would not consent to any pacific overtures until the power of Prussia had been brought down. Meanwhile, the campaign of 1761 was no more successful for the Allies than that of 1760. The Prussians remained on the defensive and the Russian Army led by Rumyantsev only succeeded in capturing the fortress of Kolberg on 25 December.

By the beginning of January 1762, Frederick II was convinced that the war was lost. The darkest of Frederick's hours came just before the dawn however, as Tsarina Elizabeth Petrovna died suddenly on 5 January. With the accession of Tsar Peter III to the Russian throne, one of Frederick's greatest admirers had assumed control of the army of his most powerful opponent.

Tsar Peter III

Born on 21 February 1728 in Kiel, Schleswig-Holstein, Karl Peter Ulrich was the only son of Karl Friedrich, Duke of Holstein-Gottorp and Anna Petrovna, eldest surviving daughter of Peter the Great. Until his adoption by Elizabeth Petrovna, he lived at the court of Holstein, then part of Denmark.

In December 1741, Karl Peter Ulrich was adopted by his aunt, Elizabeth Petrovna, then Tsarina of Russia. On 18 November 1742, Karl Peter Ulrich was received into the Orthodox Church, exchanging his original name for that of Peter Fedorovich.

By command of his aunt, the Tsarina, Peter married Princess Sophia Augusta Frederica of Anhalt-Zerbst (a minor German royal house) on 21 August 1745, who exchanged her name for that of Catherine Aleksyeevna. Their tastes were divergent and their tempers incompatible. Peter succeeded his aunt Elizabeth Petrovna as Tsar Peter III on 5 January 1762. He at once proclaimed an amnesty for the statesmen (mostly foreigners) arrested or exiled by Elizabeth after her accession. His foreign policy was the absolute reversal of that of his predecessor. At the end of February, he made peace overtures to his hero, Frederick the Great of Prussia, whom he habitually alluded to as 'the king my master.' For Frederick, this was nothing short of a miracle, as his military options had been exhausted. Russian operations against Prussia ceased on 5 May 1762 and peace was rapidly negotiated between the two states.

On 19 June, they also concluded an offensive-defensive alliance, whereby Peter restored to Prussia all the territory taken from her by Russia during the last five years. He also abrogated the treaties with France and Austria. On the domestic front meanwhile, Peter settled all the debts of his wife, Catherine, whilst conducting an affair with Countess Elizabeth Vorontsova. Catherine accepted this situation; she had her own love affair with the young guardsman, Gregory Orlov, but she resolved to depose her estranged husband and take the throne for herself.

On 9 July 1762, she led a successful coup d'état against Peter, who was sent to Ropshinskii Castle, where he was detained from 9 to 18 July, on which day he was murdered by Alexius Orlov, Theodore Baryatinski and several others. Catherine the Great had arrived on the world's stage.

BIBLIOGRAPHY

Alt, G., *Das Königlich Preussische Stehende Heer* (Berlin, 1869)

Anon, *Stammliste aller Regimenter und Corps der Königlich-Preussischen Armee fuer das Jahr 1806* (Osnabrück, 1975)

Anon, *Die Schlacht bei Minden 1759* (Minden, 1959)

Anon, *New Method of Fortification* (London, 1748)

Barcía, A.G. de, *Ensayo Cronológico para la Historia General de la Florida* (Madrid, 1723)

Bolke, E., *Preussische Fahnen 1740–1806* (Dresden, 1944)

Borresen, T., *Spanish Guns and Carriages, 1686–1800* (Yorktown, 1938)

Bourne, W., *The Arte of Shooting in Great Ordnance* (London, 1587)

Bredow, C. von, *Historische Rang und Stammliste des Deutschen Heeres* (Berlin, 1905)

Collado, L., *Platica Manual de la Artillería* (Milan, 1592)

Connor, J.T. (ed), *Colonial Records of Spanish Florida* (Deland, 1930)

Dollaczek, A., *Geschichte der Österreichischen Artillerie von den frühesten Zeiten bis zur Gegenwart* (Wien, 1887)

Eckardt, W. and Morawietz, O., *Die Handwaffen des brandenburgisch-preussisch-deutschen Heeres* (Hamburg, 1973)

Fiedler, S., *Geschichte der Grenadiere Friedrichs des Grossen* (Munich, 1981)

Foulkes, C.J., *The Gun-Founders of England* (Cambridge, 1937)

Franke, L.E., *Vorstellung der Koeniglich Preussischen Armee* (Potsdam, 18??)

Fraser, D., *Fredrick the Great* (London, 2000)

Gohlke, W., *Geschichte der Gesamten Feuerwaffen bis 1850* (Berlin, 1911)

Jany, C., *Geschichte der Preussischen Armee vom 15. Jahrhundert bis 1914* (Osnabrück, 1967)

Kimber, E., *Late Expedition to the Gates of St Augustine* (Boston, 1935)

Kling, C., *Geshichte der Bekleidung, Bewaffnung und Ausruestung des Königlich Preussischen Heeres* (Weimar, 1912)

Knötel, R. and Sieg, H., *Handbuch der Uniformkunde* (Hamburg, 1937)

Manucy, A., *Ordnance used at Castillo de San Marcos, 1672–1834* (St Augustine, 1939)

Montiano, M. de, *Letters of Montiano* (Savannah, 1909)

Morla, T. de, *Láminas pertenecientes al Tratado de Artillería* (Madrid, 1803)

Mowat, C.L., *East Florida as a British Province 1763–1784* (Los Angeles, 1939)

Müller, J., *Treatise of Artillery* (London, 1756)

Scharnhorst, D. von, 'Horse Artillery is Much Better Suited to be Used in the Reserve Than Foot Artillery' (written in 1802), in *Gerhard von Scharnhorst Private und dienstliche Schrifte* (Böhlau Verlag, Köln, Weimar, Wien, 2005)

Smith, J., *The Generall Historie of Virginia, New-Englande, and the Summer Isles* (Richmond, 1819)

Ufano, D., *Artillerie* (Roven, 1628)

Voigt, G., *Deutschlands Heere bis 1918* (Osnabrück, 1983)

_____., 'Die Bewaffnung und Ausrüstung der Armee Friedrichs des Grossen' in *Vereinigung der Freunde des Wehrgeschichtlichen Museums Schloss Rastatt* (Baden, 1986)

Archivo General de Indias

Inventories of Castillo de San Marcos armament in 1683 (58-2-2,32/2), 1706 (58-1-27,89/2), 1740 (58-1-32), 1763 (86-7-11,19), Zuñiga's report on the 1702 siege of St Augustine (58-2-8,B3), and Arredondo's 'Plan de la Ciudad de Sn. Agustín de la Florida' (87-1-1/2, ms. map).

INDEX

Anhalt, Prinz von, Hessen-Kassel (Chef IR
 Nr 11), 152
Anhalt-Dessau, Moritz, Prinz von, 265, 266,
 316, 321
Anhalt-Dessau, Leopold von (Chef IR Nr 3),
 10, 164, 165, 222, 250, 251, 265, 266, 312
Arenberg, Carl Raimund, Graf von, 267, 268,
 269, 272, 293
Aspremont-Linden, Graf, Ferdinand Carl, 36
August Wilhelm, Prinz von Preussen (Chef
 PKürR Nr 2), 191, 248, 316, 319
AUSTRIAN EMPIRE
artillery, 14, 16, 17, 42, 95, 246, 250, 263, 270,
 336
border infantry regiments
 Nr 60 Licaner, 31
 Nr 61 Ottochaner, 31
 Nr 62 Oguliner, 31
 Nr 63 Szluiner, 31, 248
 Nr 64 Creuzer, 31
 Nr 65 St Georger, 32
 Nr 66 Brooder, 32, 249
 Nr 67 Gradiscaner, 32, 249
 Nr 68 Peterwardeiner, 32
 Nr 69 1st Ansiedler, 32
 Nr 70 2nd Ansiedler, 32
dragoon regiments
 Nr 1 Erzherzog Joseph, 36, 245, 246, 268,
  274
 Nr 6 von Liechtenstein, 36, 246
 Nr 7 von Batthyányi, 36, 246, 269, 274
 Nr 9 Prinz Savoyen, 36
 Nr 13 Jung-Modena, 36, 250, 269
 Nr 18 Jung-Löwenstein, 36
 Nr 19 Hessen-Darmstadt, 36, 249, 268, 275
 Nr 28 Sachsen-Gotha, 36, 249, 270
 Nr 31 de Ligne, 37, 249
 Nr 37 Kollowrat-Krakowski, 37, 249
 Nr 38 von Württemberg, 37, 250, 262,
  268, 274
 Nr 39 von Porporati, 37
 Kohary, 38
engineers, 42
Feldjäger, 32
Grenz hussar regiments
 Nr 40 Karlstädter, 40, 248
 Nr 41 Warasdiner, 40, 248
 Nr 42 Banalisten, 40
 Nr 43 Slavonier, 40

 Nr 44 Szeckler, 41
hussar regiments
 Nr 2 Kaiser Franz I, 38, 248, 274
 Nr 11 von Nádasdy, 38, 248, 267, 275
 Nr 16 von Károly, 38, 275
 Nr 17 von Kálnoky, 38, 248
 Nr 24 Paul Anton Esterházy, 39, 248, 267,
  274
 Nr 30 von Baranyay, 39, 245, 248
 Nr 32 von Szechenyi, 39, 267
 Nr 34 von Dessewffy, 39, 248, 267, 275
 Nr 35 von Morocz, 39, 248
 Nr 36 Jazygier-Kumanier (Palatinal), 39,
  248
 von Hadick, 41
 von Splényi, 41, 248
infantry regiments
 Nr 1 Kaiser, 27, 245, 268, 274
 Nr 2 Carl, Erhzherzog von Österreich, 27,
  28, 128, 249, 274, 268, 275
 Nr 3 Carl von Lothringen, 27, 268
 Nr 4 Deutschmeister, 27, 249, 269
 Nr 5 (garrison), 27
 Nr 6 (garrison), 27
 Nr 7 Neipperg, 27, 249, 268, 274
 Nr 8 (Sachsen-) Hildburghausen, 27, 246,
  268, 274
 Nr 9 Los Rios, 27, 250, 267, 275
 Nr 10 Jung Wolfenbüttel, 27, 245, 246, 275
 Nr 11 Wallis, 27, 246, 268, 275
 Nr 12 Botta, 27, 249, 268, 274
 Nr 13 Moltke, 27, 249, 268
 Nr 14 Salm, 27, 250
 Nr 15 Pallavicini, 27, 268
 Nr 16 Königsegg, 28, 267, 274
 Nr 17 Kollowrat, 28, 246, 268, 275
 Nr 18 Marschall, 28
 Nr 19 Leopold Pálffy, 28, 269
 Nr 20 Alt-Colloredo, 28, 274
 Nr 21 Arenberg, 28, 274
 Nr 22 Hagenbash, 28
 Nr 23 Baden-Baden, 28, 249, 269
 Nr 24 Starhemberg, 28, 250, 274
 Nr 25 Piccolomini, 28, 268
 Nr 26 Puebla, 28, 249, 267, 274
 Nr 27 Baden-Durlach, 28, 246, 268
 Nr 28 Wied, 28
 Nr 29 Alt-Wolfenbüttel, 28, 314
 Nr 30 Sachsen-Gotha, 28, 250, 267, 274

 Nr 31 Haller (von Hallerstein), 28, 249, 268,
  269, 275, 321
 Nr 32 Forgách, 29, 269, 274
 Nr 33 Nikolas Esterházy, 29, 246, 268, 274
 Nr 34 Batthyányi, 29, 269, 275
 Nr 35 Waldeck, 29, 246, 268, 269, 274
 Nr 36 Browne, 29, 246, 275, 336
 Nr 37 Joseph Esterházy, 29, 246, 268, 274
 Nr 38 de Ligne, 29, 250, 257, 269, 275
 Nr 39 Johann Pálffy, 29, 269
 Nr 40 Jung-Colloredo, 29
 Nr 41 Bayreuth, 29
 Nr 42 Gaisruck, 29, 249, 269, 274
 Nr 43 Platz, 29, 250
 Nr 44 Clerici, 29, 269, 274
 Nr 45 Heinrich Daun, 29, 269, 274
 Nr 46 Macquire, 29
 Nr 47 Harrach, 30, 246, 249, 269, 275
 Nr 48 Luzan, 30, 269
 Nr 49 Kheul, 30, 268
 Nr 50 Harsch, 30, 246, 269, 274
 Nr 51 Gyulay, 30
 Nr 52 Bethlen, 30, 269
 Nr 53 Simbschen, 30
 Nr 54 Sincère, 30
 Nr 55 d'Arberg, 30
 Nr 56 Mercy-Argenteau, 30
 Nr 57 Andlau, 30, 268, 274
 Nr 58 Vierzet, 30
 Nr 59 Leopold Daun, 30, 249, 267, 275
kürassier regiments
 Nr 3 (Erzherzog) Leopold, 33, 274
 Nr 4 Erzherzog Ferdinand, 33, 246, 268, 275
 Nr 5 Emanuel Infant von Portugal, 33, 249
 Nr 8 Carl von Pálffy, 34, 246
 Nr 10 von Stampach, 34, 246, 268, 274
 Nr 12 de Serbelloni, 34, 246, 249, 268, 274
 Nr 14 O'Donell, 34
 Nr 20 von Schmerzing, 34, 249, 269, 275
 Nr 21 von Trauttmansdorf, 34, 260
 Nr 22 von Kalckreuth, 34, 268
 Nr 23 von (Zweibrücken-) Birkenfeld, 34,
  250, 269
 Nr 25 von Anhalt-Zerbst, 34, 268
 Nr 27 von Löwenstein, 34, 268
 Nr 29 von Brettlach, 35, 246, 260, 262
 Nr 33 von Anspach, 35, 245, 275
 de Ville, 35
 von Buccow, 35, 275

(Alt) Modena, 35, 249
miners 42
pioneers 42
sappers 42
HOLY ROMAN EMPIRE
Austrian-Burgundian Kreis, 44
Infanterie-Regiment Blau-Würzburg, 44,
242, 260, 263
Bavarian Kreis, 44
artillery, 45
Infanterie-Regiment Kurbayern, 44–45
Infanterie-Regiment Salzburg, 45, 49, 51
Infanterie-Regiment Varell, 45, 46, 260, 263
Infanterie-Regiment Ferntheil, 45, 46,
260, 263
Bavaria and the Palatinate, 59
Infanterie-Regiment Kurprinz, 60, 269
Infanterie-Regiment Herzog Clemens, 60
Infanterie-Regiment Minucci, 60, 270
Infanterie-Regiment Morawitzky, 60, 270
Infanterie-Regiment Preysing, 51, 60,
258, 269
Infanterie-Regiment Holnstein, 44, 60
Infanterie-Regiment Pechmann, 44, 60
Leibregiment, 60
Franconian Kreis
artillery, 47
Dragoner-Regiment Anspach, 46
Infanterie-Regiment Anspach, 46
Infanterie-Regiment Cronegk, 46, 263
Kürassier-Regiment Bayreuth, 46, 262
Rhine Electorate Kreis
artillery, 51
engineers, 51
Fusilier-Regiment Wildenstein, 48
Infanterie-Regiment Kurmainz, 47, 48
Infanterie-Regiment Kurtrier, 49
Infanterie-Regiment von Effern, 49, 50
Kurpfalz Garde zu Fuss, 50
Kürassier-Regiment Kurpfalz, 50
Kurpfalz Leib Dragoner-Regiment, 51
Leib-Infanterie-Regiment Nothaft
(Kurköln), 47, 48
Swabian Kreis
artillery, 55
Dragoner-Regiment Württemberg, 54,
262, 321
Infanterie-Regiment Baden-Baden, 51
Infanterie-Regiment von Baden-Durlach,
52, 53, 237
Infanterie-Regiment Fürstenberg, 52, 53
Infanterie-Regiment Württemberg, 53, 237
Kürassier-Regiment Hohenzollern-
Sigmaringen, 54
Upper Rhine Kreis, 55
cavalry squadron, 57
Infanterie-Regiment Hessen-Darmstadt,
55, 56, 263
Infanterie-Regiment Nassau-Weilburg,
51, 56
Infanterie-Regiment Pfalz-Zweibrücken,
57
Upper Saxon Kreis, 57
Coburg Contingent, 57
Hildburghausen Contingent, 57
Weimar Contingent, 57
Dragoner-Regiment Sachsen-Gotha, 57
Westphalian Kreis, 58
artillery, 58
Infanterie-Regiment Elverfeldt, 58
Infanterie-Regiment Mengersen, 58
Infanterie-Regiment Nagel, 58
Baden-Baden, August Georg Simpert,
Markgraf von (Chef AIR Nr 23), 28, 51
Baden-Durlach, Carl Friedrich, Markgraf
von, 43, 52, 271, 272
Baden-Durlach, Carl Wilhelm, Markgraf

von, 54, 239
Bandemer, Joachim Christian von (Chef
PKürR Nr11), 192, 247
Batthyányi, Carl Joseph, Fürst von, 36
Batthyányi-Strattmann, Adam Graf von, 29
Bayern, Maximilian, Prinz von, 60
Belling, Wilhelm Sebastian von (Chef
PHusR Nr 8), 199
Beust von (Chef PHusR Nr 9), 199
Blanckensee, Busso Christian von (Chef
Garrison PIR Nr 10), 187, 188, 189
Blanckensee, Christian Friedrich von (Chef
PDrR Nr 2), 194, 251, 267
Block, General, 255
Bonin, Bernd Eckard von (Chef Garrison
PIR Nr 9), 187
Borcke, Georg Heinrich von, 178
Botta d'Andorno, Antoniotto, 27
Brandenburg-Anspach, Friedrich Wilhelm,
Landgraf von, 35
Brandenburg-Anspach und Bayreuth,
Christian Friedrich, Markgraf von, 35
Brandenburg-Bayreuth, Christian Ernst,
Landgraf von, 37
Brandenburg-Bayreuth, Friedrich III,
Markgraf von, 29
Brandenburg-Bayreuth, Friedrich Markgraf
von (Chef PDrR Nr 5), 195
Brandenburg cuffs, 57, 140
Brandenburg, province, 320, 323, 325, 328
Brandenburg-Schwedt, Friedrich IV
Markgraf von, 320
Brandenburg-Schwedt, Friedrich Wilhelm
Markgraf von, 320
Brandenburg-Schwedt, Karl Friedrich
Albrecht von, 273, 314
Brandes, Johann Christoph von (Chef PIR
Nr 38), 177
Braun, August Wilhelm von, 177, 182
Braunschweig-Lüneburg, Friedrich August,
Prinz von, 35
Braunschweig-Lüneburg, Herzog Carl
von, 61
Braunschweig (-Alt) (PIR), 273
Braunschweig (-Jung) (PFusR), 273
Braunschweig-Lüneburg, 139
Braunschweig-Wolfenbüttel, Carl, Fürst von,
28, 247, 268
Braunschweig-Wolfenbüttel, Duchy see
Brunswick
Braunschweig-Wolfenbüttel, Friedrich Franz
Prinz von, (Chef PIR Nr 39), 172
Braunschweig-Wolfenbütten-Bevern, August
Wilhelm, Herzog von, 251, 264, 269, 300,
314, 317, 323
Braunschweig-Wolfenbüttel-Bevern,
Ferdinand Herzog von, 147, 150, 166, 167,
168, 177, 182, 189, 245, 247, 251, 255, 261,
266, 267, 272, 276, 277, 278, 300, 313, 314
Bredow, Jakob Friedrich von (Chef PKürR
Nr 9), 192, 267, 273
Breitenfeld, First Battle of, 13
BRITAIN
artillery, 138, 253
dragoon regiments
1st Royal Dragoons, 131
2nd Royal North British Dragoons, 131,
132, 278
3rd King's Own, 131
4th Princess Anne's, 131
5th Royal Irish, 131
6th Inniskilling, 131
7th Queen's Own, 129, 132
8th Conyngham's, 132
9th Wynne's, 132
10th Gore's, 132, 278
11th Honeywood's 133

12th Bowles', 133
13th Munden's, 133, 134
14th Dormer's, 133, 135
15th Elliot's, 134, 135
16th Queen's 134
17th Hale's, 136, 137
18th Light Dragoons, 136
19th Light Dragoons, 136
20th Inniskilling, 136
21st Royal Forresters, 136, 137
22nd Light Dragoons, 134, 136
Dragoon Guards
1st Queen's, 129, 278
2nd Peterborough's, 129, 130
3rd Karabiniers or Plymouth's, 129, 130
Foot Guards
1st Regiment of Foot Guards, 96, 97, 104,
105, 119
2nd Coldstream Guards, 97, 104, 105, 119
3rd Scots Guards, 97, 104, 105, 119
Horse Guards
1st/His Majesty's, 127, 127
Horse Grenadier Guards, 1st Troop,
127–128
Horse Grenadier Guards, 2nd Troop,
128–129
Life Guards, 127, 128
infantry regiments
1st Foot, 98, 100, 101, 104, 119
2nd Foot, 98, 100, 101, 104, 105, 119
3rd Foot, 98, 10, 100, 104, 105, 119, 121
4th Foot, 99, 101, 103, 104, 107, 119, 121, 305
5th Foot, 99, 101, 103, 104, 107, 119
6th Foot, 99, 102, 103, 104, 107, 119
7th Foot, 99, 101, 104, 107, 119
8th Foot, 99, 101, 104, 107, 119, 121
9th Foot, 102, 106, 107, 119
10th Foot, 102, 106, 107, 119
11th Foot, 101, 106, 107, 119
12th Foot, 102, 106, 107, 119, 277, 278,
305, 306
13th Foot, 102, 106, 109, 119
14th Foot, 101, 106, 109, 119
15th Foot, 102, 106, 109, 119, 284
16th Foot, 102, 106, 108, 109, 119
17th Foot, 101, 106, 108, 109, 119
18th Foot, 99, 101, 106, 108, 109, 119
19th Foot, 101, 108, 109, 119, 120, 121
20th Foot, 102, 106, 109, 119, 120, 128, 277,
278, 306
21st Foot, 99, 101, 108, 109, 119, 120
22nd Foot, 101, 108, 111, 119
23rd Foot, 100, 101, 108, 111, 119, 121, 277
24th Foot, 101, 108, 111, 119, 121
25th Foot, 102, 108, 111, 119, 277, 278
26th Foot, 102, 108, 111, 119
27th Foot, 100, 101, 110, 111, 119
28th Foot, 102, 110, 111, 119, 284
29th Foot, 102, 110, 113, 119
30th Foot, 102, 110, 113, 119
31st Foot, 101, 110, 113, 119, 121
32nd Foot, 101, 110, 113, 119, 121
33rd Foot, 101, 110, 113, 119, 121
34th Foot, 102, 110, 113, 119
35th Foot, 101, 110, 115, 119, 284
36th Foot, 101, 110, 115, 119, 122
37th Foot, 102, 112, 115, 119, 122, 277, 278
38th Foot, 102, 112, 115, 119
39th Foot, 101, 112, 115, 119, 252, 253
40th Foot, 101, 112, 115, 119, 284
41st Foot, 100, 101, 112, 115, 119
42nd Foot, 100, 101, 112, 115, 119
43rd Foot, 101, 112, 115, 119, 284
44th Foot, 102, 112, 117, 119
45th Foot, 101, 112, 117, 119
46th Foot, 102, 112, 119
47th Foot, 101, 112, 117, 119, 284

48th Foot, 101, 114, 117, 119, 284
49th Foot, 101, 103, 114, 117, 119
50th Foot 114, 120
51st Foot 114, 120, 277, 278
52nd Foot 114, 120
53rd Foot 114, 120
54th Foot 114, 120
55th Foot 114, 120
56th Foot 114, 120
57th Foot 114, 121
58th Foot 114, 121, 284
59th Foot 114, 121
60th Foot 114, 121, 284
61st Foot 114, 121
62nd Foot 114, 121
63rd Foot 114, 121
64th Foot, 116, 121
65th Foot, 116, 117, 121
66th Foot, 116, 121
67th Foot, 116, 121
68th Foot, 116, 121
69th Foot, 116, 121
70th Foot, 116, 121
71st Foot, 116, 121, 124
72nd Foot, 116, 121, 124
73rd Foot, 116, 121, 124
74th Foot, 116, 122, 124
75th Foot, 116, 122, 124
76th Foot, 116, 122, 124
77th Foot, 116, 122, 124
78th Foot, 116, 122, 124
79th Foot, 116, 122, 124, 290, 309
80th Foot, 118, 122, 124
81st Foot, 118, 122, 124
82nd Foot, 118, 122, 124
83rd Foot, 118, 122, 124
84th Foot, 118, 122, 124, 290
85th Foot, 118, 122
86th Foot, 118, 122
87th Foot, 118, 122
88th Foot, 118, 122
89th Foot, 118, 122
90th Foot, 118, 122
91st Foot, 118, 122
92nd Foot, 118, 122
93rd Foot, 118, 122
94th Foot, 118
95th Foot, 118
96th Foot, 123
97th Foot, 123
98th Foot, 123
99th Foot, 123
100th Foot, 123, 124
101st Foot, 123
102nd Foot, 123, 290
103rd Foot, 123
104th Foot, 123
105th Foot, 123
106th Foot, 123
107th Foot, 123
108th Foot, 123
109th Foot, 123
110th Foot, 123
111th Foot, 123
112th Foot, 123
113th Foot, 123
114th Foot, 123
115th Foot, 123
116th Foot, 123
117th Foot, 123
118th Foot, 123
119th Foot, 123
120th Foot, 123
121st Foot, 123
122nd Foot, 123
123rd Foot, 123
124th Foot, 123

Regiments of Horse
  1st Arran's, 128
  2nd Shrewsbury's, 129
  3rd Carabineers, 129
  4th Devonshire's, 129, 130
Browne, Major-General, 29, 274, 275
Browne de Camus und Mountany,
  Maximilien Ulysses von, 29, 219, 244, 245,
  272, 294, 295, 298, 299, 321
Browne, Colonel (73rd British Foot), 116
BRUNSWICK
  artillery, 64
  Dragoner-Regiment Prinz Ludwig, 63
  Garde du Corps, 63
  Husaren-Regiment von Roth, 63
  Infanterie-Regiment von Imhoff, 61, 62,
    255, 279
  Infanterie-Regiment von Stammer, 61
  Infanterie-Regiment von Zastrow 62, 255
  Jäger Corps zu Fuss, 62
  Jäger Corps zu Pferd, 63
  Leib-Regiment, 62, 64, 255
  Volontaires Auxiliaires, 62, 205
Buddenbrock, Wilhelm Dietrich von (Chef
  PKürR Nr 1), 191, 251, 266
Bülow, Johann Albrecht von (Chef PIR Nr
  46), 179, 184, 267, 274
Carl, Hessen-Darmstadt, Prinz von, 55
Carl, Lothringen, Prinz von, 260, 264, 265,
  268, 295, 296, 298
Carl, Mecklenburg-Strelitz, Prinz von, 142
Carl V (Holy Roman Emperor), 14, 21
Carl VI (Holy Roman Emperor), 7, 25, 34,
  322
Charles de Rohan, Prince de Soubise, 44,
  257, 259, 311, 321
Charles Edward Stuart, Prince (the Young
  Pretender), 303, 308
Charles Louis Victor, Prince de Broglie, 307
Charles, Marquis de Nicolai d'Osny, 89
Charles, Marquis de Marboef, 89
Charles I, King of Scotland, 97
Charles I, King of Spain see Carl V
Charles II, King of England, 97
Charles III, King of Spain, 224
Charles Sigismund, Marquis de Royans, 71
Charles XII, King of Sweden, 313
Clerici, Georg Anton von, 29, 269, 274
Coehorn, Baron Menno von, 14, 15, 218
Colbert, Jean-Baptiste, 20
Colloredo-Melz und Waldsee, Anton, (Alt)
  Graf von, 28, 246, 249, 250, 274, 296
Colloredo-Melz und Waldsee, Carl (Jung),
  29, 268
Cornwallis, Charles, 101, 305
Cronstedt, General Baron Carl, 13
Czettritz, Ernst Heinrich Freiherr von (Chef
  PDrR Nr 4), 195, 261, 267, 273
Dachenhausen, Brigadier-General, 256
Daun, Benedict, Graf von, 34, 37, 249, 268
Daun, Leopold Joseph, Graf von, 17, 30,
  36, 248, 249, 260, 264, 267, 271, 272, 274,
  275, 295, 296, 297, 298, 299, 300, 314, 316,
  318, 321
Daun, Heinrich Joseph von, 29, 269
d'Estrees, Louis-Charles-César, 254, 257
Diericke, Christian Friedrich von (Chef
  PFusR Nr 49), 181, 184, 317
Dietrich Richard von, 178
Dingelstedt, August Levin von (Chef PHusR
  Nr 4), 197
Dohna, Christoph, Graf von (Chef PIR Nr
  16), 169, 172, 205, 324
Dollaczek, 13, 14, 328
Dossow, Friedrich Wilhelm von Chef PIR
  Nr 45), 179, 183
Dreyse, Nikolaus, 11

Driesen, Georg Wilhelm von (Chef P KürR
  Nr 7), 192
Eisenstein, M., 13
Elverfeldt, Friedrich Christian Georg,
  Austrian Generalleutnant, 58
Esterhazy de Galantha, Joseph von, 25, 29,
  246, 268, 274
Esterhazy de Galantha, Nikolaus Joseph, 29,
  246, 265, 267, 268, 274
Esterhazy de Galantha, Paul Anton, 39, 248,
  274, 327
Esterhazy de Galantha, Valentin Stanislas, 90
Esterhazy family, 13, 336
Ferdinand Carl, Erzherzog, 27
Ferguson, Captain Patrick, 10
Finck, General, 296
Flanss, Kurt Friedrich von (Chef PDrR Nr
  3), 195
Forcade de Biaix, Friedrich Wilhelm von
  (Chef PIR Nr 23), 261, 267
Forgach de Ghyimes, Graf Ignaz von, 29, 269,
  274, 275
Fouqué, General, 175, 180, 205, 298
Frankfurt am Main, 43, 56, 276, 300, 308
Frankfurt an der Oder, Battle of, 13, 271,
  292, 321
Franz Stefan von Habsburg-Lothringen,
  Holy Roman Emperor, 7, 26, 307
Frederick the Great, 7, 17, 18, 61, 95, 172, 190,
  191, 205, 207, 219, 244, 248, 254, 259, 264,
  271, 283, 289, 295, 296, 298, 299, 306, 311,
  313, 314, 315, 316, 317, 318, 319, 320, 321,
  323, 324, 325, 327
FRANCE
artillery, 95
cavalry regiments
  1st Colonel Général, 79, 86
  2nd Mestre de Camp-Général, 79
  3rd Commissaire Général, 79, 83, 95, 258, 280
  4th Royal, 80, 85
  5th Du Roy, 79, 80, 258, 281
  6th Royal Étranger, 80, 84, 281
  7th Cuirassiers du Roy, 80, 83
  8th Royal Cravates, 80, 83, 257, 281
  9th Royal Roussillon, 80, 85, 258
  10th Royal Piémont, 80, 87
  11th Royal-Allemande 79, 80, 85, 280
  12th Royal Pologne, 80, 86, 258
  13th Des Salles, 81, 86, 280
  14th Royal-Picardie, 81, 83, 84
  15th Royal Champagne, 81, 85, 85
  16th Royal-Navarre, 81, 84, 86
  17th Royal Normandie, 81, 85, 263
  18th La Reine, 81, 87, 262, 282
  19th Dauphine, 81, 84, 258
  20th Bourgogne, 81, 84, 258, 281
  21st Berry, 81, 86
  22nd Royal Carabiniers, 81, 258, 282
  23rd Artois, 82, 83
  24th Orléans, 82, 84, 257
  25th Chartres, 82, 83, 86
  26th Condé, 82, 84, 258, 263, 281
  27th Bourbon, 82, 83, 262
  28th Clermont, 82, 258
  29th Conti, 82
  30th Penthièvre, 82, 84, 260, 262, 280
  31st Noailles, 82, 257, 281
  36th Saluces, 79, 86, 258, 260, 262
  37th Beauvilliers, 79, 83, 262
  38th Lastic de St-Jal, 85
  40th Archaic, 83
  41st Egmont, 80, 84
  42nd Bussy-Lameth, 80, 83, 260, 262
  43rd Chabrillan, 80, 83
  44th Grammont, 80, 85, 263
  45th Talleyrand, 80, 87, 258, 281
  46th Marcieux, 86, 281

47th Lénoncourt, 81, 86
48th Bourbon-Busset, 83, 84, 258, 262
49th Fumel, 81, 83, 84, 258, 281
50th Rochefoucauld-Langeac, 81, 85, 86, 258
51st Vienne, 81, 84, 86
52nd Moustiers, 81, 84, 86
53rd Henrichemont, 85, 258, 281
54th Viefville, 81, 87
55th Dauphin-Étranger, 81, 84
56th Dampierre, 81, 84
57th Lusignan, 81, 86, 263
58th Crussol, 82, 84
59th Maugiron, 82, 83, 86
61st Bellefonds, 82, 83, 86, 258, 281
62nd Fleury, 82, 84
63rd Clermont-Tonnerre, 82, 83
64th Descars, 84, 260, 263
65th Beuvron, 89
66th Preysac, 85
67th Montcalm, 79, 86, 263
68th Bezons, 82, 83, 263
69th Württemberg, 80, 280
Fitz-James Cavalerie, 85, 260, 262
Chevau-Légers
Aquitaine, 281
Berry, 282
Bourgogne, 281
de la Reine, 282
du Dauphin, 282
d'Orleans, 281
dragoon regiments
1st Colonel Général, 88, 257, 281
2nd Mestre de Camp Général, 88
3rd Royal, 88
4th Du Roy, 88
5th La Reine, 88
6th Dauphin, 88
7th Orléans, 88
8th Beauffremont, 88
9th Aubigné, 88
10th Caraman, 89
11th La Ferronnaye, 89
12th Harcourt, 89
13th Apchon, 89, 280
14th Thianges, 89
15th Marboeuf, 80, 89
16th Languedoc, 89
Gendarmerie
Anglais, 281
Bourguignons, 281
Berry, 282
d'Aquitaine, 281
d'Orleans, 282
Écosse, 281
de Flandres, 281
de la Reine, 282
du Dauphine, 282
Household Troops
Garde du Corps (1st Company Écosse), 66
Garde du Corps 2nd Company (1st Française), 66
Garde du Corps 3rd Company (2nd Française), 66
Garde du Corps 4th Company (3rd Française), 66
Gardes Françaises, 65
Gardes Suisses, 65
Grenadiers Royaux de Bergeret, 66
Grenadiers Royaux de Bruslan, 66
Grenadiers Royaux de Chabrilland, 66
Grenadiers Royaux de Chantilly, 66
Grenadiers Royaux de Coincy, 66
Grenadiers Royaux d'Aulans, 66
Grenadiers Royaux de Châtillon, 66
Grenadiers Royaux de la Tresney, 66
Grenadiers Royaux de Modène, 67
Grenadiers Royaux de Prugues, 67

Grenadiers Royaux de Solar, 67
hussar regiments
Bercheny Hussards, 90, 258
Polleresky Hussards, 90
Royale-Nassau Hussards, 90, 280
Turpin-Crissé Hussards, 90
infantry regiments
1st Picardie, 68
2nd Champagne, 68, 258, 282
3rd Navarre, 68, 257, 282
4th Piémont, 68
5th Normandie, 68
6th La Marine, 68, 257, 263, 309
7th La Tour-du-Pin, 68
8th Bourbonnois, 69
9th Auvergne, 69, 281
10th Belzunce, 69, 257, 281
11th Mailly, 69, 257, 262
12th Du Roi, 69
13th Royal, 69
14th Poitou, 69, 74, 258, 262
15th Lyonnais, 69, 70, 257
16th Dauphin, 69, 74, 280
17th Vaubécourt, 69
18th Touraine, 69, 74, 263, 281
19th Aquitaine, 70, 82, 282
20th D'Eu, 70
21st St Chaumont, 70
22nd Montmorin, 70
23rd Briqueville, 70
24th La Reine, 70
25th Limousin, 70
26th Royal-Vaisseaux, 71
27th Orléans, 71, 257
28th La Couronne, 71, 257
29th Bretagne, 71
30th Gardes Lorraines, 71
31st Artois, 71
32nd Rohan-Montbazon, 71, 263
33rd La Roche Aymon, 71, 257
34th La Sarre, 71, 284, 309, 310
35th La Fère, 71
36th Alsace (German), 71, 77, 257
37th Royal Roussillon, 71, 262, 284, 309, 310
38th Condé, 71, 257, 263, 282
39th Bourbon, 72
40th Grenadiers de France, 72, 257, 280
41st Beauvois, 72
42nd Rouerge, 72, 281
43rd Bourgogne, 72
44th Royal Marine, 72
45th Vermandois, 72
46th Bentheim (German), 72
47th Royal Artillerie, 72, 258
48th Royal Italien, 49th Jenner (Swiss), 72
50th Boccard (Swiss), 73
51st Reding (Swiss), 73, 258, 262
52nd Castellas (Swiss), 73, 262
53rd Languedoc, 73, 284, 311
54th Talaru, 73
55th Wittmer, 73, 262
56th Médoc, 73
57th Brissac, 73, 262
58th Vastan, 73, 282
59th Royal Comtois, 73
60th Traisnel, 73
61st Provence, 73, 258, 262
62nd Cambis d'Orsan, 74
63rd De Planta (Swiss), 74, 262
64th Rohan-Rochefort, 74
65th Nice, 69, 74
66th La Marck (German), 74, 77, 262
67th Penthièvre, 74
68th Guyenne, 69, 74, 284
69th Lorraine, 69, 74, 290
70th Flandres, 69, 74, 257, 308
71st Berry, 70, 74, 311

72nd Béarn, 74, 284
73rd Haynault, 74
74th Boulonnois, 75
75th Angoumois, 75
76th Périgord, 75
77th Saintonge, 75
78th Bigorre, 75
79th Forez, 75
80th Cambrésis, 75
81st Tournaisis, 75, 281
82nd Foix, 75
83rd Bresse, 75
84th La Marche, 75, 281
85th Quercy, 75
86th Marche, 75, 281
87th Brie, 75
88th Soissonois, 76
89th Isle de France, 76
90th Diesbach (Swiss), 76, 262
91st Courten (Swiss), 76
92nd Bulkeley (Irish), 76, 77
93rd Clare (Irish), 76
94th Dillon (Irish), 76
95th Royal Suédois, 76, 78, 258
96th Chatres, 76, 257
97th Conty, 76, 257
98th Roth, (Irish), 76
99th Berwick (Irish), 76
100th Enghien, 77, 257, 282
101st Royal Bavière (German), 77, 78, 280
102nd Salis (de Mayenfeld; Swiss), 77, 258, 262
103rd Royal Corse, 77
104th Royal Lorraine, 77
105th Royal Barrois, 77
106th Löwendahl (German), 72, 74, 282
107th Royal Écossais (Scottish), 77
108th Bergh (German), 71, 77, 281
109th Lally, 76, 77, 200
110th Nassau-Usingen (German), 77, 78
111th Nassau (German), 77, 78
112th Royal Cantabres, 78
113th Ogilvy (Scottish), 78
114th Saint Germain (German), 78
115th La Dauphine (German), 77, 78
116th Royal Pologne, 78, 262
117th Lochman-Eptingen, (Swiss), 78
118th Bouillon (German), 78, 282
119th Royal Deux-Ponts (Zweibrücken), 78, 280
120th Vierzet, (German), 262
121st Horion, 78
volunteer formations
Arquebusiers de Grassin, 91, 93, 94
Chasseurs-à-pied de Dorigny, 91
Chasseurs-à-pied de Granpré, 91
Chasseurs de Cambefort, 91
Chasseurs de Monet, 91, 92
Chasseurs de Poncet, 91
Fischer, 91, 92
Fusiliers de Montagnes, 92
Royal Cantabres, 92
Volontaires Corse, 92
Volontaires de Geschray, 93
Volontaires du Dauphiné, 93, 282
Volontaires de Flandre, 91, 93, 94, 257
Volontaires de Nassau-Sarrebruck, 93, 94
Volontaires de Schomberg, 89, 93, 95, 262, 280
Volontaires de Soubise, 94
Volontaires de Wurmser, 94
Volontaires du Hainaut, 93, 94
Volontaires Étrangers, 93, 94
Volontaires Étranger de Clermont-Prince, 94
Volontaires Royaux, 95
(Friedrich) Heinrich, Prinz von Preussen, 271, 301, 317

Fürstenberg, Joseph, Landgraf von, 43, 151, 255
Gabelentz, Georg Carl Gottlob von der, 177, 182
Gaisruck, Sigmund Friedrich, Graf von, 29, 249, 269, 274
Gessler Friedrich Leopold von (Chef PKürR Nr 4), 191, 247, 267, 273
Grant, Johann von (Chef PIR Nr 44), 179, 183
Grape, Jakob Heinrich von (Chef Garrison PIR Nr 4), 185
Gribeauval, Jean-Baptiste-Vaquette, 16
Grolman, Georg Arnold von (Chef Garrison PIR Nr 3), 185
Grothaus, General, 279
Gustav Adolf II, King of Sweden, 13
Hadley, John, 22
Hagen, General, 272
Hagenbach, Jazob Ignaz, Graf von, 28
Haller von Hallerstein, Samuel, Graf, 28, 249, 268, 269, 275
Hamilton, Duke of, 128
Hamilton-Lambert, Colonel, 116
HANOVER
artillery, 148
cavalry regiments
Dachenhausen, 144, 256
Gilten, 145, 256
Grothaus, 144, 146, 279
Hammerstein, 144, 256, 279
Hodenberg, 144, 279
Leib-Regiment, 144, 256, 279
Waldhausen, 145
Zepelin, 144
dragoon regiments
Drachenhausen, 145
Breidenbach, 145, 256
Busche, 145, 256
Bock, 145, 255
infantry regiments
Alt-Zastrow/Otten, 142
Block, 142, 255
Brunck/Estorff, 142, 255, 278
Cheusses/Dreves/Goldacker, 142
Diepenbroick/Rhöden/Mecklenburg-Strelitz, 142, 255
Druchtleben/Schulenberg, 142, 255, 280
Fabrice/Schelen, 142, 256, 278, 279
Grote/Laffert/Motte, 142, 280
Halberstadt/Fersen/Ahlefeld/Fusiliers, 140, 142
Hardenberg, 141, 142, 143, 256, 277, 278
Hauss/Linstow/Plessen, 142
Hodenberg/Behr, 142, 256
Kielmannsegg, 142, 256, 279
Knesebeck/Reden, 142, 255
Ledebour/Bock, 142, 142, 143, 255
Marschalk, Monroy, 142
Oberg/Chevallerie, 142, 143, 256, 280
Post/Sancé/Mecklenburg-Strelitz, 142, 255
Sachsen-Gotha, 140, 141, 142, 255
Scheither, 142, 255, 280
Spörken/Meding, 142, 279
Stolzenberg/Marschalk/Craushaar, 142, 255, 278
Wangenheim, 142, 279
Wrede, 142
Zandree/Halberstadt/Linsingen, 142, 143, 280
Zastrow, 142, 255, 279
light troops
Freytag's Jäger Corps, 145, 255
Legion Britannique, 146, 147, 148, 205
Stockhausen's Freikorps, 148
Hardenberg, von, 254, 255
Hardy, Sir Charles, 286
Hastenbeck, Battle of, 254
Hautcharmoy, Carl Ludwig Herault de, 178

Heinrich (Friedrich Heinrich Ludwig) Prinz von Preussen (Chef PKürR Nr 2), 191, 251, 267, 271, 301, 317, 318, 322
Hessen-Darmstadt, Carl, Prinz von (Chef PIR Nr 12), 55, 170, 263
Hessen-Darmstadt, Landgraf Ludwig VIII (Chef of ADrR Nr 19), 36, 43, 55
Hessen-Kassel, Friedrich Erbprinz von (Chef PIR Nr 48), 181, 184
Hessen-Kassel, Friedrich II, Landgraf von (Chef PIR Nr 45), 179, 183
Hessen-Kassel, Wilhelm, Prinz von, 152
HESSEN KASSEL
artillery, 153
cavalry regiments
Dragoner-Regiment Leib Nr 7, 153, 256, 279
Dragoner-Regiment Prinz Friedrich Nr 6, 153, 279
Husaren Regiment, 153, 255
Kürassier-Regiment Leib Nr 2, 152, 256, 279
Kürassier-Regiment Miltitz Nr 3, 152, 256, 279
Kürassier-Regiment Prinz Wilhelm Nr 1, 152, 256
Kürassier-Regiment Pruschenk Nr 4, 152, 279
infantry regiments
Nr 1 Leibgarde zu Fuss, 151, 255
Nr 2 Haudring, 150, 151, 255
Nr 3 Fürstenberg, 151, 255
Nr 4 Ysenburg, 151, 255
Nr 5 Leib, 151, 256
Nr 6 Grenadier, 151, 256
Nr 7 Erbprinz, 151, 255
Nr 8 Mansbach, 151
Nr 9 Prinz Carl, 152
Nr 10 Canitz, 152
Nr 11 Anhalt, 152, 255, 279
Nr 12 Hanau, 152, 255
Nr 13 Garde, 152, 279
Feldjäger, 152
Hochkirch, Battle of, 271
Hodenberg, General, 256
Hoffmann, Rudolph August von (Chef PIR Nr 44), 179, 183
Holstein-Gottorp, Georg Ludwig Herzog von (Chef PDrR Nr 9), 195, 279
Horn, Christian Sigismund von (Chef PKürR Nr 7), 192
Isenburg-Philipseich, Wilhelm Moritz II, Graf von, 57
Itzenplitz, Joachim Christian Friedrich von (Chef Garrison PIR Nr 7, 186
Joseph II, Holy Roman Emperor, 297
Jungkenn, Martin Eberhard von (aka Müntzer von Mohrenstamm) (Chef PIR Nr 44 and Garrison PIR Nr 4), 179, 183, 185
Kannacher, Ernst Ludwig von, 178
Katte, Hans Friedrich von (Chef PKürR Nr 3), 191, 247, 251, 261
Katzler, Nikolaus Andreas von Chef PKürR Nr 10), 192, 274
Kielmannsegg, von, General, 256
Kleist, Friedrich (Franz) Ulrich von (Alt Kleist) (Chef PIR Nr 27), 178, 247
Kleist, Friedrich Ludwig von, (Jung Kleist) (Chef PIR Nr 9 and Freibataillon Nr 12a and 12b), 164, 202
Kleist, Friedrich Wilhelm Gottfried Arnd von 'Green Kleist', 194, 197, 201, 202
Kleist, Georg Friedrich von (Chef PIR Nr 4), 164
Kleist, Heinrich Werner von (Chef PIR Nr 42), 179, 183
Kleist, Joachim Friedrich von, 202
Knobloch, Carl Gottfried von, 178
Kolin, Battle of, 248

Kolowrat-Krakowsky, Catejan Franz Xaverius, Reichsgraf von, 28
Kolowrat-Krakowsky, Emanuel, Graf von, 37, 269
Königseck-Rothenfels, Christian Moritz, Graf von, 28
Kreytzen, Johann Friedrich von, 177, 178, 182
Krockow, Hans Caspar von (Chef PKürR Nr 1), 191, 251, 266, 272
Krosigk, Christian Friedrich von (Chef PKürR Nr 5), 191, 251, 321
Kurssell, Heinrich Adolf von, 182
Kyau, Friedrich Wilhelm Freiherr von (Chef PKürR Nr 12), 193, 247, 251, 266, 267, 273
Lange, Christian Henning von (Chef Garrison PIR Nr 7), 186
Langermann, Adolf Friedrich von (Chef PDrR Nr 8), 195
Lattorff, Christian Friedrich von (Chef Garrison PIR Nr 6), 186, 187
Laudon, Gideon Ernst, Freiherr von, 28, 272, 275, 296, 297, 298
Lentulus, Robert Scipio Freiherr von (Chef PKürR Nr 3), 191, 247, 251, 261
Lestwitz, Johann Georg von, 178
Lettow, Ewald Georg von (Chef Garrison PIR Nr 4), 185
Leuthen, Battle of, 264
Liechtenstein, Wenzel, Fürst, 14, 16, 17, 36, 95, 246, 300
Ligne, Claudius de, Graf, 29
Ligne de, Ferdinand, Prince, 37
Leopold II, Holy Roman Emperor, 297
Linden, Christian Boguslaw von, 178
Lippe-Detmold and Schaumburg-Lippe, county, 154
Lobositz, Battle of, 244
Los Rios de Gutierez, Franz, 27
Lossow, Daniel Friedrich von (Chef PHusR Nr 5), 198, 199, 279
Luck, Georg von (Chef Garrison PIR Nr 1), 185, 186
Luckner, Nickolaus, Graf von, 147, 149
Lüderitz, David Hans Christoph von (Chef PKürR Nr 5), 191
Lützen, Battle of, 13
Malachowski, Paul Joseph Malachow von (Chef PHusR Nr 7), 199
Manteuffel, Franz Christoph von (Chef Garrison PIR Nr 11), 187, 188
Manteuffel, Heinrich von (Chef PIR Nr 17), 273
Maria Theresia, Empress of Austria, 7, 25, 43, 294, 296, 297, 298, 304
Marschall, Ernst Friedrich, Graf auf Burgholzhausen, 28, 249
Maxen, Battle of, 17, 198, 200, 292, 296, 297, 300
Meinicke, Peter von (Chef PDrR Nr 3), 195
Meyer, Carl Friedrich von (Chef PDrR Nr 6), 195
Meyerink, Dietrich Richard von, 178
Minden, Battle of, 276
Minorca, Battle of, 243
Möhring, Christian von (Chef PHusR Nr 3), 197
Moltke, Philipp Ludwig, Baron von, 27
Motte, Ernst August, Chevalier de la (Chef Garrison PIR Nr 9), 186
Motte Fouqué, Heinrich August Baron de la, 180
Münchow, Gustav Bogislav von, 178, 266
Mütschefahl, Friedrich Julius von (Chef Garrison PIR Nr 5), 185, 186
Neipperg, Wilhelm Reinhard Graf von, 27, 294
Nettelhorst, Georg Ernst von (Chef Garrison PIR Nr 8), 187, 188

Normann, Carl Ludwig von (Chef PDrR Nr 1), 194, 266
O'Donnell, Charles (Karl), 299
O'Donnell, Henry (Heinrich), 299
O'Donnell, John (Johann), 299
Oertzen, Henning Ernst von (Chef PDrR Nr 4), 195, 261, 273
Palffy ab Erdöd, Carl Paul, Graf von, 29, 248
Palffy ab Erdöd, Johann, Graf von, 29
Palffy ab Erdöd, Leopold, Graf von, 28
Palffy ab Erdöd, Rudolf, Graf von, 38
Pallavicini, Giovani Lucas von, 27
Pennavaire, Peter Ernst von (Chef PKürR Nr 11), 192, 247
Peyrl, Georg Johann, 13
Pfalz-Zweibrücken, Friedrich Michael, Prinz von der, 43
Philippsburg, siege of, 1734, 14
Plassey, Battle of, 252
Platen, Dubislav Friedrich von ('Alt-Platen') (Chef PDrR Nr 8), 195
Platen, Leopold Johann von (Chef PDrR Nr 11), 196, 250, 265, 267
Platz, Johann Anton, Graf von, 29
Plettenberg, Christoph Friedrich, Stephan von (Chef PDrR Nr 7), 195
PORTUGAL
artillery regiments
Algarve, 160
Alentejo, 160
Beira, 160
cavalry regiments
Alcantara, 160
Almeida, 160
Bragança, 160
Cais, 160
Elvas, 160
Moura, 160
dragoon regiments
Chaves, 160
Evora, 160
Olivença, 160
Penamacor, 160
infantry regiments
1st Marines, 159
2nd Marines, 159
Algarve, 159
Bragança, 159
Campoajor, 159
Cascais, 159
Castello de Vide, 159
Chaves, 159
Cortes, 159
Faro, 159
Lagos, 159
Lisboa, 159
Moncao, 159
Moura, 159
Olivença, 159
Porto, 159
Penamacor, 159
Peniche, 159
Setubal, 159
Valença, 159
Pritz, Hans Samuel von, 178
PRUSSIA
artillery, 205
dragoon regiments
Nr 1 Normann, 194, 251, 266, 267, 273
Nr 2 Blanckensee, 194, 251, 267
Nr 3 Truchess Graf zu Waldburg, 194, 261
Nr 4 Oertzen, 194, 261, 267, 273
Nr 5 Brandenburg-Bayreuth, 195
Nr 6 Schorlemmer, 195
Nr 7 Plettenberg, 196
Nr 8 Langermann, 196
Nr 9 Herzog von Holstein-Gottorp, 196, 279

Nr 10, Ludwig Graf Finck von Finckenstein, 196
Nr 11 Stechow, 196, 250, 265, 267
Nr 12 Herzog von Württemberg, 196
engineers, 206
Freikorps
Nr 1 Freibataillon le Noble, 200, 266
Nr 2 Freibataillon von Mayr, 200
Nr 3 Freibataillon von Kalben, 200, 266
Nr 4 Freibataillon d'Angelilli, 200
Nr 5 Freibataillon de Chossignon, 200
Nr 6 Freibataillon von Rapin, 200
Nr 7 Freibataillon von Wunsch, 200, 294
Nr 8 Freibataillon du Verger, 200, 273
Nr 9 Freibataillon Graf von Hort, 202
Nr 10 Freibataillon von Trumbach, 202
Nr 11a Freihusaren Jung Kleist (Friedrich Ludwig), 202
Nr 11b Freikorps von Kleist (Joachim Friedrich), 202
Nr 12a Freikorps von Kleist, 202
Nr 12b Freibataillon von Kleist (Friedrich Ludwig), 202
Nr 13 Frei-Dragoner-Regiment von Glasenapp, 203
Nr 14 Freibataillon Jeney, 203
Nr 15 Freibataillon von Schack, 203
Nr 16 Freibataillon von Heer, 203
Nr 17 Freibataillon de Bequignolles, 203
Nr 18 Freibataillon de la Badie, 203
Nr 19 Freikorps von Schony, 203
Nr 20 Freikorps von Gschray, 203
Nr 21 Von Bawr Husaren, 205
Nr 22 Legion Britannique, 146, 147, 148, 205
Nr 23 Volontaires Auxiliaires, 63, 205
garrison regiments
Nr 1 von Luck, 185, 186
Nr 2 Alt-Sydow, 185, 186
Nr 3 von Grolman, 185
Nr 4 von Grape, 185
Nr 5 von Mütschefahl, 185, 186
Nr 6 von Lattorff, 186, 187
Nr 7 von Lange, 186
Nr 8 von Nettelhorst, 187, 188
Nr 9 de La Motte, 187
Nr 10 von Blanckensee, 187, 188, 189
Nr 11 von Manteuffel, 187, 188
Nr 12 von Kalckreuth, 187, 188
hussar regiments
Nr 1 von Szekelyn, 197, 201, 250, 261, 265
Nr 2 von Zieten, 197, 265, 318, 323, 324
Nr 3 von Wartenberg, 197, 250, 265
Nr 4 von Puttkammer, 197, 250, 265, 273
Nr 5 von Ruesch/Lossow, 198, 199, 279
Nr 6 von Wechmar/Werner, 198, 250, 265, 273
Nr 7 von Seydlitz, 198
Nr 8 von Malachowski, 199
Nr 9 von Belling, 199
infantry regiments
Nr 1 Winterfeldt, 164, 165, 261, 266
Nr 2 Kanitz, 164, 165, 255
Nr 3 Anhalt-Dessau, 164, 165
Nr 4 Kalnein, Kleist (Georg Friedrich), 164, 165
Nr 5 Ferdinand von Braunschweig, 166, 167
Nr 6 Grenadiergarde, 166, 167, 247, 261, 266
Nr 7 von Braunschweig-Bevern, 166, 167, 168, 247, 251
Nr 8 von Amstell, 167, 168
Nr 9 Quadt Von Wikeradt, 167, 168, 189, 247, 261
Nr 10 von Knobloch, 167, 168, 273
Nr 11 von Below, 168, 169, 170
Nr 12 Erbprinz von Hessen-Darmstadt, 169, 170

Nr 13 von Itzenblitz, 169, 170
Nr 14 von Lehwald, 169, 170
Nr 15 Garde du Corps, 169, 170, 261, 266, 273, 314
Nr 16 von Dohna, 169, 170, 172
Nr 17 von Manteuffel, 171, 172, 247, 250, 273
Nr 18 Prinz von Preussen, 171, 172
Nr 19 Markgraf Carl, 171, 174
Nr 20 von Zastrow, 171, 174, 247
Nr 21 von Hülsen, 171, 174, 247, 251, 261
Nr 22 Prinz Mortiz von Anhalt, 171, 176, 251
Nr 23 von Forcade de Biaix, 173, 176, 266, 273
Nr 24 von Schwerin, 173, 175, 176
Nr 25 von Kalckstein, 173, 176, 250, 267, 273
Nr 26 von Meyerink, 173, 178, 261, 273
Nr 27 von Kleist, 173, 178, 247, 261, 266
Nr 28 Herault de Hautcharmoy, 173, 178, 247, 250, 251
Nr 29 von Schultze, 175, 178, 250, 273
Nr 30 von Pritz, 175, 178, 266, 273
Nr 31 von Lestwitz, 175, 178
Nr 32 von Tresckow, 175, 180
Nr 33 Baron de la Motte Fouqué, 175, 180
Nr 34 Prinz Ferdinand von Preussen, 175, 180, 273
Nr 35 Prinz Heinrich von Preussen, 177, 180, 251
Nr 36 von Münchow, 177, 182, 247, 250
Nr 37 von Kurssell, 177, 182
Nr 38 **von Brandes**, 177, 182
Nr 39 **Jung Braunschweig**, 177, 182
Nr 40 **von Kreytzen**, 177, 182, 251
Nr 41 **Graf von Wied zu Neuwied**, 179, 183
Nr 42 **Markgraf von Brandenburg**, 179, 183
Nr 43 **von Kalsow**, 179, 183
Nr **von Jungkenn Müntze**, 179, 183
Nr 45 **von Dossow**, 179, 183
Nr 46 **von Württemberg (nominal)**/ Schöning, 179, 184
Nr 47 **von Wietersheim**, 181, 184
Nr 48 **Erbprinz von Hessen-Kassel**, 181, 184
Nr 49 **von Seers**, 181, 184
kürassier regiments
Nr 1 Buddenbrock/Krockow, 191, 251, 266, 272, 273
Nr 2 Prinz von Preussen 248, 251, 267, 271, 301, 316, 317, 318, 319, 322
Nr 3 Katte/Lentulus, 191, 247, 251, 261
Nr 4 von Gessler/Schmettau, 191, 247, 266, 267, 273, 316, 317
Nr 5 Markgraf Friedrich von Brandenburg/ Krosigk/Zieten, 192, 251, 321
Nr 6 von Schönaich/Vasold, 192
Nr 7 von Driesen/Horn, 192, 273
Nr 8 von Rochow/Seydlitz, 192, 247, 251, 261, 320
Nr 9 Prinz von Schönaich-Carolath/ Bredow, 192, 267, 273
Nr 10 Gens d'Armes/Katzler/Schwerin, 193, 247
Nr 11 Leib-Karabiniers, 193, 247
Nr 12 von Kyau, 193, 251, 266, 267, 273
Nr 13 Garde du Corps/Blumenthal, 193
miners, 206
pioneers, 206
Puebla de Portugal, Antonio prince de la, 28, 249
Puttkammer, Christian Ernst von, 176
Puttkammer, Georg Ludwig von (Chef PHusR Nr 4), 197, 250, 265, 273
Puttkammer, Nikolaus Lorenz von, 317

Puttkammer, Werner Friedrich von (Chef Garrison PIR Nr 1), 185, 186
Quadt von Wickeradt, Friedrich Freiherr von, (Chef Garrison PIR Nr 8), 187, 188
Quebec, Battle of, 283
Quiberon Bay, Battle of, 20, 124, 285, 286, 289
Ramm, Friedrich Ehrentreich von, 173, 176
Retzow, Major-General, 261, 266, 271, 272, 273, 314
Rochow, Friedrich Wilhelm von (Chef PKürR Nr 8), 192, 247, 320
Rossbach, Battle of, 18, 43, 47, 49, 200, 242, 259, 264, 307, 311, 314, 316, 318, 321
Ruesch, Joseph Theodor von (Chef PHusR Nr 5), 198, 199, 279
RUSSIAN EMPIRE
artillery, 218
Cuirassier regiments
  Lieb Cuirassier Regiment of Her Majesty, 213
  Bevernsky, 213
  Kazansky, 213
  Kievsky, 213
  Minichovsky, 213
  Novotroitsky, 213
  Prince Fedorovich or Altesse Impériale, 213
dragoon regiments
  Arkhangelgorodsky, 215
  Azovsky, 215
  Ingermannlandsky, 215
  Kiev, 215
  Lutsky, 215
  Moscowsky, 215
  Nizegorodsky, 215
  Novgorodsky, 215
  Olonetsky, 215
  Permsky, 215
  Pskovsky, 215
  Revelsky, 215
  Rostovsky, 216
  Sibyrsky, 216
  Tobolsky, 216
  Troitsky, 216
  Tversky, 216
  Viatsky, 216
  Vladimirsky, 216
  Vologdasky, 216
  Yamburgsky, 216
Foot Guards
  Chevalier Guards Regiment, 208
  Guards Artillery Company, 208
  Horse Regiment, 208
  Izmailovsky Leib-Guard, 208
  Preobrazensky Leib-Guard, 208
  Semenovsky Leib-Guard, 208
Horse Grenadiers
  Astrakhansky, 214
  Kargopolsky, 213
  Narvsky, 214
  Rizhsky, 214
  Ryazansky, 214
  Sankt Peterburgsky, 214
hussar regiments
  Bolgarsky (Bulgarian), 216
  Gruzinsky (Georgian), 216
  Makedonsky (Macedonian), 216
  Moldavsky (Moldavian), 217
  Serbsky (Serbian), 217
  Slobodsky (Slovakian), 217
  Vengersky (Hungarian), 217
  Zeltiy (Yellow), 217
infantry regiments
  1st Grenadier Regiment, 209
  2nd Grenadier Regiment, 209
  3rd Grenadier Regiment, 209
  4th Grenadier Regiment, 210
  Apsheronsky, 210

Archangelogorodsky, 210
Astrakhansky, 210
Azovsky, 210
Bjelosersky, 210
Butyrsky, 210
Ingermannlandsky, 210
Kabardasky, 210
Kazansky, 210
Kegsgolmsky, 210
Kievsky, 210
Koporsky, 210, Kurinsky, 210
Ladogasky, 210
Moskowsky (1st), 211
Moskowsky (2nd), 211
Muromsky, 211
Narvsky, 211
Navaginsky, 211
Nevasky, 211
Nizhegorodsky, 211
Nizovsky, 211
Novogorodsky, 211
Permsky, 211
Pskovsky, 211
Riazansky, 211
Rostovsky, 211
Sankt Peterburgsky, 211
Schlüsselburgsky, 211
Sibyrsky, 211
Smolensky, 212
Suzdalsky, 212
Tchernigovsky, 212
Tenginsky, 212
Tobolsky, 212
Troitsky, 212
Uglitshky, 212
Velikolutsky, 212
Viatsky, 212
Vladimirsky, 212
Vologdasky, 212
Voronezhky, 212
Vyborgsky, 212
Yaroslavsky, 212
Light Horse
  Achtyrsky Free Cherkassian Kazak Regiment, 217
  Isumsky Free Cherkassian Kazak Regiment, 217
  Sumskoi Free Cherkassian Kazak Regiment, 217
  1st Chuguyevsky Kazak Regiment, 217
  2nd Chuguyevsky Kazak Regiment, 217
Observation Corps, 213
Sachsen-Eisenach, Wilhelm Heinrich, Prinz von (Chef PIR Nr 40), 182
Sachsen-Gotha, Johann August, Prinz von (Chef ADrR Nr 28), 36, 249, 270
Sachsen-Gotha-Altenburg, Herzogin Luise Dorothea von (Saxon infantry regiment in Hanoverian service), 140, 141, 142, 255, 278
Sachsen-Gotha-Altenburg, Johann Adolf, Prinz von, 221
Sachsen-Gotha-Altenburg (Saxon infantry regiment in Austrian service), 257, 282
Sachsen-Gotha-Altenburg, Wilhelm Karl Christian, Herzog von, 28
Sachsen-Hildburghausen, Joseph Maria Friedrich Wilhelm Hollandinus, Herzog, 27, 43, 246, 259, 260, 262, 274, 321
Sachsen-Teschen, Albert Casimir, Herzog von (Chef AKürR Nr 22), 34
Saldern, General, 166
Salm-Salm, Nikolaus Leopold von, 27
Salmuth aka, Bennger, Friedrich Wilhelm von (Chef PIR Nr 48), 181, 184
Saunders, Charles, 283
SAXONY
artillery, 223

Chevauxlegers
  Graf Brühl, 222, 248
  Prinz Albrecht, 219, 222 248, 267
  Prinz Carl, 222, 248
Dragoner-Regiment Graf Rutowsky, 222
Guards
  Garde zu Fuss, 189, 220
  Garde du Corps, 220
  Karabiniergarde, 219, 220, 250
  Leibgrenadiergarde, 220, 222
infantry regiments
  Königin, 219, 221
  Kurprinzessin, 219, 221, 282
  Prinz Friedrich August, 189, 221, 282
  Maximilian, 189, 221
  Prinz Xavier, 189, 221
  Prinz Clemens, 189, 221, 282
  Graf Brühl, 189, 219, 221, 222, 248, 267, 282
  Fürst Lubomirsky, 189, 221, 282
  Minckwitz, 189, 221
  Sachsen-Gotha, 189, 221, 257, 282
  Friesen, 221
  Rochow, 189, 221, 282
kürassier regiments
  Anhalt-Dessau, 222
  Arnim, 222
  Kronprinz, 222
  Leibregiment, 222
  Plötz, 222
  Vitzthum, 222
Uhlans
  Graf Renard, 223
  Graf Rudnicky, 223
Schaumburg-Lippe, Albrecht Wolfgang, General Graf zu, 154
Schaumburg-Lippe, Friedrich Wilhelm Ernst, Graf zu, 157
Schaumburg-Lippe-Bückeburg, Carabiniers, 154
Schaumburg-Lippe-Bückeburg, troops, 155, 156, 280
Scheither, Georg Heinrich Albrecht, von, 147
Schenckendorff, Balthasar Rudolf von (Chef PIR Nr 43), 179, 183
Schlabrendorff, Gustav Albrecht von (Chef PKürR Nr 1), 191, 251, 266
Schmettau, Johann Ernst von (Chef PKürR Nr 4), 266, 316, 317
Schönaich, Georg Philipp Gottlob Freiherr von (Chef PKürR Nr 6), 192
Schönaich-Carolath Johann Carl Friedrich Prinz von (Chef PKürR Nr 9), 192
Schöning, Emanuel von (Chef PIR Nr 46), 179, 184
Schorlemmer, Ludwig Wilhelm von (Chef PDrR Nr 6), 195
Meyer, Carl Friedrich von (Chef PDrR Nr 6), 195
Schulenberg, von, General, 255
Schultz, Hans Caspar Ernst von, 178
Schwerin, Friedrich Albert von (Chef PKürR Nr10), 192, 274
Schwerin, Kurt Christoph, Graf von, 176, 319, 320
Serbelloni, Johann Baptiste, Graf von (Chef AKürR Nr 12), 34, 43, 249, 268, 269, 300
Sers, Philipp Loth von (Chef PFusR Nr 49), 181, 184
Seydlitz, Friedrich Wilhelm Freiherr von (Chef PKürR Nr 8), 192, 259, 260, 261, 266, 273
Shrapnel, Henry, 15
Soubise, Sharles de Rohan, Prince de, 44, 49, 65, 219, 259, 260, 307, 308, 311, 321
Spaen, Johann Heinrich Friedrich Freiherr von (Chef PKürR Nr 12), 193, 251, 266, 267, 273

SPAIN
artillery, 228
dragoon regiments
  Batavia, 228
  Bélgica, 228
  Edimburgo, 228
  Frisia, 228
  Lusitania, 228
  Merida, 228
  Numancia, 228
  Pavia, 228
  Reina, 228
  Sagunto, 228
  Alcantara, 227
  Algarve, 227
  Andalucia, 227
  Barcelona, 227
  Bórbon, 227
  Brabante, 227
  Calatrava, 227
  Costa de Granada, 227
  Extremadura, 227
  Farnesio, 227
  Flandes, 227
  Granada, 227
  Malta, 227
  Milán, 227
  Montesa, 227
  Ordenes, 227
  Reina, 227
  Santiago, 227
  Sevilla, 227
infantry regiments
  Africa, 225
  Antiguo de Reding (foreign) 225
  Aragón, 225
  Asturias, 225
  Brabante (foreign) 226
  Bruselas (foreign) 226
  Buch (foreign) 226
  Burgos, 225
  Cantabria, 225
  Castilla, 225
  Córdoba, 225
  Corona, 225
  Dunant (foreign) 226
  Espana, 225
  Fijo de Badajoz, 225
  Fijo de Cueta, 225
  Fijo de Oran, 225
  Flándes (foreign) 226
  Galicia, 225
  Granada, 225
  Hibernia (foreign) 226
  Irlanda (foreign) 226
  la Princesa, 225
  León, 225
  Lisboa, 225
  Lombardia, 225
  Mallorca, 225
  Milan (foreign) 226
  Murcia, 225
  Napoles (foreign) 226
  Navarra, 225
  Nuevo de Reding (foreign) 226
  Príncipe, 225
  Real America, 225
  Reina, 225
  Saboya, 225
  Sevilla, 225
  Soria, 225
  Toledo, 225
  Ultonia (foreign) 226
  Vitoria, 225
  Zamora, 225
light infantry regiments
  Aragon (1st), 226

Aragon (2nd), 226
Barbastro, 226
Barcelona (1st), 226
Barcelona (2nd), 226
Campo Mayor, 226
Cataluna (1st), 226
Cataluna (2nd), 226
Gerona, 226
Navarra, 226
Taragona, 226
Valencia, 226
Spörken, von, General, 276, 277, 278
Starhemberg, Maximilian Adam, Graf von, 28, 248, 269
Starhemberg W. von, 245, 249, 268
Stechow, Christoph Ludwig von (Chef PDrR Nr 11), 196, 250, 265, 267
Stockhausen, Major von, 148
Stutterheim, Joachim Friedrich von, 178
SWEDEN
artillery, 235
cuirassier regiments
  Jämtlands, 233
  Smålands, 234
  Södra Skänska, 234
  Västgöta, 234
dragoon regiments
  Bohusläns, 234
  Karelska, 234
  Nylands, 234
Guards
  Drottningens Livregemente, 230
  Kronprinsens, 230
  Kungl Livgardet, 229
  Livdragoner, 230
  Upplands Livregemente, 230
hussar regiments
  Bla, 235
  Gula, 235
infantry regiments
  Åbolans, 231
  Älvsborgs, 231
  Björneborgs, 231
  Cronhjelmska, 231
  Dalarnas, 231
  Elimas, 231
  Hälsinge, 231
  Hamiltonska, 231
  Hessensteinska, 231
  Jämtlands, 231
  Jönköpings, 231
  Kalmar, 231
  Kronobergs, 232
  Löwnfelska, 232
  Närke-Värmlands, 232
  Nylandas, 232
  Österbottens, 232
  Östgöta, 232
  Posseska, 232
  Savolax, 232
  Skaraborgs, 232
  Södermanlands, 232
  Spenska, 232
  Tavastehus, 232
  Upplands, 232
  Västerbottens, 232
  Västgöta-Dals, 233
  Västmanlands, 233
light troops
  Böhnens, 235
  Hästjägare, 235
  Husarskyttekår, 235
  Köhlers, 235
  Schwarters, 235
tactical combined units
  Fabritius, 233
  Finnish Grenadiers, 233

1st German Grenadiers, 233
2nd German Grenadiers, 233
1st Swedish Grenadiers, 233
2nd Swedish Grenadiers, 233
Sydow, Gustav Adolph von (Jung- Sydow) (Chef Garrison PIR Nr 5), 185, 186
Sydow, Hans Sigismund von (Alt-Sydow) (Chef Garrison PIR Nr 2), 185, 186
Szekely, Michael von (Chef PHusR Nr 1), 197
Thile, Friedrich Wilhelm von, 178
Treaty of Paris, 20, 284, 302
Tresckow, Joachim Christian von, 251
Trompeter, Johann Georg, 13
Truchess, Friedrich Ludwig, Graf zu Waldburg (Chef PDrR Nr 3), 195
Unicorn (Russian gun/howitzer), 15, 218
Vasold, Heinz, Rudolf Wilhelm von (Chef PKürR Nr 6), 192
Waldeck, 43, 55, 56
Waldeck-Pyrmont, Karl August Friedrich, Fürst zu, 29, 300
Wallenstein, Albrecht von, 13
Wallis, Michael Johann, Graf von, 27
Wandewash, Battle of, 289
Wangenheim, von, General, 276, 277, 279
Wartenberg, Hartwig Carl von (Chef PHusR Nr 3), 197
Wechmar, Ludwig Anton Freiherr von (Chef PHusR Nr 6), 198
Wedell, Carl Heinrich von, 178
Werner, Johann Paul von (Chef PHusR Nr 6), 198
Wied, Heinrich Friedrich, Fürst von, 28, 245, 250, 269
Winterfeldt, Hans Carl von, 314, 322, 323
Württemberg, Carl Eugen, Herzog von, 53
Württemberg, Friedrich Eugen, Prinz von (Chef PDrR Nr 12), 196, 264, 265, 321
WÜRTTEMBERG
artillery, 240
infantry regiments
  Feldjäger zu Fuss, 239
  Füsiliers von Truchses, 237, 238, 269
  Grenadier Bataillon von Boueingausen-Walmerode, 238
  Grenadier Bataillon von Heimburg, 238
  Grenadier Bataillon Herzog, 238
  Grenadier Bataillon von Lengenfeld, 238
  Grenadier Bataillon von Plessen, 238, 269
  Kreis-Regiment, 237
  Leib-Grenadiers, 237
  Prinz Friedrich Wilhelm, 237
  Prinz Louis, 237, 269
  Roeder, 237
  Spiznass, 237, 270
  Werneck, 237, 238
cavalry regiments
  Dragoner-Regiment von Degenfeld, 238
  Feldjäger zu Pferde, 239
  Freihusaren von Glasenapp, 239
  Hussars Gorcy, 239
  Kreis Cavalry Regiment, 239
  Kürassier-Regiment von Phull, 238
  Leib-Grenadiers à Cheval, 239
Württemberg, Ludwig, Prinz von, 320
Würzburg Infanterie-Regiment Blau, 242
Würzburg Infanterie-Regiment Rot, 242
Ysenburg, Hessen-Kassel (Chef H-KIR Nr 4), 151
Zastrow, Carl Anton Leopold von (Chef PIR Nr 38), 247
Zastrow, Johann Wenzel von (Chef PDrR Nr 1) 194, 266
Zieten, Hans Joachim von (Chef PHusR Nr 2), 197, 265, 318, 323, 324
Zieten, Hans Sigismund von (Chef PKürR Nr 5), 191